THE JEFFERSONIANS

By LEONARD D. WHITE

THE FEDERALISTS

THE JEFFERSONIANS

THE JACKSONIANS

THE REPUBLICAN ERA

THE

Jeffersonians

A STUDY IN
ADMINISTRATIVE
HISTORY

1801-1829

by Leonard D. White

THE FREE PRESS, *New York*
COLLIER-MACMILLAN LIMITED, *London*

TO

LOUIS BROWNLOW

Friend and Counselor

PREFACE

On July 22, 1806, William Plumer, Senator from New Hampshire, wrote in his diary, "I have for some time wished to see a full and impartial history of the government of the United States. . . . A history of the administration of our government, its laws—of the presidents—heads of departments . . . would, if well executed, be a very useful work. There are many things in relation to this subject that are little known that would be useful to future statesmen. . . . It is a great & laborious task." Plumer never came to the point of executing his project, and Thomas Jefferson, who was urged in the same direction by Dr. Josephus B. Stewart, refused: "While in public life I had not time, and now that I am retired, I am past the time."

It was with some appreciation of Senator Plumer's remark that there were many things in relation to this subject which were little known and which might be of use if known that I began to organize the materials that led in 1948 to the publication of *The Federalists*. The present volume is a continuation of the administrative history of the general government from 1801 to 1829.

The Jeffersonian era in the field of administration was in many respects a projection of Federalist ideals and practice. The political differences between Jefferson and Hamilton turned out to be much more profound and significant than their differences in the manner and spirit of conducting the public business. Jefferson and Gallatin, moreover, inherited a going concern, and it developed that a brief twelve years had been enough to set patterns that persisted throughout the next thirty. The Federalists disappeared as a political party, but their administrative system was adopted by their political rivals.

It may be argued, indeed, that the last of the Jeffersonians in the White House, John Quincy Adams, was in truth more nearly a Federalist than a Republican. His political doctrines resembled those of Alexander Hamilton, and his ideals of administration were those of George Washington and his father, John Adams. The ambivalence reflects the duality of the Republican party and of Jefferson himself. The younger Adams was a Republican as certainly as his rival, John C. Calhoun, during the decade 1820–30; but they belonged to the "left-wing." This wing, however, could claim as direct and certain doctrinal lineage from Jefferson as the old Republicans, for Jefferson's philosophy and actions were at times contradictory.

Certain it is that the year 1829 marked the end of an era, politically and administratively. The gentlemen who since 1789 had taken the responsibility of government were driven from the scene, to be replaced by a new type of public servant and by other ideals of official action. The perfect symbol of the change was Jackson's removal of the venerable Joseph Nourse, appointed register of the Treasury by George Washington in 1789 and serving in that same office without a break until the spring of 1829.

This volume does not undertake to present the administrative history of the states or their subdivisions. This omission is a regrettable necessity which it may be hoped will be repaired by others. At the same time the states begin to peer from the wings of the stage, where their presence is necessary to illuminate the action of the principal character. The rising threat of the patronage system, the great problem of internal improvements, and the administrative relations of the two federal partners in the control of the militia compel some notice of the state authorities. The story of governmental administration in the years subsequent to 1829 will presumably require these hitherto secondary characters to take a livelier role.

The purpose of the first two chapters of *The Jeffersonians* is to set the stage by introducing the principal personalities, by suggesting the main drift of events, and by recreating some sense of the "feel of the times." The material is not new, but has been selected to provide background for the events that follow. The remainder of the volume falls into four major divisions, dealing respectively with the general administrative relationships between the executive and legislative branches; the operations of the departments, the central workshops of administration, and the fiscal system; the personnel system; and a study of some of the substantive administrative problems that were encountered. Of these the most spectacular was the embargo. The law of officers, to which some notice was given in the *The Federalists,* is not developed in this book—another omission which it may be hoped will be repaired by a student of this field.

The data on which these pages are based are almost exclusively from original sources, although I have taken advantage of available monographic works. The record of the congressional debates proved disappointing, since the reporters, being forced to summarize, usually omitted the discussion of means in favor of the arguments on policy and ends—the latter usually being far more dramatic and holding greater public interest. On the other hand the public documents, the *American State Papers,* and the House and Senate Documents and Reports, provided an immense amount of important material. This body of information is supplemented and developed by the manuscript records of the departments and agencies, for the most part in the helpful custody of the National Archives. In this study, as in its predecessor, the collected published and unpublished letters and diaries of the principal administrative figures were invaluable, giving life and color and meaning to records otherwise at times bare and without significance. One of the major tasks of the historians is to publish the collected papers of many important figures whose writings remain unknown, and to prepare more adequate collections of some whose present published works are almost fragmentary. The new edition of Jefferson's Papers, published under the editorship of Julian P. Boyd, is a welcome addition to our source material and a model for more work of its kind.

The study of administrative history during the Jeffersonian period is not facilitated by the general histories of the time. To this statement the work of Henry Adams is a necessary exception. His *History of the United States* was primarily concerned with political and diplomatic affairs, but he was sensitive to the role of administration; his biography of Albert Gallatin and his collection of Gallatin's letters are of much value, although he would not have pretended to have been wholly neutral in his point of view. Less can be said of the auto-biographies and biographies dealing with the lives of men prominent in those years; they often disregard or slight their official work. This is not to say that such important recent works as Cresson's *Monroe,* Bemis' *John Quincy Adams,* Brant's *Madison,* Wiltse's volumes on Calhoun, and others can be disregarded. The era cannot be well understood other than by mastering such works. The principal source of administrative history remains, however, in the archives, which on the whole are still untouched, awaiting the patience and diligence and insight of the scholar.

This book is dedicated in friendship and gratitude to a true Jeffersonian, Louis Brownlow. His long and distinguished career in the public service of cities, states, and nation—and overseas—has combined in skillful measure Federalist ideals of administration with Jefferson's ideals of government. The author's association with him over a period of twenty years has been a continuous and sparkling seminar in the art of administration.

I am again indebted to colleagues and friends for assistance. Substantial parts of the manuscript have been read and improved by Charles E. Merriam, William T. Hutchinson, Don K. Price, and Robert Horn. The Social Science Round Table of the Quadrangle Club has often been the convenient occasion to explore difficulties, clear up problems, and discover new leads. Lucius Wilmerding of the School for Advanced Studies at Princeton generously allowed me to read his unpublished manuscript on the history of federal accounting and in turn read my chapters on Treasury procedure. The hospitality of the Baker Library of Dartmouth College, the skillful and generous assistance of the National Archives and the Library of the University of Chicago, which had to carry the brunt of my needs, are gratefully acknowledged. Welcome grants from the Rockefeller Foundation and from Public Administration Clearing House made it possible to complete the study.

It could hardly have been completed, however, without the continued assistance of Jean Schneider. Her prodigious efforts in reading 300 volumes of House and Senate Documents, to refer to only one batch of source materials through which she made her way, her care and accuracy in putting references in order, and her unfailing capacity to spot an inadequate presentation, have all contributed heavily to my work. What errors and inadequacies remain are not her fault, nor can they be ascribed to the friends who have assisted me. The author in the last analysis *is* the author.

Chicago, June 1950.

CONTENTS

		Page
Chapter I	Thomas Jefferson and the Administrative System	1
II	The State of the Nation	16
III	The Presidency	29
IV	The President and Congress: Institutional Developments	45
V	The President and the Administrative System	60
VI	The President and the Cabinet	77
VII	Congress and the Administrative System	89
VIII	Congress and the Control of Expenditures	108
IX	Congress and Administrative Reform	117
X	The Treasury	134
XI	The Collectors	148
XII	Accountability: Paralysis and Reform	162
XIII	The State Department	183
XIV	The Domestic Business of the State Department	200
XV	The War Department	211
XVI	The Army Supply System	224
XVII	The War Department and the Army	233
XVIII	West Point and the Army Engineers	251
XIX	The Navy	265
XX	The Navy Ashore	284
XXI	The Post Office	299
XXII	Postmasters and Contractors	320

XXIII	The Office of Attorney General	336
XXIV	Personnel Administration: Theory and Practice	347
XXV	Public Service Careers	369
XXVI	The Cloud on the Horizon	386
XXVII	Jonathan Chooses to Live Snug	399
XXVIII	Public Service Ethics	412
XXIX	The Embargo: An Experiment in Peaceable Coercion	423
XXX	End of the Experiment	453
XXXI	Internal Improvements	474
XXXII	"In Regions Wide and Wild": The Management of Indian Affairs	496
XXXIII	Disposition of the Public Lands	513
XXXIV	Administrative Dualism: The Case of the Militia	528
XXXV	Republican Achievements in Administration	546
	Index	561

THE JEFFERSONIANS

CHAPTER ONE

Thomas Jefferson
and the Administrative System

Thomas Jefferson, third President of the United States, was no stranger to the national scene. Most of his life had been spent in the public service: a member of the Continental Congress and of the Virginia House of Delegates; governor of Virginia; member of Congress; minister to the court of Louis XVI; Secretary of State; and Vice President under John Adams. Jefferson was shy in appearance and low-spoken in voice. Augustus Foster, secretary of the British legation in Washington, described him as he appeared in 1804: "He was a tall man, with a very red freckled face, and gray neglected hair; his manners good-natured, frank, and rather friendly, though he had somewhat of a cynical expression of countenance. He wore a blue coat, a thick gray-colored hairy waistcoat, with a red under-waistcoat lapped over it, green velveteen breeches with pearl buttons, yarn stockings, and slippers down at the heels—his appearance being very much like that of a tall, large-boned farmer." [1]

To those who had studied his career and personality, Jefferson presented a complex character indeed as he looked beyond his immediate audience on Inauguration Day, March 4, 1801, to "the rising nation . . . advancing rapidly to destinies beyond the reach of mortal eye. . . ." [2] His happiest hours, he often

[1] Quoted in Henry Adams, *History of the United States of America during the Administrations of Thomas Jefferson and James Madison* (9 vols., New York: C. Scribner's Sons, 1889–91), I, 186.

[2] James D. Richardson, *A Compilation of the Messages and Papers of the Presidents, 1789–1910* (11 vols., New York: Bureau of National Literature, 1911), I, 321.

declared, were spent in seclusion in the company of his family; his most painful experiences had been the mortifications of the two executive offices he had already held. He was a musician, a linguist, a scientist, a philosopher, a conversationalist, an author, a lover of rural life, a gardener, an aristocrat, and an eloquent advocate of democracy. It was not surprising that he should appear to Robert Goodloe Harper as "fit to be a professor in a College, President of a Philosophical Society, or even Secretary of State; but certainly not the first magistrate of a great nation." [3]

Events were to prove that this man, blessed with a "sunny aspect" and a figure that had "a loose, shackling air" with none of that firm collected deportment which Senator Maclay had expected, combined political skill of the highest order with a hard and stubborn determination in the face of crisis. He thought administration was mostly common sense applied to concrete situations, but on the larger scene where administration, policy, strategy, and constitutional relationships were involved, he made contributions of the first order.

I

If Jefferson presented a many-sided personality to the world of art, science, philosophy, and government, he presented at least a dual personality in the realm of administration. On the one hand was the Jefferson who spoke his mind in 1796 to his disciple, Madison, then a member of Congress working for the federal improvement of the post road from Maine to Georgia. "Have you considered," he asked, "all the consequences of your proposition concerning post roads? I view it as a source of boundless patronage to the executive, jobbing to members of Congress & their friends, and a bottomless abyss of public money . . . it will be a scene of eternal scramble among the members, who can get the most money wasted in their State; and they will always get most who are meanest." [4] It was this Jefferson who in 1800 wrote Caesar Rodney, one day to be his

[3] *Papers of James A. Bayard, 1796–1815* (Elizabeth Donnan, ed.), American Historical Association, *Annual Report, 1913*, II, 25.

[4] *The Works of Thomas Jefferson* (Federal edition, Paul Leicester Ford, ed., 12 vols., New York: G. P. Putnam's Sons, 1904–5), VIII, 226–27 (March 6, 1796).

Attorney General, that the making of roads "will be a bottom-less abyss for money . . . and the richest provision for jobs to favorites that has ever yet been proposed. . . . Foreign relations are our province: domestic regulations & institutions belong, in every state, to itself." [5] It was the same Jefferson who in his First Inaugural praised "a wise and frugal Government, which shall restrain men from injuring one another, shall leave them otherwise free to regulate their own pursuits of industry and improvement, and shall not take from the mouth of labor the bread it has earned." [6]

It was a quite different Jefferson who delivered his Second Inaugural on March 4, 1805. The frugal government introduced four years earlier had borne its proper fruits. The debt was on its way to early redemption. What then to do with the more than ample revenue that the customs dues and the sale of public land would produce? Jefferson had an answer, quite contrary to the sentiments expressed in his First Inaugural. The surplus revenue, he declared, might by an amendment of the Constitution "be applied *in time of peace* to rivers, canals, roads, arts, manufactures, education, and other great objects within each State. *In time of war* . . . increased as the same revenue will be by increased population and consumption, and aided by other resources reserved for that crisis, it may meet within the year all the expenses of the year. . . . War will then be but a suspension of useful works, and a return to a state of peace a return to the progress of improvement." [7]

It was this Jefferson who consented to the purchase of Louisiana, who foresaw the establishment of great states in the new territory across the Mississippi outside the limits of the original compact, and who called forth from the Constitution powers of peaceful coercion during the embargo that rivaled the hated authority of the Alien and Sedition Acts. The "old Republicans" stood with the first Jefferson, the "new Republicans" with the second. The duality was to underlie the whole of the Republican era and to account for many of its frustrations.

The character of Jefferson's administrative theory and prac-

5 *Ibid.*, IX, 160–61 (Dec. 21, 1800).
6 Richardson, *Messages*, I, 323.
7 *Ibid.*, I, 379.

tice as the first Republican President will appear in many of the
events that comprise this volume. His significance in American
history flows much less from his contribution to the art of administration than from his convictions about democracy, liberty, and the capacity of the people for self-government. He was
a competent and conscientious executive but he had neither
the taste nor the talent for administration that was possessed
by Albert Gallatin. His was a speculative rather than an administrative mind.

Jefferson was not interested, indeed, in the normal process of
day-by-day administration. Apart from disposing of particular
cases there is hardly a reference in his public or private papers
to the management of the public business, a silence that contrasts impressively with the constant aphorisms of George Washington and the prolific propositions of Alexander Hamilton on
the art and practice of administration.

A single letter, written long after his retirement, speaks volumes. In it he referred to "the difficulties supposed to attend
the public administration." "There are no mysteries in it," he
declared. "Difficulties indeed sometimes arise; but common
sense and honest intentions will generally steer through them,
and, where they cannot be surmounted, I have ever seen the
well-intentioned part of our fellow citizens sufficiently disposed
not to look for impossibilities. We all know that a farm, however large, is not more difficult to direct than a garden, and does
not call for more attention or skill." [8] Even in Jefferson's day
such an analogy could hardly have been made by one who was
sensitive to the difficulties of keeping the machinery of the general government reasonably adequate to its tasks, modest though
they were.

Jefferson, however, was as skillful as his Federalist predecessors in using administrative means for far-reaching political
ends. His early appointment policy was designed not merely to
maintain the character and competence of government, but also
to alleviate the political bitterness that separated Americans into
two hostile camps. His refusal to keep ministers abroad for pro-

8 *The Writings of Thomas Jefferson* (Andrew A. Lipscomb and Albert Ellery
Bergh, eds., 20 vols., Washington: Thomas Jefferson Memorial Association, 1905),
XV, 112 (May 10, 1817).

fessional careers was intended not to endorse a general theory
of rotation but to ensure that our distant overseas agents should
always be sensitive to American interests and policy. His requirement of respectability as a qualification for office was not
merely to retain the function of government within the ranks
of gentlemen, but also to consolidate public respect for the new
order. His insistence upon the embargo was designed not merely
to restore the freedom of the seas, but to test "for all time" the
usefulness of economic pressure as a means of avoiding war. He
endured the insults of the newspapers for years because he considered himself

the subject of a great experiment, which was to prove that an administration, conducting itself with integrity and common understanding, cannot be battered down, even by the falsehoods of a
licentious press, and consequently still less by the press, as restrained
within the legal & wholesome limits of truth. This experiment was
wanting for the world to demonstrate the falsehood of the pretext
that freedom of the press is incompatible with orderly government.[9]

Jefferson thus saw present problems of policy and administration in the light of the distant future toward which he intended
to guide his fellow citizens.

Contradictions in Jefferson's personality and philosophy were
amply illustrated by his views on executive power. By his own
words Jefferson derived no satisfaction from the exercise of authority. Writing to Destutt de Tracy nearly two years after his
retirement from the presidency, he declared, "if I know myself,
what I have felt, and what I have wished, I know that I have
never been so well pleased, as when I could shift power from my
own, on the shoulders of others; nor have I ever been able to
conceive how any rational being could propose happiness to
himself from the exercise of power over others." [10]

Fearing power, he nevertheless found himself forced to exercise it ruthlessly. His preferences were frustrated by circumstances that compelled him to abandon his own theories. He
fought the concentration of authority through most of his early

9 Jefferson, *Works* (Federal ed.), X, 368 (Feb. 11, 1807).
10 *Ibid.*, XI, 186 (Jan. 26, 1811).

public career, but as President he exercised a mass of power in the enforcement of the embargo that exceeded the Federalists' efforts in the enforcement of the Alien and Sedition Acts.

Time brought him, as Hamilton had predicted, to the justification of the authority he wielded. In 1803 he admitted the unconstitutionality of the purchase of Louisiana, invited Congress to join in this seizure of power, and proposed that they all throw themselves on the mercy of the country.[11] In 1807 he generalized his defense for such constitutional adventures in uncompromising terms: "On great occasions every good officer must be ready to risk himself in going beyond the strict line of the law, when the public preservation requires it; his motives will be a justification. . . ."[12] That this was no mere passing opinion is assured both by his official acts and by a subsequent avowal with regard to the duties of officers of high trust: "A strict observance of the written laws is doubtless *one* of the high duties of a good citizen, but it is not *the highest*. The laws of necessity, of self-preservation, of saving our country when in danger, are of a higher obligation."[13]

Jefferson's administrative career was on the whole a tragedy, despite the congenial years in the White House before the crucial personal decision to experiment with the embargo. Each of the three great occasions when he exercised executive authority ended in what he conceived to be personal defeat and disaster, magnified by a supersensitive personality. After two years as governor of Virginia (1779–81) an inquiry into his conduct was voted by the Assembly. Although handsomely acquitted by a unanimous vote, he was so shocked by the mere fact of the in-

11 Adams, *History of the United States,* II, 84; Jefferson, *Writings* (Memorial ed.), X, 407–11 (August 12, 1803).

12 *Works* (Federal ed.), X, 347, n. 1 (Feb. 3, 1807).

13 *Ibid.,* XI, 146 (Sept. 20, 1810). In the construction of means granted by Congress for the execution of law Jefferson was equally ready, and not merely in moments of crisis, to find powers that Congress might not have provided. "It often happens that, the Legislature prescribing details of execution, some circumstance arises, unforeseen or unattended to by them, which would totally frustrate their intention, were their details scrupulously adhered to, & deemed exclusive of all others . . . the constitution gives the executive a general power to carry the laws into execution. . . . So if means specified by an act are impracticable, the constitutional power remains, & supplies them." *Ibid.,* X, 441, n. (August 11, 1807).

vestigation that he wrote Monroe, "these injuries, for such they have been since acknowledged, had inflicted a wound on my spirit which only will be cured by the all-healing grave." [14] After over three years service as Secretary of State, he resigned in defeat and bitterness, and retired to Monticello where he shunned society for four years. At the close of eight years as President, he saw his policy of peace through economic coercion in collapse, his popularity gone, and his own self-confidence so shaken that he was reduced to "an unmeddling listener," abdicating his functions as Chief Executive. It was to his honor, and to the honor of the Virginia tradition of the duty of gentlemen to govern, that a man so sensitive as Jefferson to criticism should have returned again and again to assume the burdens and labors of his time.

II

Jefferson's first administration was marked by relative quiet in foreign affairs, by steady progress in the Republican program for domestic matters, by harmony between the executive and legislative branches, and by a mellowing of the harshness of partisan strife. Its tone was caught exactly by Henry Adams: "In perfect quiet, disturbed only by rumors of war abroad, spring crept forward to summer, summer ripened to autumn. Peace was restored with Tripoli; commerce grew apace; the revenue rose to $14,000,000; the Treasury was near a surfeit; no sign appeared of check to the immense prosperity which diffused itself through every rivulet in the wilderness, and the President could see no limit to its future increase." [15]

The achievements of Jefferson's first term bore directly on his great objects of quieting party antipathy and reducing the activities and the cost of the general government. The "monarchy-minded" leaders of the Federalist party he considered beyond the power of redeeming grace; but the great mass of moderate Federalists he believed could be attached to the Republican party by forbearance and skill. To them he declared in his First Inaugural, "We are all Republicans, we are all

[14] Gilbert Chinard, *Thomas Jefferson* (Boston: Little, Brown, and Co., 1929), p. 118.
[15] Adams, *History of the United States*, III, 12.

Federalists." By the end of six years there were still Federalists, but the political success of the Republicans was decisive. Although the embargo caused some party losses, they were soon regained. John Quincy Adams, one-time Federalist and son of a Federalist President, sat in the Republican caucus of 1808, and John Adams himself voted for the Republican candidate for President in the electoral college of 1820.

Jefferson's political successes were matched by innovations in policy and administration. In quick succession the army and the navy were reduced, the excise taxes were abolished, and economy was introduced wherever possible.

Only one circumstance marred the substantial serenity of these early years, the disposal of patronage. The Republicans demanded their share of office; the Federalists denounced Jefferson's removals; and for two years the political scene was disturbed by contention over appointments. The Administration was both perplexed and harassed. The President managed a skillful course and before the end of his first term he had satisfied his supporters and blunted the outcries of his enemies. The Republicans gradually but steadily acquired control of the offices with the passage of time; the Federalists slowly passed from the public stage or held a place on it as converts to the Republican cause.

Jefferson was fortunate, too, in his official family. His Secretary of State, James Madison, modest, scholarly, and loyal, was an old friend with whom it was easy to work in the field that Jefferson particularly commanded from long experience. His Secretary of the Treasury, Albert Gallatin, had been a tower of Republican strength in the House of Representatives, was perfectly at home in both the domestic and foreign field, knew Pennsylvania politics intimately, and was to become the principal administrative figure of the federal government for twelve years. "Three more agreeable men than Jefferson, Madison, and Gallatin were never collected round the dinner-table of the White House. . . ." [16] Henry Dearborn, Secretary of War, and Levi Lincoln, Attorney General, both from Massachusetts, were loyal and congenial, if relatively subordinate associates. Robert

16 *Ibid.,* I, 191.

Smith of Maryland, Secretary of the Navy, was a problem to Gallatin, but the hostility of Smith to an austere naval policy and to Gallatin personally was kept well under control until a weaker hand took over the presidency.

Jefferson's second administration was as tempestuous as his first had been smooth. The peace that had descended upon Europe in 1802 and that had briefly released the tension on American shores was brought to an end in 1803. In 1806 British interference with American commerce and impressment of seamen started the Republicans on a policy of commercial retaliation.[17] The subsequent British blockade of the European coast, Napoleon's paper blockade of Great Britain, the British Order-in-Council blockading all ports from which the British flag was excluded, and the Milan decree in which Napoleon declared any vessel good prize that submitted to British search (1806–1807) forced the Republicans to consider war or its alternatives.

In this anxious and perplexing dilemma Jefferson decided against war. He proposed peaceful coercion of the belligerent powers by asking Congress for an embargo on foreign shipment of American products. Tension mounted during 1808 between resisting merchants and shipowners on the one hand, and a stubborn administration on the other. Power was added to administrative power, but in the end Jefferson had to yield.

There followed two years of drift, preparations for war, and finally war itself. The crisis demonstrated administrative incompetence of alarming proportions. Civilian leadership was embarrassed by Madison's incapacity and by Cabinet disunity and instability. The President lost Gallatin in 1813, when he was forced out of the Treasury Department by the Smith faction. The country was in substantial bankruptcy by 1814. The army was dominated by ancient heroes of the Revolutionary War who suffered one disgrace after another. The navy had been built and organized for harbor defense and "annoyance" of enemy shipping; it proved powerless to prevent a strangling blockade of the American coast. Public opinion was deceived by some brilliant naval encounters between individual ships and by General Jackson's victory at New Orleans, but the leaders of the country knew better.

[17] Nonimportation Act, 2 Stat. 379 (April 18, 1806).

III

The War of 1812 was the great watershed in the Jeffersonian period. The attention of the people from 1793 to 1815 had been almost wholly concentrated on the international scene, the stage of the great struggle between Great Britain and France that had such incessant consequences upon the lives of Americans. After 1815 the attention of the nation was turned inward upon its domestic problems. Americans began to think of the continent on which they lived and from which they were to carve out their destiny. "A country," said Calhoun in 1819, "so vast in its means, and abounding, in its various latitudes with almost all the products of the globe, is a world of itself. . . ."[18] This world for the first time in its history could now settle down to its own tasks of internal improvement. "Every serious difficulty which seemed alarming to the people of the Union in 1800 had been removed or had sunk from notice in 1816. With the disappearance of every immediate peril, foreign or domestic, society could devote all its energies, intellectual and physical, to its favorite objects. . . . The continent lay before them, like an uncovered ore-bed."[19]

This profound change in situation and attitude did not go unnoticed by contemporary observers. Albert Gallatin wrote Matthew Lyon on May 7, 1816, "The war has renewed and reinstated the national feelings and character which the Revolution had given, and which were daily lessened. The people have now more general objects of attachment with which their pride and political opinions are connected. They are more Americans; they feel and act more as a nation; and I hope that the permanency of the Union is thereby better secured."[20] Hezekiah Niles had already sensed the same transformation from his editorial desk in Baltimore. ". . . the people begin to assume, more and more, a NATIONAL CHARACTER: and look at home for

18 *American State Papers: Documents, Legislative and Executive of the Congress of the United States* (38 vols. in 10 classes, Washington: Gales and Seaton, 1832–61), *Miscellaneous,* II, 535 (Jan. 7, 1819).

19 Adams, *History of the United States,* IX, 173.

20 *The Writings of Albert Gallatin* (Henry Adams, ed., 3 vols., Philadelphia: J. B. Lippincott, 1879), I, 700.

the only means, under Divine goodness, of preserving their religion and liberty. . . ." [21]

A sentiment of optimism gathered strength that surmounted the depression of 1819–22. Americans, always tending to be boastful, looked upon their accomplishments with pride, mixed with amazement and unbounded expectations of the future. The editor of the *Scioto* (Ohio) *Gazette* put down any skeptics in 1827 by asking them to consider

> . . . the astonishing and progressive improvements which have and are now taking place in the world. Let them but reflect that *fifty* years ago, the powers of the steam [engine] as a mechanical agent, were unknown to the world—that *forty* years ago, the idea of a vessel being driven by the propulsion of a steam engine was not suggested—and that *fifteen* years ago, there was not one steam boat running on either the Mississippi or any of its vast tributaries. Now, the power of steam, as a mechanical agent, is applied to almost every human purpose both on the land and on the water. . . . And now, there are about one hundred and twenty steam vessels on the Mississippi and its tributaries; and upwards of 300 on the waters of the United States alone. By the construction of railroads, and the introduction of the locomotive engine upon them, *distance itself will become annihilated! and the remotest parts of this vast empire be brought within the limits of a single neighborhood!* . . . the intelligence and enterprize of the present age can effect almost any earthly project.[22]

Events were not to move at quite this exuberant pace.

After the War of 1812 there ensued a short but important period of reconstruction and reform, compressed within the years 1816 to 1820. "The war," confessed the House Ways and Means Committee, "pointed our attention to the weak points of the nation." [23] The Treasury system of accountability was reconstructed and expanded, introducing changes that were to endure in principle until 1921. The War Department was provided with a General Staff, concentrated in Washington, that remained substantially unchanged until 1903. West Point was

[21] *Niles' Weekly Register* (Baltimore), IX, 1 (Sept. 2, 1815); hereafter cited as *Niles Register.*

[22] Quoted in *ibid.*, XXXII, 301 (June 30, 1827).

[23] House Report 91, 16th Cong., 1st sess., p. 9 (April 14, 1820).

reorganized, its curriculum and discipline greatly improved, and the influence of its graduates on civil construction as well as on military leadership so firmly set that it has never been disturbed. The Secretary of the Navy was provided with professional advice and an organ for professional administration in the Board of Navy Commissioners. The State Department, for the first time in its history, got a Secretary in John Quincy Adams who was concerned with the efficiency of its operations. New energy in the Post Office under John McLean led to astonishing results in expansion, efficiency, economy, and operating surpluses.

A new generation of federal executives took charge of the departments of state—men who scarcely remembered the Revolution and who looked forward to "that destiny beyond the reach of mortal eye" that Jefferson had invoked in 1801. William H. Crawford in the Treasury, John Quincy Adams in State, John C. Calhoun in War, Samuel L. Southard in Navy, Commodore John Rodgers, president of the Board of Navy Commissioners, John McLean in the Post Office—these were men of first-rate executive ability. Under their direction and largely at their initiative the administrative machine, now over a quarter century in motion, had its first overhauling.

Reorganization bore its own good fruit. Accounting arrearages were cleared up, top management was strengthened, and new vigor ran through the executive agencies. Niles recorded the gains in fulsome praise.

. . . the whole machinery of the government proceeds in beautiful harmony, to accomplish the sublime purposes of our institutions; and, though the nation is agitated with political strife, the administration goes on quietly and resolutely, to give effect to the laws, to protect persons and property, and to increase the means or apply the resources of our country, in its majestic march to greatness. These are subjects on which the *patriot* dwells with delight. . . .[24]

IV

While these administrative events were taking place, a long struggle went on within the Republican party over major issues

[24] *Niles Register*, XXXIII, 241 (Dec. 15, 1827).

of public policy. Party did not seriously affect administration from 1801 to 1829; there were no changes in party control and the Federalist conception of a permanent public service was already strong enough when coupled with Virginian ideas of propriety to keep party demands upon administration under control. The struggle within the party, identified with two wings that were broadly termed the "old Republicans" and the "new Republicans," was, however, to have important consequences upon the relations between the legislative and executive branches. It is therefore convenient to record here the main aspects of this division of opinion.

For a few years the Federalists remained a potential danger to the Jeffersonians, but their influence rapidly waned and eventually disappeared after the evil spirit of the Hartford Convention. John Quincy Adams was prophetically correct when he declared in 1802: "The power of the administration rests upon the support of a much stronger majority of the people throughout the Union than the former administrations ever possessed since the first establishment of the Constitution. Whatever the merits or demerits of the former administrations may have been, there never was a system of measures more completely and irrevocably abandoned and rejected by the popular voice. It never can and never will be revived." [25]

The field was thus left to the Republicans, but major differences of opinion soon emerged among them. The basic original stock of Republican ideas contained such concrete proposals as rigid economy, the rapid payment of the debt, the limitation of military and naval expenditures, the reduction of administrative discretion, the reference of most matters except foreign affairs to the states, the strict construction of the powers of the general government, and the supremacy of the legislative branch.[26] Madison, Monroe, Gallatin, John Randolph, Giles,

[25] *Writings of John Quincy Adams* (Worthington Chauncey Ford, ed., 7 vols., New York: Macmillan Co., 1913–17), III, 9 (Oct. 8, 1802).

[26] Jefferson to Elbridge Gerry, Jefferson, *Works* (Federal ed.), IX, 15 (Jan. 26, 1799). This was Jefferson's statement of political faith. Cf. the forthright letter of Macon to Jefferson, April 20, 1801, Elizabeth Gregory McPherson, ed., "Unpublished Letters from North Carolinians to Jefferson," *North Carolina Historical Review*, XII (1935), 269–70, and Jefferson's reply, *ibid.*, 270, n. 43 (May 14, 1801). See also Henry Adams' masterly statement of Republican principles in his work, *John Randolph* (Boston: Houghton Mifflin, 1882), p. 33.

Burwell, Macon, and others held firmly to this body of doctrine. They became known as the "old Republicans." [27]

Policies shifted with the passage of time. Jefferson abandoned the doctrine of strict construction when he purchased Louisiana; he deserted the doctrine of legislative dominance when he imposed his leadership upon Congress. The fate of strict construction as the ruling article of Republican faith was sealed when Calhoun and a steady congressional majority sought, although in vain, to make federal funds generally available for internal improvements. The drift of Republicans away from the older doctrines had become so clear after the War of 1812 that the dominant group became identified as the "new Republicans." They included such eminent figures as Henry Clay, John C. Calhoun, John Quincy Adams, and William H. Crawford. These men were nationalist in outlook; they were facing the problems of the present and the future, and were happily unvexed with the old antipathy between supporters of England and of France that had so embittered the philosophical differences between Federalists and Republicans. They stood for the broad construction of national power, for an active employment of those powers, for a strong navy, for a well-organized army, for a United States Bank, for a tariff, for internal improvements, and for a foreign policy that looked toward the further acquisition of territory.

The new school of Republicans was in the saddle after 1817, despite Monroe's opposition to certain forms of action in constructing and maintaining internal improvements. In his first annual message John Quincy Adams accepted the broad construction theory of the Constitution, and emphasized the duty of the state to be concerned with the "moral, political, intellectual improvement" of man.[28] It was perhaps as well that Jefferson did not live to read the annual Treasury report of 1828. The pendulum had swung full circle. A Republican Secretary of the Treasury, Richard Rush, invoked none other than Alex-

---

27 Adams' characterization of Macon suggests in part the quality of the old Republicans. *Memoirs of John Quincy Adams* (Charles Francis Adams, ed., 12 vols., Philadelphia: J. B. Lippincott, 1874–77), V, 204 (Nov. 21, 1820).

28 Richardson, *Messages*, II, 311.

ander Hamilton to confirm his own policy of positive action by the general government.

. . . Such were the counsels of a departed statesman, whose name peculiarly lives in the records of this Department; who was first placed at its head, directing its operations with a forecast so luminous as still to throw a guiding light over the path of his successors. His comprehensive genius, looking into futurity, and embracing in its survey all the interests that go to make up the full strength and riches of a great empire, saw the truth, now in course of corroboration by our own experience, that the protection and increase of manufacturing labor, far from stopping the springs of our commercial power, would but multiply and diffuse them.[29]

Despite their common political views, the "new Republicans" fell into chaotic factionalism after 1820 as the contest for the election of 1824 began. Intrigue and personality drove difference of principle off the stage of public affairs. Personal politics dominated the party scene until the close of John Quincy Adams' term. After 1825 the stage was cleared as politicians and the country took station for or against Andrew Jackson. The Adams wing of the Republican party in defeat formed one nucleus of the Whigs; the Jackson wing in victory accepted the party name of Democrats. The Republican party disappeared.

[29] Senate Doc. 7, 20th Cong., 2d sess., p. 9 (Dec. 6, 1828). Although a Republican, Rush had had long personal contact with the Adams family and was not unsympathetic to their views. See J. H. Powell, ed., "Some Unpublished Correspondence of John Adams and Richard Rush, 1811–1822," *Pennsylvania Magazine of History and Biography*, LX (1936), 419–54, and LXI (1937), 26–53, 137–64.

CHAPTER TWO

The State of the Nation

The changes occurring in the first quarter of the nineteenth century have often been overlooked, dwarfed as they were by the vast developments of the second. To one who, like John Quincy Adams, could compare the America he knew in 1800 with that which he saw in 1829, these years seemed to have wrought an almost magical transformation.

Advances, indeed, had taken place during the prosperous years of the first two Presidents. When Adams landed in Philadelphia on September 4, 1801, fifty-eight days out from Hamburg, and seven years away from his native land, he observed, "The appearance of our country has very much improved since I left it in 1794. I find everywhere the marks of peace within our walls, and prosperity within our palaces—for palaces they may truly be called, those splendid and costly mansions which since my departure seem to have shot up from the earth by enchantment." [1]

During Adams' service abroad the capital had been moved from Philadelphia to Washington—a transition that left Congressmen, officials, and diplomats, accustomed to the polished society of the capital city of Pennsylvania, stranded in the open fields and marshes on the banks of the Potomac, several miles from Georgetown.[2] It was long before the new capital would have been chosen as a desirable place in which to dwell. When Richard Rush came early in 1812 to the office of comptroller, he wrote John Adams that to a Bostonian or a Philadelphian,

1 Adams, *Writings*, III, 1 (Oct. 13, 1801).
2 Cf. the brilliant description of Washington at this time in Henry Adams, *History of the United States*, I, 30–31.

Washington appeared like a "meager village; a place with a few bad houses, extensive swamps, hanging on the skirts of a too thinly peopled, weak and barren country." [3] In 1811 William Wirt asked, "What is there in the rough, unbuilt, hot and desolate hills of Washington, or in its winter rains, mud, turbulence, and wrangling, that could compensate me for all those pure pleasures of the heart I should lose in such a vicin-ity?" [4] Still, the city did emerge from the swamps of the Tiber By 1830 its population of 39,000 exceeded the ancient towns o Lancaster and Annapolis, and was beginning to encroach o neighboring Georgetown. Its indifferent reputation as a cen of infection and disease was slowly improving as the death r declined.[5] Jefferson and most heads of departments, howe had resolutely refused to remain in the capital during the summer season, and their successors followed this pruden ample.[6]

Social life was lively. It included the diplomatic corps ranking military and naval officers, the principal civilia utive officers, and members of Congress. These were the days of Dolly Madison, and not even the austerity of or the dignity of John Quincy Adams diminished the round of parties, dances, and calls.[7] Rush recorded in mer of 1812 an informality of social life that was full "Since the bustle of Congress has passed over I visit dent very frequently in the evenings, where, whether or whether like myself, his secretaries or neigh

---

[3] J. H. Powell, *Richard Rush: Republican Diplomat, 1780–185* University of Pennsylvania Press, 1942), pp. 17–18.

[4] John P. Kennedy, *Memoirs of the Life of William Wirt* (2 v Lee and Blanchard, 1849), I, 322 (August 11, 1811); hereaft *Memoirs.*

[5] *Niles Register,* XXXII, 389 (Feb. 9, 1828).

[6] Cf. King's comment of August 20, 1803, that Washingt this season from the fixed opinion that no one could pass Au there without intermittent or bilious fever. *The Life and Cor King* (Charles R. King, ed., 6 vols., New York: G. P. Putna IV, 294; and Wirt's comment on August 1, 1820: Crawfor Calhoun to the Lakes, and Thompson already in New Yo 109.

[7] Among other sources, see Mrs. Samuel Harrison Smit *of Washington Society* (New York: Charles Scribner's So

strolled in to his tea table I pass the time delightfully. . . ." [8]

The rise of the new capital city was symbolic of growth in the territory and population of the United States. The area of the United States almost exactly doubled from 1800 to 1830, thanks to the acquisition of the Louisiana Purchase and Florida. The consequences of the fortunate accident of Louisiana were endless, politically, economically, and intellectually. In 1800 almost all Americans lived east of the Alleghenies and looked out from their ports to Europe and the West Indies. By 1830 they looked easily across the Alleghenies and the Mississippi to the Rocky Mountains. They had come into possession of a continent, and no longer sat merely on the narrow shelf of the Atlantic seaboard.

The population of the country had expanded threefold. The first census (1790) showed in round figures 4,000,000 inhabitants, the fifth (1830), 12,800,000. All three great divisions of the country, which seemed to some in the 1790's destined to form three independent sovereignties, shared in this growth. New England had nearly doubled, the three middle Atlantic states (New York, New Jersey, Pennsylvania) had fallen somewhat short of quadrupling, and the south Atlantic states had doubled.

But the significant change in the seat of the population occurred across the Alleghenies, facilitated by the Cumberland road and the Erie Canal. In 1800 the territories west of Pennsylvania (Ohio, Indiana, Illinois, Michigan, and Wisconsin) could muster only 51,000 inhabitants, mere islands among hostile Indians on an open prairie. In 1830 these states and territories boasted 1,400,000 inhabitants, more than all New England in 1800. So likewise the territories west of the Carolinas and Georgia, in which the census of 1800 revealed 335,000 persons, had grown by 1830 to 1,800,000. Long fingers stretched hither, and areas that were virgin forest and prairie unknown to the census taker in 1800 appeared in the columns of 1830— Michigan, Arkansas, and Florida Territories—names strange to the school children of Massachusetts and Virginia who learned the states and their capitals when Madison took over the administration from a weary Jefferson in 1809.

Powell, *Richard Rush,* p. 38.

Immense tracts of rich land were being wrested from the wilderness. The busy village enlivened the spot "where but as yesterday the sullen bear dozed away half his existence." [9] "What a march of power and of improvement is manifested," exclaimed Hezekiah Niles in 1826 as he viewed these marks of progress. "Within the perfect recollection of middle-aged men, Ohio, and all beyond, was the home of the savage—hardly ever trodden by the foot of civilized man—now it has a third rank, because of its physical strength, among the states of the union." [10]

Jefferson himself saw the first tide of new states taking their place beside the venerable thirteen. Vermont, Kentucky, and Tennessee had been admitted before he became President, and he himself signed the bill admitting Ohio (1803). In 1812 Louisiana became a state, and as soon as the War of 1812 came to a close, in steady procession year by year came the march with a single exception from across the mountains: Indiana (1816), Mississippi (1817), Illinois (1818), Alabama (1819), Maine (1820), and Missouri (1821). This burst of energy exhausted contemporary possibilities, but the erection of new territorial governments foreshadowed new members of the federal family. Michigan Territory had been organized in 1805, Arkansas Territory in 1819, and Florida Territory in 1822.

Most Americans still lived in the country. The proportion of rural population in 1830 was calculated at 91.3 per cent.[11] The cities were, however, fastening their grip on the seaboard, progressively strengthening Jefferson's apprehension of the fate of his country.[12] The wagons, carts, stages, and other carriages which passed over the bridges into Boston in one day, or over Boston neck, were counted in 1826. They numbered 5,010.[13]

[9] *Niles Register*, XV, 1 (August 29, 1818).

[10] *Ibid.*, XXXI, 106 (Oct. 14, 1826).

[11] I.e., 11,738,000 out of 12,866,000; U. S. Bureau of the Census, *Historical Statistics of the United States, 1789–1945* (Washington: Government Printing Office, 1949), p. 25.

[12] Cf. Joseph Story to Sir William Scott, May 20, 1820: "The example of your great manufacturing cities, apparently the seat of great vices, and great political fermentations, affords no very agreeable contemplation to the statesman or the patriot, or the friend of liberty." *Life and Letters of Joseph H. Story* (William W. Story, ed., 2 vols., Boston: Charles C. Little and James Brown, 1851), I, 385.

[13] *Niles Register*, XXXI, 134 (Oct. 28, 1826).

New York by 1830 had just passed the 200,000 mark, wresting primacy from Philadelphia at 160,000. These were by far the greatest. Baltimore could command only 80,000, and Boston, which in 1800 was abreast of this southern metropolis, could muster only 60,000. The startling disclosures of the census of 1830 were not, however, the indices of growth along the seaboard, but the sudden emergence of two inland urban centers: Albany at the head of the Erie Canal, still in mortal struggle with Troy; and Cincinnati, astride the Ohio. While these were yet the only two cities of consequence in the interior, they bespoke the future.

During this quarter century the United States remained primarily a nation of farmers, although the predominance of the agricultural interest was soon to be challenged by the manufacturers of New England and the middle states. The south and the rising southwest were solidly agricultural, their economy resting almost exclusively on cotton, tobacco, rice, and other products of the soil.

The middle states, Maryland, Pennsylvania, Delaware, New Jersey, and New York, were also great agricultural sections, producing wheat, corn, cattle, hogs, lumber, and other farm commodities. Baltimore, Philadelphia, and New York City were great seaports, and commercial, banking, shipping, and insurance interests dominated such centers. Supporting them, however, lay the vast hinterland producing that which they collected, bought, sold, and shipped.

The farms of New England, often perched on hills and covered with stones, had never held the place in the economy of this section that they naturally acquired in the fertile lands around Lancaster and York or in the tidelands of the south. Commerce, trade, shipping, and the cod and whale fisheries were the foundation of Yankee prosperity. This had been nearly wrecked by French and British aggression, the embargo, and the War of 1812, and although old activities were resumed in time of peace, they were supplemented and eventually surpassed by the rise of manufactures. Daniel Webster's conversion to a protective tariff was a symbol of the changes that were taking place in the New England economy.

Across the mountains agriculture was supreme. The virgin

prairies produced with a vitality unknown to the farmers on the older land of the seaboard. The only problem was to get wheat, pork, beef, and skins to the market. The Cumberland Road, even more the Erie Canal, gave an answer to the problem, but none could guess that these improvements, the miracles of their day, were so soon to be forgotten when a new wonder shot on iron rails across the mountains and over the prairies.

The predominance of a rural population and a farmer's life naturally set high the prestige of this class of the population. In 1808 Jefferson wrote his grandson, J. W. Eppes, "I do not know whether your father intends you for a profession, or to be a farmer. This last is the most honorable and happy of all. . . ." [14]

It was not farming, however, but manufactures that captured the interest and attention of the writers of the time. "*Pittsburg,* sometimes emphatically called the 'Birmingham of America,' will probably become *the greatest manufacturing town in the world,*" Niles declared in 1814.[15] Much was also expected of Lexington, Kentucky, which in 1811 manufactured hemp to the value of $500,000. "All sorts of mechanics are prosperous; and *town lots* sell as high as they do in *Boston. . . .* Society is polished and polite." [16]

The cotton manufactory at Waltham, Massachusetts, was an especial object of interest. It was reported in 1822 to have a capital of $600,000, a work force of about 500, and an annual output of 1,820,000 yards of cloth.[17] "It cannot be denied," Niles concluded in 1825, "that our manufactures have become one of the leading interests of the country. . . ." [18]

Contemporaries were rightly impressed with the growth of manufacturing enterprises. Not, however, until interior sources of raw materials and markets were made more accessible by means of the railroad were manufactures to come into their own. The steamboat helped; but the steam locomotive was the essential foundation on which a new economy was to rise after the Jeffersonian Republicans had left the stage of public affairs.

To what extent did the Jeffersonians accept any obligation

[14] Massachusetts Historical Society, *Proceedings*, 2d series, XII (1897–99), 270.
[15] *Niles Register*, VI, 208 (May 28, 1814); *ibid.*, VIII, 141 (April 29, 1815).
[16] *Ibid.*, VI, 250 (June 11, 1814).
[17] *Ibid.*, XXIII, 66 (Oct. 5, 1822).
[18] *Ibid.*, XXVII, 337 (Jan. 29, 1825).

on the part of the general government to help its citizens? Republican doctrine tended to leave such domestic affairs to the states. Congress did, however, enact a protective tariff in 1816 for the benefit of manufacturers, a major contribution to the changing economy that was disputed by Republicans of the stricter sect. For the most part, the general government did very little beyond carrying the mail, protecting American vessels and interests abroad, maintaining external peace, and encouraging education in the new states by reserving land for school purposes.

There was no department of internal affairs, despite much talk about its usefulness. The urgent need of western farmers was for means of transportation. Hampered by doubt of constitutional authority, the general government went no further than to build the Cumberland Road and a few military and post roads, usually of little commercial value. For the shipping and fishing interests Congress was more solicitous, and more certain of its legal footing.[19] It steadily built lighthouses, placed buoys and markers, and even in modest measure pulled snags out of the Ohio and Mississippi rivers.

For the most part, the improvement of the national estate was left to the states and to private enterprise. This was the era of state-incorporated turnpike companies, hopefully, if vainly, looking for profits from tolls. It was also the era of important state enterprises in the transportation field, of which by far the greatest and the most successful was the Erie Canal.

The climate of the time was not favorable, indeed, to the extension of federal government functions or expenditures. Farmers always relied upon themselves. Merchants needed no help in finding or keeping markets in the West Indies or in the China Seas. The infant industries alone turned to the general government for protection by tariff against foreign competition; and this assistance caused no multiplication of public office. Despite the glowing paragraphs of Richard Rush's annual Treasury reports, the temper of the time was more accurately stated by Jefferson in his first annual message: "Agriculture,

[19] For the rise of the port of New York, see Robert Greenhalgh Albion with Jennie Barnes Pope, collaborator, *The Rise of New York Port, 1815–1860* (New York: C. Scribner's Sons, 1939).

manufactures, commerce, and navigation, the four pillars of our prosperity, are then most thriving when left most free to individual enterprise." [20]

These sentiments were exemplified in two concrete situations coming to a head in 1824 and 1826. The first concerned safety on steamboats. A series of disastrous explosions of steamboat boilers set in motion a demand for the inspection of boilers and the licensing of engineers. The House Committee on Commerce reported a hazardous situation. "From habitual impunity the engine workers disregard the danger, and rather than suffer a boat to pass them, will increase the pressure of the steam to a dangerous extent. In addition to this risk, accidents may occur from carelessness, inattention, or drunkenness." [21] The undisciplined character of the engineers was suggested by the written report of a witness, David Prentice, who declared, "There is also a certainty that engineers will resent any interference with their absolute rule of their engines, and some of them are not at all unlikely to encourage (if the term may be used,) their boilers to burst, to throw odium on the law." [22]

With the sound of exploding boilers in their ears, the Committee on Commerce gingerly approached their task. ". . . they entered upon the investigation of this subject, with a deep sense of its importance, and a strong conviction of the great difficulties attending any legislative interference with the management of so extensive a branch of business." [23] They proposed, nevertheless, a number of regulations: that every steamboat should be enrolled and compelled to take out a coasting license; that every boiler should be made of wrought iron or copper, not cast iron; that every boiler should be inspected and provided with two safety valves, one inaccessible to the engineer; that the valves be set at not more than one-sixth in excess of the pressure calculated to be that which the boiler was able to sustain; and that a penalty be inflicted upon any person putting an additional weight on the safety valves.

These provisions might be thought reasonable in an era more

20 Richardson, *Messages*, I, 330.
21 House Report 125, 18th Cong., 1st sess., p. 2 (May 22, 1824).
22 House Doc. 69, 18th Cong., 2d sess., p. 17 (Sept. 10, 1824).
23 House Report 125, 18th Cong., 1st sess., p. 1.

instructed in the hazards of machines. They were not congenial to the eighteenth Congress, which referred the whole matter to the Treasury for further investigation. Crawford disposed of it in one sentence: "I am of opinion, that legislative enactments are calculated to do mischief, rather than to prevent it, except such as subject the owners and managers of those boats to suitable penalties in case of disasters, which cannot fail to render the masters and engineers more attentive, and the owners more particular in the selection of those officers." [24]

The second episode concerned manpower in the shipping industry. In the middle and late 1820's it was found difficult to attract lads either to the merchant marine or to the navy. A proposal was made to require every American vessel sailing in the foreign trade to engage a prescribed number of apprentices. The Senate Committee on Commerce reported that it was "fully aware of the imposing bearings . . . of the subject . . . and of the expediency of rearing and maintaining a body of seamen. . . ." [25] The committee was also worried about "trenching upon those cardinal principles of a Republican and equal government," without which any isolated interests would be of little value. It consequently concluded that

in a free State, where every one is entitled to cultivate his own vineyard according to the dictates of his own judgment, to require that it should be done in a prescribed form, and with a specific amount of labor, or power, would appear to be an interference with individual discretion, and an encroachment on the rights of the citizen, not sustained by principle, nor warranted either by the present or future interests, or by the real or imaginary wants of the community. [26]

Contemporary views of the duty of government in a depression were a part of the same pattern. John Quincy Adams, one

24 House Doc. 69, 18th Cong., 2d sess., p. 3 (Jan. 31, 1825). The termination of the Indian trading houses in 1822 was another demonstration of correct laissez faire theory. See below, ch. 32. Deviating from the general viewpoint was an act of 1819 prohibiting masters of sailing ships from bringing from foreign ports to the United States more than two passengers per five tons and specifying a minimum amount of water and provisions for each passenger from an American to a European port. 3 Stat. 488 (March 2, 1819).

25 Senate Doc. 85, 19th Cong., 1st sess., p. 1 (May 1, 1826).

26 *Ibid.*, p. 7.

of the most intelligent men of his generation and one ready to
use the powers of the general government for national purposes,
could see no remedy "but time and patience." [27] Government,
he thought, "can do nothing . . . but transfer discontents, and
propitiate one class of people by disgusting another. . . . the
arbiters of weal and woe, the healers and destroyers, Time and
Chance, must bring the catastrophe or the cure." [28]

Republican preferences for individual enterprise, frugal government, and reliance on the states for almost the whole of the
domestic polity had the inevitable consequence of holding the
activities of the general government to a minimum. There was
some expansion of the public service from 1801 to 1829, but it
could be traced almost entirely to the growth of the country
and the increasing volume of old established business. New activities and new objects of expenditure were conspicuously
absent.[29]

The relative stability of the administrative activities of the
federal government during the three decades, 1801–1829, stands
out in comparing the objects that attracted congressional support at the beginning and end of the period. They were nearly
identical. The principal purposes for which Congress made appropriations in the 1820's that were not included in their appropriations for 1800 were surveys of roads and canals, suppression
of the slave trade, construction of the Cumberland Road, and
building a few naval hospitals. The federal government had
been unable in nearly thirty years to find means of advancing
the estate of Americans that had not been put in motion by
1800, apart from a hesitant commitment to a single highway
into the West. The system of administration consequently did
not have to accommodate itself during these years to new tasks
or unaccustomed duties. It was a period of consolidation and
of growth, not of innovation.

The bare fact of expansion of established governmental func-

[27] Adams, *Memoirs*, IV, 375 (May 27, 1819).

[28] *Ibid.*, V, 129 (May 22, 1820).

[29] Jefferson argued that public works were always less well managed than
private enterprises, and thought it unwise "to abstract the high executive officers
from those functions which nobody else is charged to carry on, and to employ
them in superintending works which are going on abundantly in private hands."
Jefferson, *Writings* (Memorial ed.), XII, 108 (July 28, 1808).

tions and activities may be recorded in some simple figures. Expenditures charged against ordinary receipts averaged from 1801 to 1810 about 9 million dollars; from 1811 to 1820, including war expenditures, nearly 24 million; from 1821 to 1830, years of peace, slightly over 16 million.[30] That is to say, normal peacetime expenditures nearly doubled, but even so failed to keep pace with the growth of population.

The principal public service maintained by the federal government was the post office. In 1800 there were 903 post offices; in 1830, 8,450. In 1800 mail was transported over 20,000 miles of post road, which by 1830 had increased to 115,000 miles. The staff of the General Post Office showed a corresponding growth. In 1800 the business was conducted with a chief clerk and five clerks; in 1828 it required a chief clerk, thirty-six full-time and seven part-time clerks.[31] By the close of John Quincy Adams' administration the Post Office employed postmasters four times as numerous as the whole body of employees (excluding the Post Office) when Thomas Jefferson assumed office in 1801.

The state of the nation in 1828, in the eyes of the old Republicans, was better than the state of its government. The nation was prosperous; the clamor for federal money for internal improvements had been withstood; the states were vigorously performing the principal public business of the people; the end of the debt was in sight; the army was a skeleton and the navy reasonably well under control.

In the eyes of the new Republicans, the state of the general government was far from what they would have had it. The common agency of the whole people was not carrying its share of the good works that were so obvious to John Quincy Adams and Richard Rush. Congress was much too occupied with investigations of the administrative system, which, according to the new Republicans, was the particular province of the executive. Offices were understaffed, and officials were underpaid.

Both old and new Republicans, and Federalists as well, if some ancients still cared to call themselves such, could take satisfaction in the physical state of the nation. The country had in

30 *Statistical Abstract of the United States, 1949*, p. 328.
31 House Doc. 62, 20th Cong., 2d sess. (Jan. 9, 1829).

1829 great assets that it lacked in 1801; vast new territory, man-power multiplied nearly by three, the Cumberland Road, the Erie Canal, the Pennsylvania waterway and inclined railroad, turnpikes and bridges, roads from Washington to New Orleans and to Chicago, as well as from Jacksonville to Portland, the steam engine at work in factories and vessels, the cotton gin bringing wealth to the south, the production of basic com-modities on a scale far beyond that of the time of Jefferson, a population full of energy and contrivance. The country had peace: "No term, indeed, of *eight* years," said Rush in 1828, "since the establishment of the government, has been so exempt from the influence of external events that disturb the regular operations of national industry and commerce, as the last eight." [32]

Public men of every political sect might rejoice in these things. Their satisfaction was arrested by the shadow of the controversy over slavery which slumbered uneasily after the harsh debate leading to the Missouri Compromise. The clash on the admission of Missouri terrified those who saw the future with imagination. In oft-quoted passages Thomas Jefferson wrote, "In the gloomiest moment of the revolutionary war I never had any apprehensions equal to what I feel from this source." [33] And on another occasion, "this momentous question, like a fire bell in the night, awakened and filled me with ter-ror." [34] John Quincy Adams, then Secretary of State, declared the Missouri Compromise "a title page to a great tragic vol-ume." [35] Neither man lived to witness the fulfillment of his fears. But this fatal issue and its twin—the nature of the Union —belong to another period and to a field of study other than public administration.

The optimism engendered by the return of peace in 1815, by improvements in transportation, and by the rise of factories spread into a renewed conviction of the superiority of American democratic institutions of government. After Monroe's return from New England in 1817, Niles exclaimed:

[32] Senate Doc. 7, 20th Cong., 2d sess., p. 8 (Dec. 6, 1828).
[33] Jefferson, *Works* (Federal ed.), XII, 157 (Feb. 7, 1820).
[34] *Ibid.*, XII, 158 (April 22, 1820).
[35] Adams, *Memoirs*, IV, 502 (Jan. 10, 1820).

. . . Behold, the peace that prevails!—the president of the United States has travelled through the eastern section of the country unguarded, save by the respect of his *fellow citizens;* the regent of *England* proceeds to his parliament in a *bullet-proof* coach; and Louis, though yet surrounded by foreign bayonets, would tremble like an aspen leaf if one man were only to stamp his foot upon the shore of France. But these are *"legitimate sovereigns."* [36]

On another occasion he declared, "The sublime problem, so long held doubtful by political casuists, is completely solved— man *is* best able to govern himself, and that of a free republic *is* the strongest system yet devised for a social compact amongst men. . . ." [37] The editor of the *Trinidad Gazette,* observing the democratic experiment from the Caribbean Sea, was moved to exclaim on reading John Quincy Adams' inaugural speech, "There is something in the rising destiny of the extraordinary republic, which forcibly arrests attention. She stands like a light and a beacon in the midst of nations. Her public documents seem intended not for herself alone; they speak to the universe." [38]

These words were not written in praise of the administrative archives of the day, unknown to the editor of the *Trinidad Gazette.* He might have concluded, nevertheless, could he have read them, that they too spoke at times in a universal language. There was no Alexander Hamilton, to be sure, but other able men practiced the administrative craft. Without the benefit of an accepted doctrine, they reconstructed the system which managed to survive the War of 1812 so well that in some instances their work endured for generations.

36 *Niles Register,* XIII, 2 (August 30, 1817).
37 *Ibid.,* XV, 2 (August 29, 1818).
38 Quoted in *ibid.,* XXVIII, 184 (May 21, 1825).

THE JEFFERSONIANS

CHAPTER THREE

The Presidency

Twelve years of combat between the Federalists and the Republicans had shaped two opposing theories about the office of President, especially in its relations to Congress. All parties and public men accepted the principle of separation of powers, but agreement ended at the edge of the Constitution. The Federalists invested the office of President with the function and responsibility of leadership in matters both foreign and domestic; they construed its powers broadly; they feared legislative encroachment on its prerogatives; they fostered its freedom of action wherever possible and minimized the accepted checks that the Constitution had placed in the hands of the people's representatives.

The Republicans saw in all this a dangerous tendency toward monarchy, and some never recovered from their conviction that certain Federalist leaders secretly plotted for an American king. The Republicans placed their faith in the people and their representatives. They believed that policy and financial proposals should originate in Congress; they feared executive encroachment; they sought to limit executive discretion, especially in expenditures; they asserted the right of the House of Representatives to deny funds to implement a treaty and thus, in a negative way, to control foreign policy; they emphasized the importance of congressional committees to such a point that Fisher Ames complained these committees had become ministers.

The Federalists, with some limitations, made effective their own theory of the executive power from 1789 to 1801. The Republicans could only resist. What would they do when on

March 4, 1801, Jefferson and his friends took over the reins of government? They now possessed the means to revise the errors of their Federalist opponents by constitutional amendment if necessary, by statutory revision, or by alterations in the custom of the Constitution.

The Republicans in fact gave no serious consideration to constitutional amendments; they made only insignificant changes in statutory requirements; they made no important *considered* changes in the custom of the Constitution. Changes of a substantial nature eventually occurred, but they grew out of circumstances of personality and events, not from attachment to a theory of executive power. The constitutional structure remained intact; the struggle between the executive and legislative branches, which was quite independent of the attitudes of particular parties, went on under the same constitutional roof. The battle now was between Republicans in Congress and Republicans in the executive branch, and between the "old" and "new" wings of the party. The Federalists, with a complete lack of logic, aided and abetted the former.

The constitutional status and form of the office of Chief Magistrate were thus untouched. Some Republicans had leaned toward a plural executive as less likely to encroach on popular liberties, but the experience of the French Directory had cured them of this preference.[1] Washington's precedent of retirement at the end of his second term converted Jefferson from his original idea of a single seven-year term.[2] The constitutional formulation of executive power was acceptable to men of all parties. The Republicans consequently felt no impulse to fundamental change in the office of President, especially since one of their own number occupied it.

The story of the presidency under four Republican Chief Executives can be summed up briefly by stating that Jefferson fully maintained in practice the Federalist conception of the executive power; that Madison lost heavily to the legislative branch and carried the presidency to one of its lowest points; that Monroe, although hard challenged by the Speaker of the House, Henry Clay, was able to maintain executive leadership

1 Jefferson, *Works* (Federal ed.), XI, 183 (Jan. 26, 1811).
2 *Ibid.*, X, 124 (Jan. 6, 1805).

in foreign policy if not in domestic affairs; and that John Quincy Adams, as thoroughly committed in principle to executive leadership as his father, was unable to carry his principle into practice. He lost all opportunity to lead when factional opponents seized control of his second Congress in 1827. Leadership under the Republicans irresistibly followed the leaders—they were Jefferson and Gallatin for eight years, but for most of the remaining twenty they were Giles, Smith, and others in the Senate; Clay, Calhoun, Lowndes, and others in the House of Representatives.

Such a summation, however, leaves much unsaid. Insight into the character and vicissitudes of political leadership and top management requires some attention to the leading events and crises of these four successive administrations.

Disregarding what the Republicans had said about executive power while in opposition, Alexander Hamilton correctly foretold Jefferson's course when he became President. ". . . it is not true . . . ," said Hamilton, "that he is an enemy to the power of the Executive, or that he is for confounding all the powers in the House of Representatives. It is a fact which I have frequently mentioned, that, while we were in the administration together, he was generally for a large construction of the Executive authority and not backward to act upon it in cases which coincided with his views." [3] Jefferson himself once described the difference between the Republicans and the Federalists as that which existed between those who would give a little more weight to the legislative and to the executive branches respectively. Party doctrine, however, was more rigid on this and other matters; and the old Republicans must have been as astonished, privately, as were the Federalists, at the march of events during Jefferson's eight years.

The suspicious attitude of the Republican rank and file toward strong leadership was congenial to the marked individualism that characterized many of their members, and had become chronic as a consequence of the opposition role that was theirs during the first decade of their existence. Success in the election of 1800 did not mellow their convictions, and it was an open

[3] *The Works of Alexander Hamilton* (2d ed., Henry Cabot Lodge, ed., 12 vols., New York: G. P. Putnam's Sons, 1903), X, 413.

question whether they could be made to act together long enough to put through Jefferson's program.[4] Jefferson was constantly worried by factional controversies within the ranks of his party, and was eventually confronted with the hard choice either of allowing faction to wreck his program and perhaps fatally weaken his party, or of taking charge of the management of Congress.[5] He chose the latter course.

The institutional developments that accompanied this decision, notably the caucus and the floor leader, are considered in the following chapter. Here it will be enough to illustrate the character and decisiveness of Jefferson's leadership by a few examples. An early case arose in Jefferson's first Congress. The House intended to inquire into Federalist fiscal methods and for this purpose set up a committee to investigate. Gallatin promptly wrote the chairman, Nicholson, suggesting that the committee might make a general call for information, or might ask specific questions, a number of which Gallatin included. Two days later Nicholson presented Gallatin the questions that the Secretary had indicated he desired to be asked.[6]

The purchase of Louisiana in 1803 provided the first severe test of executive authority. Jefferson himself was satisfied that he had no constitutional authority to purchase territory, and Republican doctrine confirmed this reading of the Constitution. The stakes were so enormous that the President finally abandoned his scruples; no mention was made of the constitutional difficulty in his message recommending approval; [7] and his party followed silently the course he marked out for them.

4 On the subject matter of this and following chapters, see the able study by Ralph Volney Harlow, *The History of Legislative Methods in the Period before 1825* (New Haven: Yale University Press, 1917).

5 Congressman William B. Grove wrote, February 25, 1803, "It is very evident the majority in our House are kept together with much difficulty. . . . They have not a man of Business & strong talents in their party. . . . If we were to be 3 months longer in Session, I firmly believe the majority would split into Violent Coteries." *The Papers of John Steele* (Henry M. Wagstaff, ed., 2 vols., Publications of the North Carolina Historical Commission, 1924), I, 368–69.

6 Lucius Wilmerding, Jr., *The Spending Power: A History of the Efforts of Congress to Control Expenditures* (New Haven: Yale University Press, 1943), pp. 56–57.

7 Richardson, *Messages*, I, 358 (Oct. 17, 1803).

The circumstances surrounding the appointment of William C. C. Claiborne to be governor of Louisiana Territory, as told by Senator Plumer, illustrate Jefferson's control of his followers and his methods of persuasion.

The question was this day taken in the Senate upon the nomination of Mr. Claiborne to be governor of Orleans, & without debate was agreed to. The opposition to this appointment was a few days since very strong; but in a private caucus it was resolved by the democrats to agree to it. After the Senate was adjourned the Vice President observed at the fire that the Senate had agreed to advise to the appointment of Claiborne when not a single Senator beleived [*sic*] he was qualified for the office. And Genl Bradley, said that the President's dinners had silenced them—& that Senators were becoming more servile.[8]

The strict followers of the Republican "sect," as parties were often called at this time, broke away in 1806 under the impulse of the erratic but powerful John Randolph, who for four years had been Jefferson's floor leader in the House. As early as 1804 Randolph had given signs of a break with the liberal construction of the Constitution forced upon Jefferson and his followers by the Louisiana Purchase. Randolph reported against the remission of duties on books for schools and colleges on the ground that imports must be uniform and that no class should have exclusive privileges. He also reported against a bill to authorize Georgetown to build a dam to improve the navigation of the Potomac, arguing that Congress had no jurisdiction since the Potomac was the joint property of the abutting states of Maryland and Virginia.[9] Jefferson called such views "metaphysical subtleties."

The major split came in 1806. The President ardently desired to acquire West Florida, and in a public message hinted war with Spain to gain his end.[10] Randolph went to the White House for consultation and learned that Jefferson really wanted two

8 *William Plumer's Memorandum of Proceedings in the United States Senate, 1803–1807* (Everett Somerville Brown, ed., New York: Macmillan Co., 1923), pp. 220–21 (Dec. 12, 1804).

9 Henry Adams, *History of the United States*, II, 208–9.

10 Richardson, *Messages*, I, 388 (Dec. 6, 1805).

million dollars to buy the territory. Randolph was enraged, believing that Jefferson was not only guilty of duplicity but that he was casting upon Congress the responsibility for a pusillanimous retreat from executive vigor.[11] The issue was fought out in a bitter debate, resulting in Jefferson's victory. John Quincy Adams, then in the Senate, remarked, "The measure has been very reluctantly adopted by the President's friends, on his private wishes signified to them, in strong contradiction to the tenor of all his public messages. His whole system of administration seems founded upon this principle of carrying through the legislature measures by his personal or official influence." [12] At a convenient moment Randolph was removed from the chairmanship of the Ways and Means Committee.

The most dramatic demonstration of Jefferson's domination was the decision to impose an embargo late in 1807, and the subsequent action, legislative and administrative, taken during 1808 to stop all movements of American ships to foreign ports.[13] The policy and the means for its execution originated not merely in the executive branch but in the mind of Jefferson himself. His Cabinet was lukewarm or in opposition. The embargo was nevertheless dutifully supported by Republicans in the House and Senate through twelve months of mounting tension, hardship, evasion, and crisis. Even in January 1809, Congress obediently accepted Jefferson's demand for more power at a time when it was evident that the policy was a failure in its external objects and a dangerous source of discord internally. The sudden collapse of the embargo policy through Republican

[11] An account of this affair, sympathetic to Randolph's position, is found in William Cabell Bruce, *John Randolph of Roanoke, 1773–1833* (2 vols., New York: G. P. Putnam's Sons, 1922), I, 224 ff. See also Henry Adams, *op. cit.*, II, 208 ff.

[12] Adams, *Memoirs*, I, 403 (Feb. 7, 1806).

[13] See below, chs. 29–30, for an account of this remarkable administrative event. The tenor of executive control over Congress during this crisis is suggested by two excerpts from the Gallatin-Jefferson correspondence. In the first Jefferson proposed the draft of new enforcement legislation and concluded, "If you will prepare something on these or any other ideas you like better . . . Mr. Newton . . . will push them through the House." Gallatin, *Writings*, I, 380 (March 30, 1808). In the second Gallatin asked Jefferson for a policy statement to guide Congress. "Both Mr. Madison and myself concur in opinion that, considering the temper of the Legislature, or rather of its members, it would be eligible to point out to them some precise and distinct course." Henry Adams, *The Life of Albert Gallatin* (Philadelphia: J. B. Lippincott, 1880), p. 377 (Nov. 15, 1808).

defection ended Jefferson's leadership and marked the beginning of a long decline in the influence of the presidency.[14]

For nearly eight years, however, Jefferson's role as President was that which Washington and the Federalists had adopted from 1789 to 1801. His methods, however, were more subtle and indirect, suited both to his own personality and to the character of his followers. He prepared the way by informal conversation, by seeking the opinions of others while imparting his to them, by deference to the coordinate branch. The secret of his success is revealed in a letter to Captain Clark in the early stages of discussion of the Lewis and Clark expedition: "I have proposed in conversation, and it seems generally assented to, that Congress appropriate 10–12,000 dollars for exploring the principal waters of the Mississippi and the Missouri." [15] His success was so great that Timothy Pickering, Federalist Senator from Massachusetts, observed that Jefferson "secretly dictates every measure which is seriously proposed and supported. . . ." [16] The presidency under Jefferson thus maintained fully the authority and prestige that it had earned under Washington and John Adams.

During the succeeding eight years of Madison's administration (1809–17), the office lost heavily in both authority and prestige. Madison was a weak executive and after the elections of 1810 he was faced with strong men in the House of Representatives. He suffered, like his successor Monroe, from allegiance to the past and to the old Republican doctrines of strict construction and relative national inactivity. New forces were stirring beneath the troubled surface of the contemporary world that neither Madison nor Monroe grasped or directed.

---

[14] Jefferson was deeply shocked by the desertion of Congress, and under the influence of this disappointment sent Madison some interesting comments on the legislative branch. "I know no government which would be so embarrassing in war as ours. This would proceed very much from the lying and licentious character of our papers; but much, also, from the wonderful credulity of the members of Congress in the floating lies of the day. And in this no experience seems to correct them. . . . The evil, too, increases greatly with the protraction of the session, and I apprehend, in case of war, their session would have a tendency to become permanent." Jefferson, *Writings* (Memorial ed.), XII, 267 (March 17, 1809).

[15] *Ibid.*, X, 431 (Nov. 16, 1803).

[16] Harlow, *op. cit.*, p. 175.

Madison's ineptitude for executive office has often been re-marked. His figure was slight, his manner quiet and reserved, his speaking voice inadequate, his force of personality moderate.[17] He had played a conspicuous and able role in the House of Representatives, especially in the first Congress, and was beyond doubt a man of superior intellectual ability. But he lacked force and driving power, and was not endowed with political insight, wisdom, or art. He was not meant to be a leader of men, but rather an expounder and student of constitutional forms. He would have been much more at home as president of the University of Virginia, later established by Jefferson, than he was as President of the United States.

Madison suffered his first major defeat at the very beginning of his administration. He intended to appoint Gallatin, then in the Treasury, to the Department of State. A coterie of hostile Senators told him that the Senate would not confirm Gallatin in this position. Madison was obliged to yield, and was forced to accept Robert Smith of Maryland, brother of Senator Samuel Smith, one of the active leaders of the hostile Senate faction. Robert Smith was both incompetent and disloyal to his chief.

Gallatin remained as Secretary of the Treasury, but he endured the steady opposition of the Smith faction. Early in 1811 he suffered a crucial defeat when the bill to recharter the United States Bank was defeated in the Senate by the casting vote of the Vice President, George Clinton. Madison apparently did not raise a hand to influence Congress on this major issue, nor to assist Gallatin in its defense. In March 1811 Gallatin offered his resignation.[18] Madison had hitherto declined to exert himself against the factional intrigues in his own party, but faced with this crisis, he removed Robert Smith from the State Department, installed James Monroe in his place, and retained the services of Gallatin.

The Smith faction bided its time. In 1813 Madison nominated Gallatin to be minister to Russia, on leave from the Treasury. Senators Smith and Giles, supported by the Federalists, refused

17 After attending a White House ball in 1810, Joseph Story wrote to his wife, "Mr. Madison seemed very little fitted for the scene. His grave and sober character and retired life lead him far from the pleasantries of a coterie." Story, *Life and Letters*, I, 196.

18 Gallatin, *Writings*, I, 495 (March 5[?], 1811).

to confirm, alleging incompatibility of a diplomatic appointment with the office of Secretary. Madison had planned to have Treasury business conducted by the Secretary of the Navy in Gallatin's absence, and Gallatin had left the country in April 1813 with this understanding. The Senate rejected the nomination on July 19, 1813, another major defeat for the President, in the midst of war. Madison yielded and nominated the relatively incompetent George W. Campbell of Tennessee to the Treasury in February 1814. Gallatin was eventually confirmed to the Russian court, having thus been forced out of Madison's Cabinet against the President's will.

Madison, like Jefferson, cherished peace. For two years (1809–1811) American relations with Great Britain and France drifted; the great experiment of the embargo had failed and Madison hopefully waited on events to bring a solution of the diplomatic crisis. Time brought him no help, but his second Congress placed him face to face with new men, principally from the south and west, who seized the initiative in foreign affairs and compelled acceptance of their war policy by a reluctant and unprepared administration. Leadership passed to the House of Representatives; the executive receded into the background.

The disastrous course of the war cast endless discredit upon the Administration, culminating in the burning of Washington in 1814. Madison and his Cabinet were obliged to flee in various directions. Probably the lowest point ever attained in the prestige of the presidency was reached during these inglorious days. Madison had to tell his Secretary of War, Armstrong, that

violent prejudices were known to exist against the administration . . . particularly against me and himself as head of the War Department; that threats of personal violence had, it was said, been thrown out against us both, but more especially against him; that . . . the temper of the troops was such as made it expedient, if possible, that he should have nothing to do with them; that I had within a few hours received a message from the commanding General of the Militia informing me that every officer would tear off his epauletts if Genl Armstrong was to have anything to do with them. . . .[19]

---

[19] *The Writings of James Madison* (Gaillard Hunt, ed., 9 vols., New York: G. P. Putnam's Sons, 1900–1910), VIII, 301 (August 29, 1814).

Threats of personal violence against a President driven from his capital and wandering about on horseback in the Virginia countryside, insubordination of troops against their commander, were events unheard of in the United States before or since.

James Monroe brought to the White House a stronger personality than that of Madison, although a capacity for leadership decidedly less than that of Jefferson. Van Buren assessed him in these terms: "Mr. Monroe's character was that of an honest man, with fair, but not very marked capacities, who, through life, performed every duty that devolved upon him with scrupulous fidelity." [20] Monroe had a strong sense of his own importance, and had been filled with ambition, military and political. Recalled by Washington from his post as minister to France, he defended his reputation by publishing a vindication of his conduct. John Randolph sought the caucus nomination for President for Monroe in 1808, and later he became governor of Virginia. In Madison's Cabinet he demonstrated vigor and decisiveness, although his energy was sometimes misdirected. He tended toward formality, and when he finally entered the White House, he introduced some of the formalism and stiffness that had prevailed under Washington.[21] He was the last President to cling to the knee breeches and buckles characteristic of the Revolutionary period. He was in more ways than one an "old Republican."

Monroe not only believed that the President should allow Congress to make up its own mind on domestic matters without influence from the Chief Executive; with an occasional exception he put his theory into practice. The greatest political issue of his day was the admission of Missouri and the status of slavery in Louisiana Territory. During all the bitter debates, he remained silent and abstained from interference in the strug-

[20] *The Autobiography of Martin Van Buren* (John C. Fitzpatrick, ed.), American Historical Association, *Annual Report, 1918*, II, 119.

[21] "People seem to think we shall have great changes in social intercourse and customs. Mr. and Mrs. Monroe's manners will give a tone to all the rest. Few persons are admitted to the great house. . . . Altho' they have lived 7 years in W. both Mr. and Mrs. Monroe are perfect strangers not only to me but all the citizens." Mrs. Samuel Harrison Smith, *The First Forty Years of Washington Society*, p. 141.

gle.[22] When the bill was finally laid on his desk he asked Cabinet advice on its constitutionality and eventually gave it his signature.[23] His course of action was perhaps politically wise, perhaps politically inevitable, but it abdicated leadership. Indeed in 1818 Justice Story, watching events from the Supreme Court, declared that "the Executive has no longer a commanding influence. The House of Representatives has absorbed all the popular feeling and all the effective power of the country." [24]

On the other major domestic issue, federal aid for internal improvements, Monroe gave Congress advance intimation of his opinion that an amendment to the Constitution would be required.[25] This warning did not prevent Congress from enacting a bill for the repair of the Cumberland Road in defiance of the President's views. Monroe vetoed the bill.[26]

Monroe, like Madison, faced powerful men in the House and Senate, particularly Henry Clay. Opposition broke out early in the field of foreign policy, Clay advocating recognition of the South American colonies of Spain then struggling for their independence. Monroe and his Secretary of State, Adams, were not yet prepared for these steps. When eventually they believed the time ripe, Monroe hesitated to use his undoubted executive power of recognition until he had asked Congress to agree to provide funds for diplomatic representatives, thus yielding executive initiative to congressional approval.[27]

Adams wrote in his diary before a year of Monroe's administration had passed, "Mr. Clay had already mounted his South American great horse. . . . Clay's project is that in which John Randolph failed, to control or overthrow the Executive by

---

[22] Cf. his letter to Jefferson in which he commented on the "menacing" situation, and indicated his reliance on the "vast portion of intelligence and virtue in the body of the people" as the means of escape from the threat to disunion. *The Writings of James Monroe* (Stanislaus Murray Hamilton, ed., 7 vols., New York: G. P. Putnam's Sons, 1898–1903), VI, 115 (Feb. 19, 1820).

[23] W. P. Cresson, *James Monroe* (Chapel Hill: University of North Carolina Press, 1946), pp. 340–50.

[24] Story, *Life and Letters*, I, 311 (March 12, 1818).

[25] Richardson, *Messages*, II, 8 (March 4, 1817); and more specifically, *ibid.*, II, 18 (Dec. 2, 1817).

[26] *Ibid.*, II, 142–44, 144–83 (May 4, 1822).

[27] *Ibid.*, II, 117, 118.

swaying the House of Representatives." [28] Visiting the President
in March 1818, he found Monroe's mind absorbed by the
"violent systematic opposition that Clay is raising against his
Administration." [29] At the end of another two years Adams observed, "One of the most remarkable features of what I am
witnessing every day is a perpetual struggle in both Houses of
Congress to control the Executive—to make it dependent upon
and subservient to them. They are continually attempting to
encroach upon the powers and authorities of the President." [30]

Monroe succeeded in timing South American recognition
and in announcing the doctrine that has become forever associated with his name. In domestic affairs, he was less successful
in positive leadership. He blocked federal funds for internal
improvement; but in the retrenchment program of 1820–22 he
was unable to protect the army and the navy from heavy cuts.
Indeed, like Madison on the Bank issue, he apparently made
no effort to come to the aid of Secretaries Calhoun and
Smith Thompson, each of whom was trying to defend his own
agency.

The presidency under Monroe suffered from two principal
handicaps. He was at odds with his party members in the House
on the constitutional authority of the general government to
undertake programs of internal improvement. His Cabinet was
torn to pieces in his second administration by internal strife
among three members, each of whom intended to succeed him:
Crawford, Calhoun, and Adams. Adams noted in his diary,
"There is slowness, want of decision, and a spirit of procrastination in the President, which perhaps arises more from his situation than his personal character." [31] At the same time, Monroe
was recognized by so astute a politician as Martin Van Buren as
a President who could not be driven. In a major conflict over a
minor issue, the appointment of the postmaster at Albany, Van
Buren asked his political friends to address a communication
to the President. He added a particular caution: "It can scarcely
be necessary for me to say, that that should be done with the

28 Adams, *Memoirs*, IV, 28 (Dec. 6, 1817).
29 *Ibid.*, IV, 70 (March 28, 1818).
30 *Ibid.*, IV, 497 (Jan. 8, 1820).
81 *Ibid.*, IV. 27 (Jan. 9, 1818).

utmost delicacy and respect. This is extremely important. If the petition should in the least degree wear the aspect of threatening or scolding, it would be ruinous." [32]

While a stronger President than his predecessor, Monroe was overshadowed by Clay in the House and by the individual ability and prominence of his able Cabinet members. He echoed Thomas Jefferson's oft expressed sentiments when writing to the sage of Monticello in 1824, "I shall be heartily rejoiced when the term of my service expires & I may return home in peace with my family. . . ." [33]

John Quincy Adams was temperamentally a man to restore the presidency to its original high estate.[34] He did not hesitate to protect his office against congressional encroachment. When approached informally by a friendly Congressman for a confidential disclosure of secret service expenditures, Adams instantly declared that the secret was enjoined upon him by the Constitution and law and that he would not divulge it.[35] He held strong convictions that it was the duty of the general government to use its powers for the common good and he was not concerned with the constitutional hesitations of his immediate predecessors. He was not content to conceal his views or to withhold his program for fear of opposition. He was familiar with the congressional scene and with the operation of the executive branch. His own self-reliance and independence of judgment confirmed him in his intention to lead Congress in an active program of governmental achievement.

In his inaugural address Adams forecast his program. It was Federalist in its conception, and boldly rejected the constitutional position of Jefferson, Madison, and Monroe. Shortly afterward in his first annual message Adams recommended a broad program of internal improvements, a national university, an observatory, scientific exploration and voyages of discovery.

---

[32] Catharina V. R. Bonney, compiler, *A Legacy of Historical Gleanings* (2d ed., 2 vols., Albany: J. Munsell, 1875), I, 375.

[33] Monroe, *Writings*, VII, 43 (Oct. 31, 1824).

[34] The admirable biography of John Quincy Adams by Professor Bemis is principally concerned with his diplomatic career. See Samuel Flagg Bemis, *John Quincy Adams and the Foundations of American Foreign Policy* (New York: Alfred A. Knopf, 1949).

[35] Adams, *Memoirs*, VII, 475 (March 15, 1828).

Congress was in no mood to respond to these sentiments. Adams had not commanded as many electoral votes as Andrew Jackson and had been elected President by the House of Representatives. He had no decisive mandate either from the country or from the electoral college. He faced opposition from the outset. Henry Clay was confirmed as Secretary of State by the votes of twenty-seven Senators against fourteen. Clay's favorite project, supported by Adams, to send envoys to the Panama Conference, was bitterly fought in the House, and so long delayed as to have become pointless. The internal improvement program encountered all the opposition that had for years delayed large-scale operations, and Adams won authorization only to survey the Florida canal route, to make stock subscriptions to the Louisville and Portland Canal and the Dismal Swamp Canal, to grant lands to Illinois and Indiana for canals to be built by these states, and to remove snags, stumps, and obstructions from the Ohio River.

Adams' second Congress marked the end of his effective influence. His opponents won control of both the House and the Senate, the first occasion on which such a division between the executive and legislative branches had occurred. Privately Adams predicted the election of Jackson in 1828, and to that event all energies were bent during Adams' last two years. The center of gravity settled again in Congress; and Congress, as Binkley well puts it, "spent its energy in a grand inquest into the conduct of the Executive." [36]

The history of the presidency during the quarter century and more from 1801 to 1829 was dictated, in short, more by personalities and events than by doctrine and theory. The Republican doctrine of legislative supremacy replaced the Federalist theory of executive leadership because, after 1809, Presidents were weak or frustrated by factional opposition beyond their control, not because Presidents avowed as a guiding principle their subordination to Congress. Jefferson succeeded by abandoning this part of his doctrine, not by waiting for Congress to discover the needs of the country and to enact laws to meet them. He assumed the leadership of Congress in defiance

[36] W. E. Binkley, *The Powers of the President* (Garden City, N. Y.: Doubleday, Doran, 1937), p. 68. The grand inquest is noted below in ch. 7.

of what he preferred theoretically as appropriate democratic practice.

The first war crisis found at the head of the government a man without talent for organizing the force of his country, for selecting its military leaders, for inspiring public confidence, or for providing national leadership. Fortunately in its succeeding military crises the country was not again to be so destitute of energy in the office of the Chief Executive. Its lack from 1812 to 1815 nearly destroyed the influence of the presidency at the time.

The heavy hand of past commitments to doctrine denied both Madison and Monroe the opportunity to lead Congress in the great domestic issue of the day—the construction of roads and canals. Congress was ripe for such leadership and would have responded to it. In the absence of positive guidance, Congress took matters in its own hands and made two major efforts to give the country what it so badly needed, despite presidential vetoes. The best that Madison could do for internal improvements was to recommend a sterile constitutional amendment. Monroe cautiously suggested a more promising lead but still advocated an amendment. Neither in war nor in peace from 1809 to 1825 did the President take the opportunities that the times provided. John Quincy Adams recognized his opportunity, indeed his duty, but could not prevail against his factional enemies.

It is of some significance to note that no President before 1829 undertook to buy leadership or legislation with patronage.[37] Congressmen were increasingly eager for influence in appointments and made some inroads on the executive domain, but the practice of using patronage to get votes in either House was rare and would have been thought corrupt. No President, naturally, was unaware of the political implications of his appointments and probably none failed on occasion to smooth the path of legislative accommodation by a suitable appointment. The institution of bartering patronage for legislation, however, did not exist.

[37] There is evidence, however, that patronage was brought to bear in connection with the Chase impeachment. Albert J. Beveridge, *The Life of John Marshall* (4 vols., New York: Houghton Mifflin, 1916–19), III, 181–82.

Nor did any President "go to the country." The facilities for such a course were almost wholly lacking, and probably none of the four Presidents whose administrations form the subject of this study possessed the personal qualities that would have made such an appeal either feasible or successful. Monroe toured the country to inspect the coast fortifications with the deliberate purpose of emphasizing their importance, but this issue was not contested by any party or faction. The interplay of policy and administration went on in relatively narrow official circles, not in general public exposition.

Despite the prestige of Virginia and Massachusetts that supported the presidency for its first forty years under Federalists and Republicans alike, the office failed to maintain the position that Washington, John Adams, and Jefferson had established. Congress on the other hand developed both an intention and a capacity to assert itself in affairs of state, not merely in the grand strategy of government but also in the lesser business of administration.

CHAPTER FOUR

The President and Congress: Institutional Developments

During the years when the presidency was undergoing the wide fluctuations in power and prestige that have just been recorded, a number of institutional developments occurred that in part reflected the rise and fall of executive leadership, and in part supported the dominance now of the executive, now of the legislative branch. Although sharp chronological boundaries cannot be set for the growth of institutions, it is clear that developments from 1801 to 1809 were designed to facilitate Jefferson's influence in Congress. It is also evident that after two years of indecision, the changes from 1811 to 1825 were designed to facilitate the will of Congress. Both chronology and the convenience of analysis and exposition thus permit the contrast of institutional growth in these two relatively compact periods.

By way of background the reader may recall that the outstanding feature of procedure in the first House of Representatives was the important part given to the Committee of the Whole.[1] The first discussion of policy and the basic decisions on policy were reached in Committee of the Whole *before* reference to a select committee for the drafting of a bill to embody these decisions. In Committee of the Whole complete freedom of

[1] On the subject matter of this chapter, see Ralph Volney Harlow, *The History of Legislative Methods in the Period before 1825;* and Wilfred E. Binkley, *President and Congress* (New York: A. A. Knopf, 1947).

debate prevailed and the full membership of the House was thus involved in the initial and formative discussion.

As party lines began to appear, this very democratic but somewhat cumbersome method of procedure was modified by the invention of the party caucus to help crystallize Federalist opinion, and by the establishment in 1795 of the standing Committee on Ways and Means. At the Federalist meetings Alexander Hamilton was frequently, if not regularly, present. Members of both Houses and of the executive branch could thus secure some degree of unity of action.

The Republicans insisted on the initiation of money bills in the House, and fought the Federalist practice of depending on the Secretary of the Treasury for fiscal plans. In the second session of the third Congress the rules were amended on Republican principles to require every proposal regarding a revenue law to be discussed in Committee of the Whole, and to forbid the House to make any increase in any tax until sanctioned by Committee of the Whole. All appropriations were likewise first to be moved and discussed in this committee.[2] The procedure was not intended to be and was not in fact conducive to executive leadership.

Hamilton withdrew from the Treasury in January 1795, and his successor did not aspire to continue Hamilton's role. When Albert Gallatin entered the House on December 7, 1795, he found, as he put it, that the "financial department in the House was quite vacant, so far at least as the opposition was concerned. . . ."[3] Gallatin became the financial mentor of the Republicans forthwith, and a consistent theory and procedure began to appear on their part. Gallatin's first move was to establish the standing Committee on Ways and Means, "to superintend the general operations of finance." The House also now appointed two standing committees, one on claims, and one on commerce, manufactures, and agriculture.

The appointment of these committees was a manifestation of Republican theory of legislative-executive relations. The members of the House, in their opinion, ought to be the mainspring

2 *Annals of the Congress of the United States*, 3d Cong., p. 881 (Nov. 13, 1794).
3 Henry Adams, *Life of Albert Gallatin*, p. 157.

of the whole system, but the House needed organization. "Just as the heads of departments were looked upon as agents of the executive, so the committees would be considered as agents of the House." [4] The Ways and Means Committee in particular was designed as a counterweight to Treasury influence.

The Federalists renewed their control of the House in 1795, more firmly in 1797, but accepted the standing committee system. In 1800, however, just in time to facilitate the fiscal operations of the Republicans, the Federalists reestablished the duty of the Secretary of the Treasury to submit annual estimates of expenditure and plans for finance.

Jefferson became President of the United States with a Republican majority requiring better organization than that to which it had been accustomed as the party of the minority. The refractory individualism of the congressional rank and file has already been noted. The quality of Mr. Jefferson's followers is perhaps symbolized in John Quincy Adams' description of one of them, William A. Burwell, for a short time Jefferson's secretary and later a member of the House from Virginia for fourteen years.

. . . He was a man of moderate talents and respectable private character, full of Virginian principles and prejudices, a mixture of wisdom and Quixotism, which has done some good and much mischief to the Union. Burwell took no lead in anything. He scarcely ever spoke; never originated a measure of any public utility, but fancied himself a guardian of the liberties of the people against Executive encroachments. His delight was the consciousness of his own independence, and he thought it heroic virtue to ask no favors. He therefore never associated with any members of the Executive, and would have shuddered at the thought of going to the drawing-room. Jealousy of State rights and jealousy of the Executive were the two pillars of Burwell's political fabric, because they are the prevailing popular doctrines in Virginia. He floated down the stream of time with the current, and always had the satisfaction of being in his own eyes a pure and incorruptible patriot. Virginia teems with this brood more than any other State in the Union, and they are far from being the worst men among us. Such men occasionally render service to the nation by prevent-

4 Harlow, *op. cit.*, p. 158.

ing harm; but they are quite as apt to prevent good, and they never do any.[5]

Faced with the necessity of combining Republican majorities into effective means of action, Jefferson shrewdly made no overt move to impose formal executive direction. Instead, with Gallatin's help, he established his outposts in Congress itself.[6] The principal innovation was the establishment of a floor leader who was recognized as the spokesman for the President. Under the Federalists, the floor leader had been an assistant to the Speaker, but not in any sense a representative of the President. Under Jefferson, floor leaders "were presidential agents, appointed by the executive, and dismissed at his pleasure." [7] They included William B. Giles, Caesar A. Rodney, John Randolph, and Wilson Cary Nicholas.[8]

Jefferson was acutely aware of the necessity for organization and leadership in the House to support his program. Writing to DeWitt Clinton in 1803 he said, "our leading friends are not yet sufficiently aware of the necessity of accommodation & mutual sacrifice of opinion for conducting a numerous assembly, where the opposition too is drilled to act in phalanx on every question." [9] When he failed to see the right man in the House to expedite its business, he did not hesitate to suggest that the right man run for Congress. At the very end of 1802 he wrote to Caesar A. Rodney, "Congress is not yet engaged in business of any note. We want men of business among them. I

---

5 Adams, *Memoirs*, V, 281 (Feb. 16, 1821).

6 The Republicans took no advantage of the office of Vice President as a potential member of the presidential team. Burr (1801–05) was in disgrace; George Clinton (1805–12) at the outset was "totally ignorant of all the most common forms of proceeding." According to Senator J. Q. Adams a worse choice for Vice President could scarcely have been made. Adams, *Memoirs*, I, 385 (Jan. 15, 1806). Clinton asked to have notice of long speeches "that he might take the opportunity to warm himself at the fire." *Ibid.*, I, 400 (Feb. 3, 1806). Elbridge Gerry served only a year, and was too old to cut any figure. Daniel D. Tompkins (1817–25) was politically prominent but not close to Monroe. Calhoun (1825–29) was himself an active candidate to succeed J. Q. Adams; each man played his own game.

7 Harlow, *op. cit.*, p. 177.

8 Cf. J. Q. Adams: "Mr. Giles continues to be our *Director*, and in general meets with little opposition to what he thinks beneficial to the public service." *Writings*, III, 104 (Jan. 5, 1805). Giles was then in the Senate. See Dice Robins Anderson, *William Branch Giles* (Menasha, Wis.: Banta Publishing Co., 1915).

9 Jefferson, *Works* (Federal ed.), X, 55 (Dec. 2, 1803).

really wish you were here. I am convinced it is in the power of any man who understands business, and who will undertake to keep a file of the business before Congress and press it as he would his own docket in a court, to shorten the sessions a month one year with another and to save in that way 30,000 D. a year." [10] Rodney had already been elected to the next Congress, with Jefferson's help, defeating the eminent Federalist James A. Bayard, and took his seat in October 1803.[11]

In the middle of his second term Jefferson was even more explicit. Writing to Wilson Cary Nicholas, he declared:

> . . . There is one subject which will not admit a delay till I see you. Mr. T. M. Randolph is, I believe, determined to retire from Congress, and it is strongly his wish, & that of all here, that you should take his place. Never did the calls of patriotism more loudly assail you than at this moment. After excepting the federalists, who will be 27., and the little band of schismatics,[12] who will be 3. or 4. (all tongue), the residue of the H of R is as well disposed a body of men as I ever saw collected. But there is no one whose talents & standing, taken together, have weight enough to give him the lead. The consequence is, that there is no one who will undertake to do the public business, and it remains undone. Were you here, the whole would rally round you in an instant. . . . Let me beseech you then to offer yourself. You never will have it so much in your power again to render such eminent service.[13]

Nicholas yielded and was elected to the House. He served from 1807 to 1809, when he resigned on account of ill health.

The floor leader was only one source of Jefferson's strength. Another was the party caucus, originated by the Federalists and now put to work by the Republicans. Beginning promptly with Jefferson's first Congress, the Republicans made regular use of this party device.[14] No records were kept and it is now impossible to retrace the respective influence of executive and con-

---

10 *Ibid.*, IX, 415–16 (Dec. 31, 1802).

11 *Dictionary of American Biography*, XVI, 82–83. Rodney had been active in Delaware politics, in 1807 became Attorney General of the United States, was elected to the U. S. Senate in 1822, and died in Buenos Aires in 1824 while serving as first American minister to the Argentine Republic.

12 I.e., John Randolph and his followers.

13 Jefferson, *Works* (Federal ed.), X, 370–71 (Feb. 28, 1807).

14 Harlow, *op. cit.*, p. 187.

gressional leaders in these conclaves. It is reasonable to presume that Gallatin played an important part, and it was alleged that Jefferson occasionally presided.[15]

The caucus was the formal aspect of the close relations that existed among the leading Republicans, whether of the legislative or executive branches. During John Adams' administration the Francis Hotel had been the convenient meeting place of Jefferson's friends; now they met at Gallatin's house. His home became the recognized headquarters of the party leaders. Macon, Randolph in the earlier years, Nicholson, Nicholas, Baldwin, and others were constant visitors. It was easy and natural for present members to gather intimately around their one-time congressional associate. Henry Adams observed that "much of the confidential communication between Mr. Jefferson and his party in the Legislature passed through this channel."[16]

Gallatin in fact worked as closely with Congress as Hamilton had done. The practice of referring policy matters to the heads of departments, that had been fought so strenuously by the Republicans in the 1790's, was revived. Thus Gallatin was asked by the House to prepare a plan for amending the duties on imports, and to digest the laws for the collection of duties and registering ships, recommending necessary alterations.[17] The Secretary of the Treasury attended committee meetings, and at times made known his preferences for committee chairmen.[18] John Quincy Adams, who was present at the meeting of the Senate Committee of Finance, January 27, 1807, noted in his diary that evening, "Mr. Gallatin, the Secretary of the Treasury, was there, who gave some explanations on particular sections of the bill. We agreed to report it without amendment."[19] At the critical moment of committee decision on the proposed two million dollar appropriation for the purchase of Florida, Gallatin met the chairman of the committee, John Randolph, at the door of the committee room.[20] Gallatin drafted a report for the Committee on Foreign Relations dealing with the embargo

15 *Ibid.*, p. 188.
16 Adams, *Life of Gallatin*, p. 302.
17 *Annals*, 7th Cong., 2d sess., p. 568 (Feb. 21, 1803); *ibid.*, p. 644 (March 3, 1803).
18 Henry Adams, *op. cit.*, p. 363.
19 J. Q. Adams, *Memoirs*, I, 447.
20 William Cabell Bruce, *John Randolph of Roanoke*, I, 227.

crisis and recommending measures for defense which the committee chairman, Campbell, presented to the House.[21]

In short, the relations between the Secretary of the Treasury and both Houses of Congress were intimate, continuous, and influential from the beginning to the end of Jefferson's administration. They were vital in facilitating the extraordinary compliance that Jefferson drew from his party followers in the two Houses. Jefferson put the end result in terms of understatement when he wrote in 1806, "In a house of Representatives of a great mass of good sense . . . principles of duty & patriotism induced . . . them . . . to vote as was right. . . ." [22]

This is a convenient point to note that executive bill drafting was known throughout the Republican regime. In 1804 Jefferson sent the draft of a bill on foreign armed vessels in American harbors to his then floor leader, John Randolph, with a covering letter that revealed some lack of equanimity on procedure.[23] A year later Jefferson and Secretary of War Dearborn worked out a bill to classify the militia by age groups, a matter in which Jefferson was deeply interested. He sent a final draft of the bill to Dearborn, adding, "Will you be so good as to communicate it to General Varnum & Mr. Bidwell? The sooner the better." [24] Senator John Quincy Adams called at Gallatin's office March 5, 1808, to show him a bill that he had reported, "with a request that he would examine it and propose such alterations or amendments as he might think proper." [25]

The practice continued under subsequent administrations. In 1818 Calhoun drafted an army bill at the request of the House Committee on Military Affairs.[26] In 1820 Crawford and Adams drafted an amendment to a bill on trade with the British colonies pending in the House, following a Cabinet discussion.[27] In 1825 Southard and Adams went over the draft of a

---

[21] Gallatin, *Writings*, I, 435 ff.; Harlow, *op. cit.*, p. 183.

[22] Jefferson to Monroe, *Works* (Federal ed.), X, 260 (May 4, 1806).

[23] *Ibid.*, X, 118–22 (Nov. 19, 1804).

[24] *Ibid.*, X, 211, n. (Dec. 31, 1805). Varnum and Bidwell were leading members of the House.

[25] Adams, *Memoirs*, I, 519.

[26] House Doc. 54, 15th Cong., 2d sess. (Dec. 22, 1818).

[27] Adams, *Memoirs*, IV, 504 (Jan. 15, 1820).

bill to establish a naval school.[28] Lesser figures than Secretaries
also submitted bills dealing with their own problems. In 1816
the commissioner of the General Land Office wrote directly to
the chairman of the House Committee on Public Lands, transmitting the draft of a bill to reprint the edition of the land laws
authorized in 1810. The destruction of the Treasury in 1814 had
consumed the available supply and not a copy was to be had at
any bookstore.[29] In at least one case a member of the Supreme
Court drafted a bill to improve the law.[30]

The floor leader, the party caucus, the intimate personal relations between members of the two branches, the willingness of
the House to accept drafts of important bills, went far to maintain effective working relations. The use of the veto power,
however, implied a breakdown of understanding. It was used
very infrequently, but with grave consequences for public
policy. The two outstanding instances were Madison's veto of
Calhoun's internal improvement bill and Monroe's veto of the
tollgate bill for repairs on the Cumberland Road. They served
to block national action in the construction of roads and canals.
Monroe's effort to enlighten Congress concerning his views on
this subject aroused suspicions that he was improperly attempting to control the free judgment of the legislative branch. As
John Quincy Adams observed, "the exercise of actual control
by the President over the opinions and wishes of a majority of
the legislature will never be very palatable in what form soever
it may be administered." [31]

Jefferson, in short, built up a highly centralized system, operated for the most part by conference, consultation, and free discussion rather than by harsher means of leadership. The development of this very machinery was to make possible, as
Harlow has demonstrated, "a radical change in the relationship
between executive and legislature." [32] If the House leaders
should get control of the machinery of caucus, floor leader, and
speakership, they would be in a position to control the whole

28 *Ibid.*, VII, 90 (Dec. 22, 1825).
29 General Land Office, Miscellaneous Letters, VI, 561 (April 18, 1816). This
series is in the National Archives.
30 Story, *Life and Letters*, I, 315.
31 Adams, *Writings*, VI, 381 (July 6, 1818).
32 Harlow, *op. cit.*, p. 192.

executive administration. Precisely this development was to occur as Jefferson left the stage. The institutions he developed were turned in the direction that Republican theory dictated.

Madison, as has already been noted, was unable to lead Congress. Two years of vacillation and floundering ensued from 1809 to 1811, followed by a remarkable reversal of form when Henry Clay and the young War Hawks appeared at the opening of the twelfth Congress, November 4, 1811. "The twelfth Congress was the very opposite of its inactive, blundering, leaderless predecessor . . . there were able, influential leaders in the House . . . [who] compelled the administration to follow their lead." [33]

One major institutional development that accompanied this transfer of the seat of power was the congressional nominating caucus. Washington and Adams had become President by reason of their situation, and the understanding of the Republicans in 1796 and 1800 to vote for Jefferson required no formal management. It seems certain, however, that a caucus of the party members of the two Houses of Congress was held by both parties in 1800 to agree on nominees for the Vice President. [34] Nominating caucuses drawn from party members in Congress were held in 1804 and regularly at four-year intervals to agree on candidates for President and Vice President until the final Republican caucus of 1824. The Republican caucus of 1808 was the first to make a vital decision. Madison was generally expected to become Jefferson's successor, but he was hated by John Randolph, who devoted himself to pushing the not unwilling James Monroe. The latter's friends, eventually perceiving that they were outnumbered, refused to attend the caucus; Madison was duly nominated and elected. Crawford's dangerous effort to seize the nomination in 1816 from Monroe became the signal for intensified opposition to the caucus, and the failure of Crawford's campaign in 1824 as the caucus nominee ended this method of nominating candidates for the office of Chief Executive.

[33] *Ibid.*, pp. 199–200.

[34] The evidence is presented in the standard work on this subject, Frederick W. Dallinger, *Nominations for Elective Office in the United States* (New York: Longmans, Green, 1897), pp. 13–21.

The operation of the congressional nominating caucus in the successive elections from 1800 through 1824 was such as always to imply and on occasion to make explicit executive subordination to congressional President-makers. "Jefferson," observed Harlow, "had made the Republican party, and as maker he ruled it. The party in its turn made Madison president, and what need was there to bow before the idol it created?"[35] In 1812 there was reason to believe that the renomination of Madison was delayed by the caucus leaders until he gave assurance of his support of congressional war policy. Monroe's second nomination was *pro forma* but the consequences of the nominating procedure were not lost on John Quincy Adams, who was already looking forward to 1824. In his diary he commented on "the numerous evils" consequent upon the congressional nominating caucus:

> . . . a practice which places the President in a state of undue subserviency to the members of the legislature, and which, connected with the other practice of re-electing only once the same President, leads to a thousand corrupt cabals between the members of Congress and the heads of the Departments. . . .
> The only possible chance for a head of Department to attain the Presidency is by ingratiating himself personally with the members of Congress; and, as many of them have objects of their own to obtain, the temptation is immense to corrupt coalitions. . . .[36]

The authority of party leaders in Congress was without doubt amplified by the operations of the nominating caucus; but it was not a continuous means of influence. The transformation of the office of Speaker, and the use of the Speaker's powers by Henry Clay, were innovations that steadily and continuously cut down the relative position of the President.[37]

Election of the Speaker had been a partisan affair since 1793, when the Federalist candidate, Theodore Sedgwick, was defeated by the newly achieved Republican majority. In 1795 and 1797 the Federalists elected their candidate, Dayton, and in

35 Harlow, *op. cit.,* p. 194.
36 Adams, *Memoirs,* IV, 242 (Feb. 3, 1819).
37 Mary Parker Follett, "Henry Clay as Speaker of the United States House of Representatives," American Historical Association, *Annual Report, 1891,* pp. 257–65.

1799 put Sedgwick in the chair. The Republicans replaced him in 1801 with Nathaniel Macon and thenceforward the contest was merely one within the Republican ranks. Down to 1811 the Speakers were "keen guardians of party interests," but neither Federalist nor Republican Speakers were the real party leaders.[38] The Speaker was still only a moderator.[39]

The election of Henry Clay as Speaker in 1811, the first of six almost unanimous selections to this office, marked a profound change in its character and in the effective leadership of the government. Clay was chosen Speaker on an issue that President Madison seemed unable to grip, and with the intention of forcing national action despite the President's incapacity to act—war with Great Britain. Clay succeeded in this purpose, and until the last day of Madison's administration the initiative in public affairs remained with Clay and his associates in the House of Representatives. He was at odds with Monroe during most of the latter's administration and carried through the House a whole series of measures that Monroe opposed with more or less force. Miss Follett concluded that from 1811 to 1825 Clay was the most powerful man in the nation.[40]

The speakership thus provided from 1811 to 1825 a center of initiative and influence either lacking in the presidency or inadequate to the times. The need of Congress for leadership was evidenced by its own incapacity from 1809 to 1811, and on the two occasions from 1811 to 1825 when Clay was not a member of the House.

The nominating caucus and the new role of the Speaker were the two principal institutions that occasioned the transfer of power from the executive to the legislative branch. The capacity of Congress to meet its broader obligations was enlarged by an inner transformation that built up the influence of the standing committees. By 1825 there were well over twenty, including six standing committees on expenditures in the various

---

[38] M. P. Follett, *The Speaker of the House of Representatives* (New York: Longmans, Green, 1896), p. 69. This principal study of the speakership contains a list of Speakers to date of publication.

[39] Hubert Bruce Fuller, *The Speakers of the House* (Boston: Little, Brown, 1909), p. 31.

[40] Follett, *Speaker of the House of Representatives*, p. 79.

departments.[41] The old system of discussion in Committee of the Whole, under slight control, was wrecked by its cumbersome procedure. The transfer of responsibility from Committee of the Whole to a substantial number of standing committees and the consequent subdivision of labor and opportunity for specialization of members' interest and competence made the House, under Clay's direction, an effective instrument of action.

The standing committees could and did serve also as a convenient means of friendly communication when friendship held sway in the highest ranges of government. Gallatin had originated the standing Committee on Ways and Means as a check on the Treasury Department, but as soon as the Federalists resumed control of the House the committee ceased to act independently. The Committee on Post Offices and Post Roads maintained good working relations with the Postmaster General except in the early years of Monroe's administration, when it launched a series of hostile investigations. During the War of 1812 Monroe, while Acting Secretary of War, constantly consulted the House Committee on Military Affairs and drew bills for it.[42] Until Clay began his independent course on foreign policy, the House Committee on Foreign Relations "was little more than the legislative agent of the department of State." [43] When cooperation between Congress and President was forthcoming, the standing committees served the invaluable function of providing the executive and legislative branches with a common body of like-minded deputies, "specialized agents of the majority." [44]

When, however, conflict raged, the committees became the ready agents of congressional leaders to impose their will on the executive. When Clay put John Randolph on the Committee on Foreign Relations in December 1819, Adams concluded, correctly enough, that the object was "to prevent anything's being done congenial to the views of the Administration." [45] In 1827 Adams' factional enemies elected the Speaker, and the Speaker fulfilled the President's expectations by ap-

---

[41] See below, ch. 7. Harlow gives a list, *op. cit.*, pp. 214–16.

[42] *Ibid.*, pp. 239–40.

[43] *Ibid.*, p. 242.

[44] *Ibid.*, p. 248.

[45] Adams, *Memoirs,* IV, 507 (Jan. 16, 1820).

pointing "four opposition to three Administration men on all the committees." [46]

Before the advent of Henry Clay, the election of Speaker was hardly an event to call for much presidential concern. By 1820 the influence of the Speaker had become so great that it was inevitable that any Administration would seek the election of a candidate friendly to its views and prepared to appoint committees that would expedite rather than hinder its program. The selection of Speaker in November 1821 appears to be the first instance in which the issue was clearly faced, but Monroe, clinging to sound old Republican doctrine on the separation of powers and the independence of Congress, declined to exert the slightest influence. Preliminary precautions taken by the Secretary of State, John Quincy Adams, quickly disavowed by the President, throw much light on the practical consequences of this point of view.

The story begins on the morning of November 29, 1821, when John W. Taylor, Speaker of the previous House and a candidate for reelection, called on Adams. They had "a free conversation" on matters political, at the close of which Taylor explicitly declared his allegiance to the Administration. Adams took this as "a promise of good behavior if he should be chosen Speaker," and outlined the President's policy as contained in his pending annual message.[47] The next morning Adams was called upon by a member of Taylor's New York congressional delegation, John D. Dickinson, who informed the Secretary of State that Taylor could not command the votes of his own delegation. "I told Dickinson that I had never on any occasion spoken to a member of Congress upon the choice of a Speaker, before or pending an election. But if the question was to turn upon the friendliness of the Speaker to the Administration, I had reason to expect that Mr. Taylor would be friendly. . . . And from various important political considerations I wished Mr. Taylor might be re-elected." [48]

Adams reported these conversations to the President and asked for advice. Monroe said "he believed the proper course

46 *Ibid.*, VII, 377 (Dec. 10, 1827).
47 *Ibid.*, V, 428–29 (Nov. 29, 1821).
48 *Ibid.*, V, 431 (Nov. 30, 1821).

would be to take no part in it at all." [49] Adams argued the contrary position and withdrew, to discover the next morning that Calhoun was strongly opposed to the reelection of Taylor, "insisting on the unnatural aspect of the Administration supporting one, who had at least always acted as its enemy, against those who had been its warm and steady friends." [50] Calhoun thought Taylor was in a coalition with Crawford and Clay and had appointed unfriendly committees during the last Congress. On the same afternoon, after a Cabinet meeting, Monroe told Adams definitely that "he had concluded to take no part whatsoever in the election of the Speaker. . . ." Adams at once declared that he would follow the same policy.[51] Taylor was defeated by Philip C. Barbour of Virginia.

Clay was elected Speaker in 1823; Taylor did not run and Barbour was easily defeated. Adams became President in 1825 and when Congress met in December he had already had several conversations with Taylor. In his diary of December 4, 1825, is the significant entry: "Mr. John W. Taylor spent the evening with me, conversing upon the prospect of the Speaker's election, and upon the composition of the committees in the event of his success. . . . With regard to the committees, I supposed he could not displace the chairmen generally, who had been such in the last Congress, but he was disposed to arrange the members so that justice may be done as far as practicable to the Administration." [52] Taylor's election on the second ballot was noted by Clay as "evidence of the strength of the Administration." [53] The election of Andrew Stevenson in 1827 by a vote of 104 to 94 was discouraging evidence of Adams' loss of strength. As he said, "This settles the complexion of the House." [54]

Whenever the choice of Speaker involved a clear contest for power between the friends and enemies of an Administration,

49 *Ibid.*, V, 432.

50 *Ibid.*, V, 435 (Dec. 1, 1821).

51 *Ibid.*, V, 436. Adams later reminded Monroe "of the proposal that I had made to him, by the use of such influence upon members friendly to the Executive as might properly be exercised, to permit . . . the re-election of Taylor as Speaker." *Ibid.*, V, 474 (Jan. 2, 1822).

52 *Ibid.*, VII, 70.

53 *Ibid.*, VII, 71 (Dec. 5, 1825).

54 *Ibid.*, VII, 367 (Dec. 3, 1827). Taylor had conferred with Adams a few days before this election. *Ibid.*, VII, 363 (Nov. 29, 1827).

it could hardly be expected that the abstract theory of separation of powers would permanently restrain a President from interfering. Monroe stood on doctrine but Adams accepted the alternative. He won, and then he lost.

The gulf between the views of a President such as Monroe and the convictions of a President such as Adams on the selection of a Speaker marked the range within which the broad relations of President and Congress fluctuated in these years of change. Jefferson maintained a firm control of Congress by holding in his hands his party majority, and thus continued the Federalist conception of leadership in the office of Chief Executive. The true Republican doctrine of congressional primacy came into its own in 1809, and the institutional developments, centering on the congressional nominating convention, the office of Speaker, and the rise of the standing committees, went far to make congressional capacity for action feasible under other circumstances than presidential leadership. John Quincy Adams was not content to remain in the shadow of Congress and undertook to renew the strength of the presidential office. That he failed was due both to political combinations against him, and to his own deficiencies in the art of leadership.

While these great movements were thus causing the fortunes of the executive branch to rise and fall and sway over a quarter century, the administrative duties and authority of the President remained substantially unchallenged, and in large measure followed their own independent evolution. To this aspect of the administrative history of the Jeffersonians we now turn.

CHAPTER FIVE

The President and the Administrative System

Variations in the President's position with respect to Congress had no counterpart inside the administrative system. The Constitution was explicit in vesting the executive power in the President. Both Hamilton and Jefferson readily accepted their subordination to Washington, and John Adams had imposed the rule of subordination on obstinate Timothy Pickering. The Republicans had no quarrel with these constitutional provisions and broadly no complaint about Federalist practice under them. The primacy of the office of Chief Executive vis-à-vis department heads and subordinate administrative authorities was common ground.

With brief hesitation the Federalists recognized Jefferson's right to appoint his own department heads. The transition was made without friction and with the courtesy of gentlemen, except for John Adams' hasty departure from Washington to avoid witnessing Jefferson's inauguration.[1]

[1] The change of party control did, nevertheless, involve considerable taking of stock by the new Administration, partly to find any evidence of maladministration by the Federalists, partly to inform heads of departments of the condition of their agencies. There was an investigation of the Treasury, and of the fires that destroyed Treasury and War Department records. Madison wrote Jefferson a week before they took office, "I take for granted one of the first steps of the new adm^n. will be to institute returns, particularly in the Navy & war dep^{ts}. of the precise state in which every circumstance involved in them, comes into the new hands. This will answer the double purpose of enabling the public to do justice both to the authors of past errors & abuses and the authors of future reforms." Madison, *Writings* (Hunt ed.), VI, 418 (Feb. 28, 1801). Republican

[60]

The political and intellectual superiority of the first Republican President over his Cabinet members would have assured his authority and their subordination, irrespective of constitutional provisions. Gallatin and Madison were the only figures of eminence among those whom Jefferson gathered about him, and their loyalty to their chief never wavered. President Madison, too, for mere intellect, overshadowed his associates, but he lacked the force of personality to ensure his moral authority. Monroe was equaled or surpassed by some members of the strong Cabinet he assembled: John Quincy Adams, Calhoun, and Crawford; and his constitutional status was far from matched by his personal authority. Adams clearly topped his department heads, none of whom apart from Clay possessed an important national position. The personal capacities of Presidents thus buttressed the constitutional position.

Foreign affairs dominated the attention of the general government from 1789 to 1815 and remained important thereafter. The competence of Presidents in this central field also helped to confirm the dominance of the Chief Executive. Every President from John Adams to John Quincy Adams, except Madison, was a specialist in foreign affairs with considerable experience abroad and constant preoccupation with foreign policy. Three Secretaries of State in succession went to the White House—Madison, Monroe, and John Quincy Adams. Clay doubtless expected he was in the direct line of succession when he became Secretary of State in 1825.

The superior administrative position of the President stands out as sharply when viewed from the vantage point of the department head. John Quincy Adams, in stating his own principles as Secretary of the State Department, put in writing what other department heads accepted in practice. He wrote to his wife, Abigail:

. . . For myself I shall enter upon the functions of my office with a deep sense of the necessity of union with my colleagues, and with a suitable impression that my place is *subordinate*. That my duty

---

reaction to John Adams was expressed in a private letter from Gallatin to his wife. "Mr. Adams left the city yesterday at four o'clock in the morning. You can have no idea of the meanness, indecency, almost insanity of his conduct. specifically of late." Adams, *Life of Albert Gallatin,* p. 265 (March 5, 1801).

will be to *support,* and not to counteract or oppose, the President's administration, and that if from any cause I should find my efforts to that end ineffectual, it will be my duty seasonably to withdraw from the public service. . . . The President, I am sure, will neither require nor expect from me any sacrifice of principles inconsistent with my own sense of right, and I hope I shall never be unmindful of the respect for his character, the deference to his sentiments, and the attachment to his person, due from me to him, not only by the relative situation which he has placed me to himself, but by the gratitude with which his kindness ought to be requited.[2]

Adams did not, however, assume that he should refrain from independent advice to the President, irrespective of the latter's preferences or opinions. Policy differences will appear in subsequent paragraphs in which Adams stoutly held to his own views. The situation was aptly illustrated in a proposed appointment of a Secretary of the Navy. Monroe had decided upon either Simon Snyder, former governor of Pennsylvania, or Smith Thompson. Adams wrote in his diary, "As he appeared to incline strongly in favor of the latter, I presented to him all the considerations which operate in favor of the other." [3] Thompson was appointed. On another occasion Adams opposed Monroe's choice for a district judge but was overruled. He noted, "by the Constitution, the responsibility for appointments rests with the President and Senate. And when a head of Department is consulted upon a nomination which he disapproves, his duty of resistance ceases when the President has decided." [4]

The problem of conflict of views on policy between Presidents and Secretaries seems not to have been contemplated by the public men who had been invited to join Cabinets before Monroe entered the State Department in 1811. Whether any of the not infrequent declinations to join Presidents' official families may have been due to policy disagreements is not known, but as a rule these refusals were due to personal, not public, considerations. The issue arose in 1811 when Madison reconstituted his Cabinet by discharging the Secretary of State, Robert Smith, and by inviting Monroe, then governor of Virginia, to

2 Adams, *Writings,* VI, 182 (May 16, 1817).
3 *Memoirs,* IV, 144 (Oct. 26, 1818).
4 *Ibid.,* IV, 445 (Nov. 23, 1819).

accept this office. Monroe had been an advocate of an understanding with Great Britain while Madison was thought to lean
toward an accommodation with France. Monroe was unwilling
to join Madison if policy commitments had already been made
that would bar further consideration of his views.

Senator Richard Brent of Virginia was the intermediary. On
receiving an intimation of Madison's intention, Monroe replied
to Brent:

> . . . Are things in such a state as to allow the adm^n to take the
> whole subject into consideration. . . . Or are we pledged by what
> is already done. . . . I have no doubt from my knowledge of the
> President & Mr. Gallatin . . . that if I come into the government
> the utmost cordiality would subsist between us, and that any opinions
> which I might entertain and express respecting our publick affairs
> would receive, so far as circumstances would permit, all the atten-
> tion to which they might be entitled, but if our course is fixed, and
> the destiny of our country is dependant on arrangements already
> made, on measures already taken, I do not perceive how it would be
> possible for me to render any service, at this time, in the general
> government.[5]

With this letter presumably before him, Madison immediately
offered Monroe the State Department, but with no comment on
Monroe's reservations.[6] In his subsequent letter of acceptance
Monroe was explicit:

> My views of policy towards the European powers are not un-
> known. . . . it was for the interest of our country, to make an ac-
> commodation with England, the great maritime power, even on
> moderate terms, rather than hazard war, or any other alterna-
> tive. . . .
> If I come into the government my object will be to render to my
> country, and to you, all the service in my power, according to the
> light, such as it is, of my knowledge and experience, faithfully, and
> without reserve. It would not become me to accept a station, and
> to act a part in it, which my judgment and conscience did not
> approve, and which I did not believe would promote the publick wel-
> fare & happiness. I could not do this, nor would you wish me to do it.

---

[5] Monroe, *Writings*, V, 179–80 (March 18, 1811).
[6] *Ibid.*, V, 181, n., Madison to Monroe (March 20, 1811).

If you are disposed to accept my services under these circumstances, and with this explanation, I shall be ready to render them. . . .[7]

Madison accepted Monroe's terms: "With the mutual knowledge of our respective views of the foreign as well as the domestic interests of our country, I see no serious obstacle on either side to an association of our labors in promoting them. . . . differences of opinion must be looked for, even among those most agreed on the same general views. These differences, however, lie fairly within the compass of free consultation and mutual concession as subordinate to the unity belonging to the Executive department."[8]

The same issue was raised in 1825 when John Quincy Adams offered Crawford the opportunity to remain in the Treasury. Crawford declined. To a friend he wrote in explanation, "I cannot, honestly, remain in the administration, differing as I do from the President on some important principles. I could not support measures I do not approve, and to go into the cabinet merely as an opponent would be as ungenerous as useless."[9]

No other correspondence involving the problem of harmony of policy between a President and a *prospective* head of a department has come to notice. Many of the men invited to this position had no strong personal views on public issues beyond the general tendencies of their party; some had no capacity for independence; those who stood on their own ground—Gallatin, Calhoun, Adams, for example—raised no issues when they entered upon their duties and accommodated their views to those of the President thereafter.

The administrative primacy of the President was confirmed during these years by two removals from Cabinet positions, following John Adams' precedent in the summary removal of Timothy Pickering. Madison's hand was forced in 1811 by Gallatin's offer of resignation. He had to choose between Galla-

---

[7] *Ibid.,* V, 182–83 (March 23, 1811). The course of events within the next year brought Monroe to favor war with Great Britain.

[8] Henry Adams, *History of the United States,* V, 372–73 (March 26, 1811); see his comments, *ibid.,* V, 373–74.

[9] J. E. D. Shipp, *Giant Days or the Life and Times of William H. Crawford* (Americus, Ga.: Southern Printers, 1909), p. 195. Letter quoted from *Southern Literary Messenger,* III, 279.

tin and Robert Smith, and decided to cast overboard his unwelcome aide in the State Department. He wrote a long memorandum on the incident. In a personal conference Madison
complained to the Secretary of State about his incompetence in
office; business had not been conducted promptly and his drafts
of correspondence were "almost always so crude & inadequate"
that the President had been obliged to rewrite them himself—
"whatever talents he might possess, he did not as he must have
found by experience, possess those adapted to his station. . . ."
Madison complained also about Smith's indiscretion in communicating confidential Cabinet proceedings, and in disclosing
to the Federalists confidential communications from ministers
abroad. He finally charged Smith with political disloyalty, coun-
teracting "abroad" measures that he had accepted in Cabinet
meetings and making disparaging remarks about the President
and the Administration. He offered Smith the mission to St.
Petersburg, but after some hesitation Smith declined and submitted his resignation.[10]

The removal of General Armstrong as Secretary of War came
as the climax of a series of incidents, culminating at the moment
of the burning of Washington in 1814. Armstrong had denied
that the British would move on Washington, had opposed preparations to meet them, and had been dilatory in executing a
Cabinet decision to make ready for an assault. When the British landed, the defense of the capital was put in the hands of
General Winder, at which Armstrong took offense and practically withdrew his cooperation. Immediately after the occupa-
tion of Washington, Madison told Armstrong that the troops
would no longer follow him, and put the question, "what was
best to be done. Any convulsion at so critical a moment could
not but have the worst consequences." [11] Armstrong offered
either to resign or to withdraw to New York to visit his family.
Madison accepted the latter suggestion. Armstrong resigned the
next morning.

Although in form these two cases were resignations, in fact
they were removals, and were recognized as such. In two other
instances, Monroe and Adams respectively contemplated a re-

10 Madison, *Writings* (Hunt ed.), VIII, 137 ff. (April 1811).
11 *Ibid.*, VIII, 300–301 (August 29, 1814).

moval but held their hands. The relations between Crawford
and Monroe deteriorated ominously until they finally broke out
in an unprecedented event that eventually came to Adams' attention and was committed to his diary. Crawford had come to
Monroe with candidates for various appointments against whom
the President raised objections.

> . . . Mr. Crawford at last rose in much irritation, gathered the
> papers together, and said petulantly, "Well, if you will not appoint
> the persons well qualified for the places, tell me whom you will
> appoint, that I may get rid of their importunities." Mr. Monroe
> replied with great warmth, saying that he considered Crawford's
> language as extremely improper and unsuitable to the relations be-
> tween them; when Crawford, turning to him, raised his cane, as in
> the attitude to strike, and said, "You damned infernal old scoun-
> drel!" Mr. Monroe seized the tongs at the fireplace for self-defence,
> applied a retaliatory epithet to Crawford, and told him he would
> immediately ring for servants himself and turn him out of the house;
> upon which Crawford, beginning to recover himself, said he did not
> intend, and had not intended, to insult him, and left the house.
> They never met afterwards.[12]

Toward the close of his administration, Monroe wrote to Wirt,
without mentioning this encounter but referring generally to
the lack of harmony that existed between Crawford and himself, that "it comported better with the principles of our govt,
& with my own character, to permit him to remain than to
remove him. . . ."[13] Monroe was undoubtedly influenced by
the knowledge that Crawford was an active candidate for the
presidency and did not care to be responsible for the consequences of a removal upon the ultimate outcome of the struggle
to enter the White House.[14]

---

[12] Adams, *Memoirs,* VII, 81 (Dec. 14, 1825). According to J. H. Powell, the
incident took place early in 1825. Powell, *Richard Rush,* p. 181.

[13] Monroe, *Writings,* VII, 39 (Sept. 27, 1824).

[14] Crawford remains one of the less-known figures of American public life,
due in part to the lack of a good biography, which in turn is foreclosed by the
loss of his private papers by fire. Gallatin thought he had a powerful mind, a
most correct judgment, and an inflexible integrity, and hoped he would become
President. Adams, *Life of Albert Gallatin,* p. 598. Calhoun, a political rival, declared there had never been a man in American history who had risen so high,
of so corrupt a character or upon so slender a basis of service. Adams, *Memoirs,*
V, 497 (April 22, 1822). John Quincy Adams, another rival, believed Crawford

Adams was sorely tempted to remove his Postmaster General, John McLean, whom he believed, rightly or wrongly, to be guilty of political disloyalty and an active partisan of General Jackson. He refrained, probably in part on grounds of principle, in part on grounds of political expediency. As to the latter, McLean was a prominent Methodist and Adams was warned that his removal would alienate the Methodists. As to the former, Adams sincerely accepted, indeed he went beyond Monroe's views on the matter of partisan loyalty of Cabinet heads. Monroe declared, after his retirement, "No person at the head of the govt. has, in my opinion, any claim to the active, partizan exertions of those in office under him. Justice to his public acts, friendly feelings, and a candid & honorable deportment towards him, without forgetting what is due to others, are all he has a right to expect. . . ." [15] Adams tolerated McLean even though he believed the Postmaster General was actively supporting his principal rival.

An important phase of the relations of department heads to the President, again illustrating the superiority of the Chief Executive, was thrust into the center of Cabinet attention in 1819. The issue was whether department heads in making reports to Congress had a responsibility to reflect the opinions of the President rather than their own.[16] Calhoun, an ardent advocate of internal improvements, had been called upon by the House to recommend roads and canals for military purposes. At this time Monroe was holding the view that Congress had no power to legislate or appropriate for internal improvements. Faced with this awkward situation the President called a Cabinet meeting. Adams' account follows.

. . . Mr. Calhoun read the report. The President's question was, whether it could be made to the House consistently with his declaration in the message at the commencement of the last session, that, in his opinion, Congress had not the power by the Constitution to make

---

nothing more than a shrewd manipulating politician. His administrative record revealed first-class ability and appeared at its best in the Report of the Four Secretaries in 1816.

[15] Monroe, *Writings*, VII, 128–29 (Dec. 5, 1827).

[16] The issue is the same as that now recognized in the duty of departments to clear their legislative proposals with the President through the Bureau of the Budget.

laws and to incur expense for purposes of internal improvement.
The President expressed an opinion that the call of the House directly upon the Secretary of War for this report was itself irregular,
and not conformable to the spirit of the Constitution of the United
States, the principle of which was a single Executive. . . . And as
the heads of Departments were executive officers under the President,
it was to be considered whether the President himself was not
responsible for the substance of their reports.[17]

Adams, who sympathized with Calhoun's views on internal
improvements, nevertheless defended the President's position
on the duty of department heads. "I thought," he wrote in summarizing his response to Monroe's question, "there would be an
obvious incongruity and indecency that a head of Department
should make a report to either House of Congress which the
President should disapprove. . . ." [18] Calhoun apparently took
the same line, for Adams recorded that "he readily agreed to
omit the passages in which there were intimations of a duty in
Congress to make internal improvements," and in the first
draft had expressly stated that he did not enter into the question
of constitutional authority.[19]

This situation was in contrast with one of long standing, quite
remarkable in its character, viz., the transmission of annual estimates to Congress directly by the Secretary of the Treasury
without intervention of the President. The practice had been
initiated by Hamilton and continued during the whole of
Washington's and John Adams' administrations.[20] In a later
chapter it will appear that Gallatin discussed the estimates, especially for military and naval purposes, with Jefferson and expected Jefferson to determine controversial points. After the
unsettled period of military defense and war that ran from 1811
to 1815, the estimates were compiled in the Treasury, but without any effort by either the Secretary of the Treasury or the

17 Adams, *Memoirs,* IV, 217 (Jan. 12, 1819).

18 *Ibid.,* IV, 217.

19 *Ibid.,* IV, 218. The report is printed in *American State Papers: Miscellaneous,*
II, 533–37.

20 Leonard D. White, *The Federalists: A Study in Administrative History*
(New York: Macmillan Co., 1948), pp. 323–26.

President to review departmental requests or the policy contained in them. The estimates continued to go directly from the Treasury to Congress.

The matter was privately discussed by Monroe and Adams in 1820. Monroe had first become aware of the practice in 1812 when Gallatin made a report to Congress "the tendency of which was exceedingly unfavorable to the measures then contemplated by Mr. Madison." Monroe asked Madison how it had been permitted to appear. Madison replied that it was unexpected and displeasing to him, and that he had not seen it before it was presented to the House. He added, according to Monroe's account as recorded by Adams, that "from the practice having originated with General Hamilton, it was supposed that there were considerations of delicacy for its being withheld from the President until after having been presented to Congress." [21]

The matter arose again in 1820 when Adams, in the course of a long conversation with the President, asked whether any plan had been matured for meeting a deficiency that had been announced in the annual Treasury report. Monroe replied that he did not know. Crawford had made the annual report without showing it to him and he was ignorant of Crawford's financial program.[22] Adams was astonished and declared that he thought the practice "altogether inconsistent with the spirit of the Constitution," and one that "ought immediately to be changed." Monroe asked Adams to look into the law and expressed his own opinion that the practice was wrong. Apparently nothing was done, for in 1824 Adams again reported in his diary that Monroe "spoke much of the annual Treasury reports being made directly to Congress without being previously communicated to the President." [23] Nor is there any evidence that Adams changed the practice when he became President.

A delicate point concerning the President's duty to intervene in the case of disability of a department head arose with respect to the Secretary of the Treasury, William H. Crawford. A seri-

21 Adams, *Memoirs,* IV, 501 (Jan. 8, 1820).
22 *Ibid.,* IV, 501.
23 *Ibid.,* VI, 439 (Dec. 10, 1824).

ous paralysis affected Crawford in the autumn of 1823. For nearly a year he lay in seclusion, almost blind and quite incapacitated.[24] He took no steps to resign his official station or to ask Monroe to appoint an Acting Secretary. At a Cabinet meeting June 21, 1824, the Secretary's disability was brought to notice and the President was asked if he knew what the state of the Treasury Department was. Monroe replied that he had only a general knowledge from the reports of the comptroller.[25] The next day he told Adams that, if necessary, he would appoint an Acting Secretary and that he intended to name Adams.[26]

The business of the Treasury had been authenticated by the use of a facsimile of Crawford's signature, since he was unable to sign his name. "Much comment" ensued on the part of Calhoun, Southard, and Wirt. Adams believed that many warrants had been paid without any signature from Crawford, the facsimile having been applied subsequently.[27] Attorney General Wirt held the use of facsimile legal, if the mind and sight were competent,[28] but Calhoun took the opposite view.[29] Doubtless many Treasury decisions were made in fact without cognizance of the Secretary.[30] By August 1824 Crawford was able to call on the President, and on November 10, 1824, he attended a Cabinet meeting.[31] But in December Monroe was still handicapped by Crawford's incapacity to meet the President's requirements.[32] He did not, however, disturb Crawford in the possession of his office, although the act of May 8, 1792, clearly authorized him to make an acting appointment in case of sickness.[33]

The law and Constitution alike prescribed that in theory the whole business of the executive branch, domestic and foreign,

---

24 *Dictionary of American Biography*, IV, 529.

25 Adams, *Memoirs*, VI, 390 (June 21, 1824).

26 *Ibid.*, VI, 394 (June 22, 1824).

27 *Ibid.*, VI, 400 (July 10, 1824).

28 *Opinions of the Attorneys General of the United States* (House Doc. 123, 26th Cong., 2d sess., 1841), pp. 500–503 (July 5, 1824).

29 Adams, *Memoirs*, VI, 399 (July 7, 1824).

30 One such is recorded in *ibid.*, VI, 401.

31 *Ibid.*, VI, 405 (August 4, 1824); VI, 426 (Nov. 10, 1824).

32 *Ibid.*, VI, 438.

33 1 Stat. 279, sec. 8.

be performed by the President or at his direction.[34] This doctrine was declared by the organic departmental acts and was generally recognized. To an astonishing degree, the President personally participated in matters large and small. Jefferson set the actual Republican pattern by adopting Washington's rule on the transmission of departmental correspondence to him for approval.[35] This practice, as Jefferson told his department heads, preserved unity of object and action and enabled the President to discharge his responsibility. That this method imposed a heavy burden upon the Chief Executive was certain, even in a relatively simple age, but it was a burden that Jefferson, Madison, Monroe, and John Quincy Adams accepted as part of their duty.

Thus we find Jefferson instructing Gideon Granger on the problem of post-road river crossings in the western wilderness. "I would propose that all streams under 40. f. width not fordable *at their common winter tide* shall be bridged; & over all streams not bridged, a tree should be laid across, if their breadth does not exceed the extent of a single tree." [36] On another occasion he approved an increase of pay of $150 to an Indian agent.[37] Early in his administration Gallatin authorized an expenditure of $600 to repair a leaky hospital roof in Norfolk as an emergency matter that would normally have gone to the President.[38] Jefferson frequently complained about the pressure of business and in 1806 put in one sentence a classic observation: "It is not

[34] Early opinions of the Attorney General began to define presidential powers in the area of administration. See, for example, *Opinions of the Attorneys General* (1841 ed.), p. 590 (Feb. 17, 1828); p. 668 (Jan. 10, 1829); p. 853 (Dec. 28, 1831).

[35] Jefferson, *Works* (Federal ed.), IX, 310–12 (Nov. 6, 1801). His description of procedure is reprinted in full in White, *The Federalists*, pp. 35–36. He took pains to keep a careful record of his correspondence. "I am in the habit of noting daily, in a list kept for that purpose, the letters I receive daily, by the names of the writers, and dates of time and place, and this has been done with such exactness, that I do not recollect ever to have detected a single omission." Jefferson to U. S. Senate, April 8, 1808, *American State Papers: Miscellaneous,* I, 921.

[36] MS., Library of Congress, Papers of Gideon and Francis Granger, 1800–1864, Letter No. 11 (August 9, 1806).

[37] *The Territorial Papers of the United States* (Clarence Edwin Carter, ed., 16 vols., Washington: Government Printing Office, 1934–48), VII, 168 (Jan. 19, 1804); hereafter cited as *Territorial Papers.*

[38] Gallatin, *Writings,* I, 81 (August 9, 1802).

because I do less than I might do, but that I have more to do than I can do." [39] There is no evidence, however, that either he or Madison understood the administrative ailment from which they suffered.

Monroe was bothered by the petty responsibilities of attending to the presidential household but tried in vain to secure release from them. As he was about to leave the White House he sent Congress "a few remarks . . . founded on my own experience, in this office." Beyond a certain limit, he wrote, no one can go, and if inferior details are forced upon the attention of the President he loses time to devote to matters of higher importance. The higher duties of his office, said Monroe, "are sufficient to employ the whole mind, and unceasing labors, of any individual. . . ." Among these duties he cited the message to Congress, the replies to calls for information, personal contact with members of Congress, and the "supervision and control of the several departments so as to preserve efficiency in each, and order and consistency in the general movement of the Government." [40] He suggested the desirability of aid to the President, perhaps the first statement of this need. Congress gave him no aides, and the broad stream of detail flowed steadily on.

John Quincy Adams, too, was in need of help. He had no disposition to protect himself, however he might suffer from intrusion. The number of idle visitors, total strangers, increased until they became an almost daily annoyance.[41] The President was becoming an object of attention like the exhibits in the Patent Office. His prize case, however, but one of a different order, was Dr. George P. Todson.

Todson first appeared on December 16, 1826, in company with Senator Findlay of Pennsylvania to ask reappointment as an assistant surgeon in the army, a post from which he had been

---

39 Jefferson, *Writings* (Memorial ed.), XIX, 150 (Jan. 16, 1806).

40 House Report 79, 18th Cong., 2d sess., pp. 23–25 (Jan. 18, 1825).

41 Adams, *Memoirs*, VII, 446 (Feb. 23, 1828). As Secretary of State he had had much experience with importunate persons. One such came to ask for a loan of $500. *Ibid.*, IV, 76 (April 9, 1818). While President another stranger came to ask fifty or sixty dollars to get home. Adams "did not perceive the propriety" of providing him with money. *Ibid.*, VII, 302 (July 4, 1827).

removed by court martial.[42] Adams had already gone over the proceedings twice, had declined to reverse the verdict, and had heard from Todson's counsel "that Todson had come to the most cool and inflexible determination to murder me." [43] In the interview Adams told the one-time army surgeon that he could do nothing for him, especially under a threat of assassination. "Todson . . . somewhat faintly said he had given up the idea," and left the White House. Adams reflected upon a number of threats and assassinations of others, and called upon Heaven to preserve him from any weakness.[44]

Five days later Todson came back to ask Adams for money to pay his lodgings bill and his passage to New Orleans, and to declare that his intention to assassinate Adams was "absurd," since he had learned that the President had kindly feelings toward him. Adams declined the request for a loan.[45] On March 15, Todson called again at the White House, this time to ask remission of the court-martial fine of forty-seven dollars. To this Adams agreed.[46] On March 21 he requested further favors, and received Adams' advice to return to his profession.[47] On the 27th he came to tell Adams that he "was about forming a matrimonial connection with a young lady" whose parents showed reluctance on account of his discharge from the army. Adams remained firm.[48] In May he came to ask for a vacant clerkship in the War Department; Adams passed him on to the Secretary.[49] In June Adams recommended him to the navy as a surgeon to accompany a naval vessel returning Negroes to the African colony.[50] With considerable reluctance Southard yielded, and Dr. Todson sailed for Africa, doubtless much to Adams' satisfaction. In December he returned, bringing a certificate in his favor and a report on the colony.[51] Next June Adams

42 *Ibid.*, VII, 209 (Dec. 16, 1826).
43 *Ibid.*, VII, 210.
44 *Ibid.*, VII, 212–13.
45 *Ibid.*, VII, 216.
46 *Ibid.*, VII, 239.
47 *Ibid.*, VII, 244–45.
48 *Ibid.*, VII, 248–49.
49 *Ibid.*, VII, 282–83.
50 *Ibid.*, VII, 285.
51 *Ibid.*, VII, 378.

sought to send Todson off with a company of displaced Indians.[52] Such was the burden one man cast upon the President of the United States.

The President's task was the heavier because no one of them had proper assistance.[53] Congress allowed a private secretary and no more. Detail of clerks from the departments was unknown and would doubtless have been criticized in Congress. Monroe retained his brother, Joseph, as his private secretary, and Adams for a while employed his son, John. The President, like the heads of departments, toiled incessantly, working with his own hands.

The Republicans, like their predecessors, left no loose ends of administration unconnected with the departments and independent of presidential direction. Secretary of State Monroe expressed the common opinion in a letter to Congressman Adam Seybert on the status of the Patent Office. He declared:

I have always thought that every institution, of whatsoever nature it might be, ought to be comprised within some one of the departments of Government, the Chief of which only should be responsible to the Chief Executive Magistrate of the Nation. The establishment of inferior independent departments, the heads of which are not, and ought not to be members of the Administration, appears to me to be liable to many serious objections.[54]

Republican leaders were perhaps specially alert to keep a strong hand on naval commanders, in the interest both of international comity and of civilian authority. In 1827 Congress gave thought to establishing a line of communication across the Isthmus of Panama, in order to expedite orders to the American fleet in South Pacific waters. The House Committee on Naval Affairs took occasion to emphasize executive authority. "Indeed, it is desirable at all times, that our Navy should act under the immediate instruction of the Executive, as far as practicable,

---

[52] *Ibid.*, VIII, 31.

[53] In 1824 Adams complained of irregularities in the President's office due "above all, from his want of an efficient private Secretary." *Ibid.*, VI, 374 (June 3, 1824). Two sons-in-law assisted Monroe at one stage, Gouverneur and Hay.

[54] Monroe, *Writings*, V, 203 (June 10, 1812); also in *American State Papers: Miscellaneous*, II, 192.

and that as little be left to the discretion of the officers as circumstances will allow." [55]

The spirit of relations between Republican Presidents and department heads suggested less subordination than that prescribed by the constitutional rule, except in the field of foreign policy. Constitutional doctrine confirmed Adams' view that heads of departments were subalterns, but Presidents did not treat them as such. Presidents and Secretaries normally formed a team, small enough to be a workable unit. The President headed the team, to be sure, but he drove with a light rein. A department head was substantial master of his own agency. The President, indeed, was informed by his Attorney General that his power to take care that the laws should be executed did not imply that he could in person execute the law himself.[56]

Although the facts suggest that Presidents demanded much less of their department heads than the Constitution allowed, they do not modify the underlying relationship of authority and subordination that the Constitution and Federalist practice had established. In the last analysis, Presidents decided what they chose to deal with in the administrative framework and made the decisions. The stronger the President, the more definitely this subordination would weigh on either an active or an ambitious department head. Robert Smith, Secretary of the Navy under Jefferson, was restive in the face of Jefferson's unwillingness to ready the navy for war, but he dared not proceed without authority. He revealed his discomfort in a letter to W. C. Nicholas, his brother-in-law.

My ambition is at an end. . . . We have established theories that would stare down any possible measures of offense or defense. . . . the President cannot recommend (although he now sees the necessity) any augmentation of the army. Nay *I*, even *I*, did not dare to bring forward the measure until I had first obtained his approbation. Never was there a time when executive influence so completely governed the nation.[57]

[55] House Report 56, 19th Cong., 2d sess., p. 1 (Jan. 24, 1827).
[56] *Opinions of the Attorneys General* (1841 ed.), p. 471 (Oct. 20, 1823).
[57] Henry Adams, *John Randolph*, p. 206. The letter was written January 9, 1807.

We may conclude therefore that no doubt arose in the minds of the Jeffersonians concerning the administrative supremacy of the President. The department heads were responsible to him. The executive power remained where the Constitution had placed it.

CHAPTER SIX

The President and the Cabinet

Presumably one of the most flexible institutions of the general government, the Cabinet showed little capacity for institutional development under four successive Republican Presidents. The functions and composition of the Cabinet had been settled initially by experience under Washington and John Adams. They remained substantially unchanged during the Jeffersonian period. This additional quarter century of experience had the effect of stabilizing the character of the American Cabinet for all the years that have followed, making due allowance for the innumerable shades of variety that inevitably occur from year to year.

Public men in 1801 might properly have asked themselves whether, under new leadership that deprecated the consolidation of power, the Cabinet might not evolve into the kind of autonomous council that was debated in the Constitutional Convention as a useful check to a potentially dangerous executive. No such tendency appeared, partly because Presidents were now Republican, friends of liberty, and darkly antimonarchical; partly because Jefferson and his successors had no more intention to dissipate authority in fact than had John Adams. The Cabinet became no balancing council.

Jefferson left a brief description of Cabinet procedure in his day.

. . . The ordinary business of every day is done by consultation between the President and the Head of the department alone to which it belongs. For measures of importance or difficulty, a consultation is held with the Heads of departments, either assembled, or by taking their opinions separately in conversation or in writing. The latter is most strictly in the spirit of the constitution. . . . This was General Washington's practice for the first two or three years of his administration, till the affairs of France and England threatened to embroil us, and rendered consideration and discussion desirable. . . . I practised this last method, because the harmony was so cordial among us all. . . .[1]

The systematic Gallatin tried to have Jefferson hold a regular weekly Cabinet meeting: "otherwise they will be only occasional, and, as we have already experienced, often omitted."[2] The President did not fall in with this suggestion.

By 1807 grave matters of business were piling up so as to require a modification in Cabinet routine. Jefferson's letter to Gallatin described the difficulty and the President's manner of meeting it.

Something now occurs almost every day on which it is desirable to have the opinions of the heads of departments, yet to have a formal meeting every day would consume so much of their time as to seriously obstruct their regular business. I have proposed to them, as most convenient for them, & wasting less of their time, to call on me at any moment of the day which suits their separate convenience, when, besides any other business they may have to do, I can learn their opinions separately on any matter which has occurred, & also communicate the information received daily. Perhaps you could find it more convenient, sometimes, to make your call at the hour of dinner. . . . You will always find a plate & a sincere welcome.[3]

In one way or another Cabinet members were called into consultation on all important questions. No instance has come to notice in which a Cabinet officer complained that decisions were made without notice on which he believed he should have been consulted.

[1] Jefferson, *Works* (Federal ed.), XI, 137–38 (March 5, 1810); *ibid.*, X, 414 (June 12, 1807). On occasion a file would circulate for separate opinions.

[2] Gallatin, *Writings*, I, 59 (Nov. 9, 1801).

[3] Jefferson, *Works* (Federal ed.), X, 452–53 (July 10, 1807). Cabinet meetings were called quite informally. Cf. Adams' diary entry of October 21, 1818, "Stopped at Mr. Wirt's office and gave him notice of the meeting at the President's house, which I had forgotten to do yesterday. He immediately went with me. . . ." Adams, *Memoirs*, IV, 140–41. Learned calculated that about 180 Cabinet meetings were held during the eight years of Monroe's administration. Henry Barrett Learned, "Some Aspects of the Cabinet Meeting," Columbia Historical Society, *Records*, XVIII (1915), 109. Adams' Cabinet met less frequently, *ibid.*, XVIII, 112.

The single piece of Cabinet business of most common occurrence was foreign negotiations. Cabinet procedure in this area was described by Adams while dealing with the Spanish envoy, Vivés, for the acquisition of Florida.

. . . On receiving a note from Vivés it is immediately translated by J. H. Purviance, the only translator for the Department. I then take the translation to the President, and, after a conversation with him, prepare the draft of an answer, according to my own ideas, which I take to the President. He assembles the members of the Administration, by whom the draft is discussed. Alterations, additions, or omissions are proposed, after which the note is finally prepared and sent.[4]

CABINET UNITY

Experience was to confirm the difficulty of maintaining harmony among Cabinet members, the lack of which had caused both Washington and Adams so much trouble. The combination of a strong and skillful President and a Cabinet free from high ambition would work, as Jefferson demonstrated. A strong President and a Cabinet containing only one ambitious member whose place promised fulfillment of his hopes would also work, as the experience of John Quincy Adams revealed. A weak President and restless or mediocre Cabinet members produced much disharmony from 1809 to 1817, and a reserved President harassed by strong and competing Cabinet members resulted in mounting official chaos under Monroe.

The character of the four Cabinets serving successively under Jefferson, Madison, Monroe, and Adams varied from one extreme to another. Jefferson succeeded in maintaining harmony and unity among his advisers. His well-known description of the relative calm that was maintained in Cabinet discussions is adequate testimony of his success.

. . . The third administration, which was of eight years, presented an example of harmony in a cabinet of six persons, to which perhaps history has furnished no parallel. There never arose, during the whole time, an instance of an unpleasant thought or word between the members. We sometimes met under differences of opinion, but

4 Adams, *Memoirs*, V, 75 (April 26, 1820).

scarcely ever failed, by conversing and reasoning, so to modify each
other's ideas, as to produce an unanimous result. Yet, able and
amicable as these members were, I am not certain this would have
been the case, had each possessed equal and independent powers.
Ill-defined limits of their respective departments, jealousies, trifling
at first, but nourished and strengthened by repetition of occasions,
intrigues without doors of designing persons to build an importance
to themselves on the divisions of others, might, from small begin-
nings, have produced persevering oppositions. But the power of decision in the President left no object for internal dissension, and
external intrigue was stifled in embryo by the knowledge which in-
cendiaries possessed, that no division they could foment would
change the course of the executive power.[5]

At another time he stated, "in truth all measures of importance
were the measures of all." [6]

Madison's Cabinet was a failure from the outset.[7] Due to
Senate opposition, as already noted, he was unable to place
Gallatin in the State Department and had Robert Smith imposed upon him in this important office at a crucial time. He
was unable to hold a Cabinet together. He had two Secretaries
of State, four Secretaries of the Treasury, four Secretaries of
War, three Attorneys General, and four Secretaries of the Navy.
He succeeded in picking, or having thrust upon him, four who
were incompetent (Smith, Campbell, Hamilton, and Eustis),
and two who were insubordinate (Armstrong and Granger).
The dissension between Gallatin and Smith increased so as to
cause a watchful Jefferson much misgiving. ". . . I hope that
the position of both gentlemen may be made so easy as to give
no cause for either to withdraw." [8] To this end he recommended
written instead of oral opinions to the President: "It is better

5 Jefferson, *Works* (Federal ed.), XI, 185 (Jan. 26, 1811).

6 *Thomas Jefferson Correspondence Printed from the Originals in the Collections of William K. Bixby* (Worthington Chauncey Ford, ed., Boston, 1916), p. 181
(July 10, 1809). See also Jefferson, *Works* (Federal ed.), X, 241, for a corresponding
statement. Jefferson perhaps minimized Gallatin's irritation with the Secretary
of the Navy, Robert Smith, and on the embargo Jefferson secured acquiescence
rather than agreement. He was, however, constantly on the alert to thwart Federalist efforts to create differences in his Cabinet, which he asserted had taken
place successively with respect to Secretaries Madison, Dearborn, and Gallatin.
Ibid., X, 294 (Oct. 12, 1806).

7 Henry Adams, *John Randolph*, p. 235.

8 Jefferson, *Works* (Federal ed.), XI, 137 (March 5, 1810).

calculated . . . to prevent collision and irritation, and to cure it, or at least suppress its effects when it has already taken place." [9] The Cabinet, like the presidency, suffered a severe decline during these eight years.

Taken man for man, Monroe's Cabinet was one of the strongest that any President had assembled.[10] It was unknown since the days of Washington to find in a single Cabinet men as able and nationally known as John Quincy Adams, Crawford, Calhoun, and Wirt. Stability returned, too; there was only one Secretary of State, one Secretary of the Treasury, and one Secretary of War during the two terms of Monroe's service as President.

While the administration began with evidences of harmony, the internal situation soon began to deteriorate in the face of competition to succeed Monroe. At the start of his second term, the Cabinet broke asunder amidst open and jealous warfare between Crawford, Calhoun, and Adams. President Monroe wrote Madison in 1822, "I have never known such a state of things as has existed here during the last Session, nor have I personally ever experienced so much embarrassment and mortification. . . . There being three avowed candidates in the administration is a circumstance which increases the embarrassment. The friends of each endeavour to annoy the others. . . ." [11] Joseph Story wrote Jeremiah Mason, "The whole Cabinet is by the ears. All are candidates, and as I hear, they are quite shy of each other. I imagine that consultations are merely formal and advice rarely given in concert." [12]

On many important matters, indeed, advice was far from unanimous. A three-hour Cabinet meeting on January 9, 1818, found Adams and Calhoun advising the President not to return Amelia Island to Spain, contrary to Monroe's intention; Crawford, Crowninshield, and Wirt advising its return. Adams observed:

[9] *Ibid.*, XI, 138.
[10] See Charles M. Wiltse, *John C. Calhoun: Nationalist, 1782–1828* (Indianapolis: Bobbs-Merrill, 1944), pp. 142 ff. for an interesting description of Monroe's Cabinet members; and also Samuel Flagg Bemis, *John Quincy Adams*, pp. 251–53.
[11] Monroe, *Writings*, VI, 286 (May 10, 1822); cf. a similar letter to Jefferson *ibid.*, VII, 11 (March 22, 1824).
[12] Adams, *Writings*, VII, 207, n. 1 (Feb. 21, 1822).

The President . . . was very apparently affected by the conflict of sentiment among his advisers. . . . We parted, leaving the question yet undetermined and the President not a little embarrassed. These Cabinet councils open upon me a new scene and new views of the political world. Here is a play of passions, opinions, and characters different in many respects from those in which I have been accustomed heretofore to move.[13]

Repeated Cabinet meetings to determine American policy concerning Jackson's seizure of Pensacola in Spanish Florida revealed Adams arguing stubbornly against the President and the whole Cabinet. In the end the President's draft of a note to Spain was approved "precisely on the grounds of the President's original sketch." [14] Later in the same year the Cabinet split evenly on a British proposal concerning impressment, Crawford and Wirt against Adams and Calhoun. "The President ultimately found a middle term, upon which he concluded, after expressing his regret that he was obliged to decide between us, equally divided in opinion as we were." [15] Discord mounted with every year.

Adams' own Cabinet was a relative success. Apart from Clay, its members were not men of strong ambition, and Clay was well placed in the State Department to satisfy his hope of succeeding Adams. All were deferential to the President, but after two years it became apparent that he would not succeed himself. Adams, nevertheless, was able to hold his Cabinet intact for four years; the only break occurred when Barbour, nine months before Adams retired, became minister to Great Britain. The inherent forces of disintegration in any Cabinet were thus

13 Adams, *Memoirs*, IV, 36–37 (Jan. 9, 1818). Adams' private views of his Cabinet colleagues and other personalities were often astringent. Clay, he thought, was "essentially a gamester," with a vigorous intellect but "a very undigested system of ethics." *Ibid.*, V, 59 (April 6, 1820). He found Clay's temper impetuous and his ambition impatient. *Ibid.*, V, 325 (March 9, 1821). Adams' distaste for Crawford was intense. He described Calhoun as the only man in the Monroe administration who had a philosophical turn of mind. *Ibid.*, V, 221 (Dec. 27, 1820). Calhoun was, according to Adams, "a man of fair and candid mind, of honorable principles, of clear and quick understanding, of cool self-possession, of enlarged philosophical views, and of ardent patriotism . . . above all sectional and factious prejudices. . . ." *Ibid.*, V, 361 (Oct. 15, 1821).

14 *Ibid.*, IV, 114 (July 20, 1818).

15 *Ibid.*, IV, 149 (Oct. 30, 1818).

avoided by Adams, but he was acutely conscious of their existence.

With the hard experience of dissension in the Cabinets of both the first and second Presidents much in his mind, Jefferson had declared just before he took office, "It is certain that those of the Cabinet Council of the President should be of his bosom confidence." [16] Failure to maintain this maxim weakened Madison and Monroe. But Presidents found that personal confidence had at times to be balanced against geographical considerations and factional power.[17] Each of the Republican Presidents sought to represent the four major geographical sections—east, central, southern, and western—although Monroe was not successful, and Jefferson was handicapped by numerous refusals to enter his Cabinet, especially in the Navy Department.

POLITICAL AND ADMINISTRATIVE ASPECTS
OF THE CABINET

The Cabinet was an institution basically political in its character. The occasions on which it was consulted usually involved political matters in both the partisan and policy meanings of the term. Each individual member was in charge of large administrative operations; each consulted the President individually where he needed counsel or support. When the heads of departments gathered collectively in the White House, it was not to discuss the conduct of departmental business, but to debate constitutional issues, policy, or partisan matters on

16 Jefferson, *Works* (Federal ed.), IX, 186 (Feb. 20, 1801).

17 Madison commented on this proposition in a letter written long after his retirement: "Besides the more essential requisites in the candidate, an eye must be had to his political principles and connexions, his personal temper and habits, his relations of feelings towards those with whom he is to be associated; and the quarter of the Union to which he belongs. . . . Add to the whole, the necessary sanction of the Senate; and what may also be refused, the necessary consent of the most eligible individual. . . ." Madison, *Writings* (Hunt ed.), IX, 278, n. (Feb. 1827). Monroe held ". . . that a head of a Department (there being four) should be taken from the four sections of the Union, the East, the Middle, the South and the West. . . . Each part of the Union would be gratified by it, and the knowledge of local details and means, which would be thereby brought into the Cabinet, would be useful." Monroe, *Writings*, V, 347 (Dec. 14, 1816). Adams recorded in his diary as he was about to become President, "The members of Congress all advise variously for the formation of a Cabinet. . . ." *Memoirs*, VI, 509 (Feb. 12, 1825).

which the President required their counsel. The Cabinet did not become a specifically administrative agency for the government as a whole, as, for example, the Board of Navy Commissioners did for the Navy Department.

The business of the Cabinet was as wide ranging as the business of the government, but certain matters, especially foreign affairs, were apt to absorb the greater part of Cabinet attention. Troublesome appointments occasionally found their way into Cabinet meetings. General Van Rensselaer's appointment to the Albany post office provided an excellent example.[18] Exceptional administrative events came to the attention of the Cabinet also, matters such as the scandal over tea duties in Philadelphia.[19] The fundamentally political character of the Cabinet as an institution is revealed in one of its characteristic functions, consideration of the President's messages.

Messages. The Cabinet was particularly useful to Presidents in preparing the annual message to Congress. This document regularly embodied the President's policy and recommendations and, although seldom as forthright as John Quincy Adams' first message, nevertheless was usually a state paper of importance. Its discussion furnished an invaluable annual occasion for a review of events and for welding the Cabinet, if possible, into a single composite body. Each of the four Republican Presidents used the Cabinet extensively for advice at this point. Jefferson declared of his annual message of 1805, "there was not a single paragraph in my message to Congress, or those supplementary to it, in which there was not an unanimity of concurrence in the members of the administration." [20] The preparation of John Quincy Adams' first two messages will serve as a convenient exposition of practice.

Adams wrote his own first draft, based in part on the annual reports that now came in regularly from the departments, and in part on suggestions conveyed to him orally by heads of departments. On November 21, 1825, he began reading sections of the first draft to members of the Cabinet as they happened

18 See below, ch. 22.
19 See below, ch. 11.
20 Jefferson, *Works* (Federal ed.), X, 242 (March 22, 1806). For Monroe's practice, see Adams, *Memoirs*, IV, 25 (Nov. 28, 1817).

into the White House.[21] On November 23 he read the whole
message to the Cabinet, and both Clay and Barbour raised objections.[22] A second Cabinet meeting on November 25 devoted
four hours to the message, which Adams now read paragraph by
paragraph, Clay and Barbour making various suggestions.
Barbour would suppress all reference to internal improvements;
Clay would discard Adams' support for a university. "Clay good-
humoredly remarked this alternate stripping off from my draft;
and I told them I was like the man with his two wives—one
plucking out his black hairs, and the other the white, till none
were left." [23] A third Cabinet meeting took place the next day.
Clay proposed to eliminate references to the university and the
new executive department, the Patent Office, and the list of
proposed internal improvements. Rush stood by the President's
draft. Barbour reluctantly withdrew his objections to the subject of internal improvements; Southard said scarcely anything;
and with numerous concessions and much redrafting Adams
concluded the discussion.[24]

Preparation of the second annual message introduced an innovation that gave Adams some concern. Clay and Barbour
proposed that, after the message had been read to the Cabinet,
they would take it off for private consideration. After the Cabinet meeting on November 29, 1826, Adams consequently gave
the draft to Barbour, but with some trepidation. "I have consented," he wrote, "to this mode of scrutinizing the message,
because I wish to have the benefit of every objection that can
be made by every member of the Administration. But it has
never been practised heretofore, and I am not sure that it will
be a safe precedent to follow. . . . there may be some danger
in placing the composition of it so much under the control of
the Cabinet members, by giving it up to a discussion entirely
among themselves." [25] Barbour and Clay again joined in objecting to some passages, Rush stood by the President, and
Southard apparently remained silent.[26] All agreed, however,

21 *Ibid.*, VII, 57–58.
22 *Ibid.*, VII, 59.
23 *Ibid.*, VII, 61.
24 *Ibid.*, VII, 62–63.
25 *Ibid.*, VII, 189–90. He continued the practice in 1827. *Ibid.*, VII, 363.
26 *Ibid.*, VII, 191.

that in the last instance the President decided what to include
in his messages to Congress and the particular form of the
language.[27]

Secrecy of cabinet discussions. Another symbol of the political
character of the Cabinet was the rule of secrecy concerning its
deliberations. This rule, accepted from the outset without any
dissent, came into public attention when Crawford, long retired from national affairs, revealed the Cabinet debates on
Jackson's military actions in Pensacola, Florida. His disclosures
resulted in a resounding quarrel between Calhoun, then Vice
President, and Jackson, who sat in the White House.

Some unknown person informed James A. Hamilton (son of
Alexander Hamilton and friend of Jackson) that Crawford had
made a statement concerning the Pensacola affair. Jackson asked
Hamilton for permission to see the letter in which it was contained. Hamilton apparently went to Senator John Forsyth of
Georgia, a strong Jackson man, who wrote Crawford and received from him a long statement, asserting that Calhoun argued
in Cabinet to punish Jackson for acting beyond his orders.
Forsyth promptly showed the letter to the President.

The resulting break between Calhoun and Jackson does not
concern us at this point. Crawford, however, had revealed in a
letter, that he knew would instantly get into circulation, the
substance of a Cabinet discussion:

. . . My apology for having disclosed what passed in a cabinet
meeting is this: In the summer after that meeting, an extract of a
letter from Washington was published in a Nashville paper, in
which it was stated that I had proposed to arrest General Jackson,
but that he was triumphantly defended by Mr. Calhoun and Mr.
Adams. This letter, I always believed, was written by Mr. Calhoun,
or by his directions. It had the desired effect. General Jackson became extremely inimical to me, and friendly to Mr. Calhoun.[28]

In the course of a long letter to Jackson, Calhoun referred to
Crawford's breach of confidence. "I am not at all surprised," he

27 Monroe did not consult the Cabinet on his veto message defeating tollgates
on the Cumberland Road to secure money for repairs, alleging lack of time.
Ibid., V, 516 (May 4, 1822).
28 *The Works of John C. Calhoun* (Richard K. Crallé, ed., 6 vols., New York:
D. Appleton, 1854–61), VI, 360.

wrote, "that Mr. Crawford should feel that he stands in need of an apology for betraying the deliberations of the cabinet. It is, I believe, not only the first instance in our country, but one of the very first instances to be found in any country, or any age, that an individual has felt absolved from the high obligation which honor and duty impose on one situated as he was." [29] Calhoun's indignation was sharpened by the mortal wound which Crawford's indiscretion had caused.

There is no doubt that a traditional, if ill-defined, obligation to secrecy regarding Cabinet discussions had become well fixed. Calhoun wrote to Wirt for confirmation of his own position. Wirt replied, "I should not feel myself at liberty to disclose the proceeding of any cabinet meeting without the concurrence of the President and of all the members who attended it; but as your inquiry relates to your own course only, and I can speak of that without involving any one else, I see no impropriety in doing so at your request." [30] Calhoun also wrote to John Quincy Adams, who had earlier received a letter from Crawford on the Cabinet meeting in question. Adams wrote Calhoun with reference to Crawford's letter, ". . . as it related to transactions sacredly confidential in the cabinet of Mr. Monroe, I have not thought myself at liberty to furnish a copy of it without his permission, even to Mr. Monroe. . . ." [31]

Crawford denied Calhoun's whole position on the matter of Cabinet secrecy, both as to practice and as to propriety. His views can best be put in his own words.

I shall first notice your observations upon the disclosure of the secrets of the cabinet, which you say is the first that has occurred, at least in this country. Do you really believe this assertion, Mr. Calhoun? How did the written opinion of Messrs. Jefferson and Hamilton, on the first bank bill, ever see the light? How were the facts and circumstances which preceded and accompanied the removal of Edmund Randolph from the state department, by General Washington, disclosed and made known to the public? . . . While a cabinet is in existence and its usefulness liable to be impaired, reason and common sense point out the propriety of keeping its

29 *Ibid.*, VI, 372.
30 *Ibid.*, VI, 428.
31 *Ibid.*, VI, 433.

proceedings secret. But after the cabinet no longer exists, when its usefulness cannot be impaired by the disclosure of its proceedings, neither reason, common sense, nor patriotism, requires that those proceedings should be shrouded in impenetrable darkness. The acts of such a cabinet become history, and the nation has the same right to a knowledge of them that it has to any other historical fact. . . .

. . . Since the dissolution of Mr. Monroe's cabinet I have not felt myself restrained from disclosing any fact that transpired in it. While it existed I disclosed none of its secrets. . . .[32]

Crawford was justified in pointing to the particular instances supporting his position. They occurred, however, very early in Cabinet history, and the practice of succeeding years had confirmed the rule of reticence with respect to Cabinet proceedings. The rule was important in order to secure freedom of exchange of views and to protect individual Cabinet members from charges of vacillation or subservience as positions were mutually accommodated to each other in the course of discussion.

As we look back over the operation of the Cabinet from Jefferson through John Quincy Adams the principal conclusion to be drawn is that it did not develop into a specifically administrative agency. Its business was primarily concerned with foreign affairs, with an occasional constitutional question, with policy matters and advice on the annual message, and with such administrative problems as rose above the departmental level because they had become charged with political or partisan consequences. The Cabinet remained under the Republicans what the Federalists had made it in the formative years.

[32] J. E. D. Shipp, *Giant Days*, pp. 238–39, 247 (Oct. 2, 1830).

CHAPTER SEVEN

Congress and
the Administrative System

By the close of John Quincy Adams' administration, Congress had become far more active in dealing with the administrative system than it had under the Federalists, or indeed under Thomas Jefferson. This evolution was in accordance with Republican theory, but more important than theory was the appearance of strong men in the House, and the continuation in public affairs of staunch old Republicans such as John Randolph and William B. Giles, congenitally suspicious of executive power. Of much importance also were the disturbances within the Republican party which, after Jefferson, set one faction in the legislative branch at the official throats of another in the executive. Beyond this it must be recognized that the House began to take seriously its inherent responsibility of holding executive officers accountable for their conduct of the public business. These were the years when the investigating function of legislative committees, recognized under Federalist auspices, really came into full vigor.

Behind the daily incidents of interchange between the executive agencies and Congressmen and their committees, it is possible to disengage some of the practices and institutional forms that spelled out a new diligence on the part of the legislative branch. While on the one hand Congress was asserting itself, on the other it continued to fear executive encroachment on its independence. As a defense, it sought, although in vain, to erect stronger barriers than those set down explicitly in the Constitu-

[89]

tion against presidential appointment of members of Congress to lucrative official posts. At the same time, the early sensitivity of Republicans to dependence on executive sources of information (then Federalist) diminished as Republicans took possession of these springs from which aid could be summoned. However, through a whole series of aggressive acts, Congress reached out after 1810 to establish a much more energetic influence upon the daily conduct of executive business. It demanded better sources of information, it corrected irregularities, especially through investigating committees, and the House provided itself with standing committees on the expenditures of the departments and agencies. These matters are the subject of our present attention.

CONGRESS SEEKS TO PROTECT ITSELF

Important constitutional principles were involved in securing the independence of the House and Senate against executive influence. One phase of this matter had been safeguarded in the Constitution, wherein it was declared: "No Senator or Representative shall, during the time for which he was elected, be appointed to any civil office under the authority of the United States, which shall have been created, or the emoluments whereof shall have been increased during such time; and no person holding any office under the United States, shall be a member of either House during his continuance in office." [1]

This protection to the independence of the people's representatives had been put to use in several cases by the Republicans.[2] It did not, however, prevent the President from selecting members of Congress for appointment to executive position, excepting to new offices and those whose salary had been augmented during their term of office, or prevent him from appointing Congressmen after their terms had expired. Thus also the independence of the House might be suborned, and several attempts, all vain, were made to tighten the constitutional provision.[3]

1 Art. I, sec. 6.
2 House Doc. 30, 15th Cong., 1st sess. (Jan. 5, 1818).
3 See House Res. 10, 17th Cong., 1st sess. (March 28, 1822); House Report 82, 16th Cong., 1st sess. (Jan. 24, 1820); House Res. 5, 19th Cong., 1st sess. (Dec. 13, 1825); and Senate Doc. 52, 19th Cong., 1st sess., p. 6 (March 1, 1826). A complete

Some Congressmen saw that their independence might be undercut not only by the promise of appointments but also by the award of government contracts. Jefferson was acutely aware of the possible scandals that might arise from competition for contracts by members of Congress, but from a different point of view. He privately wrote Gallatin, ". . . I am averse to giving contracts of any kind to members of the Legislature." [4] Both branches therefore readily concurred in the contract law of 1808.[5]

By its terms Congressmen were forbidden to execute any contract with the United States under penalty of a fine of $3,000 and the voidance of the contract. Every contract entered into with the government was required to specify that no member of Congress should be admitted to any share in it. Executive officers were forbidden, directly or indirectly, to enter into any contract with a member, and an annual statement of all contracts made by Treasury, War, Navy, and the Post Office was required.

The House debates left no doubt concerning the object of this legislation. Its author, Burwell Bassett of Virginia, based it on the fundamental principle of maintaining "the purity of the Representative body." [6] One of its principal supporters, Nathaniel Macon, declared that "this body should be as pure as purity itself, and therefore . . . its members should have no concern with the public money." [7] Representative Troup declared that unless some bill of this sort were adopted, "the time is not far distant when this House will become, what the British House of Commons are, a corrupt, servile, dependent, and contemptible body. We had better have no Legislature, than one composed of contractors, placemen, and pensioners." [8] These remarks were made in the knowledge that Senator John Smith of Ohio held large contracts with the War Department

---

list of appointments of Congressmen to executive posts from 1789 to 1825 is found in House Doc. 77, 22d Cong., 2d sess.; and from 1825 to 1833 in House Doc. 76, 22d Cong., 2d sess.

4 Jefferson, *Writings* (Memorial ed.), XI, 165 (March 20, 1807).
5 2 Stat. 484 (April 21, 1808).
6 *Annals,* 10th Cong., 1st sess., II, 1466 (Jan. 15, 1808).
7 *Ibid.,* II, 1469.
8 *Ibid.,* II, 1618 (Feb. 16, 1808).

and Representative Matthew Lyon of Kentucky had a number of contracts with the Postmaster General.[9]

In 1826 President Adams asked the Attorney General, William Wirt, whether the public contract law would bar the employment of members of Congress as assistant counsel to the district attorneys. Wirt replied in the affirmative.

The policy of the law is to prevent the exercise of executive influence over the members of the Congress by the means of contracts; and whether the contract be for the service of a lawyer, a physician, or a mail-carrier, an army purveyor, or a turnpike-road maker, it seems to me to be equally within the policy and the mischief of the law. . . . a succession of single engagements is quite as mischievous as a contract *in solido.* . . .[10]

If we may accept the testimony of John Quincy Adams, there was considerable office seeking among members of Congress. In 1821 he declared, "About one-half the members of Congress are seekers for office at the nomination of the President. Of the remainder, at least one-half have some appointment or favor to ask for their relatives." [11]

There is no evidence that the independence of Congress was substantially affected by thirst for office on the part of Representatives and Senators. No President from Washington to John Quincy Adams, as has been noted, depended on patronage to facilitate passage of his legislative program. Congressmen, however, continued to declaim against such executive threats to the purity of their deliberations, doubtless from various motives.

CONGRESS DEPENDS ON EXECUTIVE INFORMATION

Despite the undercurrent of jealousy that ran continuously between the legislative and executive branches, Congress regularly depended on the latter for information concerning proposed legislation. Furthermore it never hesitated to take the initiative in asking for this type of assistance, notwithstanding early Republican opposition to references of pending matters

9 House Report 81, 17th Cong., 1st sess., p. 5 (March 29, 1822).

10 *Opinions of the Attorneys General* (1841 ed.), p. 575 (July 18, 1826).

11 Adams, *Memoirs,* V, 238 (Jan. 18, 1821). For particular instances, see *ibid.,* V, 207–8, 291; VI, 309; VII, 118.

to the heads of departments. Substantially all major legislation and much minor legislation were based on administrative reports, giving facts and opinions for the guidance of Congress. Some examples, large and small, will illustrate the practice.

In 1803 the House asked Gideon Granger, the Postmaster General, whether it would be expedient to require the more extensive use of stages or covered wagons for the transportation of the mail.[12] In 1808 Gallatin presented his masterly report on roads and canals in response to a congressional request.[13] Many reports were made by the War Department on military organization, especially after the War of 1812. At the request of both Houses, John Quincy Adams prepared his great report on weights and measures.[14] In 1823 the House asked for information concerning the improvement of the post road to New Orleans.[15] In 1825 the Treasury was invited to present information on further measures to prevent smuggling on the northern frontier.[16] In 1826 the Navy Department gave the House information on establishing a line of communication between the Atlantic and the Pacific across the Isthmus of Panama.[17] The list might be extended indefinitely.

The significance of this procedure stands out in the acknowledgment in 1826 of the House Select Committee on Increase of the Tariff on Spirits. The committee started out independently to organize its material and report.

. . . They, however, soon discovered the difficulties, as well as delays of this mode, and in an interview which they requested of the Secretary of the Treasury, for the purpose of consultation, that gentleman expressed a willingness and a readiness to afford the committee all the facilities for this information which the records of the Treasury Department could furnish. Accordingly, the various points were committed to writing and presented to the Secretary.[18]

To what extent these requests for information were privately instigated by the departments themselves, in order to initiate

12 *American State Papers: Post Office*, p. 29.
13 *American State Papers: Miscellaneous*, I, 724.
14 Adams, *Memoirs*, V, 290 (Feb. 22, 1821).
15 *American State Papers: Post Office*, p. 111.
16 Senate Doc. 22, 18th Cong., 2d sess.
17 *American State Papers: Naval Affairs*, III, 21.
18 House Report 225, 19th Cong., 1st sess., p. 1 (May 19, 1826).

discussion of legislation that they thought desirable, is impossible to determine. It is highly probable that this process was taking place in view of the strong leadership that Jefferson and Gallatin exerted in Congress for nearly eight years, and in view of the weight of influence exerted by department heads such as Calhoun, McLean, or Crawford. In any event requests for facts represented a normal part of the interplay between Congress and the executive departments. The latter acted in this respect somewhat in the capacity of staff aides to committees of Congress, none of which had any assistance of their own.[19]

CONGRESS SUPERVISES THE EXECUTIVE BUSINESS

Both Federalists and Republicans recognized Congress as the "grand inquest of the nation." This function was long established in Parliament and accepted without question in 1792 when the House investigated the causes of the defeat of General St. Clair.[20] Much more than investigation was involved, however, as Congress began to find its place in a Republican scheme. Regular annual departmental reports were established as a means of informing Congress and the people; special reports multiplied as administrative irregularities came to the attention of Congressmen; congressional interest in particular cases increased under pressure from constituents; and six standing committees on public expenditures were established to reduce costs and increase efficiency. Republicans, however, like their predecessors, refused to yield executive discretion on the submission of papers upon demand from either House.

Call for papers. In the precedent-making case of the call for the papers relating to the Jay Treaty, President Washington had asserted the power of the executive to refuse to transmit papers

19 No assertion by the old Republicans of legislative supremacy went so far as to exclude some statutory delegation of rule-making power to the executive branch. Powers constitutionally conveyed to the Chief Executive were thus supplemented, and particular authorities to make rules and regulations were conferred at times directly upon the heads of departments or agencies. Some early legislation was eventually replaced by executive rules, notably the Naval Regulations. See John Preston Comer, *Legislative Functions of National Administrative Authorities* (New York: Columbia University Press, 1927), especially ch. 3.

20 White, *The Federalists*, pp. 80–81.

if not in the public interest.[21] The precedent stood during the Republican era, and was occasionally put to work.[22] In 1825 Monroe refused to send the House papers concerning charges against Commodore Stewart and a political agent, Prevost, stationed in Peru. His remarks have a permanent interest.

. . . It is important that the public servants in every station should perform their duty with fidelity, according to the injunctions of the law and the orders of the Executive in fulfillment thereof. . . . It is due to their rights and to the character of the Government that they be not censured without just cause, which cannot be ascertained until, on a view of the charges, they are heard in their defense, and after a thorough and impartial investigation of their conduct. Under these circumstances it is thought that a communication at this time of those documents would not comport with the public interest nor with what is due to the parties concerned.[23]

Normally, however, a call for papers resulted in prompt compliance. The *American State Papers* provide an abundance of examples from every department.

Annual reports. One significant guide to congressional interest in administration was the extension and regularization of reports required from executive officers. In the early years periodical departmental reports were not prepared and were not required by law, except in the Treasury Department. By the end of the Jeffersonian era, every department submitted an annual report which was transmitted to Congress with the President's annual message and referred to the appropriate House committee. These reports, supplemented by many special reports prepared at the request of the House or Senate, became one of the principal means of informing Congress concerning every aspect of the public business.[24] The call for special reports also became in part an agency for harassing the Administration,

21 *Ibid.,* p. 63.

22 The Republicans were forced to retreat from the position they had taken in 1796 when they were the party of opposition. Cf. the indignant remarks of Federalist Senator Plumer, *Memorandum,* p. 24 (Oct. 24, 1803).

23 Richardson, *Messages,* II, 278 (Jan. 10, 1825).

24 Many of them are printed in the *American State Papers* and after 1815 in the House and Senate Documents and Reports. Many were never printed. These are now in the National Archives.

a procedure for which precedent was readily available in the last years of Hamilton's tenure of the Treasury.

From year to year the House published a list of the reports required to be made to it. An analysis of the list for 1822, rearranged in chronological order, shows something both of the content of the reports and of the evolution of their character.[25] In the Federalist years, twelve regular reports were required of the executive departments. With one exception, they were exclusively financial or informative in character, such as the annual report on the state of finances, or the returns of registered seamen. The annual statement of the emoluments and expenditures of officers employed in customs, however, was designed to control administrative expenses.[26]

No further reports of this character were required until 1808, when Congress gave emphatic notice of its interest in what executive officers were about. New legislation required annual statements of all contracts made by Treasury, War, Navy, and the Post Office, and by the collectors of customs.[27] The next year Congress asked for annual reports of official accounts remaining unsettled for more than three years, in a drive to curb delinquents.[28] It also required particular statements of payments made for miscellaneous claims and for contingent fund expenses of the War and Navy Departments, in an effort to reduce discretionary expenditures.[29] The new emphasis was definitely on control.

After the War of 1812 other regular reports were required, the character of which suggested congressional intent to watch closely the public business. In 1817 all accounts not settled at the end of one year were required to be reported.[30] In 1818 the Senate asked for an annual statement of the condition of the public buildings.[31] In the same year Congress asked for an annual report showing the names of all clerks employed in the

25 House Doc. 1, 17th Cong., 2d sess. (Dec. 2, 1822).
26 1 Stat. 704, sec. 2 (March 2, 1799).
27 2 Stat. 484, sec. 5 (April 21, 1808).
28 2 Stat. 535, sec. 2 (March 3, 1809).
29 *Ibid.*, sec. 5.
30 3 Stat. 366, sec. 13 (March 3, 1817).
31 *Senate Journal,* 15th Cong., 1st sess., p. 112.

departments, with the emoluments of each.[32] In 1820 it sought to tighten up appropriation procedure by requiring War and Navy reports of balances available under each heading.[33] In 1822 Congress asked for the names of all Indian agents, the state of their accounts, and a list of delinquents.[34] Another type of report, required whenever the contingency arose, and directly concerned with congressional control of the use of funds, was initiated in 1809. Congress required the President to report to it, in the first week of each session, what transfers of money had been authorized from one branch of expenditure to another.[35]

Special reports on alleged irregularities. From time to time Congress called upon departments to justify their specific administrative actions, the implication being that statutory requirements and conditions had been disregarded. These requests were relatively uncommon during the Federalist period. They became more frequent after 1815. They were designed to expose what some member or members of Congress believed to be maladministration or malfeasance. The power to ask questions and require an answer, without the formality of an investigation, was often enough in itself to correct dubious practices or to initiate remedial legislation. Some examples will illustrate the beneficial consequences.

In December 1820 the House appointed a committee to inquire by what authority the ordnance department had made loans of powder and lead to private individuals. The committee report exposed a curious state of affairs.[36] In 1821 the House Committee on Military Affairs asked the War Department what army officers were employed as clerks and what extra compensation had been allowed them. Calhoun's answer led directly to a committee recommendation prohibiting the practice.[37] In 1823

[32] 3 Stat. 445, sec. 9 (April 20, 1818).

[33] 3 Stat. 567, sec. 2 (May 1, 1820).

[34] 3 Stat. 682, sec. 3 (May 6, 1822).

[35] 2 Stat. 535 (March 3, 1809). Particular notice is not given to other annual reports primarily concerned with producing information of the state of the nation. A list of the more important would include an abstract of the tonnage of U. S. vessels (1792); militia returns (1803); patents issued (1812); passengers arriving in the United States (1819); statistics of commerce and navigation (1820).

[36] *American State Papers: Military Affairs*, II, 287 (Feb. 7, 1821).

[37] House Report 61. 16th Cong., 2d sess. (Feb. 13, 1821).

the House asked each department to what newspapers it subscribed at the public expense. The publication of the list was
enough in itself to curb what apparently was a minor type of
patronage. The War Department alone subscribed to thirty-
one newspapers and periodicals, a list probably reflecting deference to editors rather than a passion for the daily news.[38] In
1823 the Engineer Corps was required to report whether money
appropriated in 1820, 1821, and 1822 had been expended on
the several fortifications as required by law.[39] In 1824 the House
called upon the President to inform its members whether legal
proceedings had been instituted against prize agents, delinquent
in their accounts, and whether certain directions of Congress
had "of late been enforced." [40] These *ad hoc* reports fulfilled
somewhat the same function as the question hour in the House
of Commons.

CONGRESS INVESTIGATES

A more pointed aspect of legislative supervision over administrative affairs appeared in the work of the various investigating
committees.[41] These were typically select committees, authorized
to look into some specific matter where incompetence, illegality,
or scandal was suspected. They were designed less to lay the
foundation for new legislation than to correct specific errors or
malpractices. They normally presumed charges or evidence of
fault and often were hostile in intent. They were quite infrequent before 1815, but became almost an annual occurrence
for nearly ten years thereafter.

The power to investigate rested in part on the authority of
the House to impeach. A number of investigations were made
as preliminary to impeachment proceedings, including those
against Judge John Pickering, 1803,[42] and Justice Samuel Chase,

---

[38] The War Department list is contained in House Doc. 68, 17th Cong., 2d
sess. (1823); other lists are contained in documents of this Congress.

[39] House Doc. 72, 17th Cong., 2d sess., p. 5 (Feb. 17, 1823).

[40] House Doc. 153, 18th Cong., 1st sess., p. 7 (April 23, 1824).

[41] On this topic see Marshall E. Dimock, *Congressional Investigating Committees* (Baltimore: Johns Hopkins Press, 1929); Ernest J. Eberling, *Congressional
Investigations* (New York: Columbia University Press, 1928), chs. 1–2.

[42] *Annals,* 8th Cong., 1st sess., pp. 380, 1097.

1804.[43] The failure of the Chase trial foreclosed the use of impeachment to control the operations of either the judicial or the executive branch until the impeachment of President Johnson in 1868.

The power to investigate was an obvious means of imposing congressional discipline upon an administrative officer. One of the earliest applications of such discipline occurred just at the close of the Federalist period when complaints of excess of power were made against Winthrop Sargent, governor of the Mississippi Territory. A House committee considered documents, including a long defense by Sargent, and concluded that he and the territorial judges had misconceived their legislative power. The committee also concluded that there was no cause for further proceedings.[44] Two years later Sargent was again investigated on charges of illegal arrest. The House committee found that the arrest was in fact irregular and oppressive, but could do no more than refer the complainant to a court.[45] The conduct of Judge Harry Innis of Kentucky in connection with the Burr conspiracy was looked into by a House committee in 1808, but no ground for impeachment was discovered.[46]

New energy flowed into Congress after the War of 1812 and a sequence of investigations of administrative affairs occurred quite unparalleled in previous experience. A substantially complete list of investigations from 1815 to 1826 demonstrates both the activity of Congress and the broadening scope of the investigating power.

1815—expenses of the state militia
1816—defalcation by Colonel Thomas
1816—army expenditures on the northern frontier
1816—fiscal affairs of the Post Office
1818—conduct of General Jackson in the Seminole War
1818—conduct of clerks in the executive departments
1818—fees exacted by a district attorney
1819—illegal executions in the army

[43] *Ibid.*, pp. 806, 1124.
[44] *American State Papers: Miscellaneous*, I, 233 (Feb. 19, 1801).
[45] *Ibid.*, I, 361 (Nov. 28, 1803).
[46] *Ibid.*, I, 922 (April 19, 1808).

1819—embezzlement by a clerk of court
1819—failure of a judge to hold court
1820—illegal loans of powder to private individuals
1821—administration of the Post Office
1822—affairs of the Post Office
1822—War Department contract with Mix
1823—refusal of a judge to admit an attorney to practice
1823—alleged suppression of documents by Gales and Seaton
1823—conduct of superintendent of Indian trading houses
1824—conduct of Secretary of the Treasury in making deposits of money
1826—administration of the War Department by John C. Calhoun

The content of these investigations need not require attention at this point; those which have special significance are dealt with elsewhere. For present purposes it is sufficient to record that in the decade from 1815 to 1825 the power to investigate became well fixed as an important means by which Congress discharged its duty of supervising the conduct of administration. Where necessary, these committees were granted power to send for persons and papers.

It may be noted in passing that congressional inquiries began to reflect the special interest of individual members in field establishments located within their districts or state. The War Department, proposing to move an Indian agency from Fort Wayne to the Great Miami reservation, received a strong protest from Senator James Noble and Representative O. H. Smith. Lewis Cass, governor of Michigan Territory, wrote the Indian agent that he thought the Indiana delegation should decide the question.[47] The House Committee on Indian Affairs recommended the assignment of Indian agents in 1827.[48] The War Department was interrogated in 1827 on the removal of troops from certain fortifications.[49] Congressional inquiries on the apportionment of appointments to West Point bore the imprint of the same type of interest.

Congressmen were already being driven to the departments by their constituents. John McLean was in Congress for only a

47 Senate Doc. 189, 20th Cong., 1st sess. (May 1, 1826).
48 House Report 86, 19th Cong., 2d sess. (Feb. 22, 1827).
49 House Doc. 46, 20th Cong., 1st sess., p. 5 (Dec. 22, 1827).

brief period, but long enough to record this trend in the relations of Congress and the executive branch. "During the last winter, I never was more industriously engaged than in attending to the private business of others, when the house was not in session. There were three western mails a week, by which my principal letters were received—these often amounted to between 30 and 40, generally on business, which required my attention at the different offices." [50]

The taste for putting questions and making investigations grew upon members of Congress, reflecting their new sense of participation in public affairs, their realization of factional advantage in embarrassing political opponents, and their appreciation of the usefulness of such activity in impressing their constituents. The departments were hard put to it during the sessions, and on occasion had to plead incapacity to produce the information desired. The problem of congressional self-discipline was raising its head.

The six committees on public expenditures. On February 24, 1814, the House of Representatives created a standing Committee on Public Expenditures.[51] Two years later (March 30, 1816), in connection with the reorganization of 1816, it established six standing committees on expenditures, one respectively for the State, Treasury, War, Navy, and Post Office Departments, and one on public buildings. These committees bespoke the intention of Congress to follow the operations of the various agencies continuously and consistently. They came into existence under the House leadership of Henry Clay, and reflected the intention of Clay and his friends "to take control of the government." [52]

[50] John McLean, *Letter on the Compensation Bill* (Richland, Ohio, May 28, 1816), p. 10. Cf. comment of Congressman Mills ". . . I have been constantly engaged in attending to some private business for my *constituents* and friends, who think they have a right to call on me for that purpose." Letters of Elijah H. Mills, Massachusetts Historical Society, *Proceedings*, XIX (1881–82), 15 (Dec. 30, 1815).

[51] Originally the House Committee on Ways and Means performed all the duties peculiar to it, plus those of the Committee on Public Expenditures and of the six standing committees on expenditures in the several departments. "Until the appointment of these six additional Standing Committees, the duties imposed on the Committee on Public Expenditure must have been too arduous and multifarious ever to have been performed with effect." House Report 116, 20th Cong., 1st sess., p. 2 (Jan. 31, 1828).

[52] Ralph Volney Harlow, *History of Legislative Methods*, p. 216.

They also reflected an emerging phase of institutional growth and a new balance between the two coordinate branches of government.

The six standing committees on expenditures had a function different from that of other standing committees of the House dealing with the same departments, and different from the newly established offices of the five auditors. The House Committee on Post Offices and Post Roads, for example, was concerned with the Post Office, as was the Committee on Expenditures in the Post Office. The former was concerned with postal legislation, the establishment of post roads, postal revenue, and in general with post office policy. The Committee on Public Expenditures in the Post Office was responsible for watching the conduct of business, for criticizing laxness, and for the use of funds.

It would have been easy for the committees on expenditures to have encroached on the work of the auditors. It was generally understood, however, that the committees had nothing to do with the settlement of accounts, although they might criticize an expenditure made or an account settled on the ground that undesirable practices were involved in the transaction. The rule was well stated by the Committee on Expenditures in the Navy: "The best security against the misapplication of the public money, will be found in the integrity and vigilance of the officer who has the examination and settlement of the accounts." [53]

The general Committee on Public Expenditures set up in 1814 and continued alongside the six departmental committees was, however, at some loss to define its own field of action. In a report in 1828 it took ground that brought it close to the function of auditing. The committee described its duty as being to ascertain:

. . . 1st, Whether the money thus appropriated has been drawn for the specific object designated in the law, making the appropriation. 2dly, whether any more has been drawn, than may have been authorized by the law. 3dly, whether the money has been drawn from the Treasury on the requisition of proper officers of the Department . . . leaving it to the committee on the particular Department to ex-

[53] House Report 45, 18th Cong., 2d sess., p. 2 (Jan. 28, 1825).

amine whether that Department has properly applied the money thus placed at their disposal; whether the vouchers for its disbursements are regular; and whether the expenditure has been made with due regard to economy, and in good faith for the public service.[54]

The actual work of this committee had in fact been largely taken over by the six standing committees on public expenditures.

These committees did not make regular annual reports and were apparently somewhat sporadic in their activities. In 1821 John Quincy Adams recorded that hitherto he had heard nothing of the committee upon the Department of State except its appointment.[55] They were, however, all stimulated by the economy drive of 1820–1822.

The character of the work of the committees on public expenditures, and the quality of their supervision over the departments, may best be judged by two examples.[56] For the first case we select the report of the Committee on the Accounts and Expenditures of the War Department for 1822.[57] The committee asked first whether the departmental expenditures were justified by law. This question gave opportunity to discuss the practice of extra compensation to officers detailed occasionally to clerical duties, which this committee endorsed. Secondly, the committee inquired whether the expenditures were supported by vouchers "establishing their justness," giving occasion to criticize various small items in the contingent expenses such as the purchase by officers of books having no connection with their official duties. Thirdly the committee queried whether the disbursements were made in conformity with the appropriation laws. The only issue raised under this head was a purely technical matter of the status of an appropriation for $60,000 for work at Fort Calhoun, one of that interminable class of questions that arise from ambiguity in appropriation language.

Next, the committee asked what further provisions were nec-

[54] House Report 116, 20th Cong., 1st sess., p. 2 (Jan. 31, 1828).

[55] Adams, *Memoirs*, V, 227 (Jan. 3, 1821).

[56] Cf. the constructive report on the Patent Office by the Committee on Expenditures of the Department of State. House Report 86, 17th Cong., 2d sess. (Feb. 7, 1823).

[57] House Report 105, 17th Cong., 1st sess. (May 1, 1822).

essary for the proper and economical disbursement of the public money. Its recommendations were prefaced by an interesting comment, the purport of which has too often been obscured in congressional committees: "They are persuaded that, under the most vigilant and judicious administration, there will occasionally be some mismanagement, some waste, some peculation; and the most that can be effected, is to lessen the temptations and the facilities to these malversations; to provide for their early detection; and for indemnity to the public when detected." [58] With this statesmanlike declaration, the committee went on to assert that while "mere accountability" was complete, there was room for improvement in economy. The committee strongly urged that fortifications and other permanent works be built under army direction, not by contract. It recommended also that a government agent, in whose hands were placed large advances of money, should be required to deposit these funds in a bank in his name as an officer. It also advised dividing the contingency fund into specific subheads to be placed under the control of a single clerk for all the War Department bureaus.

The committee finally addressed itself to the matter of retrenchment. It endorsed the position of the Secretary of War that his department could not conduct its business efficiently with a lesser number of clerks or with a lower standard of compensation. Finally the committee referred to the need for more effective means of recovering money from defaulters, suggesting that prosecution be transferred to the Attorney General. This committee evidently took its duties seriously.

The Committee on Expenditures in the Navy Department gave special attention in 1825 to the navy contingent fund.[59] It asserted that this fund had "at all times, been liable to abuses," but agreed that "a discretionary power must necessarily reside in the head of the Department, and much must depend upon the vigilance" of the responsible officers.[60] "As little latitude, how-

---

[58] *Ibid.*, p. 3.

[59] House Report 45, 18th Cong., 2d sess. (Jan. 28, 1825); excerpts from p. 2.

[60] This statement may be compared with one made by the House Committee on Public Lands in 1824: "In all legislation, much must necessarily be left to construction, and the sound discretion of those charged with the administration of the laws." House Report 130, 18th Cong., 1st sess. (May 26, 1824).

ever, should be allowed to the discretion of the officer as is consistent with the good of the service. . . ." The committee commented on traveling expenses and extra allowances unauthorized by law but depending on usage for their justification. It criticized the volume of expenditure on the contingency fund growing out of the frequent occurrence of courts martial and courts of inquiry, and expressed the hope that a new rule requiring authorization by the Secretary of the Navy would reduce their number and expense.

These examples suggest that the committees on expenditures were mainly concerned with characteristic administrative problems of efficiency and economy.[61] They were distinctly not concerned with substantive policy. On the whole they succeeded in avoiding particular claims and accounts, claims indeed being referred to various committees dealing with this perplexing subject. Only a full examination of the reports of expenditure committees, many of which were not published but most of which are available, would permit a judgment as to their capacity to rise above factional advantage and as to the broad wisdom of their recommendations.

The six committees on expenditures found their task both arduous and responsible. The members of the Committee on Expenditures in the State Department reported in 1828 that they had found it impossible "to enter into a critical examination of the justness of the multiplied items" in a certain account, and, if practicable, it "would consume more time than the Committee could promise to devote to it, consistently with their other duties."[62] The Committee on Expenditures of the War Department observed in 1822, "The committee will now take occasion to remark, that the duties prescribed to them, to be completely executed, require much time and labor. . . . They

---

[61] In 1828 the House declined to set up a standing committee on retrenchment to investigate the manner of discharging the public business. Such a committee, it was said, should be raised only on allegation of mismanagement. Past experience induced the belief that a committee thus "armed with general inquisitorial powers" would first excite odium and "soon fall into disuse and contempt." House Report 240, 20th Cong., 1st sess. (April 26, 1828).

[62] House Report 226, 20th Cong., 1st sess., p. 4 (April 5, 1828). The Committee on Naval Expenditures asserted in 1825 that to do their task properly would require "a total abandonment of their legislative duties." House Report 45, 18th Cong., 2d sess. (Jan. 28, 1825).

think it highly desirable, that the duties should be performed in the early part of the session, that the legislature may thereby be able to correct abuses, if they exist, and if they do not, to remove unfounded causes of distrust, and restore the public confidence; for, next to the evil of having a wasteful and corrupt government is the belief that we have one." [63] No better statement of the general object and purpose of the six standing committees could have been made.

The evidence leaves no doubt that a new spirit of enterprise and a different sense of responsibility animated Congress after the close of Jefferson's administration, and notably after the achievement of peace in 1815 gave the country opportunity to look at its domestic institutions. Fisher Ames, who was cast down by the tentative assaults of congressional committees on executive discretion in the days of the Federalists, would have been appalled at their restless activity in the administration of James Monroe, could he have lived to witness the scene. He would have concluded indeed that the six standing committees on expenditures had become ministers, and he would have been deeply alarmed at the succession of select committees to look into all sorts of executive conduct. He would have thought the energy of government lost in the combinations of the committee rooms.

Ames, however, would not have been an acceptable guide even to his own generation. Congress had its part to play in administration, as well as in policy and politics, and that part could be constructive. There was evidence enough that the public service required inspection, and effective inspection originated in considerable measure from the representatives of the taxpayer. In the administrative reforms following peace in 1815, Congress played a constructive role; and it was due to Congress that a major retrenchment program was put into effect to meet the consequences of the depression of 1819–1822.

The administrative process was not expedited, to be sure, and the burden of Secretaries was not lightened by the energy that Congress directed toward the executive branch. Both branches began to feel more heavily the pressure of constituents claiming

63 House Report 105, 17th Cong., 1st sess., p. 5 (May 1, 1822).

various rights and privileges—land, pensions, claims, relief, settlement of accounts, remission of forfeitures, appointment to West Point, trading licenses with the Indians, and contracts of divers sorts. Presidents and Secretaries had more work and more interruption by reason of the rising activities of Congressmen and their committees. All this, however, was a part of the price of democratic government, and Republicans in executive office could hardly complain.

CHAPTER EIGHT

Congress and the Control
of Expenditures

As the party of the opposition, the Republicans had fought consistently to strengthen the control of Congress over the use of funds by executive officers. They wanted an executive responsible to Congress and consequently favored the least possible discretion in the use of funds. Put in other terms, they favored specific appropriations to which the heads of departments would be bound. They were also concerned with economy, and did not trust the spending proclivities of subordinate agents. Both Republicans and Federalists had been puzzled as to where exactly to draw the line between executive discretion and congressional control. The Republicans leaned toward strict specification of appropriations and close executive responsibility. In this battle Gallatin had been the principal Republican leader.[1]

After 1801 as the government of the day the Republicans stood by their guns, but with responsibility they tended to lean less energetically in favor of stringent congressional control, and events conspired to render it difficult to achieve Gallatin's ideal. Nevertheless, he did not waver in his convictions, and steadily urged Congress to impose greater limitations upon the freedom of his colleagues and himself in the use of funds. His

1 White, *The Federalists,* ch. 26; Lucius Wilmerding, Jr., *The Spending Power,* chs. 1–2; in this section I have borrowed freely from Wilmerding. For many of the documents, see Fred Wilbur Powell, compiler, *Control of Federal Expenditures: A Documentary History, 1775–1894* (Washington, D. C.: Brookings Institution, 1939).

colleagues, especially Robert Smith in the Navy Department, were less convinced of the administrative soundness of the Treasury position. The experience of these twenty-eight years demonstrated clearly enough that, given responsibilities to discharge, the departments would find ways and means of action even at the cost of evading congressional dictates on the expenditure of funds. John Randolph became so pessimistic about the possibility of control that he was prepared to appropriate in a single lump sum for each department! Congress, however, persisted in the Republican tradition.

ITEMIZATION

The issue first to present itself was the form of the appropriation act. Gallatin promptly invited Jefferson to ask Congress for its cooperation along the lines of Republican theory.[2] In his first annual message Jefferson recommended prudence "by appropriating specific sums to every specific purpose susceptible of definition; by disallowing all applications of money varying from the appropriation in object or transcending it in amount; by reducing the undefined field of contingencies and thereby circumscribing discretionary powers over money. . . ."[3] Congress took no action despite a concurring report from a House committee.[4] The discussion, however, revealed that both Federalists and Republicans accepted the doctrine of specific appropriations in principle, and that the latter were not disposed to be doctrinaire in its application. ". . . we want specific appropriations," declared Nicholson, "but when we specify we ought to take care that we do not go too far."[5]

Faced with the responsibility of governing, Republicans began to think more realistically about the value of specific itemization in the appropriation acts. The pattern which they followed during the years of their ascendancy turned out to be the same as that which Republican-Federalist argument had settled upon in earlier years. The degree of itemization varied

2 Gallatin, *Writings*, I, 68; see also *ibid.*, I, 73.

3 Richardson, *Messages*, I, 329. Hamilton promptly defended the Federalist position in the Lucius Crassus letters, *Works* (Lodge ed.), VIII, 246 ff.

4 *American State Papers: Finance*, I, 752–54.

5 *Annals*, 7th Cong., 1st sess., p. 1246 (April 24, 1802).

among the three great annual appropriation acts for (a) the "support of Government," i.e., the civil list, (b) the army, and (c) the navy, respectively. The first of these was well itemized and closely controlled; the latter two were lump sums, with wide latitude for official discretion.

Practice may be illustrated by excerpts from the appropriation acts of 1806. The following items were in the act "for the support of Government." [6]

For compensation to the Secretary of State, clerks and persons employed in that department	$12,560
For the incidental and contingent expenses of the said department	4,200
For expense of stationery, printing, and incidental and contingent expenses of the comptroller's office	800
For purchasing books, maps and charts for the use of the treasury department	400

The compensation item of $12,560 was in fact not an unrestricted fund. It was exactly enough to pay the clerks in the State Department on the existing establishment. It granted no freedom to the Secretary except as a clerkship might fall vacant —a rare event. With these characteristic items may be compared a few larger authorizations, such as $98,000 for the allowance to invalid pensioners, $81,000 for the maintenance and support of lighthouses, beacons, and stakeage, and $120,000 toward completing the surveys of public lands in Ohio, Indiana, and Mississippi.

The navy appropriation act stood in sharp contrast, consisting of only twelve heads contained on less than a single page.[7] By way of illustration, Congress authorized expenditures of $291,000 for pay and subsistence of officers, and pay of seamen; $157,000 for provisions; $411,000 for "repairs of vessels, store rent, pay of armorers, freight and other contingent expenses," and $60,000 for "the expense of navy yards, docks and other improvements," and for the pay of navy-yard employees. The

[6] 2 Stat. 384 (April 18, 1806).
[7] 2 Stat. 398 (April 21, 1806).

pay and subsistence items gave little latitude, since they were calculated on a known naval establishment. On the other hand the items of $411,000 for repairs and other contingent expenses, and of $60,000 for the maintenance of yards and docks were wide open, leaving almost uncontrolled discretion in the Navy Department. The military establishment appropriation was equally broad in its terms.[8]

It is an extraordinary fact that despite Republican commitment in theory to specific appropriations, the character of the three basic authorizations for the civil list, the army, and the navy remained the same throughout the years from 1801 to 1829. The appropriation acts of 1827 used the same enactment formula, and contained substantially the same standard items as those of 1806. The area of administrative discretion remained as broad; the difference was merely in the greater amounts appropriated.

So far as closer itemization of army and navy expenditures was concerned, therefore, Congress made little progress in extending its control over the executive branch. Republicans tacitly agreed that executive discretion was necessary to good administration, and declined to hamper their freedom of action, despite Gallatin's consistent appeal to theory. Jefferson on this point was shrewder. He wrote his Secretary of the Treasury in 1804 in terms which demonstrate that the President was well content with the substance of Federalist practice.

It is true that this appropriation is usually made on an estimate, given by the Secretary of State to the Secretary of the Treasury, and by him reported to Congress. But Congress, aware that too minute a specification has its evil as well as a too general one, does not make the estimate a part of their law, but gives a sum in gross, trusting the Executive discretion for that year and that sum only; so in other departments, as of war for instance, the estimate of the Secretary specifies all the items of clothing, subsistence, pay, etc., of the army. And Congress throws this into such masses as they think best, to wit, a sum in gross for clothing, another for subsistence, a third for pay, etc., binding up the Executive discretion only by the sum, and the object generalized to a certain degree. The minute details of

8 2 Stat. 408 (April 18, 1806).

the estimate are thus dispensed with in point of obligation, and the discretion of the officer is enlarged to the limits of the classification, which Congress thinks it best for the public interest to make.[9]

In this same letter Jefferson also observed, "The sum appropriated is generally the exact amount of the estimate, but not always."

BINDING CHARACTER OF THE APPROPRIATION ACT

While the Republicans in Congress were content to appropriate for army and navy in lump sums, they nevertheless insisted that whatever terms were written into the appropriation act should be precisely observed by the executive departments. On this point Federalists and Republicans were inclined to agree, but Federalist practice, especially in the armed services, denied their assertions of principle. The Secretaries of War and Navy stubbornly construed their appropriations, in whatever form, as "in gross." The issue focused on the language of the appropriation act. The Federalists used language which made the items less than obligatory; the Republicans preferred, and for a short interval imposed, language which was intended to make the items binding. The battle of the enacting clauses, to use a term employed by Heinlein,[10] was quickly terminated under the new regime in favor of Gallatin's formula: "the following sums be, and the same hereby are respectively appropriated." [11] This became the standard pattern throughout the period under review.[12] The formula was not powerful enough, however, to prevent evasions by Republican department heads —other than Gallatin.

Gallatin was strict in the use of funds appropriated to the Treasury Department. Every specification was to him a binding directive from which he never varied. In 1809 he could declare to the House of Representatives that "so far as relates to the expenditure of the monies . . . under the direction of this

9 Jefferson, *Writings* (Memorial ed.), XI, 6 (Feb. 19, 1804).

10 J. Clare Heinlein, "The Administrative Theory and Practice of Albert Gallatin," unpublished doctoral dissertation, University of Chicago, 1948.

11 2 Stat. 183 (May 1, 1802).

12 Cf. the enacting clause of the appropriation act of January 6, 1829, 4 Stat. 323.

Department, there is no instance within my knowledge in which the agents have exceeded or blended the appropriations." [13]

The use of funds in both the War and Navy Departments presented special problems. Here it was much more difficult to estimate exactly the sums required for various types of expenditure or to stand on the appropriation act, since in part disbursements depended upon the movement of troops or vessels and other considerations which could not be wholly foreseen. The Board of Navy Commissioners put their case well in 1829, in a report to Jackson's Secretary of the Navy.

The estimates upon which the appropriations are founded are prepared with all the care and accuracy of which the fallible judgment of man will admit. Yet, after all, they are but *estimates;* and until it shall be given to us to foresee the events of futurity, the fluctuations in the markets of the world, and the casualties of the ocean, we shall never arrive at precise accuracy in our calculations as to the expense of a navy employed in every known sea, and experiencing the vicissitudes of every known climate. A degree of accuracy, sufficient for practical purposes, may be gained; and this is all that can be reasonably expected. Yet, even in this case, it will be found that some items in the estimate are too low, others too high; but take the whole together, and they may prove sufficient.

The Board of Navy Commissioners freely admitted that "the principle which confines the application of navy appropriations to the particular objects for which they are made . . . has . . . in numerous instances, been violated in practice" and declared themselves "fully satisfied that the intention of the law of 1809, in its provisions as to the application of specific appropriations, has never been carried into full effect in any one year since the enactment." [14]

RESTRICTIONS ON TRANSFERS

The problem of adjusting expenditures to needs had been met by the Federalists by construing the military and naval establishment appropriations as in gross. This solution was obviously open to abuse, and clearly reduced the authority of Con-

[13] Wilmerding, *The Spending Power,* p. 63.
[14] *American State Papers: Naval Affairs,* III, 400.

gress. The Republicans' first idea of reform through narrowly itemized appropriation acts was not pursued. Their second attempt, to enforce the binding character of the appropriation language, failed in practice where expenditures were heaviest, i.e., in War and Navy. Their third attempt was to restrict the use of one fund for the purposes of another by requiring tighter procedures on transfers. This solution was enacted into law in 1809.[15]

The essential features of the statute relevant here were two. Congress flatly declared that "the sums appropriated by law for each branch of expenditure in the several departments shall be solely applied to the objects for which they are respectively appropriated, and to no other." This imperative injunction was followed by the necessary loophole for the transfer of funds from one branch to another:

> . . . *Provided nevertheless,* that during the recess of Congress, the President of the United States may, and he is hereby authorized, on the application of the secretary of the proper department, and not otherwise, to direct, if in his opinion necessary for the public service, that a portion of the monies appropriated for a particular branch of expenditure in that department, be applied to another branch of expenditure in the same department, in which case a special account of the monies thus transferred, and of their application, shall be laid before Congress during the first week of their next ensuing session.

Congress thus sought to curtail the unrestricted use of funds within departments by requiring the formal action both of the Secretary and the President for any variations from the terms of the appropriation act, and to discourage such variations by requiring a prompt report of each of them.

This statute may be interpreted either as a victory or as a defeat for the partisans of congressional control. On the one hand the binding character of items was reaffirmed, and exceptions were authorized only under extraordinary circumstances, approved by the supreme executive authority. On the other hand, the necessity of departure from the items was formally recognized by Congress. Randolph asserted that Gallatin was

[15] 2 Stat. 535 (March 3, 1809).

opposed to the transfer privilege, and Randolph himself considered the act "as a sort of death-warrant" to Jeffersonian principles.[16] The act was a compromise between Gallatin's position and that of the Secretary of the Navy, Robert Smith. The provision confining expenditures to the objects and amounts specified by law reflected Gallatin's influence and was presumably declaratory of existing practice; the provision allowing transfers reflected the influence of Smith and sanctioned what was perhaps already being done covertly.[17]

In 1817 Congress limited executive discretion still further by prohibiting any transfers of sums appropriated for certain purposes—fortifications, arsenals, armories, customhouses, docks, navy yards, or buildings of any sort, munitions of war, or the pay of the army and navy.[18] Three years later Congress made another attack on the control of transfers in the War and Navy Departments, this time by specifying affirmatively, and in narrow terms, what transfers the President could make, and banning all others.[19] Congress also forbade the transfer of funds for the service of one year to that of another, or the transfer of funds by War and Navy after they had initially drawn on their appropriation accounts.[20]

DEFICIENCIES

Faced with these restrictions on transfers, and faced also with responsibilities for operating their departments, the administrative agencies were forced to find other means of carrying on. One already of long standing was to incur a deficiency, asking Congress to make it good in the next fiscal year. Secretary of War McHenry came in for severe criticism for a $50,000 deficiency in his contingent fund of 1797, but Congress eventually supplied the money.[21] After 1820 deficiencies became chronic in some appropriation heads, each new appropriation being mortgaged to pay previous obligations.[22] Forbidden to

[16] *Annals*, 16th Cong., 1st sess., I, 787 (Dec. 23, 1819).
[17] Wilmerding, *op. cit.*, p. 76.
[18] 3 Stat. 390 (March 3, 1817).
[19] 3 Stat. 567, sec. 5 (May 1, 1820).
[20] *Ibid.*, sec. 4.
[21] Wilmerding, *op. cit.*, p. 45.
[22] *Ibid.*, p. 99.

transfer funds, the Navy Department invented the practice of "borrowing" from surpluses in well-placed accounts, later repaying from subsequent appropriations. Another device was simply to defer payment when funds ran out, requiring suppliers and others to wait for their cash.[23]

These practices were particularly unfortunate because they lent themselves readily to concealment and to confusion. The confusion was augmented because reports of expenditures to Congress were based not on the actual expenditure of disbursing officers, but on issues of funds to them. For example, an agent asked for $10,000 under "pay of the Navy," a fund which was exhausted; it was sent to him from the appropriation for "provisions" and was reported to Congress under that head. The most flagrant case was the use year after year of money collected from officers and seamen for their hospital care which was entered correctly on the books, but actually used for navy pay.[24] It followed that reports comparing expenditures with appropriations conveyed information which was far from reality. "On the surface all was regular; beneath there was nothing but confusion." [25]

The tug of war between Republicans in Congress and Republicans in the executive branch thus ended in a clear-cut victory for neither. The old Republicans, symbolized by Gallatin and John Randolph, steadfastly insisted on reducing executive discretion in the expenditure of public money to the single item of contingencies, which it was their further object to reduce to the smallest possible amount. The necessity of government, however, overrode these limitations. In the War and Navy Departments especially, executive discretion remained the rule. The balance in fiscal affairs between the executive and legislative branches remained about where the Federalists had left it.

23 *Ibid.*, pp. 103–4.
24 See below, ch. 20.
25 Wilmerding, *op. cit.*, p. 103.

CHAPTER NINE

Congress and Administrative Reform

The War of 1812 offered conclusive demonstration of the inadequacy of the prevailing administrative system, civil and military. Congress, with considerable executive guidance, responded to the desperate need of the day by providing the legislative foundation for a comprehensive administrative reorganization, the first of its kind. Other improvements were made by executive direction. The net result was to lay new administrative foundations, none of which required reworking for a quarter century and some of which lasted for a hundred years.

The detail of this reorganization movement, especially the reform of the system of accountability, is presented in subsequent chapters dealing with the respective departments. Here it is sufficient to note the general achievements of a remarkable two years, 1815–1817.

ADMINISTRATIVE REORGANIZATION

The first major reorganization occurred in the navy. The Secretary of the Navy had had no professional assistance of any kind, and even in peacetime had been swamped with a mass of trivial details. Congress in 1815 gave him a new agency for professional advice, the Board of Navy Commissioners, and took from his shoulders the burden of building, equipping, and manning ships, and supervising yards and docks. The Secretary of the Navy gained some time to consider naval policy and the most effective deployment of naval power.[1] The Board continued for over a quarter century.

Corresponding aid came to the Secretary of War in 1816, following preliminary legislation that carried the army through the War of 1812. Congress established a General Staff, stationed it in Washington, and thereby gave the civilian Secretary of War relief from buying hats and blankets and flintlocks. This type of General Staff existed until replaced by its modern version in 1903.[2]

The accounting system, already feeble, broke down under the mass of claims arising out of the War of 1812. An able Report by the Four Secretaries laid the foundation for a major Treasury reorganization that was written into law in 1817.[3] It remained substantially unchanged until 1921.

The Attorney General, who had been little more than a private member of the bar with the government as one of his clients, finally succeeded in 1817 in establishing an office of the Attorney General, with a room, a clerk, and a record book, from which was to develop the Department of Justice.

In the State Department John Quincy Adams found disorder and arrearages when he took over in 1817. Within two years he had introduced system and order, fixing forms that in some cases have persisted in departmental practice to the present time. Here reorganization did not need legislation, but proceeded under the impulse of a man who himself was the essence of system.

The spirit of reform was in the air. West Point was given new and superior leadership in the person of Major Thayer, and new sources of support and advice in a Board of Visitors. The quality of West Point instruction was radically improved. The very modern concept of standardization was grasped and made the foundation for new naval construction. The coast fortifications were found inadequate, and Congress approved a ten-year plan for a new system.

It is both impossible and unnecessary to assign exact responsibilities for this successful drive for administrative reorganiza-

1 See below, ch. 19.
2 See below, ch. 17.
3 See below, ch. 12.

tion to the executive or the legislative branch. Both had their share. Congress performed its responsibility well and in its reforming legislation showed an effective appreciation of administrative needs.

RETRENCHMENT

The financial consequences of the War of 1812 were disastrous to Gallatin's program for the liquidation of the public debt. By 1812 it had been reduced to $45,000,000; in 1815 it stood at $99,000,000.[4] In 1819 a depression overtook the country. Congress was faced with shrinking income and the choice between new taxes or reduction of expenditure. It made the easy choice of the latter alternative, unhampered by the economic doctrines of a later century. Its difficulties in enforcing retrenchment were a forecast of much subsequent history. They suggested that the only means of major reduction was to cut substantive programs; and that the only programs then susceptible of reduction were those of the army and navy.

The story opened in 1818 when the Senate asked the Treasury Department for a list of useless officers of customs.[5] The Treasury accepted with alacrity the opportunity to improve a situation that was obviously unsatisfactory to it. Crawford submitted, without comment, reports from various collectors recommending reductions.[6] The collector of Baltimore remarked with reference to the numerous collection districts established by law, that "some of them, it is probable, have been inserted at the suggestion of members of Congress, who have usually had a view to the accommodation of their neighborhood and counties. . . . it appears that much is hazarded by the numerous small ports of entry and delivery. . . ."[7] The port of Folly Landing was one of these, in which the Treasury believed that injury ensued to the revenue. The collector of Norfolk reported, "I have very long entertained the opinion . . . that we have, by far, too many collection districts. . . ."[8] They afford, he declared,

[4] *American State Papers: Finance,* III, 21–23.
[5] Senate Doc. 188, 15th Cong., 1st sess. (April 15, 1818).
[6] Senate Doc. 27, 15th Cong., 2d sess. (Dec. 2, 1818).
[7] *Ibid.,* p. 6.
[8] *Ibid.,* pp. 8, 10.

"very great facilities for smuggling. . . ." Crawford consequently was able to recommend the suppression of a small number of customs establishments, but the reduction in cost was trifling.

At the same moment the House asked Calhoun what reductions could be made in the military establishment, opening up a long series of events that were to culminate in a heavy attack on the size of the army. In his able report Calhoun defended the size and efficiency of the military establishment, and argued that improvement in management was a responsibility of the executive branch which Congress should forego.[9]

By 1820 the fiscal situation had become worse. The House Committee on Naval Expenditures addressed a long series of questions to the Secretary of the Navy, all pointing toward the reduction of expenditures and concluding with a noteworthy exhortation: "It cannot fail to escape our observation, that the popularity won for the navy by the valor of our officers and seamen during the late war, can only be maintained, in time of peace, by exhibiting that branch of our national defence as an example to others of judicious management." [10] The Secretary of the Navy made a polite and judicious, if noncommittal reply, observing that

> . . . there is no retrenchment in the public expenditure which requires a legislative act; but all such as can be made, in the exercise of my official authority, and in directing the best mode of economy, shall receive every attention and exertion in my power to afford, compatible with the good of the service and the public interest. . . . I fully coincide with your observations relative to the navy generally, and the means of preserving its popularity, by the prudent management of its fiscal operations; and no effort shall, on my part, be wanting to secure to this branch of the national defence a continuance of the public favor, which its efficiency and bravery obtained for it during the late war.[11]

These appeals to departments were buttressed by an ominous report of the House Committee on Ways and Means, April 14, 1820.

[9] House Doc. 36, 15th Cong., 2d sess. (Dec. 14, 1818).
[10] House Doc. 87, 16th Cong., 1st sess., p. 3 (Jan. 13, 1820).
[11] *Ibid.*, p. 6.

From the extraordinary depression of commerce within the last three years, the stagnation of our navigation, the depreciation in the value of our exports, the corresponding depreciation in the value of property of every description, and the serious embarrassments under which every branch of industry now labors, economy and retrenchment in expenditures of every citizen are imperiously required. The finances of the nation being seriously affected by those causes, there would seem to arise a corresponding obligation on the part of the government to retrench its expenditures, and economise its means.[12]

The committee called upon the President to prepare a plan for reductions "in the various branches of public expenditures," but the House did not accept its recommendations.

The time for action came when Congress reassembled in November 1820. Two major reductions were imposed on the army and the navy respectively. The army was reduced to four regiments of artillery and seven regiments of infantry, and the scale of operations of the corps of engineers was diminished; the construction of fortifications was cut from an annual rate of $800,000 to $202,000 plus an unexpended balance of about $100,000, and Congress specified the forts on which this sum was to be spent; the appropriation for the Indian department was cut in half.[13] The navy had been authorized to spend $1,000,000 annually in the construction of new ships. This amount was reduced to $500,000 per annum.[14] Congress thus was able to require a substantial reduction in expenditures, but only by reducing the scale of substantive programs: the size of the army, the building of forts, Indian expenditures, and the construction of ships.

It may be noted that there were no important citizen groups prepared to come to the defense of either the uniformed forces, fortifications, Indians, or the construction of ships. The principal interested group was the contractors, and they were not in favor with Congress. Practically the only resistance to these cuts came from the departments. Calhoun fought hard to save the

[12] House Report 91, 16th Cong., 1st sess., p. 10.

[13] 3 Stat. 615 (March 2, 1821); 3 Stat. 633 (March 3, 1821).

[14] 3 Stat. 642 (March 3, 1821). Cf. the resolutions offered by Representative Cobb, November 22, 1820 (House Res. 6, 16th Cong., 2d sess.).

army, but in vain.[15] He was given no previous knowledge of the
congressional reduction imposed on Indian expenditures. The
other source of resistance was the House Committee on Naval
Affairs which brought in a report opposing the slow-down in
naval construction.[16] President Monroe apparently was merely a
disinterested bystander, an attitude doubtless induced in part
because the army reduction became involved in the political
struggle between Calhoun and Crawford.[17]

At the next session of Congress two further attempts were
made at retrenchment, each of which ended in confusion and
frustration. A select committee on retrenchment was set up in
the House, which to the general consternation promptly brought
in a report to reduce the compensation of Congressmen. ". . .
the committee," so read the report, "are unanimously of opinion, that, in the great and good work of retrenchment, Congress
ought to be the first to set an example to the balance of the nation, and begin with themselves. . . ." The committee consequently recommended "a return to good old principles, which,
for some years past, have been lost sight of." [18] This was true
old Republican doctrine, however unpalatable to the new elements in the party. Few Congressmen liked to reduce their not
excessive pay, but a substantial majority dared not vote against
the proposal. Debate ran for over a week, and motions to recom-
mit or to lay on the table were repeatedly defeated before the
bill was finally disposed of by a motion to lay on the table,
carried "by a large majority" *without a division.*[19] This symbolic sacrifice to the cause of economy thus miscarried.

Not much more was achieved by the second attempt, which
took the form of a direction to the heads of the departments to
report "the number of officers and messengers retained in their
respective departments, and whether any of them, and, if any,

15 Charles M. Wiltse, *John C. Calhoun: Nationalist*, pp. 225 ff.

16 House Report 74, 16th Cong., 1st sess., p. 3 (March 7, 1820).

17 Adams, *Memoirs*, V, 237–38 (Jan. 18, 1821). Monroe wrote privately to
Madison, "Under the pretext of economy, attempts have been made, and in some
instances with success, to cut up that system [i.e., the army] in many important
parts, and in fact to reduce it to a nullity." Monroe, *Writings*, VI, 286–87 (May
10, 1822).

18 House Report 95, 17th Cong., 1st sess., p. 2 (April 20, 1822).

19 *Annals*, 17th Cong., 1st sess., II, 1782 (May 3, 1822).

how many of them are unnecessary, inefficient, or engaged in other pursuits or professions in no wise relating to the public service; and, also, whether they cannot adopt a more efficient as well as a more economical organization of their respective departments." [20]

The replies were not encouraging. For his own office clerks, Secretary Crawford stated, "They are all efficient, and necessary for the correct and prompt discharge of the duties of the office. . . ." With regard to other branches of the Treasury establishment he reported that "a reduction of the number will be found to be practicable in some of the offices. This, however, will depend more upon the character and conduct of the principal officers of the Department, than upon legislative enactments." [21] For his own office he asked for one additional clerk. Peter Hagner, third auditor, reported that he had actually discharged five clerks due to progress in clearing up unsettled accounts.[22] John McLean, then land commissioner, cautiously answered, ". . . I find some of the clerks more efficient than others, but I might do injustice by saying, that any of them are inefficient. . . . the number cannot be lessened . . . without prejudice to the public service." [23] The treasurer replied rather tartly, ". . . I have the honor to state to you that none of the officers now employed in my office are either unnecessary or inefficient. . . ." [24]

The War Department reported that it could dispense with three clerks in the bounty land and pension offices. It discovered only one inefficient clerk, Colonel Henley, "who is seventy four years of age, and has been in the service of the United States, except an interval of twelve years, from the year 1775, up to the present day. . . . From his age, he is incapable of performing the duties of a Clerk, but, from his recollection of Revolutionary events, he is useful in the examination of Revolutionary claims." [25] The fourth auditor, Constant Freeman, also discovered one inefficient clerk. John Craven commenced his of-

20 *House Journal,* 17th Cong., 1st sess., p. 464 (April 16, 1822).
21 House Doc. 4, 17th Cong., 2d sess., pp. 3–4 (Dec. 2, 1822).
22 *Ibid.,* p. 8.
23 *Ibid.,* pp. 10–11.
24 *Ibid.,* p. 12.
25 House Doc. 5, 17th Cong., 2d sess., p. 4 (Dec. 2, 1822).

ficial duties in 1799 and was then eighty-one years of age: "he has been one of the best clerks in the office, but age has impaired his strength; he is, however, now, one of the most attentive, and does all in his power." [26]

As to improved organization, the general tenor of the replies is adequately suggested by three examples. Calhoun reported, " 'A more efficient or economical organization' of the Department, it is believed, cannot be adopted." [27] Return J. Meigs declared, "The Postmaster General does not perceive that any advantages or economical change can be made in the organization of his office, excepting by the employment of two additional Clerks." [28] The Secretary of Navy replied, ". . . I am not aware of any mode, by which it could be rendered more efficient, or economical." [29]

It could hardly be said that in this effort at economy and efficiency Congress was even moderately successful except by reducing the scale of the army and navy. The early improvement in the economic condition of the country caused the great retrenchment drive to evaporate.[30] Furthermore, the election of 1824 was on the doorstep.

Three general observations seem warranted by the experience of this drive for retrenchment. First, the rate of expenditure could be substantially reduced by Congress if it was prepared to cut substantive programs. Second, no department was likely to admit in response to a questionnaire that it was either inefficient or uneconomical. Third, it was easier to reduce substantive programs when no important group outside the government was adversely affected.

The matter of retrenchment appeared again in 1828, but the circumstances suggested strongly that the object of the House inquiry was to embarrass the Administration and to lay a part of the foundation for the 1828 campaign rather than to improve the public service. The chairman of the select committee was James Hamilton, a strong Jackson man. The committee made its report on May 15, 1828; Congress adjourned May 26th. The

26 House Doc. 4, 17th Cong., 2d sess., p. 10.
27 House Doc. 5, 17th Cong., 2d sess., p. 4.
28 House Doc. 7, 17th Cong., 2d sess., p. 5 (Dec. 2, 1822).
29 House Doc. 6, 17th Cong., 2d sess., p. 5 (Dec. 2, 1822).
30 Data on outside employment of clerks are presented elsewhere; see ch. 28.

committee criticized severely the administration of the State
Department under Henry Clay, of the Treasury under Richard
Rush, and of the War Department under James Barbour; the
Navy escaped with a few adverse comments on the costs of
courts martial; the Post Office under John McLean, by many
supposed to be a Jackson man, received the committee's praise.
President Adams was accused of maintaining a government
press.[31]

He, at least, had no doubt about the intent and purpose of
this retrenchment report. Commenting on a bill giving the
President discretionary power to build a breakwater at the
mouth of the Delaware River at a cost of five or six millions,
he wrote, "This discretionary power and control over public
money singularly contrasts with the report of the Retrenchment
Committee, containing near one hundred and fifty pages of in-
vective upon every Department of the Government, except the
Post Office, for extravagance and waste of public money." [32]

THE SENATE AND THE APPOINTING POWER

John Adams had felt the force of Congressmen's interest in
appointments, and had been obliged in considerable measure
to yield to it. Every one of his Republican successors struggled
with the same problem. The net result by 1829 was to lessen only
slightly the President's initiative in the field of appointments.
Various lines of reform were proposed; none were enacted into
law, but practice continued to define the relative place of the
President and Congress.

Jefferson believed that the role of the Senate in confirmation
should be limited. Writing in 1803 to Gallatin, he said:

. . . I have always considered the controul of the Senate as meant
to prevent any bias or favoritism in the President towards his own
relations, his own religion, towards particular states &c. and perhaps
to keep very obnoxious persons out of offices of the first grade. But
in all subordinate cases I have ever thought that the selection made
by the President ought to inspire a general confidence that it has
been made on due inquiry and investigation of character, and that
the Senate should interpose their negative only in those particular

31 House Report 259, 20th Cong., 1st sess. (May 15, 1828).
32 Adams, *Memoirs*, VIII, 7 (May 23, 1828).

cases where something happens to be within their knowledge, against the character of the person and unfitting him for the appointment.[33]

Jefferson stood firmly on Washington's precedent against yielding to a Senate request for the reasons for his nomination.[34]

The practice of consultation with state delegations was continued under the Republicans, but with considerable flexibility. Some New York Senators and Representatives were consulted on replacements in the port of New York, but disagreement led Jefferson to ask the opinion of Governor Clinton.[35] According to John Quincy Adams, Jefferson attempted to strengthen his hand by making acting appointments during congressional recess, thus presenting the Senate with a sort of *fait accompli*.[36] In 1808 Jefferson withheld an appointment as marshal in North Carolina until he could hear from the state delegation.[37] Gallatin talked with the Rhode Island delegation on appointments in Providence.[38] Madison drily remarked to Alexander Dallas that if fit persons could not be found for a vacant collectorship, he would wait for the meeting of Congress, "which always promises information on such points." [39] John Quincy Adams consulted personally with the Maine delegation to ascertain their wishes for marshal.[40]

Particular incidents taken from different stages of the Jeffersonian era will illustrate the tendency of Congressmen to share in the President's power to nominate to other than major posts. In 1804 the Senate was so quiescent that John Quincy Adams, still a Federalist, wrote in his diary, "The co-operation of the Senate in all appointments is at present a mere formality, and a very disgusting formality." [41] Within a month he had to record a different situation. The Senate rejected Jefferson's nominee

---

33 Jefferson, *Works* (Federal ed.), IX, 444 (Feb. 10, 1803).

34 *Ibid.*, X, 217–18 (Jan. 1806).

35 *Ibid.*, IX, 254 (May 17, 1801).

36 Adams, *Writings*, III, 83 (Dec. 11, 1804).

37 Jefferson, *Works* (Federal ed.), XI, 26 (April 2, 1808).

38 Gallatin, *Writings*, I, 451 (Feb. 4, 1809).

39 George Mifflin Dallas, *Life and Writings of Alexander James Dallas* (Philadelphia: J. B. Lippincott, 1871), p. 443.

40 Adams, *Memoirs*, VI, 359 (May 26, 1824).

41 *Ibid.*, I, 320 (Dec. 11, 1804).

as consul to Santo Domingo; the individual came from Maryland, and Maryland's Senator, General Smith, according to Adams, "appeared dissatisfied that this appointment had been made *without consulting* him." [42] Senator Plumer put the opposition of Smith on other grounds, that the nominee was a subject of Great Britain and of doubtful reputation.[43] The Senate rejected Jefferson's nominees on other occasions. In 1806 it refused confirmation of Joseph Wilkinson as collector of the port of Detroit, and of Joseph Thomas as a justice of peace for the District of Columbia.[44] General Wilkinson was confirmed as governor of Louisiana Territory in 1806 by the close vote of 17 to 14 and on the same day John B. C. Lucas was confirmed as territorial judge, 16 to 15.[45] Return J. Meigs, later Postmaster General, was refused confirmation as judge of Michigan Territory.[46] No information has been secured to reveal the grounds for the Senate's action.

The relative position of Senators and the President under Monroe was sharply defined in a case opened up by Senator Ninian Edwards of Illinois. Monroe had nominated Philip Foulke as register of the land office at Palestine, Illinois, but in consequence of objections made by Edwards the nomination was not acted upon. At the opening of the next session, Edwards addressed a letter to the President explaining the grounds of his opposition and in effect asking for the nomination of a resident of the Palestine region.[47] Edwards also suggested to Crawford that he and his fellow Senator, Judge Thomas, then rivals, should each be allowed to select two of the four land officers to be appointed. Crawford replied that "the proposition was deemed by the President inadmissable, as it would, in fact, be a transfer of the right of nomination vested by the Constitution in the President to the Senators of the State." [48] The Attorney

---

42 *Ibid.*, I, 340 (Jan. 29, 1805).

43 *Plumer's Memorandum*, p. 254.

44 *Journal of the Executive Proceedings of the Senate of the United States of America*, II, 13 (Jan. 3, 1806); hereafter cited as *Senate Executive Journal*.

45 *Ibid.*, II, 18 (Jan. 27, 1806).

46 *Ibid.*, II, 59 (Nov. 18, 1807).

47 E. B. Washburne, ed., *The Edwards Papers* (Chicago Historical Society's Collection, Vol. III, 1884), p. 166 (Dec. 22, 1820).

48 *Ibid.*, p. 167, n.

General, William Wirt, followed up with a further exposition of the President's views.

. . . I do not understand, however, that he feels himself *bound* by the recommendations of the senators of the state in which the office is to be filled, even when the senators concur. In such a case he has great respect to their opinion, but he considers himself at perfect liberty to put a different character in nomination, without giving just cause of offence to them. The constitutional act of nominating is *his;* he ought to be free, therefore, to nominate whom he pleases. Were he *bound* even by the joint recommendation of the senators, the nomination would cease to be the act of the President —it would be that of the senators; while by the Constitution, the responsibility would still rest with the President. You can not but admit the correctness of this view of the subject; and I am told that the practice of the senators is in strict conformity with it; they wait till the President calls on them to express their opinion, and retire respectfully from any further interference with the nomination, but with full liberty to exercise their rights, in turn, as senators when the nomination is sent in, and they have to vote on its confirmation. The President asks no sacrifice of the rights of senators in opposing and rejecting his nominations, and why should they seek to narrow his freedom in making his nominations? [49]

In the tense case of the appointment of Solomon Van Rensselaer to the Albany post office (1822), nearly the whole New York delegation in both Houses sought to impose their will upon the Postmaster General and President Monroe, but without success since the appointment did not require confirmation.[50] Protection of army officers against discharge on reduction of force also engaged the attention of Congress. Monroe's careful program of army reduction in 1822 was upset, certain favorite officers were required to be retained, and the President was put to much embarrassment.[51]

Congress also reached out to secure recognition of the rule of state apportionment of appointments to West Point and to the post of midshipman. When the rule was established, the practice quickly followed of allowing the state delegation,

49 *Ibid.,* pp. 167–68, n. (Jan. 11, 1821).
50 See below, ch. 22.
51 Monroe, *Writings,* VI, 287–88 (May 10, 1822); Adams, *Memoirs,* V, 527 (May 13, 1822).

friendly to the Administration, to suggest the appointment. By 1825 an outside observer could write that heads of departments were being told by Congressmen, "You have so many in employment from such a state. . . . We are fairly entitled to preference now." [52]

The Tenure of Office Act of 1820 was a powerful engine in the development of congressional influence in appointments.[53] The nature and effect of this legislation are dealt with in a later chapter.[54] Here it is sufficient to record that the terms of a large number of officers of intermediate grade, such as collectors, navy agents, paymasters, and others, hitherto held during good behavior, were set to expire at the end of four years. Nominations to these offices required confirmation by the Senate. The consequence was to multiply the occasions for Congressmen to insist on their preferences for appointment. Although both Monroe and Adams resisted, the tendency was to increase congressional standing in patronage. "The Senate," as Adams recorded, "was conciliated by the permanent increase of their power, which was the principal ultimate effect of the Act, and every Senator was flattered by the power conferred upon himself of multiplying chances to provide for his friends and his dependants." [55]

It would be easy, however, to overestimate the influence of the Senate in the selection of personnel. The number of vacancies was relatively small, due to the prevailing rule of service during good behavior. Lesser officers and employees did not require senatorial approval and were posted on nomination of chief clerks, auditors, collectors of customs, and other intermediate officials, and approved by the head of the appropriate department. The executive branch consulted members of both Houses from time to time with reference to the character and qualifications of prospective appointees, but Presidents and Secretaries got advice also from friends and political associates outside of Congress. The letters from the Secretary of the Treas-

[52] Augustus B. Woodward, *The Presidency of the United States* (Washington City: D. Van Veghten, 1825), pp. 53–54. This is a pamphlet of 79 pages.
[53] 3 Stat. 582 (May 15, 1820).
[54] See below, ch. 26.
[55] Adams, *Memoirs*, VII, 424 (Feb. 7, 1828).

ury to Congressmen, which after 1829 were full of patronage matters, were almost silent on appointment problems under Jefferson, Madison, Monroe, and John Quincy Adams.[56]

We may conclude that, while executive leaders called on members of Congress for information and advice, Senators stood in 1829 about where they found themselves in 1801 so far as a recognized right of initiative in appointments in their respective states was concerned. William Wirt was substantially correct, so far as the evidence that has come to attention is concerned, in his statement of practice. The Senate of course retained full freedom of action and for various reasons occasionally refused confirmation of presidential nominations.

Benton's Report. The ideological climax to this encroachment on presidential and executive discretion in selecting persons for appointment came in 1826, in a partisan document inspired by Senator Thomas H. Benton. The Senate, unfriendly to Adams throughout his whole term, set up a select committee to "inquire into the expediency of reducing the Patronage of the Executive Government of the United States." The hostile tone of the committee report is revealed in the following passage:

In coming to the conclusion that Executive Patronage ought to be diminished and regulated . . . the Committee rest their opinion on the ground that the exercise of great patronage in the hands of one man, has a constant tendency to sully the purity of our institutions, and to endanger the liberties of the country. This doctrine is not new. A jealousy of power, and of the influence of patronage, which must always accompany its exercise, has ever been a distinguished feature in the American character.[57]

Benton's remedy was sixfold: to limit the number and require the publication of the names of newspapers selected to publish the laws; to limit the application of the Tenure of Office Act to defaulters; to require confirmation of the appointment of postmasters; to distribute by law appointments to the Military Academy; to apply the same rule to the selection of midship-

---

56 MS. National Archives, Treasury Department, Letters and Reports to Congress, Series E, *passim.*

57 Senate Doc. 88, 19th Cong., 1st sess. (May 4, 1826).

men; and to prevent dismissal of army and navy officers at the pleasure of the President.[58] An unfortunate gap in Adams' diary prevents reporting his views on this document, but it must have gone hard with a President who of all others had refused to take advantage of his authority and who believed that the whole mass of customhouse patronage had been thrown against him.

Benton's Report brought no changes in the President's authority, and doubtless was not intended to do so. It is significant, however, not merely as a campaign document, but also as a frank recognition of the power available to a party and its leaders in deciding the outcome of elections. It pointed to the future, not to the past.

THE REPUBLICAN BALANCE OF POWER

A combination of unforeseeable circumstances contrived first to deny and then to affirm Republican doctrine on the relations that ought to exist in a democratic system between the legislative and executive branches of government. How tenuous both Republican and Federalist doctrine was, appeared during the eight years of Jefferson's administration. During these years Jefferson acted in contradiction to Republican theory at many points. He did not allow Congress that freedom of deliberation he had praised while in opposition, but dominated its movements and guided it to the course of action he deemed right. He did not subdue the executive power, but pushed it to an extreme in the enforcement of the embargo acts. He consciously cultivated institutions within the House, notably the caucus and the floor leader, to facilitate his wishes. He encouraged his able Secretary of the Treasury, Albert Gallatin, to intervene at any stage of legislative deliberation to ensure the "proper" consideration of administration policy. He did not restrain federal power, but acted on the theory of liberal construction. Coerced by events, he adopted the Federalist position at crucial points, which proved his eminence as a statesman and his indifference to a narrow consistency of theoretical views when faced with practical problems. The Federalists, with equal unconcern for consistency, threw themselves into opposition and rejected all

[58] Thomas Hart Benton, *Thirty Years' View* (2 vols., New York: D. Appleton. 1854-56), I. 80-82.

that Hamilton had taught them on the relations of the executive branch to Congress.

Events and personalities caused a profound reversal when James Madison succeeded the founder of the first Republican party. Jefferson's own domination had collapsed, and the current of executive-legislative relations was reversed for a generation. Congress became the dominant partner, whether in war or peace. The center of initiative and leadership passed to the House. It was concentrated in the office of Speaker, and was supported by the nominating caucus, the legislative caucus, and the standing committees.

The Jeffersonian period was one in which Congress and the executive continued to explore and solidify the many day-by-day contacts that circumstances made inevitable. The growth of party cohesion first facilitated these relations; but as the Republican party split, the influence of faction hindered good working relations. Through the institution of regular annual reports Congress kept itself better informed. By means of select committees it looked into allegations of mismanagement and official delinquency. The standing committees on the expenditures of the respective departments symbolized congressional intent to discharge its responsibility for the supervision of administrative management.

The latent hostility of the two branches of government that John Adams had forecast was evident enough during the Jeffersonian period. Congress ate into executive influence. Free choice of executive personnel on the part of the President had lost ground under old John Adams; it lost heavily when Madison found it impossible to select his own Cabinet; and it was potentially subject to new threats with the passage of the Tenure of Office Act. Congress reached out into the special domain of the executive branch, foreign affairs, and contested the initiative in foreign policy with both Madison and Monroe.

Despite these skirmishes and some major victories on the part of the legislative branch, the constitutional position of the executive was unchallenged. Its initiative in most administrative business was accepted and indeed even protected by congressional committees that shrank from the burden of detail. Force of circumstances compelled the transaction of government business by the executive branch. The aggression of Congress was directed toward capturing the initiative in policy, to a lesser degree toward securing compliance in appointments, and in large measure to the sheer struggle on the part of powerful men in Congress for dominance on the national scene.

CHAPTER TEN

The Treasury

Four men presided over the Treasury Department during the four presidencies claimed by the Jeffersonians: Albert Gallatin, one of the principal leaders of the Republican party from its inception; Alexander J. Dallas, an able lawyer born of humble parents in Jamaica; William H. Crawford, an ambitious politician from Georgia; and Richard Rush, son of the famous physician, Benjamin Rush, at once son and grandson of a signer of the Declaration of Independence.[1] All of these were men of stature, and Gallatin ranks as perhaps the ablest administrator of the Republican years.

ROLE OF THE TREASURY IN PUBLIC POLICY

Alexander Hamilton and Oliver Wolcott typified two distinct roles that the Treasury Department might play in the governmental scheme.[2] Hamilton took full advantage of the fact that every phase of public policy involved finance to throw himself into foreign affairs, military business, and domestic problems with little regard for the sensibilities of his Cabinet colleagues. Wolcott limited the function of the Treasury and his own role in the government to the collection of revenue, the settlement of accounts, and the performance of such matters as the sale of land that had been delegated to the Treasury by law. Hamilton thought in terms of policy and its effective management throughout the government and used the Treasury where pos-

[1] This list omits George Washington Campbell, who held the office for a few months in 1814.

[2] On the subject of this and the following chapters dealing with the departments, see Lloyd Milton Short, *The Development of National Administrative Organization in the United States* (Baltimore: Johns Hopkins Press, 1923).

sible to improve it; Wolcott was quite content to deal only with the matters that came to his desk.

Jefferson had suffered from Hamilton's conception of the role of the Treasury, and it might be supposed that he would have taken care to instruct Gallatin on the etiquette of interdepartmental relations. There is no record that he did so; and Gallatin promptly resumed the role that Hamilton had played.[3] He was the fiscal and administrative architect of Jefferson's administration. For general fiscal policy Jefferson was responsible, but for its details and management Gallatin had a free hand. He advised the President on army and navy estimates, and together they worked out the figures that Jefferson communicated to the departments. Gallatin took the initiative in determining naval policy.[4] He stood with Jefferson for a reduction of the army. He was influential in the field of foreign policy. He made recommendations for the American embassy in Madrid.[5] He advised Jefferson on appointments to the federal bench,[6] and to the territorial governments.[7] He helped pick an Attorney General.[8] He proposed a candidate for marshal in New York.[9] He remained active in Pennsylvania politics and advised the President on national political currents. He did not intervene in departmental administration outside the Treasury beyond giving hints to Jefferson, and in this respect he was less meddlesome than his great predecessor. The concept of the Treasury Department held by Gallatin was, however, substantially the same as that held by Hamilton; and Jefferson took full advantage of Gallatin's wide-ranging mind and influence.

Gallatin, like his first predecessor, had the qualities of a great administrator. Both men had a national point of view and could work without the limitations of state loyalties that influenced most of their contemporaries. Both men had a taste and capacity for planning and a skill in administrative invention. Gallatin's plans were largely devoted to finance, and were suc-

---

3 Henry Adams, *Life of Albert Gallatin*, pp. 267–492.
4 Gallatin, *Writings*, I, 252–53 (Sept. 12, 1805).
5 *Ibid.*, I, 217 (1804).
6 *Ibid.*, I, 177 (Feb. 15, 1804); and *ibid.*, I, 230.
7 *Ibid.*, I, 202 (August 20, 1804).
8 *Ibid.*, I, 202; *ibid.*, I, 208 (Sept. 18, 1804); *ibid.*, I, 219 (Jan. 1805).
9 *Ibid.*, I, 305 (August 7, 1806).

cessfully pursued until foreign complications interrupted the reduction of the debt. They were also devoted to a national scheme of internal improvements, which illustrated both his statesmanship and his political shrewdness. His skill in administrative inventiveness was admirably exemplified in the discovery of legal means to build the Cumberland Road.

Both Hamilton and Gallatin were men endowed with exceptional energy and drive. Gallatin became the leader of the Republicans in Congress under the Federalist regime by reason of his capacity for work and his consequent command of facts. He was relentless in his steady drive for cutting expenditures. He would not trifle with delinquent collectors of public money: "The last six months that a man who is not fit for the office remains in it are always those during which confusion of accounts and delinquency either take place or increase beyond bounds." [10] It was Gallatin who, almost singlehanded, carried the administrative burden of enforcing the embargo.

Gallatin was both independent and loyal. He never hesitated to give Jefferson and Madison opinions contrary to theirs. He opposed Jefferson on his removal policy, on the building of dry docks, on the need for a constitutional amendment to justify the purchase of Louisiana, and on the embargo of 1807, and tempered Jefferson's views on other matters. He ignored a passive Madison in his fight for the second United States Bank. When, however, the President had decided upon the course of public policy, Gallatin never hesitated to throw all his energies into its execution. John Quincy Adams declared that Gallatin had "in his character one of the most extraordinary combinations of stubbornness and flexibility that I ever met within man." [11] Pennsylvania Senator Jonathan Roberts wrote that he was "truly a great man, in quickness, versatility, & clearness, & profundity of conception." [12] While Gallatin's reputation rests on his eminence as a financier, he deserves also to be remembered as one of the great American administrators. [13]

[10] *Ibid.*, I, 176 (Feb. 11, 1804).

[11] Adams, *Writings*, V, 238 (Dec. 16, 1814).

[12] "Memoirs of a Senator from Pennsylvania: Jonathan Roberts, 1771–1854," *Pennsylvania Magazine of History and Biography*, LXII (1938), 239.

[13] Henry Adams, *Life of Albert Gallatin*, pp. 491–92.

His successors were men of lesser mold. The Treasury, hampered by Congress in its own fiscal policy and overwhelmed by the business of the war, lost ground. George Washington Campbell, Secretary for seven months in 1814, was a failure.[14] Alexander J. Dallas, incumbent for two years (1814–16), was an able lawyer but left no mark on the administrative system.[15] William H. Crawford (1816–25) held the office long enough to make an important contribution to its organization; but for months he was so incapacitated by a severe stroke that he could not sign his name to the necessary papers; and at least for the last four years of his service he devoted himself principally to his campaign to succeed Monroe, with whom, to complete the destruction of Treasury influence, he had a mortal quarrel. Adams' Secretary of the Treasury, Richard Rush, was a man of wide experience, diplomatic and legal,[16] but not a man to impose upon others either his views or his authority.

Apart, therefore, from the twelve years of Gallatin's administration, the Treasury Department occupied a role not different in principle from that of State, War, or Navy. It was important in its own right but after 1812 asserted no special position in relation to the President or heads of departments. No Secretary of the Treasury after Hamilton, not even Gallatin, followed his example of administrative "empire-building."

WORK AND ORGANIZATION

The substantive tasks of the Treasury from 1801 to 1829 were well defined. During the first decade every effort was concentrated on reducing the debt; during the second decade the dominant problem was to finance the War of 1812 and to restore financial confidence at its close; the third decade was principally concerned with debt reduction and with depression

[14] A summary of a doctoral dissertation, "The Public Career of George Washington Campbell," by Weymouth Tyree Jordan (Vanderbilt University) is printed in the *East Tennessee Historical Society's Publications*, No. 10 (1938), pp. 3–18. Most of Campbell's public life was spent in Congress as a member from Tennessee. He has the distinction of being the first Cabinet member "from over the mountains."

[15] Dallas, *Life and Writings*. This volume contains a valuable selection of Madison's letters bearing on administration not published elsewhere.

[16] J. H. Powell, *Richard Rush*, chs. 2 and 7.

financing from 1819 to 1822. The revenue system throughout
was based on customs, although internal excises were resumed
from 1813 to 1817 as a part of war financing, otherwise managed by loans. The protective tariff of 1816 and the general
prosperity of the country (briefly interrupted by the depression
of 1819–22) facilitated achievement of the broad ends of the
financial program. Customs revenue approximated $20,000,000
annually; public lands added something like $1,000,000 more.
Expenditures from 1817 to 1829 fluctuated from just under
$15,000,000 to $21,000,000. The debt was rapidly reduced and
finally extinguished in 1835, thus realizing Gallatin's absorbing
passion.

The Treasury as an administrative agency both gained and
lost ground from 1801 to 1829. It gained by a great increase of
its business in the settlement of accounts arising out of the War
of 1812, and by the expanding volume of customs collections.
It lost by reason of the growing independence of the Post Office from general Treasury supervision and the reduction in
personnel caused by the repeal of the direct taxes. It lost more
by the rise of the War Department as the active center of major
substantive programs. By 1820 the War Department under
Calhoun had definitely become the prime instrument for carrying out the positive constructive programs of the general government.

Treasury nevertheless remained an important organization,
although it is a striking fact that through 1829 it gained almost
no new functions or activities over and beyond those for which
it was responsible in 1801. The collection of customs and tonnage dues, with all the complexities of enforcing the law upon
shippers and importers, and the audit of accounts, remained
the central core of its duties. The sale of public land, a modest
enterprise until about 1810, became a more extensive and complex operation. The network of collectors of internal revenue
was abandoned in 1802, revived from 1813 to 1817, and given
up again at the opening of Monroe's administration. The lighthouses remained under Treasury supervision, as well as the
hospitals for seamen. In all this there was nothing new. Change
was in magnitude, not in substance.

The dominant administrative job of the Treasury was the

collection of revenue. While the dimensions of this task inevitably expanded with the physical growth of the country and with the increasing volume of international trade, the nature of the operation remained the same. The organization of a customhouse remained unaltered. The procedures for securing payment of customs remained substantially unchanged, with the same provisions for remission of fines and forfeitures by appeal to the Secretary of the Treasury. Means for compelling the submission of accounts of collectors were tightened up, but were not modified in principle. Administrative inspection of customhouses was unknown in 1801 and was equally unknown in 1829. Each customhouse was a self-contained establishment, in the great ports of considerable magnitude, untroubled by Washington. The number of collection districts in 1801 was 82. In 1826 the number was 95, reflecting in part new districts in Louisiana and Florida, in part some expansion in Maine, New York, and North Carolina. In general the collection districts remained remarkably stable during these twenty-eight years.

The Treasury pay roll, due to Republican vigilance and the repeal of the excise taxes, was actually less in 1826 than in 1801, despite considerable increase in volume of work other than excise. In 1801 Secretary Wolcott turned over to Gallatin an establishment comprising 78 persons in the headquarters offices, 707 in the customs service, and 500 in internal revenue, a total of 1,285. In 1826 the number of clerks and messengers in Treasury headquarters had more than doubled (181), an increase due to the auditing business. The number in the customs service had increased to 894 and the internal revenue service had been liquidated. The total Treasury staff was 1,075.[17]

Secretaries of the Treasury had little personal assistance in their daily routine. They were saved by the existence of offices, corresponding to bureaus, that carried on certain blocks of business. Thus the excise taxes were administered by the commissioner of revenue; purchasing was done by the purveyor until the office was abolished in 1812 and its functions transferred to the War Department; land business was conducted after 1812 by the General Land Office; lighthouses were super-

---

[17] For 1801 figures, see *American State Papers: Miscellaneous*, I, 260–319; for 1826 figures, Senate Doc. 88, 19th Cong., 1st sess., pp. 47 ff. (May 4, 1826).

vised by the commissioner of revenue and after 1820 by the fifth auditor; and the collection of foreign commerce statistics was a duty of the register.[18] The settlement of accounts was in the hands of the comptrollers and auditors. The absence of personal assistance and of professional advice on fiscal matters is, nevertheless, a striking fact. The Secretary of the Treasury had an immense burden, apart from the special tasks that went to his subordinates, and he had to carry it alone.

In short, the Treasury as an administrative agency was in 1829 about what it was in 1801, except in the volume of its transactions.[19] Its role in the larger framework of government varied, as already suggested, with the personality of the Secretary of the Treasury. It remained true, nevertheless, as Hamilton had written, that fiscal affairs touched all others, and Treasury continued as a major partner in the administrative team.

TREASURY CONTROL OF ESTIMATES AND EXPENDITURES

One impact of the Treasury upon the other departments, foreseen by Hamilton, was the review of their annual estimates. Another was the settlement of their accounts. Over the first the Secretary of the Treasury might have exerted considerable influence, and Gallatin moved in this direction. Over the second, also, early practice did not exclude the participation of the Secretary of the Treasury and the heads of departments, despite the independent position of the comptroller within the Treasury Department.[20] The government-wide influence of the Secretary of the Treasury was, however, more likely to come from his connection with the annual estimates.[21]

"The reduction of the public debt was certainly the principal object in bringing me into office," wrote Gallatin to Jefferson in the late autumn after the latter's retirement to Monticello.[22] How far was Gallatin's success in this respect due to his influence upon the estimates? Gallatin recognized that

18 3 Stat. 541 (Feb. 10, 1820).
19 For a criticism and defense of the Treasury Department in 1828 by the majority and minority members of the House Select Committee on Retrenchment see House Report 259, 20th Cong., 1st sess., pp. 19–23 (May 15, 1828).
20 See below, ch. 12.
21 On this topic see especially Wilmerding, *The Spending Power*, chs. 3–4.
22 Henry Adams, *Life of Gallatin*, p. 409 (Nov. 8, 1809).

reduction of the debt necessarily involved control of expenditures, and before he became Secretary of the Treasury he informed Jefferson of the necessity of reductions in the War and Navy Departments. He added, "The most eligible mode of making the reduction . . . must be the result of a strict investigation by the gentlemen who understand the subject." [23]

The gentlemen from whose understanding Gallatin needed most were Robert Smith, Secretary of the Navy, and Henry Dearborn, Secretary of War. Dearborn cooperated to Gallatin's satisfaction, but Smith was a constant source of fiscal annoyance to the savings-minded Secretary of the Treasury. The pressure brought by Gallatin on Smith from 1801 to 1809 was probably the source of the hostility to Gallatin in the Senate, where sat Secretary Smith's brother, General Samuel Smith of Maryland.

Gallatin's statutory authority over estimates was based on the organic Treasury Act of 1789, fortified in 1800 by a final gesture of the Federalists directing the Secretary of the Treasury to lay before Congress estimates of receipts and expenditures at the commencement of every session.[24] Preparation of the estimates began about three months before their submission to Congress with a request from the register of the Treasury, Joseph Nourse.[25] "I have the honor to apply to you," wrote Nourse to Madison, "at the request of the Secretary of the Treasury, for the usual Estimates of your Department, of monies to be included in a general appropriation, for the services of the ensuing year. . . ." [26]

To what extent Nourse transmitted instructions from the Secretary of the Treasury or the President to the heads of departments and agencies as to the over-all amount or the substance of their estimates is obscure. In the Gallatin Papers, Heinlein discovered the following letter from Nourse to Gallatin, "Be prepared to favor me with your directions in respect to an application to the heads of departments and offices, for

[23] Gallatin, *Writings,* I, 25 (March 14, 1801).

[24] 1 Stat. 65 (Sept. 2, 1789) and 2 Stat. 79 (May 10, 1800). For background see White, *The Federalists,* pp. 323–26.

[25] See J. Clare Heinlein, "The Administrative Theory and Practice of Albert Gallatin" (University of Chicago, 1948).

[26] Gallatin Papers, Library of Congress, I, 222 (Oct. 3, 1803).

their estimates for an appropriation of monies for the ensuing year." [27] Probably this communication is best understood as a formal request to ask for the estimates rather than as a request for a statement of Gallatin's budgetary policy. Nowhere in Gallatin's published correspondence is there evidence that he gave the departments instructions as to the amount of their estimates, although he did give directions on the form of segregating deficiency requests.[28]

The first phase of the budget-making process was completed when Nourse transmitted the consolidated estimates to the Secretary of the Treasury. Gallatin's real influence on the budget was exercised during the interval between receipt of the consolidated estimates and the submission of his annual report to Congress. It was brought to bear through the President, with whom Gallatin doubtless had informal conferences on his colleagues' figures. It was Jefferson, however, who dealt with the heads of departments, informing them of such corrections as he deemed necessary. The decisive factor of Jefferson's decision was illustrated in Gallatin's note to him in 1803. "The corrected navy estimates are much wanted. Whatever you shall decide shall be recommended to the Committee of Ways and Means." [29]

Consideration of navy estimates revealed Treasury influence at its peak. The rate of naval expenditure had been reduced from about three million in 1800 to about one million dollars in 1801–2, but Gallatin pressed for further reductions. Writing to Jefferson he severely criticized the 1803 naval estimate for contingencies and proposed to reduce it from $40,000 to $10,000. In the same letter he declared that he could not "discover any approach towards reform" in the Navy Department, and criticized what he called "loose demands for money" for naval expenditures.[30] In the autumn of 1803 he advised Jefferson that "the large item of repairs for vessels may be postponed till next year," [31] a favorite savings device. The next spring he pushed Jefferson again on total expenditures and on naval esti-

[27] Gallatin Papers, New York Historical Society, Box IX (Sept. 7, 1807).
[28] Gallatin to Robert Smith, *ibid.*, Vol. XVI (Nov. 1805).
[29] Jefferson Papers, Library of Congress, Vol. CXXIX, No. 22,265 (Jan. 29, 1803).
[30] Gallatin, *Writings*, I, 117.
[31] *Ibid.*, I, 162.

mates. "In every arrangement not connected with this Department which may be adopted, I have but one observation, which is to request that the Treasury may not be pressed this year beyond our former calculations. . . . I allow three hundred thousand dollars to the Secretary of the Navy for the equipment of the four additional frigates: he wants four hundred thousand dollars; but that is too much. . . ." [32] In 1805 Gallatin was putting on the screws in order to keep in the Treasury adequate funds to meet an installment of the French debt. He told Jefferson that the War Department had assisted much better than the Navy. His feelings rose to the surface as he closed his letter with this passage: "On this subject, the expense of the navy greater than the object seemed to require, and a merely nominal accountability, I have, for the sake of preserving perfect harmony in your councils, however grating to my feelings, been almost uniformly silent; and I beg that you will ascribe what I now say to a sense of duty and to the grateful attachment I feel for you." [33]

Secretary Smith must have found his relations with the Treasury full of annoyance. The navy was professionally outraged both by the drastic reductions in the number of ships afloat, and by Jefferson's policy of building inexpensive gunboats fit only for defensive purposes. Smith was caught between the force of professional naval opinion and Gallatin's insistence on reducing the debt by cutting expenditures—at navy expense. As we have already seen, Smith was very restive toward the end of Jefferson's administration when war with Great Britain seemed imminent and naval preparations were still denied in the light of Treasury policy.

Jefferson's views both on the navy and on the reduction of the debt were parallel to those of Gallatin, and Smith was obliged to yield. The extent of Gallatin's influence on navy estimates is suggested by the following brief note from the President to him in 1807.

If you could call on me conveniently this forenoon, Mr. Smith will meet you here with an entire readiness to modify his estimate to our

[32] *Ibid.*, I, 191 (May 3, 1804).
[33] *Ibid.*, I, 234 (May 30, 1805).

mutual liking. I am not familiar enough with the subject to explain
to him the alteration desired. Give me a few moments' notice, that
I may get him here. Affectionate salutations.[34]

At the opening of Madison's administration, Gallatin claimed
the right to advise the President on the general level of expenditures, in favor of a balanced budget. He recognized that in time
of war control of estimates and expenditures would be practically impossible, since "all the resources of the country must
be called forth to make it efficient. . . ."[35] But even as war
overtook the country, he still kept his mind on conserving its
resources. "There are but two practicable ways of diminishing
the expenditure: 1, by confining it to necessary objects; 2, by
introducing perfect system and suppressing abuses in the necessary branches."[36]

Gallatin recognized that a review of the estimates of his colleagues raised the problem of their responsibility for the management of their departments and for the public policy to be
pursued by the Administration. On matters of policy he was
entitled to speak as a member of the Cabinet, and did so freely.
On matters of the departmental responsibility of his colleagues,
he wrote Jefferson, early in Madison's administration:

. . . I do not pretend to step out of my own sphere and to
control the internal management of other Departments. But it
seems to me that as Secretary of the Treasury I may ask that, whilst
peace continues, the aggregate of the expenditure of those Departments be kept within bounds such as will preserve the equilibrium
between the national revenue and expenditure without recurrence
to loans. I cannot, my dear sir, consent to act the part of a mere
financier, to become a contriver of taxes, a dealer of loans, a seeker
of resources for the purpose of supporting useless baubles, of increasing the number of idle and dissipated members of the community, of fattening contractors, pursers, and agents, and of introducing in all its ramifications that system of patronage, corruption, and rottenness which you so justly execrate.[37]

These were strong words!

34 *Ibid.*, I, 357 (Oct. 17, 1807).
35 *Ibid.*, I, 465 (Nov. 8, 1809).
36 *Ibid.*, I, 528–29 (autumn 1812).
37 *Ibid.*, I, 465–66 (Nov. 8, 1809).

No evidence has come to attention to suggest that during this period any President or Secretary of the Treasury other than Jefferson and Gallatin sought to dictate the amount of money appropriate for the various departments and agencies to ask from Congress. Nourse compiled the figures prepared by the departments, the Secretary of the Treasury transmitted them to Congress. No one apparently expected from the executive branch any coordination or general over-all consideration in the interest of a balanced program.

In some respects the estimating process could be precise and specific. Thus the estimates for pay of clerks could be stated exactly in each of the departments and offices; the number of clerks was small and their emoluments were stable. In other areas the estimates were not much more than informed guesses. Nathaniel Frye, chief clerk of the War Department in 1818, sent in an estimate for Calhoun's inspection and asked for "indulgence for any inaccuracies it may be found to contain, as it has been drawn up hastily, amidst continual interruptions of other business of the department, and as some of the materials . . . are not so perfect as I could have wished." [38] The quartermaster general, new to his office, sent in figures for transportation that he described as "hypothetical." [39] According to a statement made in 1820, every quartermaster estimate during the administrations of Jefferson and Madison was contained in a single sentence.[40] The Secretary of the Navy declared in 1822 that from the nature of expenditures for navy yards and contingencies it was "utterly impossible to make an estimate with any tolerable certainty." [41] No trace of executive pressure for greater precision in estimates was evident, and Congress was unable to go far beyond what the departments produced in the less settled aspects of administrative affairs.

Little evidence has been encountered to indicate how closely congressional committees inspected the estimates. An entry in Adams' diary suggests that in 1808 the examination was casual.[42]

[38] Senate Doc. 65, 15th Cong., 2d sess., p. 27 (Oct. 3, 1818).
[39] *Ibid.*, p. 52.
[40] House Doc. 84, 16th Cong., 1st sess., p. 21 (Jan. 14, 1820).
[41] House Doc. 70, 17th Cong., 1st sess., p. 6 (Feb. 17, 1822).
[42] Adams, *Memoirs*, I, 507 (Jan. 25, 1808).

It was on the eve of war that Gallatin suggested a modern means of expenditure control, monthly allotments. Writing to Madison March 17, 1812, he proposed "requesting the Secretaries of the War and Navy Departments to prepare estimates of the probable monthly expenditures," and asked Madison to take the initiative: ". . . the whole management should be the result of general concert and be matured under the sanction of the President." [43] Madison apparently declined to impose this plan on his department heads, and in any event the demands of war would have made the scheme impossible at that time.

A year later Gallatin, on his own motion, dictated an emergency allocation of funds. He told the War Department it could have $13,220,000 and the Navy $4,500,000 for the last nine months of 1813. "Should that distribution be objected to, the President must decide, and the alterations which he may direct will be obeyed. . . ." He also told the two service departments that they could not requisition more than one-ninth of these sums for any month, unless they secured from the President a special order; and he added that any such special advances would be deducted from the following month.[44]

War brought fiscal confusion and near bankruptcy; normal processes in budgeting and appropriation disappeared; and the return of peace found the Treasury in the hands of a Secretary, William H. Crawford, who was unlikely to jeopardize his political ambitions by a display of administrative authority over his Cabinet colleagues. Peace also found the departments in the hands of men who were unlikely to submit to Crawford's judgment of their needs.

It was a matter of chagrin to Jefferson that he found it impossible to change Hamilton's department and fiscal system. Writing to Dupont de Nemours in 1802, he said, "When this government was first established, it was possible to have kept it going on true principles, but the contracted, English, half-lettered ideas of Hamilton, destroyed that hope in the bud. We can pay off his debt in 15. years: but we can never get rid of his financial system. It mortifies me to be strengthening principles which I deem radically vicious, but this vice is entailed on us

[43] Madison Papers, Library of Congress, Vol. XLVIII, No. 4718.
[44] Gallatin, *Writings*, I, 536–37 (April 17, 1813).

by the first error." [45] Jefferson would have amalgamated the offices of comptroller and auditor and reduced the register to a clerk of accounts, "and then the organization will consist, as it should at first, of a keeper of money, a keeper of accounts, & the head of the department." [46] Gallatin was wiser in these matters than Jefferson, and with respect to the civil departments generally, including the Treasury, asserted that here "by far . . . less abuse has been practised; . . . the reason is, that . . . it has been most closely watched, and any increase attempted but with caution and repelled with perseverance." [47]

Gallatin's theory and practice of finance as the controller of policy and administration in the general government and the failure of his successors to achieve his position were eloquently generalized by Henry Adams. "The Treasury," wrote Adams, "is the natural point of control to be occupied by any statesman who aims at organization or reform. . . ." Both Hamilton and Gallatin found their keenest anxieties not in their own department, but in "that effort to control the whole machinery and policy of government which is necessarily forced upon the holder of the purse." Writing in 1879 Henry Adams declared that there were only these two examples that could serve as perfect models for study of the meaning of practical statesmanship under the American system.[48]

[45] Jefferson, *Works* (Federal ed.), IX, 344, n. (Jan. 18, 1802).
[46] *Ibid.*, IX, 360–61 (April 1, 1802).
[47] Gallatin, *Writings*, I, 66 (Nov. 1801).
[48] Henry Adams, *Life of Albert Gallatin*, p. 267.

CHAPTER ELEVEN

The Collectors

One of the principal administrative problems that vexed the Treasury under the Republicans was to enforce accountability upon federal agents either collecting or disbursing public money. Before embarking upon this matter, finally brought to a satisfactory conclusion, it is convenient to devote some pages to the collectors of customs, perhaps the most important single body of federal agents dealing directly with citizens. Their history and character tell much about the quality and essence of the Jeffersonian system. More than this, they were in many instances colorful figures, important in their own right.

The collector of Baltimore in 1818 made a not unjust summary of their official status. ". . . the collectors," he wrote, "must be considered as watchmen for the community, reporters to the government, promulgators of the law, and generally acting an auxiliary part in behalf of the whole." [1]

The collectors were the backbone of the Treasury Department during both the Federalist and Jeffersonian periods. Even when direct taxes were reintroduced from 1813 to 1817, the collectors, rather than the internal revenue officials, were responsible for the great bulk of the revenue. In the great crisis of the embargo, 1807–09, they were the chief enforcement agents. The connections of the government with the mercantile interests were principally through the collectors, whose discretionary judgment on the sufficiency of importers' securities formed a delicate balance between convenience to the importers and protection to the revenue.

The collectors in the larger ports, moreover, tended to be

1 Senate Doc. 27, 15th Cong., 2d sess., pp. 6–7 (June 10, 1818).

[148]

confidential advisers to the government on local trends of opinion, on maneuvers of party and faction, and on qualifications of prospective appointees.[2] From this fact it followed that the collectors were politically influential, an influence strengthened by their power to appoint a numerous subordinate staff—measurers, weighers, gaugers, and others.

The collectors holding office on March 4, 1801, had been selected by Washington or Adams, and were Federalists. They quickly came under Jefferson's attention. During the first session of the seventh Congress (1801–02), the Senate confirmed fifteen new collectors, including Gelston (New York), Bishop (New Haven), and Whipple (Portsmouth, New Hampshire). In the second session (1802–03), thirteen additional ports received new collectors, including five immediately north of Boston in the homeland of the Essex Junto. Several large ports still remained in the hands of Federalist collectors—Boston, Philadelphia, Baltimore, Norfolk, and Charleston. Boston was held by General Benjamin Lincoln, a Revolutionary hero the displacement of whom would have been dubious politics and who in any event cooperated fully with Gallatin. Not until 1809 did a Republican, Henry Dearborn, retiring Secretary of War, become collector of this port. The Philadelphia collectorship fell into Republican hands in 1803 when the Senate confirmed General Peter Muhlenberg, former member of Congress and brother of Frederick Muhlenberg, first Speaker of the House. In Baltimore, Robert Purviance was replaced in 1806 by Republican Gabriel Christie, also a former member of the House. Norfolk had already been acquired in 1804; two years later Simeon Theus took over Charleston.[3]

These and other changes having been consummated, the new collectors settled down to the uninterrupted enjoyment of their office, no party or factional change threatening their positions until the election of Andrew Jackson. Long tenure of office was

[2] In the smaller ports, too, they were likely to be politically active. Traveling through Rhode Island in 1801, Josiah Quincy discovered his landlord in Warren engaged "in deep political discussion with Mr. Fessenden, the schoolmaster, and Mr. Phillips, who was at once the principal village trader, its custom-house officer, Postmaster, and printer." Massachusetts Historical Society, *Proceedings,* 2d series, IV (1887–89), 124–25.

[3] Data from *Senate Executive Journal,* Vol. I.

common, and where interrupted by death or disability the
office sometimes passed on to a son of the incumbent. Cases
drawn from the larger ports illustrate the high degree of stability.[4] In Portland, Maine, Jefferson appointed Isaac Ilsley in
1803; he served until removed by Jackson in 1829. Joseph
Whipple was collector of Portsmouth, New Hampshire, from
1789 to 1798, when he was removed by Adams for gross partisanship and other causes; Jefferson restored him in 1802 and he
served until his death in 1816. His successor remained in office
from 1816 to 1829. Boston had only three collectors from 1789
to 1829—General Benjamin Lincoln, who finally resigned in
1809, worn out by the embargo; General Henry Dearborn; and
his son Henry A. S. Dearborn. William Ellery was collector of
Newport, Rhode Island, from 1790 until his death in 1820 at
the age of ninety-three. He was succeeded by his son, Christopher
Ellery, who held the office until 1834.[5] In New Haven, Samuel
Bishop (the subject of the famous remonstrance by the merchants) died in 1803, a year after his appointment, and was
succeeded by his son, Abraham Bishop, who served until 1829.
David Gelston held the New York collectorship from 1802 to
1820, being succeeded by Jonathan Thompson who was cut off
by Jackson in 1829. John Steele was collector in Philadelphia
from 1808 to 1827.[6] James McCulloch held the Baltimore collectorship from 1808 to 1836.[7] Perhaps the most extraordinary

4 Data drawn from *ibid.* The dates in the text are those of Senate confirmation; in some cases there had been a previous short recess appointment.

5 *Dictionary of American Biography*, VI, 86. An unsuccessful effort was made
to unseat William Ellery in 1801. Aaron Burr was consulted in the case. Burr
to Jonathan Russell, May 22, 1801, in Massachusetts Historical Society, *Proceedings*, XLVII (1913–14), 294–95. The Ellery family was a notable one; two
of William Ellery's grandsons were Richard Henry Dana and William Ellery
Channing.

6 Steele sometimes signed his correspondence J. Steele, John Steele, and Jno.
Steele. He should be distinguished from John Steele of North Carolina, who
was comptroller of the Treasury from 1796 to 1802.

7 Both John Quincy Adams and Monroe suspected McCulloch of collusion in
clearing vessels engaged in piracy and slave trading, but no action was taken
either to investigate or to remove. Adams, *Writings,* VII, 59 (August 2, 1820).
Crawford said that the old man was "perfectly honest" but had become an
enthusiast in the cause of the South American Republics and could not be
relied upon where their interests were involved. Crawford thought "McCulloch
ought to have been removed long ago. . . ." Adams, *Memoirs,* V, 154 (June 19,
1820).

case of official longevity was that of James Gibbon of Richmond, Virginia, appointed surveyor of the customs in 1789, inspector in 1792, and collector in 1800, serving as such until his death in December 1831.

If we may judge from the record of the Philadelphia customhouse, subordinate employees enjoyed the same permanence of tenure as their superior officers. In connection with an investigation in 1826, every inspector reported among other matters the date of his appointment. David Rose had entered the service in 1789, Robert Hopkins in 1793, and three others before 1800. Four had secured office in the next decade, and nine during the second decade of the nineteenth century. Of twenty inspectors, only three had been recently selected.[8]

Appointments as collector were usually initiated by Gallatin but were cleared with Jefferson. Members of Congress were frequently, but not always, consulted.[9] For positions on the northern shore of Massachusetts, the advice of Captain Crowninshield, later Secretary of the Navy, was regularly taken.[10]

In 1807 Gallatin had Duval, a Marylander, write to "the most conspicuous Republicans" of the county in which was situated the port of Snowhill, Maryland, for recommendations of a successor to a delinquent collector.[11] For intermediate positions in the collector's office, Jefferson sometimes made his own inquiries of personal or political friends. In most of these appointments Gallatin proposed and Jefferson decided.[12]

Membership in the Republican party was a prerequisite to nomination as a customs officer. Jefferson wrote Gallatin in the summer of 1801, "we must be inflexible against appointing Federalists till there be a due portion of Republicans introduced into office."[13] The selection of Deacon Samuel Bishop as col-

8 House Doc. 137, 19th Cong., 1st sess. (March 23, 1826), *passim*.

9 Gallatin to Jefferson, August 10, 1801, Gallatin, *Writings*, I, 30–31; Gallatin to Jefferson, June 21, 1803, *ibid.*, I, 123, reporting recommendations from two Massachusetts Congressmen on the position of naval officer at Newburyport; Gallatin to Jefferson, Feb. 4, 1809, *ibid.*, I, 451, stating that Gallatin had consulted two of the Rhode Island delegation on a vacancy in Providence.

10 *Ibid.*, I, 85 (August 14, 1802); *ibid.*, I, 182 (March 28, 1804); and *ibid.*, I, 192 (May 11, 1804).

11 *Ibid.*, I, 356 (Sept. 2, 1807).

12 For illustrations, see *ibid.*, I, 36; 60; 85; 92.

13 *Ibid.*, I, 37 (August 14, 1801). Cf. Adams' comments in 1825, *Memoirs*, VII, 93.

lector of the port of New Haven, with the expectation of the succession of his son, Abraham, an ardent Republican, was perhaps an exaggerated but not exceptional case. Abraham Bishop graduated from Yale in 1778 at the age of fifteen. After a European tour from which he returned, according to Yale's President Stiles, "full of Improvement and Vanity," he became clerk of various local courts in New Haven and a bold agitator for the Republican cause. To the Federalists he gave a Phi Beta Kappa address, "On the Extent and Power of Political Delusion," a campaign document calling forth a reply, probably from Noah Webster, one of his Yale classmates, entitled, "A Rod for the Fool's Back." [14]

With respect to subordinate customs officers, appointed by the collectors but subject to approval by the Secretary of the Treasury, Gallatin originally proposed to instruct the collectors that "the door of office be no longer shut against any man merely on account of his political opinions, but that whether he shall differ or not from those avowed either by you or by myself, integrity and capacity suitable to the station be the only qualifications that shall direct our choice." [15] At the moment the collectors and their aides were Federalists. Gallatin intended only to ask them to divide the appointments—"which in the large ports are really numerous, influential, and sometimes lucrative." Jefferson asked that the instruction be postponed, and apparently it was never circulated. Republicans not only became eligible, but preferred.

Beyond correct party affiliation, Gallatin and Jefferson sought men of integrity and ability, gentlemen prominent in their communities—qualities that were equally sought earlier by the Federalists.[16] Referring to a Virginia port, Gallatin declared, "The successor should have integrity, keenness, and firmness." [17] Gallatin was delighted with the recommendation of Abraham Bishop for collector of New Haven: "he has a very sedate appearance, which from what I had heard of his character, I did

14 Franklin B. Dexter, "Abraham Bishop, of Connecticut, and his Writings," Massachusetts Historical Society, *Proceedings,* 2d series, XIX (1905), 190–99.

15 Gallatin, *Writings,* I, 28–29 (July 25, 1801).

16 Local residence was normally expected. Cf. Madison to Dallas concerning the handicap of its absence, Dallas, *Life and Writings,* p. 429 (May 24, 1815).

17 Gallatin, *Writings,* I, 44 (Sept. 7, 1801).

not expect. Before he mentioned his name I mistook him for a clergyman." [18] Jefferson's choice for collector of the port of Georgetown, John Barnes, was the "owner of a superb estate and many slaves" who lived in "princely style among the gentry of that period." [19] He held this office until his death in 1826 at the age of ninety-six. The Republicans were handicapped in selections for this field of operations, since, as Gallatin complained, "first-rate merchants we have not." [20]

Collectorships were highly prized, especially in the larger ports where the income from fees was handsome. Wilson Cary Nicholas resigned as United States Senator from Virginia in 1804 to become collector of Norfolk. Captain William Jones, Secretary of the Navy, 1813–14, became naval officer of the port of Philadelphia in 1824 and collector in 1827. Even the smaller ports called forth lively competition in the event of a vacancy. In 1805 Gallatin forwarded to Jefferson several letters "in favor of John Kittredge as collector of Gloucester vice Gibault, who is dying, but not to my knowledge yet dead." [21] The net earnings in 1827 of collectors in a few of the larger ports may be noted by way of example: Boston, $4,001.80; New York, $4,411.29; Philadelphia, $4,584.42; Charleston, $2,-962.05.[22] Department heads received a salary of $6,000 a year.

At the same time, the collectors were exposed to considerable risks in the conduct of their office. They were vested with large power over the movement of ships and the valuation of goods, and Congress did not intend these powers to be used with impunity for the distress or persecution of the commercial class. Collectors were liable before the ordinary courts for official acts that were subject to challenge. The case of David Gelston illustrated the vexations that might fall upon collectors.

Gelston was "a merchant . . . of respectable abilities and unimpeachable integrity," an active New York politician who had been surrogate of New York City, a state senator, a member of the New York Council of Appointment, and a protégé of

[18] *Ibid.*, I, 140 (August 20, 1803); see also *ibid.*, I, 138.
[19] Cordelia Jackson, "John Barnes, a Forgotten Philanthropist of Georgetown," Columbia Historical Society, *Records*, VII (1904), 39–48.
[20] Gallatin, *Writings*, I, 139 (August 20, 1803).
[21] *Ibid.*, I, 240 (August 17, 1805).
[22] Senate Doc. 141, 20th Cong., 1st sess. (March 17, 1828).

James Monroe.[23] Jefferson appointed him collector of the port of New York in 1802.[24] By official declaration "he was a most faithful and vigilant officer." [25] During his eighteen years' service the government's share of forfeitures recovered in the port of New York was $139,582.01; an equal sum went to informers and customs officers, principally the latter. Gelston's own share amounted to $37,523.40.[26] His vigilance thus brought him large financial rewards, but also trouble and anxiety that did not cease with his death. His executors were still seeking satisfaction in 1834.

Upon settling Gelston's accounts subsequent to his retirement in 1820, the Treasury found a balance due the government of $44,818.61. He disputed the correctness of the Treasury settlement and claimed various items disallowed by the auditor. The central claim was the case of the *American Eagle*. Information had been brought to Gelston that, contrary to the law of 1794, this vessel was fitting out as an armed ship for the use of one of the St. Domingo chiefs in rebellion against France. Gelston hesitated to act on the evidence at hand. As the House Committee of Ways and Means stated in 1818, he showed "a prudent, and, if they were untaught by subsequent events . . . an extreme reluctance to incur the responsibility involved in the seizure of the vessel. While any thing was left to the discretion or judgment of Mr. Gelston, he inquired, examined, reported, but made no seizure. . . ." [27] In July 1810 Gelston received a positive instruction from the President to seize the ship. He followed this order, but the federal district judge restored the *American Eagle* to her owner and refused to give a certificate of probable ground of seizure.

Without this protection Gelston was promptly sued in the

23 Howard Lee McBain, *DeWitt Clinton and the Origin of the Spoils System in New York* (New York: Columbia University Press, 1907), p. 34; Monroe, *Writings*, III, 274 (March 23, 1801); *ibid.*, V, 101 (Feb. 7, 1809).

24 *Senate Executive Journal*, I, 403, 405. The date of his appointment is erroneously given as 1807 in House Report 276, 23d Cong., 1st sess. (Feb. 21, 1834).

25 *Ibid.*, p. 1. There was some early complaint that he was not sufficiently attentive to the claims of fellow Republicans for local printing patronage. Letters of James Cheetham, in Massachusetts Historical Society, *Proceedings*, 3d series, I (1907–8), 60–62.

26 House Report 276, 23d Cong., 1st sess., pp. 5–6.

27 House Doc. 169, 15th Cong., 1st sess., p. 1 (March 21, 1818).

New York State courts for damages and the owner secured a verdict for $107,369.43. The case went through appeal, and finally came to the Supreme Court of the United States.[28] The lack of a certificate of probable cause was fatal to Gelston at every turn. Congress finally came to the rescue, appropriating $130,000 to meet the judgment.[29]

The case of the *American Eagle* was only one of many in dispute between Gelston and the accounting officers of the Treasury. In the case of the brig *Laguada* Gelston suffered damages and costs in the amount of $2,737.64 because the witness on whom he relied to support his seizure refused to testify. The judge declined to grant a certificate of probable cause. To complete Gelston's undoing, all the papers were burned in Washington in 1814. The Committee on Claims declined to recommend relief, and laid down an important dictum.

. . . While the Government has important rights which are to be duly regarded, the citizen has his rights, which should not be overlooked nor forgotten in our zeal to enforce the laws. If an officer will wantonly and without probable cause seize upon the property of an individual who is engaged in carrying on a lawful commerce, he ought to be made to respond in the courts of justice for the injury inflicted, without the most remote prospect that he will be remunerated by the Government whose laws he has violated by oppressing one of her citizens.[30]

Gelston of course acted on information that he thought adequate, and under the spur of pressure from Washington. His zeal and good intentions availed him not.

On the whole Gelston's executor fared badly before the Committee on Claims. His case was ruined by the burning of the Treasury papers in the British assault in 1814, and neither auditors nor the Committee on Claims would listen to settlements not based on written evidence. Even though no one sug-

---

[28] 3 Wheaton 245 (1818). At one stage Gelston was in imminent danger of being thrown in jail for lack of adequate security. Gallatin, *Writings*, I, 674 (Dec. 12, 1815).

[29] Appropriation Act, 3 Stat. 418 at 423 (April 9, 1818); other claims were not settled until 1842 when Congress authorized $36,157.40 to be paid his legal representatives, 6 Stat. 854 (August 11, 1842).

[30] House Report 276, 23d Cong., 1st sess., p. 2.

gested that Gelston had been guilty of misappropriation of funds or misfeasance of any kind, he gained nothing from his reputation as a diligent and honest collector. The case leaves the impression that other collectors would act prudently, if at all, guided by the principle of settlement in the Gelston affair.[31]

The normal relations of the Secretary of the Treasury and the collectors were carried on by (1) *regular reports* of imported goods, collections of imposts and tonnage dues, registration of vessels, suits to collect on defaulted bonds, and the like; (2) *correspondence* on particular problems as they arose from time to time; (3) *circulars of instructions* issued by the Secretary to the collectors, interpreting the revenue laws and the duties of the collectors and their subordinates; (4) *particular directions* from the Secretary on special matters. The routine reports and much correspondence went usually to the commissioner of the revenue or to the comptroller of the Treasury. Gallatin sent samples to Jefferson on one occasion for his information, but for the most part did not even see this class of papers himself.[32]

The embargo crisis intensified communication between the Treasury and the collectors. They were given extraordinary powers, and needed advice, direction, and support. Gallatin poured out an unceasing stream of letters during the emergency, giving them specific directions in some cases, stating the intent of the law in others, and encouraging everyone to his full en-

---

[31] The troubles of Gelston were paralleled by those of William Otis of Barnstable. Despite positive assurances from the government of protection, he was found liable to the owners of the schooner *Ann* in the amount of over $3,000. His farm was sold; he was removed in 1814 with other suits pending, and became so discouraged that for a time he fled the country. In 1828 he got a favorable report from the House Committee on Claims for indemnity, House Report 244, 20th Cong., 1st sess. (May 5, 1828); and in 1829 congressional authority to be paid principal and interest on amounts approved by the President. 6 Stat. 396 (March 2, 1829). Cf. also the case of Josiah Hook, collector of the Penobscot district, who seized a drove of cattle he thought were headed to the enemy. The owner sued for damages, recovered judgment, and was sustained by the higher court. The House Committee on Claims declined, ten years after the event when it finally considered Hook's petition, to make good his losses. House Report 46, 18th Cong., 1st sess. (Jan. 24, 1824). The committee was, however, reversed in part by Congress, which appropriated $1,165 to cover his legal expenses. 6 Stat. 302 (May 18, 1824).

[32] Gallatin, *Writings*, I, 58 (Nov. 9, 1801).

deavor. One is struck by the fact that the only means of communication during this long crisis was by circular and letter. Gallatin had no one to send to the collectors as his personal representative; collectors did not go to Washington for advice and information, nor were they ever called into consultation as a group; there were no roving customs inspectors who as a matter of course were consulting with and assisting them.

The pattern of relationship between the collectors and their headquarters remained unchanged to 1829. A system of inspection was proposed, but despite examples in the War Department and the General Land Office no action was taken. The collectors in 1829 as in 1801 were self-contained outposts, operating under instructions that were designed to reduce discretion to a minimum, but still with a large degree of autonomy.

Standards of integrity in the collectors' offices, which had been set at a high level by Hamilton and Wolcott, remained firm during the Jeffersonian period. A few New England collectors sabotaged the embargo acts, but apparently only one (New Bedford) was removed for his unfaithfulness. On the whole the collectors, naval officers, surveyors, and subordinate staffs gave a gratifying demonstration of integrity, often under difficult circumstances. They were able to stand on their record when at times they petitioned for an increase in emoluments, hinting darkly at the temptations laid before underpaid officials.

Two or three unusual cases will illustrate occasional exceptions to these generalizations. The first involved a troublesome son-in-law of John Adams, Colonel William S. Smith,[33] whom Adams had appointed surveyor of the port of New York.[34] With other prominent public figures he became involved in the plot of Francesco de Miranda to fit out an expedition in New York against the Spanish possessions in South America. Since this enterprise was in violation of the laws of the United States, it was the clear duty of Smith to report his information and to defeat the adventure. Instead he advised Miranda with refer-

[33] See White, *The Federalists*, pp. 251, 278–80.
[34] The nomination was contested in the Senate and finally approved by a vote of 18 to 8. *Senate Executive Journal*, I, 384 (Feb. 21, 1801).

ence to securing the ship *Leander* and, with his active aid, Miranda bought arms and supplies and enlisted men.[35]

When the matter was brought to the attention of the State Department, Jefferson hesitated to take Madison's advice to remove Smith, whereupon Gallatin joined Madison in urging summary action. "The honor of government and the peace of the country seem to require an explicit mark of disapprobation and disavowal, and retaining in public service an officer who, by his own declaration, has been guilty of an outrage against the law of nations which endangers the peace of his country, and of a direct violation of a positive statute, will be considered by Spain and France as an evidence of our connivance. . . ." Gallatin went on to expose Smith's character as an agent of the customs:

> . . . I may add that Colonel Smith is a bad officer; that he does not attend to the duties of his office; that he has presented fallacious statements of his emoluments, with intention of keeping a portion which by law ought to be paid in the Treasury, and that he has not even paid what he acknowledged to be due. I know that the delicacy of removing, under all circumstances, a near connection of the late President of the United States made you anxious to overlook every inferior breach of duty in that officer; and those are now mentioned only to show that he is not entitled from his general official conduct to any special indulgence.[36]

Smith was removed and tried in New York. To Gallatin's disgust he was acquitted—"the verdict of acquittal," he declared, "being so glaringly contrary to law and evidence." [37] Jefferson declared himself satisfied with the result. "I had no wish to see Smith imprisoned; he has been a man of integrity and honor, led astray by distress." [38]

There is evidence that toward the end of the Republican period there was laxity in the administration of some of the customhouses. The fraudulent withdrawal of tea from the Philadelphia customhouse by a well-known China merchant, Edward Thomson, was a dramatic example. On November 22, 1825,

35 Henry Adams, *History of the United States*, III, 189–96.
36 Gallatin, *Writings*, I, 293–95 (March 11, 1806).
37 *Ibid.*, I, 306 (August 7, 1806).
38 *Ibid.*, I, 306 (August 15, 1806).

the elderly collector of Philadelphia, John Steele,[39] wrote the Secretary of the Treasury, "I have the painful task to perform of announcing to you the failure of Edward Thomson . . . by which I fear the United States will sustain a very heavy loss; I am the more inclined to think so from information I received on Sabbath afternoon, which affords strong ground to suspect a premeditated fraud." [40] Subsequent intelligence revealed that Thomson had fraudulently withdrawn imported teas on which the unpaid duties amounted to $857,247.60.[41] Rush immediately consulted the President, who directed his friend, Samuel Harrison Smith, to make a thorough investigation.[42]

The report by Smith revealed inefficiency of long standing, due to the warehouse system as well as to the indifference of some employees. Thomson had apparently been withdrawing tea surreptitiously without payment of duties for several years, by various modes. As the teas were unloaded from the ship by porters, they were placed temporarily on the pavements near the wharves while awaiting transportation to the official storehouses to which they were destined until released by a customs officer. They were not subject to close watch and parcels were taken forthwith to packets destined for New York, Boston, or Baltimore. On other occasions the drays loaded with tea, "watching their opportunity," would pass the government storehouse and carry off the boxes to parts unknown.[43] The residue was eventually brought into the storehouses and secured by double locks, one key taken by the customhouse official and one by the importer. No inspection and record of the amount of tea actually stored were made. Later when the importer wished to

[39] Cf. J. Q. Adams, "Steele, at Philadelphia, from the state of his health, has for more than a year been unable to perform his duty." *Memoirs*, VII, 163 (Oct. 28, 1826).

[40] House Doc. 137, 19th Cong., 1st sess., "Letter from the Secretary of the Treasury . . . in relation to Fraud Practised, or Attempted, upon the Revenue Laws of the United States," p. 21 (March 23, 1826).

[41] *Ibid.*, p. 13.

[42] Adams, *Memoirs*, VII, 96 (Dec. 30, 1825). Smith had been induced by Jefferson to move to Washington in 1800, where he became the Republican editor of the *National Intelligencer* (1800–10), and later commissioner of the revenue, an office that had made him familiar with the customs service. *Dictionary of American Biography*, XVII, 343–44.

[43] House Doc. 137, 19th Cong., 1st sess., p. 97.

enter the stores, the customs inspector, if busy, loaned him the customhouse key! Under cover of permits "for taking out a small number of chests, a large number were withdrawn" when the inspector was busy at a distance.[44]

The system of warehousing lent itself to evasion. There were in Philadelphia at this time seventy-one storehouses scattered over the city to meet the convenience of merchants, and in the confusion of unloading vessels it was impossible to watch what was going on. The naval officer, William Jones, put his finger on the difficulty. He testified:

The root of the evil appears to me to be in the ware-housing system. . . . The numerous arrivals nearly at the same time, particularly of large cargoes from China, perhaps to 30 or 40 different consignees, scattered over the surface of this large city, each desirous to store his goods contiguous to his seat of business, together with the rapid transportation of all these in every direction, at the same time, creates such a diversity of calls upon the officers of inspection, as must, at such times, render it extremely difficult, if not impracticable, to answer to those calls, and at the same time to inspect the landing of the cargoes.[45]

Of negligence there was no doubt, but there appeared to be no collusion or corruption among the customs clerks. Smith reported to Rush:

I am happy to add that so far as my knowledge extends, but one opinion prevails in Philadelphia of the integrity of all the officers in the Custom House, as well as their dispositions, by all proper means, to accommodate the mercantile interest by a prompt and obliging discharge of their duty. . . . An indignant feeling at the recent scenes is universally expressed, accompanied, however, with an exoneration of all the officers of the customs from any criminal participation in them.[46]

Gallatin, shortly after he came to the Treasury, had ironically commented on "the general relaxation, which pervaded the internal administration of this and every other department

44 *Ibid.*, p. 15.
45 *Ibid.*, p. 83.
46 *Ibid.*, p. 19.

during the reign of energy. . . ." [47] One gains the impression
that levels of efficiency tended to sink, partly, it may be, by
reason of the unwillingness of any President or Secretary of the
Treasury to remove superannuated or mediocre officials and
employees.

The record of the collectors over a period of more than a
quarter century was, nevertheless, with occasional exceptions,
an honorable one. Early in his administration Jefferson wrote
privately to John Page that, with proper precautions against un-
trustworthy clerks, "these officers are the best in the U. S." [48]
They passed through the embargo crisis with credit to themselves, excepting a few on the New England coast who yielded
to local sentiment. Even here they stoutly enforced Jefferson's
rules in most instances, at peril of costly and annoying suits. In
the larger ports the office was a desirable one both on account
of its income and its standing in commercial and social circles.
In the smaller ports as well it added status to its incumbent.

As the stable years of Republican ascendancy lengthened,
collectors and their subordinates grew gray in office, and with
the passage of time they tended to become careless in the conduct of customhouse business. Like other federal agents, many
were slow in rendering their accounts. Perhaps inevitably they
became involved to some extent in the great national political
campaigns of 1824 and 1828. The standards set by Gallatin were
admirable, but there were signs by 1828 that the collectors had
suffered both by circumstances and by the absence of proper
supervision from less able Secretaries of the Treasury.

[47] Gallatin, *Writings*, I, 31 (August 10, 1801). Gallatin found that the collector
of Cherrystone, a small Virginia port, "the worst delinquent on the list," had
rendered his last account as of December 31, 1796, *ibid.*, I, 44.

[48] Jefferson, *Works* (Federal ed.), IX, 352 (Feb. 20, 1802).

CHAPTER TWELVE

Accountability:
Paralysis and Reform

The Federalist system of accountability of public officers for money was elaborate and was designed to safeguard the public against malfeasance of any kind. It included the requirement of bonds and sureties, regular submission of accounts and vouchers, double examination first by the auditor and then by the comptroller, and judicial process for collecting sums due either from collectors or disbursing agents. The system had fallen into the hands of Treasury accounting officers who gave a rigid construction to its regulations. It imposed heavy burdens upon the auditor and the comptroller; and their offices were the largest in the Treasury Department.[1] It was also a source of much annoyance to many persons in high station and low.

The Republicans continued the system without any immediate change. The Federalist comptroller, John Steele, stayed on for nearly two years; the auditor, Richard Harrison, served from 1791 until his resignation in 1836; and the accounting clerks were not disturbed in their offices. The same rigid principles were applied.[2]

Gradually, however, the system broke down in the face of an increasing load of business and a lack of aggressiveness in proceedings against delinquent collectors and disbursing agents.

[1] White, *The Federalists*, ch. 27.
[2] In the preparation of this chapter, I have been greatly assisted by the courtesy of Mr. Lucius Wilmerding, Jr., who kindly allowed me to read his unpublished manuscript, "A History of the Accounting System of the United States."

A mass of unsettled claims quickly piled up, and procedure was lacking to dispose of those hopeless in nature; they were filed away unsettled and forgotten until Congress eventually required a statement of their number and amount.

The system broke down not merely because it was too restricted to deal with the business it faced. The procedure was hampered by the necessity of going to the courts both to compel accountable officers to render their accounts, and to collect amounts due. This judicial safeguard of the interests of officials was cherished by Republicans, and it was only after long delay and repeated executive recommendations that the system was altered at this crucial point.

THE SYSTEM OF ACCOUNTABILITY

A skeleton description of the structure of the system of accountability in terms of the officers involved includes:

(1) *The accounting officers:* the comptroller, the auditor, and until 1817, the War and Navy Department accountants, who functioned as auditors.

(2) *The officers accountable:* of whom the principal classes were ministers and other agents abroad; army and navy paymasters and navy pursers; deputy commissaries, quartermasters, and navy agents acting as purchasing officers; collectors of customs, and excise tax collectors from 1813 to 1817; land office receivers; Indian agents; prize agents; marshals and clerks of court; postmasters; and on occasion the President of the United States.[3]

The essential elements of the system can be stated briefly, although a complex mass of detail grew up around them. Officers collecting money were required to make regular returns, usually quarterly, and to deposit their collections either in a convenient bank or directly with the Treasury. In the former case the money was available for payment of government obligations in the neighborhood and was customarily so employed at

---

[3] ". . . as to the foreign intercourse fund, the President is emphatically the disbursing officer of the Government. . . ." *Opinions of the Attorneys General* (1841 ed.), p. 470 (Oct. 14, 1823). This chapter excludes consideration of the Post Office which, until 1836, was a self-financing agency; also the special problem of property accountability in the army and navy; and the special case of the General Land Office.

the direction of the Secretary of the Treasury. Officers collecting money were under bond, and they and their sureties were liable to suit for failure to pay in funds collected.

Disbursing officers normally received advances from the department they served, subject to an accounting. They were required to take evidence of all sums disbursed and at regular intervals to submit their accounts to the department, with the supporting documents. In some departments the accounts were examined forthwith, before being submitted to the auditor; in others they were sent directly to the auditor. He examined the records and required appropriate evidence to support each and every expenditure. His examination resulted in a "settlement," in which items disallowed, if any, were charged to the disbursing officer. The file was then transmitted to the comptroller, who reviewed the settlement and stated the final balances.

The auditor's duties were original, the comptroller's revisionary and appellate, but each officer was independent of the other. The auditor, like the comptroller, was appointed by the President, with the consent of the Senate, and the comptroller had no authority to discipline or remove him, although of course he could overrule the auditor's decisions. The comptroller could also direct the auditor forthwith to state and settle an account, an authority which enabled the comptroller to bring up any claim for immediate revision and final settlement. This was an exceptional authority and was not used to govern the normal course of the auditor's business.

The rigidities of the system of accountability, from the point of view of an official desiring to get an early and fair settlement, had long been subject of adverse notice. After John Quincy Adams returned from his diplomatic mission in 1801, he was elected to the United States Senate, and sought to get his diplomatic accounts settled. He started with the Secretary of State, October 24, 1803, with whom he "had some conversation . . . relative to the settlement of my accounts. . . . But he still makes difficulties beyond what I conceive to be reasonable or proper." [4] On the 26th he advanced to the auditor, "and showed him the documents which had been required for the settlement

---

[4] Adams, *Memoirs*, I, 265.

of my accounts." [5] On November 7th he pushed forward to the Secretary of the Treasury, and "conversed with him respecting the settlement of my accounts, in which I presume all the difficulties are now removed." [6] On November 17th he called on the auditor, but his accounts were not ready.[7] Finally on January 10, 1804, he secured his final settlement.[8] Relatively speaking this was a model of expedition, due beyond doubt to the fact that Adams was a figure of standing, a Senator, on the spot, persistent and stubborn. Lesser figures, and some prominent ones not so strategically placed, found interminable difficulties.[9] Indeed the Attorney General formally stated that "it was no unusual thing for a person found a debtor by the rules of evidence which governed the accounting officers, to request that he might be sued for the supposed balance, in order that he might have the benefit of the more liberal rules of evidence which prevail in courts of law." [10]

BREAKDOWN OF THE SYSTEM

Systems of accountability, however, do not break down because individuals are incommoded. This system broke down, as already noted, because it was overwhelmed with business, and because it lacked adequate means of compulsion upon reluctant officers accountable. Information on the first of these problems became available in 1816 in an able report transmitted by Benjamin Huger, chairman of a select committee of the House to examine the subject of unsettled balances.[11]

The War of 1812 had piled up accounts in huge stacks, over-

---

[5] *Ibid.*, I, 266.

[6] *Ibid.*, I, 272.

[7] *Ibid.*, I, 273.

[8] *Ibid.*, I, 286.

[9] The rigidities were of long standing. In 1795 Representative Wadsworth declared after getting a settlement that "he would not go through such a business again for twenty times the balance that he recovered. Many people had in despair given up the attempt." *Annals,* 3d Cong., p. 1173 (Feb. 4, 1795). Boudinot "had been put to the utmost difficulties." *Ibid.,* p. 1224 (Feb. 14, 1795).

[10] *Opinions of the Attorneys General* (1841 ed.), p. 449 (March 20, 1823). For the trouble encountered by the city of Baltimore in recovering expenses incurred at the time of the British invasion in 1814 (still pending in 1827), see House Doc. 39, 20th Cong., 1st sess. and House Report 218, 20th Cong., 1st sess.

[11] *American State Papers: Finance,* III, 123 (April 24, 1816); see also *American State Papers: Miscellaneous,* II, 396 (Dec. 9, 1816).

laying the dusty accumulations of the previous decade. The
Huger Committee had anticipated difficulty in exploring these
papers, but they were literally overwhelmed. "They found
themselves advancing into a labyrinth, the intricacies of which
increased at every step they progressed." There was "a great
mass of unsettled accounts in the Department of State; nor is
it easy to anticipate, under the present organization, when they
can be finally acted upon and settled." [12] Comptroller Joseph
Anderson stated, "The accounts of the General Land Office are
greatly in arrears; some of them remain unsettled from seven
to ten years. These accounts are intricate, and generally very
large; from ten to fifteen days is required for the best accounting clerk to examine one of them." [13] There was an arrearage
in the War Department accounts running back to 1798.[14] The
accounts of the Indian department, "without a solitary exception," had remained unsettled since 1798.[15] No Post Office
accounts had been settled from 1810 to 1817.[16] For the Treasury, which was in the best shape, no accounts had been settled
from June 1815 to the close of 1816.

This is a convenient point to note that no adequate procedure was developed under the Jeffersonians to clear the
Treasury books of hopeless accounts.[17] Congress authorized
some relief from the rigid rules of the accounting officers in
1823 by directing the third auditor, who handled War Department accounts, to admit expenditures arising before July 1,
1815, for which regular vouchers could not be produced, if
their unavailability could be demonstrated to the accounting
officers; if the evidence submitted was the best the nature of the
case would permit; and if it were of such a character as to be
received in courts of law. If differences of opinion should de-

12 *American State Papers: Finance*, III, 123 (April 24, 1816).
13 *Ibid.*, III, 127.
14 *American State Papers: Miscellaneous*, II, 397.
15 *Ibid.*, II, 397.
16 Senate Doc. 74, 15th Cong., 1st sess., p. 22 (Dec. 22, 1817).
17 An early proposal for equitable cases, made by the Huger Committee in
1816, suggested an administrative tribunal consisting of the Secretary of the
Treasury and the comptroller, with power either to pass upon the accounts or
report them to the House. *American State Papers: Finance*, III, 124 (April 24,
1816).

velop in these special cases between the third auditor and the second comptroller, the Secretary of War gave a conclusive decision.[18] In 1825 the fourth auditor, Tobias Watkins, begged for "some legislative provision to authorize me to relieve the files of the office from a mass of accounts against persons long since *deceased* or *insolvent;* and against others, from whom there is not even the remotest prospect of recovering a cent." [19] Congress gave no relief.

The embarrassments caused by this mass of arrearages were doubled by the cumbersome methods of enforcing submission of accounts and collection of balances due the government. The system for securing accountability had been fixed by the organic Treasury Act of 1789, and by legislation of 1795 and 1797. The act of 1795 required a lawsuit to compel officers to submit their accounts and vouchers. The person accountable was entitled to a period up to twelve months to submit his vouchers, and in default the comptroller was authorized, in his discretion, to bring suit to ensure submission of the account. The courts were the only means of compelling this initial step to bring the vouchers and accounts to the auditor.[20] The actual payment of amounts eventually found due could be enforced only by recourse to the courts for a second time. The act of 1797 strengthened the position of the United States as debtor by requiring early court action on suits instituted, by making the United States a preferred creditor, and by causing writs of execution to run in any state or territory against the delinquent.[21] The lawsuit, however, remained the essential requirement both to compel the submission of accounts and papers and to collect sums due the government. It was the basic weakness of the system.

The inadequacy of these judicial remedies became increasingly apparent. Josiah Quincy told the House in 1810 that the "tendency of these defects in the law has been to render receivers of public moneys negligent in rendering their accounts,

[18] 3 Stat. 770 (March 1, 1823).
[19] House Doc. 107, 18th Cong., 2d sess., p. 4 (Feb. 7, 1825).
[20] 1 Stat. 441 (March 3, 1795).
[21] 1 Stat. 512 (March 3, 1797).

and to expose the officers of the treasury to inconvenience in compelling settlement." [22] In 1816 Comptroller Joseph Anderson reported to Congressman Huger, "There is no period fixed at which ascertained balances are sued for. . . . In important cases the Secretary of the Treasury is always consulted." In minor cases the discretion of the comptroller, advised by the district attorneys, governed action—or more often inaction.[23] The heads of departments declared:

The want of power to compel those to whom the collection or disbursement of the public money has been confided to render their vouchers and settle their accounts when required has already contributed to swell the list of unsettled accounts. . . . The conviction on the part of an officer that his accounts cannot or will not be settled for years presents a certain degree of impunity to embezzlement, and powerfully tempts to the commission of it. The necessity of resorting to an action at law to enforce the settlement of accounts, or to recover money embezzled by an officer, ought to be avoided. . . .[24]

The matter was again brought to the attention of Congress in 1818 by Crawford, who repeated that "the most serious obstacle to the prompt settlement of the public accounts, is the want of power to compel delinquent officers to render their accounts and vouchers." What made the matter worse was that if a single quartermaster should withhold his vouchers, the account of the quartermaster general (including all other quartermasters) had to be suspended.[25] ". . . the means of coercing a settlement are extremely defective." Congress still remained unmoved.

Two years later Crawford once again notified Congress of this crucial weakness. "The evils described in these reports have been increasing and will continue to increase, until an appropriate remedy shall be provided. Immense sums will be lost in the settlement of the accounts which accrued during the late war, for the want of an efficient remedy against defaulting

22 *American State Papers: Finance*, II, 415.
23 *Ibid.*, III, 126.
24 *American State Papers: Miscellaneous*, II, 398.
25 Senate Doc. 74, 15th Cong., 1st sess., p. 6 (Jan. 22, 1818).

officers." [26] This time Congress responded with legislation authorizing summary process, the details of which are noted below.[27]

Before this effective means was applied to coerce officials to render their accounts promptly, however, years had passed during which other schemes had been tried out. Gallatin asked Jefferson in 1801 to put in his first message to Congress a request for greater fiscal safety, "by rendering every person who receives public moneys from the Treasury as immediately, promptly, and effectually accountable to the accounting officer (the Comptroller) as practicable." [28] Jefferson responded favorably but the matter was not pressed. Congress eventually tried publicity as a morally coercive device, then reconstructed the auditing machinery, and finally authorized summary administrative process.

Publicity. This sequence of reforms turned the screws more and more upon the delinquent fiscal officers, as mild measures proved ineffective. The first scheme was to enforce compliance by publicity. The comptroller was directed in 1809 to lay before Congress an annual statement of accounts in the Treasury, War, and Navy Departments that remained unsettled more than three years.[29]

In response to a resolution of the House (April 20, 1808) Gallatin had submitted a list of balances due the day before the President signed the "publicity" measure.[30] It may be presumed

26 House Doc. 73, 16th Cong., 1st sess., p. 3 (Feb. 11, 1820). In 1820 Calhoun wrote David B. Mitchell, former governor of Georgia and at the time Indian agent, to get information on two advances of $5,000 each for road construction, one in 1816 and one in 1818, of which the Treasury had apparently lost all record. *Correspondence of John C. Calhoun* (J. Franklin Jameson, ed.), American Historical Association, *Annual Report, 1899*, II, 177–78.

27 3 Stat. 441, sec. 8 (April 20, 1818). A special problem that throws light on the character of the times was encountered in the effort to provide a legal remedy against banks which failed to pay their notes when held by the government. The first case revealed that by the laws of the state in which suit was brought there was no process by which a corporation could be brought into court! House Doc. 73, 16th Cong., 1st sess., p. 3.

28 Gallatin, *Writings*, I, 68 (Nov. 1801).

29 2 Stat. 535, sec. 2 (March 3, 1809).

30 *American State Papers: Finance*, II, 356–64 (March 2, 1809).

that leading members of Congress were aware earlier of its contents. On the whole the disclosures were not spectacular. In twenty-five cases judgments had been obtained or suits were pending—a number not calculated to impress Congress with the activity of the comptroller. The report as printed in the *American State Papers* covered eight pages of open accounts, for the most part held up for lack of vouchers, "informal vouchers," or "suspended" in the office of the comptroller. Among them was the name of John Adams, with an unsettled account of $12,898 for the accommodation of his presidential household, "certified to have been applied, but no specific account rendered." James Monroe had an unsettled account of $18,195.46 "supposed to be due for salary." [31] Timothy Pickering stood charged for two sums of $383,045.67 and $54,003.76 respectively, eight years after he ceased holding the office of Secretary of State.[32] Samuel R. Franklin, late paymaster of the 10th regiment of infantry, had absconded, owing the government $69,978.21. The number of embezzlements, on this record, was small. The open accounts were due generally to the slow operation of the system and to honest differences of opinion, not to delinquency.

The weakness of the publicity system quickly became apparent. It resulted in much embarrassment to men of integrity in stations high and low who found themselves on a public list of defaulters and embezzlers. A House committee in 1816 recognized that the unregulated publication of unsettled balances was to be regretted. "Nor can it fail to be peculiarly painful and aggravating to the feelings of honest and honorable men, to find themselves in such company, and held up to the public under at least the appearance of having committed like frauds

[31] Monroe was upset over this affair and wrote a long defense to Senator Richard Brent of Virginia in which he remarked, "I own I expected from M.r Duval, in case he made any mention of my name, without communicating with me, such a statement, as would have placed the aff.r in a just light before the publick." Monroe, *Writings*, V, 118 (Feb. 25, 1810).

[32] Until an account was finally closed, no matter how small the sum in dispute, the Treasury considered the individual a debtor for the whole amount. *Annals*, 7th Cong., 1st sess., p. 1275 (May 1, 1802). Pickering actually was not indebted to the government but it was not until 1810 that his account was finally settled. See Charles W. Upham, *The Life of Timothy Pickering* (4 vols., Boston: Little, Brown, 1867–73), IV, 162–69.

upon the Government." [33] In the reorganization act of 1817
Congress reduced this evil by directing the comptroller, in his
annual statement of three-year-old unsettled balances, to distinguish those where the difficulty was one of form which ought
equitably to be removed by Congress.[34] The publicity scheme
apparently had little if any value in hastening the settlement
of balances of those officials who were reluctant to submit to
an accounting.

Reorganization: the reforms of 1817. The second and the
major stage in reform came shortly after the close of the War
of 1812. The movement was concerned primarily with the reduction of arrearages, but it also dealt with the means of putting
pressure on delinquent officials, and moved out into broader
realms by proposing again a Home Department. Procedure in
developing the plan of reform was significant. The Senate required the Secretaries of the four departments to report jointly
a plan to insure annual settlements and more certain accountability. The House was not invited to concur, and the President
was by-passed, although as a matter of form the report was submitted by Madison. This document, the first essay in administrative reorganization, will be referred to as the Report of the
Four Secretaries.

The plan was developed by Crawford, who wrote Gallatin:
"In my office, and that of Treasurer, the amounts [sic] had not
been balanced from June, 1815. In every other Department it
was worse. . . . To remain in the Treasury under such circumstances afforded no prospect of gaining reputation, but a
certainty of losing what little might have been previously
acquired." [35] The Report was also signed by Monroe, Crowninshield, and George Graham, Acting Secretary of War.[36] It was a
state paper of major importance whose principal features, with

33 *American State Papers: Finance,* III, 124 (April 24, 1816).
34 3 Stat. 366, sec. 14 (March 3, 1817).
35 Gallatin, *Writings,* II, 24 (March 12, 1817).
36 *American State Papers: Miscellaneous,* II, 396–99 (Dec. 6, 1816). Debates on
this measure were barely noticed in the record. *Annals,* 14th Cong., 2d sess., p.
1034 (Feb. 26, 1817). The second session of the 14th Congress was dominated
by two controversial issues, the compensation bill to repeal a previous increase
in Congressmen's salaries, and the internal improvements bill that was vetoed by
Monroe.

two exceptions, were adopted by Congress in the legislation of
1817. We note first the findings of the Four Secretaries and
then their recommendations and the resulting legislation.

The Four Secretaries found first that the delay in settling
accounts was due in part to the excessive load imposed upon
them as heads of departments. They therefore recommended a
new department, to be called the Home Department, that would
include the supervision of territorial governments, the construction and maintenance of national highways and canals, the
General Post Office, the Patent Office, and the Indian department. Congress declined to move along this line.

The Secretaries found in the second place that the "leading
feature of the organic laws of the Departments, that the settlement of public accounts should exclusively rest with the [Treas-
ury] Department," had been substantially abandoned when
the army and navy accountants were established in the 1790's.
They declared that responsibility should rest either in the
departments or in the Treasury, and joined in stating their conviction in favor of the latter. They recognized what had become
universally apparent, that more manpower had to be applied
to the task. They consequently recommended (1) that the offices of war and navy accountants and the superintendent general of military supplies be abolished; (2) that the "primary
and final settlement of all accounts be made in the Treasury
Department"; and (3) that the auditing and settlement staff
be enlarged by four additional auditors, one additional comptroller, and one solicitor, the latter to be responsible for
prosecution of delinquent officers.

The Secretaries found in the third place that judicial process
to compel submission of vouchers was cumbersome, slow, and
ineffective. They recommended summary process against any
delinquent officers on the model already provided for the collectors of internal revenue: i.e., seizure and sale of real and
personal property of the delinquent and of his securities.[37] This

[37] *American State Papers: Miscellaneous*, II, 399. Some light is thrown on one
aspect of the problem by a report of 1824 from the Treasury. "Mr. Parke Walton's
defalcation was discovered by the examiner of the land office, in November 1819.
He was permitted to remain in office a short time, in consequence of an assurance given by him to the Hon. Mr. Williams, one of the Senators from Mississippi,

was too strong medicine for Congress! In a supplementary report the Secretaries advised against allowing any judicial review of a final settlement, keeping open the possibility of an appeal to Congress.[38]

With the exception of the recommendations in favor of a new department, summary process, and a solicitor, Congress accepted substantially the whole program proposed by the Four Secretaries. The terms of the act of March 3, 1817, provided that all claims and accounts were to be settled in the Treasury Department.[39] The offices of accountants in the War and Navy Departments, and the office of superintendent general of military supplies were consequently abolished. One additional comptroller and four additional auditors were created and their respective duties specified. The first comptroller continued (for a few years) to possess authority to superintend the recovery of debts and to direct suits and legal proceedings. The Secretary of the Treasury was admonished to cause all accounts to be settled within a year, but was given no additional authority to secure this goal. The comptroller was authorized to discontinue publication of three-year delinquents after three listings, and, as already indicated, was allowed to distinguish cases where arrearage was merely a matter of form.[40] He was also instructed

that he would bring up his books, and pay over the deficiency by the first of March following. He did not comply with this promise, however, and was removed on the 23d May, 1820." He had made way with over $54,000 (House Doc. 149, 18th Cong., 1st sess., p. 3).

38 *American State Papers: Miscellaneous*, II, 417–18 (Dec. 31, 1816).

39 3 Stat. 366, sec. 2.

40 It is of some interest to note that Gallatin had foreseen the main lines of this reform. He understood the need for prompt rendering of vouchers and early settlements. He proposed a second auditor in 1802 (*American State Papers: Finance*, I, 757). He recommended that the settlements made by the army and navy accountants be reported directly to the comptroller, omitting the intermediate inspection of the auditors. (Nicholson Papers, Library of Congress, Manuscript Division, II, 1143, April 27, 1801). See also for a later reference to the same idea, *American State Papers: Finance*, II, 336 (Feb. 4, 1809). The same object (i.e., two instead of three revisions) was reached by abolishing the army and navy accountants in 1817. He opposed the plan for two independent comptrollers (Gallatin to Macon, April 23, 1816, Gallatin Papers, New York Historical Society, Vol. XVIII). He repeatedly recommended an express statutory requirement of quarterly accounts from all officials in the United States and annual accounts from others (*American State Papers: Finance*, II, 417).

174   THE JEFFERSONIANS

to publish annually a list of officers who failed to make settlements required by law.[41]

The distribution of work among the five auditors and two comptrollers was so arranged as to effect a complete separation of military and civil accounts. Accounts of military expenditures, by far the most voluminous, went to the second and third auditors; accounts of naval expenditures went to the fourth auditor; and all statements of accounts made by them were revised by the second comptroller. The first auditor dealt with all accounts accruing in the Treasury Department; the fifth auditor handled those accruing in the State Department, the Post Office, and the Indian office; and their settlements went to the first comptroller. Although the Four Secretaries had discreetly suggested the wisdom of allowing the President to reallocate the auditing business in the light of experience, Congress went no further then than to permit him to assign certain War Department business to either the second or the third auditor.

These reforms of 1817 did not interfere with departmental examination of accounts before submission to the Treasury for settlement. The duties of the departmental accountants were transferred to the new auditors, but the principle of prior administrative examination of accounts was left intact. The War Department was apparently the only one in which an administrative examination was regularly enforced. The procedure was described by Calhoun in 1822. ". . . one principle pervades the whole organization—to hold the head of each subordinate department [for example, ordnance or quartermaster] responsible for the disbursements of his department. All advances are made on his recommendation, founded on precise estimates; and all accounts are rendered to him, and, before they are audited, are minutely examined by him and approved." [42]

The new system and the added manpower produced results. Peter Hagner, the third auditor, was an indefatigable and conscientious official. Upon taking over his office in 1817 he found it necessary "to open a correspondence with every receiver of

41 For the first such annual list, see House Doc. 73, 15th Cong., 2d sess. (Dec. 31, 1818).

42 *American State Papers: Military Affairs*, II, 345 (Feb. 11, 1822).

public money. Volumes have been filled with such letters, and by these and other means a most successful result was produced. . . ." [43] In 1820 he remarked that "much time and labor is also consequent to an arrangement which requires the Auditor to conduct all the correspondence in relation to every account received in the office, some idea of the extent of which may be formed, when it is stated that, since the establishment of the office, twenty-three letter books have been filled with the letters written on the business of the office." [44] On his own motion, as already noted, he discharged five of his clerks in 1822 since the business relating to the old accounts had so far diminished.[45] Two years later he told Congress that his current achievements in reducing the amount of money outstanding were small in proportion to his earlier efforts, but added that "the difficulties in effecting settlements increase, as the number of accounts lessens. . . ." [46]

Achievements fell into two classes: the liquidation of old accounts pending in 1817, and the settlement of current accounts arising after the introduction of the new organization.

Notable improvement was recorded in the War Department with respect to *current* accounts. In his annual report for 1823 Calhoun recorded with evident pride that order, accuracy, economy, and accountability had been introduced into every branch of the military service.

. . . the accounts have been made up with accuracy, and transmitted with promptitude to the proper Departments for settlement, and have there been settled without delay. . . . the result has been,

43 House Doc. 10, 16th Cong., 2d sess., p. 6 (Nov. 20, 1820).

44 *Ibid.*, p. 6.

45 House Doc. 4, 17th Cong., 2d sess., p. 8 (Nov. 26, 1822).

46 House Doc. 110, 18th Cong., 2d sess., p. 4 (Dec. 18, 1824). This is the same conscientious Peter Hagner who fell in with John Quincy Adams on his regular morning walk, March 10, 1831, and of whom Adams wrote in his diary, "He told me he had ten children, and had never lost one; and that he always made it a practice to prevent their getting their feet wet, and to make them wear flannels." *Memoirs*, VIII, 340. Peter Hagner and his son, Alexander B. Hagner, an associate justice of the Supreme Court of the District of Columbia, enjoyed the distinction of being acquainted with every President of the United States from Washington through Wilson. See Alexander B. Hagner, *A Personal Narrative of the Acquaintance of My Father and Myself with Each of the Presidents of the United States* (Washington, D. C.: privately printed, 1915).

that, of the entire amount of money drawn from the Treasury in the year 1822, for Military service, including the Pensions, amounting to $4,571,961.94, although it passed through the hands of no less than 291 disbursing Agents, there has not been a single defalcation, nor the loss of a cent to the Government; and that the whole has been accounted for at the Treasury, except a small amount, which remains in the hands of the disbursing agents, ready to be applied to the object for which it was drawn.[47]

The current accounts of the Treasury Department also were in good shape, and indeed had never fallen into such disrepute as those of the army and navy.

A general view of the auditors' relative success in dealing with "new" accounts after 1817 was given in a statement of 1822. From March 4, 1817, to September 30, 1822, the Treasury had become accountable for over 96 million dollars, of which 8.8 million dollars remained unsettled on the latter date. The War Department had drawn 16 million dollars of which the second auditor had settled all but 2 million, and 17 million dollars of which the third auditor had cleared all but 4 million. The Navy Department had drawn 15 million dollars, of which 4.5 million remained unsettled. The navy accounts were normally slow in settlement where they involved pursers and officers at sea for prolonged periods.[48] The greater part of these balances were in regular course of settlement.

To clear up arrearages accumulated before 1817 was a more difficult matter, and years were required to bring them to substantial settlement.[49] In 1822, five years after reorganization, Joseph Anderson made a progress report to accompany Mon-

[47] Senate Doc. 1, 18th Cong., 1st sess., Documents accompanying the Message of the President, p. 3 (Nov. 29, 1823).

[48] *American State Papers: Finance*, IV, 2. For a list of pursers and navy agents in arrears in 1823, see Senate Doc. 33, 18th Cong., 1st sess. (Feb. 11, 1824).

[49] The loss of papers in 1814 when the British army burned a number of public buildings in Washington was of course a great handicap. A letter of Joseph Nourse, the register, will illustrate the difficulty. ". . . the books with the vouchers are not at this time in existence; they were placed for security, and also *for privity*, in an iron chest, in the fire-proof of the Treasury building. The clerk who had more immediate charge of them on the 24th of August, 1814, when the late enemy made an eruption in this city, was at his military post on the field of action, and the fire-proof not resisting the flame, the papers were all consumed." (March 6, 1816, House Doc. 134, 15th Cong., 1st sess., p. 15).

roe's message to Congress.[50] The Treasury still had on its books old accounts pending on March 3, 1817, amounting to $836,-917.80. This sum consisted of nearly three hundred personal accounts "which have been accumulating since the commencement of the government." The second auditor, who had inherited old army accounts exceeding five million dollars in amount, had cleared all but $321,598.74, of which most had been reported for suit. The third auditor was still in the woods. He had inherited another $40,000,000 of old army accounts, had cleared over $35,000,000 and still was struggling with something over $4,000,000. This sum comprised more than two thousand personal accounts, including some as remote as 1792. The fourth auditor was also far behind, despite much progress. He had acquired navy accounts amounting to over $14,000,000, and in 1822 still was examining old accounts whose total exceeded $4,000,000.

. . . This consists of balances which have been accumulating since the first establishment of the Navy Department, in 1798, and which are due from persons not now in service, and of whose place of residence, or of whose solvency or insolvency, nothing is known. In some cases, confused and informal accounts have been rendered by persons indebted to a very large amount; in others, the parties have been either lost at sea, or killed in action, and no accounts whatever rendered. A considerable part, also, consists of sums advanced to prize agents, who have rendered no accounts for settlement. . . .[51]

We may conclude that by the reorganization of the auditing machinery an administrative crisis of large magnitude was successfully resolved. In 1816 a sort of paralysis had been imposed on the accounting services as a consequence of the fiscal operations of the War of 1812. Existing resources and organization were totally inadequate to deal with the situation. Congress asked the executive branch for a plan; the Four Secretaries presented a plan; Congress adopted its central features; and within a decade the crisis had been surmounted.

On compelling the submission of accounts. These large reforms in accounting machinery out of the way, Congress began

[50] *American State Papers: Finance*, IV, 1 (Nov. 26, 1822).
[51] *Ibid.*, IV, 1–2.

to pay heed to repeated executive recommendations to secure submission of accounts and collection of balances due. The first remedy, to post the names of delinquents, had proved a failure, and reluctantly Congress turned to stronger administrative measures.

By way of exception to the normal reliance on a lawsuit to compel submission of accounts, already described, the district supervisors of the excise tax had been authorized in 1798 to issue a summary administrative process, known as a warrant of distress, against delinquent collectors of the excise tax and their sureties.[52] The warrant was issued directly to the marshal, who was then authorized to sell the goods and chattels of the delinquent. The courts were not involved. This procedure was renewed in the excise tax law of 1813, but the warrant was issued by the comptroller.[53] A further pressure was put on the excise tax collector by forfeiture of his bond for failure to render his accounts for more than three months, or to pay over money collected.[54]

In 1820 this mode of action became the rule for all *collectors* of public money, after a decade of persuasion by the executive branch. Congress directed the President to appoint an officer of the Treasury to act as agent for the recovery of sums due to the United States.[55] The agent was authorized to issue a warrant of distress to the United States marshal against "any collector of the revenue, receiver of public money, or other officer who shall have received the public money before it is paid into the treasury of the United States," who failed to render his account or pay over the money as prescribed by law. This law did not, however, affect *disbursing officers* to whom advances had been made for public purposes.

A rider to the appropriation act of 1822 brought additional pressure to bear on all persons accountable, including the disbursing officers. The salary of any person in arrears to the

52 1 Stat. 597, sec. 15 (July 14, 1798).

53 3 Stat. 22, sec. 28 (July 22, 1813).

54 3 Stat. 82, sec. 5 (August 2, 1813).

55 3 Stat. 592 (May 15, 1820). The constitutionality of this law was affirmed many years later in a suit growing out of the defalcations of Samuel Swartwout, collector of New York under Jackson. *Murray's Lessee* v. *Hoboken Land and Improvement Company*, 18 Howard 272 (1855).

United States was to be withheld until he had accounted for and paid in to the Treasury all sums for which he was liable. Recognizing that in some cases failure to account was due to honest differences of opinion, the act further provided that upon demand of the officer prompt action must be taken by the Treasury agent to secure a judicial determination of the issues.[56]

Further means to secure a settlement were provided in 1823. Every accountable officer was required to make quarterly returns within three months from the close of the quarter if resident within the United States, and six months if resident abroad. Any officer failing to account was to be promptly reported to the President and dismissed from the public service, unless he could make his peace with the Chief Executive.[57]

Two separate but related systems to enforce accountability consequently developed. The first was directed against all *collectors* of public money (of whom the collectors of customs were the principal group); it was summary administrative action in the form of a distress warrant issued by the comptroller, authorizing the seizure and sale of the delinquent's property. The second was directed against the *disbursing officers,* as well as collectors, and involved withholding of salary. A third, discharge from office, was also directed against both classes. The original single dependence upon a suit at the instance of the comptroller was thus replaced by much more effective administrative remedies; but actual collections of balances due from *disbursing officers* still could only be forced by a suit at law.

These reforms produced good results, especially in the War Department. In 1826 the paymaster general reported that "every cent advanced within the time embraced in this report, has been accounted for, that could be required or expected. . . ."[58] In the same year the second auditor, who settled War Department

[56] 3 Stat. 668, sec. 2 (April 30, 1822); 4 Stat. 246 (Jan. 25, 1828).

[57] 3 Stat. 723 (Jan. 31, 1823). This act also forbade advances of money in any case except where specifically directed by the President. Until 1823 there apparently was no law requiring submission of accounts at stated periods, but regulation and custom had fixed the quarter as the usual interval. The Huger Committee stated in 1816, "it would seem not less expedient to oblige all foreign ministers and public agents to send in a regular and semi-annual account current. . . ." *American State Papers: Finance,* III, 123.

[58] Senate Doc. 1, 19th Cong., 2d sess., p. 186 (Nov. 27, 1826).

accounts, reported, "I have the satisfaction to state that, in this office, not a single officer has failed to make the settlement required by law." [59] In 1827 the commissary general of purchases declared, "it affords me great satisfaction to state, that every account due on the 30th September, save one, has been received, and those are of an officer whose duties, in consequence of the recent disturbance by the Winnebago Indians, were too arduous and multifarious to give that attention to his accounts . . . which under ordinary circumstances, he undoubtedly would have done." [60] The Secretary of the Navy declared, "The disbursing officers have exhibited punctuality and faithfulness. . . ." [61] Summary powers were, however, seldom brought into play. The House Committee on Claims declared in 1832 that they had rarely if ever been exercised.[62]

Stephen Pleasonton, Treasury agent. In 1820, as already noted, Congress authorized the President to designate a Treasury agent to superintend the collection of debts to the United States. President Monroe designated the fifth auditor, Stephen Pleasonton. His letters and directions are preserved in the National Archives.[63] They provide a fascinating record of adjusting the law to the circumstances of the case. The standard form of administrative action, of which the pages of this volume are full, is illustrated in the following letter from Pleasonton to the United States attorney for Ohio.

I transmit, herewith, authenticated copies of the account and bond of John McDougal, late Paymaster to the Militia of the state of Ohio, exhibiting a balance of 16,811 01/100 dollars due from him to the United States, for the recovery of which, with interest, you will be pleased to institute suit against the principal and his sureties without delay. Mr McDougal's residence is believed to be at Chilicothe, Ohio.[64]

Mercy tempered justice to a degree, however, despite congressional pressure to clean up old accounts. Indulgences were

[59] House Doc. 136, 19th Cong., 2d sess., p. 4 (Dec. 7, 1826).

[60] Senate Doc. 1, 20th Cong., 1st sess., p. 82 (Nov. 26, 1827); see also *ibid.*, p. 92.

[61] *Ibid.*, p. 212.

[62] House Report 511, 22d Cong., 1st sess., p. 2 (July 5, 1832).

[63] MS. in National Archives, Treasury Department, 5th Auditor's Office, Letters on Debts and Suits, No. 2.

[64] *Ibid.*, p. 14 (July 9, 1821).

forthcoming where the government's interest seemed secure. Thus another Ohio militia paymaster, Henry H. Evans, was granted a stay of proceedings on September 17, 1820, and nearly a year later Pleasonton extended the days of grace. "A letter has just been received from Mr Evans, stating that the balance due by him to the United States will be settled very soon, and praying that a little more indulgence may be granted. If his sureties will give their assent, in writing, to the indulgence, and the costs of suit which have accrued be paid . . . you may direct a stay of further proceedings until the 1st of October next." [65] Occasionally a settlement would be reached by which the delinquent officer would consent to repayment by deductions from his salary as it became due.[66] In the case of Lieutenant Redmond, Pleasonton agreed to pay jail fees to the extent of eighty dollars, thus presumably expediting the release of a delinquent officer who had suffered the full penalties for failing to clear his accounts.[67]

General Winder, whose feeble military capacities had been revealed in the brief Washington campaign of 1814, presented one of those "delicate" cases. Pleasonton wrote the General:

. . . I discovered among the papers received from the Comptroller . . . an authenticated copy of an account adjusted by the Third Auditor, on which a balance appeared to be due from you of $4,484 85/100, for the recovery of which suit was required to be instituted. The performance of this unpleasant duty I have deferred to this period, in the hope that you would have had it in your power to discharge this balance; and it would give me great pleasure to be able further to delay it by an assurance from you that the money will in a short time be paid.[68]

With respect to indulgences on customhouse bonds, a somewhat analogous case, he wrote the collector of Norfolk: "You will . . . exercise a sound discretion, both as it regards the interest of the individuals and that of the public; always bearing in mind that it is not the wish of the Executive Government,

[65] Pleasonton to John C. Wright, U. S. attorney, July 6, 1821, *ibid.*, p. 10.
[66] Pleasonton to Peter Hagner, July 26, 1821, *ibid.*, p. 43.
[67] Pleasonton to Tench Ringgold, marshal, Sept. 10, 1821, *ibid.*, p. 101.
[68] Pleasonton to General William H. Winder, Sept. 6, 1821, *ibid.*, p. 96.

by precipitate or harsh measures, to involve individuals in unnecessary sacrifices." [69]

Pleasonton did not, however, trifle with procrastinating evaders. A collector of direct taxes, Harry Smith, pleaded for indulgence, after four years of delay since suit was instituted against him. "If M̲r̲ Smith and his sureties," he wrote, "are subjected to sacrifices, by a sale of their property at the present time, it is to be ascribed not to the rigor of the Treasury, but to his apparent indifference. . . ." [70] After reading hundreds of letters, one reaches the conclusion that the transfer of prosecuting power from the first comptroller to the fifth auditor and the pressure brought by Congress for more vigorous action produced favorable results, but that when one gentleman had to deal with another in a business disagreeable to both there was a wide margin of tolerance. Summary action was likely to be less than summary, and some debts remained uncollected pending improvement in the fortunes of the debtor—always to be hoped for, if not always achieved.

[69] Pleasonton to James Johnson, August 7, 1821, *ibid.*, p. 64. Cf. a letter from Joseph Anderson to the sureties of Thomas B. Hall, one-time collector of internal revenue in Maryland, "the United States did not wish to run the party to any unnecessary expense. The object of the Government being to obtain the payment of the money in the mildest manner, within the shortest time practicable, under all the circumstances of the case, and in that mode which should conduce most to the convenience of the sureties." MS. in National Archives, Records of the Comptroller, File Box 1068. The sureties were General Samuel Ringgold and Colonel Otho H. Williams.

[70] Pleasonton to William B. Rochester, August 31, 1821, Fifth Auditor's Office, Letters on Debts and Suits, No. 2, pp. 88–89.

CHAPTER THIRTEEN

The State Department

The importance of the State Department was due not to the complexity and significance of its administrative problems but to the magnitude of the interests confided to its care. As an administrative organism it was of much less interest than either Treasury, War, Navy, or the Post Office, but John Quincy Adams could rightly claim that the "important and critical interests of the country are those the management of which belongs to the Department of State." [1] Moreover the Secretary of State was in a way to become the natural successor to the presidency. The office had therefore a political interest of primary significance.

THE PRESIDENT, THE CABINET, AND THE
SECRETARY OF STATE

The Constitution was explicit in vesting all executive powers over foreign affairs in the President. The office of Secretary of State was not mentioned. In the organic act of 1789 establishing the State Department the subordination of the Secretary was equally explicit; he was to perform such duties as should be entrusted to him by the President.

Both Washington and John Adams were their own Secretaries of State in all essential particulars. The times were arduous and the infant Republic had to thread its way through unexplored passages. Washington had to decide policy as between Jefferson and Hamilton, and later had to watch the dispatches of Timothy Pickering, too likely to be written in uncompromising terms.

[1] Adams, *Memoirs*, IV, 241 (Feb. 3, 1819).

John Adams made crucial decisions of foreign policy himself, on occasion without even consulting his Secretary of State, and eventually summarily removed him for lack of confidence.

Both constitutional requirement and practice were thus clear when the Republicans took over power in 1801. The Republicans easily fell in with precedent. Jefferson appointed Madison as Secretary of State, and for eight years close harmony prevailed between the two men primarily responsible for foreign policy. It has been said that perhaps no President and his Secretary of State ever worked together with as complete understanding as Jefferson and Madison.[2] Jefferson had served for years at the French court, while Madison had never been abroad; and it was natural for Jefferson to make the great decisions himself.

When Madison became President, he sought to appoint Albert Gallatin to the State Department but had to yield to Senate opposition by nominating Robert Smith. After two years of incompetence, which compelled Madison to become his own foreign secretary to a burdensome and annoying degree, and of political disloyalty which could not be mistaken, Madison removed Smith and invited Monroe to the office. For the first time the relationships between the Secretary of State and the President were explored in the course of the negotiations leading to Monroe's acceptance in an exchange of letters that has already been noted.[3]

Madison continued his activity in the foreign field. Both he and Monroe were concerned in an undercover enterprise to feel out the prospects of peace in 1813. "Light-horse Harry" Lee had made his way to Barbados, at the intervention of Madison and with a pass from the British naval officers, to recover from wounds received in the Baltimore riots of June 1812. He had a more important errand, to initiate informal negotiations with Sir George Beckwith, governor of Barbados and the first representative of the British government to the United States. Lee opened the exchange of views with a letter asking Beckwith

---

[2] Charles E. Hill, "James Madison," in Samuel Flagg Bemis, ed., *The American Secretaries of State and Their Diplomacy* (10 vols., New York: A. A. Knopf, 1927–29), III, 8.

[3] See above, ch. 5.

for information; Beckwith replied after a month suggesting "a sound Principle" of peace; Lee responded more decisively a month later, offering to hasten to Washington and back again, to which Beckwith replied in a sufficiently sympathetic tone to enable Lee to cast aside his reserve.

Lee now wrote Beckwith, "From my personal knowledge of the President and Secretary of State, with both of whom, I held various conversations, before my departure from Home, on the subject of Peace, I can venture to assert . . . that no event is more dear to the President's heart, than the immediate restoration of Peace on honorable Terms." He proceeded to offer the heads of a treaty of peace. Beckwith replied immediately, but on the subject of impressment was uncompromising. Lee left at once for home.[4]

Monroe went to the White House fully equipped by early diplomatic experience and by six years of service as Secretary of State to play a leading role in foreign policy. He and his Secretary of State, John Quincy Adams, made an effective team, but Monroe remained in control. In the negotiations leading to the acquisition of Florida, Adams took the brunt of a tortuous affair. The Monroe Doctrine was apparently initially proposed by the President at a Cabinet meeting, of the importance of which Adams had no private notice, but the ultimate form of the pronouncement was fixed upon in the light of Adams' views.[5] These eight years were notable in the diplomatic history of the United States. Florida was acquired from Spain; treaties were negotiated with Great Britain, France, and Russia; diplomatic missions were sent to the new South American Republics; and the Monroe Doctrine was announced to the European world. Adams, indeed, declared: "Of the public history of Mr. Monroe's administration, all that will be worth telling to posterity hitherto has been transacted through the Department of State."[6]

President Monroe kept in his own hands the appointment of

---

[4] "Major-General Henry Lee and Lieutenant-General Sir George Beckwith on Peace in 1813," *American Historical Review*, XXXII (1926–27), 284–92.

[5] Dexter Perkins, "John Quincy Adams," in Bemis, *op. cit.*, IV, 69–71.

[6] Adams, *Writings*, VII, 316 (Oct. 7, 1822).

foreign ministers, following the established practice of his predecessors.[7] Although he consulted his Secretary of State, John Quincy Adams, he also dealt with others. Adams complained privately about his lack of influence: ". . . there is much machinery at work respecting the appointments under the Department of State, of which I am not informed. . . ." [8] To one of his confidants he declared that he had been very cautious in recommending persons for appointment. "The President kept it very much in his own hands. There had not been a single appointment of any consequence, even in my own Department, made at my recommendation, nor one that I approved." [9]

When Adams took over the State Department, Monroe explained to him that it was the practice "to communicate in confidence to all the heads of Departments every important circumstance occurring in our foreign concerns, and also to the Chairman of the Committee of Foreign Relations. . . . This . . . had been found very useful to the Government." [10] The House Foreign Relations Committee also kept in touch with Adams.[11]

When Adams became President it was inevitable that he should follow the pattern of presidential responsibility that had been so well established. Most of his life had been spent in diplomatic circles; and his temperament was not one to trust another—especially a Secretary such as Henry Clay whose personal habits and tastes were so at variance with his own austere Puritanism. Adams made his own selections for the diplomatic service, but Clay was influential in guiding Adams' policy in South American affairs.[12] Clay, in the diplomatic field, was overshadowed by the President. The period closed, as it had begun, with an undisputed primacy of the President over the domain of the Department of State.

7 Jefferson nominated Pinkney as minister to Great Britain in 1806 without consulting the Cabinet. Henry Adams, *John Randolph,* p. 190.

8 Adams, *Memoirs,* IV, 193 (Dec. 16, 1818).

9 *Ibid.,* IV, 307 (March 18, 1819). For his critical views of John Forsyth, minister to Spain, see *ibid.,* IV, 262–63.

10 *Ibid.,* IV, 31 (Dec. 26, 1817).

11 *Ibid.,* IV, 183 (Nov. 28, 1818).

12 Theodore E. Burton, "Henry Clay," in Bemis, *op. cit.,* IV, 115–58.

ORGANIZATION AND ACTIVITIES

When John Marshall turned over the State Department to James Madison in 1801 its staff numbered one chief clerk, seven cierks, and a messenger.[13] Twenty years later the size of the office had increased by only two clerks, an assistant messenger, a laborer and two watchmen.[14] The work had greatly increased in volume, but only one new activity had fallen under its care, and that an incidental one, the preparation of the biennial register listing all civilian and military personnel and known as the *Blue Book*.[15] Secretary of State Henry Clay set out the duties of the department in 1826 under fifteen heads. Of these the most important were:

1. Correspondence with fourteen American ministers, two claims agents, and one hundred and ten consuls
2. Correspondence with from ten to fourteen foreign ministers resident in Washington
3. Issuing passports, and sea letters and Mediterranean passports for ships
4. Compiling lists of passengers arriving in the United States, and of registered seamen
5. Examination of departmental accounts and application of funds for distressed seamen.

The duties of the department in its capacity as a Home Office were time consuming, but relatively of secondary importance. They included:

1. Reports to Congress, on calls for information
2. Correspondence with governors, judicial officers, marshals, and United States attorneys
3. Preservation of public papers, and printing and distribution of the laws
4. Supervision of the Patent Office
5. Supervision of the census

[13] White, *The Federalists*, p. 136.

[14] House Doc. 3, 17th Cong., 2d sess., p. 3 (Dec. 2, 1822). The duties of each clerk were described briefly in House Doc. 194, 15th Cong., 1st sess., pp. 5–6 (April 13, 1818).

[15] *Official Register of the United States*. The first edition of this now rare but invaluable publication appeared in 1816, the second in 1817, and biennially thereafter. See also Peter Force, *The National Calendar* (1820–1836).

6. Compiling the biennial register of officers
7. Authentication of documents, keeping records of pardons, and remission of fines and forfeitures
8. Custody of the Great Seal and recording of commissions.

The concentration of all responsibility for these varied activities in the person of the Secretary subjected him to great
pressure. The Four Secretaries in their 1816 Report joined in
asking Congress for all-round relief by the creation of a new
department.[16] Monroe, soon to leave the State Department for
the White House, concurred in the recommendation, although
it would have taken from his jurisdiction the supervision of the
territorial governments and the Patent Office. Occupied as he
was, he nevertheless did not propose to yield the principal responsibility for the district attorneys and marshals, nor for the
supervision of the census. Congress took no action, and Adams
was to find, with his predecessor, that the duties of the department were more than he could perform.[17] After a year in office,
Henry Clay also told Congress that "there are too many and too
incompatible duties devolved upon the Department." "The
necessary consequence of this variety and extent of business, is,
that it lessens responsibility, or renders the enforcement of it
unjust." Going beyond Monroe, Clay was ready to relinquish
the whole range of domestic activities.[18]

Why it did not occur to any Secretary of State to propose an
assistant secretary who could take the initial responsibility for
the domestic affairs of the department or for aid in foreign
affairs remains a puzzle. In different forms the precedent for
professional assistance had been established in War and Navy
immediately after the War of 1812 came to an end. In State
there was no professional aid whatever. The Secretary was the
only one who could exercise judgment on policy matters.[19]

16 *American State Papers: Miscellaneous*, II, 398.
17 Adams, *Writings*, VI, 354 (June 22, 1818).
18 House Report 232, 19th Cong., 1st sess., p. 5 (Feb. 16, 1826).
19 In 1825 an active-minded citizen, A. B. Woodward, proposed a reorganization
of the State Department to meet this problem, forecasting accurately the future
development of the department. He recommended eight geographical desks,
each headed by an undersecretary, "because the situations will all exact extraordinary attainment, and high respectability." A. B. Woodward, *The Presidency of the United States*, especially pp. 74–79.

Writing to his mother, Abigail, soon after he became Secretary of State, Adams described the "routine of the ordinary business of the Department where I am stationed which requires nothing but my signature; yet even that occasions no trifling consumption of time." He continued, "But there is business enough which cannot be committed to clerks or performed by them. . . . Business crowds upon me from day to day requiring instantaneous attention, and in such variety that unless everything is disposed of just as it occurs it escapes from the memory and runs into the account of arrears." [20] That the office was managed on the basis of memory suggests the failure of Adams' predecessors, and of his own chief clerk, to develop a useful system of office management.

The essential task of the Secretary of State was to assist the President to define foreign policy in all its aspects, large and small, and to carry it forward in particular negotiations. In overt form this task was performed by instructions to and correspondence with American agents abroad, and by conversation and the exchange of notes with foreign ministers stationed in Washington. Adams found the "duty of giving instructions to Ministers and public agents abroad as the most important and difficult of the functions of a Secretary of State." [21] He performed this essential task alone, and declared that it was "perhaps the most laborious and difficult part of the duties of the State Department to hold at once the threads of our different relations with all the European powers." [22]

The department was apparently not well served by its clerks. Adams appointed Daniel Brent as his chief clerk. Brent had been a clerk in the department for many years and "was strongly recommended by Mr. Monroe and Mr. Rush; had many years' experience of the business of the office; was a man of forty years of age, or upwards, and of the most respectable character." [23] Brent's character did not include skill in office manage-

[20] Adams, *Writings*, VI, 227–28 (Nov. 2, 1817).
[21] Adams, *Memoirs*, V, 143 (June 7, 1820). Adams wrote out all instructions in his own hand (*Writings*, VI, 233, n. 2).
[22] *Memoirs*, V, 338 (April 4, 1821).
[23] *Ibid.*, IV, 27. Brent had a farm two hours' drive beyond Washington where he once entertained Adams, Calhoun, Colonel Freeman, and Pleasonton of the

ment, and Adams frequently complained about the loss of papers and the lack of system.[24] "One of the greatest inconveniences that I suffer," he confided to his diary, "is the necessity of attending to the minutest details, and of superintending with incessant vigilance even the routine of the office."[25] His patience nearly gave out in 1821 when Brent overlooked some crucial papers in the correspondence with Great Britain on the slave trade that were to be submitted to Congress. After the British minister, George Canning, had called the omission to Adams' attention, he personally examined the file and quickly discovered the missing reference. "This accident," wrote Adams in his diary, "is one of those which many times have happened from the complicated cause of my own inattention, Brent's inaptitude, and the want of method in the arrangement of business and disposal of papers in the Department. . . . I ought to have examined the whole file . . . myself. . . ."[26]

One of his clerks, John B. Colvin, was discharged by Adams for "neglect of duty and grovelling vices." Monroe told Adams of his own forbearance to dismiss Colvin, said that he was guilty of treachery to Secretary Robert Smith and had been kept always on nonconfidential work. Colvin was a political writer in the newspapers, first opposing Monroe, then supporting him after his election. After Colvin's discharge he busied himself, in Adams' words, "by lampooning me from that day to this in the City Gazette. He had rung all the possible changes [charges] of falsehood against me, from the basest lie to the most insidious misrepresentation."[27]

In an office as small as that of the State Department, and as overwhelmed with business and papers, the ineptness of Brent

---

auditor's office, and Gales and Seaton, the publishers (*ibid.*, VI, 46). He occasionally brought political information to Adams (*ibid.*, VI, 384).

24 "Another source of continual confusion and embarrassment to me is the want of order in keeping the files of papers in the office." *Ibid.*, IV, 364 (May 15, 1819); cf. *ibid.*, IV, 443–44. Adams devised a systematic index to diplomatic papers that was in use as late as 1915 (*ibid.*, IV, 98; *Writings*, VI, 327, n. 1).

25 *Memoirs*, V, 144 (June 7, 1820). This entry was made after nearly three years in the office, an interval of time that suggests how strongly the Republicans held to their principle of removing only for serious cause.

26 *Ibid.*, V, 234 (Jan. 9, 1821).

27 *Ibid.*, VI, 288 (April 10, 1824).

and the untrustworthiness of Colvin were serious handicaps. But the greatest lack was the absence of a person of stature who, in the role of an assistant secretary of state, could have shared the responsibility of the office.

FISCAL AND ADMINISTRATIVE AFFAIRS
OF THE STATE DEPARTMENT

Without doubt one of the most annoying administrative problems of the State Department under the Jeffersonians was the settlement of the accounts of the department and its agents abroad. There was both some laxity on the part of the latter and some unnecessary rigidity on the part of the auditor and comptroller. The result was endless delay, much confusion, great annoyance, and some injustice.

The standing heads of the State Department appropriation for foreign affairs during the whole Republican period dealt with (1) salaries and outfits; (2) contingent expenses for the missions abroad, and departmental expenses at home; and (3) relief of distressed American seamen abroad. With respect to salaries, the exact amounts were annually appropriated and there was no discretion in the use of the funds and no problem in the settlement of accounts. Claims for outfits (a single money payment) rested on custom and were at times disputed. With respect to distressed seamen, the money was paid to American consuls on vouchers rendered, and accountability raised few problems. The contingent fund charged with the expenses of foreign missions gave rise to much trouble; it was here that the carelessness of ministers in supplying evidence of expenses and the absence of supervision by the department caused delay and confusion in reaching settlements.

The procedure of settlement of the accounts of foreign ministers was described by the comptroller, Gabriel Duval, in 1810. Upon their return from abroad agents rendered their accounts to the State Department and where a balance appeared against them they were subsequently called upon by the comptroller to submit their statements to him. This call seems to have been quite casual; Duval said it was governed by "a knowledge of the character and circumstances of the agent, the nature of his service, and the probability of the result of a settlement of his accounts." [28] In 1816 a House committee reported that the submission of accounts by foreign agents had been left "very much to the individual himself to do or not, as he judged proper, and instances are not wanting of those in high and responsible situations who have never furnished any account whatever of their expenditure, or of the moneys which have passed through their hands." [29] We may presume, however, that few adopted the high tone of Samuel Sitgreaves, who was in London from 1798 to 1801 securing settlements under the Jay Treaty, and who indignantly told the comptroller that it "could not have been expected, that I should keep or render an account or vouchers for the numberless items of detail which enter into the expenses of a gentleman abroad." [30]

The length of time between expenditure and settlement on the return of the foreign agent at the end of his mission, combined with the difficulty of rectifying mistakes or deficiencies in vouchers, made settlements "always difficult, and sometimes impracticable." They would have become impossible apart from an understanding between the Secretary of State and the comptroller, already noted, by which (after 1801) the settlement was made by the Treasury "under the direction of the Secretary of State." He furnished statements of salary and allowances for contingent and other expenses, and decided "on the principles of settlement," leaving the Treasury "little more to do than to arrange and give form to the account" and make the necessary calculations.[31]

Even with this margin of tolerance, large amounts hung in suspense for long periods of time. A report in 1809 showed unsettled accounts of David Humphreys, late minister at Madrid, amounting to over $122,000; of Robert R. Livingston, late minister at Paris, amounting to over $60,000; of James Monroe, for disputed salary, in the sum of $18,195.46; of Charles Pinckney, late minister at Madrid, for nearly $60,000—"informal accounts rendered, without vouchers"; and of William Smith, late min-

28 *American State Papers: Finance*, II, 416 (Feb. 28, 1810).
29 *Ibid.*, III, 123 (April 24, 1816).
30 *Ibid.*, II, 416 (Feb. 28, 1810).
31 *Ibid.*, III, 125–26 (March 14, 1816).

ister at Lisbon, for over $34,000 supposedly due for salary. In the list were such ancient accounts as that of C. W. F. Dumas, "agent under the old Government; dead." [32]

John Quincy Adams exerted a useful influence upon the gentlemen who served abroad. He lectured Alexander Hill Everett, chargé d'affaires at The Hague and later minister to Spain, in caustic terms.

For a public officer of the United States abroad punctuality is a quality as essential as integrity, and in the general estimation of the people of this country inseparable from it. Delinquency in regard to public money fixes irretrievable ruin almost always upon a man's fortune, and universally upon his reputation. It never fails to shed a portion of his disgrace upon his friends, and to cast obloquy upon the administration which employed him. . . . As you value your reputation, your integrity, and your *understanding* correct your habit of inattention to pecuniary concerns. And if you cannot roughly, inflexibly, permanently correct it, let me advise you for your own account and entreat you for mine, to renounce all thoughts of entering again upon the career of public life. If you must travel the road to ruin, take at least a private path and not the thoroughfare, where your fall will be the blush of your friends, the triumph of your enemies, the scorn and derision of the public, and the bitter disappointment of your country.[33]

Adams took energetic steps to reform State Department expenditures in other directions as well. In 1819 he noted in his diary that "great abuses have been creeping into the pecuniary affairs of the Department, which have produced disorders in its accounts and a consequent dissatisfaction in Congress. Mr. Monroe and Mr. Madison, while in the Department, made it a principle to leave all these questions unsettled." Adams clamped down on irregular allowances to ministers traveling abroad on public ships, a reform which, as he said, brought him "into a disagreeable collision with every Minister going abroad." [34] He tackled the accounts of the department for contingent expenses (an account separate from the contingent expenses for foreign intercourse) which he found had been kept "in a very loose and

32 *Ibid.*, II, 358 (March 2, 1809).
33 Adams, *Writings*, VI, 222–24 (Oct. 15, 1817).
34 Adams, *Memoirs*, IV, 352 (April 26, 1819).

slovenly manner." He told one of his clerks, Bailey, to get an account book and instructed him how to make the entries. Good results were forthcoming, for in 1822 the House Committee on the Expenditures of the State Department reported that the accounts of the contingency fund were regularly kept, that the expenditures were made with fidelity and economy, and that they were unable to suggest any subject of retrenchment.[35] This was indeed a truly remarkable event!

JOHN QUINCY ADAMS

Adams was not only sensitive to fiscal reforms in State Department operations; he was a good detail man who in a later age would have been recognized as a first-class administrative analyst. "The only possible means of transacting much business of complicated character is by some methodical course of arrangement," he wrote his mother.[36] ". . . I feel incessantly," he noted in 1820, "the want of method—systematical arrangement. I am endeavoring to introduce it gradually. . . ."[37] After eight years of official life in Washington, he noted in his diary, "There is much to correct and reform, and the precept of diligence is always timely." [38]

A partial list of his reforms as Secretary of State is indicative of his superior administrative capacity. Soon after taking office, he initiated a minute book in which were recorded the letters received. He worked out an index of diplomatic and consular correspondence. He directed the printers who published the laws and treaties to send in their accounts promptly. For two years he had not been able to ascertain the state of his printing accounts.[39]

He discovered in 1819 that the act of September 15, 1789, requiring the Secretary of State to have the laws recorded in books, had been neglected for years. "I determined that this part of my duty should no longer be omitted, and gave Mr.

[35] House Report 106, 17th Cong., 1st sess. This was the contingency fund for departmental expenses.
[36] Adams, *Writings*, VI, 228 (Nov. 2, 1817).
[37] Adams, *Memoirs*, V, 143 (June 7, 1820).
[38] *Ibid.*, VI, 540 (April 1825).
[39] *Ibid.*, IV, 366–67 (May 19, 1819).

Brent some directions for carrying it into effect." [40] He wrote
new instructions to the marshals for taking the census.[41]

To secure a current record of public officers he caused copies
of the *Register* to be bound with blank interleaves, on which
was to be recorded every personnel change.[42] He was soon at
work inserting lists of names in his own hand—as he agreed,
wasting his time. In 1826 he put into operation a plan by which
young men were attached to each of the consulates in Barbary
for a three-year period, to learn the Turkish and Arabic languages and the lingua Franca, "with a view to have persons
among our public officers versed in those languages." [43] This is
probably the first in-service training course in the history of
the Republic, apart from the military.

Adams could not reform himself, especially at that point
where it was most important. He could not delegate readily to
others. On major issues, indeed, there was no one in his department to whom he could delegate—since there was no assistant
of professional stature to whom he could turn. The department
in 1825, as in 1795, was a department of clerks. The conduct of
foreign affairs was a personal function of the Secretary of State
and the President. The Secretary was in an exact sense of the
term the department.

He consequently had a harried and unsatisfactory official
existence. "A hurly-burly day," he noted on May 21, 1819, "by
which denomination I designate that class of days which I have
already noticed in this journal, days of continual and unexpected interruptions, by persons successively calling at the office and by a multitude of letters and voluminous dispatches
received from various quarters. It is *distraction* of the character
which Dr. Rush, in his work upon the mind, describes as naturally leading to madness." [44]

Adams was highly introspective and entered in his diary
many critical evaluations of his own personality. "My self-

40 *Ibid.*, IV, 435 (Nov. 9, 1819).
41 *Ibid.*, V, 135 (May 30, 1820).
42 *Ibid.*, V, 152 (June 15, 1820); "Further improvements to methodize this part
of the business of the Department are to be thought of," he wrote in his diary
of this date.
43 *Ibid.*, VII, 106 (Jan. 19, 1826).
44 *Ibid.*, IV, 368.

examination this night," he once recorded, "gave rise to many mortifying reflections. . . . Pride and self-conceit and presumption lie so deep in my natural character, that, when their deformity betrays them, they run through all the changes of Proteus, to disguise themselves to my own heart. I often see and often condemn my faults." [45] "I am," he said, "by nature a silent animal, and my dear mother's constant lesson in childhood, that children in company should be seen and not heard, confirmed me irrevocably in what I now deem a bad habit." [46] "The operations of my mind are slow, my imagination sluggish, and my powers of extemporaneous speaking very inefficient. But I have much capacity for, and love of, labor, habits on the whole of industry and temperance, and a strong and almost innate passion for literary pursuits." [47] "Literature has been the charm of my life, and, could I have carved out my own fortunes, to literature would my whole life have been devoted. I have been a lawyer for bread, and a statesman at the call of my country." [48]

Adams was not a sociable man, and his aversion to society was doubled by jealousy of his own time. He was a man with an extraordinary sense of order and method, and a prodigious capacity for work. His early days as United States Senator were not burdensome; he rose at seven, wrote in his chamber until nine, and after breakfast walked to the Capitol, a distance of two and one-half miles. He was home at four, dined, and sat with his family until eleven, the hour for bed.[49] As Secretary of State he was to enjoy no such leisure. Winter weather delayed his hour of rising, he could scarcely write at all in the morning, his indispensable business ran in arrears, and sometimes crowded him "almost to distraction." [50]

Adams was governed by two deep-seated sentiments; a strong feeling of responsibility for the discharge of his public duties, and a passionate sense of independence. ". . . the first duty of

45 *Ibid.*, I, 276 (Dec. 4, 1803).
46 *Ibid.*, V, 165 (July 15, 1820).
47 *Ibid.*, V, 220 (Dec. 25, 1820).
48 *Ibid.*, V, 219–20 (Dec. 25, 1820).
49 *Ibid.*, I, 269 (Oct. 1803).
50 *Ibid.*, IV, 33 (Dec. 1817)

a public officer is to the government, and consists in the discharge of the trust committed to him. . . ." [51] The treatise on weights and measures was one of his great monuments to duty —as well as to industry. His pressure on Monroe to move against politically well-placed collectors who were suspected of corruption was for him an inevitable course of action, however distasteful. "It sickens me to the heart to be forced to act in this case; but a duty paramount to every other consideration urges me, and I will not shrink from it." [52] His determination to receive anyone who wished to call upon him, for reasons important or trivial, was based on a sense of duty that overcame his sense of good administration. In 1824 he recorded, "My time is chiefly worn out with visitors, of whom the number personally received in the course of the month has been two hundred and sixty-four. I never exclude any one." He added, "But necessary and important business suffers by the unavoidable waste of time." [53]

Writing in 1818 to Francis Calley Gray he set out his philosophy with respect to office. "My theory of accordance between the duties of self respect, and devotion to the public according to the genius of our institutions, is this. The individual owes the exercise of all his faculties to the service of his country. Whether he shall serve his country in a public capacity, should in the first instance be determined by the country (through its constitutional organs) and not by the individual. He ought not to obtrude, nor even to offer himself directly or indirectly, nor to use by himself or his friends any means whatever to obtain an appointment." [54] He repeated these views

51 Adams, *Writings*, VI, 230 (Nov. 4, 1817).
52 Adams, *Memoirs*, V, 170 (August 19, 1820).
53 *Ibid.*, VI, 370 (May 1824).
54 Adams, *Writings*, VI, 413 (August 3, 1818). Cf. a letter to Alexander Hill Everett, March 16, 1816, in which he advises Everett how to seek his public fortune. ". . . resume your station at the Bar. Take an interest and exercise an influence in the public affairs. You must steel your heart and prepare your mind to encounter multitudes of political enemies, and to endure all the buffetings without which there is no rising to distinction in the American world. When the knaves and fools open upon you in full pack, take little or no notice of them, and be careful not to lose your temper. Preserve your private character and reputation unsullied, and confine your speculations upon public concerns to objects of high and national importance. . . . Let your conduct be at once

when the struggle for the presidency in 1824 was already in full tide. "At a very early period of my life . . . I formed the determination never to solicit, or by any act of mine direct or indirect to endeavor to obtain, any office of honor, profit, or trust, in the gift of my countrymen; but to stand ready to repair to any station which they through their constitutional authori‑ ties might think proper to assign to me." [55]

As the campaign for the presidency took shape in 1822, Adams' refusal to seek the office withstood all pressure. His expressions of disdain for office seeking became more and more astringent and his assertions of independence more and more emphatic—at times almost hysterical. In early summer, 1822, he wrote to Robert Walsh, "I make no *bargains*. I listen to no overtures for *coalition*. I give no money. I push for no appoint‑ ments of canvassing partisans to office. This utter inability to support my own cause passes among the caucus mongers for simplicity approaching to idiotism." [56]

In October his wife Louisa wrote from Quincy to urge him to spend a week in Philadelphia with political friends. His answer betrayed the tension under which he was laboring, as well as his proud self-reliance.

. . . My friends at Philadelphia are not the only ones who send me kind messages to inform me that unless I mend my manners, I shall never be President. Well, and what then? There will be candidates enough for the Presidency without me, and if my delicacy is not suited to the times, there are candidates enough who have no such delicacy. It suits my temper to be thus delicate. Do they call it aristocratic hauteur and learned arrogance? Why, so be it, my worthy friends and approved good masters. It is not then cringing servility, nor insatiate importunity.

. . . Do my friends in Philadelphia suppose me so totally blind to what is passing around me, as not to see what my situation is, or not to foresee what its result must be? Do they suppose that, while I see *all* the avenues to the temple preoccupied one by one, and a crowd rushing to the gate, already stifling one another, I expect to

bold, resolute, and wary; preserve inflexibly your personal independence, even while acting in concurrence with any party, and take my word for it, you will not need to go in search for public office, at home or abroad." *Ibid.*, V, 540–41.

[55] *Ibid.*, VII, 192 (Jan. 7, 1822).

[56] *Ibid.*, VII, 272 (June 21, 1822).

obtain admission by standing still? Or do they think me besotted enough to believe that I could, if I would, turn the current of public opinion in my favor by a week's visit to Philadelphia? Tell them that I am going by another road and to another temple. That if they must have a President to whom they dare speak, and if they dare not speak to me, they must vote for another man. That I am *not* bound to be President of the United States, but that I *am* bound to perform the duties of Secretary of State so long as I hold that office, and that Washington and not Philadelphia is the place where those duties must be performed.[57]

Adams' character was based on stern New England Puritanism, and this foundation was admirable for success in the field of administration. His dour talent for introspection revealed to him his own weaknesses, and his sense of obligation prodded him to their correction. His courage and independence preserved him from embarrassing commitments, and throughout his long career he remained free to do his duty as he discovered it. Adams' ambitions were political, despite his lack of qualification for popular leadership; his achievements in the executive branch were largely diplomatic and administrative in character.

[57] *Ibid.*, VII, 315–16, 318 (Oct. 7, 1822).

CHAPTER FOURTEEN

The Domestic Business of
the State Department

Despite the opinion of Secretaries Madison, Monroe, Adams, and Clay that the domestic business of the State Department should be transferred to a new agency, Congress preserved its reputation for economy by refusing to embark upon an additional opening for expenditures. Adams took more seriously than his predecessors the "interior correspondence" for which he was responsible. Here, in more or less intimate contact with the Secretary of State, was to be found such continuing business as the publication of the laws, the maintenance of the library, recommendations to the President on pardons, and occasional claims; special tasks such as the preparation of the report on weights and measures; the supervision of the census; and the almost independent business of the Patent Office.

Publication of the laws. The selection of newspapers for the publication of the laws became charged with political consequences. The privilege was sought for by newspaper publishers, and editors sympathetic to the party and faction in power expected the awards.[1] The often tense atmosphere in which this phase of the department's responsibilities was discharged is amply illustrated in selections from John Quincy Adams' diary.

. . . The appointment of the printers, three in each State, now rests with the Secretary of State. Pindall patronized and earnestly

[1] "Letters of William Duane," Massachusetts Historical Society, *Proceedings,* 2d series, XX (1906–7), 257–394.

recommended a partisan printer in his own district. A competitor of opposite politics happened to be more strongly recommended by the District Judge and Marshal and the Postmaster-General, and was appointed. So Pindall undertook to get the law repealed. He first moved for a committee to enquire, of which he was of course appointed Chairman. Then he moved for a list of all the printers appointed for the four last sessions of Congress, with an estimate of the expense. . . . he now writes to enquire what has been for the last two years the expense of printing the laws in the pamphlet form. . . . Colvin . . . thought it a very insidious call for an opinion, and quite suited to bring down a hornet's nest of printers upon me throughout the Union. . . . I saw the propriety of giving him [Pindall] a wary as well as an honest answer.[2]

A year later a Pennsylvania politician, James S. Stevenson, came to urge reappointment of the *Statesman*. Adams said that by a standing rule of the department the paper would be reappointed as a matter of course "unless some representation to the contrary should be made by the delegation from the State." Stevenson reported that the local Congressman, Baldwin, might recommend another paper, but that the majority of the delegation favored the *Statesman*, and that "the democratic party in that part of Pennsylvania would be totally averse to a change." Stevenson added that Baldwin was out of favor in state politics. Adams assured him that he would make no change without giving notice so that the Pennsylvania delegation could state their wishes.[3]

In the midst of the anxious days before Adams' election to the presidency by the House of Representatives, John Scott, member from Missouri, called on the Secretary of State

and gave me a list of the printers whom he wished to have appointed for printing the laws in Missouri. . . . Scott explained to me his causes of complaint against me, which consisted only in my having appointed several years since one newspaper to print the laws in Missouri, which was politically opposed to him. He appeared to be satis-

2 Adams, *Memoirs*, V, 16 (March 9, 1820). James Pindall was a Federalist member of the House from Virginia.

3 *Ibid.*, V, 394 (Nov. 13, 1821). For other incidents of the same sort, see *ibid.*, V, 265.

fied with the assurances that I gave him, that I had not in that, or any other instance, acted with intentions unfriendly to him.[4]

The retrenchment drive of 1820–22 hit at the arrangements for publication of the laws from several points of view. A House committee reported that the cost, as fixed by the law of 1818,[5] was too high. Publication in newspapers was alleged to be of relatively little use, since few read and none preserved them. The choice of newspapers was criticized—two papers had been appointed in New Haven, Lexington, and Natchez while none had been selected in Richmond, Lancaster, or Louisville. The publication of Indian treaties, at heavy expense, was said to provide small public benefit. Finally the committee declared that the law had an "evident tendency to confer on the State Department a direct patronage and influence (useless or pernicious) over many of the 69 presses, which the government has taken into its employment." [6] Despite these strictures and the prospect of saving $15,000 Congress clung to the printing privilege.

Library. After years of neglect, Adams put the departmental library, initiated in 1790 by Jefferson, on its feet. Following the British invasion of 1814, the library had been reduced "almost to nothing," in part for "the want of system in the administration of the Department. . . . There were no regulations for keeping it; anybody took out books from it, and no one was responsible for the return of them." Adams set aside rooms for the library, had shelves put in, charged the youngest clerk in the department, Thruston, with its custody, set up regulations, and began again to collect the laws of the various states.[7] The library interested him so greatly that he tarried late one afternoon and was locked in by the watchman.[8]

Pardons. Another domestic duty of the Secretary of State was

4 *Ibid.*, VI, 473 (Jan. 21, 1825). In 1826 Clay sent Congress a list of newspapers in which the laws were published in 1824 and 1825, and authorized for 1826. House Doc. 41, 19th Cong., 1st sess. (Jan. 16, 1826).

5 3 Stat. 439 (April 20, 1818).

6 House Report 78, 16th Cong., 1st sess. (March 20, 1820).

7 Adams, *Memoirs*, V, 168–69 (August 11, 1820).

8 *Ibid.*, V, 173 (Sept. 2, 1820).

to advise the President on applications for pardons.[9] The Secretary of the Treasury was directly responsible for deciding applications for remission of fines and forfeitures incurred for violation of the revenue laws; and the Secretaries of War and Navy respectively for recommendations on decisions of courts martial. Adams was impatient with pleas for hardened criminals. Mail robbers he thought should never be pardoned.[10] The friends of a criminal convicted of murder in Alexandria managed to get direct access to President Monroe, who ordered a last-minute reprieve on the alleged ground of idiocy. "I have no doubt," Adams indignantly wrote in his diary, "it is a gross imposition. . . . the moment a man is sentenced to die for these offences that strike at the very existence of human society, religion, humanity, family influence, female weakness, personal importunity, pious fraud, and counterfeit benevolence all join in a holy league to swindle a pardon from the Executive. The murderer is pumped and purged into a saint, or certified into an idiot." [11]

Adams himself was not wholly proof against appeals for mercy, however. Bridget Smith came to ask for a pardon for her brother, imprisoned for slave trading. "Miss Smith operated with the usual female weapon, a shower of tears. It seldom fails to disconcert my philosophy. . . . I promised to do my best to obtain his release, though in his own person he has very little claim to mercy or even to compassion." [12]

Report on weights and measures. A heavy extracurricular task was imposed on the Secretary of State by a request from Congress for a report on weights and measures, following the work done by Hamilton and Jefferson in the early years of the Republic. Adams began his studies in 1817, but found the burden of other duties so great that it was not until February 22, 1821, that he was able to send his report to Congress. It had been a millstone around his neck. In October 1819 he confided

9 A full summary of prosecutions for offenses against the United States and of pardons, 1789–1829, is available in House Doc. 146, 20th Cong., 2d sess. (Jan. 26, 1829).
10 See below, ch. 21.
11 Adams, *Memoirs*, V, 168 (July 27, 1820).
12 *Ibid.*, VI, 52 (August 10, 1822).

to his diary, "Two hours by candle-light" on the report; in August 1820, "I now sit down, the moment after rising, to my task, in which I write slowly, with great difficulty, and much to my own dissatisfaction." [13] It was a masterly work and despite Adams' misgivings he recorded, ". . . I have no reason to expect that I shall ever be able to accomplish any literary labor more important to the best ends of human exertion, public utility, or upon which the remembrance of my children may dwell with more satisfaction." [14]

Adams had recommended severe penalties upon all federal officials, such as customhouse agents, who were negligent in using certified weights and measures that Congress might approve. Congress preferred to rely on an official sense of duty, and no new legislation was forthcoming. So far as influence upon the states was concerned, a House committee proposed to give each of them "one model of each standard," to be used at its discretion.[15]

Census. The fourth census (1820) fell under Adams' direction, and became, as he said, "one of the most urgent objects of attention." Asking for copies of instructions to the marshals for the previous enumerations, he discovered to his astonishment that "there was not a line to be found upon the subject on the records of the office." [16] Colvin had been in charge of the third census, and from him Adams learned that the instructions for 1810 had been printed in the *National Intelligencer*.[17] Although they had thus been preserved (with no thought from the State Department), Adams found them not of much use, and set out to prepare new ones; "each census ought to be an improvement upon that last preceding it," he declared.[18] He proposed columns "from which the general and particular healthiness of the climate and longevity of the inhabitants

13 *Ibid.*, IV, 425; V, 171.

14 *Ibid.*, V, 291 (Feb. 22, 1821). The report was published in House Doc. 109, 16th Cong., 2d sess. (Feb. 22, 1821), and in *American State Papers: Miscellaneous*, II, 656. In the large format of the *State Papers*, the report occupied 48 printed pages, with appendices of 45 more.

15 House Report 44, 17th Cong., 2d sess. (March 11, 1822).

16 *Memoirs*, V, 130 (May 24, 1820).

17 The 1810 instructions were copied verbatim from those of 1800 by Colvin, and signed by Robert Smith without alteration. *Ibid.*, V, 134 (May 30, 1820).

18 *Ibid.*, V, 130.

might be demonstrated. . . ." [19] He worried, however, about increasing the work of the census takers who would get no more compensation: "This will probably produce obstacles to the execution of the law. . . ." [20] To aid the next census, he directed a special record to be kept of all correspondence dealing with this one, and also a memorandum book, to include every incident of importance in the progress of the enumeration.[21]

The orderly and systematic mind of John Quincy Adams must have been deeply frustrated by his experience with the fourth census. Despite an extension of time for returns from the marshals to September 1, 1821, they had not all been received in mid-December. The marshals had a good excuse for their failure; the compensation allowed by law for assistants was so inadequate that competent enumerators could not be obtained. The marshal of the Alabama district told Adams that he was sensible of the many imperfections of his returns, and deplored the loss of about one-fourth of his counties through failure to submit returns in time. Census papers were "handed from one private conveyance to another" for want of mails.[22] Fortunately better results were obtained in the older parts of the country. An effort was made to gather data on manufactures, and in 1823 a supplementary report on this novel subject was submitted. Adams had to note the imperfection of the returns, due principally to the unwillingness of manufacturers to impart their secrets.[23]

The Patent Office. Although the Patent Office remained an appendage of the State Department, it was something of an orphan. Madison admitted, in his cautious manner, that he had not been able to give the Patent Office "all the attention which it is, at all times, my desire to bestow on any portion of the public duties confided to me." [24] John Quincy Adams had an intuitive attraction for the field of science and invention and inevitably began to think of ways and means to make the Patent

[19] *Ibid.*, V, 135.
[20] *Ibid.*, V, 135.
[21] *Ibid.*, V, 148 (June 10, 1820).
[22] House Doc. 4, 17th Cong., 1st sess., p. 7 (Dec. 18, 1821).
[23] House Doc. 90, 17th Cong., 2d sess., p. 3 (Feb. 27, 1823).
[24] *American State Papers: Miscellaneous*, II, 192 (June 10, 1812).

Office more useful. With regret he was forced to admit that he would never find time to follow this interest. "Every day starts new game to me . . . but the hurry of the hour leaves me no time for the pursuit of it. . . ." [25] Clay also told Congress that he could not give attention to this part of his department.

The legislative history of the Patent Office from 1801 to 1829 was practically nil.[26] It went its way under the charge of an extraordinary character, Dr. William Thornton, and a single clerk, William Elliot. The principal question that came to the attention of Congress was the preservation of models deposited by inventors. Adequate space was lacking, and Thornton was apparently indifferent. Representative Seybert reported in 1812 that the west wing of Blodgetts Hotel (which had been acquired for joint use of the Post Office and Patent Office) was in disrepair; that the models were badly arranged; that all was chaos.[27] The situation had not improved in 1823. Another House committee found that many of the 1,800 models deposited in the office were in "a decayed or injured condition," and recommended an appropriation to permit the regular employment of an "artist" to keep them in repair.[28] The work of the office gradually outgrew the capacities of the superintendent and his clerk; they solved their problem by neglecting matters that could be postponed. Clay found that almost none of the patents that had been issued had been recorded (an omission that had escaped Adams' sharp eye), and employed two extra part-time clerks to bring up the arrearages.[29]

25 Adams, *Memoirs*, IV, 352 (April 26, 1819).

26 An early list of patents is printed in *American State Papers: Miscellaneous*, I, 423 (Feb. 22, 1805). The first patent was granted to Samuel Hopkins, July 31, 1790, for an improved process of making pot and pearl ashes. An annual list appeared regularly in subsequent years in the House Documents.

27 *American State Papers: Miscellaneous*, II, 188 (June 12, 1812). Senator Plumer had found the same situation in 1807. "The floor & shelves are covered with models thrown together without any order or regularity. The books lie in an irregular confused pile on shelves & window stools covered with dust. . . . Dr. Thornton . . . has too long been guilty of great negligence." *Memorandum*, p. 556 (Jan. 3, 1807).

28 *American State Papers: Miscellaneous*, II, 1040 (Feb. 7, 1823). In this report may be found a topical list of models; nail-cutting machines headed the list with 95, pumps claimed 66, and ploughs 65.

29 House Report 232, 19th Cong., 1st sess., p. 7 (Jan. 14, 1826). Cf. Report of the Select Committee on Clay's Report on the Patent Office, House Report 99, 19th

Interest in the Patent Office grew under the Jeffersonians as the needs of the country for better mechanical equipment became more and more apparent. Representative Seybert was extravagant in his appreciation of its possibilities in 1812, but he was an exceptional Congressman.[30] As the Jeffersonian period came to an end it was written of the Patent Office:

. . . it claims attention on higher ground: It is a repository of national ingenuity. It affords an interesting display of the progress of the useful arts, and of the inventive faculties of man: It holds out incentive to industry; a premium to ingenuity; a powerful stimulus to improvements in the arts and manufactures; the comforts and embellishments of life: and therefore, as a means of national improvement, is highly entitled to national regard.[31]

When Jackson became President a discrepancy in the number of patents actually issued and the number for which fees were collected, resulting in an apparent deficit of over $4,000, caused a temporary furor. The explanation by William Elliot disclosed the paternal spirit with which Thornton administered the agency.[32] "During many years of his superintendence," explained Elliot, "he conceived himself to be invested with, and exercised freely, much discretionary power in the issuing of patents; for he held it as a maxim . . . that the patent law was made solely for the 'encouragement of authors and inventors'; and not to collect revenue; and therefore, when any mistake or omission took place in issuing patents, whether by the inventor or the office, he would order a new one to be issued, without the payment of an additional patent fee. . . ."[33]

Dr. Thornton was one of those rare characters who came close to the eighteenth century ideal of the perfect man, at home in

---

Cong., 2d sess. (March 1, 1827), containing Thornton's plea for aid (Nov. 28, 1826), a detailed statement of expenditures for 1825 and 1826, and an account of the new record of patents begun in 1825.

[30] Adam Seybert was an important figure in the early history of science in the United States. *Dictionary of American Biography*, XVII, 2–3.

[31] House Doc. 38, 21st Cong., 1st sess., p. 8 (Dec. 22, 1829). Cf. an article, "The Patent Office," *North American Review*, XXIII (1826), 295–303.

[32] Under the Federalists, the Secretary of State took a direct personal responsibility, which gradually fell into the hands of a patent clerk; see White, *The Federalists*, pp. 136–39.

[33] House Doc. 38, 21st Cong., 1st sess., p. 3 (Jan. 16, 1830).

any field of knowledge and in any situation, competent in the arts but also a man of affairs, intellectually alert to the great interests of his time. "Full of talent and eccentricity, a Quaker by profession, a painter, a poet, and a horse-racer," he was not quite the equal of the immediate Jeffersonian circle—Rittenhouse, Benjamin Rush, Barton, Priestley, Peale, and Paine [34]—but he was acquainted with most of them and enjoyed the friendship of Washington, Jefferson, and especially James and Dolly Madison.

Thornton was born in a tiny member of the Virgin Islands, Jost van Dyke, in 1759, and took his degree in medicine in 1784 at Aberdeen University. He arrived in New York in 1787, settled in Philadelphia, and in 1789, entirely destitute of any professional training in architecture, took first prize for his design of a building for the Library Company of Philadelphia. He became actively associated with John Fitch in a crude invention of the steamboat, preceding Fulton.[35] After two years in the Virgin Islands following his marriage Thornton hurried back to Philadelphia with the winning designs for the Capitol, and from 1794 to 1802 he was one of the commissioners of the District of Columbia. During these years he designed several well-known private houses and later was consulted by Jefferson on the design for the University of Virginia.

In 1802 Thornton was appointed by Jefferson as clerk in the State Department in charge of patents, an office which, under the more impressive title that he assumed, superintendent of patents, he held until his death in 1828. His official duties were far from occupying his mind. He drew and painted with facility. He wrote three unpublished novels. He was awarded a gold medal by the American Philosophical Society for a publication entitled, *Cadmus: or, a Treatise on the Elements of a Written Language*. In it he included the first American essay on the education of the deaf. He advocated the abolition of slavery and was active in the American Colonization Society. He tried to establish a national university in Washington. He became a leading advocate of the liberation of South America and visual-

[34] Daniel J. Boorstin, *The Lost World of Thomas Jefferson* (New York: Henry Holt, 1948).

[35] Adams, *Memoirs*, IV, 351.

ized a union of the two continents in a tract, *Outlines of a Constitution for United North & South Columbia*. He collected funds for the Greeks.[36]

There was something of Alexander Hamilton in his management of a crisis. The story went around that when the British had captured Washington and were about to discharge a cannon into the Patent Office, Thornton placed himself before its mouth and declaimed, "Are you Englishmen or only Goths and Vandals? This is the Patent Office, a depository of the ingenuity of the American nation, in which the whole of the civilized world is interested. Would you destroy it? If so, fire away, and let the charge pass through my body." [37]

Thornton's own account was less dramatic but to the same general effect. After saving the Patent Office, he found that the mayor had fled the city, and promptly took charge, as justice of the peace. He ordered the navy-yard gates to be shut and stopped every plunderer. He visited the English prisoners and gave thanks in the name of the city to the local physician, Doctor James Ewell, who had attended them. He appointed a commissary to secure their provisions. He gave orders to the English sergeant in their command. These things done, the mayor arrived. "I informed him," wrote Thornton, "of all I had done, and stated that I then delivered over to him all the authority I had, from the duty of office, assumed." [38] Two days before he had galloped around the Maryland countryside with Monroe on his futile scouting expedition.

Thornton s passion for the freedom of the Americas gave play to his bad judgment on matters political.[39] He acted as intermediary between the British minister and certain adventurers who proposed to seize Florida, and under a pseudonym described their plan in the *National Intelligencer*. Adams

[36] *Dictionary of American Biography*, XVIII, 504–6; Adams, *Memoirs*, VI, 324 (May 10, 1824).

[37] George W. Evans, "The Birth and Growth of the Patent Office," Columbia Historical Society, *Records*, XXII (1919), 109–10.

[38] *Ibid.*, XXII, 111–13. Quoted from Dr. Thornton's statement in the *National Intelligencer* of Sept. 7, 1814.

[39] Had Adams not dissuaded him, he would have distributed 1,500 handbills against Crawford in the 1824 presidential campaign in New York. Adams, *Memoirs*, VI, 413.

quickly learned of these activities, called Thornton to his office where he discovered Thornton's connections with South
American patriots, which Thornton said, were "in his view very
important." [40] Adams promptly took this information to President Monroe and the next day conveyed Monroe's views to
Thornton. Monroe "thought this interposition utterly incompatible with the duties of his office," and intimated his displeas-
ure that Thornton had not consulted him. The superintendent
of patents was much upset and asked to see Monroe. The President, however, sent back word through Adams that he would
not talk with Thornton on anything but patents, "and very
little upon them." [41] Two years later Thornton's liberating
enthusiasm was undiminished and his political judgment still
unimproved. He was then seeking an appointment as agent to
any part of South America. Adams finally had to tell him that
as an ardent South American patriot he was disqualified. Thornton "thought that very strange, for in his opinion it was precisely
that which made him peculiarly fit for the Agency." [42] Such was
the many-sided near-genius who with one clerk performed the
whole Patent Office business, after a fashion, for over a quarter
century.

40 *Ibid.*, IV, 53 (Feb. 7, 1818).
41 *Ibid.*, IV, 54 (Feb. 13, 1818); *ibid.*, IV, 55 (Feb. 14).
42 *Ibid.*, IV, 528 (Feb. 17, 1820).

CHAPTER FIFTEEN

The War Department

The War Department was responsible for two large and bothersome administrative operations: the management of army business and on a lesser scale the conduct of Indian affairs. In both there was a mixture of civilian and military influence that was at times difficult to reconcile. So far as the army was concerned, the American experiment, seeking to maintain a standing army in a republican state without danger to popular institutions, was unique. This novel aspect of military affairs was celebrated by the editor of the *North American Review* in 1826.

. . . The mere fact, that our military establishments have been the result of popular legislation, has a novelty in it, which should command attention. In the older countries of the world, the army forms an essential part of the royal authority, and is often augmented or diminished without reference to the wishes, ability, or wants of the people.

Our venerable fathers, in framing the constitution of the United States, reversed the principles upon which military establishments had been founded for ages. . . . the military force of the country . . . should be the offspring of the same popular and deliberate legislation, which originates every other measure connected with the general good.[1]

Unfortunately Congress, although responsible for the military system, did not prove competent under the leadership of Jefferson and Madison to erect an organization adequate to its tasks.

[1] "Army of the United States," *North American Review*, XXIII (1826), 245–74, at 245–46. This is the first discussion of the military policy of the United States in a journal of opinion that has come to our notice.

The election of Thomas Jefferson in 1800 and the appointment of Albert Gallatin as Secretary of the Treasury in 1801
foretold little glory for the professional soldier. Jefferson spoke
in his inaugural address in favor of "a well-disciplined militia,
our best reliance in peace and for the first moments of war."
His European observations had long before confirmed his antipathy to a standing army. He knew that it could become an
instrument of tyranny and the essential support of monarchy, to
say nothing of its weight against the authority and influence of
the states. He consequently proposed to reduce the regular army
to the bare minimum needed to police the frontier and to guard
the arsenals. He held out no assurance to officers or men for
permanent employment, and favored no higher ranks or salaries
than absolutely necessary.[2] Moreover he believed that a standing
army was impossible to maintain in the comfortable condition
of American life. Even in the worst year of the War of 1812 he
wrote Monroe, "It is nonsense to talk of regulars. They are not
to be had among a people so easy and happy at home as ours. We
might as well rely on calling down an army of angels from
heaven." [3]

In 1801 circumstances validated up to a point Jefferson's
willingness to depend on a "well-disciplined militia," if he could
have been assured of such. The crisis with France had been
resolved, the Provisional Army into which Hamilton had poured
his abundant energy had been disbanded, and the protection of
the frontier against the Indians was the only concrete military
mission. Future embarrassments with both France and Great
Britain could not be foreseen, and in any event the Atlantic
Ocean and five weeks of sailing lay between the young Republic
and its potential enemies.

[2] James Ripley Jacobs, *The Beginning of the U. S. Army, 1783–1812* (Princeton, N. J.: Princeton University Press, 1947), pp. 244–45.

[3] Jefferson, *Works* (Federal ed.), XI, 436–37 (Oct. 16, 1814). Jefferson had,
however, moved a long way toward Washington's position favoring a truly de-
pendable militia. He accepted the idea of a classified militia, in which only the
younger men would be thrown into active service while the older men did
garrison duty and supply service. In 1813 he wrote Monroe, "We must . . .
make military instruction a regular part of collegiate education. We can never
be safe till this is done." Jefferson thus forecast the military education programs
of the land-grant colleges. Jefferson, *Writings* (Memorial ed.), XIII, 261 (June
18, 1813).

The Republicans consequently proceeded with sanguine determination to put the army on a minimum footing of peace. The basic legislation of 1802 authorized an army of one regiment of artillerists, and two regiments of infantry, with a full strength of about 3,350 officers and men. All officers and men supernumerary to this establishment were to be discharged, with a modest bonus.[4] An army with ten general officers assigned to three regiments hardly promised either a military career or a threat to civil institutions.

This was the regular army during almost the whole of Jefferson's administration. At its end the crisis in foreign affairs stirred Congress to some more adequate means of defense. Provision was made in 1808 for five additional regiments of infantry, one regiment of riflemen, one regiment of light artillery, and one regiment of light dragoons, to be enlisted for the term of five years;[5] further provision was made for arming and equipping the militia;[6] and attention was given to strengthening the coast fortifications. All this, as the event was to prove, appeared more impressive as legislation than in execution.

It must be recorded at the outset that the administration of army affairs before 1812 was wretched, and that while more adequate means of management were provided by Congress in 1812 and 1813, much too late, the record remained wretched throughout the conflict with Great Britain. The handicaps to effective army management from 1801 to 1812 were nearly insuperable. They stemmed from popular distrust of a standing army, which was part of the Republican ideology, and from the determination of the Republicans to economize on current expenditures until the debt was discharged. The Resolution of the Continental Congress of June 2, 1784, offered by Elbridge Gerry, had not been forgotten in 1801:

And whereas standing armies in time of peace, are inconsistent with the principles of republican Governments, dangerous to the liberties of a free people, and generally converted into destructive engines for establishing despotism. . . .
Resolved, That the commanding officer be . . . directed to dis-

4 2 Stat. 132 (March 16, 1802).
5 2 Stat. 481 (April 12, 1808).
6 2 Stat. 490 (April 23, 1808).

charge the troops now in the service of the United States, except 25 privates, to guard the stores at Fort Pitt, and 55 to guard the stores at West Point and other magazines, with a proportionate number of officers. . . .[7]

In 1802 Gallatin wrote his wife, "The distribution of our little army to distant garrisons where hardly any other inhabitant is to be found is the most eligible arrangement of that perhaps necessary evil that can be contrived. But I never want to see the face of one in our cities and intermixed with the people."[8]

Even in 1818 John C. Calhoun, then Secretary of War, had to give deference to this public attitude while combating it. Reporting to Congress his views on the further reduction of the army, he wrote,

. . . a reduction of the expense of our present establishment cannot be made, with safety to the public service, by reducing the army. In coming to this conclusion, I have not overlooked the maxim that a large standing army is dangerous to the liberty of the country, and that our ultimate reliance for defence ought to be on the militia. . . . To consider the present army as dangerous to our liberty partakes, it is conceived, more of timidity than wisdom. Not to insist on the character of the officers, who, as a body, are high-minded and honorable men, attached to the principles of freedom by education and reflection, what well-founded apprehension can there be from an establishment distributed on so extended a frontier, with many thousand miles intervening between the extreme points occupied? But the danger, it may be said, is not so much from its numbers as a spirit hostile to liberty, by which, it is supposed, all regular armies are actuated. This observation is probably true when applied to standing armies collected into large and powerful masses; but, dispersed as ours is over so vast a surface, the danger, I conceive, is of an opposite character—that both officers and soldiers

[7] *Journals of the Continental Congress, 1774–1789* (34 vols., Washington: Government Printing Office, 1904–37), XXVII, 518, 524.

[8] Henry Adams, *Life of Gallatin*, p. 304 (July 7, 1802). The sentiments of the old Republicans were suggested by a motion of John Randolph as the army was being readied for war in 1812, authorizing the President to employ the army in time of peace on the construction of roads, canals, or other works of public utility. A large majority thought this would degrade the army to something like the status of Maryland felons. *Annals*, 12th Cong., 1st sess., I, 720 (Jan. 10, 1812).

will lose their military habits and feelings, by sliding gradually into those purely civil.[9]

Both the fear of a standing army and the military necessity of scattered posts to protect the frontier delayed the development of an effective administrative system, especially for supplies. The system from 1802 to 1812 lacked integration, responsibility, unity, and energy, and was utterly inadequate for even the most modest military operations.[10] There were no central agencies of the War Department or the army for procurement, for record keeping, or for control, other than the accountant and the clerks who copied figures and letters. The War Department in 1812, indeed, comprised only the Secretary of War and a dozen clerks.

Until 1812–1813 the system was not only embryonic; its faults were not easily cured merely by the reforms instituted during the War of 1812. While everyone complained about the sins of the contractors, no one prosecuted them for their knavery. While it was admitted that stores were lost and wasted, no one was able to introduce an effective method of control. While the Secretary of War was kept in the dark from lack of field reports, no one seemed concerned to enforce the obligation of field commanders to supply exact information. While in the early months of war, field officers lacked powder and ammunition, no one seemed competent to place these necessities on the front line. When Congress enacted remedial laws in 1812, it was so timid about giving power to the military arm that it finally created a dual, overlapping, and competing system of supply which was an administrative impossibility on its face.

These were matters that experience and intelligence could correct. A more fundamental handicap to effective army man-

[9] *American State Papers: Military Affairs*, I, 779 (Dec. 11, 1818). Cf. the editor of the *North American Review* in the article on the army already cited: "Jealousy of military power has ever been a practical feeling in this country." The people "regarded soldiers as useless and even dangerous, when not required for immediate service." *North American Review*, XXIII, 246.

[10] Lynton Keith Caldwell commented on "Jefferson's reluctance to insist upon an energetic, well-organized federal administrative system" which "had left a legacy of military incompetence in the Army and administrative ineptitude in the War Department." *The Administrative Theories of Hamilton and Jefferson* (Chicago: University of Chicago Press, 1944), p. 179.

agement and to the successful prosecution of campaigns, one that could not be readily improved, was the miserable system of overland communications. Supplies had to be moved in the interior mostly over roads. Roads were poor at best and almost impassable at worst. Distances were great. Given the state of the means of communication from 1800 to 1830, it may be doubted whether it would have been physically possible to mount an effective campaign on any substantial scale. Even where integrity, good will, and harmony of purpose prevailed, nature, not yet subdued by man, interposed stupendous obstacles. At this point, the constitutional scruples and the economizing spirit of the old Republicans handicapped the warlike ambitions of their western members.

CIVIL AND MILITARY LEADERSHIP IN THE WAR OF 1812

War was declared against Great Britain on June 18, 1812. Two weeks earlier, the chairman of the Senate Committee on Military Affairs, Joseph Anderson, asked the Secretary of War how many troops had been raised under the legislation of 1808 and whether they were sufficiently equipped and disciplined for immediate service. The inspector general was forced to admit that he had received almost no recent returns from the forty-eight recruiting districts and could not state the strength of the army; and as to its readiness for combat, he declined to make answer, "not having inspected the troops newly raised." The best figure available shows, on the eve of war, a force of 6,744 men, stationed at twenty-three different forts and posts, in detachments of usually less than 200 men each. About 900 were stationed at New York, of an estimated 3,000 needed to man the works defending this harbor.[11]

The land strategy of the War of 1812 centered on the conquest of Canada. The campaign was a failure.[12] The naval strategy was directed toward harassing British shipping and protecting American vessels. Many captures were made by privateers, and in single-ship encounters American naval vessels scored some brilliant victories. The superior weight of the British navy, however, soon made itself felt, and during most

11 *American State Papers: Military Affairs*, I, 319–20.
12 *Ibid.*, I, 439, "Causes of the Failure of the Army on the Northern Frontier."

of the war the American coast was subject to a tight blockade that kept American frigates confined in the coves of Chesapeake Bay. The bold talk of the War Hawks in 1812 concealed an extraordinary incapacity for warlike endeavor. The country was sorely unprepared whether from the point of view of finance, of military readiness, of competent leadership, of national unity, or of administrative capacity to sustain a large-scale military operation. The only calculation of forces that could have assured victory to even the most sanguine observer was either a European stalemate or an English defeat; and when Napoleon surrendered, these calculations suddenly became worthless.

The success of military enterprise depended not only on such matters as the quality and quantity of troops and equipment, skill in the disposition and use of forces, accurate intelligence concerning the enemy, and morale. It depended also on effective leadership and top management, proper relations between high civilian and military personnel, and the undramatic and humble task of providing supplies to troops in the field. These are problems of administration, and the conduct of the war revealed great deficiencies in such essentials.

The Secretary of War in 1812 was William Eustis, an army surgeon during the Revolutionary War who practiced in Boston and maintained a lively interest in local and national politics as a Republican. He represented his party in Congress from 1800 to 1805 and was commissioned Secretary of War on March 7, 1809, to help secure a desirable geographical balance in Madison's Cabinet. In the words of Major Jacobs, "he was essentially a military tinker. . . . He concerned himself with details so much that he lost track of missions and principles." [13] He "had only a second-rate mind that dwelt on petty things; most of the time he thought in terms of schemes rather than principles. He had a kind of smartness, but no real ability. . . . he always consulted the oracles of his party before making any military decision . . . as secretary of war, he was a piddling incompetent." [14]

---

[13] Jacobs, *Beginning of the U. S. Army*, p. 363.

[14] *Ibid.*, p. 383; cf. Henry Adams, *History of the United States of America*, VI, 168, 206, 392, 395, 396. Crawford characterized Eustis as a "Secretary of War, who, instead of forming general and comprehensive arrangements, for the or-

After six months of defeat on the Canadian border, Eustis resigned, December 3, 1812. Monroe was ambitious to succeed to the War Department and acted as its head for a few weeks, pro tempore, but Madison nominated John Armstrong to take this heavy responsibility. Armstrong had been in the diplomatic service, was active in New York politics, and had an eye on the presidency. He came into the Cabinet, openly critical of Virginia and its statesmen, without the confidence of the President, barely confirmed by the Senate, and opposed by the jealous Monroe who, at the end of a year, wrote Madison recommending his summary removal.[15] Armstrong was, nevertheless, the first strong Secretary of War, and promptly began a reorganization of the high command that swept out the elderly Revolutionary War generals and brought new men to the front. Henry Adams declared that the "energy thus infused by Armstrong into the regular army lasted for half a century." [16] He was hampered by a long accumulation of army deficiencies, by unfriendly Cabinet associates, and by a widely held suspicion that he was building a political machine with his army appointments.

Armstrong was assisted by a so-called General Staff, of which more is said below. Its members did not inspire confidence. Crawford, watching events from Paris, wrote Gallatin, also abroad, "For God's sake, when you return, endeavor to rid the army of old women and blockheads, at least on the general staff." [17] The adjutant general, Thomas H. Cushing, was in such poor health that he could scarcely attend to his duties. Major Jacobs characterized the inspector general, Alexander Smyth,[18] as "just a commonplace braggart without redeeming qualities." The quartermaster, Morgan Lewis, was a man of character who had, however, only a microscopic conception of

---

ganization of his troops and for the successful prosecution of the campaign, consumes his time in reading advertisements of petty retailing merchants to find where he may purchase one hundred shoes or two hundred hats. . . ." *Ibid.*, VI, 395.

15 Monroe, *Writings*, V, 275–77 (Dec. 1813).

16 Adams, *History of the United States*, VII, 409.

17 Gallatin, *Writings*, I, 583 (Sept. 22, 1813).

18 Madison later said of Smyth that "his talent for military command was equally mistaken by himself, and by his friends." *Writings* (Hunt ed.), IX, 278, n. (Feb. 1827).

his office, and his branch of the army was gravely inadequate. The adjutant and inspector, A. Y. Nicoll, made merely a modest contribution. Robert Brent, the paymaster, was competent for peacetime routine, but during the war the Treasury failed so completely to provide him with funds that several bodies of troops mutinied for lack of pay.[19]

The field commanders, with a few exceptions, were also incompetent, often politically minded, and as a group were "either to bring disgrace to the army or to fade away into innocuous obscurity." The tiny army thought appropriate by Jefferson had given no opportunity for military training or experience in the management of troops, but better judgment in appointments might have saved some military disasters.

Madison's lack of judgment in selecting field commanders was never more completely illustrated than in the case of the unfortunate William H. Winder. No general, wrote Henry Adams, "showed such incapacity as Winder either to organize, fortify, fight, or escape. When he might have prepared defences, he acted as scout; when he might have fought, he still scouted; when he retreated, he retreated in the wrong direction; when he fought, he thought only of retreat; and whether scouting, retreating, or fighting, he never betrayed an idea." [20] Such harsh and melancholy judgment could be made of many of the commanders upon whom Madison relied in the first year of the war to conquer Canada and impose peace upon His Majesty's Government. Andrew Jackson, Jacob Brown,[21] and Winfield Scott were among the few military figures to emerge with credit from three years of war on land, mostly confined to minor engagements between insignificant forces.

In his later years Madison privately admitted his mistakes

19 Jacobs, *op. cit.,* pp. 384–85; *American State Papers: Military Affairs,* I, 497.
20 Adams, *History of the United States,* VIII, 153.
21 General Jacob Brown, Quaker, school teacher, surveyor, and county judge in Ohio was a fascinating character who after the War of 1812 made the army his career. He became general in chief in 1821 and was much involved in presidential politics in 1824. He continued to advise Adams on politics during his years in the White House. Upon Brown's death in 1828, Adams wrote in his diary: "General Brown was one of the eminent men of this age and nation. Though bred a Quaker, he was a man of lofty and martial spirit, and in the late war contributed perhaps more than any other man to redeem and establish the military character of his country." Adams, *Memoirs,* VII, 447 (Feb. 24, 1828).

in choosing generals. "Selections for office, always liable to error was particularly so for military command at the commencement of the late war. The survivors of the Revolutionary band who alone had been instructed by experience in the field were but few; and of those several of the most distinguished, were disqualified by age or infirmities, or precluded by foreknown objections in the advisory Branch of the appointing Department" [i.e., the Senate].[22]

The events attending the British capture of Washington revealed the greatest confusion as to the proper function of the commander in chief, the Secretary of War, other members of the Cabinet, and the general commanding in the field. Madison was more aware of the impending danger to the capital, still a village, than Secretary Armstrong, who declined to take any preparatory measures. Madison did not, and probably could not, impose his will upon his Secretary. The city was left defenseless. Early in July 1814, the Cabinet finally decided to organize a new military area, the Potomac district. Madison appointed General Winder in command, over the objection of the Secretary of War, who henceforth took the ground that the responsibility for the protection of the city was Madison's, not his.

When the British landing force was nearing Washington on a hot summer day, August 23, 1814, Madison rode out to review the American troops; then on horseback he followed Winder from place to place a couple of days, for what military or official purpose can hardly be imagined.[23] He nearly rode into the British lines on the day of the battle of Bladensburg. Having appointed a rendezvous with his Cabinet at Frederick, Maryland, in case of disaster, he fled his capital in another direction and again began to follow Winder toward Baltimore as the British moved in that direction after the sack of Washington.

[22] Madison, *Writings* (Hunt ed.), IX, 277, n. (Feb. 1827).

[23] Earlier in the summer, Rush observed the President visiting "in person, a thing never done before, all the offices of the departments of war and the navy, stimulating every thing in a manner worthy of a little commander in chief, with his little round hat and huge cockade! He is wonderfully animated and firm inflaming the young officers about him by his remarks." Powell, *Richard Rush*, p. 42.

The President was "greatly shaken" by the disaster, and in Henry Adams' words, "showed his prostration by helplessness." He dealt indecisively with Armstrong, who finally rode away and under pressure from Madison resigned as Secretary of War. Madison could not make up his mind to fill the vacancy even temporarily with Monroe, who ardently desired the office, until Monroe made a direct application. As commander in chief, the President was irresolute, weak in his judgment of men, unaware of his proper function, and incapable of giving direction to the course of events.

James Monroe, while still Secretary of State, entertained no doubt as to his own military capacity and had no hesitation in offering to supply the vigor that was lacking. Faced with the impending engagement with the British, he promptly mounted his horse and set off on a long scouting tour, August 19–20. With the other Cabinet members he appeared on the battlefield at Bladensburg and, although destitute of military rank or authority, altered the disposition of General Stansbury's troops without his knowledge. After the defeat of the American forces Monroe rode back to Washington, agreed to an evacuation of the city, crossed the Potomac into Virginia, and eventually caught up with Madison.[24] "As a scout," wrote Henry Adams, "the Secretary of State's services were hardly so valuable as those of a common trooper, for he was obliged to be more cautious; as a general, his interference with the order of battle at Bladensburg led to sharp criticisms from General Stansbury . . . and to the epithet of 'busy and blundering tactician' from Armstrong."[25] Monroe completely abandoned his function as a member of the Cabinet and assumed a role for which there was no justification beyond personal ambition.

The ineptitude of the American forces was perhaps never more fully displayed than in the events surrounding the arrival of a regiment of Virginia militia to defend the national capital. They appeared in the late afternoon of the day before the Brit-

24 For a contemporary account of the scene in Washington see "Diary of Mrs. William Thornton. Capture of Washington by the British," Columbia Historical Society, *Records*, XIX (1916), 172–82.

25 Adams, *History of the United States*, VIII, 151.

ish marched into the city. The militia came unarmed and required guns, flints, and ammunition. Their commander called on Madison who after a short conversation sent him to the Secretary of War. Armstrong told him to report the next morning to Colonel Carberry, in charge of military stores. Colonel Carberry had gone out to his country seat the night before. "After several hours spent in most painful waiting for his return," on the following morning, orders were given by General Winder (Carberry being still absent) to supply the Virginia militiamen. "The arms were dealt out at last, but without flints, and, instead of throwing them out by handfuls, they were actually counted out, one by one, as if they had been so many guineas; and . . . after counting out a considerable number the man employed in this economizing business, fearing he had miscounted, insisted upon counting them over again." [26] The Virginia militia never reached the battlefield.

Jefferson himself bore bitter testimony to the incapacity of the military arm when he wrote Monroe in 1815 after he had taken over the War Department. "I much regretted," he told his younger Virginia friend, "your acceptance of the war department. Not that I know a person who I think would better conduct it. But, conduct it ever so wisely, it will be a sacrifice of yourself. Were an angel from Heaven to undertake that office, all our miscarriages would be ascribed to him. Raw troops, no troops, insubordinate militia, want of arms, want of money, want of provisions, all will be charged to want of management in you." [27]

But apart from the incapacity of men, it was the lack of system and comprehension of the function of top executives and commanding officers in a military situation that is impressed upon the mind. Neither the President, nor the Secretary of State, nor the Secretary of War, nor General Winder seemed to possess any general ideas as to their proper roles under the circumstances. All were irresistibly drawn to the field of battle, where none of them should have been. No one of them per-

[26] James Ewell, "Unwelcome Visitors to Early Washington," Columbia Historical Society, *Records,* I (1897), 58–59.

[27] Jefferson, *Works* (Federal ed.), XI, 445 (Jan. 1, 1815).

formed correctly the function which his office imposed upon him. No one had what Washington or Hamilton would have instantly supplied, a reasoned conception of function and duty that would have provided an intelligent means of coping with the emergency.

CHAPTER SIXTEEN

The Army Supply System

Great though the deficiencies of leadership, civilian and military, may have been during the War of 1812, they were more than matched by the faults of the supply system. The Federalists had concentrated the army supply function in the Treasury, but by 1798 they had become convinced that such a dual scheme led to confusion and irresponsibility. They gave the War Department the authority to purchase, but under the incompetent McHenry the results were far from satisfactory.

Jefferson's peacetime military establishment made no provision for a quartermaster general or commissary. The paymaster of the army and his assistants were put in charge of the clothing of the troops. Three military agents and several assistant agents, stationed one at each military post, were given the duty to feed the army, to purchase, receive, and forward all military stores and other articles for the troops, as well as Indian goods.[1] The law of 1808 providing for an additional military force increased the number of agents, but did not change the system, which was recognized to be gravely deficient.[2] The Secretary of War was obliged personally to perform the duties of a quartermaster general, for which he was unlikely to be either competent or in possession of the necessary time or resources of information. Colonel A. Parker, retiring from active service in late 1809, told Secretary Eustis that the quartermaster department should be restored, and alleged that more than $100,000 had been lost in a few years by its abolition.

[1] 2 Stat. 132, secs. 3, 17 (March 16, 1802).
[2] 2 Stat. 481 (April 12, 1808).

Agents, he said, had been employed who were "perfectly igno-rant of military affairs." [3]

On the very eve of the war Congress finally bestirred itself recognizing, as Nathaniel Macon told the House, that "it was impossible to go to war without a Quartermaster General; for there is no man has so much to do about an army as this of-ficer." [4] The House insisted upon both a quartermaster general —an army officer to receive and distribute supplies—and a commissary general, a civilian to purchase supplies, a man "well acquainted with mercantile concerns." These officers, argued Congressman David R. Williams, "are a check upon each other; one being the purchaser, and the other the distributor of sup-plies; whereas, if they were united in one person, frauds to any amount might be committed without the possibility of detec-tion." [5]

The measure finally enacted was a masterpiece of legislative ineptitude. The quartermaster general was authorized "to pur-chase military stores, camp equipage and other articles requisite for the troops." [6] The commissary general of purchases was authorized "to conduct the procuring and providing of all arms, military stores, clothing, and generally all articles of supply requisite for the military service of the United States." [7] Each was thus authorized to duplicate the work of the other and neither had authority over the other. The Secretary of War was put in a position to arbitrate between these potential rivals, but it took additional legislation a year later to clarify this confusion. [8]

Congress also established an ordnance department, with a commissary general of ordnance, an assistant commissary gen-eral, four deputies, and as many assistant deputies as the Presi-dent might direct. The duties of the department in time of peace were supervisory—to inspect ordnance and powder, to

3 *American State Papers: Military Affairs*, I, 257–58 (Nov. 29, 1809).

4 *Annals*, 12th Cong., 1st sess., I, 802 (Jan. 17, 1812).

5 *Ibid.*, I, 795–96 (Jan. 16, 1812).

6 2 Stat. 696, sec. 3 (March 28, 1812).

7 *Ibid.*, sec. 5.

8 2 Stat. 816, sec. 5 (March 3, 1813), provided that the Secretary of War be authorized to prescribe the species of supplies to be purchased respectively by the commissary general and the quartermaster general.

supervise the construction of ordnance carriages and apparatus, and to receive semiannual returns from superintendents of military stores and keepers of magazines and arsenals.[9] By the end of the War of 1812, however, the commissary general of ordnance was letting contracts for the manufacture and supply of ordnance, ammunition, and powder, in effective control of purchasing authority that had also been delegated by Congress in 1812 both to the quartermaster general and the commissary general.[10]

The problem of keeping some control over the issue, use, and accountability of supplies was a baffling one. Congress undertook to provide means to this end by establishing, March 3, 1813, the office of superintendent general of military supplies, a civilian office under the direction of the Secretary of War.[11] The duties of the superintendent were to keep accounts of all military stores, to prescribe forms of returns to be rendered by all agents concerned with supplies, to audit and settle their accounts, and to report to the Treasury for recovery of delinquent accounts. Madison appointed to this office Richard Cutts, a lame-duck Congressman from Massachusetts.

The problem of accountability for army property nevertheless remained unsolved. The quartermaster general, Thomas Jesup, made an illuminating report in 1824, in which he ob-

---

[9] 2 Stat. 732 (May 14, 1812).

[10] The government manufactured small arms, ammunition, and gun carriages at its armories and arsenals, but contracted for the manufacture of cannon both for the army and navy. Some small arms were also made by contract, notably with "Mr. Whitney, of Connecticut." The government was the principal outlet for the sale of arms, and a close relationship developed between the War Department and the few successful arms manufacturers. Price of small arms was regulated by the cost of manufacture in the government arsenals. Competitive bids were not invited by the War Department, for reasons explained in 1825 in a report from Colonel Bomford to the Secretary of War. "All the existing cannon foundries, as well as the manufactories of small arms, had been established under assurances, of continued support from the Government, if their terms, and the quality of their work, should prove satisfactory. . . . The experience acquired in a practice of many years, enables them to furnish ordnance of a more safe and durable description, and of a better quality, generally, than could be expected from new establishments." Senate Doc. 2, 19th Cong., 1st sess., p. 39 (Nov. 29, 1825). See also House Doc. 23, 18th Cong., 1st sess., p. 7 (Dec. 31, 1823).

[11] 2 Stat. 816. The office was apparently terminated by the army establishment act of 1816.

served, "During the late war, as well as previous to it, there may be said to have been no accountability for public property . . . no effort appears to have been made to enforce accountability for clothing until 1816. . . . The Pay Department was charged with enforcing the new system; but its principles, though plausible in theory, were found in practice . . . to be entirely inapplicable. . . . It is a fact worthy of notice, that, while our statute books abound with laws relating to *money* accountability, there is scarcely a line in relation to that of *property*." [12] Jesup proposed a plan which Congress approved in 1826.[13] The quartermaster general was authorized to prescribe a system of accountability for all clothing and equipage issued to the army. All issue officers were directed to preserve these supplies from waste or damage, and were made personally liable for any deficiencies that could not be explained to the satisfaction of the Secretary of War.

To a degree, and tardily, these changes met some of the essential requirements for army management. They failed, however, to touch another urgent need, the control of the army contractors. The normal system of procurement, both before and after the quartermaster and commissary legislation of 1812, was based on purchase by private contractors in accordance with agreements made between them and the Secretary of War or his representatives. The contractors supplied posts, garrisons, and armies in the field directly, in accordance with the terms of their contracts. Only when they failed to deliver could a field commander purchase for his immediate needs. Contracts were normally made to supply troops in a given military district or for specified posts or campaigns. Ten or more such annual contracts, at times running over $100,000 each, were common in peacetime.[14] The system was not conducive to ef-

12 House Report 4, 18th Cong., 2d sess., pp. 3, 4 (Feb. 9, 1824).

13 4 Stat. 173 (May 18, 1826).

14 In 1818 the commissary general of subsistence entered into 20 contracts with 14 contractors for particular army posts. The smallest of these was just under $3,000, the largest, for New Orleans, over $109,000. The contract with Sterrett Ramsay for the post of Baltimore is typical.

857 barrels of port, at $19		$16,283.00
1,786 bushels of peas or beans, at $1.50		2,679.00
2,296 barrels of flour, at $9		20,664.00

fective supply, and in the years of war it proved to be one of the gravest hindrances to military operations.[15]

Evidence on the delinquencies and failures of the army contractors began to pour in from the field without delay as military operations began in 1812. Captain William King inspected the Twelfth Regiment of Infantry stationed near Buffalo in the early autumn and made the following report.

The muskets are good, but some few of them are out of repair. No gun slings have been furnished; neither has there been a sufficiency of screw-drivers, worms, picks, or brushes, supplied. The knapsacks are very bad, as are likewise the canteens. The regiment has only about twenty-three rounds of ball cartridge, and not two flints per man; and there is no ammunition in store at this place. The cartridges are many of them very bad.

. . . All the men are without coats. . . . The tents are very bad. . . . The surgeon complains that he is without medicine, hospital stores, or surgical instruments. Colonel Parker states that he receives good provisions for his regiment.[16]

The inspector's report on the Fourteenth Regiment noted: "The arms of this regiment are in infamously bad order. . . . The tents never were good. . . . All the men are without coats, and many without shoes or stockings; and have been obliged to mount guard, during the cold and stormy weather which we have had for a week past, barefooted, and in their linen jackets and overalls. . . . The Lieutenant Colonel states that the regiment is supplied with very bad provisions."[17] Brigadier General Smyth wrote General Dearborn from the Buffalo encamp-

400 barrels of whiskey, at 55 cents per gallon	$7,040.00
143 hundredweight of soap, at 10 cents per pound	1,601.60
6,000 pounds of candles, at 19 cents	1,140.00
250 bushels of salt, at 70 cents	175.00
4,000 gallons of vinegar at 25 cents	1,000.00
	$50,582.60

American State Papers: Military Affairs, I, 848. The ration was fixed by law from time to time; see 2 Stat. 132, sec. 6 (March 16, 1802) for example. Subsequently the President was authorized to alter it, 3 Stat. 426, sec. 8 (April 14, 1818). Monroe did so, on the advice of the surgeon general.

15 Jacobs, *Beginning of the U. S. Army*, p. 349.
16 *American State Papers: Military Affairs*, I, 491 (Oct. 5, 1812).
17 *Ibid.*, I, 492 (Oct. 5, 1812).

ment, "I do not expect the contractor to supply us with provisions. I received a number of returns from Lewistown, 'unfit for duty for want of provisions.' " [18] About two weeks later he wrote Dearborn again, "the want of salt meat, of ovens, and exposure to cold, until lately without winter clothing, has produced dysenteries and other diseases. Our hospitals are filled with sick and wounded. . . ." [19] On November 7, 1812, Colonel Winder reported to General Smyth, "We are literally starving on this end of the line for bread"; Major Armistead reported from Fort Niagara, "my greatest concern is the want of provisions"; and General Tannehill, "there is no flour to be drawn." [20]

In 1814 Congress asked Monroe whether any other mode of supplying the army could be devised. Monroe requested three army officers to present their views of the contract system. Their statements condemned it without qualification. General Scott declared, "The interests of the contractor are in precise opposition to those of the troops. . . . It would be endless to trace the petty villainies which contractors are daily tempted to commit, to the prejudice of the troops. . . ." [21] General Gaines was more specific and equally emphatic.

The sub-contractor at Wilmington has not furnished a day's rations for near two weeks past. The sub-contractor at Billingsport, New Jersey, as well as the one at Marcus Hook, our principal encampment, have, in defiance of my frequent orders and threats, and contrary to their contract, contrived to palm upon the troops the coarsest and cheapest provisions, and such as are often damaged. . . . if I were called before Heaven to answer, whether we have not lost more men by the badness of the provisions, than by the fire of the enemy, I should give it as my opinion that we had. . . .

Original contractors seem to be a privileged order of men. . . . They take care to secure to themselves at least one cent per ration, leaving a second, and sometimes a third order of miserable under contractors to perform the duties, and each of these must calculate on making money. Thus the contract, after being duly entered into

18 *Ibid.*, I, 494 (Oct. 24, 1812).
19 *Ibid.*, I, 497 (Nov. 9, 1812).
20 *Ibid.*, I, 509 (Nov. 7, 22, Dec. 1, 1812).
21 *Ibid.*, I, 600 (Dec. 1814).

at Washington, is bid off, until it falls into the hands of men who are forced to bear certain loss and ultimate ruin, or commit frauds, by furnishing damaged provisions; they generally choose the latter, though it should tend to destroy the army. I know the opinion of no officer on this subject, who does not think with me.[22]

It must not be assumed, however, that all contractors were knaves. The record of John H. Piatt proves that honorable and capable men were also among those who supplied the army. Piatt was a merchant in Cincinnati who, from "close application to business and economy" had amassed a considerable fortune by 1812 which was in turn augmented by a contract to supply General Hull's army. On January 26, 1814, he entered into a contract with the Secretary of War to supply rations to troops within Ohio, Kentucky, and Michigan Territory. Almost immediately "the face of affairs underwent a change, more violent, more rapid, and the fulfilment of its stipulations more disastrous, than the most gloomy imagination could have anticipated." [23] The price of provisions more than doubled, the demand for rations increased, and the government was unable, in December 1814, to meet bills contracted by Piatt to the amount of $210,000. The inability of the government to meet these obligations broke the contract, and Piatt was urged to withdraw from it, with the prospect of large profits on subsequent operations, since he had control of most of the stocks of provisions throughout the area.

On January 10, 1815, after consulting with Monroe, Piatt wrote his agent, Hugh Glenn, to continue to meet the terms of the agreement.

. . . my duty as a citizen, and the confidence reposed in me since the declaration of war, compels me to continue the supply of the army. . . It is incompatible with the duty of a public agent, in any capacity, to take an advantage of the embarrassments of his Government. You will therefore continue the supply of the army, and meet every wish of the general commanding, with the utmost promptitude in your power, disregarding any necessary expense. I

22 *Ibid.*, I, 600–601.
23 House Report 21, 18th Cong., 1st sess., p. 2 (Jan. 9, 1824).

shall rely solely on the liberality of my Government for remuneration for any losses I may sustain.[24]

The outcome was financial ruin for Piatt, a lingering controversy with the second auditor that had not come to an end when death overtook Piatt, and the final intervention of Congress to force a liberal settlement for his estate.

The select committee of 1824 which reported on the case found that Piatt had performed his contract throughout with punctuality; that "this was an instance of unexampled fidelity"; that it was fully proved, "that Mr. Piatt was not only a man of activity and zeal, but of the most lofty patriotism"; and that he had sacrificed his fortune and health to the cause of his country.[25]

Bad as the contract system was, Congress made no change in it during the War of 1812. The alternative supported by Generals Scott and Gaines and by Colonel Fenwick was direct purchase by army officers. General Gaines wrote Monroe, "Commissioned officers only should be employed in this duty; men who stand most solemnly pledged to serve the United States honestly and faithfully, and to obey orders; men who may be cashiered or capitally punished by military law, for neglect of duty, or for fraudulent practices." [26]

Peace came in 1815, and in organizing the peacetime military establishment Congress finally recognized in part the army recommendations with reference to supply. The army purchasing department was continued under the direction of the commissary general of purchases, assisted by as many assistant commissaries of issue and military storekeepers as the establishment of 10,000 men required.[27] Supplies continued to be bought on contract, apart from emergencies, on public notice, but hence-

24 *Ibid.*, pp. 20–21; for earlier documents on the case see House Doc. 15, 17th Cong., 2d sess. (Jan. 3, 1823); and House Report 102, 17th Cong., 2d sess. (March 3, 1823). See also Senate Doc. 104, 16th Cong., 2d sess., and Senate Doc. 117, 16th Cong., 2d sess.

25 House Report 21, 18th Cong., 1st sess., p. 2. Two relief acts were passed in favor of Piatt, 6 Stat. 245 (May 8, 1820) and 6 Stat. 314 (May 24, 1824). The latter authorized payment of $63,620.48 to his heirs.

26 *American State Papers: Military Affairs*, I, 601 (December 1814).

27 3 Stat. 297, sec. 5 (April 24, 1816); and 3 Stat. 426 (April 14, 1818).

forth to be delivered in bulk, after inspection, to stipulated depots, and thence distributed by the quartermaster general.

The essential improvement lay in removing from the contractors the responsibility of delivering and issuing the rations to field commanders; in requiring delivery in bulk at certain depots where adequate inspection was feasible; and in removing from the contract price the hazards and costs of transportation to the field, thus encouraging more responsible bidders. John C. Calhoun told Congress in 1818 that this system was adequate to the cheap and certain supply of the army, although it would be necessary to expand and modify it in time of war. "The ordinary supplies," wrote Calhoun, "ought to be by contract on public proposals. By a judicious collection of provisions at proper depots, combined with an active and energetic system of transportation, it would be seldom necessary to resort to any other mode of purchasing." [28]

Contracts were henceforward made for the army by four principal agencies: the commissary general of subsistence, for rations; the ordnance department, for arms and ammunition; the commissary general of purchases, for clothing; and the engineer department, for labor and materials for fortifications. The system worked well for the remainder of the Republican period, and the reorganization may be justly appraised as at least a peacetime solution of the problem of supply.

28 *American State Papers: Military Affairs*, I, 781 (Dec. 11, 1818).

CHAPTER SEVENTEEN

The War Department
and the Army

Both the War Department and the Navy Department differed from the civil agencies of the federal government by reason of the special status of the uniformed forces. So far as the Treasury or the Post Office were concerned, there was merely a single undifferentiated hierarchy running from the Secretary to the customs inspector, or from the Postmaster General to the humblest rural postmaster. The State Department with its foreign service stood in a midway position, since the physical and chronological separation of the minister abroad gave him an independence of action that differed from the dependence characteristic of Treasury or Post Office agents. The War Department and the Navy represented still another situation.

In its broad outline, the differentiation between the War Department and the United States Army was sharp and decisive. The department was civilian, and beyond the Secretary, comprised only clerks and bookkeepers.[1] The army was uniformed, and comprised a hierarchy of commanding officers and men subject to military discipline. The army spoke often of honor and glory; the department, in clerical silence, found no equivalent motivations. The department was nevertheless theoretically supreme, and the army readily acknowledged its constitutional

[1] It is of interest to note that before Calhoun every Secretary of War except Samuel Dexter and William H. Crawford, who held the office briefly, had had military experience. Calhoun was the first civilian Secretary to impress himself upon the department and the army.

[233]

subordination to the civil power. The Secretary of War was directly served both by the War Department and the army, and of course was responsible for the operations of both. The structural difference between the War Department and the army was striking, especially after the reforms of 1816.

THE WAR DEPARTMENT

The War Department clerks, about twenty in number in 1821, were engaged in correspondence, record keeping, and dealing with accounts and claims of former officers and men.[2] Most of them had a specific standing assignment in the subject matter of which they became specialists, such as the allowance of military pensions or the grant of military bounty land. All worked under the immediate direction of the chief clerk.

The War Department was responsible for the management of Indian affairs and had two civilian agencies for this purpose. The office of superintendent of Indian trade was established in 1806 and terminated in 1822. The bureau of Indian affairs carried on all other business with the natives. Both offices maintained a civilian field service.[3] There was also a superintendent of the buildings of the War and Navy Departments. None of these agencies had anything to do with military affairs. Before the War of 1812 the accountant of the War Department constituted a part of the civilian organization, acting in effect as an auditor. This office was transferred in 1816 to the Treasury.

The central responsibility of the War Department was therefore discharged by a single office comprising a small number of clerks. None of them had professional, political, or administrative standing. The Secretary of War, so far as the immediate civil organization of the department was concerned, stood practically alone in the management of military affairs.

Before 1812 the Secretary also lacked military agencies permanently located in Washington to assist him in army management. The miniature army organized by the Republicans in 1802 made no provision for staff officers, nor did the legislation of 1808, increasing the size of the military establishment. The

[2] The record of departmental business is preserved in the National Archives, Records of the Office of the Secretary of War, Letters Sent, Military Affairs.
[3] See below, ch. 32.

army was fed, clothed, housed, documented, and kept in health by the commanding officers of garrisons and detachments and their subordinate officers. The Secretary thus had no professional advisers, civil or military. On the eve of hostilities in 1812 the Secretary of War was not only the head of the department, attending as such to the claims of pensioners, the grant of military land warrants, and the supervision of Indian agents; he also had to act in a strictly military capacity as adjutant general, quartermaster general, commissary general, paymaster, and as appellate authority for review of courts martial, besides "the more troublesome business of members of Congress, who crowd the offices from morning to night, and who can never be turned off unsatisfied." [4]

In the face of impending hostilities Madison recommended relief by the creation of two assistant secretaries,[5] aides described in the House as persons to help the head of the department "not only with their hands, but with their minds"; [6] men who could "relieve the Secretary of War from the details of the various branches of his department, that he may have the command of his time and his mind to attend to the general superintendence of the whole. . . ." [7] It is of some significance that Madison recommended civilian support for the Secretary, as well as the military assistance that was forthcoming.

The hostility of members of the House to this sorely needed reform was intense, and significant of much "old Republican" theory. Congressman Williams "could not but believe there were thousands of individuals perfectly adequate to the correct arrangement and prompt execution of all the duties of the Department." [8] Congressman Tallmadge could "find no justification . . . to tax the Treasury with six thousand dollars additional salaries, or sinecures, for services which could be performed by able, competent clerks. . . ." [9] John Randolph hinted darkly at the prospect of a corresponding bill for the

4 *Annals,* 12th Cong., 1st sess., II, 1362 (April 30, 1812).
5 Richardson, *Messages,* I, 499 (April 20, 1812).
6 *Annals,* 12th Cong., 1st sess., II, 1355 (April 30, 1812).
7 *Ibid.,* II, 1365.
8 *Ibid.,* II, 1358.
9 *Ibid.,* II, 1372.

Navy Department. "This system," he declared, "if pursued, will effectually create all our great departments of Government into sinecures." [10]

In vain did the friends of the Administration support Madison. Troup declared, correctly enough, "In the wretched, deplorably wretched organization of the War Department, it was impossible either to begin the war or to conduct it. In its present organization, it was a mere counting-house establishment. . . ." [11] McKim argued, "There will be no economy in making the Head of this extensive Department a man of labor, in the drudgery of the business; he should be a man of leisure, his mind at ease, and his attentions given to . . . a general superintendence of the entire concerns of the Department; to see that every thing is done correctly, to the best advantage, and in due time. . . ." [12] The friends of a frugal government prevailed in the House.[13] Relief to the overworked Secretary came not through civilian aides but from the provision of a military General Staff. A parallel evolution was to occur in the Navy Department where an exactly analogous administrative vacuum existed until filled, in 1816, by the Board of Navy Commissioners.

THE GENERAL STAFF

Army organization before 1813, as already noted, was extremely simple. Top military management offices were completely lacking; the army consisted of small self-sufficing scattered posts mostly on the frontier under the control of local commanders. Even the simple Federalist pattern of central mili-

10 *Ibid.*, II, 1368.

11 *Ibid.*, II, 1359.

12 *Ibid.*, II, 1374.

13 A substantial part of the administrative weakness of the War Department was thus specifically due to a timid Congress, worried about military power. Madison was quite justified in recounting some congressional failures. ". . . the first provision of the two vital Departments, the Commissary's and Quarter Master's, was so inadequate, that the War office, otherwise overcharged, was obliged for some time to perform the functions of both. It was only after repeated failures and a lapse of months that a Commissary General could be obtained on the terms offered by the law. Nor ought it to be omitted that the recommendation of a greater number of General Officers . . . was rejected in the first instance. The same may be remarked as to two auxiliary appointments in the war office, now substantially provided for under other names in the organization of the military establishment." Madison, *Writings* (Hunt ed.), VIII, 264 (Sept. 30, 1813).

tary direction had been abandoned. Early disasters in the northwest finally prompted Congress to strengthen the army by creating a General Staff.[14] The basic act of 1813 contained the first legislative use of the term, although its content was different from that given it nearly a hundred years later. The Secretary of War was authorized to prepare general regulations, specifying the duties and powers of its members. These regulations contained the fundamentals of army management, as distinct from military operations and exercises.

Neither the legislation nor the regulations defined the concept or function of the General Staff as a collective organ, and indeed it did not act as such. Armstrong's report to Congress, December 27, 1813, however, indicated precisely what officers were included, and the regulations of May 1, 1813, defined their particular duties.[15] The General Staff included the adjutant and inspector general and his two immediate assistants, the inspector general and the assistant adjutant general; the quartermaster general; the commissary general of ordnance, two deputy commissaries of ordnance, and the assistant commissary of ordnance; the paymaster of the army; and the assistant topographical engineer.

At this time there were nine military districts, each provided with its own staff. These staffs included the commanding general of the troops in the district, and the responsible military and civil heads of what would now be called (in civilian terms) the auxiliary services: adjutant generals, inspector generals, assistant quartermaster generals, engineers, deputy commissaries of ordnance, surgeons, judge advocates, chaplains, paymasters, deputy commissaries of purchases, and military storekeepers. This enumeration indicates that the term, General Staff, was understood in 1813 to refer to the principal officers, both military and civil, who were concerned with the housekeeping functions of the army.[16]

---

[14] 2 Stat. 819 (March 3, 1813).

[15] *American State Papers: Military Affairs,* I, 385–92.

[16] "Rules and Regulations of the Army of the United States," May 1, 1813, *ibid.,* I, 425 ff. The legislation of 1813 also provided for a physician and surgeon general, and an apothecary general, both civilians and neither members of the General Staff.

With the end of hostilities Congress asked for advice from the Secretary of War concerning the future organization of the General Staff. Crawford suggested its continuation on the same footing as during the war. "The experience of the two first campaigns of the last war," he wrote, "furnished volumes of evidence upon this subject. . . . The stationary staff of a military establishment should be substantially the same in peace as in war. . . ." He also urged a General Staff in each of the two military divisions set up by the general order of May 17, 1815.[17] Congress responded favorably in the legislation of April 24, 1816.[18] The vote was decisive, 96 to 22, but unfortunately the record of the debate was not informative.

The staff agencies, brought together in Washington during the war emergency, settled down in the capital city in ready contact with the Secretary of War after peace had been restored. The regulations of the subsistence department stated in 1818 that "the commissary general of subsistence, will be stationed at Washington, and will have a general superintendence of his department." [19] In 1820 Calhoun informed the House, "Experience has proved that, in time of peace, the chief of the corps [of engineers] should be stationed at the seat of Government, to superintend, under its immediate control, the great and important duties assigned to the corps." [20] After the reduction of the army in 1821, the major general was stationed in Washington "in order to render the military organization more complete . . . *thus bringing the military administration of the army, as well as its pecuniary* . . . under the immediate inspection and control of the government." [21]

Officers attached to the General Staff quickly became the professional advisers of the Secretary. Military boards were frequently set up to make investigations and draft recommendations. For example, we note the report of General Bernard and

<hr>

17 *American State Papers: Military Affairs,* I, 636 (Dec. 27, 1815).
18 3 Stat. 297.
19 House Doc. 36, 15th Cong., 2d sess., p. 30 (Dec. 14, 1818).
20 *American State Papers: Military Affairs,* II, 75.
21 Senate Doc. 1, 17th Cong., 2d sess., p. 24 (Nov. 27, 1822). Italics supplied by author. The army reduction act of 1821 established one major general, who by rank thus became the commanding officer of the whole army. 3 Stat. 615, sec. 5.

Major McRee on the course of instruction at West Point,[22] the elaborate reports on fortifications presented from 1818 to 1821 and summarized in 1821 by General Bernard, Captain J. D. Elliott of the navy, and Major Totten;[23] and the report on a western armory made by Colonel McRee, Colonel Lee, and Captain Talcott.[24] Calhoun also received a succession of valuable reports from the individual heads of the army management branches.

In 1818 Calhoun told Congress that the staff, as organized in 1816, combined simplicity with efficiency, and was considered to be superior to that of earlier periods.

. . . no part of our military organization requires more attention in peace than the general staff. It is in every service invariably the last in attaining perfection; and, if neglected in peace, when there is leisure, it will be impossible, in the midst of the hurry and bustle of war, to bring it to perfection. It is in peace that it should receive a perfect organization, and that the officers should be trained to method and punctuality. . . . With a defective staff, we must carry on our military operations under great disadvantages, and be exposed, particularly at the commencement of a war, to great losses, embarrassments, and disasters.[25]

One consequence of the War of 1812 was thus to enlarge and make permanent the management branches of the United States Army. Although these housekeeping services were designated collectively as the General Staff, the term as understood by Crawford and Calhoun and by the army did not signify a central planning agency concerned with strategy and coordination. In this early form the General Staff carried through the Mexican War, the War between the States, and the Spanish-American War, being finally replaced by the contemporary view of a General Staff in 1903.

Inherent in these developments was the origin of the bureau system within the War Department. Bureau organization meant specialization of function, separately organized as such, with assigned authority to operate under the general oversight of the

[22] *American State Papers: Military Affairs*, I, 834 (1819).
[23] *Ibid.*, II, 304 (1821).
[24] *Ibid.*, II, 731 (1825).
[25] *Ibid.*, I, 780 (Dec. 11, 1818).

head of the department. It also necessarily implied the appointment of officers who had the competence and standing to take responsibility for making decisions under a broad delegation of authority. It involved the emergence of a team for the conduct of the work of the department, and the end of a single, direct, and immediate responsibility of the civilian head of the department for all matters that took place within the agency. It implied eventually the consideration of relationships between "persons of eminence" in important military posts and their superior, the Secretary of the department. It marked the cleavage between an organization consisting of a head with clerks, and one comprising a head with professional associates able to share responsibility.

The *National Intelligencer* caught the spirit and meaning of these innovations. ". . . the principal office of each branch of the military service will be stationed at the seat of government, forming bureaus under the secretary of war, so constituted as to give precision, energy and promptness to the army machinery. . . . no one can doubt the good policy of congress in affording the means . . . to carry this arrangement into operation." [26] The reform of military administration had well begun.

STAFF AND LINE

The army, while recognizing its subordination, nevertheless cherished its autonomy and its internal freedom from civilian interference. The recommendations of General Scott and others for a purely military supply system, already noted, furnished one example. The resounding conflict between Monroe, Calhoun, and General Jackson furnished another, and raised important issues of relationship between the department and army, and between headquarters staff and field commanders.[27]

By way of introducing this episode, we may note that during most of the Jeffersonian period there was no single commander of the army. During the War of 1812 there were command-

26 Quoted in *Niles Register*, XIV, 224 (May 23, 1818).
27 The issue had been smoldering for several years. In 1815 Madison noted that military commanders had complained of orders from the War Department given directly to inferior officers within their districts, even though made known at the same time to them. Madison to Dallas, May 15, 1815, Dallas, *Life and Writings*, p. 418.

ing generals of geographical divisions, each of whom reported directly to the Secretary of War, and the peacetime establishment of 1816 provided for a commanding general of the northern and southern military divisions respectively. They had no common military superior. One was finally provided in 1821 in the office of the major general, first occupied by General Jacob Brown. The term, division, meant a geographical area for military purposes, not a portion of the army. Each division was divided into military districts.

Late in 1816 the War Department instructed Major Long, a topographical engineer assigned to the southern division, of which Andrew Jackson was commanding general, to report to Washington. No copy of the order was sent to Jackson, who learned about it only from a subsequent report made by Long, transmitted to him through the adjutant general's office in Washington. Jackson immediately asked for an explanation.[28] George Graham, Acting Secretary of War, reported the circumstances, but closed his letter with this uncompromising comment: "It is distinctly to be understood, that this department at all times exercises the right of assigning officers to the performance of special duties, at its discretion." [29] This proposition was not congenial to Jackson, who complained about the channels through which the orders went, and his own lack of knowledge of them.

About five weeks later, on the very day of Monroe's inauguration, Jackson proceeded to lay the issue before the new President, objecting to the right "assumed by the Secretary of War to direct the Topographical Engineers to perform special duties, the manner in which they shall report, and even directing them to report to an independent department, and all this without the knowledge of the commanding Genl."

. . . Such a doctrine, is a violation of all military etiquette, and subversion of every principle of subordination, and could only

28 *Correspondence of Andrew Jackson* (John Spencer Bassett, ed., 7 vols., Washington, D. C.: Carnegie Institution of Washington, 1926–35), II, 273 (Jan. 14, 1817); Spaulding noted that the Secretary of War was following the bad habit acquired by the department during the War of 1812. Oliver Lyman Spaulding, *The United States Army in War and Peace* (New York: G. P. Putnam's Sons, 1937), pp. 148–49.

29 Jackson, *Correspondence*, II, 274–75 (Feb. 1, 1817).

originate in an inexperienced head, perfectly unskilled in military matters. . . .

Admit for a moment this modern doctrine, and you destroy all subordination, deprive, at the pleasure of the Secretary the Commanding Genl . . . of the services of his best Officers . . . and that too without his knowledge. . . .

. . . the duties and labour of a Topo: Engineer are alone important to the Officer directing the operations of an Army: it can be of no benefit to him that the Topography of a Country has been obtained and locked up in the War Department, or even, which is more ludicrous, instead of being reported to him, reported to the chief of Engineers. It is the correct knowledge of the Topography of a country that enables the commander of an Army to strike the enemy with certainty and effect, and act with promptness and success; for this purpose that part of the General Staff was created by law and attached to the Division, and made subordinate to the orders of their Commanders, and cannot be removed without their knowledge and consent, unless it is by establishing in the person of the Secretary of War a Tyrant superior to the law, whose will is the constitution, his caprice the law.

. . . Every military order must pass through the regular channel. . . .[30]

Monroe was faced with an awkward situation, given the well-known character of General Jackson. He delayed an answer but delay did not ease the problem. On April 22, 1817, Jackson issued a divisional order prohibiting any officer under his command from obeying any order emanating from the War Department "unless coming through him as the proper organ of communication," i.e., through the office of the commanding general of the division.[31] Thus the issue was inescapably joined.

President Monroe took charge of the ensuing correspondence. In early August he wrote a hasty note to Jackson from Sackett's Harbor, stating, "The principle is clear, that every order from the dept. of war, to whomever directed, must be obeyed. I cannot think that you are of a different opinion. . . ." On this letter Jackson noted, "This is to be filed, and the further explanation waited for. . . ."[32] To Monroe he wrote, immediately

---

[30] *Ibid.*, II, 281–82 (March 4, 1817).
[31] *Ibid.*, II, 291; order printed in *Niles Register*, XII, 320 (July 12, 1817).
[32] Jackson, *Correspondence*, II, 319 (August 4, 1817).

upon receipt of the letter, ". . . I will continue to support the Government in all respects when the orders of the War Dept. do not, in my opinion, go to infringe all law and strike at the very root of subordination and the discipline of the Army," and hinted broadly at his resignation if the President failed to concur in his position.[33]

Monroe finally worked out his views in a long letter to Jackson early in October 1817. Referring to Jackson's order of April 22, he said:

. . . This order involves the naked principle, of the power of the Executive, over the officers of the army, in such cases, for the department of war cannot be separated from the President. . . . The orders of the dept are therefore the orders of the President. . . .

According to my view of the subject, no officer of the army, can rightfully disobey, an order from the President. . . .

If the question is examind on military principles, it appears to me, that all those principles require a short and prompt obedience to the orders of the Chief Majistrate. I do not think that any officer of either of our divisions, would disobey an order from its commander. . . .

Whatever may be said of the right of a commander of a district and division, to command within his district and division, applies with full force to the President as Commander in chief of the army. In that character, he is present every where, and no officer, can, in my judgment, rightfully disobey his order, provided it be conveyd to him, thro the dept of war, or other proper channel. . . .

The commander of a district, is, it is true, charg'd with its defense . . . but still he is no further responsible, than for the faithful application of the means committed to him for the purpose, by the Executive. The whole means provided by law . . . are committed to the Executive. . . . He must therefore be the judge how those means are to be applied, and have full power to apply them . . . as he may find expedient. . . .

As to the policy of exercising the power to the full extent of the right, of giving orders, invariably, to officers in any division, without passing them thro' the commander of the division, I am far from advocating it. In general, I think that the practice, should be otherwise, and be deviated from, in cases, of urgency only, of which, the dept. should be the judge. . . . in all cases, when departed from, the commander of the district should be promptly advisd of it, and a copy of the order sent to him.[34]

Upon receiving this communication Jackson yielded to the extent of withdrawing his order of April 22, induced by "the conciliatory features" of Monroe's letter and by the expectation of new regulations "which may tend to harmonize the Army and keep up subordination." "I would barely remark," he wrote the President, "that cases of necessity, creates [sic] their own rule, and where they really exist, forms [sic] an exception from the Genl. rule—altho' not expressed always implied—hence I have never complained of any order being issued in cases of necessity, when I was immediately advised thereof—nor is it a source of real complaint." [35]

A further exchange of conciliatory letters caused Jackson to withdraw his proposed resignation, and Calhoun proceeded to draft the new regulations. The general order was framed in these terms.

As a general rule, all orders will issue, in the first instance, to the commanders of division. In cases where the nature of the duty to be performed, and the public interest may require it, orders will issue directly to officers commanding departments, posts, or detachments, and to any officer attached to the division; but in such cases, a copy of the orders will be transmitted to General of division, for his information.[36]

This sensible arrangement thus terminated a controversy that had raged for a full year, and according to Jackson adopted "the principles I contended for, and on which my famed Genl. order was predicated." The incident is significant for more reasons than the single issue that precipitated it. The doctrine of the supremacy of the department over the army was again affirmed, and in terms of concrete application. The authority of the department to shift "staff" officers, in this case a topographical engineer, from one commanding general to another was clarified. The right of the central staff department to control the assignment of the field staff officers (as against the field

34 Ibid., II, 329–31 (Oct. 5, 1817).
35 Ibid., II, 332–33 (Oct. 22, 1817).
36 Dated December 29, 1817; reprinted in ibid., II, 343, n. 1.

commanding general) was implicitly confirmed. At the same time the normal channel of communication through the line was accepted by all concerned.

Another aspect of the general relationship of the department to the army came to the front in 1819. The assistant surgeon generals and the post surgeons were required to report directly to the surgeon general in Washington.[37] They were negligent in the discharge of this duty and in the summer of 1819 Calhoun wrote an informal but strong letter to Jackson on the subject. It appeared that Jackson had ordered all the post surgeons to send their reports to the assistant surgeon general in his division (and under his command) instead of directly to Washington. Calhoun asked Jackson to "modify" this regulation, since it was in part the cause of delay. Calhoun wrote:

. . . It certainly would be perfectly agreeable to me to order all reports to pass through the Headquarters of the Divisions, were it not for the delay which would in many instances result; and, which as experience proves in this case is inconsistant with the proper management of the department. It is certainly important that the Commanding General as well as the Government should be kept promptly informed of whatever effects his command; but this can be effected consistently with the correctest principles, by ordering a duplicate of such reports as may be thought adviseable by the Commanding General to be made to his headquarters.

Calhoun concluded his "informal" letter by expressing the hope that he would be relieved "from the necessity of determining whether I shall permit the orders of the Government to be habitually neglected, or resort to the proper means of enforcing them. Should the alternative be presented I will not hesitate to do my duty." [38] Strong words to address to Andrew Jackson, soon to enter the arena of national politics where Calhoun was already well placed!

[37] A general order of April 21, 1818, provided, "All orders and instructions relative to the duties of the several officers of the Medical Staff, will be issued through the Surgeon General, who will be obeyed and respected accordingly." Reprinted in Harvey E. Brown, compiler, *The Medical Department of the United States Army from 1775 to 1873* (Washington, D. C.: Surgeon General's Office, 1873), p. 109.

[38] Calhoun, *Correspondence,* pp. 160–62 (August 10, 1819).

JOHN C. CALHOUN

The War Department acquired dynamic and intelligent leadership in the person of John C. Calhoun. After graduating from Yale in 1804, Calhoun studied law in Connecticut and was admitted to the bar in his native state in 1807. In the next year he was elected to the South Carolina House of Representatives, and in 1810 to Congress. With hardly a break he remained in public life until his death in Washington in 1850. His principal administrative experience covered eight years (1817–25) as Secretary of War. His administrative record was outstanding.

Calhoun accepted Monroe's invitation to the Cabinet as a part of his preparation for the presidency, realizing that he must demonstrate his ability to administer laws as well as to make them.[39] He quickly showed capacity of a high order and a ready understanding of the administrative art. His mind ranged far beyond the present to new and challenging responsibilities of the future. He saw matters in the large but at the same time recognized that "the minute and constant attention to details" was "indispensable to a perfect administration." [40] He was endowed not only with energy, working at times fourteen or fifteen hours a day, but also with self-confidence.[41] During his eight years of office, the War Department replaced the Treasury as the dynamic center of government operations.

Calhoun was governed by three basic ideas about administration: concentration of authority at the center; definite responsibility in all the parts of his organization; and eminence in the capacities of his immediate assistants. He completed the movement to bring the heads of all the army agencies into Washington, and established in peacetime the office of commanding general as the single center of army command. The office of inspector general, the eye and ear of the Secretary of War, he considered one of the most important means of concentrating

[39] Charles M. Wiltse, *John C. Calhoun: Nationalist,* pp. 140–41.
[40] Senate Doc. 1, 18th Cong., 1st sess., Documents, p. 3 (Nov. 29, 1823).
[41] Calhoun's colleague, Wirt, described him in 1824 as a "most captivating man. . . . the very character to strike a Virginian;—ardent, generous, high-minded, brave, with a genius full of fire, energy, and light. . . . He is, at present, a little too sanguine, a little too rapid and tenacious. . . ." Wirt, *Memoirs,* II, 185.

authority in the military establishment. "On the skill, the industry, firmness and impartiality of the Inspr General, the discipline and condition of the troops must, to a considerable extent, depend. If he is known to possess the requisite qualifications, very few officers would venture to neglect their duty. . . ." [42] With respect to the medical staff, he declared it must remain unsatisfactory " 'till its duties are brought to a centre." [43]

His views on responsibility in the subordinate ranks were written into the army regulations of 1818. Their intent was described by Calhoun in these terms: "the regulations propose to carry a minute and rigid responsibility into every branch of the military disbursements. . . . one principle pervades the whole organization—to hold the head of each subordinate department responsible for the disbursements of his department." [44]

It fell to Calhoun to appoint the first surgeon general.[45] He selected Joseph Lovell, a Harvard medical school graduate who proved to be an outstanding choice. Lovell became surgeon of the Ninth Infantry in 1812 at the age of twenty-four, only one year away from his professional training. He was in the army service until his death in 1836. By 1817 he was the chief medical officer of the northern department, where he showed both interest in and aptitude for medical administration.[46] He became surgeon general in 1818 at the age of thirty and served continu-

42 Calhoun, *Correspondence,* p. 194 (August 18, 1821).

43 *Ibid.,* p. 133 (Feb. 5, 1818).

44 *American State Papers: Military Affairs,* II, 345 (Feb. 11, 1822).

45 There is a good account of the early history of the medical service in Harvey E. Brown, compiler, *The Medical Department of the United States Army from 1775 to 1873.* See also P. M. Ashburn, *A History of the Medical Department of the United States Army* (Boston: Houghton Mifflin, 1929). Basic legislation was the act of March 2, 1799 (1 Stat. 721); see also the 1814 Regulations for the Medical Department (Brown, *op. cit.,* pp. 94–98), and the revised Regulations of 1818 (*ibid.,* pp. 110–21). Before 1812 the medical department consisted only of a few garrison and regimental surgeons and their mates, stationed at isolated posts and having no professional head. The office of physician and surgeon general was established by the act of March 3, 1813, but was terminated March 3, 1815. The office of surgeon general was established in 1818.

46 There is a brief account of Lovell and his professional work in the army in Brown, *op. cit.,* pp. 108–10. One of the best known members of the medical corps was Dr. William Beaumont, who made the famous experiments on the stomach of Alexis St. Martin. See Jesse S. Myer, *Life and Letters of Dr. William Beaumont* (St. Louis: C. V. Mosby, 1939).

ously until 1836. It was Lovell who initiated daily weather reports from all medical officers, hoping to find some correlation between weather and army diseases.[47] He campaigned against the use of alcohol, and eventually succeeded in eliminating the rum ration.[48] His first report, November 16, 1818, was an able analysis of the central problem of feeding the army and of the consequences to health from an inadequate ration.[49] He met Calhoun's test, "a medical character of eminence."

Calhoun not only picked able men, he stabilized the top management of the army. The Army Register for 1825 showed the date of appointment to the office then held for each of the responsible officials.[50] The list was impressive. The head of every one of the management agencies of the army served continuously through the eight years of Calhoun's leadership, an experience conducive both to expertness, teamwork, and morale.

Aided by his chief clerk, Major Christopher Van Deventer, and an able corps of army officers, Calhoun completed the General Staff and gave the army the form of top organization that lasted through the Civil War.[51] He rejuvenated West Point and established an artillery school at Fortress Monroe. He submitted to Congress the first systematic and rational plan of coast defense. He maintained civilian control over the army and handled judiciously such difficult personages as Generals Jackson and Scott, although finally estranged from the former. He perfected the supply system and improved the ration while

---

[47] This was in close accord with the medical philosophy of the time. Jeffersonian interest in draining swamps was due to the belief that their noxious gases caused disease.

[48] *Dictionary of American Biography*, XI, 440–41.

[49] *American State Papers: Military Affairs*, I, 804–7.

[50] *Ibid.*, II, 837. The quartermaster general was Thomas S. Jesup, whose reports were models of administrative sense; for example: "The best test of the efficiency of a department, is to be found, not in minor details, but in general results" (Senate Doc. 1, 18th Cong., 1st sess., p. 10, Nov. 22, 1823); "Besides, the experience of every Department proves, that the only way to ensure strict accountability, is, to confine officers to the duties of their own branches of service—to compel them to perform them, and positively to prohibit their interference with those of others" (*ibid.*, p. 11); ". . . for the best guarantee the nation can have, for the proper application of its funds, will be found in the honor, intelligence, and abilities, of its officers" (*ibid.*, p. 12).

[51] The general pattern of organization was a guide both to the navy and to the post office. Wiltse, *op. cit.*, p. 297.

diminishing the cost. He pushed for higher pay for the staff officers. He cleared up nearly $45,000,000 of unsettled accounts and reduced an annual loss of 3 per cent of disbursements to substantially nothing.[52] He supported the reform of army rules and regulations prepared by General Winfield Scott. He pushed army posts to the Rocky Mountains and encouraged the use of steamboats for army transport. He cultivated science through officer personnel. In a series of masterly reports he instructed Congress and the American people on the role of an army in peace, on army management, and on military policy.[53]

When he retired in 1825, the General Staff subscribed to a testimonial of respect in which they declared, "The degree of perfection to which you have carried the several branches of this department, is believed to be without parallel." Calhoun acknowledged this tribute in a brief letter in which he summed up his principles of organization: "Believing that the utility of a military establishment depended much more on organization and science, than on numbers, my efforts have been directed to give to ours the best possible organization, and the highest degree of science; to which, I have endeavored to add the most exact accountability and rigid responsibility in the disbursements, as being indispensable to the morality and efficiency of the army." [54] In 1827 he wrote John Ewing Calhoun "whatever may have been the irregularity in the first instance in consequence of the previous disorder, I left it [the War Department] in the most perfect condition." [55] This was no idle boast; eight

[52] Senate Doc. 1, 18th Cong., 2d sess., p. 57 (Dec. 3, 1824); also noted in *American State Papers: Military Affairs*, II, 450 (Nov. 27, 1822).

[53] Calhoun's principal reports are found in the following citations: *American State Papers: Military Affairs*, I, 773, on the manufacture of arms; I, 779, on the reduction of the army; I, 834, on the extension and perfection of military training; II, 33, on the protection of the western frontiers; II, 75, on the Military Academy; II, 188, on the role and organization of the army in peacetime; II, 199, transmitting a system of martial law, field service, and police; II, 345, on the system of accountability; II, 698, on a national system of roads and canals for military and other purposes. This record calls to mind the concentrated activity of Alexander Hamilton in the Treasury, 1789–95.

[54] *Niles Register*, XXVIII, 37–38 (March 19, 1825).

[55] Calhoun, *Correspondence*, p. 241 (Jan. 31, 1827). This opinion was shared by Niles, who noted in his *Register* of March 27, 1824, "Judging by the various reports . . . from the war department, the order and harmony, regularity and promptitude, punctuality and responsibility, introduced by Mr. *Calhoun* in

years under Calhoun had transformed an administrative wreck to a well-managed, smooth-working, and acquisitive organization.

every branch of the service, has never been rivalled, and perhaps, cannot be excelled—and, it must be recollected, that he brought this system out of chaos."
Niles Register, XXVI, 50.

CHAPTER EIGHTEEN

West Point
and the Army Engineers

The act fixing the peacetime establishment of the army in 1802 authorized the President to organize a corps of engineers to consist of not more than twenty officers and men, to be stationed at West Point in the state of New York, and to constitute a military academy.[1] Over twenty-five years of discussion and plans thus finally came to modest fruition.[2]

European precedent had made the idea of a military academy familiar to army officers. As early as 1776 Henry Knox wrote, "We ought to have academies, in which the whole theory of the art of war should be taught." [3] The Revolutionary War was brought to an end, however, by a self-taught army drilled by French, Polish, and Prussian officers. The matter dropped from sight until Washington in 1793 raised the question in the Cabinet. Jefferson objected "that none of the specified powers given by the constn to Congress would authorize this," [4] and Washington consequently made only a very guarded allusion in his message of December 3, 1793. In his last message, however, he set out concisely the basic theory of a military academy

[1] 2 Stat. 132, secs. 26–28 (March 16, 1802).

[2] Edward S. Holden, "Origins of the United States Military Academy, 1777–1802," *The Centennial of the United States Military Academy at West Point, New York, 1802–1902* (2 vols., Washington: Government Printing Office, 1904), I, 201–22; Sidney Forman, *West Point* (New York: Columbia University Press, 1950).

[3] Quoted in James R. Jacobs, *Beginning of the U. S. Army*, p. 285.

[4] Jefferson, *Works* (Federal ed.), I, 330 (Nov. 23, 1793).

and invited Congress to provide such an institution. "However pacific the general policy of a nation may be, it ought never to be without an adequate stock of military knowledge for emergencies. . . . a thorough examination of the subject will evince that the art of war is at once comprehensive and complicated, that it demands much previous study, and that the possession of it in its most improved and perfect state is always of great moment to the security of a nation." [5] Congress remained indifferent.

The first concrete plan for a military academy came from Alexander Hamilton and was presented to Congress in 1800 by Secretary of War McHenry. "If a farmer would secure his flocks," said Hamilton, "he must go to the expense of shepherds; if preserve his crops, he must enclose his fields. . . . military science, in its various branches, ought to be cultivated with peculiar care, in proper nurseries. . . . To avoid great evils, we must either have a respectable force always ready for service, or the means of preparing such a force with certainty and expedition." [6] He proposed a *Fundamental School* to give basic instruction for all branches of the army and navy; a *School of Engineers and Artillerists;* a *School of Cavalry and Infantry;* and a *School of the Navy.* The plan, based on the French military academy, was worked out in masterly strokes, with ample provision for practical application of theoretical knowledge. Congress still remained indifferent.

By a curious turn of the wheel, it fell to Jefferson, who in 1793 had denied constitutional power to establish a military academy, to approve the legislation bringing one into existence.[7] The scale was tiny, far from the impressive institution that Hamilton had sketched. The chief army engineer became ex officio superintendent of the academy. The faculty comprised, in addition, a professor of mathematics and a professor of drawing and French. The students pored over Hutton's *Mathematics,* Enfield's *Philosophy,* Vauban's *Fortifications,* and Sheet's *Artil-*

[5] Richardson, *Messages,* I, 202–3 (Dec. 7, 1796).

[6] *American State Papers: Military Affairs,* I, 133; Jacobs, *op. cit.,* p. 294.

[7] 2 Stat. 132 (March 16, 1802). There is a good account of the early development of the academy in *American State Papers: Military Affairs,* II, 75; and in House Doc. 104, 17th Cong., 1st sess. (March 30, 1822).

lery. The cadets comprised men from the ranks, usually sons of army officers, and civilians, all appointed by the President but at first without the blessing of any minimum qualifications.[8]

The standards and accomplishments of the early academy were not impressive. Until 1817 "there was but little system or regularity." [9] The army engineers who presumably were to give instruction were often absent on detail; more advanced students had to help instruct their younger members; the civilian faculty was unstable; discipline was difficult to maintain; and the morale of the cadets was low. In 1808 Lieutenant Colonel Jonathan Williams, who had been superintendent since the foundation of the academy, urged its reorganization and removal to Washington. ". . . the military academy, as it now stands, is like a foundling," declared Williams, "barely existing among the mountains, and nurtured at a distance out of sight, and almost unknown to its legitimate parents. . . . Had it been so attached to the Government . . . as to be always with it, always in sight, and always in the way of its fostering care, it would probably have flourished, and have become an honorable and interesting appendage to the national family." [10] Williams recommended that the academy be placed under the immediate direction of the President, that it take in the junior officers of the navy and, on a tuition basis, youths who might wish for such an education. He anticipated that the latter would move into the state militia, to its great advantage. "There is nothing," he declared, "more fascinating to youth than excellence in arms. . . ."

Secretary of War Eustis was not impressed with these observations. He had no use for the professional soldier, assigned the young men at West Point to various army units, and cut off the scanty flow of cadets to the academy. On the day when Congress declared war, the Military Academy stood empty.

Congress, however, was of a different mind than Eustis, and in April 1812 authorized an expansion of the number of cadets

8 Jacobs, *op. cit.*, pp. 298–300.

9 House Doc. 104, 17th Cong., 1st sess., p. 7 (March 30, 1822).

10 *American State Papers: Military Affairs*, I, 229–30 (March 14, 1808). This dim view was echoed by Gallatin. Referring to West Point in 1810, he said: "It is now worse than none." Gallatin, *Writings*, I, 494 (Nov. 30, 1810).

to 250, enlarged the faculty, directed the course of training to include all the duties of a private, noncommissioned, and commissioned officer, and required each cadet before his appointment by the President to be "well-versed in reading, writing, and arithmetic." [11] Congress also improved the prospect of a commission by authorizing a brevet appointment for graduates as supernumerary officers with pay until a vacancy developed. An appropriation of $25,000 was made for buildings and a library.[12] The academy remained at West Point.

By the close of the War of 1812 the Military Academy had become an accepted institution and, as part of the peacetime military establishment, a new set of regulations was issued for its governance.[13] A four-year course of study was required, including a review of English, and French, Latin, and Greek (for those who had previously studied these foreign languages); *mathematics,* including logarithms, algebra, plane and solid geometry, trigonometry, and the doctrine of infinite series; *drawing,* with special reference to fortification; *philosophy,* in the sense of mechanics, physics, chemistry, electricity, and astronomy; *engineering,* with special reference to military requirements; *geography; history; ethics;* [14] and *military instruc-*

[11] The need for some prerequisites for admission was admitted ruefully in a letter from Secretary Crawford to General Joseph G. Swift, May 2, 1816. "As it appears that impositions, shameful in their nature, and great in their extent, have been practised upon the department, by the friends of cadets, improperly admitted, you are requested to forward, with the least possible delay, the names of all cadets who have not, at this time, the legal qualifications. . . . The regulation which places the letter of appointment in the hands of the academical staff, to be delivered to the Cadet, after being found by examination, qualified for admission, will it is hoped, effectually prevent the recurrence of the evil, which has been seriously felt for some time past." National Archives, War Department Records, Military Book 9, p. 1.

[12] 2 Stat. 720 (April 29, 1812). By 1826 the library contained about 4,000 volumes (*North American Review,* XXIII, 273, n.). The present plan of allotting a certain number of appointments to each member of the House of Representatives was instituted in 1843 (*Centennial of the U. S. Military Academy,* I, 227).

[13] The rules and regulations, adopted January 1, 1815, were published in *American State Papers: Military Affairs,* II, 77–80.

[14] Geography, history, and ethics were "all annexed to the office of chaplain," and in 1826 it was noted that "it does not appear that these studies are largely attended to at any time." *North American Review,* XXIII, 269. In 1826 the Board of Visitors, described below, recommended an end to studies useful merely for the "character of an accomplished citizen," that had crept into the curriculum:

tion, so arranged as to "least interfere with their other academic duties." Each professor was directed not to interfere with any other department, and was made fully responsible for his own.

The selection of cadets was an official act of the President, advised by the Secretary of War. Although minimum requirements were set up by law in 1812, cadets were admitted "without the least regard to their age or qualifications." There was some suspicion that appointments were granted usually to "the sons of the most wealthy or most influential persons in the United States." [15] The inspector general of the army frankly admitted that before 1817, "the institution was filled with students, who were more or less unfit for their situations." [16] By the mid 1820's this deficiency had been substantially remedied.

Postwar admission procedure began with a letter of application, filed in the office of the chief engineer in Washington. [17] In February or March about one hundred applicants were selected for probational appointment. In June they reported to West Point for an examination by the academic board, success in which completed probational admission. [18] In the following January they took a strict qualifying examination, at which about one fourth failed and were reported to the War Department for separation. [19]

The faculty was not authorized to separate an incompetent scholar, once past the probationary stage, but was required to

---

English grammar, geography, history, rhetoric, national law, constitutional law, and political economy. Senate Doc. 1, 19th Cong., 2d sess., p. 259 (June 24, 1826).

15 *Niles Register*, XXII, 33 (March 16, 1822). The Marine Corps suffered from the same handicap. Colonel Henderson complained in 1824 that "young men without merit, or any qualification indeed whatever for military life, file as honorable testimonials of character in the department, as the most worthy," and reported nearly half of those receiving commissions had been dismissed for worthlessness or ungentlemanly conduct. Senate Doc. 44, 18th Cong., 2d sess., p. 29 (Nov. 23, 1824).

16 House Doc. 104, 17th Cong., 1st sess., p. 7 (March 30, 1822).

17 Letter from General Alexander Macomb, inspector of the Military Academy, December 15, 1826, reprinted in *Niles Register*, XXXI, 279–80 (Dec. 30, 1826).

18 At this point nearly all were accepted. Senate Doc. 1, 19th Cong., 2d sess., p. 252 (June 24, 1826).

19 *Ibid.*, p. 253. Entrance requirements were still very low; the Board of Visitors recommended that no cadet be admitted who did not understand English grammar and geography—a sufficiently modest improvement in academic standards! *Ibid.*, p. 263.

report the case to the Secretary of War with a statement of his "general inclination, temper, and habits . . . and especially whether his propensities impel him to the profession of arms." The President then determined whether the cadet should be dismissed or retained. Book learning obviously had to compete with martial ardor in the formation of the officer corps. A summary statement issued in 1824 disclosed that from 1818 to 1823 inclusive, 555 cadets had been admitted and 314 had been discharged "or permitted to depart." [20]

The standards for selection were ingenuously described in 1828 by the Secretary of War.

. . . one of the leading considerations inducing a preference, is the claim of the applicants on the ground of public services rendered by their ancestors. I eagerly seize the opportunity of cancelling a debt of gratitude by the appointment of the descendants of those who have been thus distinguished by such services, *civil* or *military*. And although poverty, the rest being equal, has a decided preference, yet I have not thought it just or politic to confine appointments exclusively to the poor.

. . . In making selections, I have received, and treated with great respect, the recommendations of the members of Congress, as well as respectable private citizens. . . .[21]

The rule of apportionment was early in vogue. Secretary of War James Barbour merely defined prevailing practice when he stated in 1828, "I determined to appoint a cadet from every Congressional district, and two from each State. . . ." [22] He hoped also to achieve a fair distribution between the country and the populous cities, the latter having had an undue share. Hezekiah Niles recanted from his earlier charges of favoritism, agreeing that the appointment of cadets had become "fairly and liberally made." [23]

The academy came into its own after the War of 1812. Although it remained on the banks of the Hudson, it became a national institution well placed in the public eye. The new spirit in the academy was exemplified not only in the energy of

20 House Doc. 111, 18th Cong., 1st sess., p. 8 (Jan. 31, 1824).
21 House Doc. 167, 20th Cong., 1st sess., pp. 3–4 (Feb. 28, 1828).
22 *Ibid.*, p. 3.
23 *Niles Register*, XXX, 334 (July 8, 1826).

Major Sylvanus Thayer, appointed superintendent in 1817, but also by the unfailing support it received from Calhoun. His general views were expressed in a report to the House of Representatives in 1820.

. . . It ought never to be forgotten that the military science, in the present condition of the world, cannot be neglected with impunity. It has become so complicated and extensive as to require for its acquisition extensive means, and much time to be exclusively devoted to it. It can only flourish under the patronage of the Government, and without such patronage it must be almost wholly neglected.[24]

A Board of Visitors was authorized by the rules and regulations of 1815, and made its first report in 1817. The Board consisted of "five gentlemen versed in military and other science," the superintendent being chairman, and was required to make two reports annually of the actual state and progress of the institution. According to the rules of 1815 each cadet was examined orally twice a year before his professors, the Board of Visitors, "and such other literary gentlemen as may be invited to attend." [25]

By 1826 a scheme of competition was introduced into the method of instruction which was warmly approved by the Board of Visitors. Each class was divided into sections "according to the talents, previous acquirements, and ambition of the cadets." After the semiannual examination the cadets took their seats in order of merit, including "general conduct." It was supposed that, as a result, every one who aspired to distinction would be led to vigilance over his daily deportment. Report on the best and most deficient cadet in each section was sent weekly to Washington. Two successive failures at the examinations resulted in dismissal. The Board of Visitors expressed public gratitude to the superintendent and staff "for having introduced so powerful, yet so simple an instrument of emulation and discipline. . . ." [26]

By the middle 1820's the Board of Visitors was regularly mak-

[24] *American State Papers: Military Affairs*, II, 76 (Feb. 23, 1820).

[25] *Ibid.*, II, 77; the number on the Board of Visitors was later increased by adding more civilians.

[26] *North American Review*, XXIII, 272–73.

ing complimentary reports on West Point. In 1826 the Board declared, "the country has great reason for congratulation in the condition and management of its Military Academy." [27] In 1827 the Board expressed its unfeigned satisfaction: "The Military Academy of West Point is now invested with a reputation worthy of the times and of the Republic. . . ." [28] In 1828 the Board found: "The moral discipline of the institution is perfect; the avenues to vice are closed, and the temptations to dissipation seem to have been vigilantly guarded against." [29] This happy situation seems, however, to have tried the faculty to the utmost, for the Board report of 1829 asserted that "to keep the Cadet, in all things, and at all times, to his duties, is a task which admits of no relaxation, is never agreeable, and frequently becomes odious." It was so odious, indeed, that officers would neither seek such employment or remain in it longer than they were obliged.[30]

The school, however, was making a favorable impression on the public mind. In the *North American Review* of October 1826 we read: "It is scarcely possible for any troops to attain the power of manoeuvring with greater precision. . . . The institution has acquired a wide and honorable reputation, and is deservedly in favor both with the people and the government." [31]

The value of West Point to the army soon inspired plans for a second institution to provide practical training at a postgraduate level, particularly for the artillery. Calhoun raised the issue in 1819 and repeated his recommendation in 1820.[32] General Jesup declared in 1823: "Without such an establishment, uniformity of discipline cannot be expected; nor can the Government be sufficiently acquainted with the character, capacity, and attainments, of its officers. . . ." [33] In 1824 Calhoun ordered

[27] Senate Doc. 1, 19th Cong., 2d sess., p. 264 (June 24, 1826).

[28] Senate Doc. 1, 20th Cong., 1st sess., p. 75 (June 21, 1827).

[29] Senate Doc. 1, 20th Cong., 2d sess., p. 60 (June 1828).

[30] Senate Doc. 1, 21st Cong., 1st sess., p. 102 (June 1829).

[31] *North American Review*, XXIII, 271-72. In his annual report for 1828, Secretary of War Barbour wrote: "The Military Academy, it is believed, has conquered all the prejudices against it. . . ." Senate Doc. 1, 20th Cong., 2d sess., p. 19 (Nov. 24, 1828).

[32] House Doc. 88, 16th Cong., 1st sess., p. 7 (Feb. 23, 1820).

[33] Reprinted in House Doc. 124, 19th Cong., 2d sess., p. 9 (Nov. 5, 1823).

an artillery school to be established at Fortress Monroe, to
consist of ten companies of artillery assembled from different
garrisons and posts and known as the "Artillery Corps for Instruction." [34] A scheme of rotation was designed to pass the
whole artillery corps through this training school. The handicaps of its dispersion were thus in part overcome.[35] After two
years' experience General Jacob Brown discovered "results . . .
so obvious and salutary" as to remove all doubts of the utility
of the new institution.

However feeble the initial contribution of the Military
Academy may have been, its establishment was of the greatest
symbolic value. It was premised, however uncertainly, on the
concept of the military service as a career. The academy was a
recognition of the fact that the military art was not the job
of an amateur but one that required training and experience
for its proper performance. The government accepted responsibility for training its own servants, the first instance of this
kind in the United States. In the academy was laid the foundation for the first organized professional body in the public service, the precursor of an essential element in the expanding functions of government during the middle and latter part of the
nineteenth century. The institution reflected the philosophy of
military preparation that Hamilton had put in words in 1800.

The art of war, which gives to a small force the faculty to combat
with advantage superior numbers, *indifferently instructed,* is subjected to mechanical, geometrical, moral, and physical rules; it calls
for profound study; its theory is immense; the details infinite; and
its principles rendered useful only by a happy adaptation of them
to all the circumstances of place and ground, variously combined,
to which they may be applicable.[36]

From the academy came many of the officers who led American forces in the Mexican War of 1846, and many of the officers who fought on both sides of the War between the States.
It was truly ironic that this institution was brought into being
by the signature of Thomas Jefferson, who hated war, loved

[34] *Ibid.,* pp. 7–8 (April 5, 1824).
[35] *American State Papers: Military Affairs,* II, 699.
[36] *Ibid.,* I, 142 (Jan. 31, 1800).

peace, and had denied the constitutional power of the federal government to create such an agency.

THE ARMY CORPS OF ENGINEERS

The peacetime military establishment set up by the Republicans in 1802 was notable both for the rigor of its economy and for the authorization of the Military Academy and the corps of engineers.[37]

The army engineer officers had for their prime duty the construction of fortifications, and until 1812 this business, although on a modest scale, occupied their principal attention. A second duty was to train young engineers at West Point, but this was a much less congenial task than the construction of military works in the field. From the outset it was understood that the army engineers might also be detailed to civil public works. Hamilton, in the report submitted by McHenry in 1800, declared: "Their utility extends to almost every department of war, and every description of general officers, besides embracing whatever respects public buildings, roads, bridges, canals, and all such works of a civil nature." [38] War emergency caused the supplementary organization of a group of topographical engineers,[39] originally numbering sixteen, who were placed under the supervision of the engineer corps in 1818.

The unhappy experiences of the War of 1812 convinced Congress that systematic protection of the coast was essential to the safety of the country, and in 1816 it launched a major program for coast fortification with an appropriation of $838,000.[40] By 1829 over $8,500,000 had been appropriated to complete these military works.[41] A Board of Engineers was constituted, com-

[37] 2 Stat. 132 (March 16, 1802).

[38] *American State Papers: Military Affairs,* I, 143 (Jan. 31, 1800). An excellent account of the organization of the corps of engineers is found in *Niles Register,* XXIX, 157 (Nov. 5, 1825). The organization was identified in the legislation of 1802 as a corps of engineers, but terminology settled on engineer corps and engineer department.

[39] 2 Stat. 819 (March 3, 1813).

[40] 3 Stat. 330 (April 29, 1816). This act also appropriated $115,800 for new buildings at West Point, and $22,171 for maps, books, and instruments for the academy.

[41] See exhibit in House Doc. 75, 21st Cong., 1st sess. (March 9, 1830).

prising two high-ranking members of the corps and a navy captain, to examine the whole line of the seaboard. By 1821 this Board had substantially completed its work. It developed a national plan, embracing, as its members declared, "every naval and military consideration. . . ." [42] The coast survey, originally assigned to the Swiss scientist, Ferdinand Hassler, was transferred to the engineer corps.

The preparation of the system of fortifications absorbed the energy of the engineer corps for about six years. Actual construction commenced as rapidly as sites and surveys were settled, and from January 1, 1817, to September 30, 1824, the engineer corps had expended over $3,000,000, about 70 per cent as much as all such expenditures from 1789 to 1817, including the war years.[43] The program was closely followed in Congress and without. It served to fix favorable attention on this body of professional engineers, the more so since the works of first priority were in the neighborhood of the great population centers: Boston, New York, Baltimore, Norfolk, Charleston, Savannah, and New Orleans.[44]

New impetus was given to the engineer corps by legislation enacted in 1824 providing funds for surveys of internal improvements,[45] and by annual rivers and harbors appropriations.[46] The President was authorized to have made surveys and plans for such roads and canals as he deemed of national importance, from the point of view of commerce, defense, or the transportation of the mails. The corps of engineers was designated as the agency to do the work. A Board of Engineers for Internal Improvements was organized, comprising General Simon Bernard, Lieutenant Colonel Totten, and an eminent civil engineer in private practice, Jonathan L. Sullivan. Soon the topographical engineers, as Niles put it, were found "scattered over the in

[42] House Doc. 98, 16th Cong., 2d sess., p. 5 (Feb. 7, 1821).

[43] *American State Papers: Military Affairs*, III, 248–50 (1824).

[44] See *American State Papers: Military Affairs, passim*, for a whole series of reports on fortifications and policy.

[45] 4 Stat. 22 (April 30, 1824). The general treatment of the problems, constitutional and administrative, arising out of the program of internal improvements is found below, ch. 31.

[46] See, for example, 4 Stat. 175 (May 20, 1826).

terior of our country, finding the summit levels of our mountains, or tracking the route for vast lines of intercourse through our forests, swamps, and valleys." [47]

The Board plunged into a mass of work, based on Gallatin's plan of internal improvements submitted in 1808. It rendered its first report in 1825. The engineers had explored the country between the Potomac and Ohio Rivers, the prospective site of the Chesapeake and Ohio Canal; between the Schuylkill and Allegheny Rivers, the site of Pennsylvania's competitive route to the West; between the Delaware and Raritan, and Boston harbor and Narragansett Roads, the two northern links in Gallatin's north-south inland waterway channel; and between the Ohio River and Lake Erie. Part of this work was done in direct cooperation with the canal commissioners of Pennsylvania and New Jersey. [48] From these reports President James Monroe contemplated "results of incalculable advantage"— subject to a constitutional amendment. [49]

The report of the engineer department for 1828 presented an impressive list of works in progress. [50] Fourteen projects of fortification were passed in review, thirty-seven works of civil construction were under way, eight surveys had been made by special direction of Congress, and twenty surveys had been pushed forward at the direction of the President. In addition aid was given to two private enterprises, the Baltimore and Ohio Railroad, and the South Carolina Canal and Rail Road Company.

The shortage of engineers became severe as demands mounted for the threefold requirements of fortifications, surveys for internal improvements, and calls from state governments and private enterprise. The *North American Review* correctly stated the situation.

47 *Niles Register*, XXIX, 122 (Oct. 22, 1825).
48 House Doc. 83, 18th Cong., 2d sess., pp. 9 ff. (Feb. 3, 1825).
49 *Ibid.*, p. 3.
50 Senate Doc. 1, 20th Cong., 2d sess., pp. 39 ff. (Nov. 19, 1828). The immensity of potential construction, for the time, was revealed in a report of December 1830, showing works commenced involving the expenditure of $3,700,000; works surveyed and estimates completed, $49,300,000; and works partially surveyed, $51,200,000. House Report 77, 21st Cong., 2d sess., pp. 19–26.

The profession of a civil engineer is scarcely known among us. . . . To construct a canal, it would hardly be thought necessary now to employ a regular engineer. Digging a wide ditch, blasting rocks and laying a few short walls for locks, are things of every day's experience. . . . In the construction of roads, a proposition to employ a professed engineer would excite laughter.

. . . No school has been opened, no board of works created, no society of engineers established, nor any constant, profitable employment offered in the United States for the encouragement of this highly valuable but unaspiring profession.[51]

The prestige of the army engineers, associated with the improving quality and esteem of West Point, rose rapidly and climbed high. The engineers were visibly engaged in good works, military and civil, urgently needed in every part of the country. The only major constructive program of the federal government was that in the hands of the engineers. The Secretary of War declared in 1828, "There are, probably, no expenditures of the government which come so directly home to the interests and feelings of the great body of the people of the United States, or which are viewed with more lively and unqualified satisfaction, than those which relate to public improvement. . . ."[52] The integrity and competence of the engineers were unquestioned, and the regularity of system that Calhoun had imposed bore its proper fruit. The most signal mark of approbation was to come late in 1829 after Jackson had become President and Eaton, Secretary of War. The new Secretary wrote of the engineer corps: "Intelligent and skilful, these branches of service have been confided to them, and the fidelity of execution every where displayed, is a manifestation of their worth and value to the country. . . ."[53]

The reorganization of the War Department was in retrospect one of the major administrative contributions of the Republican period. The reconstruction was forced by circumstances, not by a theoretical attachment of Republicans to armed power. The new Republicans, to be sure, were nationalist in tone, but

[51] *North American Review*, VIII (1818–19), 13, 15.
[52] Senate Doc. 1, 20th Cong., 2d sess., p. 19 (Nov. 24, 1828).
[53] Senate Doc. 1, 21st Cong., 1st sess., p. 24 (Nov. 30, 1829).

their aspirations looked fully as much to a navy as an army, and they, too, were unable to surmount the general illusion that a militia could be an effective instrument of action.

The improvement in army organization and administration was immense. The gulf between the condition of the army as it stood in 1810 and in 1825 was as astonishing as it was gratifying. In 1810 the army had no top organization, no commander, no General Staff, neither quartermaster nor commissary nor medical corps. It was unable to enforce accountability on its agents and was miserably served by its contractors. It offered no career to young men warmed by military ardor, and no prospects to enlisted men who were drawn from elements, as one observer put it, whose removal from circulation served "to purify society."

The hasty improvisations of 1812 and 1813 began the process of reform that was institutionally completed between 1816 and 1818. The size of the standing army was tripled; a General Staff was established; its members were brought together on permanent station in Washington; the Military Academy was reinvigorated. Above all, the army was given peacetime tasks to perform in the construction of fortifications and in surveys for internal improvements that were important and prestige-making, and that furnished adequate foundations for a military career. Administrative system was introduced which clarified responsibility, made effective accountability a matter of routine, and greatly improved the service rendered by the army contractors. Men of first quality, such as Lovell in the medical department, Thayer at West Point, Jesup in the quartermaster general department, Macomb in the engineers, responded to the opportunity and themselves strengthened the new order. But the central contribution was made by a civilian, hoping that he was training himself for future executive responsibilities in the White House, John C. Calhoun.

CHAPTER NINETEEN

The Navy

The full impact of the Jeffersonians' passion for economy and for the reduction of the debt fell upon the navy. Managed by the War Department until 1798, the navy finally acquired independence of the land forces only to become the object of an economy drive launched by Gallatin in 1801—a drive that, combined with Jefferson's addiction to small gunboats as the principal naval ship, nearly wrecked the program that had been instituted by John Adams and the New England Federalists.

Neither Federalists nor Jeffersonians grasped the lesson of the naval aspects of the Revolutionary War, i.e., to secure protection against blockade required a strong naval force able to command the high seas at least in the vicinity of the American coast. The Federalists were committed to privateers and to "annoyance" of enemy vessels by swift but single ships of war. The Jeffersonians limited themselves to the means of driving enemy vessels out of American harbors, bays, and rivers if they became too audacious in raiding our shores. The gunboat was the visible symbol of this view of naval policy.

The times hardly lent themselves to such limited concepts of naval policy, justifiable only in the hope, year by year postponed, that peace and reason would return to a world rent by revolution and national conflict. The United States had recently passed through a naval quasi-war with France, and in Jefferson's administration had to maintain a fleet in the Mediterranean to quiet the Barbary powers. The danger of war with either France or Great Britain hung like a dark cloud over both Jefferson and Madison—a conflict in which sea power would clearly be vital if not decisive. But Republicans, in secure con-

trol of Congress, declined until the very eve of war materially
to strengthen the navy or the Navy Department. Indeed, the
House of Representatives in 1809 voted to authorize the President to lay up such of the naval vessels as he thought proper.[1]
Nearly a year later the House voted to reduce both the army
and the navy by an impressive vote: 77 out of about a hundred
members against the army, 63 against the navy.[2]

These views of naval policy grew out of various considerations, of which fiscal policy was one of the most important. As
soon as Jefferson was well settled in the White House, Gallatin
wrote him concerning the necessity of a great reduction in the
navy estimates.[3] In 1802 Jefferson wrote Gallatin, "It is of the
utmost importance . . . to diminish our expenses; this may be
done in the Naval Department." [4] In 1803 the Secretary of the
Treasury would have cut the slender force on the high seas in
half, leaving only one frigate and two or three small vessels.[5]

Jefferson concurred in these views, holding that not only was
a navy expensive to build but also expensive to maintain. He
asserted that either the existing ships would be entirely rotten
in six or eight years, or they would cost three or four million a
year in repairs.[6] As an old man he clung to these views, writing
to John Adams from Monticello, "Yet a navy is a very expensive
engine. . . . a nation who could count on twelve or fifteen
years of peace, would gain by burning its navy and building a
new one in time." [7]

The naval views of both Jefferson and Gallatin were also
deeply affected by their desire for peace. Jefferson feared that
collisions between naval vessels might erupt into war.[8] Gallatin
in 1798 had given voice to an eloquent and moving vision of a
happy, peaceful, and unarmed America. ". . . I had conceived,"

---

1 *Annals,* 11th Cong., 1st sess., p. 394 (June 23, 1809).

2 *Ibid.,* 11th Cong., 2d sess., p. 1879 (April 16, 1810).

3 Gallatin, *Writings,* I, 25 (March 14, 1801).

4 *Ibid.,* I, 98 (Sept. 13, 1802).

5 *Ibid.,* I, 162 (Oct. 6, 1803); cf. *ibid.,* I, 191, 234, 357.

6 Jefferson, *Works* (Federal ed.), IX, 416 (Dec. 31, 1802).

7 *Ibid.,* XII, 269 (Nov. 1, 1822). Cf. an early similar view of John Quincy
Adams, written to his father in 1811, and called by himself "political heresy."
J. Q. Adams, *Writings,* IV, 240 (Oct. 14, 1811).

8 Jefferson, *Works* (Federal ed.), XII, 270.

he told the House of Representatives, "that our distance from the European world might have prevented our being involved in the mischievous politics of Europe, and that we might have lived in peace without armies and navies and without being deeply involved in debt. . . . I had conceived it would have been our object to have become a happy and not a powerful nation, or at least no way powerful except for self-defence." [9]

Animated by these views on peace and economy, the Republicans took full advantage of an act signed by John Adams as he left Washington.[10] The Federalists had proposed to dispose of smaller vessels built by Stoddert from 1798 to 1800 and to concentrate on frigates. Even they proposed to keep only six frigates in service, seven others to be laid up in convenient ports. For naval expenditures in 1801 they appropriated just over three million dollars, including the marine corps.[11] Jefferson promptly laid up the frigates and curtailed naval expenditures at every point. Work on dry docks and shore installations was suspended, commissioned officers and seamen were laid off, purchasing agents and navy-yard employees were reduced in number. Expenditures for 1802 dropped to just under one million dollars.

The positive aspects of Jefferson's naval policy began to take shape in 1805. They were defensive in nature, and in form consisted of the building of a considerable number of gunboats designed strictly to repel marauders on the coast. They were vessels about fifty feet in length, fitted with oars as well as sails, and armed with one or two medium-sized cannon. They

[9] Henry Adams, *Life of Albert Gallatin*, pp. 218–19. These views were later summarized in *Niles Register*, XXI, 114 (Oct. 20, 1821):

"The old republican party . . . of which I had the honor to be a zealous member, generally was . . . opposed to a large naval establishment. The chief grounds of objection [were]

"1. The mighty patronage given thereby to the executive power, and the raising up of an interest that does not enter into the *common feelings* of the people at large. . . .

"2. The disposition, created by power, to enter on war. . . .

"3. The great expense of building and maintaining a navy, and supporting the officers and men. . . ."

[10] 2 Stat. 110 (March 3, 1801).

[11] 2 Stat. 122 (March 3, 1801).

cost only a few thousand dollars apiece. Congress authorized
25 in 1805, an additional 50 in 1806, and 188 in 1807.[12]

Service on the gunboats was intensely unpopular, and in no
way could supply effective training for a naval force able to sail
the high seas. The gunboat policy has been condemned by
most professional students of naval affairs, although some captains supported it at the time.[13] Jefferson made his own defense
of these vessels after he left the presidency, in the early years
of the War of 1812. Writing to Madison in favor of more gunboats for southern waters, he said:

. . . I am not unaware of the effect of the ridicule cast on this
instrument of defence by those who wished for engines of offence.
. . . I know, too, the prejudices of the gentlemen of the navy, and
that these are very natural. . . . But . . . it is impossible not to
see that all these vessels [i.e., seagoing ships] must be taken and
added to the already overwhelming force of our enemy; that even
while we keep them, they contribute nothing to our defence, and
that so far as we are to be defended by anything on the water, it
must be by such vessels as can assail under advantageous circumstances, and under adverse ones withdraw from the reach of the
enemy. This, in shoally waters, is the humble, the ridiculed, but
the formidable gun-boats.[14]

12 Harold and Margaret Sprout, *The Rise of American Naval Power, 1776–1918*
(Princeton: Princeton University Press, 1939), p. 58. A useful compilation of
naval laws was published in 1826 with the title, *Laws of the United States in
Relation to the Naval Establishment, and the Marine Corps* . . . (Washington:
Davis and Force, 1826). The work by Dudley W. Knox, *A History of the United
States Navy* (New York: G. P. Putnam's Sons, 1936), is principally concerned
with naval events and their relation to political affairs. Naval administration
has been studied by Charles Oscar Paullin. The basic bibliographical and reference work is Robert Wilden Neeser, *Statistical and Chronological History of the
United States Navy, 1775–1907* (2 vols., New York: Macmillan Company, 1909).

13 At the very moment that the Republicans embarked upon the gunboat
policy, both Gallatin and Jefferson were facing the probability—if not the desirability—of a seagoing navy. Cf. Gallatin, *Writings*, I, 252–53 (Sept. 12, 1805).
In 1806 Jefferson wrote his Salem merchant-friend, Jacob Crowninshield: "But
the building some ships of the line instead of our most indifferent frigates is not
to be lost sight of. That we should have a squadron properly composed to prevent the blockading our ports is indispensable. The Atlantic frontier from
numbers, wealth, & exposure to potent enemies have a proportionate right to
be defended with the Western frontier, for whom we keep up 3,000 men."
Jefferson, *Works* (Federal ed.), X, 267 (May 13, 1806).

14 *Ibid.*, XI, 288–89 (May 21, 1813). For Admiral A. T. Mahan's estimate of
Jefferson's naval policy, see his *Sea Power in Its Relations to the War of 1812*
(2 vols., Boston: Little, Brown, 1905), I, 291.

The act for the gradual increase of the navy in 1816 marked the culmination of the drift away from the early small-navy views of Jefferson and his advisers.[15] Congress authorized the construction of nine 74's, twelve 44's or better, and three steam batteries, and appropriated one million dollars for each of the next eight years for this purpose. This act was, in the view of John Quincy Adams, "the introduction of a system to act upon the character and history of our country for an indefinite series of ages. It was a declaration of that Congress to their constituents and to posterity that it was the destiny and duty of these confederated states to become in regular process of time and by no petty advances a great naval power."[16] Truly these were prophetic words.

ORGANIZATION

The administrative organization of the Navy Department and its shore facilities were inevitably neglected before 1812 as a necessary consequence of Republican thrift. The civilian branch of the department consisted of the Secretary and his office, and the accountant and his clerks. Secretary Robert Smith (1801–1809) managed with three clerks during most of his term;[17] the accountant before the War of 1812 had less than ten. The Secretary had no professional aides or advisers in his office; he was the department; whatever had to be authorized or done, he authorized and did. To him reported the civilian superintendents or naval commandants of six navy yards, as well as a fluctuating and widely scattered number of navy agents. Each ship was usually an independent unit, its commander re-

[15] 3 Stat. 321 (April 29, 1816).
[16] Richardson, *Messages*, II, 362 (Dec. 5, 1826).
[17] The Jeffersonian Secretaries of the Navy were Robert Smith, a Baltimore merchant with good political connections who was Jefferson's fifth choice (1801–1809); Paul Hamilton, a South Carolina planter who knew little of naval affairs and who was induced to resign on the eve of the War of 1812 (1809–1812); William Jones of Philadelphia, a merchant who knew the sea and ships and who had ideas about organization and management (1813–1814); Benjamin W. Crowninshield of Salem, Massachusetts, a merchant who finished out Madison's administration and carried over into Monroe's (1815–1818); Smith Thompson of New York, a lawyer who served until his appointment to the Supreme Court in 1823; and Samuel L. Southard of New Jersey, perhaps the ablest of the group, who was appointed by Monroe and carried through by John Quincy Adams. Further notice of some of these men is found in the text.

ceiving orders directly from the Secretary. Financial affairs of the ship were in the hands of pursers, appointed by the President with the consent of the Senate, officials who by reason of frequent long absences were difficult to control. The system was as simple and as embryonic as could well have been imagined. When faced with the emergency of war, it proved as inefficient as would have been expected.[18]

Given the naval policy that the Republicans proclaimed, it is no wonder that Jefferson had much trouble in persuading anyone to become Secretary of the Navy. He first offered the post to Robert R. Livingston of New York. Upon his declination, Jefferson next invited General Samuel Smith of Baltimore. The basis of his invitation is of interest. "You will bring us," he wrote Smith, "the benefit of adding in a considerable degree the acquiescence at least of the leaders who have hitherto opposed. Your geographical situation too is peculiarly advantageous. . . . But what renders it a matter not only of desire to us, but permit me to say, of moral duty in you, is that if you refuse where are we to find a substitute?" [19]

Smith nevertheless declined and Jefferson turned next to John Langdon of New Hampshire. Langdon declined; so did William Jones of Philadelphia. Jefferson then prevailed on General Smith to perform the duties of the office unofficially, while Henry Dearborn was made Acting Secretary. Smith was a member of the House and feared to lose his seat if he accepted either an official commission or salary. Early in May Jefferson wrote Gouverneur Morris, "I believe I shall have to advertise for a Secretary of the Navy." [20] In June the vacant post was again offered to Langdon, in vain. Finally Jefferson accepted Robert Smith, brother of Samuel Smith.[21] The new Secretary was a

18 By 1826 the central office had expanded to include seven clerks, in addition to those employed by the Board of Navy Commissioners, numbering six. The office of accountant had been transferred to the Treasury. By this time the volume of communications was considerable, involving dealings with "three squadrons abroad, five extensive building establishments, five recruiting stations, about eight hundred officers, and many hundred pensioners. . . ." House Report 232, 19th Cong., 1st sess., p. 14 (Jan. 21, 1826).

19 Jefferson, *Works* (Federal ed.), IX, 207–8 (March 9, 1801).

20 *Ibid.*, IX, 251 (May 8, 1801).

21 For Monroe's corresponding difficulty in getting a Secretary of War, see Wiltse, *John C. Calhoun: Nationalist,* pp. 138–39.

Princeton graduate, a lawyer by profession and active in public affairs, having served several terms in the Maryland legislature. Henry Adams characterized him as a "Baltimore gentleman, easy and cordial, glad to oblige and fond of power and show, popular in the navy, yielding in the Cabinet, but as little fitted as Jefferson himself for the task of administering with severe economy an unpopular service." [22] His differences with Gallatin have already been noted. Smith dealt with routine and with details; Jefferson and Gallatin with policy and finance.[23]

Madison introduced his own Secretary of the Navy, Paul Hamilton of South Carolina. Hamilton was a planter, with no special knowledge of naval affairs, who instructed his chief clerk to observe a wholesome economy, to "watch well the behaviour of our officers; attend also to the Navy Yard at Washington; 'tis a sink of all that needs correction . . . ; I have only to add my firm persuasion that you will do your duty for your own sake and our Country's. . . ." [24] He proved unfit for the administration of the department in time of crisis and resigned on December 31, 1812. He was succeeded by William Jones, whom Jefferson had sought in vain to accept the office in 1801.

A native of Philadelphia, Jones fought both on land and sea in the Revolutionary War. After some years spent in Charleston, where his social success exceeded his commercial fortunes, he returned to Philadelphia and engaged in the China trade. He was an ardent advocate of war with Great Britain and became Secretary of the Navy in January, 1813. With great

[22] Adams, *History of the United States*, I, 222. John Randolph held Smith in contempt. In 1807 he called at the navy office for information on the estimates. "I propounded a question to the head of the department; he turned to the clerk like a boy who cannot say his lesson, and with imploring countenance beseeches aid. . . . This pantomime was repeated at every new item, until, disgusted, and ashamed for the degraded situation of the principal, I took leave. . . . There was not one single question relating to the department that the Secretary could answer." Adams, *John Randolph*, pp. 208–9. For a more sympathetic view, see Charles C. Tansill, "Robert Smith," in Samuel Flagg Bemis, ed., *The American Secretaries of State and Their Diplomacy*, III, 151–97; and George E. Davies, "Robert Smith and the Navy," *Maryland Historical Magazine*, XIV (1919), 305–22.

[23] Charles Oscar Paullin, "Naval Administration under Secretaries of the Navy Smith, Hamilton and Jones, 1801–1814," *Proceedings of the United States Naval Institute*, XXXII (1906), 1289–1328 at 1300.

[24] *Ibid.*, p. 1307.

energy he took on almost every detail of provisioning, supplying, arming, manning, and giving strategic direction to the naval forces. In his later years Madison praised Jones highly. "I do not hesitate," he wrote, "to pronounce him the fittest Minister who had ever been charged with the Navy Department. With a strong mind, well stored with the requisite knowledge, he possessed great energy of character and indefatigable application to business." [25] Jones had an inventive and innovating mind; to him we owe the first major proposal on Navy Department organization.[26]

NAVY DEPARTMENT REORGANIZATION

The impact of war on the Navy Department revealed its administrative inadequacy, contrasting with the brilliant exploits of individual commanders. These victories caused a profound reversal of public sentiment concerning the navy. A resurgent nationalism bore the navy high into public favor. The tone of postwar opinion is reflected in the exuberance of John M. Niles: "The enterprise, activity, skill, bravery and success of the infant navy of the United States, was without any example, and the naval events of the war, without [sic] scarcely an exception, were not only highly creditable to the skill and courage of American seamen, but reflected the greatest honour upon the national character." [27] Even President Monroe, an eye witness to the sack of Washington, could tell Congress in 1824, "Our armies and Navy signalized themselves in every quarter where they had occasion to meet their gallant foe. . . ." [28] Republicans and Federalists united in determination to create a powerful navy.

It is difficult, indeed, to appreciate the change in Republican attitude on the subject of the navy even in the first three years of Madison's administration. The President certainly was not re-

25 *Letters and Other Writings of James Madison* (4 vols., published by order of Congress, Philadelphia: J. B. Lippincott, 1865), III, 563 (Feb. 1827).
26 See Kenneth L. Brown, "Mr. Madison's Secretary of the Navy," *United States Naval Institute Proceedings*, LXXIII (1947), 967–75, for an account of Secretary Jones' activities.
27 John M. Niles, *The Life of Oliver Hazard Perry* (2d ed., Hartford: Oliver D. Cooke, 1821), p. 61.
28 Richardson, *Messages*, II, 223 (Jan. 30, 1824).

sponsible, for he took no leadership in the matter. Federalists must have rubbed their eyes in 1812 when a Republican House Committee on Naval Policy, advocating a naval program for ships of the line of 88 guns and frigates of 52 and 42, used this language:

. . . it is with something like exultation, as republicans, that they present a species of national force that, whilst it will best subserve the national defence, can operate least on the national liberty. It is a bright attribute in the history of the tar, that he has never destroyed the rights of the nation. . . . Thus aided by economy, and fortified by republican principle, your committee think they ought strongly to recommend that the fostering care of the nation be extended to the naval establishment.[29]

The movement for reform and reorganization began in 1813 when Secretary Jones asked for a naval purveyor to relieve him of the load of details that, as he said, diverted his attention from "the great and efficient objects of the establishment." [30] The conduct of the War of 1812 and the opposition of congressional economizers prevented the elaboration of Secretary Jones' proposals until 1814. At the direction of the Senate he then presented a major program of reorganization, the object of which was "to provide a practical, efficient, and economical system, with as much individual and collective responsibility as may be attainable. . . ." [31] Since the plan furnished the basis for the reorganization of 1815, and occasioned a revealing discussion of administrative principles by the navy captains, it will be useful to identify its principal features.

From the professional point of view this report was an extraordinary document, certainly the most significant that had come from the department since its foundation. Strategically Jones recognized the error of both Federalist and Jeffersonian theories, and advocated the concentration of naval power in fleets of ships of the line. Such a concentration, Jones argued, would free our waters from invasion and our coast from blockade; paralyze enemy efforts on the North American continent;

29 *American State Papers: Naval Affairs*, I, 276 (Nov. 27, 1812). A year before Langdon Cheves of South Carolina had begun to instruct the House. *Ibid.*, I, 247.
30 *Ibid.*, I, 285 (Feb. 2, 1813).
31 *Ibid.*, I, 320–24 (Nov. 15, 1814).

make unnecessary a vast military establishment; and eliminate the need of repeated and irregular calls on the militia to repel enemy raids. This kind of a navy, he urged, would be both cheap and efficient, if "cherished by a well digested, energetic, and liberal system."

The system proposed by the Secretary of the Navy was based on the doctrine of standardization in the construction and equipment of ships—"the most important branch in the civil administration" of the navy's affairs. In a passage of very modern connotation, Jones advocated the doctrine of standardization and interchangeability of parts, a program already well advanced. He declared, "This strict similarity should be carefully preserved, upon every principle of convenience, economy, and efficiency." [32] He urged, with his predecessors, the collection of timber and the maintenance of dockyards, foundries, smitheries, and armories. He advocated a permanent career service. "If we examine . . . the nature, extent, and importance, of the objects involved in the administration of naval affairs . . . we may learn to appreciate . . . the life of study, observation, and experience, required to arrive even at moderate attainments in a science which . . . is the most complicated, critical, and interesting, that has ever engaged the attention or influenced the destinies of nations." He consequently recommended a naval academy.[33]

To ensure an adequate force of seamen, he cautiously recommended compulsory naval service to supplement voluntary enlistments. "In my view there would be nothing incompatible with the free spirit of our institutions, or with the rights of individuals, if registers, with a particular descriptive record, were kept in the several districts, of all the seamen belonging to the United States, and provision made by law for classing and calling into the public service, in succession, for reasonable stated periods, such portions or classes as the public service might require. . . ."

The administrative structure of the department was boldly reconstructed in Jones' recommendations. ". . . the executive branch . . . should be conducted by persons of enlarged views,

32 *Ibid.*, I, 321.
33 *Ibid.*, I, 322, 323.

collectively combining all the practical knowledge, and professional intelligence, which these important diversified, and comprehensive subjects, obviously require." [34] To secure such management, the Secretary of the Navy proposed a board of inspectors—three naval officers and two persons skilled in naval affairs —to be appointed by the President and confirmed by the Senate. To the board would be delegated "the general superintendence and direction of the affairs of the navy, under the instructions from, and powers delegated by, the President of the United States, and authority over all the officers, agents, and persons, employed under the Navy Department. . . ." It was to report to the Secretary matters for improvement of the navy; to prepare estimates; to make contracts and purchases; to give instructions to superintendents of naval districts; and to prepare comprehensive regulations on all aspects of naval administration for the approval of the President.[35]

The proposed board of inspectors and its relation to the Secretary became the principal matters of discussion. The Senate Committee on Naval Affairs sent Jones' report to each of the naval captains for their views and comments.[36] Replies were exceedingly interesting. Substantially all opposed any but naval officers on the board, which in their opinion should be reduced to three. Most objected to the assignment of particular duties to members of the board and favored collective responsibility. Most implied or stated explicitly their lack of confidence in the civilian Secretary; "it might happen," said Captain Bainbridge, "that the Secretary of the Navy would not be a nautical character." [37]

The establishment of a navy board with a broad delegation of authority was naturally approved by the captains. The relations of such a board to the Secretary of the Navy, however, puzzled them. Four combined in a recommendation that the

34 *Ibid.,* I, 322.

35 *Ibid.,* I, 323.

36 The House Committee on Naval Affairs found three basic causes of abuses in naval affairs: (1) the excessive and laborious duties of the Secretary; (2) the irresponsibility of subordinate agents; and (3) the great latitude allowed commanders in altering, repairing, and furnishing their ships. *Ibid.,* I, 354 (Jan. 9, 1815).

37 *Ibid.,* I, 355.

Secretary serve as presiding officer, and the members as his counselors, while also exercising the powers proposed to be delegated to them.[38] Captain Evans, observing that not much was left to occupy the time of the Secretary, flatly recommended the abolition of the office and the control of the Navy Department by a board dominated by naval officers.

Upon the whole, it is my opinion that the duties and powers of the Secretary of the Navy, as they now exist, and all the duties and powers that it is necessary should be invested in a Navy Department, would be most advantageously settled in a board, to consist of five members and a secretary; one to be selected by the President, for his abilities as a statesman, who should preside at the board, and the remaining four to be selected by the same authority, from the officers of the Navy.[39]

The idea of replacing the civilian Secretary with a professional board was apparently much in the air. A few years later Madison, then in retirement, approved such a plan and gave President Monroe his views. Monroe did not, however, concur, and would not even give an appointment as Acting Secretary to a man in naval uniform.[40]

The reform legislation of 1815 established a Board of Navy Commissioners, consisting of three officers not below the rank of post captain and appointed by the President with senatorial confirmation. The Board was attached to the office of the Secretary of the Navy and, under his superintendence, discharged "all the ministerial duties of said office, relative to the procurement of naval stores and materials, and the construction, armament, equipment, and employment, of vessels of war, as well as all other matters connected with the naval establishment of the United States." The Board, with the consent of the Secretary, was authorized to prepare regulations for presidential approval to secure uniformity in the construction and equipment of vessels and responsibility of subordinate agents, and to prepare the annual estimates. Congress required the Board's rules

[38] *Ibid.*, I, 356.

[39] *Ibid.*, I, 357.

[40] Adams, *Memoirs*, IV, 133 (Oct. 15, 1818). Monroe offered Commodore John Rodgers the secretaryship on condition of resigning as chairman of the Board of Navy Commissioners, but Rodgers declined. *Ibid.*, IV, 141, 144.

and regulations to be laid before it. The act concluded by declaring that "nothing in this act shall be construed to take from the Secretary of the Navy his control and direction of the naval forces of the United States, as now by law possessed." [41]

It may be argued that this was a better balance than that suggested by Secretary Jones or that desired by the navy captains. Its terms were sufficiently ambiguous, however, to cause immediate disagreement on the respective authority of Secretary and Board, finally requiring the intervention of the President.

Madison appointed as first members of the Board Captains John Rodgers, Isaac Hull, and David Porter, Rodgers presiding by virtue of seniority. The Board, as a matter of right, at once requested the Secretary of the Navy, Crowninshield, to communicate to it "the destination of a squadron." Crowninshield refused. The claim of the Board amounted to the assertion of the right to control the movements of the fleet and the personnel of the navy.[42] After a sharp exchange of letters the matter was laid before Madison, who, with his customary clarity, defined the respective functions of each party.

The Navy Board, he observed, was attached to the office of the Secretary of the Navy, the "regular organ of the President" for dealing with navy business. The Board had no independent power but was subject to the superintendence of the Secretary. At the same time, the Secretary could employ no other agency for the discharge of the functions allotted to the Board. Madison concluded with a delicate emphasis on the "candor, cordiality, and confidence, which distinguish those whom the law associates . . . I flatter myself that the law will go into its due effect with the advantages to the public service for which it was enacted." [43]

41 3 Stat. 202 (Feb. 7, 1815).

42 Charles Oscar Paullin, "Naval Administration under the Navy Commissioners, 1815–1842," *Proceedings of the United States Naval Institute*, XXXIII (1907), 609–10. Dallas' comments to President Madison are of some interest. "The occurrence was anticipated, and stated to Mr. Jones when he showed me his plan. It appears to me a plain case in favor of the Secretary of the Navy; but a case of some delicacy. The style of the Board was improper, even if their claims were correct." Dallas, *Life and Writings*, p. 426 (May 20, 1815).

43 Madison to Crowninshield, June 12, 1815, Madison, *Letters* (Congressional ed.), II, 604–6; cf. Madison to Dallas, May 30, 1815, Dallas, *Life and Writings*, p. 431.

This appeal to candor, backed by a clear declaration of presidential understanding of relative powers and duties, apparently had its desired effect. The history of Board relationships with successive Secretaries appears to have been smooth, on the whole, down to the termination of the Board in 1842.[44]

The actual powers of the Board of Navy Commissioners were restricted to the supply of the navy; the building, repairing, and equipping of ships; and the superintendence of navy yards, naval stations, and dry docks. The Secretary of the Navy retained control of appointments and detail of officers, the movement of ships, and the discipline of personnel. Naval policy remained in the hands of the civilian Secretary.

While the Board of Navy Commissioners relieved the Secretary of the Navy of one class of detail, it left in his hands the direct performance of a mass of business concerning naval personnel and the movement of ships. The flow of letters from the Secretary of the Navy to ship captains and commandants of navy yards reveals an astonishing volume of detail that the head of the department continued to perform himself.[45]

The content of typical letters written by captains to the Secretary in 1820 suggests the kind of matter that he dealt with. Captain Isaac Hull, commandant at the Charlestown Navy Yard, asked approval of the transfer of Lieutenant William Berry to Portsmouth. The commander of the station at Whitehall on Lake Champlain reported the death of a gunner, "an assiduous and a worthy man." Captain Samuel Angus reported that the navy agent at New York was out of funds and would be obliged to stop recruiting. Lieutenant Commander Rousseau reported the capture of a privateer; Captain Sinclair reported the desertion of a sailor; Captain Downes reported that he loaned some cordage to the brig *Macedonian*.[46]

On his side the Secretary of the Navy engaged in a varied

[44] Paullin, "Naval Administration under the Navy Commissioners," *op. cit.*, XXXIII, 610–11.

[45] Manuscript letter books in the National Archives. For letters from captains to the Secretary, a series of volumes entitled "Captains' Letters"; for letters from the Secretary to the captains, a series marked "Officers of Ships of War," with appropriate dates.

[46] Navy Department: Captains' Letters, 1820, Volume I, *passim.*

course of letters to the captains. He ordered Captain Shaw to open a rendezvous at the Charlestown Navy Yard to recruit one hundred seamen. He asked Lieutenant Conklin to explain an unsettled account. He directed Dr. Cutbush to receive a seaman in the Naval Hospital. He dispatched a sum of money by Commander Bainbridge to the United States vice consul at Genoa. He assured Lieutenant Finch that every attention would be given to his claim for promotion. He congratulated Lieutenant Commander Stockton of the U.S. ship *Erie* on his safe arrival at New York "at this boisterous season." He authorized pursers to carry in stock for officers' purchase razor strops, suspenders, buttons, looking glasses, and tape.[47] On February 18, 1820, he wrote Bainbridge:

The friends of Jacob Deakeyne, a Marine on board the U. S. Ship Guerriere in the Mediterranean, being very respectable and anxious that he should be discharged . . . ; with a view to their gratification, I have to request, that you will on assuming the command of the Squadron in that Sea, send the said Individual home in the first public vessel that may be returning to the United States.[48]

Before Jackson's administration only one suggestion was made to alter the Navy Board. It was a proposal brought forward in 1820 to make the Secretary of the Navy the presiding officer of the Board. The effect of this arrangement would have been to destroy the independent power of decision of the Secretary and to make him the prisoner of his professional colleagues. The House committee, to whom the matter was referred, perceived this tendency and declined to endorse it. The members reported:

The committee are not advised whether the resolution contemplates the Secretary to be a constituent part of the Board, and at the same time possessed of the control and superintendence of its proceedings, or merely the presiding officer, with a casting vote. In the latter case, the benefit to be derived from the superintendence of one officer over others, under distinct responsibilities, as well as the circumspection naturally resulting from such responsibility,

47 Navy Department: Officers of Ships of War, Volume XIII, *passim.*
48 *Ibid.*, XIII, 458.

would be entirely lost. In the former case, the Commissioners would be little more than advisory, and, in that proportion, bereft of responsibility.[49]

The success and value of the Board were considerable in its day. It brought the best available professional advice to the Secretary of the Navy. It relieved him in part of a heavy and increasing burden of daily routine. It was an early solution of the general problem of administrative devolution, of which the second stage in the Navy Department was the bureau system introduced in 1842. The Navy Board gave an immediate impulse and new energy to naval business.[50] It had the disadvantages of all operating commissions, and lacked adequate means for securing rotation of membership. Paullin summarized its virtues and limitations.

As an administrative organ the Board of Navy Commissioners was moderately successful. It displayed both the good and bad qualities of a plural-headed executive. Its acts were conservative and deliberate. The principles and information upon which it acted were well-considered. Its advice to the Secretary of the Navy when drawn from its professional knowledge was valuable and judicious. As its members were not specially trained in the art of shipbuilding, it sometimes blundered in naval construction. Its work often lacked expedition. Since each member had to reach a decision on all questions presented to it, it was sometimes slow in reaching a conclusion. When its members failed to agree, it gave forth discordant advice. Unfortunately, many of the problems that the board by reason of its professional information was best able to solve did not fall to it, but to the Secretary of the Navy.[51]

Hezekiah Niles gave an informed, if nonprofessional contemporary view: "There is no establishment appertaining to the government of more practical utility . . . than the board of navy commissioners—for it is composed of *practical* men who know 'all about' the matters over which they have a controul. . . ."[52]

---

[49] *American State Papers: Naval Affairs*, I, 675 (May 1, 1820).

[50] See MS. in National Archives, Navy Commissioners Office, Letters to the Secretary of the Navy, No. I, *passim*, for an obvious record of energy and dispatch.

[51] Paullin, "Naval Administration under the Navy Commissioners," *op. cit.*, XXXIII, 641.

[52] *Niles Register*, XX, 103 (April 24, 1821).

NAVAL PERSONALITIES

Before turning to an account of the shore establishment we may pause to note a few men who played a prominent part in naval administration. Adams' Secretary of the Navy, Samuel L. Southard, was a Jerseyman, son of a Congressman, a graduate of Princeton, and a lawyer by profession.[53] From 1815 to 1820 he was an associate justice of the New Jersey Supreme Court. In 1821 he was appointed to a vacancy in the United States Senate and from there came to the Navy Department in 1823, by appointment of his old friend, James Monroe. He served as Secretary of the Navy until the inauguration of Jackson, became governor of New Jersey in 1832, and was elected to the United States Senate in 1832 and 1838, serving from 1833 to 1842, the year of his death.

Southard was a vigorous and effective Secretary. He pushed forward the construction of navy hospitals and rescued the navy hospital fund from a quarter century of worse than neglect. He advocated a thorough survey of the whole coast of the United States, a naval criminal code, improvement in navy officer rank, the reorganization of the marine corps, and the establishment of a regular line of communication from Washington to the Pacific across the Panama Canal. His state papers were crisp and courageous.[54] He sought in vain, with his predecessors, to establish a naval academy.

Continuity in the management of naval affairs was supplied by Charles Washington Goldsborough who, with the exception of two years (1813–1814), served the department from its establishment in 1798 to 1843. Goldsborough was a member of a distinguished Federalist family of Maryland. His cousin, Charles Goldsborough, the last Federalist governor of Maryland (1818–1819), had served as a Federalist member of Congress from 1804 to 1817. Charles Washington Goldsborough was first appointed to the department by his fellow Marylander, Benjamin

---

53 There is a sketch of Southard in Lucius Q. C. Elmer, *The Constitution and Government of the Province and State of New Jersey. . . .* (Collections of the New Jersey Historical Society, Vol. VII, 1872), 201–34.

54 See, for example, the reports on the hospital fund cited below in ch. 20 and his report to John Quincy Adams in 1825. Senate Doc. 2, 19th Cong., 1st sess., pp. 93 ff. (Dec. 2, 1825).

Stoddert, was continued as a clerk under Jefferson, and in 1802 became chief clerk, retiring from this position in 1843. Paullin described him as one of the most important officials of the department.

To Goldsborough we owe what is perhaps the first professional publication by a member of the permanent civil service, *The United States Naval Chronicle,* a volume of over four hundred pages published in 1824.[55] One of his sons, Louis M. Goldsborough, entered the navy and rose to the rank of rear admiral, commanding the Atlantic Blockading Squadron in the early years of the Civil War.[56] Another son, John Rodgers Goldsborough, attained the rank of commodore, U.S. Navy.[57]

The quality of naval administration was much affected by the attitude and experience of the members of the Board of Navy Commissioners, high-ranking "sea dogs," for the time being housed on land. They were an able group, proud individualists, jealous of rank and position, and whether on land or sea accustomed to command and obedience. One of the best known was Captain John Rodgers, whose character and personality were put in heroic terms by Senator Benton.

. . . He was to me the complete impersonation of my idea of the perfect naval commander—person, mind, and manners; with the qualities for command grafted on the groundwork of a good citizen and good father of a family; and all lodged in a frame to bespeak the seaman and the officer.

His very figure and face were those of the naval hero. . . . His person was of the middle height, stout, square, solid, compact; well-proportioned; and combining in the perfect degree the idea of strength and endurance with the reality of manly comeliness— the statue of Mars, in the rough state, before the conscious chisel had lent the last polish.[58]

Paullin described the type of naval officer upon whom the duties of administration were to fall after 1815 in a passage

[55] Charles W. Goldsborough, *The United States Naval Chronicle* (Washington: James Wilson, 1824).

[56] *Dictionary of American Biography,* VII, 365–66.

[57] *Appleton's Cyclopaedia of American Biography,* II, 673.

[58] Thomas Hart Benton, *Thirty Years' View,* II, 144; see also Charles Oscar Paullin, *Commodore John Rodgers* (Cleveland: Arthur H. Clark, 1910).

which would doubtless require some modification to portray the off-ship personality of the early naval commander.

The typical commodore of the Old Navy was a law unto himself. He was a most austere and august personage, bluff, proud, pompous, reserved, and self-willed. "The little tyrant," Commodore David Porter called him, "who struts his few fathoms of scoured plank." Wrapped up in his own notions of dignity, he associated but little with his officers, a "solitary being in the midst of the ocean." [59]

These were the men who were to build and sail a navy sufficient to place the United States securely among the naval powers.

[59] Paullin, "Naval Administration under the Navy Commissioners," *op. cit.*, XXXIII, 629.

CHAPTER TWENTY

The Navy Ashore

The mission of a navy is performed on the high seas, but its management is carried out for the most part ashore. Even the tiny force allowed by Jefferson and Gallatin required an embryonic shore establishment concentrated at the navy yards and revolving about the superintendents of yards and the navy agents.

The demand for economy and the hope for peace during the first decade of the century had their effect upon the shore establishment as well as on the size of the navy afloat. The supporting shore organization was "sadly defective." All the navy-yard facilities had deteriorated under ten years' neglect. The navy had not a single dry dock and had to clean and repair hulls by the slow and expensive process of heaving down. Timber stocks were depleted and stores were inadequate.[1] "In the winter of 1811–1812," Paullin concluded, "on the eve of the war with Great Britain, the Navy Department was unprepared in every essential means, instrument, and material of naval warfare." [2]

One element of the shore establishment ardently desired by the Navy Department was sought in vain, an academy corresponding to West Point. Secretary Jones proposed a naval academy in 1814 for instruction in mathematics and experimental philosophy, the science and practice of gunnery, the theory of naval architecture, and mechanical drawing.[3] With hardly an exception the ranking naval officers concurred in the plan. Secretary Thompson renewed the recommendation in

[1] Harold and Margaret Sprout, *Rise of American Naval Power*, pp. 76–77.

[2] Paullin, "Naval Administration under Secretaries of the Navy Smith, Hamilton and Jones," U.S. Naval Institute, *Proceedings*, XXXII (1906), 1317.

[3] *American State Papers: Naval Affairs*, I, 323.

1822.[4] Two years later Secretary Southard told Congress, "Instruction is not less necessary to the navy than to the army." [5] In 1826 Maryland stepped forward to propose Annapolis as a suitable site,[6] but it was not until 1845 that Secretary Bancroft finally organized the Naval Academy. Meanwhile elementary instruction, academic and professional, was provided on shipboard and at some of the navy yards. For the most part the character and professional skill of young naval officers under the Jeffersonians were formed in the salty school of firsthand experience.[7]

THE NAVY YARDS

Early management of the extemporized shore facilities of the Navy Department was distinguished neither by skill nor foresight. The arrangements for building the first six frigates authorized by Congress in 1794 were badly planned. New wharves to accommodate the ships were constructed at public expense, but on the private ground of the shipbuilders.[8] The yards were so small that thousands of dollars were wasted in moving timber from place to place. The first wharf built at New York for the frigate *President* was in water too shallow to permit the ship to be launched; a second wharf was required. The old yard at Boston was surrounded by wooden houses, constituting a fire hazard of dangerous proportions.[9]

Stoddert and Adams boldly seized the occasion early in 1801 to remedy past errors by purchasing land for yards and by commencing them "on a scale as if they were meant to be permanent." [10] Six navy yards were quickly acquired from January

4 *Ibid.*, I, 816.

5 *Ibid.*, I, 1005.

6 *Ibid.*, II, 623.

7 Captain W. D. Puleston, *Annapolis: Gangway to the Quarterdeck* (New York: D. Appleton-Century, 1942) has sketched the early education of midshipmen. See also Park Benjamin, *The United States Naval Academy* (New York: G. P. Putnam's Sons, 1900).

8 *American State Papers: Naval Affairs*, I, 86.

9 *Ibid.*, I, 87.

10 The yard of John Langdon at Portsmouth was used up to 1800 for naval construction. Walter E. H. Fentress, *Centennial History of the United States Navy Yard, at Portsmouth, N. H., 1775–1875* (Portsmouth: O. M. Knight, 1876), p. 33.

to March 1801 at Portsmouth, Charlestown, New York, Philadelphia, Washington, and Norfolk. By October 1801, over a quarter million dollars had been invested in these places.

This decisive action for a shore establishment proved beyond the capacity of the Jeffersonians to reverse. Jefferson suspended or delayed further expenditure on the yards, and in 1802 Robert Smith apparently expected that Congress would require some of them to be sold.[11] The chairman of the House Committee on Naval Affairs, Samuel L. Mitchill, reported that he could find no authority in law or appropriation for the purchase of the yards and asserted that almost $200,000 had been illegally disbursed.[12] The sites, however, had been selected by the leading naval constructor of the time, Joshua Humphreys, and after some hesitation they were retained as public property. Only one additional yard was needed through the administration of John Quincy Adams—that established at Pensacola in 1825 as a substitute for the naval station at New Orleans.

Naval officers eventually came to the opinion that the government had more yards than were needed and were obviously worried over political pressure for an increase of their number.[13] In May 1828 the Senate asked the Navy Department to report whether a new yard between Cape Hatteras and Florida would be advantageous. Secretary Southard replied: "Our error is in having too many; and if other causes, obvious in their character, and arising principally from the nature of our confederation, do not prevent, the time will come . . . when two or three naval establishments and depots . . . will provide for most of our wants. . . . the proposed addition to the number of our

---

[11] *American State Papers: Naval Affairs*, I, 84 (March 10, 1802).

[12] *Ibid.*, I, 103 (April 27, 1802).

[13] Navy Department correspondence in 1801 already suggested political influence in naval matters. A letter to the navy agent at New York, Daniel Ludlow, June 11, 1801, contained the following passage, "When Mr. Langdon arrives, it may be thought proper to sell the present navy yard. I wish you would see him as he comes through New York. . . ." Langdon presumably was the recently retiring Senator from New Hampshire, to whom Jefferson had offered the Navy Department. On October 28, 1801, Ludlow received a further communication from the Navy Department, containing this passage: "The members of Congress from your State may, possibly, give the preference to a different place from that at present contemplated, and I do not wish the subject entangled in any unnecessary difficulties." *Ibid.*, I, 88.

navy yards would not, at this time, promote either economy . . . or energy in our naval operations." [14]

Secretary Southard thought also that the six original yards had not been too wisely selected. He told John Quincy Adams in December 1825 that "the greater part, if not the whole, of our Navy Yards, are badly located; and that a very large proportion of the public money, which has been, and continues to be, expended upon them, might have been saved, by a wiser location at the commencement." [15] Both Portsmouth and Charlestown enjoyed good natural facilities, but they were too near each other. Charlestown was generally rated very high, along with Norfolk; Philadelphia was hampered by ice in the winter and Washington was remote from supplies of skilled labor. Jefferson nevertheless favored the Washington yard as being close to the watchful eye of government. He caused the ships laid up in ordinary to be brought to the eastern branch of the Potomac, where, as he said, they would require "but one set of plunderers to take care of them." [16]

The heads of some navy yards early in Jefferson's administration were civilians, but they were gradually replaced by naval officers. No civilian served as head of a yard after 1813, and the title was correspondingly altered from superintendent to commandant.[17] Among the yard commandants Captain Thomas Tingey was one of the best known. Tingey was ordered to the site of the Washington Navy Yard in January 1800 and served as its commandant under Jefferson, Madison, Monroe, and John Quincy Adams. He was the first naval officer to establish a home in the new capital. Endowed with a great fondness for society, he took an active part in balls, banquets, and receptions, and established the naval circle solidly in Washington.[18] Almost without exception Tingey's official letters were in his own hand-

14 *Ibid.*, III, 276 (Dec. 26, 1828).

15 Senate Doc. 2, 19th Cong., 1st sess., p. 95.

16 Paullin, "Naval Administration under Secretaries of the Navy Smith, Hamilton and Jones," *op. cit.*, p. 1298; there is an account of the Washington Navy Yard by Paullin, "Washington City and the Old Navy," Columbia Historical Society, *Records*, XXXIII–XXXIV (1932), 163–77.

17 Paullin, "Naval Administration under Secretaries of the Navy Smith, Hamilton and Jones," *op. cit.*, p. 1315.

18 Paullin, "Washington City and the Old Navy," *op. cit.*, p. 165.

writing, even in his late service when "the unmistakable quiver
of weakening age is plainly revealed in the manuscript." He
resigned in 1829 at the age of seventy-eight, realizing as he said,
"I am incapable of the lively energy of a youthful seaman and
require some relaxation." He died within two weeks.[19]

The competence of navy-yard personnel was excellent. When
in 1816 Congress authorized the gradual increase of the navy,
the Secretary decided to build the new ships at the navy yards,
rather than by private contract. Experience showed that better
vessels could be built by the government than by private shipbuilders.[20] In 1825 Secretary Southard noted in his annual report, "Building by contract has been abandoned, as inexpedient
and expensive, for many years past, and ought not to be resumed
but by the express direction of Congress. This direction has
been, more than once, attempted, and always refused. . . ."[21]

The small corps of naval constructors assumed great importance and included some of the leading naval architects. Henry
Eckford and Christian Bergh had charge of naval construction
on the Great Lakes, and Eckford was the naval constructor at
New York from 1817 to 1820. Later he built ships for Turkey
and established a navy yard there. Samuel Humphreys, son of
the Federalist naval authority, Joshua Humphreys, was chief
naval constructor from 1826 to 1846.[22]

Navy artisans, however, began to cause concern as they complained about the inadequacy of their wages. An event which
may have been the first threat of a strike in a public establishment is recorded in a letter of Secretary Robert Smith at Washington to Commander Preble, then stationed at Portland,
Maine. The letter tells the story.

The blacksmiths at the yard here, being a dissatisfied set of men,
are complaining of their wages, & have said that unless we encrease

[19] Henry B. Hibben, *History of Washington Navy-Yard,* Senate Ex. Doc. 22,
51st Cong., 1st sess. (1890), pp. 64–65.

[20] Paullin, "Naval Administration under the Navy Commissioners," U.S.
Naval Institute, *Proceedings,* XXXIII (1907), 614–15.

[21] Senate Doc. 2, 19th Cong., 1st sess., p. 102 (Dec. 2, 1825). There is an interesting account of naval construction and costs in a report by Rodgers, Senate Doc.
12, 17th Cong., 2d sess. (Dec. 31, 1822).

[22] Paullin, "Naval Administration under the Navy Commissioners," *op. cit.,*
p. 635.

them they will leave the yard on the 1st April next—If they should do this, it would most probably detain the frigate Chesapeake & the ship Wasp. . . .

I wish to avoid such a situation in future, & shall therefore dismiss all the complaining men as soon as publick convenience will permit —& I wish to introduce in their place a set of orderly, hard working fellows, & I have determined to resort to your country for them. If practicable, which I cannot doubt, procure us six prime black-smiths . . . if you should *know* them all to be first rate workmen, & orderly, quiet men who will continue satisfied with their wages, & give us their constant services, you may engage to give each of them 180 cents p^r day.[23]

No further record has come to light concerning the fate of the dissatisfied men working on the *Chesapeake* and the *Wasp*. Their power position was weak.

DRY DOCKS

The efforts of the navy to secure a dry dock ran into a series of frustrations extending over a quarter century. The Federalists appropriated $50,000 for two docks in 1799 but never proceeded with the enterprise beyond a report on sites made by Joshua Humphreys.[24] The appropriation act for 1801, the last work of the Federalists, carried $500,000 for completing navy yards, docks, and wharves, but the new Administration spent nothing on the dock project.[25] Jefferson's interest in the subject was exhausted in a plan for a huge dry dock on the eastern branch of the Potomac in which could be permanently stored, high and dry, the majority of the frigates then a part of the navy.[26] Congress was dubious about the practicality of this scheme and declined to appropriate funds.

The navy entered the War of 1812 without a single dry dock. Secretary Paul Hamilton reported to Congress in December 1811: "To repair our vessels we are compelled to heave them down—a process attended with great labor, considerable risk, and loss of time," as well as inconvenience to the carpenters and

23 Library of Congress, Manuscript Division, Edward Preble Papers, XIX, 4265 (March 13, 1807).
24 1 Stat. 622 (Feb. 25, 1799); *American State Papers: Naval Affairs*, I, 89.
25 2 Stat. 122 (March 3, 1801).
26 *American State Papers: Naval Affairs*, I, 104–8 (Dec. 28, 1802).

the danger of straining the frame of the ship.[27] Congress finally appropriated $100,000 for a dockyard in 1813, much too late to permit construction to be undertaken during the war.[28] The war ended where it began so far as docks were concerned.

The Board of Navy Commissioners made a strong plea for docks in 1821, but the temper of Congress was then in favor of retrenchment, not expansion.[29] Secretary Southard finally persuaded Congress to authorize two dry docks, at Charlestown and Norfolk respectively, the construction of which was begun in 1827 and completed in 1833.[30] Thus finally came to fruition a long struggle, in which Congress twice authorized dry docks only to have circumstances defeat the requirements of the navy; in which Secretaries, the Board of Navy Commissioners, special boards of inquiry, and naval officers all concurred in asserting over and over again the need for such a facility, although differing as to where it should be placed; and in which finally the Secretary of the Navy had to shame Congress into action by observing in an official report: "It is a remarkable circumstance, that, holding the rank which we do among the naval Powers, we should not have one dock for the repairs of the vessels in which we take so much pride; and that we are, in this respect, behind every other nation, however inferior in naval strength." [31]

NAVY AGENTS

The purchase of materials for construction and maintenance of ships, dockyards, and facilities required direction from a departmental representative on the spot. These civilians were known from Federalist times as navy agents, and although their number was somewhat diminished in the early years of Jefferson's administration, they proved to be so useful that additional agents were soon required. As their number in-

27 *Ibid.*, I, 249 (Dec. 3, 1811).

28 2 Stat. 821 (March 3, 1813); *American State Papers: Naval Affairs*, I, 366.

29 *Ibid.*, I, 735 (Jan. 18, 1821); for discussion of the question see *ibid.*, I, 366, 434, 486, 735, 1032.

30 Southard's convincing report, summarizing early reports and recommendations is in *American State Papers: Naval Affairs*, I, 1032; the congressional authorization, 4 Stat. 242 (March 3, 1827).

31 *American State Papers: Naval Affairs*, I, 1032 (Jan. 3, 1825).

creased, the difficulty of adequate supervision by a Secretary, who himself had to supervise, mounted until it presented a serious administrative problem. Relief was found in the Board of Navy Commissioners.

The War Department, while in charge of naval matters before 1798, appointed naval agents at Portsmouth, Boston, New York, Baltimore, and Norfolk; at Philadelphia the purveyor and the principal naval constructor performed similar duties. The first Secretary of the Navy, Benjamin Stoddert, added another half dozen. The principal duty of these agents, then and later, was to purchase naval supplies of all sorts—timber, canvas, and other material for building and equipping ships; cannon, powder, and the like for armament; provisions, clothing, and other necessities for the crew.[32] The first navy agent for the District of Columbia was William Marbury, whose name later became famous as the complainant in *Marbury* v. *Madison*. The navy agent at New York in 1818 was Robert Swartwout;[33] one of his two securities was John Swartwout, bearing a family name that was to earn indignity and contempt in the 1830's when Samuel Swartwout embezzled over one million dollars as collector of the port of New York.

While the principal duties of the navy agents were concerned with procurement, they became the handy men of the department, much as the marshals had become the handy men of the government under the Federalists.[34] Thus we find agent Marbury in 1800 charged with finding quarters for the department in the new capital on the Potomac;[35] the navy agent at New

32 Charles Oscar Paullin, "Early Naval Administration under the Constitution," *Proceedings of the United States Naval Institute*, XXXII (1906), 1017–18. For an analysis of the status and duties of the office, see *Opinions of the Attorneys General* (1841 ed.), p. 220 (Sept. 1819).

33 *American State Papers: Naval Affairs*, I, 588.

34 Navy agents were used from time to time as recruiting officers. The navy had difficulty in manning its ships. It was national policy to maintain the supply of seamen by bounties to fishing vessels (House Doc. 101, 16th Cong., 2d sess.), but competition from private merchantmen left the navy at a disadvantage in the labor market. The whole subject was treated in an able report by Secretary Southard in 1828 (Senate Doc. 207, 20th Cong., 1st sess., May 23, 1828).

35 Paullin, "Early Naval Administration under the Constitution," *op. cit.*, p. 1020.

Orleans acting in 1809 as commandant of the station; [36] agent James Morrison in Kentucky handling insurance; [37] and others locating good live oak and red cedar timberland in the south.[38] There were also navy agents abroad, stationed at various ports in the Mediterranean. The firm of McKenzie and Glennie of London was the financial agent of the Navy Department for payments to the Mediterranean fleet.[39]

The unsolved problem of adequate accounting and reporting of navy agents was tackled by the Board of Navy Commissioners as a matter of high priority. By departmental circular in 1817 the navy agents were required to make returns every three months, and generally complied with the regulation.[40] The day was, however, already late.

The state of the accounts of Theodorick Armistead, agent at Norfolk, Virginia, was calamitous. In 1819 he had standing against him almost $250,000 and it was accepted that the government would take a considerable loss. The accounts of John Bullers in New York showed over a half million dollars balance due.[41] These revelations induced a recommendation for higher bonds, hitherto usually set at $20,000 by executive direction, but no legislation appears to have been enacted. The establishment of the Board of Navy Commissioners provided the regulations and administrative supervision necessary to prevent subsequent difficulties.

NAVAL HOSPITALS

The parsimonious and at the same time paternal attitude of Congress toward its naval officers and seamen is revealed in an amusing passage from a contemporary report of the House Committee on Naval Affairs:

. . . their attention had been called by the Secretary to navy hospitals. . . . It remains for your committee to state, their conviction of the propriety of the Secretary's suggestions, and to congratu-

---

[36] *American State Papers: Naval Affairs*, I, 203.

[37] *Ibid.*, I, 203.

[38] 3 Stat. 347 (March 1, 1817).

[39] Paullin, "Naval Administration under Secretaries of the Navy Smith, Hamilton and Jones," *op. cit.*, p. 1295.

[40] *American State Papers: Naval Affairs*, I, 588.

[41] *Ibid.*, I, 588, 589.

late the House that the opportunity is offered to ameliorate greatly the situation of a meritorious portion of citizens, without recurring to the public treasury. Of all classes of society, seamen require most the paternal foresight of Government. Habit, which tyrannizes over man in every situation, makes the sailor ever regardless of to-morrow; like the infant, he requires a guardian, or old age brings with it miserable poverty. On this principle, our Government, as well as others, have, from seamen's wages, raised a fund for marine hospitals, with guardian care setting apart a portion of the earnings of health for a support in sickness and decrepitude.[42]

The story of the mismanagement of the navy hospital fund is a minor scandal, as well as a commentary on the consequences of diffusion of responsibility in an ex officio board. The narrative begins in 1799 when Congress required monthly deductions of twenty cents from the pay of naval officers, seamen, and marines to provide temporary relief and maintenance in case of their sickness or disability, and to provide navy hospitals from any surplus.[43]

These deductions were regularly made and put into navy funds but no surplus was devoted to the construction of navy hospitals. In 1811 Congress passed an act establishing an overhead hospital organization,[44] an ex officio board consisting of the Secretary of the Navy, the Secretary of the Treasury, and the Secretary of War, designated "by the name and style of Commissioners of Navy Hospitals." The commissioners accepted collections from the pay of officers, seamen, and marines, and also $50,000 "out of the unexpended balance of the marine hospital fund"—an estimate of the deductions already made from navy personnel from 1799 to 1811 but never applied to their object. The commissioners were directed to purchase sites and erect hospitals, as well as provide a permanent asylum for "disabled and decrepid navy officers, seamen and marines."

42 *Ibid.*, I, 227 (Feb. 26, 1810).

43 1 Stat. 729 (March 2, 1799); and parallel act for seamen privately employed, 1 Stat. 605 (July 16, 1798). The management of this simple type of medical insurance was committed to the collectors of the various ports; they received deductions and made payments to local physicians and householders who boarded the sick or disabled, or in such large cities as Boston, New York, Philadelphia, and others, to local hospitals.

44 2 Stat. 650 (Feb. 26, 1811). Deductions from 1811 to 1821 are shown in House Doc. 8, 17th Cong., 1st sess. (Dec. 19, 1821).

The deductions continued to be made, but instead of applying them to the purposes prescribed by law, they were used for current navy pay without interruption from 1811 to 1824. It eventually appeared that $119,712.95 had thus been misapplied. Southard directed the fourth auditor to segregate future deductions from January 1, 1824.[45] The House of Representatives got wind of this extraordinary situation in 1822, and asked for a report.[46] The commissioners admitted that the deductions for naval personnel had been absorbed in the pay of the navy, and submitted to Congress "whether justice does not require that this fund should be made good, and applied without delay to the establishment of naval hospitals." [47]

Without waiting for congressional action the Hospital Commissioners, after a decade of inaction and misapplication of funds, began to perform their duty. In September 1823 they purchased a site for a hospital in Chelsea, Massachusetts; in May 1824, a site in Brooklyn, New York; in June 1826, a site for an asylum in Philadelphia; and in 1827, a site for a hospital near Norfolk.[48] The House of Representatives asked for a further report in 1827 and the commissioners minced no words. They stated:

. . . It is a painful fact that although the law, designed to provide hospitals and an asylum for our seamen, has been in operation nearly twenty-eight years, and deductions from their pay constantly made during all that time, yet, in consequence chiefly of the state of the funds, not one building for their accommodation and comfort has been erected. The effect upon the feelings of our officers and seamen may well be imagined. The commissioners are assured that it has been one powerful cause of the difficulties sometimes encountered in procuring seamen for our public vessels.[49]

[45] *American State Papers: Naval Affairs,* III, 18.

[46] Secretary Crowninshield had informed the House in 1818 that no hospitals had been constructed for lack of funds and somewhat weakly argued that "no neglect is justly imputable, for every accommodation and medical aid has been afforded to the sick, in temporary hospitals, commensurate with the means, and so far as circumstances have permitted." House Doc. 74, 16th Cong., 1st sess., p. 12 (Jan. 15, 1818).

[47] *American State Papers: Naval Affairs,* I, 853 (Jan. 6, 1823); also in House Doc. 54, 19th Cong., 2d sess.

[48] *American State Papers: Naval Affairs,* III, 14.

[49] *Ibid.,* III, 15.

Congress still took no action to restore the fund, but addressed a further inquiry to Southard in December 1828. The Secretary of the Navy in his report was even more pointed. He asked for full repayment, with interest due. He asserted that not one man had ever received advantage from the hospital fund.

The government kept and *used the money,* to which it had no possible right. It belonged to the officers, seamen and marines, from whom it was taken by the power of the law. . . . The government surely does not need, nor can it wish to receive, a charitable dona- tion of the use of money from a band of poor seamen and marines. . . .

In addition, I beg leave to add, that the government has never given a cent to create hospital establishments for the navy. In no other country, and under no other civilized government, is this the fact.[50]

The Committee on Naval Affairs belatedly fell in with the spirit of these observations and recommended an appropriation to cover the whole amount due, reckoned by Southard as $195,- 351.81, but by the committee as $167,759.37. By the act of May 24, 1828, Congress had appropriated $46,217.14, the bal- ance of the $50,000 presumably transferred in 1811; and on March 2, 1829, a further appropriation of $125,000 was made to the hospital fund.[51] Congress declined, however, to accept Southard's invitation to add the United States to the list of civilized countries that made an appropriation, other than de- ductions from pay, for naval hospitals.

The record of hospital construction was far from impressive. Progress was slow and in 1829 it did not appear that a single institution had been completed. The Hospital Commissioners recommended their own abolition and the transfer of their au- thority to the Secretary of the Navy. They intimated that the Philadelphia asylum had been planned "with a liberality bor- dering on extravagance," [52] and the description of "a marble portico of eight Ionic columns, three feet each in diameter" on the Schuylkill, and of "a bold Doric portico of ten columns, accessible by twenty steps that stretch ninety-two feet, the whole

50 *Ibid.,* III, 299 (Jan. 22, 1829).
51 4 Stat. 304 and 4 Stat. 360.
52 *American State Papers: Naval Affairs,* III, 480 (Jan. 16, 1830).

length of the portico," at Norfolk, could give rise to doubt as to the proper application of the building fund.[53]

Naval medical personnel. The medical service was slow in finding a suitable administrative organization. The Navy Register for 1821 showed 47 surgeons and 43 surgeons' mates, afloat and ashore.[54] They were subject to the orders of the commander of their ship, or the commandant of the navy yard or station. They had no professional supervision, had no place in the central organization of the Navy Department, and did not form a medical corps. They were merely isolated representatives of the medical profession, practicing their art on the members of the crew or establishment to which they were assigned. Secretary Thompson had sought to remedy this lack of organization by recommending in 1819, "the designation of some officer to be placed at the head of this class of officers, and who should have the immediate superintendence of this branch of the service. . . ."[55] Congress was not responsive.

In 1824 an element of central control of the medical service was introduced by establishing a board of surgeons to examine candidates for appointment or promotion. Secretary Southard informed Congress that the result had been most gratifying. "The character of the corps has been elevated, and now contains men inferior to none of their age in merit and acquirement."[56]

Congress regularized these arrangements in 1828 and took the first step toward introducing an administrative structure in the navy medical service.[57] It provided for the appointment of a

53 *Ibid.*, III, 482, 483 (Dec. 1, 1829). The third floor of the asylum at Philadelphia contained, among other accommodations, "chambers for the officers and governor, or manager, of the institution; apartments for the insane, bath rooms, closets, &c., &c."

54 *Ibid.*, I, 702.

55 *Ibid.*, I, 618 (Dec. 29, 1819).

56 *Ibid.*, III, 160–61. Southard had support from the House in this improvement. A year earlier the House Committee on Naval Affairs reported they were convinced that appointments in the medical service had been unsatisfactory and that many of the best had "abandoned the service in disgust" over poor pay and prospects. House Report 63, 17th Cong., 2d sess. (Jan. 20, 1823). In 1827 Niles made a strong plea for better pay for navy medical officers. *Niles Register,* XXXII, 146–47 (April 28, 1827).

57 4 Stat. 313 (May 24, 1828); *American State Papers: Naval Affairs,* III, 129.

"Surgeon of the Fleet" for every fleet or squadron; directed him to approve all requisitions for medical and hospital stores and to inspect their quality; and to consult with surgeons on ships and transmit medical records to the Navy Department. As to the quality of personnel, Congress required every candidate for assistant surgeon to pass an examination given by a board of naval surgeons, and every promotion to the rank of surgeon to be based on at least two years of service at sea and an examination before the board.

Secretary John Branch, who succeeded Southard when Jackson became President, asked Congress to appoint a surgeon general of the navy to take administrative responsibility for the medical service. Congress failed to act, and both before and after the Jeffersonians, the surgeons of the navy, as Branch put it, were "under no guidance whatever in the discharge of their professional duties, except their own discretion or pleasure." [58]

The Federalists could claim with some justice that they had initiated all the elements of the shore establishment which, after 1815, the Republicans set about to strengthen and to use. The first impulse of the Jeffersonians to dismantle ships and shore organization was only well started when events overseas delayed and then reversed their plans. After 1815 the Republicans accepted what had then become a national, not merely a party, policy. Postwar expenditures of a million a year for ten years to build a navy obviously meant, as John Quincy Adams put it, an intent to become a great naval power. The shore establishment grew in size and perfection as the navy expanded, for it required an effective land base as well as fast-sailing, straight-shooting ships on the high seas.

The principal administrative improvement was the creation of the Board of Navy Commissioners, a body broadly analogous to the army General Staff. While neither of these agencies possessed the central planning and preparatory functions that characterized the later evolution of staff bodies, both gave needed professional support to the civilian heads of the two defense departments. In each case civilian and military authori-

[58] *Ibid.,* III, 490 (Jan. 26, 1830).

ties found difficulties of mutual adjustment. No doubt can remain, however, that the country was better served by these administrative innovations than it could have been by the simple and undeveloped structures that preceded the reforms of the new Republicans.

CHAPTER TWENTY-ONE

The Post Office

The story of the post office establishment from 1801 to 1829 could well be written in terms of mud, toil, hazard, and achievement. Under the Federalists the chief concern was the great mail route from Maine to Georgia; under the Republicans the post office turned its face west, through Pittsburgh to Cincinnati, Louisville and Nashville, along the Great Lakes from Buffalo to Cleveland and Chicago, and southwest to that distant but vital port, New Orleans. Westward lay the future, but westward also lay mountains, swamps, mud, and Indians.

The post office followed closely on the heels of pioneers; where stagecoaches could not go, sulkies might; and where sulkies became impossible, the mail went forward by horse. The political importance of the West made the circulation of intelligence a matter of deep concern of which the Jeffersonians were fully aware. Gideon Granger, Jefferson's Postmaster General, declared in 1810, "From the nature of our Government, it becomes a matter of the highest importance to furnish the citizens with full and correct information. . . .[1] Congress concurred in this view, and with almost unfailing regularity, year by year, extended the post roads into regions more and more remote. The annual designation of post roads, indeed, became one of the earliest congressional perquisites and a useful claim for reelection.

The postal system worked out by the Federalists was taken over without change by their successors. Jefferson was deeply suspicious of the post office employees, whom he repeatedly ac-

---

[1] *American State Papers: Post Office,* p. 42 (Feb. 21, 1810).

cused both before and after 1801 of prying into his letters,[2] but Gideon Granger, Republican successor to the Federalist regime, did nothing to control their curiosity. The system comprised the General Post Office in Washington, an expanding army of "deputy postmasters" in each city and village, and hundreds of contractors who carried the mail from place to place for a stipulated annual sum.

Despite the almost unbelievable handicaps of miserable roads and absent bridges, the carriage of the mails on the schedules then possible steadily improved in regularity. Laxness in administration and accountability, observable to a degree in all government agencies under Jefferson and Madison, and exaggerated by the events of the War of 1812, was reduced under Monroe and Adams, and was attacked with special vigor and success by John McLean. So remarkable were McLean's achievements, indeed, that in a spontaneous expression of sentiment, Congress showed its appreciation by increasing his salary—perhaps the only such event in the administrative history of the federal government and certainly unique to 1829.

"There is no branch of the Government," wrote the Postmaster General in 1828, "in whose operations the people feel a more lively interest than in those of this Department; its facilities being felt in the various transactions of business, in the pleasures of correspondence, and the general diffusion of information. In the course of every year no inconsiderable amount of the active capital of the country, in some form or other, passes through the mail." [3]

This sentiment was echoed by the House Committee on Post Office and Post Roads in 1829, in language which reflected an embryonic interest in the efficient operation of the public business, in contradistinction with its earlier preoccupation in safeguarding the public liberties.

A well regulated mail establishment is an indispensable requisite to a free Government, and to the commercial, agricultural, and manufacturing interest of an enterprising and growing people. Every

[2] For illustrations of Jefferson's complaints, see Jefferson, *Works* (Federal ed.), IX, 85, 89, 393; X, 474, 498.

[3] *American State Papers: Post Office*, p. 183 (Nov. 17, 1828).

buyer and seller should be informed of the state of the market, at home and abroad, with the greatest possible certainty and expedition. This can only be accomplished through the operations of the mail, regulated and directed by a discriminating mind, intimately acquainted with the local interest of the country. Every part must harmonize like a well regulated machine, which, though complicated in its structure, has no disorder in its movements.[4]

Gideon Granger, Postmaster General from 1801 to 1814, was born in Connecticut in 1767.[5] His father and his son, like himself, were graduates of Yale and lawyers by profession. Granger early became an active politician, holding a seat in the Connecticut General Assembly, with the exception of two years, from 1792 to 1801. He became a Republican in 1798. In October 1801 Jefferson offered him either the office of auditor or treasurer, for neither of which did he appear to have any special qualifications.[6] He doubtless owed his appointment as Postmaster General to his political availability. In 1810 he sought a place on the Supreme Court, but he was accused of "Yazooism" and was out of favor with the South. The President commented on "his bodily infirmity with its effects on his mental stability. . . ."[7] Madison continued Granger in office but removed him summarily in 1814 for political insubordination. He had also been suspected of some connection with Burr.[8] Senator Jonathan Roberts declared "Grainger was too selfish, to warrant confidence."[9] He was primarily interested in the political movements of his time,[10] but gave a reasonably satisfactory administration to the post office.[11]

[4] House Report 65, 20th Cong., 2d sess., pp. 3–4 (Feb. 3, 1829).

[5] *Dictionary of American Biography*, VII, 483–84.

[6] Library of Congress, Papers of Gideon and Francis Granger, 1800–1864, Letter No. 5.

[7] Madison, *Writings* (Hunt ed.), VIII, 111 (Oct. 19, 1810).

[8] Granger Papers, Letter No. 17.

[9] "Memoirs of a Senator from Pennsylvania: Jonathan Roberts, 1771–1854," *Pennsylvania Magazine of History and Biography*, LXII (1938), 240.

[10] See his defense of the Republican party, December 15, 1808: *An Address to the People of New England* (Washington: Dinmore and Cooper, 1808; Algernon Sidney, pseudonym).

[11] Jefferson wrote him a testimonial in 1810, referring to the "able & faithful direction of the office committed to your charge." Granger Papers, Letter No. 14 (Jan. 26, 1810). For Jefferson's friendly endorsement in 1814, see Jefferson, *Works* (Federal ed.), XI, 389.

Return Jonathan Meigs, his successor, was also a Connecticut Yankee by origin, a graduate of Yale, 1785, who studied law and in 1788 moved to Marietta, Ohio. He became active in public life, a judge of the territorial government in 1798, a member of the legislature in 1799, and first chief justice of the Ohio Supreme Court in 1803. In 1808 he was elected to the United States Senate, from which he resigned in 1810 to become governor of Ohio. He was energetic in the western campaigns of the War of 1812 and in 1814 became Postmaster General in recognition of his war activities, serving until 1823. His talents and tastes were political rather than administrative.[12]

Meigs enjoyed the dubious distinction of recommending that "no book ought ever to be sent by mail, even if letter or packet postage was paid on it." Books, he observed, were usually bound with leather and had the hardness of blocks of wood which injured letters and wore out the wrappers on newspapers. He criticized the Secretary of State for sending "a number of cartloads of books" through the mail in 1822. He proposed that books be distributed like merchandise, to "some considerable commercial town" and thence to any settled part of the country. ". . . there is no necessity of burdening the mail with such as are intended either for public or private use." [13] These ideas hardly suggest an innovating or enterprising spirit.

The successor to Meigs, John McLean, overshadowed both his predecessors and his successors. His career is so significant and so controversial that it will be dealt with at greater length in a later section.

EXPANSION AND GROWTH, 1801–1829

The size of the post office establishment was inevitably fixed by the population of the country and by its distribution. Policy, however, could play within limits of substantial proportions, and especially under the administration of McLean policy favored vigorous expansion by plowing back surplus revenue into new routes. Granger had been more cautious, and both Granger and Meigs in fact made some payments of surplus into

[12] *Dictionary of American Biography,* XII, 509–10.
[13] *American State Papers: Post Office,* p. 112 (Feb. 21, 1823).

the Treasury. Not so McLean: "I say now, as I have always said when speaking on the subject, that I do not consider an efficient administration of the Department is shown by the annual balance in its favor. Its funds should be actively employed in extending the operations of the mail." [14] The record of expansion is shown in the following table.[15]

TABLE I

GROWTH OF UNITED STATES POST OFFICE, 1790–1829

Year	Number of Post Offices	Miles of Post Roads	Number of Clerks in the General Post Office
1790	75	1,875	–
1795	453	13,207	4
1800	903	20,817	7
1805	1,558	31,076	9
1810	2,300	36,406	12
1815	3,000	43,748	15
1820	4,500	72,492	21
1825	5,677	94,052	27
1829	8,004	115,000	38

From 1823 to 1827 there were "ingrafted on the establishment an amount of revenue, and accommodation in post offices and transportation of the mail, greater than the entire mail establishment in the Union in 1800. . . . an increase unparalleled in the annals of the Department. . . ." [16] An estimate of the number of letters carried showed a markedly greater volume of business. In 1801 the estimate ran to 2,240,000; in 1810, 3,860,000; in 1820, 8,890,000; and in 1829, 13,650,000.[17] In 1828 McLean reckoned about 26,956 employees, including the small central office, the postmasters and their clerks, the contractors and their drivers. To carry the mail there were needed 2,879 carriages of various descriptions and 17,584 horses.[18] These fig-

14 *American State Papers: Post Office*, p. 324 (March 31, 1829).

15 *Ibid.*, p. 253.

16 *Ibid.*, p. 146.

17 Wesley Everett Rich, *The History of the United States Post Office to the Year 1829* (Cambridge: Harvard University Press, 1924), pp. 182–83.

18 *American State Papers: Post Office*, p. 184; a tabulation of existing post routes in 1825 disclosed about 1,280, on the larger number of which mail was carried only once a week.

ures were not unnoticed by some politicians of the time.

Among post offices, rated by postal receipts, were giants and dwarfs. The post office at Washington, D.C., was one of the largest, but on the basis of postal receipts it was outranked, since it had to handle a mass of franked mail. The other great offices (1827–28) were New York ($124,000), Philadelphia ($80,000), Boston ($52,000), and Baltimore ($43,000). Among the dwarfs we may note such curiosities as Flushing, New York, whose net postage sales in 1828 amounted to $58.65; Middlebury, Connecticut, $9.70; Smyrna, Ohio, $5.08; and Mercer's Bottom, Virginia, eighteen cents.[19]

In the New York office, which employed 24 persons, the number of mails made up daily in 1828 was 150, involving in the course of a week between fifty and sixty thousand letters. The packet ships brought in considerable mail; the Liverpool packet from 1,500 to 2,500 letters, the London about 500, the Havre from 600 to 1,200. "The labor in this office," said the *New York Journal of Commerce,* "is arduous, and the utmost activity, accuracy, and civility, are required to expedite business, and do justice to the citizens and to strangers who throng there for letters."[20]

ORGANIZATION OF THE GENERAL POST OFFICE

The General Post Office in 1802 consisted of the Postmaster General, one assistant postmaster general, Abraham Bradley, Jr., seven clerks, and a messenger.[21] In 1829, Bradley was still assistant postmaster general, his brother Phineas was also an assistant postmaster general, and the establishment was well organized into appropriate subdivisions, employing approximately thirty-eight clerks. The Postmaster General was the active head of the organization.

The responsibility of the Postmaster General at the close of the twenties was relatively great; he disbursed about $1,000,000 annually for the conveyance of the mail and nearly $500,000 to

19 *Ibid.,* p. 184.

20 Reprinted in *Niles Register,* XXXV, 118 (Oct. 18, 1828). In 1826 Niles noted that between 6,000 and 7,000 ship letters came in to the New York office in one afternoon. *Ibid.,* XXX, 239 (June 3, 1826).

21 *American State Papers: Miscellaneous,* I, 305.

the postmasters. Their dispersion in every part of the Union added to the labor of control, and the degree of public interest required the most unceasing diligence on the part of the central administration. The daily correspondence of the Postmaster General amounted to about six hundred communications, incoming and outgoing. He made from five to ten appointments every day, investigated charges, and decided many legal questions. He was required to judge of the expediency of giving additional mail accommodations and "to correspond on almost numberless topics connected with his Department." [22]

To assist him, the business of the General Post Office had gradually been divided into three general and distinct branches, not including the office of chief clerk. These were concerned respectively with finance, appointments, and mail contracts.[23] The finance branch included three bookkeepers who kept accounts with postmasters and contractors; a solicitor's office which collected balances due and prosecuted delinquents; a pay office; an examiner's office in which remittances were received and accounts settled to the number of about 32,000 a year; and a register's office which kept records and prepared accounts for the Treasury. One clerk was kept busy registering and filing alphabetically the letters received by the department.

The appointments branch was organized into three subdivisions, geographically.[24] Here the clerks read letters and memorials concerning applications, collected and prepared material on each case, examined bonds and oaths of office, and made out letters of appointment. Here also for convenience were placed the dead letter office and an "office of instruction," which circulated decisions of the Postmaster General, and gave special

---

[22] *American State Papers: Post Office*, p. 145 (Jan. 11, 1827). There is an excellent account of the work of the General Post Office in *Niles Register*, XXX, 243-44 (June 3, 1826), borrowed from the *National Intelligencer*. The volume of correspondence falling to the Postmaster General early aroused the compassion of Granger's friends in the Senate. Senator Bradley offered to increase his salary in 1803 by reason of his expanding duties: "He is frequently obliged to write all night till one oclock in the morning." Senator John Smith of Ohio declared, "The postmaster General has wrote *two quires & three sheets* of paper in one day in his office. . . ." William Plumer, *Memorandum*, p. 74 (Dec. 6, 1803). The House repelled this assault on the Treasury.

[23] *American State Papers: Post Office*, pp. 222-23.

[24] For regions, see *ibid.*, p. 255.

directions to postmasters in tracing lost letters and in detecting "depredators."

The contract branch advertised for proposals for carrying the mails, watched the performance of the contractors, filed contracts and bonds, and maintained information on mail routes. The office of the chief clerk was concerned with general supervision, correspondence, keeping accounts with the banks, and preparation of statements for the President and Congress. The simple and undifferentiated office of 1801 had obviously undergone an administrative transformation as the volume of business grew with the years.

EQUIPMENT AND PROCEDURES

Wherever the volume of travel was adequate, coaches were strongly preferred by the Post Office Department as the means of conveyance.[25] The mail was carried inside the coach, protected from the elements. The presence of passengers also deterred either carriers or robbers from depredation. The coaches were heavy, lumbering affairs and in wet weather often proved impossible to pull over the miry roads. In 1815 "A Friend to Improvement" complained that the mail and other coaches "should be so miserably wanting in every thing, for the comfort of the traveller. . . . nothing seems to have been aimed at but speed. . . ."[26]

A well-known description of the decorations of a mail coach was written by Habersham in 1799.

The body painted green, colors formed of Prussian blue and yellow ochre; carriage and wheels red lead mixed to approach vermillion as near as may be; octagon panel in the back, black; octagon blinds, green; elbow piece, or rail, front rail and back rail, red as above; on the doors Roman capitals in patent yellow, "United States Mail

[25] For one of many such statements, we may quote Granger. "I cannot agree with you in opinion, that it is preferable to convey a mail, by sulkies rather than by a stage . . . when a mail is transported by a stage, a business vehicle is furnished for the Citizens of that part of the Country thro' which it runs & the Travellers ordinarily constitute a security to the mail. Their solicitude also to expedite their Journey generally contributes to expedite its arrival." Granger to Reverend Nathaniel Irwin, March 23, 1811, in Madison Papers, MS., Library of Congress, XLIV, 50.

[26] *North American Review*, I (1815), 15.

Stage," and over those words a spread eagle of a size and color to suit.[27]

Where the roads would not permit a coach, or where passenger revenue was slender, the mail might be carried in sulkies, light two-wheeled vehicles requiring only a single horse. Jefferson's sulky used in traveling from Monticello to Washington is still preserved at Monticello. Across the Mississippi transportation was on horseback; and for years the mail overland to New Orleans was carried in this way. When the load became too heavy, a led horse carried the surplus. By 1828 coaches and sulkies and riders on horses were carrying mails at four or five miles an hour under good conditions. To the fellow citizens of John Quincy Adams, this achievement seemed to deserve the highest approval.

The system of handling mail had undergone only one important change since Granger took over in 1801 from Habersham. Under the Federalists, the mail portmanteau was opened at every post office, local mail taken out and new mail put in. The improvement consisted in separating the "through" mail from the local mail.[28] Under the new system forty-eight offices (in 1823) were designated as "distributing offices." To each of them were carried in special portmanteaus, called principal mail bags, all letters destined for the section in which the office was located. The postmaster receiving such a principal mail bag would then direct each letter along the proper route within his section. In turn he would make up packets for other districts to go into principal mail bags which were opened only at the distributing points. Special locks were placed on the principal mail bags. The system made for greater certainty, speed, and security.[29]

Another innovation was to use steamboats for carriage of the mail. Congress committed itself to this experiment in 1813, provided the Postmaster General could be satisfied of regular transportation.[30] By 1815 masters and crews of steamboats were carrying mail privately, for their own profit, to an extent that

[27] Quoted in Rich, *History of the U.S. Post Office*, p. 98.
[28] 2 Stat. 592, sec. 5 (April 30, 1810).
[29] *American State Papers: Post Office*, p. 113 (Dec. 24, 1823).
[30] 2 Stat. 805 (Feb. 27, 1813).

led Congress to make further specific prohibition of this practice.[31] In 1823 all waters on which steamboats regularly passed from port to port were declared post roads, thus extending the government postal monopoly over the waterways.[32]

In 1825 Congress authorized personal delivery of letters by city carriers, a practice already well established by custom.[33] For this service, the carrier collected two cents for each letter and the postmaster one cent. Personal letter boxes in the post office were discussed but not introduced until a later period. McLean also considered placing a letter box in Chatham Square, New York City, in which letters could be mailed.[34] The slowness of the ordinary mails was so annoying to the commercial interest and to newspaper publishers that they began to send special messengers, especially for the delivery of market information. In 1825 the Post Office Department instituted "Express Mail" between the leading commercial centers, the forerunner of special delivery service.[35] In 1828 McLean proposed another innovation: "It may be advantageous to the public and the Department, at some future time, for it to become the insurer of moneys transmitted in the mail. . . ." [36] The post office obviously was not merely expanding its routes; it was searching for better service to its constituents.

THE REGULARITY AND SECURITY OF THE MAIL

A perennial problem of the Postmaster General was to secure the prompt delivery of mails by the contractors, particularly at junction points and the end of their routes. They were harassed by bad weather, muddy roads, lazy and bibulous drivers, and an endless series of accidents for which they could not be blamed. Despite particular complaints, Hezekiah Niles was prepared in 1816 to bear "a general good testimony of the fidelity and care with which the business of this interesting and extensive establishment" was conducted.[37] Two years later he wrote, "the

---

[31] 3 Stat. 220 (Feb. 27, 1815).
[32] 3 Stat. 764, sec. 3 (March 3, 1823).
[33] 4 Stat. 102, sec. 36 (March 3, 1825); Rich, *op. cit.*, p. 104.
[34] *Ibid.*, p. 105.
[35] *Ibid.*, p. 101.
[36] *American State Papers: Post Office*, p. 184 (Nov. 17, 1828).
[37] *Niles Register*, X, 201 (May 25, 1816).

great business of the general post-office is managed with the regularity of the machinery of a clock. . . ." [38] He was in a position to know.

The means at the disposal of the government to apprehend mail robbers were inadequate, and Timothy Pickering had been more than once obliged to declare his chagrin. In 1808 Jefferson commented on the fact that robbery of the mail had become "so frequent and great an evil." [39] After the close of the Napoleonic Wars, various desperate characters came to the New World and a wave of attempts upon the mail ensued. Congress became alarmed and in 1819 asked Postmaster General Meigs for advice. He was obviously disturbed at the expense of providing the armed guards suggested by the Senate committee: "even the stage fare of the guards would be very expensive." After pointing out that the guard "would possess a complete power over the mail carrier and the mail; and, if unfaithful, might effect the most extensive depredations on its contents," he asked, "In fine . . . who is to guard the guards?" He concluded with an interesting bit of rhetoric.

It may not be desirable in this nation to see the employment of an armed physical force to protect the operations of civil Government, to the distrust of the civic virtues and moral energies of the people, unless in cases of emergency, and unless the efforts of those virtues and energies should fail of their proper consequences, and demonstrate that a reliance on them would be fruitless and deceptive. [40]

Congress was silenced if not convinced.

Losses continued, but the zeal of the Post Office Department in pursuing the criminals was great. Meigs asserted in 1819 that for five years not a single robbery had taken place in which the culprits were not apprehended, convicted, and punished. [41] A clever bit of official detective work caught the postmaster at Newbern, Virginia, with stolen funds in his possession. [42] In 1826 occurred "the most alarming and extensive robbery of the mail" that had yet happened, somewhere between Philadelphia

38 *Ibid.*, XV, 134 (Oct. 24, 1818).
39 Jefferson, *Writings* (Memorial ed.), XII, 222 (Dec. 28, 1808).
40 *American State Papers: Post Office*, p. 63 (Feb. 10, 1819).
41 *Ibid.*, p. 63.
42 *Niles Register*, XXV, 229 (Dec. 13, 1823).

and Baltimore.[43] Four persons were involved, including two stage drivers. They and one accomplice sat on the driver's seat with the mail bag under their feet. As the stage proceeded, they cut open the bag and dropped on the road such letters as they supposed of value. The fourth accomplice, on horseback behind the stage, picked up the loot. One of the drivers was apprehended, confessed, and the other parties were secured.[44] Niles concluded after this episode that some way of affording additional security for the great mails was needed: "for it appears that the certain and swift destruction of all who have robbed them, is insufficient to check the spirit of new adventurers, to get money or find a gallows." [45] In 1826 a guard was appointed to attend the mail between Philadelphia and New York.[46] Congress threw in its advice, by recommending the purchase of a quantity of new model receptacles designed by Richard Imlay —copper cases, secured in iron chests by inside locks and sliding bars, which could not be violated "without much hammering and noise." [47]

By 1825, McLean was able to give reassuring evidence on the increasing safety of the mails.[48] Contributing to this improvement was the use of stagecoaches over a larger number of routes. Contributing also was presidential reluctance to pardon mail robbers. Two brothers named Hare had an irresistible attraction toward the hidden riches of the mail bags. One was convicted and executed. The other received a ten-year sentence, and sent in repeated petitions for a pardon. President Adams expressed his policy in these words: "Mail-robbery is one of those offences the full punishment of which in this country ought perhaps never to be remitted, and the sentence of ten years' imprisonment was, in this case, itself a very mitigated penalty." [49]

43 *Ibid.*, XXX, 17 (March 11, 1826).
44 *Ibid.*, XXX, 48 (March 18, 1826).
45 *Ibid.*, XXX, 17.
46 *Ibid.*, XXXI, 96.
47 *American State Papers: Post Office*, p. 93.
48 *Ibid.*, p. 138.
49 Adams, *Memoirs*, VII, 197 (Dec. 5, 1826).

CONGRESS AND THE POST OFFICE

During the Jeffersonian period the attention of Congress was fixed on the post office steadily and at times anxiously. The needs of an expanding population were of natural interest to Congressmen, and the authorization of added mail routes or service to a congressional district was a concrete evidence of industry and official attention. Congress strictly held to the rule that had been so strongly but vainly contested by the Federalists, reserving to itself the designation of routes.[50] It did not, however, seek to lay hands on post office appointments by requiring senatorial confirmation, although members of both Houses were active and at times insistent with their advice.[51]

The interest of Congress was directed into three channels: legislation, investigation, and claims. Legislation fell into two principal categories: the annual law prescribing new mail routes, and two revisions of the organic Post Office Act.[52] Congress also prohibited the employment of Negroes, fixed postal rates and franking privileges, altered the compensation of postmasters, provided fire engine protection to the departmental office in Washington, and protected the governmental monopoly in the carriage of the mails. None of this legislation was of major importance; the developments of these decades came through administrative action rather than through legislation.

Congress was, however, alert to detect and reveal official delinquency, and repeatedly looked into the affairs of the department. Gideon Granger himself was the object of an investigation.[53] The interim report of the select House committee reflected perfectly the attitude of the old Republicans toward executive officers.

50 Congress was finally persuaded to allow the Postmaster General to abandon routes whose receipts failed to equal one fourth of the costs. 4 Stat. 95, sec. 2 (March 3, 1825).

51 For appointment practice, see the following chapter.

52 2 Stat. 592 (April 30, 1810); 4 Stat. 102 (March 3, 1825).

53 According to Senator Plumer two charges were "whispered" against Granger: first, that he had used his office to persuade Duane to support the Yazoo claim; second, that he had refused to contract with a Federalist low bidder and had awarded the mail route to a Democrat at nearly three times the cost. Plumer, *Memorandum*, pp. 485–86 (April 17, 1806).

While the committee regret the situation of a public officer, laboring under the suspicious appearance of a constitutional scrutiny into his conduct, yet, in a government like ours, where watchfulness of men in office is the surest guarantee of the preservation of the liberty of the people, the public functionaries must yield their feelings to the general benefit, and endure a temporary inconvenience as an honorable sacrifice to the freedom of our institutions.[54]

The inquiry was eventually postponed indefinitely.[55]

In an investigation in 1816 the committee found no delinquency. An investigation in 1821 turned on the compliance of the Postmaster General with various formalities of law, such as lodging duplicate contracts with the comptroller of the Treasury, rendering quarterly reports and lists of contracts, and the like. The committee found a number of apparent failures, but Postmaster General Meigs made a vigorous and sensible defense, based on the realities of an administrative situation which made exact compliance an impossibility.[56]

An investigation in 1822 was apparently initiated in part from rumors of preference in granting contracts. The committee cleared the department on this count, but commented adversely on the mode of settlement of accounts (which was promptly altered), and on the excessive number of clerks employed in some of the larger post offices. The committee confessed itself unable to ascertain whether suits against delinquent postmasters had been brought within the appointed time, "as well from the multiplicity of Deputy Postmasters" as from lack of records.[57] These and other investigations and reports on more limited matters suggest that Congress was taking seriously its duty as guardian of the public business. Compliance with legal requirements, rather than efficiency and economy, was the central theme of the three major investigations; efficiency and economy peeked through the window but did not enter the committee rooms.

[54] *American State Papers: Post Office*, p. 40 (April 17, 1806).
[55] *Annals*, 9th Cong., 1st sess., pp. 831–33 (March 21, 1806); *ibid.*, p. 1116 (April 21, 1806).
[56] *American State Papers: Post Office*, pp. 77–90 (Feb. 28, 1821).
[57] *Ibid.*, pp. 97–98 (April 29, 1822).

The third major interest of Congress was in dealing with individual claims of postmasters, contractors, and their sureties, and occasionally citizens who complained of losses through post office negligence. These were often full of interest but did not affect post office policy or administration.

The post office was inevitably an institution that attracted the people's representatives. Local in its operations, it could be seen and appreciated by constituents. Simple in its activities, it did not require the sophisticated talents that were needed to debate foreign policy, tariff for protection, or the affairs of the United States Bank. Any Congressman could feel himself at home here, and claim, with some justification, that he could prescribe the post roads in his district from personal knowledge better than the President of the United States, or pick a postmaster among his constituents better than the Postmaster General.

JOHN MCLEAN: HYPOCRITE OR STATESMAN?

By almost universal testimony, John McLean was the ablest man to hold the office of Postmaster General since 1789. Whether or not he used the patronage of his department to defeat John Quincy Adams in the election of 1828 remains to this day in dispute. Adams was convinced of his treachery. McLean steadily denied Adams' suspicions, and wrote more eloquently than any man of his time against partisanship in appointments.

McLean was born in New Jersey in 1785, the son of a Scotch weaver who after some wandering finally settled on a farm near Lebanon, Ohio. In 1801 the young McLean went to Cincinnati and was indentured for two years to the law clerk of the Hamilton County Court, reading law with Arthur St. Clair, son of General St. Clair. McLean was admitted to the bar in 1807 and soon entered politics, being elected as a Republican to Congress in 1812 and reelected unanimously in 1814. In 1816 he retired from Congress to become a member of the Ohio Supreme Court, and then returned to Washington in 1822 as commissioner of the Land Office. In 1823, at the age of thirty-eight, he was appointed Postmaster General, and in 1829 to the United States Supreme Court.[58]

McLean infused new energy and vitality into the post office from 1823 to 1829. His policy was one of expansion and improvement of service, efficiency and strict accountability of postmasters and contractors, and maintenance of high ideals of integrity and responsibility. He reduced costs and increased efficiency to the point of converting an annual deficit of about $100,000 to a surplus of the same amount, that he put into postal extensions. He collected over $40,000 a year in post office receipts that had hitherto been concealed. He introduced regular reports. John Quincy Adams did not fail to recognize McLean's ability, however doubtful he might become of his loyalty. In 1827 he wrote in his diary: "Mr. McLean . . . is perhaps the most efficient officer that has ever been in that place." [59] All factions of the Republican party joined in approval of the bill to increase his salary to Cabinet level.[60] The House Committee on Post Office and Post Roads declared in 1827, "The great amount of additional mail accommodation and revenue is not the only advantage which the public have derived from a vigilant administration of the Department. There is a degree of regularity and energy in all its operations, which is highly beneficial to the country." [61] In a decade that included such able men in high administrative posts as Calhoun in the War Department, Colonel Thayer at West Point, Rodgers in the Navy, and Adams in the State Department, McLean fully held his own.

McLean had political ambitions as well as administrative talents and moved easily in political circles. In 1816 he aided Monroe in securing the presidency; [62] in 1822 he quietly sup-

[58] *Dictionary of American Biography*, XII, 127–28; Francis P. Weisenburger, *The Life of John McLean: A Politician on the United States Supreme Court* (Columbus: Ohio State University Press, 1937).

[59] John Quincy Adams, *Memoirs*, VII, 343 (Oct. 23, 1827). Cf. *ibid.*, VII, 363 (Nov. 30, 1827). His biographer wrote, "It is probable that McLean's best talents were as an administrator." Weisenburger, *op. cit.*, p. 47.

[60] *American State Papers: Post Office*, pp. 145–46.

[61] *Ibid.*, p. 146.

[62] Weisenburger, *op. cit.*, p. 35.

ported Calhoun; [63] in 1824 he supported Adams; [64] in 1825 he opposed Crawford and later Clay; [65] during 1826 and 1827 he kept up a lively correspondence with friends in the west on political trends and information; [66] by 1827 he was believed by some to be a Jackson man; in 1831 he declined the presidential nomination of the Anti-Masonic party, but kept a steady gaze on the White House for nearly thirty years.[67]

McLean's appointment to the Land Office was due to Calhoun's influence, although the office was in the Treasury at the head of which was Crawford. His appointment to the Post Office Department was apparently due to the same support. Adams continued him in office, although aware of this personal friendship for a political rival.

By the spring of 1827 Adams noted the "opinion abroad" that McLean was hostile to the Administration, and despite McLean's disclaimers, declared, "His conduct is ambiguous. . . ." [68] By November both Clay and Barbour were complaining that McLean was "using perfidiously the influence and patronage of his office . . . against the Administration." [69] By the spring of 1828 (the year of election), Adams was convinced of McLean's duplicity in the use of patronage to defeat him for reelection. "The evidences of McLean's double-dealing, and the treachery to the cause of the Administration, have multiplied upon me till it would require the credulity of January in the tale to believe him honest or faithful." [70]

These harsh words were written in the midst of a violent controversy over McLean's pending appointment to the office

63 *Ibid.*, p. 32.

64 Adams, *Memoirs,* VI, 323.

65 *Ibid.*, VI, 488.

66 The Papers of John McLean, Library of Congress, Manuscript Division, Vols. I, II, *passim.*

67 *Dictionary of American Biography,* XII, 128.

68 Adams, *Memoirs,* VII, 275 (May 23, 1827).

69 *Ibid.*, VII, 349 (Nov. 7, 1827), and VII, 355 (Nov. 16, 1827).

70 *Ibid.*, VII, 544 (May 17, 1828). Shortly afterward he wrote in his diary, "The conduct of Mr. McLean has been that of deep and treacherous duplicity. . . . he has been three years using the extensive patronage of his office in undermining it [i.e., the Administration] among the people." *Ibid.*, VIII, 2 (June 3, 1828).

of postmaster in Philadelphia. In this case the least that can be said is that McLean used poor judgment. His action could have been readily interpreted as giving aid and comfort to Adams' political enemies. Adams so construed it.

As early as October 1826, the President had spoken to McLean of complaints against the Philadelphia postmaster, Richard Bache, but then and later McLean declared there were no grounds for his removal.[71] Finally on April 16, 1828, McLean went to the White House, informed Adams that Bache had again become delinquent and was to be removed, and that "he proposed to appoint Thomas Sergeant in his place." [72]

Adams pressed McLean on this selection and discovered that the Postmaster General had consulted Congressman Samuel D. Ingham of Pennsylvania, a Jackson man who was to become Secretary of the Treasury, and George Mifflin Dallas, mayor of Philadelphia, soon to be appointed district attorney by Jackson. The mortal affront conveyed by these names can only be fully understood in the light of an entry in Adams' diary six years earlier, "The Franklin Gazette, of Philadelphia, under the direction of R. Bache, G. M. Dallas, T. Sergeant, and Ingham, in concert with Rogers, opened immediately upon me, and had kept up ever since an insidious fire against me." [73] Adams acidly told McLean that "the deportment of these two men towards the Administration, and personally towards myself, made them singular counsellors for appointments to office under me." [74] The President might well have concluded that his Postmaster General, by an intrigue with his enemies, had succeeded in deeply offending his friends in Philadelphia.

McLean stoutly denied any conduct hostile to Adams, and in private letters asserted his loyalty to the Administration. In the summer of 1827 he wrote a long letter to a friend in Lebanon, Ohio, stating his position.

Some may conjecture that, my not engaging personally in the present contest, arises from objections to Mr. Adams, or a wish for the election of Gen. Jackson. Such is not the fact. I refrain from tak-

71 *Ibid.*, VII, 162 (Oct. 26, 1826); VII, 282 (May 30, 1827).
72 *Ibid.*, VII, 509 (April 16, 1828).
73 *Ibid.*, VI, 42–43 (July 8, 1822).
74 *Ibid.*, VII, 533.

ing an active part in the contest, because I conscientiously believe that the officers of the general government who hold in their hands an extensive patronage, ought not to engage in the canvass. . . .

. . . let the Post Master General, become an electioneering partisan, and suspicion will be attached to all his movements. He will not be able to sustain himself. The grounds of attack are everywhere. Every letter that is missent, delayed or lost through the mail, is charged to want of integrity in the Department. . . .

. . . What is to be the consequence, if every officer of the federal government must take an active part in the election of the President. The country will be continually agitated on that subject—confidence in the purity of the administration will be greatly impaired, and the contest will be carried on and decided with a reference to persons, more than principles. . . .

. . . So long as I hold an office under the general government, and especially my present office, I will never take, personally, an active agency in a presidential election. . . .

. . . I have never intimated or stated an objection to the reelection of Mr. Adams, or a wish that Gen. Jackson might succeed. I have defended both of them when unjustly assailed in my presence. This I shall continue to do. . . .[75]

In the summer of 1828 McLean exchanged a remarkable series of letters with Edward Everett, then a rising political figure in Massachusetts.[76] Everett maintained that it was folly not to prefer political supporters in making appointments to office, high and low, putting in its most palatable form the theory of rotation that was soon to become the platform of the Jacksonian Democrats and the alarm of the old Republicans. McLean rejected this view with an almost religious fervor. He wrote to Everett that patronage was a sacred trust, committed by the people to the hands of their agents to be used for the public benefit.[77] He declared that "qualification, merit and public sentiment, should combine to favour the successful applicant." He asserted that if the principle of favoritism were introduced, the struggle for office would be perpetual, and no

[75] Library of Congress, Manuscript Division, Papers of John McLean, II, 251 (August 19, 1827).

[76] John McLean-Edward Everett Letters in Massachusetts Historical Society, *Proceedings,* 3d series, I (1907–8), 360–93.

[77] *Ibid.,* p. 366.

higher motive would influence the combatants. The result
would be to let political integrity slip down to the grasp of
the lowest political intriguer.[78]

"Give me," said the Postmaster General, "the moral force
of the country, and I care little about office-hunters. . . . If I
did not believe that the people possess enough of virtue, intelligence and patriotism, to sustain this policy, I should despair
of the permanency of our institutions." [79] It is difficult to reconcile sentiments such as these with a course of conduct that
Adams considered to be political treachery. Many years later
McLean wrote to John Teesdale, "I stated to Mr. Adams, that,
as Postmaster-General, I would have nothing to do in making
him President, or General Jackson; that I would devote my
whole energies to serve the public." [80]

McLean's course of conduct when Jackson became President
supported his assertions of political neutrality in the post office.
Jackson asked him to make removals to find room for his
political friends. McLean refused. Jackson offered to transfer
him to another department. McLean declined. Jackson then
offered him a seat on the Supreme Court, and this appointment
he accepted. In letters written well after the event, McLean
described his position and that of General Jackson.

. . . When General Jackson invited me to remain at Washington,
I told him that I had not done anything to advance his election,
but that, in the discharge of my official duties, I had been actuated
by no other motive than to promote the public interests. He
approved of my course; but it was found before his administration
commenced that I could not take one step with them. The bench
was offered to me, and I accepted it.[81]

Was John McLean a hypocrite, as Adams firmly believed, or
a statesman? Calhoun's biographer, Charles M. Wiltse, concluded that he was innocent of the charges of abusing the patronage.[82] The biographer of Richard Rush declared in rather

[78] *Ibid.*, p. 367.
[79] *Ibid.*, p. 388.
[80] Sept. 26, 1846. William Salter, ed., "Letters of John McLean to John Teesdale," *Bibliotheca Sacra*, LVI (1899), 717–40 at 724.
[81] *Ibid.*, p. 720 (July 9, 1846).
[82] Wiltse, *John C. Calhoun: Nationalist*, p. 358, n. 17.

general but certainly correct terms that McLean refused to make the postal service a spoilsmen's paradise.[83] Senator Jesse B. Thomas of Illinois accepted at face value McLean's declaration of loyalty to the Administration.[84] It is well known, further, that Adams possessed a suspicious temperament and tended to brood over his contemporaries. Even after the Philadelphia episode when Adams' convictions were fully settled, he wrote in his diary that McLean had played his game "with so much cunning and duplicity" that Adams could fix upon no positive act that would justify his removal.[85] This suggests that McLean could claim with some show of reason that his error was one of judgment, not of political immorality.

The evidence that has come to hand is insufficient to permit a firm judgment on McLean's course of conduct. In the highly charged political atmosphere from 1827 to 1828, it was easy to misinterpret motives and to misunderstand adherence to principles that brought political handicaps to an Administration fighting to save itself. My interpretation of McLean's official actions is that he held the views and acted the part of the statesman. He was sufficiently unsatisfactory to the politicians in 1826 so that they sought to create a new judgeship in the Supreme Court with the understanding that McLean would be appointed to it.[86] He refused to cooperate with Jackson in removing postmasters to make room for Jackson men, and was sent upstairs by Jackson to the Supreme Court in 1829.[87] He made a serious error of judgment in the Philadelphia post office case, which could plausibly be interpreted as political disloyalty—but which can also be construed as bad judgment. His Methodism and his uprightness of character combined to make unlikely the sort of duplicity of which Adams was convinced he was guilty. McLean's sentiments on the appointing power were those of a statesman, and his record of action so far as it remains for inspection suggests a close conformity with his views.

83 J. H. Powell, *Richard Rush,* p. 180.

84 Adams, *Memoirs,* VII, 536.

85 *Ibid.,* VIII, 51 (July 7, 1828).

86 Charles Warren, *The Supreme Court in United States History* (3 vols., Boston: Little, Brown, 1923), II, 143, n. 1.

87 Adams, *Memoirs,* VIII, 109–10 (March 9, 1829). Adams commented on McLean: "He declined serving as the broom to sweep the post-offices."

CHAPTER TWENTY-TWO

Postmasters and Contractors

In the smaller cities and villages postmasters were relatively humble citizens who performed a useful public service for their neighbors without thought of preferment or view of future ambition. In the large cities postmasters occupied a more prominent position and were usually selected from among persons of standing in the community. Some had been politically successful and retired to a relatively quiet administrative post; some were politically ambitious; others were gentlemen who had a taste for the public service.

Solomon Southwick, whose removal from the Albany post office caused widespread reverberations, had had a long political career. The son of a Newport, Rhode Island, printer whose devotion to the Revolutionary cause had wrecked his fortunes, he began life at sea. In 1791 he became a printer's apprentice in New York City, removed to Albany where he became junior partner in a strong Republican paper, the *Albany Register,* and by 1803 was elected clerk of the New York State Assembly. He held one political office after another until he became postmaster in 1815. He was removed in 1822, having become insolvent by reason of speculation in real estate and carelessness in his accounts. After two subsequent attempts at the governorship, both unsuccessful, he turned to religion.[1]

His successor, General Solomon Van Rensselaer, was a Revolutionary patriot, a member of Congress, and a scion of the powerful Van Rensselaer family of upper New York. For twenty years in the forty-year period from 1789 to 1829, the

[1] *Dictionary of American Biography,* XVII, 413–14.

Albany district had been represented in Congress by a member of this family, which was equally active in the affairs of the state. Solomon Van Rensselaer epitomized the up-state New York country gentleman. Of his anticipated appointment he wrote, "by abandoning politics, with a strict regard to my duty, I may sit down in comfort, peace and quietness with an affectionate family the rest of my precarious days." [2]

General Theodorus Bailey, postmaster of New York from 1804 until his death in 1828, had been in the House of Representatives for four terms and was beginning a term as Senator when he resigned to take the post office appointment. Senator Michael Leib of Pennsylvania also resigned his seat in the Senate in 1814 to become postmaster of Philadelphia. John S. Skinner, postmaster of Baltimore from 1816 to 1837, and third assistant postmaster from 1841 to 1845, was perhaps best known as the founder of *The American Farmer* in 1819, the first continuous successful agricultural periodical in the United States. He was a great agricultural publicist, carrying on these activities for over twenty-five years outside his working hours as a public official.[3] While postmaster he became involved in South American conspiracies that once led to his indictment, and to a critical evaluation by John Quincy Adams.

. . . He is a man of mingled character, of daring and pernicious principles, of restless and rash temper, and yet of useful and honorable enterprise. Ruffian, patriot, and philanthropist are so blended in him that I cannot appreciate him without a mingled sentiment of detestation and esteem.[4]

A different type of postmaster presided over the Richmond office. Dr. William Fouchee died in harness at the age of seventy-five: "a highly respected and much beloved gentleman." [5] He was succeeded by a former governor of Virginia, James Preston.[6]

2 Catharina V. R. Bonney, *Legacy of Historical Gleanings,* I, 370.

3 *Dictionary of American Biography,* XVII, 199–201.

4 Adams, *Memoirs,* IV, 515–16 (Feb. 1, 1820).

5 *Niles Register,* XXVII, 16 (Sept. 4, 1824).

6 *Ibid.,* XXVII, 64 (Sept. 25, 1824). Niles thought it worth while in 1821 to record that of 4,030 postmasters all were born in America except 161, and of 481 mail contractors all were native born except 20. *Ibid.,* XIX, 312 (Jan. 6, 1821).

POSTMASTER APPOINTMENTS

Postmasters had been appointed since Washington's day by the Postmaster General.[7] This practice was continued throughout the Jeffersonian period, and it was unusual for the Postmaster General to consult the President, or to be called in by him to receive executive advice. This gulf between President and Postmaster General occasionally caused violent disturbances. As factional contest sharpened during the 1820's, it became more and more difficult to allow the Postmaster General full freedom of action.

Jefferson, indeed, advised Madison to take hold of the situation. He wrote:

. . . The true remedy for putting those appointments into a wholesome state would be a law vesting them in the President, but without the intervention of the Senate. That intervention would make the matter worse. Every Senator would expect to dispose of all the post offices in his vicinage, or perhaps in his state. At present the President has some controul over those appointments by his authority over the Postmaster himself. And I should think it well to require him to lay all his appointments previously before the President for his approbation or rejection.[8]

Voices were raised in Congress at the same time in favor of senatorial confirmation of presidential nominations—the very plan that Jefferson feared. Charles Jared Ingersoll declaimed against the patronage of the Postmaster General: "unless some remedy be applied to this evil, and that without delay, we are in danger of a new order of Jesuits, in this country, with an unlimited General at their head, to dictate his orders, and enforce them. . . ."[9] Congress, however, took no action. Even the Tenure of Office Act of 1820 left the appointment of postmasters where it had been, with the Postmaster General.

That postmasters would normally be selected from Republicans was taken for granted. The sentiment of the times was reflected by a correspondent of Gideon Granger who wrote from upper New York in these words.

[7] For early practice, see White, *The Federalists,* ch. 15.
[8] Jefferson, *Works* (Federal ed.), XI, 392 (March 10, 1814).
[9] *Annals,* 13th Cong., I, 865 (Jan. 7, 1814).

. . . That a Post office would be useful at that place . . . is admitted. But the proposed Post-Master *Seymour* . . . is the last man deserving any favor from this Government. He is not only an opponent of the administration, which however I think ought to be sufficient, but he is an old *tory* of the most violent and malignant class.

. . . I would recommend to your consideration *Asa Hickox* Esqr . . . who is as honest and correct in his private capacity as he is in his political principles.[10]

The Postmaster General consulted various sources of information, and made his own inquiries of persons residing in localities where a vacancy had to be supplied. Representatives and Senators were regular advisers. Persons prominent in the affairs of state, county, or city were asked independently for their views of applicants. One branch of the General Post Office was occupied by the never-ending task of collecting files on prospective nominees. The recommendations of persons prominent in public life and party councils were of special value, but there is also evidence that the Postmaster General made an independent decision.[11]

The independent exercise of this power was, however, a dangerous privilege. Gideon Granger declined to accept Madison's remonstrances against the intended appointment of Senator Michael Leib of Pennsylvania, one of the President's leading political opponents. Leib became postmaster of Philadelphia, but Granger ceased to be Postmaster General. Madison did not even deign to notify him that he was sending to the Senate the nomination of his successor, Return J. Meigs, Jr. John McLean had his own troubles as the result of appointing Thomas Sergeant to the Philadelphia post office. McLean made the appointment, but at the cost of losing Adams' confidence and at the peril of losing his own office.

The complications of postmaster appointments were well illustrated when it became necessary early in 1822 to replace the Albany postmaster, Solomon Southwick, for delinquency in his

10 Library of Congress, Papers of Gideon and Francis Granger, Letter No. 23 (Jan. 16, 1814).

11 An interesting case is reported in *Niles Register*, XXXVI, 365 (August 1, 1829).

accounts. Twenty-two members of the New York delegation, representing a variety of factions and both parties, recommended General Solomon Van Rensselaer, then holding a seat in the House of Representatives, and a Federalist. Postmaster General Meigs, doubtless suspecting trouble, called the matter to the attention of Monroe, who said that he had no objection but wished to consult the Secretary of the Navy, Smith Thompson, a New Yorker. Thompson protested in the strongest manner, and promptly informed Van Buren, Senator from New York, and Vice President Tompkins, also a New Yorker. According to Adams' account, Tompkins was so exasperated that he "broke out into the most violent language against the President himself, and in presence of a person who he must have known would report all he said to him." [12]

Van Buren asked for delay in making the appointment and began to bring all possible pressure to bear on Meigs from the New York Republicans.[13] The Van Rensselaer family, backed by Governor De Witt Clinton, took equally strong measures to defend their candidate. Van Buren and Vice President Tompkins put the issue squarely before the Postmaster General: "we had flattered ourselves, with the hope that for new appointments at least (all other matters equal) a preference would be given by every department of a republican administration to its republican supporters." [14]

Monroe was in an awkward position, caught between the New York Senators, Van Buren and King, the Vice President and the Secretary of the Navy on the one hand, and the House delegation on the other, although its members showed signs of weakening under Van Buren's pressure. Monroe called a Cabinet meeting for advice. Wirt and Crawford condemned Meigs for having ever laid the case before the President, but argued that under the circumstances, Monroe would have to decide. Adams defended Meigs, and reminded the Cabinet that Madison

[12] Adams, *Memoirs,* V, 479 (Jan. 4, 1822).
[13] The whole episode may be traced in detail in correspondence published in Catharina V. R. Bonney, compiler, *A Legacy of Historical Gleanings,* Vol. I, 369-93; and in *Niles Register,* Vol. XXI (1822), *passim.* The incident began December 25, 1821, when news of Southwick's pending removal leaked out, and closed on January 7, 1822, when Meigs appointed Van Rensselaer.
[14] Bonney, *op. cit.,* I, 391.

had removed Granger for appointing Leib postmaster at Philadelphia. Adams also argued that the President ought to retain
the right to intervene in postmaster appointments upon occasion. To which Crawford retorted that if the appointments were
to become a responsibility of the President, then confirmation
by the Senate should be required. Calhoun agreed with Adams.[15]

Monroe refused to intervene. Meigs wrote a brief note to
Van Buren and Tompkins, regretting that he had not been able
"to accord with your views and opinions," [16] and appointed
Federalist Van Rensselaer. Van Buren declared privately, "We
have been shamefully treated by the post-master-general in this
matter," but absolved Monroe from blame.[17] Van Buren sought
to avenge this defeat in 1829 when he became Secretary of State.
Threatened with removal, Van Rensselaer betook himself to
Washington, called upon President Jackson, and prepared to
tear open his shirt to show the wounds he had received in fighting for his country. He was instantly confirmed in his office.[18]

These cases suggest what an abundance of evidence would
prove, that the post-office prizes were not being overlooked by
the politically active members of the country. Competition for
appointment to the larger post offices was keen by the 1820's.
When rumors of a vacancy in the Albany office began to spread
in 1821 Governor Clinton wrote, "a Scramble will take place
for the spoil." [19] In 1825 Senator Elijah H. Mills of Massachusetts wrote his wife on a Sunday evening, "I have been all day
engaged in reading and collecting letters of recommendation
and applications for the office of post-master, so unexpectedly
vacated by the sudden death of my old friend, Daniel Wright."
He named eleven, all his personal friends, and added, "you will
perceive the embarrassments in which I am placed." [20]

15 Adams, *Memoirs*, V, 480–82 (Jan. 5, 1822).

16 *Niles Register*, XXI, 360 (Feb. 2, 1822).

17 Bonney, *op. cit.*, I, 383 (Jan. 10, 1822).

18 Carl Russell Fish, *The Civil Service and the Patronage* (Cambridge:
Harvard University Press, 1904), p. 118.

19 Bonney, *op. cit.*, I, 369 (Dec. 25, 1821).

20 Letters of Elijah H. Mills, Massachusetts Historical Society, *Proceedings*,
XIX (1881–82), 45 (Jan. 2, 1825).

TENURE

Postmasters held office at the pleasure of the Postmaster General, being appointed for no specific term and possessing no protection in law against removal. Apart from the first two years of Jefferson's administration, however, they enjoyed the benefit of a tradition of tenure during good behavior, very broadly construed. Removals were usually confined to the serious offense of gross carelessness, or worse, in accounts.

Until Jefferson achieved a due proportion of office for Republicans, i.e., until 1803, the postmasters were in an exposed position. Granger took an ambiguous course. On one occasion he wrote:

To remove people from the subordinate offices for a difference of opinion is both unjust and impolitic,—unjust; because the Deity and not Government gave man his rational faculties, and the free use of them and the elective franchise ought to be secure from party bars. Impolitic; because a wise Government would soothe, not irritate, because the contrary rule would change the Government from being the common father of the people and bring it down to the humble head of a party.[21]

At the same time he stated in a letter printed by the *New York Evening Post* that, in the light of recent events, "it occurred to me that some removals would become necessary, as well to effect an equal participation and enjoyment of office by the two great classes of citizens who are designated by the terms of Federalists and Republicans as to preserve and maintain confidence in the department." [22]

Some postmasters were removed to make way for Republicans; and after 1803, as vacancies occurred, they were filled with Republicans. With the passage of time and the decline of the Federalists, the postmasters naturally became predominantly Republican. Their tenure was not disturbed by party oscillation. The rule on postmaster removals that was established by John McLean confirmed the practice during the Jeffersonian

21 Quoted in Wesley E. Rich, *History of the United States Post Office*, pp. 128–29.

22 March 2, 1802, quoted in *ibid.*, p. 129.

period, apart from the earliest years. McLean wrote a member of Congress in these forthright terms.

> . . . I have adopted a rule to remove no postmaster without substantial cause, and then not until he shall have had an opportunity to meet the charges against him. This will make a removal of the highest consequence to the office. As it will be understood that the ground on which a removal is made, is that he is not entitled to public confidence. I can see no reason why the character and interests of Postmasters should not be treated with as much respect as other officers of the government. A removal without substantial objection against the individual must be productive of pernicious consequences to the public, as the fear of it cannot stimulate to a careful discharge of duty.[23]

Stability was the order of the day, from the assistant postmaster general, Abraham Bradley, to the postmasters in the 8,000 offices stretching from Maine to New Orleans and across the Mississippi. The consequence was that in the larger offices postmasters became a type of career executive.

ACCOUNTABILITY

For many years the General Post Office was incapable of securing accounts promptly from postmasters and of enforcing their liability to turn in their postal collections. How serious and widespread this problem was did not become public until 1824 when Congress required a statement from the Postmaster General containing the names of defaulters for the sixteen years prior to July 1, 1823. We may suspect that McLean inspired the request.[24] He became Postmaster General in 1823 and must have discovered a situation for which he would not have cared to take responsibility. The 1824 list of delinquent postmasters, which contained apparently only the names of

---

[23] August 13, 1823; quoted in Weisenburger, *Life of John McLean,* p. 43.

[24] Although Congress was on the trail in 1820; see "Letter from the Postmaster General transmitting a Report of the names of Persons who were indebted to the Post Office Department. . . ." House Doc. 111, 16th Cong., 2d sess. (Feb. 3, 1821). This list, covering 234 pages, was useless to Congress because it included every one whose accounts were unsettled, whether delinquent or not. Congress made a second attempt to locate the defaulters in 1822, but found it "a fact difficult to ascertain." *American State Papers: Post Office,* p. 98 (April 29, 1822).

actual defaulters,[25] was astonishingly large, just over two thousand among about six thousand postmasters. Most of the defalcations were small, amounting to five dollars, sixty-two dollars, occasionally a few hundred dollars. Some of them, however, were considerable. The postmaster of Savannah, Georgia, Philip Box, surpassed his fellows with an indebtedness of $16,412.07; defalcation seemed to have been the rule in this city, for two earlier postmasters of Savannah were also in arrears, one for over $3,000, another for $1,000. Twenty-nine postmasters were in default for sums over one thousand dollars.

Further examination of the 1824 list demonstrates, however, that the position was due in many cases not to moral turpitude but either to honest differences of opinion as to small amounts in arrears or to failure on the part of the General Post Office to devote itself seriously to the task of collection. It would be unreasonable to charge the postmaster of China Grove, South Carolina, with embezzlement in the amount of $4.15, or the postmaster of Scholharie Kill, New York, with stealing $1.66, or the postmaster of Wind Gap, Pennsylvania, of absconding with forty-four cents. Of the whole list of 2,093 delinquent postmasters, nearly 1,400 owed sums of less than fifty dollars.

These figures suggest that the Postmaster General needed a simpler, and less expensive, means of collection than a lawsuit —his only recourse. To secure these debts would have cost far more than the debts themselves. Collection was a specific duty of the Postmaster General and in order to ensure diligence on his part, Congress had made him personally liable for defalcations. The House committee initiating the 1824 list consequently asked to be informed of the amount charged against the Postmaster General. McLean replied curtly that "no sum . . . has been charged . . . against the Postmaster General." [26] In his annual report for 1824 McLean stated that "unremitting exertions" had been made to collect balances due, but that no suits had been instituted where both the postmaster and his sureties were found to be insolvent.[27] In his report for 1825 he

25 House Doc. 144, 18th Cong., 1st sess. (April 7, 1824), pp. 1–90. The comptroller of the Treasury's list of three-year delinquents did not include postmasters.

26 *Ibid.*, p. 3.

27 *American State Papers: Post Office*, p. 118 (Nov. 30, 1824).

declared that the quarterly returns of postmasters were then being made with "great punctuality." [28]

The principal problem of accountability was not the prosecution of exceptional cases but rather the administrative task of getting regular financial reports from 8,000 postmasters. The vast majority lived in small communities, and were performing a service to their neighbors for a niggardly compensation. They were much more concerned with their daily private affairs than with filling out official forms. Even here McLean made much progress.

One means of enforcing compliance would have been to send inspectors from headquarters to visit and examine the affairs at least of the larger offices. This means was apparently neither conceived nor discussed. Agents were employed from time to time to apprehend mail robbers, but not to discover dishonest or negligent postmasters.[29]

THE CONTRACTORS

When the government put the post office on new foundations in 1792, it might have chosen to establish its own stage lines and riders, but no one proposed such an innovation. With two exceptions the mail was carried for the government by private citizens entering into contracts with it. An agreement was made with each of them designating the routes (already authorized by Congress), specifying the frequency and time of delivery of the mail, the means of carriage—stagecoach, sulky, or horseback —the penalties for failure, and the amount of compensation. The number of contractors on December 31, 1821, was 693 for 1,048 routes; [30] by 1828 the number approximated 2,000.

The two exceptions to the contract system may be noted briefly. Service between Philadelphia and Baltimore became so

[28] *Ibid.*, p. 138 (Nov. 24, 1825).

[29] One of the best known agents was Chester Bailey, also a contractor for the mail route from Philadelphia to New York. "No agent," Meigs declared, "has ever served this Department more faithfully or usefully than Mr. Bailey has done; he has been the means of prosecuting to conviction more offenders against the Post Office law, within the last ten years, than all other persons in the United States unconnected with this Department." *Ibid.*, p. 102 (April 1822); see also *ibid.*, p. 97.

[30] *Ibid.*, p. 98.

unsatisfactory that Habersham established a line of government stages in 1799. In response to a Senate inquiry in 1802, Granger reported that the mail had been carried "with unexampled regularity and despatch, within the body of a carriage, in a box prepared for that purpose, less liable to be chafed and injured, and secured from robbery and inclement weather." He added that the fare of travelers on the stage line had fully defrayed the expense of the establishment, and that the profits were estimated at about $11,000 for three years.[31]

The second government stage line was set up in 1810, between Philadelphia and New York. The delivery on this line had become so irregular that Granger bought public stages and horses, through Chester Bailey as agent, and retained Bailey to superintend the line. The improved service met Granger's "most decided approbation." Meigs advertised for bids when he became Postmaster General in 1814, but decided to retain the government stage, for reasons full of contemporary interest. The line, he said, "operated as a check upon contractors, both in repressing exorbitant demands, and stimulating contractors to a faithful discharge of their duty." Thus early did the central concept of yardstick regulation appear in federal practice. This line was finally sold to Bailey in 1816.[32]

The process of contracting was relatively simple. Before an existing agreement expired the department advertised for offers. Holders of the expiring contract were normally anxious to secure a renewal, and to be free from ruinous underbidding. Their attitude was well expressed in a communication from John Tayloe.

Owning so much property on the road, in the stage way, and finding it impossible to be back by the 18th of September, when your contracts are to be closed, I am induced, by letter, to forward you my proposals for the same.

I will carry your mails from Alexandria to Dumfries, and back again, on the same terms, low as they are, as I have heretofore done, namely for $1,800 a year. . . . Should any person or company offer on lower terms, which will be ruinous, yet, from the great expense I have been at in erecting houses on the road, and the improvement

[31] *Ibid.*, pp. 21–22.
[32] *Ibid.*, p. 102.

of the stage line, I trust, as an old contractor, and a faithful one, too, you will give me permission to take it, when I say I will carry it lower for you than any other person.[33]

Offers or bids were usually brief and simple. "I will carry the mail from Washington to Alexandria . . . for the sum of $800 a year." "I propose to carry the mail of the United States from Washington City to Fredericksburg, agreeably to your advertisement . . . at the rate of $3,700 per annum." [34] The process of making awards was arduous and time-consuming. In 1827 McLean told John Quincy Adams that for a fortnight he had been at his office from early morning until night, working on contracts, even having his dinner sent there from his house.[35]

Not much evidence has appeared to show that contractors or bidders took advantage of their congressional connections, but that some did not overlook this asset is clear from the correspondence of Duff Green, later a figure in the Jackson administration. Green was badly in debt and wrote his brother-in-law, Senator Ninian Edwards, for help in getting the mail route from Franklin to Liberty. "Urge this on the Post-Master General and by all means secure me this contract." [36]

The terms of mail contracts are illustrated in an agreement between the Post Office Department and George Williams on September 20, 1813. The two parties mutually covenanted that Williams would carry the mail from Washington to Fredericksburg, Virginia, and return, every day, for $825 a quarter. The rest of the contract was devoted to penalties for delay and failure; two dollars for each hour delay, double the sum due for a single trip if connections were lost with depending mails, five dollars for passing an office, and so on. The General Post Office retained the right to require the discharge of any carrier upon reasonable complaint, and to annul the contract under certain circumstances.[37] Contracts were commonly for one year, but at times were made for longer periods. With the permission of the department, contracts could be sold, and in 1822 rumors were

---

33 *Ibid.*, p. 78 (August 30, 1813).
34 *Ibid.*, p. 78.
35 Adams, *Memoirs*, VII, 344 (Oct. 25, 1827).
36 *The Edwards Papers* (E. B. Washburne, ed.), p. 214 (Dec. 10, 1823).
37 *American State Papers: Post Office*, p. 79.

circulating that contracts had been improperly obtained for profit on a resale. A House committee found no evidence to support this charge.[38] Contracts were let after advertisement, usually but not always to the lowest bidder.

Contractors were expected to reside in the neighborhood of their routes in order to give them proper supervision. On this point a *cause célèbre* occurred in 1826. Duff Green, whose appeal to Senator Edwards has just been recorded, held a contract in Missouri. McLean learned that he was planning to remove to Washington and consequently sent him the following letter.

It is desirable that all who have any agency in the operations of this Department should, as far as practicable, devote their personal attention to the same. This is considered as indispensable, so far as postmasters are concerned, and it is the policy of the Department to apply the same rule to contractors. I am aware that the control over those who transport the mail must, necessarily, be far less effective in this respect than over postmasters, as the contract fixes the conditions, and that of personal superintendence is not included among them. But it is not doubted that the personal attention of contractors insures greater regularity and energy in the conveyance of the mail, and has a tendency to elevate the character of the Department.[39]

Duff Green replied with some heat, protesting against any right of the Postmaster General to select his place of residence, and informing the department that he intended to dispose of his interest in the route, for reasons that might well have alarmed McLean.

I was induced to do this, because, having determined to become the editor of a newspaper, the object of which was to expose the abuse of the patronage of the Government, I was unwilling to subject myself to the charge of sharing that patronage.

. . . I regret to see an admission coming from you, which goes so far to strengthen the prevailing opinion, that every man who refuses to give in his adhesion to the present dynasty shall be proscribed. . . . although it is my fixed purpose to use all lawful and honorable means to prevent the re-election of Mr. Adams, it

38 *Ibid.*, p. 97.
39 *Ibid.*, p. 148 (April 13, 1826).

is not therefore proper that I should be denied the rights of a citizen.[40]

Fortunately for the equilibrium of the post office, there were few Duff Greens among the contractors, and few difficulties in keeping contractors in the vicinage of their routes.

McLean drove the contractors hard. In 1823 he warned them that any failure to convey the mail under cover, or to deliver it on time would result in a fine. "And if this remedy should prove ineffectual, the conveyance will be placed in other hands." [41] In 1825 he sent out a circular declaring:

. . . No obstacles, which human exertions can overcome, shall excuse a failure. Any want of energy, in this respect, will first be noticed by the highest pecuniary penalty; and, for a second failure, the contract will be forfeited.

. . . Whatever may be the condition of the route, no trip should be lost. . . .[42]

In the contracts for 1826 and thereafter McLean introduced the rule of a penalty for every failure "without regard to the cause producing it." He also increased the fine for failure to connect with a depending line, through any want of exertion, to forfeiture of the contract at the discretion of the department.[43] Given the often legitimate reasons for delay, this penalty permitted the department a measure of discipline that was in principle extreme, and that could hardly have been ventured under the less energetic disposition of previous administrations.

We may leave the contractors by reporting an incident full of human interest. The story is told by John Quincy Adams, then President of the United States.

Mr. Clay came, and introduced the committee of the mail contractors, who had passed a written resolution that they would in a body visit the President and the Secretary of State, and they enquired at what time I could with convenience receive them. As some of them were going away to-morrow morning, I fixed upon four o'clock this afternoon. They then came in procession, upwards

40 *Ibid.*, pp. 148–49 (April 15, 1826).
41 *Niles Register*, XXIV, 308 (July 19, 1823).
42 *Ibid.*, XXVII, 341 (Jan. 29, 1825).
43 *American State Papers: Post Office*, p. 144.

of a hundred in number. I received them in the winter parlor, shook hands with them all, and, at the suggestion of Mr. Clay, who said they would perhaps be glad to see the house, showed them the rooms on the lower floor and those above, with the exception of the bedchambers. There was cake and wine served to them, and I drank success to them all, through highways and byways. Their visit was over in about half an hour. These are persons from all parts of the Union, who at this time of the year come to offer proposals of contracts for carrying the mails. . . . This, I believe, is the first time that they have assembled and acted as a body.[44]

It was also probably the first time that a President of the United States gave a personally conducted tour of the White House to a body of humble citizens, seeking contracts with the government.

The story of the post office during the first thirty years of the century was in some respects a dramatic one. The conquest of the open spaces of the Mississippi Valley by post riders, struggling through forests, swamps, and mud was a never-ending test of courage and determination. The increase in the number of routes and the miles of post roads was beyond all past experience. The post office, by virtue of its magnitude as well as the importance of its function in furnishing citizens "with full and correct information," steadily carried more weight—and was steadily drawn closer to the political vortex from which McLean succeeded for his time in preserving it.

The administrative structure of the General Post Office showed the characteristic quality of specialization that was also a feature of the management of army and naval affairs. The basic elements of the postal system stood intact: the General Post Office with its clerks, the postmasters, and the contractors. The transformation of the postal service derived not from reorganization but from the force of a single individual, Postmaster General from 1823 to 1829, John McLean. The change is put in a single sentence in one of his circulars: "If two horses to a cart do not give sufficient force, four should be applied." [45]

McLean was not merely a driver, he knew how to draw out

---

44 Adams, *Memoirs*, VII, 340–41 (Oct. 18, 1827).
45 *Niles Register*, XXVII, 341 (Jan. 29, 1825).

exertions by the more subtle qualities of leadership. He wrote to the postmasters and contractors:

Each one should consider himself so far identified with the department, as to participate in the elevation of its character, and his increasing efforts should be directed to so desirable an object. The postmaster general acknowledges with a high degree of satisfaction, the efficiency of many thousands of those who are connected with him in the discharge of arduous and responsible duties. . . .[46]

The post office was acquiring a corporate spirit.

[46] *Ibid.*, XXXIII, 90 (Oct. 6, 1827).

CHAPTER TWENTY-THREE

The Office of Attorney General

The Federalists left the Attorney General in 1801 an officer without an office, a legal adviser without a clerk, a prosecutor with no control over the district attorneys, a counsel who earned the larger share of his professional fees from his private clients. By the end of the Jeffersonian period the passage of time, the pressure of work, and the contributions of William Wirt had created an office of dignity and respect, although *sui generis* in several particulars.

Until 1814 the office of Attorney General was where the Attorney General happened to be. When Levi Lincoln went to Massachusetts, the office went with him. When Caesar A. Rodney left for Delaware, the office left, too; and no legal business could be transacted, except by mail, until the absent Attorney General returned. William Pinkney never took up residence in Washington, living in Baltimore during the two years he served in this capacity. Madison was embarrassed by his absence and in 1814 the House of Representatives instructed its Judiciary Committee to consider legislation requiring the Attorney General to reside at the seat of government. Pinkney promptly resigned, although Congress enacted no legislation. Richard Rush, his successor, was told by Madison to live in Washington.[1]

The requirement that the Attorney General reside in Washington changed the character of the office. The Attorney General had always been considered a member of the Cabinet, but now he was able to attend meetings regularly. Being on the spot increased the number of calls for his opinions and the occasions

[1] Homer Cummings and Carl McFarland, *Federal Justice: Chapters in the History of Justice and the Federal Executive* (New York: Macmillan, 1937), p. 78.

for informal advice; his business more than doubled. The increasing amount of Supreme Court litigation also symbolized the changing stature of the office.[2]

Residence was only the first step in the creation of an office. As Monroe explained to Congressman Lowndes in 1817, "The office has no apartment for business, nor clerks, nor a messenger, nor stationary, nor fuel allowed. These have been supplied by the officer himself, at his own expense." [3] Over some opposition on grounds of economy, Congress took the second step in 1818 by authorizing the Attorney General to appoint one clerk at $1,000,[4] and in 1819 to spend $500 for contingencies.[5] Wirt took another step in 1817 by setting up a simple system of records, consisting of an Opinion Book and a letter book.[6] In 1818 he asked Nourse to provide furniture, the list of which would amuse any practicing attorney of a later generation: ten book presses, a press for public papers and letter books, a map and chart stand, a writing desk and seat for his clerk, six chairs, two washstands, a stone pitcher and tumblers, and one water table.[7] The office began to be visible.

For twenty years the duties of Attorney General had been administered with an indifference to records and precedents that is remarkable. When Wirt became Attorney General in 1817 he found nothing.

. . . my first inquiry was for the books containing the acts of advice and opinions of my predecessors: I was told there were none such. I asked for the letter-books, containing their official correspondence: the answer was, that there were no such books. I asked for the documents belonging to the office . . . but my inquiries resulted in the discovery that there was not to be found, in connection with this office, any trace of a pen indicating, in the slightest manner, any one act of advice or opinion which had been given by

---

[2] *American State Papers: Miscellaneous*, II, 418–19.

[3] *Ibid.*, II, 419. In 1817 Rufus King contemptuously called this "an office composed of scraps & offals from other Depts." King, *Correspondence*, VI, 46.

[4] 3 Stat. 445, sec. 6 (April 20, 1818).

[5] 3 Stat. 496 at 500 (March 3, 1819).

[6] The first printed collection of opinions of the Attorneys General was issued in 1841. House Doc. 123, 26th Cong., 2d sess. (March 3, 1841).

[7] Cummings and McFarland, *op. cit.*, p. 81.

any one of my predecessors, from the first foundation of the federal government to the moment of my inquiry.[8]

As might be anticipated, he also found none of the laws of the several states, the omission of which he called "a serious practical evil."[9]

Although the office of Attorney General thus took form after the War of 1812, its competence was narrowly interpreted by the very man who put it on its feet. William Wirt refused to recognize "the government" in general as his client, but construed his responsibility narrowly to requests for opinions emanating from the President and the heads of departments alone, and to the prosecution of cases only in the Supreme Court. When he came to Washington he found that he was called on for opinions by committees of Congress, by the district attorneys, by collectors of customs and internal revenue, by the marshals, and by courts martial.[10] He began a steady course of curtailment to the strict range of duties prescribed by law. These duties he discovered to include only "to prosecute and conduct all suits in the Supreme Court in which the United States shall be concerned, and to give his advice and opinion upon questions of law when required by the President of the United States, or when requested by the heads of any of the departments, touching any matter that may concern their departments."[11]

Starting with the principle that "the influence of every office should be confined within the strict limits prescribed for it by law," he declined to give opinions to state officials, subordinate federal officers, civil and military, and private persons.[12] He also curtailed the practice of requests from congressional com-

8 Wirt, *Memoirs*, II, 62; also in somewhat different text in *American State Papers: Miscellaneous*, II, 590.

9 Wirt, *Memoirs*, II, 63.

10 *Ibid.*, II, 63.

11 1 Stat. 73, sec. 35 (Sept. 24, 1789). A House committee asserted in 1822 that the War Department had employed counsel other than the Attorney General, instancing a member of the House and of the Senate. House Report 81, 17th Cong., 1st sess., p. 6 (March 29, 1822).

12 Cummings and McFarland, *op. cit.*, pp. 82, 83.

mittees asking for his legal advice, especially on claims.[13] To one of them he wrote:

The Attorney General is sworn to discharge the duties of his office *according to law*. To be instrumental in enlarging the sphere of his official duties beyond that which is prescribed by law, would, in my opinion, be a violation of this oath. . . .

. . . believing, as I do, that, in a Government purely of laws, it would be incalculably dangerous to permit an officer to act, under color of his office, beyond the pale of the law, I trust I shall be excused from making any *official* report on the order with which the House has honored me.[14]

Wirt was governed by good Republican doctrine in construing narrowly his own powers. He was also influenced by the lack of means to accomplish more than his strict duty. "I am convinced," he declared in 1818, "that no single unassisted individual, whatever may be his strength, his habits of industry, or the system and celerity of his movements, could discharge, in a manner satisfactory either to himself or the nation, the vast load of duties . . ." which were in the process of piling up from all quarters. To carry the load would require the Attorney General to abandon his private practice, and Wirt hinted that lack of time for private practice was in part responsible for the frequent resignations of his predecessors.[15]

Wirt found the office "no *sinecure*. I have been up 'till midnight, at work, every night, and still have my hands full." [16] In 1821 he wrote his friend, Judge Carr:

During the last Supreme Court I was very much engaged. I was forced to lose my wonted sleep, and had not a moment for exercise. The Court kept me constantly engaged till four o'clock: I had then to hasten home to dinner, and, immediately afterwards, to sit down to my papers till ten, eleven and twelve at night—then up again at three or four in the morning, and with merely time enough to take breakfast, off, as rapidly as my carriage could drive me, to the Capitol, at eleven.[17]

13 *Ibid.*, p. 86.
14 *American State Papers: Miscellaneous*, II, 575 (Feb. 3, 1820).
15 Wirt, *Memoirs*, II, 64.
16 *Ibid.*, II, 73.
17 *Ibid.*, II, 121.

This regime was well after he had freed himself of calls not required by law. In the summer of 1820, indeed, he was almost the *de facto* head of the government. Monroe had gone, Crawford, Calhoun, and Thompson had followed him; Wirt and John Quincy Adams alone were in Washington. "Thus," wrote Wirt, "three departments will be in the hands of subalterns, who will stand in daily need of the Attorney General to help them through their difficulties." [18]

The narrow construction of his powers by Wirt necessarily forbade the extension of his supervisory authority over the district attorneys, leaving these law officers in an independent and anomalous position. Failing to create a Home Department in 1789, Congress confided the general supervision of the district attorneys to the State Department. In a very casual way Jefferson and his successors instructed the attorneys on cases involving international law, foreign ministers and consuls, and the relations of the United States to other countries or their nationals. Much business, however, arose from the navigation and revenue laws, and in 1789 Congress had authorized the comptroller to direct prosecutions for all debts due the United States.[19] By clear implication and subsequent practice the district attorneys thus became subject to the comptroller's instructions for this class of cases, as well as the fifth auditor's instructions after 1820 in cases involving delinquent collectors of revenue. They also assisted the Postmaster General in suits against delinquent postmasters and their sureties, and in the prosecution of offenses against the mails. The attorneys might, therefore, receive instructions from three major federal agencies, to none of which they were clearly responsible.

Edmund Randolph, as Attorney General, had complained about this situation during Washington's administration, but to no avail. Subsequent efforts up to 1829 to clarify control over the district attorneys also failed. By 1828 there were pending over 3,000 lawsuits against delinquent public officers; they were initiated by the fifth auditor, but Wirt ruled that the district

---

[18] *Ibid.*, II, 109.

[19] 1 Stat. 65 (Sept. 2, 1789); this duty, as already noted in ch. 12, was transferred to the fifth auditor in 1820, 3 Stat. 592 (May 15, 1820), and to the solicitor of the Treasury in 1830.

attorneys could not expect advice from the fifth auditor or from him on law questions. His opinion on this point is significant.[20]

The district attorney for the western district of Virginia had transmitted to the fifth auditor in 1823 the record of a pending case involving the accountability of a public agent, with a request for instructions from the Attorney General. Wirt declined to give instructions, on the same ground taken in declining opinions to congressional committees, and also because to do so would be to perform the duties of district attorneys "in all other cases, in which, for their own ease, they may call for such aid. . . ." Wirt recognized, of course, that the Treasury Department might call for his opinion in a proper case, and to defend his position he was consequently required to show that the district attorney could not call on the Treasury Department for instructions of this sort. His argument left the district attorneys with no possibility of professional assistance.

. . . The Treasury Department sends to the district attorneys all orders for suits, and puts them in possession of all the facts and evidence necessary for the prosecution of those suits. But here, I apprehend, the duties of the department stop; and it is no part of those duties to prescribe to the district attorney *the form of the action, or the form of the pleadings:* these are referred exclusively to his own learning; and it is for this reason that he is required to be a person *learned in the law.*

. . . To what kind of *direction* and *instruction,* then, would the law have looked . . . but directions and instructions *when,* and *against whom* and *for what amount,* to institute suits; *when to press the collection,* and *when to indulge;* . . . *what compromises to accept; when to acquiesce in the decisions of the courts below; and when to appeal,* &c.; always leaving to the learning of the law officer the direction of all measures *merely technical and professional?* [21]

Wirt might have built up considerable control over the district attorneys through the fifth auditor, but his view of the responsibility of his office and of the function of the fifth auditor made this impossible. One suspects that his opinion was based not merely on legal considerations, but on the physical impos-

---

[20] *Opinions of the Attorneys General* (1841 ed.), p. 460 (April 11, 1823).
[21] *Ibid.*, pp. 461–62.

sibility of handling the mass of business that a contrary view might have imposed on him. He frankly said in this opinion, *"Lex non requirit impossibilia,"* but he apparently did not think of the alternative of building his office up to new needs. Both Hamilton and Randolph would have seized this alternative.

The private income of the Attorney General from other professional engagements came in for hostile scrutiny by the House of Representatives in 1822, in circumstances that would now seem extraordinary. The House learned that Wirt was being paid fees for appearing as United States counsel in certain cases, over and above his salary of $3,500, and asked Monroe for information. The President submitted a statement showing two fees in 1818 of $1,500 and $1,000 respectively and three smaller fees in later years, but declared that these payments were in accordance with precedent, being for services not required by the duties of the office.[22] The House committee to which the matter was referred sustained these transactions.

Where such occasional aid can be afforded by the Attorney General without interference with his proper duties . . . there is no objection to his being employed upon the ordinary professional footing—of receiving a compensation for the services required. . . . it was never understood or intended that the office was to deprive the officer of the right to employ his professional talents and learning for his own benefit, where that could be done without prejudice to the faithful performance of his stated duties. . . .

. . . Where compensation has been allowed to the Attorney General, it has been for services rendered which did not belong to his office, which he was in no manner bound to perform, and for which, therefore, if he did perform them, he was entitled to be paid as any other professional man would be.

The committee indeed asserted that the only alternative to this arrangement would be the appointment of legal advisers "upon a scale to embrace every possible contingency, (with adequate salaries and emoluments,) which, if it be at all practicable, would be onerous and wasteful. . . ."[23]

[22] Richardson, *Messages,* II, 128; the message and documents are printed in *American State Papers: Miscellaneous,* II, 930–33.

[23] *Ibid.,* II, 931.

The Attorneys General from 1801 to 1829, with the possible exception of William Wirt, were men who devoted most of their lives to the public service in successive positions of leadership in state and nation. They were statesmen, in the accepted use of the term, rather than lawyers, although both Pinkney and Wirt were distinguished members of the bar and all were practicing attorneys. Public service, however, was the principal aspect of their careers.

Levi Lincoln had been an active Republican politician in Massachusetts before he became Attorney General in 1801, and after returning to his native state in 1805 he served as lieutenant governor and governor.[24] John Breckenridge of Kentucky was attorney general of his adopted state, a member of the state House of Representatives from 1797 to 1801 and of the United States Senate from 1801 to 1805.[25] He served as Attorney General of the United States from 1805 until his death in December 1806. Caesar A. Rodney of Delaware was a member of the state assembly from 1796 to 1802, when he came to Congress. After his service as Attorney General (1807–1811), he became a major in the United States Army, and at the close of the War of 1812 a member of the state senate. In 1817–1818 he was a member of the South American Commission, later was elected in succession to the House of Representatives and the Senate and became minister to Argentine in 1823.[26]

William Pinkney of Maryland, one of the most spectacular Attorneys General who has ever held the office, started his political career in the Maryland legislature (1788–1792) and in the state Executive Council (1792–1795). From 1796 to 1804 he was in London as commissioner to settle claims under the Jay Treaty, and after a short sojourn in his native land, where he promptly became attorney general of Maryland, he returned to London as minister to the Court of St. James (1807–1811). He served as United States Attorney General from 1812 to 1814, was elected to Congress in 1815, and went to St. Petersburg as

24 *Dictionary of American Biography*, XI, 262–63.
25 *Ibid.*, III, 6.
26 *Ibid.*, XVI, 82–83.

American minister in 1817. He held a seat in the United States Senate from 1819 to his death in 1822.[27] He was admittedly "the most talented versatile advocate of his time," but was possessed of a passion for success at the bar and for applause that made him appear affected and extravagant. Wirt thought he had "nothing of the rapid and unerring analysis of Marshall," but rather a dogmatizing absoluteness that gave him "a sort of papal infallibility." [28]

As a lawyer, Pinkney was without doubt, as Wirt himself later declared, endowed with "great force of mind, great compass, nice discrimination, strong and accurate judgment"; [29] but as administrative head of the legal branch of the government, William Wirt was not only his superior, but the first Attorney General to sense the needs of the office. The son of a Swiss tavern keeper in Bladensburg, Maryland, Wirt was left an orphan at the age of eight. He was eventually admitted to the Virginia bar, and with Jefferson's endorsement secured his first public office as clerk to the Virginia House of Representatives.[30] He rose rapidly in the private practice of the law and became a national figure as one of the counsel for the government in the trial of Aaron Burr. In his early years Wirt thought of going to Kentucky, but refrained, learning "that there was no *cash* in that state." [31] He went instead to Norfolk, from whence he wrote, "If a fortune is to be made by the profession in this country, I believe I shall do it." [32] He declined Jefferson's suggestion to enter the House of Representatives in 1808, for financial considerations.[33] Shortly after becoming Attorney General he wrote his friend, Pope, "The salary, you know, is very low, only three thousand dollars. There is a talk of raising it.

27 *Ibid.*, XIV, 626–28.
28 Wirt, *Memoirs*, I, 403.
29 *Ibid.*, II, 138.
30 Jefferson wrote, "He is a person of real genius and information, one of the ablest at the bars in this part of the country, amiable & worthy in his private character, & in his republicanism most zealous & active." The Jefferson Papers in Massachusetts Historical Society, *Collections*, 7th series, I (1900), 67 (Nov. 26, 1799).
31 Wirt, *Memoirs*, I, 99.
32 *Ibid.*, I, 134.
33 *Ibid.*, I, 228.

I wish it may not end in talk." [34] John Quincy Adams asserted that Wirt appeared to think more about his salary than of any other subject.[35]

Wirt was not possessed of ambition for the role of a public man. Through his letters ran an undercurrent of concern for security and financial success, and certainly in his early years he had both literary tastes and ambitions. His first published book, *Letters of a British Spy,* had a considerable success, and later he wrote *Sketches of the Life and Character of Patrick Henry.* His biographer in the *Dictionary of American Biography* asserted that, "His one ambition was to acquire a competency and retire to the country to live a life of literary ease." [36] He himself declared:

. . . there is not enough iron in my composition for a public character; I mean, for a politician aiming at glory. Nor do I regret it. . . .

As to the office which I have received, it was not, trust me, either the supposed honor attached to it nor any ulterior promotion to which it might be supposed to lead, that induced my acceptance. . . . it was the single object of bettering the fortunes of my children, by pursuing my profession on more advantageous ground. . . . Nor am I vain and foolish enough to aim at anything higher. I am already higher than I had any reason to expect. . . .[37]

His own political judgments were neither pronounced nor shrewd. There is little evidence that he thought seriously about Republican doctrine; he accepted it. He did not understand the value of geography in balancing a Cabinet and declared he would be "no more governed by residence, than I would by the color of a man's hair." [38] He deprecated the Washington round of official and ceremonial visits, although possessed of a highly sociable character.[39] In 1831 he accepted the nomination of the Anti-Masonic party for the presidency—an act both out of character and far from an astute estimate of the political situation.

34 *Ibid.,* II, 70.
35 Adams, *Memoirs,* IV, 82 (April 28, 1818).
36 *Dictionary of American Biography,* XX, 418–21.
37 Wirt, *Memoirs,* II, 67.
38 *Ibid.,* I, 322.
39 *Ibid.,* II, 32–33.

All this is to say that Wirt was much more concerned with financial and professional success than with a public career. These qualities of his character were fully compatible with a sound administrative record of twelve years as Attorney General. Two years before he entered this office he wrote to his nephew, a young lawyer, the rules of conduct that would lead him to success; they were obviously Wirt's own guides and well reveal some of the qualities that made him both an able lawyer and an able administrator. The rules were the epitome of system and prudence. They prescribed a fixed plan of life as to business and exercise; promptness in answering letters and care in filing them; regular accounts; a simple style of speaking, always unflurried: "learn to assume the exterior of composure and self-collectedness, whatever riot and confusion may be within"; and the maxim, "Live in your office." [40]

Wirt succeeded in creating a visible administrative entity in place of an unanchored though long-established office. He set precedents defining its scope and jurisdiction. He organized for the first time a record system, and left for his successor a complete account of his opinions. He participated in three of the great cases under the Marshall Supreme Court: *McCulloch* v. *Maryland*, the *Dartmouth College Case*, and *Gibbons* v. *Ogden*. Although disinterested in securing control over the district attorneys, Wirt nevertheless laid the foundation on which, much later, the Department of Justice was to rest.

[40] *Ibid.*, I, 394–95 (August 29, 1815).

CHAPTER TWENTY-FOUR

Personnel Administration:
Theory and Practice

The inauguration of Thomas Jefferson was not only an anxious moment for Federalist officeholders; it was also one of the important events in the formation of the ideals and practice of officeholding in the federal government. The same issue was put in 1801 as reappeared in 1829, and superficially in even more decisive form, for Jefferson had defeated a party while Jackson had defeated only a faction of the party to which both he and his predecessor gave allegiance. The temptation to removal of Federalists was great and the expectations of Republicans were high. The whole country waited to see what would happen upon the first transfer of the power to govern from one party to another.

THE REPUBLICAN DILEMMA

The Federalist leaders naturally gave thought to the problem of statecraft that was involved, hoping something could be saved from the disaster of 1800. They generally agreed that Jefferson should have the privilege of appointing his department heads, but they stood firmly on the ground that the rank and file were beyond party bounds, servants of the nation, neutral in partisan debate, and deserving to be continued without interruption in their respective offices. In the negotiations that took place in the critical choice between Jefferson and Burr, the Federalists sought reassurances from Jefferson on these points, but without success.[1] Their position was fatally weakened by their own marked preference for Federalists in the latter years of Washington's administration and the whole of John Adams'. Jefferson later declared, "Out of about six hundred offices named by the President there were six Republicans only when I came into office, and these were chiefly half-breeds." [2]

Jefferson's sense of political justice required preference to Republican applicants for federal office. On the other hand he was concerned with the long-term political advantages to be derived from weaning away the moderate Federalists to the Republican party. This consideration specified caution not to offend them by numerous removals of their fellow partisans. He was also anxious to lessen the gulf between the suspicious and intolerant sections of American opinion, and this object also spelled caution.

The policy of the new Administration, affected by these somewhat conflicting forces, went through a transitional period of about two years, and then settled down into practices that much resembled those of the Federalists. Jefferson did not adopt a theory of rotation in office, but he did find ways and means in these years to satisfy the clamor of his followers. The transition over, he found it possible to continue the high standards of selection established by Washington—but strictly within the ranks of the Republican party. The withering-away of the Federalists postponed a second trial of the patronage problem until 1829.

INTERIM PERIOD OF ADJUSTMENT

Jefferson suffered acutely in discharging his duty to nominate and appoint to public office, caught as he was in a hard dilemma between his own sense of right, which dictated no disturbance to gentlemen who had conducted themselves discreetly, and his followers' open expectations of reform, reward, and punishment.[3] He entered upon his task with no illusions, telling

[1] Jefferson, *Works* (Federal ed.), IX, 179 (Feb. 15, 1801); cf. Adams, *Memoirs,* I, 428 (April 3, 1806), asserting that a pledge had been given by Jefferson.

[2] Jefferson, *Works* (Federal ed.), X, 393–94 (May 19, 1807).

[3] Cf. a letter to Jefferson from two New York Republicans, June 1, 1801. "We wish to observe, however, that the people of this City and State look to the new administration with full Confidence for a thorough Change in the different

Monroe in February 1801, that he had "reason to expect in the outset the greatest difficulties as to nominations." [4] He wrote to Levi Lincoln:

. . . I had foreseen, years ago, that the first republican President who should come into office after all the places in the government had become exclusively occupied by federalists, would have a dreadful operation to perform. That the republicans would consent to a continuation of everything in federal hands, was not to be expected, because neither just nor politic. On him, then, was to devolve the office of an executioner, that of lopping off.[5]

The difficulties he foresaw were not slow in swarming around his head. Three weeks after taking the oath of office he wrote Benjamin Rush that he was giving great offense to his friends in failing to remove Federalists and that the "torrent has been pressing me heavily, & will require all my force to bear up against. . . ." [6] At the close of his first term he wrote that if he had hundreds to nominate instead of one, it would be no "bed of roses. You would find yourself in most cases with one loaf and ten wanting bread. Nine must be disappointed, perhaps become secret, if not open enemies." [7] In the middle of the second term the proportions had become worse: "Every office becoming vacant, every appointment made, *me donne un ingrat, et cent ennemis.*" [8] He did not escape "schismatic divisions in the medical fraternity" when appointing Dr. Benjamin Water-

---

offices, so as to exclude obnoxious characters, those who were enimical to the revolution, or have since become hostile to the Constitution and to the principles and progress of republican government. . . . a measure of this sort is absolutely necessary to preserve that republican majority in this State which has contributed so essentially towards placing you in that elevated situation which you now hold. . . ." Letters of James Cheetham, Massachusetts Historical Society, *Proceedings*, 3d series, I (1907-8), 42-43. Note also a letter from Elbridge Gerry: ". . . it is therefore incumbent on you, Sir, as expeditiously as circumstances will permit, to clear the augean stable of its obnoxious occupants. . . ." Gerry made it clear, however, that he referred only to the "inveterate enemies" of republicanism. *Some Letters of Elbridge Gerry of Massachusetts, 1784-1804* (Worthington Chauncey Ford, ed., Brooklyn, N. Y.: Historical Printing Club, 1896), p. 24 (May 4, 1801).

4 Jefferson, *Works* (Federal ed.), IX, 179 (Feb. 15, 1801).
5 *Ibid.*, IX, 289 (August 26, 1801).
6 *Ibid.*, IX, 232 (March 24, 1801).
7 *Ibid.*, X, 123 (Nov. 26, 1804).
8 *Ibid.*, X, 342 (Jan. 13, 1807).

house to the Marine Hospital in Boston, but, as he confided to Dr. Benjamin Rush, "My usage is to make the best appointment my information and judgment enable me to do, and then fold myself up in the mantle of conscience, and abide unmoved the peltings of the storm. And oh! for the day when I shall be withdrawn from it; when I shall have leisure to enjoy my family, my friends, my farm and books." [9]

In performing this unpleasant duty, this "office of hangman," Jefferson, like Washington, was governed by long-range considerations of statesmanlike proportions. "There is nothing I am so anxious about as good nominations, conscious that the merit as well as reputation of an administration depends as much on that as on it's measures." [10] Success in administration was not moreover his principal goal; he was even more anxious to reduce the tensions growing out of the bitter party warfare of the last eight years.

. . . The greatest good we can do our country is to heal it's party divisions & make them one people. I do not speak of their leaders who are incurable, but of the honest and well-intentioned body of the people. I consider the pure federalist as a republican who would prefer a somewhat stronger executive; and the republican as one more willing to trust the legislature as a broader representation of the people, and a safer deposit of power for many reasons. But both sects are republican, entitled to the confidence of their fellow citizens.[11]

Jefferson deliberately set out "to obliterate, or rather to unite the names of federalists & republicans" by means of his appointment policy, and, aided by many other circumstances, he succeeded in his program. "The way to effect it is to preserve principle, but to treat tenderly those who have been estranged from us. . . ." [12]

Hence Jefferson determined, before his inauguration, not to disturb Adams' officeholders for political reasons alone: "no

9 Jefferson, *Writings* (Memorial ed.), XI, 412 (Jan. 3, 1808). He never quite achieved his early hope that "Time, prudence, and patience will perhaps get us over this whole difficulty." *Works* (Federal ed.), IX, 225-26 (March 24, 1801).

10 *Ibid.*, IX, 248 (April 8, 1801).

11 *Ibid.*, IX, 281 (July 23, 1801).

12 *Ibid.*, IX, 205-6 (March 8, 1801).

man who has conducted himself according to his duties would have anything to fear from me, as those who have done ill would have nothing to hope, be their political principles what they might." [13] To Monroe he wrote three days after entering the White House, "deprivations of office, if made on the ground of political principles alone, would revolt our new converts, and give a body to leaders who now stand alone." [14] And to one of his congressional supporters he declared, "Malconduct is a just ground of removal: mere difference of political opinion is not." [15]

Jefferson was trying to preserve what good Republicans everywhere were committed to cherish: the right of the citizen to his own opinions, to freedom of speech, and to equality in opportunity to serve the commonwealth. No terms could be more forthright than those in which he revealed these deepest purposes. "The right of opinion shall suffer no invasion from me. Those who have acted well have nothing to fear, however they may have differed from me in opinion. . . ." [16]

By the summer of 1801, however, the air was full of complaint from Republicans and Federalists alike. Jefferson, eagerly awaiting an opportunity to declare his principles and policy, found the occasion in a remonstrance from the merchants of New Haven against the removal of the collector of customs at this port. His carefully composed, and now famous, New Haven letter was intended to make public the considered policy of the Administration.

. . . If a due participation of office is a matter of right, how are vacancies to be obtained? Those by death are few; by resignation, none.[17] Can any other mode than that of removal be proposed? This is a painful office; but it is made my duty, and I meet it as such. I proceed in the operation with deliberation & inquiry, that it may

13 *Ibid.*, IX, 177 (Feb. 14, 1801).
14 *Ibid.*, IX, 204 (Feb. [i.e., March] 7, 1801).
15 *Ibid.*, IX, 225 (March 24, 1801).
16 *Ibid.*, IX, 242 (March 29, 1801).
17 In 1803 he confided to William Duane, in an effort to keep him quiet, that "Many vacancies have been made by death and resignation, many by removal for malversation in office and for open, active and virulent abuse of official influence in opposition to the order of things established by the will of the nation." *Ibid.*, X, 23 (July 24, 1803).

injure the best men least, and effect the purposes of justice & public utility with the least private distress; that it may be thrown, as much as possible, on delinquency, on oppression, on intolerance, on incompetence, on ante-revolutionary adherence to our enemies.

. . . It would have been to me a circumstance of great relief, had I found a moderate participation of office in the hands of the majority. I would gladly have left to time and accident to raise them to their just share. But their total exclusion calls for prompter correctives. I shall correct the procedure; but that done, disdain to follow it, shall return with joy to that state of things, when the only questions concerning a candidate shall be, is he honest? Is he capable? Is he faithful to the Constitution? [18]

This policy statement left open the exact meaning of a due proportion. In March 1801 Jefferson spoke of the restoration of "something like an equilibrium in office," after which *"Tros Tyriusque nullo discrimine habetur."* [19] By 1803 he had settled on the relative numbers of the two parties as the proper criterion,[20] but whether to apply the rule state by state or within the nation as a whole long remained a perplexing and unsettled problem. Until a due proportion was attained Jefferson decided to appoint only Republicans. As soon as John Adams was well on his way to Quincy, the President told Monroe, "I have given, and will give only to republicans, under existing circumstances." [21]

The crux of the matter in 1801 and 1802 lay in the availability of vacancies to which appointment of Republicans could be made, and here Jefferson was put to his hardest trials. The early years of his administration were years of retrenchment, substantially reducing the number of offices that had been hitherto available. His original idea was to depend on "deaths, resignations, & delinquencies." [22] To these aids to Republicans, he added several others, particularly "the new appointments which Mr. A crowded in with whip & spur from the 12th of

---

[18] *Ibid.,* IX, 273–74 (July 12, 1801).
[19] *Ibid.,* IX, 230 (March 24, 1801).
[20] *Ibid.,* IX, 471, n. (June 1, 1803).
[21] *Ibid.,* IX, 204 (March 7, 1801).
[22] *Ibid.,* IX, 401 (Oct. 25, 1802). The number of removals for delinquency was expected by Jefferson to be small, probably not twenty. *Ibid.,* IX, 231 (March 24, 1801).

Dec. when the event of the election was known . . . until 9. o'clock of the night at 12. o'clock of which he was to go out of office." These appeared to Jefferson an outrage to decency and so far as they were vulnerable he treated them as nullities.[23] Removals for misconduct affected Federalists and Republicans alike; the President had to remove the brother of a leading Republican, Elbridge Gerry, later Vice President, for carelessness in his accounts as collector.[24] By 1802 Jefferson was removing Federalist officeholders "most marked for their bitterness and active zeal in slandering and in electioneering. . . . such officers as shall afterwards continue to bid us defiance shall as certainly be removed, if the case shall become known." [25] In the Massachusetts election of 1802 he put Levi Lincoln on the watch:

. . . Your present situation will enable you to judge of prominent offenders in your State, in the case of the present election. I pray you to seek them, to mark them, to be quite sure of your ground, that we may commit no error or wrong, and leave the rest to me. . . . I think it not amiss that it should be known that we are determined to remove officers who are active or open mouthed against the government, by which I mean the legislature as well as the executive.[26]

One additional group of federal officials was marked out by Jefferson for removal, as a departure from his normal allegiance to the triple test of honesty, competence, and loyalty to the Constitution—the attorneys and marshals. "The courts being so decidedly federal & irremovable, it is believed that republican attorneys & marshals, being the doors of entrance into the courts, are indispensably necessary as a shield to the republican part of our fellow citizens. . . ." [27] Even here Jefferson retained

[23] *Ibid.*, IX, 237 (March 27, 1801).
[24] *Ibid.*, IX, 390–91 (August 28, 1802).
[25] *Ibid.*, IX, 392–93.
[26] *Ibid.*, IX, 401–2 (Oct. 25, 1802).
[27] *Ibid.*, IX, 223 (March 23, 1801). Jefferson accused the marshal of Pennsylvania of packing the jury in a capital case with persons who either avowed or were known to be determined to condemn, and suspected others of the same offense. *Ibid.*, IX, 231 (March 24, 1801). In April 1801, he asked Archibald Stuart to recommend an attorney and a marshal for the western district of Virginia: "Pray recommend one to me, as also a marshal; and let them be the

some incumbents. By midsummer 1803 he reckoned that out of a total of 316 offices subject to appointment and removal by him, only 130 were held by Federalists.[28]

During the transitional period Jefferson thus sought to follow the tradition of Washington, but modified by a sort of pernicious political activity rule directed against his most obnoxious opponents. Faced with a hard and novel choice between principle and party expediency, he established a doctrine that was politically expedient in the narrower sense,[29] that brought him success in his more distant objects, and that left many Federalist officeholders in quiet possession of their jobs. Jefferson was not a spoilsman and, as will be seen at a later point, was revolted by the Tenure of Office Act of 1820. He raised a standard that in retrospect commands honor, and by his prudence delayed for a generation the practice of rotation in federal office, already breaking into state circles.

REPUBLICAN PERSONNEL PRACTICE

It was against the background of the special condition of party overturn and the normal condition of a lively appetite for office that Jefferson and his Republican successors worked out their appointment practice. No machinery for making appointments had ever been set up, or indeed even been thought of. Not only was there no central appointment office; only the Post Office Department had an agent to advise its head on the replacement of subordinates. A clerk was usually in charge of letters of application, which were filed for consideration against

most respectable & unexceptionable possible; and especially let them be republican. The only shield for our Republican citizens against the federalism of the courts is to have the Attornies & Marshals republicans." *Ibid.*, IX, 248.

28 *Ibid.*, X, 23 (July 24, 1803); also in Gallatin, *Writings*, I, 131. An occasional Federalist actually received an appointment, for example Benjamin Tupper, receiver of public monies at the Marietta land office. He had been recommended by two leading Republicans. "Letters to Jonathan Russell, 1801–1822," Massachusetts Historical Society, *Proceedings*, XLVII (1913–14), 294–95.

29 A private exchange of correspondence between two leading Federalists confirmed Jefferson's success. "I do not think," wrote Theodore Sedgwick to Rufus King on December 14, 1801, "that Mr. J—n has lost any influence by his removals from office. There is nothing more mischievous & monstrous than the principle . . . on which this conduct rests. . . . And yet there is a wonderful tranquillity prevailing on the avowal and practice of this conduct." King, *Correspondence*, IV, 35.

the day when a vacancy might occur. Department heads continued to make their own selections of clerks and subordinates without reference to the President. By law the appointment of postmasters remained the prerogative of the Postmaster General, despite misgivings and occasional crises.[30] On the other hand, the principal offices were filled by the President usually with the advice and consent of the Senate. This rule was especially strong in the foreign service. The balance between Presidents and the Senate in this joint responsibility has already been described.[31]

Party affiliation. Like his predecessors, Jefferson knew that the reputation and success of his administration and the prospects of his party depended heavily upon prudence and skill in choosing persons for office. He consolidated his party in power by confining his appointments, with rare exceptions, to his adherents. No one of the four Republican Presidents, indeed, was free to appoint persons still loyal to the lingering remnants of the Federalist party. Madison, as we have seen, had to consider party background in choosing his generals during the War of 1812. The temper of the times, under both Monroe and Adams, was not sufficiently an era of good feeling to make possible a choice between Republicans and their one-time powerful opponents.[32] Both Monroe and Adams regretted this, but Adams recognized that party feeling was "powerful everywhere, and will be so for many years to come."

. . . And it is upon the occasion of appointments to office that all the wormwood and the gall of the old party hatred ooze out. Not a vacancy to any office occurs but there is a distinguished federalist started and pushed home as a candidate to fill it—always well qualified, sometimes in an eminent degree, and yet so obnoxious to the Republican party that he cannot be appointed . . . without

30 See above, ch. 22.
31 See chs. 3, 9.
32 For Monroe's attitude, see Adams, *Memoirs*, VI, 128 (Jan. 12, 1823); and *ibid.*, VI, 494 (Feb. 4, 1825), quoting Monroe: ". . . General Izard was a federalist, and he wished on his own retirement to give some token of his disposition to conciliate that class of our citizens. He regretted that it had not been in his power to show the same disposition more frequently in his appointments. He had gone as far as was possible without forfeiting the confidence of his own supporters and thereby defeating the very object that he had at heart."

offending one-half of the community—the federalists, if their associate is overlooked; the Republicans, if he is preferred. To this disposition justice must sometimes make resistance and policy must
often yield.[33]

Respectability. Within the party circle, however, Republican
standards were high. Their choice fell upon persons from the
same reputable social class of gentlemen upon whom the Federalists had depended. In one of his letters to Gallatin about a
man proposed for a position on the "eastern shore" of Virginia
Jefferson wrote, "His family has been among the most respectable on that shore for many generations. . . ."[34]

Respectability was indeed a frequently recurring theme in
Jefferson's comments on officeholding. "Pray write me your
opinion, which appointment would be most respected by the
public. . . ."[35] Great was his satisfaction in considering Sump-
ter for the first civil governor of Louisiana. "I think I have selected a governor for Louisiana, as perfect in all points as we can
expect. Sound judgment, standing in society, knolege of the
world, wealth, liberality, familiarity with the French language,
and having a French wife."[36] Describing his selection for surveyor of lands south of Tennessee, he wrote Claiborne, "He is
a Quaker, a sound republican, and of a pure and unspotted
character. In point of science, in astronomy, geometry and
mathematics, he stands . . . second to no man in the United
States. . . . the candor, modesty and simplicity of his manners
cannot fail to gain your esteem."[37] "Mr. Hall's having been a
member of the Legislature, a Speaker of the Representatives,
and a member of the Executive Council, were evidences of the
respect of the State towards him, which our respect for the State
could not neglect."[38]

The tradition of respectability and standing in the community set by Jefferson was followed by Madison, Monroe, and

[33] *Ibid.*, VII, 207–8 (Dec. 13, 1826).
[34] Gallatin, *Writings*, I, 60 (Nov. 12, 1801).
[35] Jefferson, *Works* (Federal ed.), IX, 248, n. (April 25, 1801).
[36] *Ibid.*, X, 27 (July 31, 1803).
[37] Jefferson, *Writings* (Memorial ed.), X, 394–95 (May 24, 1803).
[38] *Ibid.*, XI, 53 (Oct. 9, 1804). This letter is almost identical in content with
Washington's message to the Senate defending his nomination of Fishbourn. See
Richardson, *Messages*, I, 58–59 (August 6, 1789).

Adams, although Presidents weaker than Jefferson had more trouble in withstanding pressure from politically powerful sources. Monroe was plagued by the furious competition among his Cabinet members for the succession and sought to play the role of a neutral in making appointments.

> . . . In the appointment to office, I have been forc'd either to distribute the offices among the friends of the candidates, to guard myself against the imputation of favoritism, or to take my own course, and appoint those whom I knew & confided in, without regard to them. Had I pursued the former, the office in my hands, for two or three years of the latter term, would have sunk to nothing. I therefore adopted the latter, and have steadily pursued it. . . .[39]

John Quincy Adams consistently reappointed incumbents at the expiration of their terms, irrespective of their factional affiliation. Where new appointments were to be made, he selected persons of known qualifications and standing in the community, friendly to his Administration.[40]

A corollary of the preference for gentlemen was to take for granted that their sons would be equally respectable and entitled to preference in the line of succession. A number of such instances were well known: Henry Dearborn and his son; William Ellery and his son; Abraham Bishop and his son; Page and his son, and others. Calhoun became concerned about this tendency and wrote Monroe in 1819 with respect to a vacant collectorship where a son was an applicant:

> . . . It is certainly painful to do an act, which may leave the family of the late Collector in want, yet the tendency to the hereditary principle from this very cause in the inferior offices of our country merits great consideration. What is humanity now, may in the course of one or two generations ripen into a claim on the government.[41]

Nepotism. Jefferson was as staunch against preference to his family connections as Washington. To George Jefferson he wrote:

[39] Monroe, *Writings,* VII, 11 (March 22, 1824).

[40] Cf. the somewhat unsympathetic interpretation of Adams' record by the biographer of Calhoun: Charles M. Wiltse, *John C. Calhoun: Nationalist,* pp. 327, 361.

[41] Calhoun, *Correspondence,* pp. 163–64 (Sept. 14, 1819).

. . . The public will never be made to believe that an appointment of a relative is made on the ground of merit alone, uninfluenced by family views; nor can they ever see with approbation offices, the disposal of which they entrust to their Presidents for public purposes, divided out as family property. . . . It is true that this places the relatives of the President in a worse situation than if he were a stranger, but the public good . . . requires this sacrifice.[42]

Adams also took high ground with respect to the appointment of his relatives, appearing in much more favorable light than some other prominent Republicans. The comptroller of the Treasury, Joseph Anderson, became intent on finding a place for his son, Alexander. After an obscure intrigue to have Adams appoint him chief clerk in the State Department, Anderson bluntly told Adams that unless Alexander was found an office in State the comptroller would remove Adams' brother-in-law, William S. Smith, from the comptroller's staff to make room for him.[43] Adams promptly declined to take a family relation into his own office or to recommend any to another department. Smith was dismissed, but was quickly appointed to a position with the same salary in the office of the second auditor, William Lee. The episode was an annoying one; Adams wrote in his diary, "Smith and his wife, and all the family, were up in arms against me about it; but I thought my resolution right, and adhered to it." [44] In 1819 Adams was approached by a Kentucky Representative, George Robertson, to urge the appointment of John Pope as district attorney of Kentucky. Pope had married the sister of Adams' wife. Adams declined to make the suggestion to Monroe, "having made it a principle to avoid recommending to the President any of my family relations. . . ." [45]

Lesser figures found it more difficult to resist family preferences. Joseph Nourse found places for several members of his family, leading to Jackson's *bon mot* that when he became President he would clean out the Noursery.[46] Abraham Bradley

42 Jefferson, *Works* (Federal ed.), IX, 238–39 (March 27, 1801).
43 Adams, *Memoirs*, IV, 9–10 (Sept. 23, 1817).
44 *Ibid.*, IV, 26–27 (Dec. 6, 1817).
45 *Ibid.*, IV, 230 (Jan. 25, 1819).
46 Anne Hollingsworth Wharton, *Social Life in the Early Republic* (Philadelphia: Lippincott, 1902), p. 106.

found a good berth in the post office for his brother Phineas. Gabriel Duval, one-time comptroller, wrote Henry Clay from the Supreme Court bench to ask a place for his third son, two already holding public office.[47] General Dearborn resigned what was said to be the best office in New England, the collectorship of the port of Boston, to his son. One of his sons-in-law was collector of the port of Bath, Maine, until he died, when he was succeeded by another son-in-law. He resigned in turn in favor of his brother. Niles remarked, "verily, verily, there has been too much of such doings in the United States." [48] John Quincy Adams agreed. When Judge Thruston came to ask a commission in the marine corps for his son, Adams reminded him that not only did the Judge himself hold an office for life, but that already one son was a "high-salaried clerk" in the State Department and another an officer in the army. ". . . . I intimated to the Judge that I sometimes heard complaints that too many places were accumulated in families." [49]

Veterans. No statutory privileges for veterans with respect to civilian offices were established by the Jeffersonians. Military service, nevertheless, counted favorably in the selection of officials and subordinate employees, especially in the customs service. Individual applicants were likely to emphasize their exploits in the Revolutionary War or the War of 1812 to excite sympathy and such appeals might bear fruit. Secretary of the Navy Hamilton wrote an order to Captain Tingey, in command of the Washington Navy Yard, as follows: The bearer "is an old revolutionary officer for whom I wish to make some provision in the Navy Yard. He is too old to labor now, and he must not want. You will consider of some place in which his fidelity may be of use to the public, and report the same to me." [50] There was, of course, no organization of veterans to press their collective interest.

The issue was temporarily acute in 1815–16, when the army

47 *The Works of Henry Clay* (Calvin Colton, ed., 6 vols., New York: A. S. Barnes & Burr, 1857), IV, 127 (Sept. 2, 1825).

48 *Niles Register,* XX, 321 (July 21, 1823).

49 Adams, *Memoirs,* VII, 346 (Oct. 26, 1827).

50 Charles Oscar Paullin, "Naval Administration under Secretaries of the Navy Smith, Hamilton and Jones," U. S. Naval Institute, *Proceedings,* XXXII (1906), 1320.

was in the process of reduction to peacetime status and many officers had to be released. Dallas was involved in this operation and sent a revealing letter to Madison. "Conversing with Mr. Monroe and Mr. Crowninshield," he wrote, "we agreed that some attention should be paid to our gallant officers, when vacancies in civil stations occurred." [51] From the beginning of the government, army officers had been appointed to such positions as collectors of customs, naval officers and surveyors, internal revenue officers, and commissioners of loans, but the rank and file carried no preference with them. As the Revolutionary patriots grew old, their places were taken by officers serving in the War of 1812. This policy was, however, not written into statute. Pensions, not offices, were the means of testifying to the gratitude of the country for military service.

Apportionment. Prudence suggested to Federalist and Republican Presidents alike the desirability of filling important posts —Cabinet, diplomatic, and judicial, especially—from different parts of the country. Jefferson found three members of his Cabinet in New England, an obvious evidence of intent to reassure that part of the country. Monroe's Cabinet represented east, middle, and south, while the Post Office Department was in the hands of westerners; and Adams' department heads were well distributed, although New England had no representative. In 1823 Monroe told Secretary of State Adams that he wished to distribute the new South American diplomatic posts "to citizens of the different parts of the Union." [52]

An apportionment rule was also applied to subordinate offices. "Virginia is greatly over her due proportion of appointments in the general government," Jefferson wrote apologetically to a fellow Virginian, "and tho' this has not been done by me, it would be imputed as blamed to me to add to her proportion. So that for all general offices persons to fill them must for some time be sought from other states, and only offices which are to be exercised within the state can be given to its own citizens." [53] The departmental clerks, although subject to no formal rule,

[51] Dallas, *Life and Writings*, p. 136 (March 13, 1815).
[52] Adams, *Memoirs*, VI, 127–28 (Jan. 12, 1823).
[53] Jefferson, *Works* (Federal ed.), IX, 350–51 (Feb. 20, 1802), and *ibid.*, IX, 352–53, n.

were drawn from various sections, but near-by Maryland and Virginia tended to produce the largest numbers.[54]

The rule of apportionment of cadets to West Point has already been noted. An analogous practice gradually developed with respect to the appointment of midshipmen, but to keep a proper balance proved more difficult. As early as 1808 Secretary of the Navy Smith wrote that Virginia had her full quota, but despite care an undue share of midshipman appointments went to Virginia, Maryland, and the District of Columbia.[55] Early in 1823 pressure mounted from states in arrears, causing Secretary Thompson to state formally the rule that governed appointments: "to apportion them among the several states, according to the ratio of representation in Congress, when the applicants were unexceptionable as to character and qualifications for the service." [56] The House Committee on Naval Affairs supported navy practice and executive discretion, declaring that a legislative apportionment would be highly pernicious in its operation.[57] Pressure continued, nevertheless, and Southard was required in 1828 to answer a House inquiry on what rule had been adopted "to equalize the honor and advantage" of naval appointments. He made a strong defense of established practice, while admitting that an exact proportion had not been obtained.[58] An angry member of the House complained to Southard in 1827 that his candidate for purser had not been appointed, "intimating that no appointment could be obtained for a person from Rhode Island." Southard knew his distribution and told President Adams that of thirty-two pursers, Rhode Island already had four.[59]

In the appointment of army medical officers preference was usually given to applicants who came from states without members in this corps. In 1826 a New York doctor was informed

[54] *Official Register of the United States, 1816, 1817, et seq., passim.* A number showed foreign origin: England, Ireland, Scotland, Germany, Switzerland, France, and the West Indies.

[55] Paullin, "Naval Administration under Secretaries of the Navy Smith, Hamilton and Jones," *op. cit.*, pp. 1302, 1320.

[56] House Report 92, 17th Cong., 2d sess., p. 3 (Jan. 25, 1823).

[57] *Ibid.*, p. 2.

[58] *American State Papers: Naval Affairs*, III, 158 (March 12, 1828).

[59] Adams, *Memoirs*, VII, 350 (Nov. 10, 1827).

that his prospects were poor since there were over two hundred names on file of which one-fourth were from his state. A Connecticut physician was told that his prospects were good, as he was the only applicant from this state.[60]

Local residence. The local residence rule that had been so precisely stated by Timothy Pickering was scrupulously observed by Jefferson. "Where an office is local we never go out of the limits for the officer," he advised Caesar A. Rodney.[61] Practice at a later date was illustrated in a letter from President Monroe to Jefferson in 1820.

. . . Wherever territory is to be sold, within a *State,* the Senators oppose, the appointment of the officers intrusted with it, of persons from other States, an opposition which is now extended even to Indian agencies. The number of applicants, too, for every office, is so great, & the pressure from the quarter interested, so earnest, that it is difficult in any case to be resisted.[62]

Local claims to local offices of the federal government, buttressed by the political interests of Congressmen in their constituents, became well-nigh irresistible.

Examinations. Both the army and the navy introduced formal examinations as a part of the process of selecting their professional personnel. The army medical corps was the first to develop a test system. The initial official step was apparently taken in 1814, when the regulations for the medical department provided that "no candidate will hereafter be appointed in the medical department of the army, who shall not have received a diploma from a respectable medical school or college, without first passing the examination of an army medical board."[63] The first such board was ordered for the examination of Dr. Brown, November 8–9, 1814, and others were set up from time to time.[64] The regulations also forbade army surgeons to engage in private practice.

The navy moved in the same direction. The House Commit-

60 Harvey E. Brown, *Medical Department of the United States Army*, p. 129.
61 Jefferson, *Works* (Federal ed.), X, 323 (Dec. 5, 1806).
62 Monroe, *Writings*, VI, 114–15 (Feb. 7, 1820).
63 Brown, *Medical Department of the United States Army*, p. 97.
64 Data supplied by courtesy of Army Medical Library, Washington, D. C.

tee on Naval Affairs reported in 1823 that they were "fully convinced that appointments in that branch of service [i.e., medical] have hitherto been made with too little discrimination, and that many have entered it, who, on a due examination of their competency, would have been rejected." [65] The navy took prompt action. In May 1824 it established a board of "old and skillful surgeons, for the examination of those who should apply for the appointment of surgeon's mate, or for promotion as surgeon, and to recommend to the President no one who had not submitted to an examination, and been declared, by that board, to be qualified . . . by his talents, acquirements, and character." [66] *Ad hoc* examining boards were set up from time to time, resulting in marked improvement. The first board, which convened in Philadelphia in the summer of 1824, comprised five navy surgeons. Niles reported, "It is understood that their attention will be directed to moral character, and scientific and professional attainments." [67]

The scheme of examination for West Point cadets, introduced about 1818 and subsequently extended by a stiff examination at the end of a six-months qualifying period, has already been noted. An effective system of probation and examination was also in effect for midshipmen that apparently commenced in 1819.[68] Lads and young men from fourteen to twenty years of age were appointed on a showing of "a sound constitution, correct habits, and good English education." [69] They were sent six months at sea, "strictly on trial," and were given "permission to retire" unless their conduct was correct and they gave promise of usefulness. After this first weeding out, on a practical test, the survivors continued in the service for five years, three at sea. They were then required to take another test for promotion to lieutenant.

---

[65] House Report 63, 17th Cong., 2d sess., p. 2 (Jan. 20, 1823).

[66] *American State Papers: Naval Affairs,* III, 160; Paullin, "Naval Administration under the Navy Commissioners," U. S. Naval Institute, *Proceedings,* XXXIII, 634. Such a board had been recommended in 1815 by Captain Tingey. *American State Papers: Naval Affairs,* I, 359.

[67] *Niles Register,* XXVI, 252 (June 19, 1824).

[68] *American State Papers: Naval Affairs,* II, 23; Paullin, "Naval Administration under the Navy Commissioners," *op. cit.,* p. 634.

[69] *American State Papers: Naval Affairs,* III, 160.

. . . This examination is rigid, and those unfit, from their habits or ignorance, cannot pass it. Failing once, a second opportunity is offered, and upon a second failure, they are dismissed or permitted to resign. . . . This examination affords a second opportunity to relieve the public from those who are unfit for advancement to the higher grades. It is not very probable, under these arrangements, that improper or incompetent persons will pass the ordeal, and become commissioned officers.

Southard testified that "no general regulation has ever produced better effects upon the industry, habits and intelligence of any class of officers. . . ." [70] The first such examination was held in 1819 before a board consisting of Commodores Rodgers, Bainbridge, and Chauncey, and the Reverend Mr. Felch. Twenty-five candidates appeared, of whom twelve were rejected.[71]

The Secretary of the Navy was so convinced of the value of examinations, indeed, that he proposed one to eliminate older naval officers unfit for promotion.

. . . Another and a rigid test ought to be provided, of which the officers should have full warning, as well as time and opportunity to prepare for it. Such a test will be found in an examination conducted on proper principles, both as to character and skill. . . . it cannot be doubted that it will produce a beneficial effect on the habits and industry of all.[72]

This recommendation was not pressed, but it is full of interest, revealing a care for the professional competence of the navy on the part of its civilian leadership that was precedent-making.

So far as civilian employment was concerned, no one thought of a system of examinations. Individual applications, with letters of recommendation, and appointment on the basis of personal knowledge or confidence in testimonials were the order of the day.

THE OFFICE SEEKERS

Competition for office was severe during the years from 1801 to 1829, and the reserve that had often marked office seeking

70 *Ibid.*, III, 160.
71 *Niles Register*, XVII, 104, 144 (Oct. 1819).
72 *American State Papers: Naval Affairs*, III, 160.

under the Federalists became an ever more distant memory.[73] Officeholding was apparently congenial to American tastes.

Demands for appointment fell most heavily on Jefferson, but all his Republican successors felt the oppressive weight of office seekers. In turn, Jefferson, Madison, Monroe, and John Quincy Adams suffered their importunities and privately recorded their own apprehensions. Congressmen hovered around the executive offices to gain what they could for their friends; and if we may believe the hostile evidence of Adams, his rival, Crawford, assiduously cultivated the attention of place hunters who could help him to the White House.[74]

To Jefferson the scramble for office was a deep source of concern. Watching the rise of Republican fortunes from his vantage point as Vice President in 1799, he expressed his fears to Tench Coxe, himself an inveterate officeholder. "We are not incorruptible; on the contrary, corruption is making sensible tho' silent progress. Offices are as acceptable here as elsewhere, & whenever a man has cast a longing eye on them, a rottenness begins in his conduct." [75] Looking back on what he thought was Federalist profligacy, he remarked in 1803 with reference to places under John Adams:

. . . These had been so numerous, that presenting themselves to the public eye at all times & places, office began to be looked to as a resource for every man whose affairs were getting into derangement, or who was too indolent to pursue his profession, and for young men just entering into life. In short it was poisoning the very source of industry, by presenting an easier resource for a livelihood, and was corrupting the principles of the great mass of those who passed a wishful eye on office.[76]

The stream of applications from Jefferson's Republican friends may be illustrated by a few cases. One of the earliest requests was from Joseph Whipple, who had been removed by

---

[73] On rare occasions an appointment was made without solicitation. Edwin Lorrain became naval officer for New Orleans in 1814. It was an unexpected favor, of which he wrote, "I didn't even know of the vacancy." *The Papers of Archibald D. Murphey* (William Henry Hoyt, ed., 2 vols., Publications of the North Carolina Historical Commission, 1914), I, 68 (May 1, 1814).

[74] Adams, *Memoirs*, V, 482; *ibid.*, VI, 3.

[75] Jefferson, *Works* (Federal ed.), IX, 70 (May 21, 1799).

[76] *Ibid.*, IX, 450–51 (Feb. 19, 1803).

Adams as collector of Portsmouth for offensive partisanship. Early in April 1801, he addressed the new President:

. . . I will take the liberty to add that, should it be your pleasure, I should esteem a re-establishment to the office which I held (that of Collector of the Customs for Port of Portsmouth) as a healing specific to a wound maliciously inflicted through the influence of the enemies of our country's peace and independence: I do not solicit this, Sir, from pecuniary considerations; it proceeds from an earnest wish founded on political principles to participate in the execution of the government under the administration and the enjoyment of the felicity of a justifiable triumph over your enemies and the enemies of our country.[77]

Whipple had some claim for consideration. He was reappointed.

Less congenial to Jefferson's sense of propriety was the type of office seeking illustrated in correspondence from Solomon Southwick, later postmaster at Albany, who, unable to accept an appointment as marshal, proposed his brother-in-law. "It would perhaps increase his influence in Society, tend to his advantage as printer of the *Albany Register* (in which I shall not dissemble that I am privately concerned) and aid the Republican cause." [78] Even more distasteful must have seemed those not infrequent applications sent forward in anticipation of the death of the incumbent. By way of example, Horatio Turpin addressed the President of the United States in these terms:

MR. VANDERVALL the present postmaster at Richmond has been in a declining state of health for 12 months past and I have been lately informed is now confined to his bed and cannot live but a little time. by his death that office will become vacant and having no acquaintance with Mr. Granger [the Postmaster General] have to solicit the favour of your friendly aid in obtaining that birth for me.[79]

Horatio Turpin was not the only prudent individual to take time by the forelock.

John Quincy Adams early reached the conclusion that "although there is nothing dishonorable or unjust in the pursuit

77 Jefferson, *Correspondence from Bixby Collections* (W. C. Ford, ed.), p. 83 (April 9, 1801).

78 *Ibid.*, p. 84 (April 11, 1801).

79 *Ibid.*, p. 144 (June 1, 1807).

of public office, I always have considered and yet consider it as a passion, which requires great moderation, self-management and control." [80] In later years Adams suffered much from applicants who showed no moderation, self-management, or control. After some years of experience he wrote in his diary, "There is something so gross and so repugnant to my feelings in this comorant appetite for office . . . that it needed all my sense of the allowances to be made for sharp want and of the tenderness due to misfortune to suppress my indignation." [81] To his wife, Louisa, he wrote:

Your advice to treat all place hunters courteously is excellent, but you know there is a Scylla as well as a Charybdis. One of the first objects of those worthy citizens is to obtain a *promise*, and many of them are not at all scrupulous in their modes of address to that end. Some ask it with downright importunity, others like elderly maiden ladies construe a civil word and even a smile into a promise, and then if not on the first possible occasion gratified, charge one with giving delusive hopes and expectations. It is the bent of my nature to be rather more willing to be thought harsh than insincere.[82]

Jefferson's convictions on the principles that should attend the exercise of the appointing power, corresponding closely to those of his predecessors, were held also by his Republican successors. Jefferson was occasionally disposed by friendship to find places for particular individuals, John Page, a lifelong Virginia friend, and Philip Reibelt, a newcomer with a charming wife, serving as examples.[83]

Exceptions to principle and policy occur in any system, and we need not allow favors to Page, Reibelt, and others to obscure the standards that the Republicans announced and generally

---

[80] Adams, *Writings*, IV, 183 (August 20, 1811).

[81] Adams, *Memoirs*, V, 24 (March 18, 1820). Hezekiah Niles had become so impatient by 1823 that he lumped officeholders and office seekers together, calling them "the meanest class of all the mean classes." *Niles Register*, XXIV, 241 (June 21, 1823).

[82] Adams, *Writings*, VII, 296 (August 23, 1822). A couple of weeks earlier he had written Louisa, "A place or a subscription is the object of all the new acquaintance that I make. . . ." *Ibid.*, VII, 288.

[83] For the Page case, see Jefferson, *Works* (Federal ed.), IX, 351; 354–55, n.; 355, n.; and the Jefferson Papers in Massachusetts Historical Society, *Collections*, 7th series, I, 120–24. For the Rcibelt case, see *Territorial Papers*, IX, 563, n. 56; 671; 687; 728; 729; 808.

maintained. Their selections for office were made within the ranks of the Republican party, but they were confined to gentlemen who were men of integrity, who had the confidence of their community, and were "respectable" in the eyes of their neighbors. The Republicans were as sensitive as other gentlemen to the evil of favoring friends and relatives, and as other politicians to the value of balanced tickets for the administration at large and to the rule of local residence in local offices. They, like the Federalists, reflected the predispositions of their social class; and, since both came from the same social class, with varying rural-urban emphases, their views on officeholding were much alike. Standards of appointment from 1789 to 1829 conformed to a single pattern.

CHAPTER TWENTY-FIVE

Public Service Careers

The spirit of the Federalist system favored continuity of service from the highest to the lowest levels. John Adams retained Washington's Cabinet members, and the whole range of important accounting and operating officials as well as employees in subordinate positions remained on their jobs. No property right in office was ever established or seriously advocated, but permanent and continued employment during good behavior was taken for granted.

Jefferson, Gallatin, and other important Republicans accepted this policy, barring Cabinet appointments and the foreign service. It was not, therefore, a party doctrine, but an opinion common to the gentlemen of both parties that the same comptrollers and auditors, clerks and customs inspectors, land agents and navy pursers should serve the government, no matter what the fortunes of the two political parties. The Republicans, to be sure, were forced to depart from their convictions during the interim period of adjustment from 1801 to 1803, but despite this, a large number of moderate Federalists quietly kept at their work. The name of Washington was continued in the public service by his relative, Lund Washington, and by the latter's son, Peter Grayson Washington. Death and resignations due to ill health or advanced age were the normal conclusions of an official career.

The situation was due not to law but to practice. Until 1820 the law specified tenure at the pleasure of the appointing authority in almost every type of employment and official post except the marshals, for whom a four-year term had been prescribed by the Federalists. The report of Senator Benton in

1826 gave complete evidence on this point.[1] Holding office at the pleasure of the President were department heads, the whole diplomatic and consular service, the two comptrollers and five auditors, the Board of Navy Commissioners, the superintendent of Indian affairs and eighty-four Indian agents and subagents, the collectors, and a miscellaneous lot of officials such as the keepers of the archives in East and West Florida and the commissioner of public buildings in Washington. The great mass of subordinates held office or employment at the pleasure of the head of the department. The chief clerks, the clerks, and messengers; the numerous subordinate customs staff including clerks, inspectors, weighers, measurers, and gaugers; postmasters, assistant postmasters, and their clerks all fell into this class.

The Tenure of Office Act of 1820 altered the legal situation by specifying four-year terms for most officers concerned with the collection or disbursement of public funds, especially the collectors, naval officers, and surveyors in the customs service and the army and navy paymasters.[2] A few other officials had specific terms. Thus the governors of Michigan and Arkansas Territories were appointed for three years, and the justices of the peace in the District of Columbia for five.[3]

Security of tenure and life service were therefore not protected by law. The statutes made substantially the whole of the administrative service responsible to the President, either directly or through the heads of departments. Policy and tradition combined in practice to build a working superstructure of service during good behavior on this legal foundation of service at pleasure or for specified terms.

CAREER SERVICE

Justice Story forecast a true career service, specifically in the judicial branch but in principle elsewhere. Arguing for an improvement in official compensation, he wrote of this reform, "It will hold out a motive for ambitious young men to qualify themselves for these offices, and secure to the Government a

---

[1] Senate Doc. 88, 19th Cong., 1st sess. (May 4, 1826); hereafter cited as Benton's Report.

[2] 3 Stat. 582 (May 15, 1820). This act is dealt with in the following chapter.

[3] Benton's Report, *passim*.

succession of men, whose talents and virtues shall place them in the first rank in the profession." [4] Particular instances of life-long careers have already been noted in connection with the work of the departments. Some may be recalled here: Joseph Anderson, first comptroller from 1815 to 1836; Richard Cutts, superintendent general of military supplies and second comptroller from 1817 to 1829; Peter Hagner, clerk, principal clerk, and third auditor, continuously employed from 1792 to 1849; Stephen Pleasonton, clerk and fifth auditor from 1800 to 1855; Charles Washington Goldsborough, whose service in the Navy Department as clerk and chief clerk was interrupted only for two years from 1798 to 1843; Abraham Bradley, assistant post-master general from 1802 to 1829; William Thornton, head of the Patent Office from 1802 to 1827; and Joseph Lovell, surgeon general from 1818 to 1836.

The Nourse family was one of the best known in official circles in Washington during both the Federalist and Republican years.[5] Joseph Nourse, a Virginian, was appointed register of the Treasury by Washington in 1789 and remained in this post until removed by Jackson in 1829. In 1805 he bought and occupied the house now known as Dumbarton House, and later moved into the country, building a new home on what is now the site of the Washington Cathedral. Here he entertained his friends, among them Jefferson, Madison, Monroe, and John Quincy Adams. One son, Major Charles J. Nourse, became chief clerk of the War Department. The *Washington Directory* of 1822 listed in addition to Joseph Nourse and Major Charles J. Nourse, the following members of the family: Joseph R.—a clerk in the register's office; Col. Michael—chief clerk in the register's office; and John R.—clerk in the register's office.[6]

The Nourses were long associated with another official family, the Brents. The Brent family and their immediate connections played a prominent part in Republican circles, both political and administrative. Among the sons of the elder Robert Brent

[4] Story, *Life and Letters*, I, 302 (1816).

[5] Grace Dunlop Peter, "Unpublished Letters of Dolly Madison to Anthony Morris Relating to the Nourse Family of the Highlands," Columbia Historical Society, *Records*, XLIV–XLV (1944), 215–39.

[6] Judah Delano, *The Washington Directory* (Washington: William Duncan, 1822), p. 62.

were four—Daniel, John, Robert, and William—who chose the public service as a career. Daniel began his government work as a Treasury clerk under Alexander Hamilton, was appointed marshal of the District of Columbia by Jefferson in 1802 and again in 1803, became a clerk in the State Department, and eventually the chief clerk, and completed his public service as United States consul in Paris. John had a less impressive career, serving as collector and inspector of the port of Nanjemoy. William, too, was less conspicuous, but had a useful career as clerk of the several courts of Washington, D. C. Robert was perhaps most in the public eye—the first mayor of Washington by appointment of Jefferson, ten times renewed to cover the years 1802–1812. While mayor he was also paymaster of the United States Army, 1808–1819, justice of the peace, judge of the orphan's court, and a member of the school board. In 1815 he became the first president of the Patriotic Bank in Washington. He was one of "very few private gentlemen" to have a house in Washington in 1804.

Robert Brent, the father, had a sister, Jane, who married Richard Graham, scion of an influential and wealthy Virginia family. Two sons were born of this union who also had important public careers. John Graham served an apprenticeship in the foreign service in Madrid, and eventually became chief clerk of the State Department (1807–1817). In 1817 he went on a South American mission for Monroe, and in 1819 became the United States minister to the Portuguese government, then in exile in Brazil. He was highly praised both by Madison and Monroe as "among the most worthy of men, and most estimable of citizens . . . [with] a purity of character, a delicacy of sentiment, and an amenity of temper & manners, exceeded in no instance" to which Madison could refer.[7] His brother, George, served in the Virginia Assembly where he made the acquaintance of Madison and Monroe, became chief clerk in the War Department, and later commissioner of the General Land Office until his death in 1830. Three cousins therefore held chief clerkships: John Graham and his successor, Daniel Brent, in State; and George Graham in the War Department.

[7] Madison, *Writings* (Hunt ed.), VIII, 390.

The administrative Brents also had their family connections in Congress. Richard Brent (an uncle) served in the House of Representatives from Virginia in the fourth, fifth, and seventh Congresses, and was Senator from 1809 until his death in 1814.

Republicans were definitely opposed to careers in one branch of public affairs, the diplomatic service. Despite the long years abroad of such notable characters as John Quincy Adams, doctrine strongly preferred short terms. This view was expressed often by Jefferson, was endorsed by Monroe, and approved by Adams. While Secretary of State he wrote:

> . . . It was a maxim of Mr. Jefferson's, which I find is also approved by Mr. Monroe, that Americans, and especially young Americans, should for their own sake, as well as for that of their country, make no long residences in a public capacity at the courts of Europe. He thought the air of those regions so unfriendly to American constitutions that they always required after a few years to be renovated by the wholesome republican atmosphere of their own country. The practice of the present administration will be altogether conformable to these principles.[8]

Individual examples of life service, such as the Brent family, are repeated in the history of particular bodies of officials or employees. One of the most important was the group of collectors of customs, whose record has been set out in previous pages.[9] The district attorneys, who might have been supposed peculiarly vulnerable, showed remarkable stability of employment in most states and districts.[10] Jefferson removed some but declined to make a clean sweep. Pierrepont Edwards carried on in Connecticut until 1805, Joseph H. Davies of Kentucky served until 1807, Benjamin Woods of North Carolina until 1808, and Thomas Parker in South Carolina from 1792 to 1821. Instances of long tenure could be cited from all parts of the country. Delaware was the most striking; George Read, Jr., was ap-

---

8 Adams, *Writings*, VI, 357 (June 22, 1818).

9 See ch. 11.

10 Some light is thrown on the district attorney's office by the following excerpt from a "substitute," the episode occurring in 1817. "John Rodman, District Attorney of New York, being obliged by feeble health to pass the winter in the South, employed me to perform the duties of his office during his absence. The compensation for these services, both arduous and painful, was $50." *Reminiscences of James A. Hamilton* (New York: Charles Scribner & Co., 1869), p. 57.

pointed United States attorney in 1789 by George Washington and died in office in 1836. Connecticut had only two district attorneys from 1789 to 1829; South Carolina, two from 1792 to 1831. In New Jersey, Joseph McIlvane served in this capacity from 1804 to 1824, when he was elected to the United States Senate. In New Hampshire, Daniel Humphreys held the office from 1804 to 1828. The expiration of terms, even after the Tenure of Office Act of 1820, bore no relation to a change in the White House. Changes were incident to resignation, death, appointment to a judgeship, or election to Congress. A corresponding record has already been revealed among the postmasters.

Benton's Report of 1826 provided substantiating data with respect to navy surgeons and pursers. Despite unsatisfactory conditions in the navy medical service, it appeared that of the thirty-nine surgeons in service in 1826, one had been appointed in 1799, five in the decade 1800–1809; twelve in the next five years (1810–14), nine in the following five (1815–19), and twelve since 1820.[11] Of forty-two pursers, exactly one half had been appointed in the five years 1810–1814; ten had gone on duty from 1815 to 1819; and ten had been appointed in 1820 or later.[12] The navy agents, who held responsible posts, showed a similar record of continuous service. George Harrison began in 1799; Beatty and Randall in 1810; Binney and Riddle in 1812; and others from 1816 to 1825.[13]

If we turn our attention to the subordinate staff, we discover again the fact of continuous service over many years. From an official report in 1818 [14] the following record appears among the clerks in the office of the fourth auditor, formerly the navy accountant's staff: Thomas H. Gillis, chief clerk—"This gentleman has been twenty years clerk in the Navy Department"; George M. Daniel—"He has been nineteen years in the service of the Navy Department"; Joseph Mechlin—"He has been nineteen years in service"; John MacDaniel—"He has been eighteen years in service"; Ezekiel MacDaniel—"His term of service has

11 Benton's Report, p. 122.
12 *Ibid.,* p. 123.
13 *Ibid.,* p. 135.
14 House Doc. 194, 15th Cong., 1st sess., pp. 36–37 (April 13, 1818).

been twelve years"; Henry Forrest—"Period of service, fourteen years"; "Mr. Craven is a respectable old man. . . . He has
been nineteen years in service." Many of these, it will be observed, go back to the administration of John Adams. One instance has been noted in which a young man deliberately set
out for a Treasury career. Joseph Chambers of Salisbury, North
Carolina, entered the comptroller's office in 1797 "with a view
to qualify himself for public business by acquiring a familiar
knowledge of the forms and principles of accounting at the
Treasy." [15]

The investigation of the Philadelphia customhouse in 1826,
already noted, showed life service to be the rule in the subordinate customs staff.[16] The record of employment among the
craftsmen showed the same pattern.[17] Among the navy carpenters at work in 1826, one had been employed in 1814, one in
1815, one in 1818, three in 1820, and one each in 1821, 1822,
and 1823. Among the sailmakers, one had worked since 1813,
one since 1817, one since 1819, and others were employed in
the years from 1821 to 1825.

THE PROBLEM OF SUPERANNUATION

Stability and continuity thus became as conspicuous features
of the public service under the Republicans as under the
Federalists. Employment legally at pleasure became in practice employment during good behavior. A government career,
however, brought few of the advantages that came with later
years except security and status. The case of Samuel Gordon
demonstrated some of its early limitations.

Gordon was the driver of a mail stage from Albany to
Schenectady. On March 2, 1804, he was overtaken by a violent
snow storm, which prevented the movement of the stage. Faithful to his duty he took the mail on his back and on foot conveyed it to its destination. "From the violence of the storm and
a cold which it produced, he wholly lost his eye sight, and had
become dependent upon public charity." He asked for an in-

15 John Steele, *Papers*, I, 247–48 (1802).
16 See ch. 11.
17 Benton's Report, p. 133.

valid pension. Granger sent the following communication to the House.

The petitioner is highly commendable for his exertions, and the unfortunate result is to be regretted. But it does not appear to the Postmaster General that this case is to be distinguished from that of other citizens who have been disabled while engaged in their ordinary pursuits.

The circumstance occurred in a settled country, where there is already provision for the unfortunate poor, and where there is no occasion to encourage persons to enter into the public service with the hope of pensions, in case of disability. The case of Webb, which probably gave rise to this petition, is materially different; by passing through the Indian nations he was exposed to extraordinary hazard from the savageness of their habits, and his wound and disability proceeded from that extraordinary source of injury; his disability also occurred where there was no provision for the poor, and not within any State jurisdiction, and Congress were, of course, the only regular authority to whom he could apply for relief.

The Postmaster General is, therefore, of opinion that Samuel Gordon ought not to be provided for by Congress.[18]

Consequences, good and ill, flowed from the fact of life employment. One result was to encourage close personal relations among the gentlemen who comprised an agency or office. "No one who has not experienced it," said Thomas L. McKenney, head of the Indian office, "can know how strong the ties become between the head of a department and his clerks, provided there is mutual zeal, and a corresponding intelligence, to carry on the business entrusted to each, in his sphere." [19]

Another consequence was that the important positions of middle management were held by men progressively advanced in years, in many instances less and less able to perform their duties effectively. Collector John Steele of Philadelphia was a case in point. The laxness disclosed in his establishment in 1826 was in part due to his age and incapacity, making him unable to cope with an increased volume of business or to suggest necessary alterations in storehouse facilities.[20] Collector

18 *American State Papers: Post Office*, p. 43 (March 23, 1810).
19 Thomas L. McKenney, *Memoirs, Official and Personal* . . . (2 vols., New York: Paine and Burgess, 1846), I, 23–24.
20 See above, ch. 11.

Benjamin Lincoln remained in office in Boston long after he was equal to its responsibilities; he, indeed, would have retired earlier but for Jefferson's insistence on his continuance in office.

Another consequence was that the efficiency of the service was lowered by retaining superannuated clerks and subordinates. In 1827 Secretary Rush called the Treasury "the octogenarian department," and complained bitterly about being ground down with his duties as "head overseer, and journeyman too." [21] In 1828 Rush and the treasurer came to the White House for Adams' advice regarding the treasurer's chief clerk.

> . . . It is ostensibly held by a man named Samuel Brooks, who in process of time has become perfectly superannuated, and for more than a year past has never even attended at the office. He is poor, and has no other means of subsistence than his salary. The late Treasurer, Dr. Tucker, who had been for at least ten years before his death past the age of active service, unwilling to adopt the harsh measure of turning Brooks adrift upon the world in the last stage of life, authorized one of the inferior clerks to perform the duties of Chief Clerk, deducting from Brooks's salary the difference between that of the Chief Clerk, which is seventeen hundred dollars, and that of a copying clerk, of eight hundred dollars, the last of which only was paid to Brooks, and the remainder to Mr. Dashiel, who performed the duties of Chief Clerk.[22]

It was a perplexing case and as Adams said, "We had much conversation upon the subject." The President advised to continue the arrangement only for that fiscal year.

Adams had also to hear the personal appeal of a Land Office clerk, dismissed at the age of seventy-three. "He has almost totally lost his memory, and has long been unable to perform any duty at the Land Office; but his removal from it has placed him in a pitiable condition, and his appeal to me was pathetic, not without tears." [23] The President could not offer him prospect of continuance in his job.

Robert Brent, paymaster general in the War Department, had been a helpless paralytic for a year before he resigned in 1819; his chief clerk, Frye, did all the business of his principal as well

21 Clay, *Works*, IV, 186 (Dec. 18, 1827).
22 Adams, *Memoirs*, VIII, 68 (July 30, 1828).
23 *Ibid.*, VII, 250 (March 29, 1827).

as his own.[24] William Essenbeck had been employed as a messenger for more than twenty-four years, "and is still retained in public service as assistant messenger, on half pay." [25] This was in effect a pension to a worthy but no longer useful employee. Probably most offices could have duplicated situations like these.

In the armed services, life work again was the normal expectation, subject to the vicissitudes of the periodic reductions in staff caused by congressional retrenchment drives. Commander John Rodgers was in the navy from 1798 to 1837; [26] Captain Thomas Tingey from 1798 until his retirement a few days before his death in 1829 at the age of seventy-eight.[27] The failures of the early campaigns of the War of 1812 were due in part to the lack of energy of aging Revolutionary War generals whom time had elevated to the highest ranks. Superannuation was a problem in both the civil and military branches, but how to deal with it was beyond the grasp of that generation.

Congressmen looked at the problem but held their hands. The House Committee on Naval Affairs reported in 1823:

. . . Advantage might be supposed to accrue to the public service, by striking from the list of officers some whose age or infirmities render them no longer useful; but a power of so much delicacy ought never to be exercised by legislation. If its policy or justice were admitted, the Executive is the only organ of the constitution, which, in the discharge of such a duty, possesses the competent means of information, and which ought, therefore, to assume the responsibility.[28]

Congress, however, stated no policy and established no system. The executive could remove officers, civil and military, but the act of removal denoted fault or delinquency and was wholly inappropriate as a means of dealing with men who had given a lifetime of loyal and effective service to the government. Congress remained in a quandary; and the aged incompetents remained a charge on the pay roll.

24 *Ibid.*, IV, 369 (May 21, 1819); *ibid.*, IV, 408 (August 11, 1819). Frye had married the sister of John Adams' wife. *Ibid.*, IV, 408.

25 Senate Doc. 46, 15th Cong., 1st sess. (Jan. 7, 1818).

26 *Dictionary of American Biography*, XVI, 75–77.

27 *Ibid.*, XVIII, 560–61.

28 House Report 63, 17th Cong., 2d sess., p. 2 (Jan. 20, 1823).

THE POWER TO REMOVE

The stability of the federal service was reflected in the very modest use of the power to remove. The power was conceded to be vested in the executive branch and was not limited by Congress. It was employed with great reluctance by Federalists and Republicans alike. Even during the transition period from 1801 to 1803 Jefferson removed only a relatively small number, mostly persons who had been improvidently appointed at the last minute by Adams or who were conspicuous by their open opposition to the new regime. This was the only occasion when removals were made for party reasons from 1801 to 1829.

According to Fish, in the course of eight years Jefferson removed 109 officers out of 433 in the presidential class.[29] These included Adams' midnight appointments, of which there were 40; marshals, who were thought to be unreliable as a class, and a few attorneys, 11 in all; and 26 collectors of customs. Granger removed some postmasters, and Republican collectors in some cases removed subordinate customs clerks, but generally the Republicans waited on time, and time fulfilled their needs.

Madison removed twenty-seven presidential officers during his eight years in the White House.[30] Almost without exception they were officers collecting the revenue. Madison was under some pressure after the War of 1812 to find civil employment for supernumerary military officers, but declined to disturb the civil service. He was prepared to favor meritorious and indigent officers, but only where a removal could be justified "by legitimate causes." [31] Crawford once remarked that Madison could not bear to turn men out of office for "simple incapacity." [32]

Monroe also removed twenty-seven civil officers in his eight years in the White House. One-third were in the foreign service, all consuls with a single exception; one-third were collectors

---

[29] Carl Russell Fish, "Removal of Officials by the Presidents of the United States," American Historical Association, *Annual Report, 1899*, I, 65–86 at 70.

[30] *Ibid.*, p. 71; House Doc. 132, 26th Cong., 1st sess., p. 10 (March 13, 1840), reports names and offices of seventeen.

[31] Fish, *Civil Service and the Patronage*, pp. 54–55.

[32] Philip Jackson Green, "The Public Life of William Harris Crawford, 1807–1825," p. 154 (MS., Ph.D. thesis, University of Chicago, 1935).

of revenue.[33] Adams thought Monroe much too lenient, governed by momentary feelings rather than by "steady and inflexible principle."

. . . He is universally indulgent, and scrupulously regardful of individual feelings. He is perhaps too reluctant to exercise this power at all. He rather turns his eyes from misconduct, and betrays a sensation of pain when it is presented directly to him. . . . I should look for a little more vigilance to observe, and a little more rigor to control, the faults of Executive officers.[34]

Adams removed only twelve, in a service which had expanded considerably since 1816.[35]

The case of Adams is particularly instructive, because he was under greater pressure to use the removal power than any of his predecessors excepting Jefferson. Henry Clay strongly advised him to clear his political enemies out of public office. ". . . so long as the election was pending," said Clay, "every man was free to indulge his preference for any of the candidates; but after it was decided, no officer depending upon the will of the President for his place should be permitted to hold a conduct in open and continual disparagement of the Administration and its head." [36]

Adams demurred. Removal merely on the ground "that it was the pleasure of the President, would be harsh and odious—inconsistent with the principle upon which I have commenced the Administration, of removing no person from office but for cause." A removal unjustifiable before public opinion, Adams thought, would "indicate an irritable, hasty, and vindictive temper, and give rise to newspaper discussions, of which all the disadvantage would fall upon the Administration." To those who urged him to sweep away his opponents and provide their places for his friends, he replied that such a course was incon-

33 Fish, "Removal of Officials," *op. cit.*, p. 72.
34 Adams, *Memoirs*, V, 158 (June 23, 1820). Adams' judgment on Monroe was confirmed within six weeks, when Monroe admitted he suspected the Baltimore customs officers of winking at the slave trade and piracy operations out of Baltimore, but declined either to investigate or remove. Monroe to Adams, August 11, 1820, Adams, *Writings*, VII, 60, n. 1.
35 Fish, "Removal of Officials," *op. cit.*, p. 73.
36 Adams, *Memoirs*, VI, 546 (May 13, 1825).

sistent with his concept of the public good: "An invidious and inquisitorial scrutiny into the personal dispositions of public officers will creep through the whole Union, and the most selfish and sordid passions will be kindled into activity to distort the conduct and misrepresent the feelings of men whose places may become the prize of slander upon them." Adams ended the passage in his diary by observing, "Mr. Clay did not press the subject any further." [37] The modest number of removals suggests beyond question that the power to remove was confined to cases of moral delinquency.

PROFESSIONAL FOUNDATIONS: LAW, MEDICINE, ENGINEERING

In 1826 Niles listed the number of graduates from the sixteen American colleges that produced about two-thirds of the college graduates of that day. There were 439 in 1823 and 517 in 1826.[38] He also reported that "twelve hundred young gentlemen were prepared for the profession of medicine, six hundred for law, and five hundred for the ministry" in 1825, meaning presumably that these numbers were enrolled at the time in professional courses of study.[39] He gave no figures for engineering, the study of which was then confined to West Point.

The study of law was the usual foundation for the careers of men in important positions in the federal service. All four Republican Presidents studied law as young men and John Quincy Adams practiced law for a brief period in Boston. In the House of Representatives in 1822 were 97 lawyers, among 190 whose occupations were reported; 59 were farmers and planters, and 15 were physicians.[40] The Attorney General and district attorneys were required by statute to be "learned in the law." A legal training was thought most desirable for the comptrollers and auditors.[41] Comptrollers Duval, Anderson, and Cutts all came up through the law. Auditors, however, were more likely to have advanced by promotion from the office of clerk or auditing clerk.

37 *Ibid.*, VI, 546–47.
38 *Niles Register*, XXXI, 158 (Nov. 4, 1826).
39 *Ibid.*, XXX, 234 (June 3, 1826).
40 *Ibid.*, XXII, 177 (May 18, 1822).
41 Gallatin, *Writings*, I, 103 (Oct. 26, 1802).

There were good reasons for the eminence of lawyers in the early public service. Their training and experience accustomed them to close analysis of legal documents, and a considerable part of the business of administration was necessarily concerned with the interpretation of statutes, regulations, and appropriation acts. Lawyers moreover lived in a world of controversy and argument, and public office is inevitably a center of conflicting interests. Despite much feeling against the legal profession as interested fomenters of discord, the leaders of the bar in the various states enjoyed a high standing in the community.[42] From their ranks came both the federal and state judges of the supreme and intermediate courts. Lawyers therefore readily became the principal professional group in the public service.

The medical profession in government service expanded during the first three decades of the century, principally in the army and navy. The regime of examinations that was introduced toward the end of the period was designed to raise the level of competence and professional interest. The surgeons' reports that were required in the 1820's marked the origin of the collection of medical data and of research that a century later was to have flowered into a great scientific enterprise.

It was in the Jeffersonian period that the engineers came into their own. We have already noted the foundation and improvement of West Point and the organization of the engineer corps. After 1816 they were the most acclaimed body of professional men in the public service, despite their limited numbers. They remained, however, engineers. They did not move over into statecraft nor escape the bounds of the War Department for administrative careers elsewhere in the federal government.

The total number of professionally trained civil servants was

---

[42] Jefferson was contemptuous of lawyers. In the midst of the embargo crisis he wrote Gallatin, "It is well known that on every question the lawyers are about equally divided . . . and were we to act but in cases where no contrary opinion of a lawyer can be had, we should never act." *Writings* (Memorial ed.), XII, 168–69 (Sept. 20, 1808). At about the same time he referred to "a half-sighted lawyer" who might object to a commission signed in blank. *Ibid.*, XII, 171 (Oct. 16, 1808). In 1815 he wrote to Thomas Leiper complaining about procrastination in Congress. "How can expedition be expected from a body which we have saddled with an hundred lawyers, whose trade is talking?" *Works* (Federal ed.), XI, 479 (June 12, 1815).

small.[43] There were probably not more than fifty men with law degrees in the executive branch, about sixty navy surgeons and a lesser number of army surgeons, and about sixty civil and topographical engineers. A few persons had training in science or mathematics, but they were not necessarily employed as scientists or mathematicians.

OFFICIAL AND EMPLOYEE ORGANIZATIONS

The tradition of permanent service during good behavior was favorable to the growth of collective action among persons holding the same type of employment. Common interests united small groups to secure as a body what they had not been able to gain as individuals. For the first time there was a meeting of professional officers on their salary problem, and an association of government clerks appeared on the administrative scene.

The unsatisfactory situation of the surgeons and assistant surgeons of the United States Navy became so acute that a number of them held a meeting in Philadelphia to prepare a memorial to Congress. It was transmitted by a committee to John C. Calhoun, Vice President, and president of the Senate on January 12, 1828. "We appeal," declared the committee, "to the good sense and sound judgment of the national legislature . . . for that relief which we humbly conceive is founded on the most correct views of the service, and in the best policy of the country." [44] The surgeons asked for an improvement in pay and approved the system of medical examinations to which reference has been made. Congress responded favorably to the well-written petition, which showed among other things that the Republic of Mexico paid its naval surgeons more than three times the salary enjoyed in the United States Navy. An improved pay scale was authorized.[45] There is no record of any further meetings of this *ad hoc* organization.

Thirteen army captains memorialized the Senate and House

---

43 At one time Jefferson hoped for the early development of Robert Fulton's submarine, and forecast a "corps of young men trained to this profession." Jefferson, *Works* (Federal ed.), X, 477, August 16, 1807.

44 *American State Papers: Naval Affairs*, III, 131.

45 4 Stat. 313 (May 24, 1828). See also *American State Papers: Naval Affairs*, III, 128 (Jan. 12, 1828).

in 1826 for an increase in their pay. The Senate Committee on Military Affairs accepted the memorial and made a favorable report.[46] Congress raised the captains' pay ten dollars a month in recognition of their increased responsibility for clothing, arms, and accoutrements.[47]

Somewhat more permanent was the Provident Association of Clerks, in the District of Columbia. This beneficiary association was incorporated by act of Congress, February 15, 1819, for a period of fifteen years.[48] Its purpose was to make grants to the families of deceased members from annual contributions of ten dollars each. The officers made a report in 1832, summarizing their activities and requesting renewal of their charter.[49] The Association then had sixty-nine members who in fifteen years had contributed something over $7,000. Payments to the families of deceased members exceeded $4,300. The expenses of administration were gratifyingly slight; in fifteen years they amounted to $288.45. The president of the Association in 1834 was Charles Washington Goldsborough, chief clerk of the Navy Department.

The charter was renewed in 1832 [50] but the bank failures of 1836 and the panic of 1837 brought the Association to its knees. In 1836 it petitioned Congress for a grant "to relieve the association from its embarrassments, and enable it fully to accomplish the salutary and benevolent purposes for which it was incorporated." [51] Congress made no grant but gave it power to invest its funds more freely.[52]

These organizations can be considered as forerunners of the active unions of federal employees that were to make their appearance by the close of the century. They suggest the recognition of a common economic interest, and the application of

46 Senate Doc. 33, 19th Cong., 1st sess. (Feb. 9, 1826).
47 4 Stat. 227 (March 2, 1827).
48 6 Stat. 218. There is evidence that the Association was already in existence in 1817, since there was an appeal for payment of subscriptions in the *Daily National Intelligencer* of May 15, 1817. See Leonard D. White, *Introduction to the Study of Public Administration* (2d ed., New York: Macmillan, 1939), p. 426, n. 1.
49 House Doc. 211, 22d Cong., 1st sess. (April 20, 1832).
50 6 Stat. 504 (July 9, 1832).
51 House Doc. 71, 24th Cong., 1st sess. (Jan. 18, 1826).
52 6 Stat. 681 (July 2, 1836).

collective means of securing these interests: petition to Congress and private aid through a beneficiary association. They reflect the stability and permanence of employment which became a settled feature of the Jeffersonian period. Had that stability continued without interruption, it is possible that the incorporation of the Provident Association of Clerks would be remembered as an initial step in a scheme of social security.

CHAPTER TWENTY-SIX

The Cloud on the Horizon

On January 30, 1811, Josiah Quincy, a member of the House from Massachusetts, delivered an address on the influence of place and patronage.[1] It was an exquisite piece, whimsical, sly, pointed, and prophetic. The evil to which he was addressing himself was the loss of congressional independence to executive patronage, not the consequences of what later became known as the spoils system. The analogy was, however, close, and Quincy's comments were not irrelevant to tendencies which could be discerned before the end of the Jeffersonian era.

The evil, said Quincy, "has its origin in that love of place which is so inherent in the human heart that it may be called almost an universal and instinctive passion. It cannot be otherwise; for so long as the love of honor and the love of profit are natural to man, so long the love of place, which includes either the one or the other or both, must be a very general and prevalent impulse." [2] He spoke, as he said, not merely to his colleagues, "but also for the purpose of attracting the attention of the public to the subject . . . unless it [i.e., reform] have the aid of external pressure, *it will stick in the passage*." [3]

The timing of Quincy's speech, in the second year of Madison's first administration, was not propitious. It was hardly a moment to worry about protecting Congress against executive machinations, for never had the influence of the Chief Executive been so low and seldom were fewer places to be filled by

[1] Edmund Quincy, ed., *Speeches Delivered in the Congress of the United States by Josiah Quincy, 1805–1813* (Boston: Little, Brown, 1874), pp. 227–44.
[2] *Ibid.*, p. 234.
[3] *Ibid.*, p. 229; italics author's.

what Quincy called "an interchange, strictly speaking, of good offices" between the executive and legislative branches. Postwar expansion, however, put a new aspect on the face of things, and intense rivalry for success in the election of 1824 pushed the issue of patronage into a new focus. The shadow of things to come was visible in the Tenure of Office Act of 1820.

TENURE OF OFFICE ACT

The evidence seems conclusive that this enactment was the work of William H. Crawford. In 1828 Adams wrote in his diary that the act "was drawn up by Mr. Crawford, as he himself told me. It was introduced into the Senate by Mahlon Dickerson, of New Jersey, then one of his devoted partisans. . . ." [4]

The act itself was brief.[5] It provided that the principal officers concerned with the collection or disbursement of money should be henceforth appointed for fixed terms of four years, and that the commissions of present incumbents should expire at stated intervals, not later than September 30, 1821. The classes of agents affected were district attorneys, collectors of the customs, naval officers and surveyors of the customs, navy agents, receivers of public money for lands, registers of the land offices, paymasters in the army, the apothecary general, the assistant apothecaries general, and the commissary general of purchases. Not affected were pursers, Indian agents, postmasters, or any of the accounting and clerical officers and employees stationed in Washington.[6]

Crawford's motives have been the subject of different interpretations. Whether he was animated by a desire to make accountable officers more accountable or nonpartisans more partisan is a subject of dispute. In previous chapters there appears ample evidence to show that more effective methods of accountability were needed,[7] and it has been suggested that the objects

4 Adams, *Memoirs*, VII, 424 (Feb. 7, 1828).
5 3 Stat. 582 (May 15, 1820).
6 The law further prescribed that the President could increase bonds required for these or other disbursing officers in the army or navy; and that the commissions of all officers employed in collecting the revenue should be made out and recorded in the Treasury.
7 See above, ch. 12.

of this reform were the same as those which had caused Congress for four years to give almost constant attention to the improvement of fiscal methods.[8]

The President signed the act immediately upon its presentation toward the close of the session. According to Adams, "Mr. Monroe unwarily signed the bill without adverting to its real character. He told me that Mr. Madison considered it as in principle unconstitutional. . . . Mr. Monroe himself inclined to the same opinion, but the question had not occurred to him when he signed the bill." [9] The President apparently had not been warned by his advisers and had not surmised that the bill was possibly an engine for Crawford's use.

However this may be, the potential danger was quickly perceived by the elder statesmen. Tench Coxe took immediate advantage of the rich openings by petitioning his old friend, Thomas Jefferson, who sent the letter to Madison with these prescient comments.

. . . This is a sample of the effects we may expect from the late mischievous law vacating every four years nearly all the executive offices of the government. It saps the constitutional and salutary functions of the President, and introduces a principle of intrigue and corruption, which will soon leaven the mass, not only of Senators, but of citizens. It is more baneful than the attempt which failed in the beginning of the government, to make all officers irremovable but with the consent of the Senate. This places, every four years, all appointments under their power, and even obliges them to act on every one nomination. It will keep in constant excitement all the hungry cormorants for office, render them, as well as those in place, sycophants to their Senators, engage these in eternal intrigue to turn out one and put in another, in cabals to swap work; and make of them what all executive directories become, mere sinks of corruption and faction. This must have been one of the midnight signatures of the President, when he had not time to consider, or even to read the law; and the more fatal as being irrepealable but with the consent of the Senate, which will never be obtained.[10]

[8] The principal defender of this thesis is Carl Russell Fish. See his article, "The Crime of W. H. Crawford," *American Historical Review*, XXI (1915–16), 545–56. For the opposite view, see Charles M. Wiltse, *John C. Calhoun: Nationalist*, p. 211, n. 1.

[9] Adams, *Memoirs*, VII, 424–25 (Feb. 7, 1828).

[10] Jefferson, *Works* (Federal ed.), XII, 174–75 (Nov. 29, 1820).

Madison concurred in these dark opinions of Jefferson: "The law . . . is pregnant with mischiefs such as you describe. . . . If the error be not soon corrected, the task will be very difficult; for it is of a nature to take a deep root." [11] John Quincy Adams declared, "A more pernicious expedient could scarcely have been devised." [12]

The political consequences of the Tenure of Office Act soon appeared. Less than a year after its passage Adams observed General Dearborn, collector of customs at Boston, in Washington to protect his interests against "prowling here to supplant him in his office." Adams drily noted that the principle of rotation was "more congenial to republicans out of than to those in office." [13]

Toward the end of his administration, Monroe sent in a number of nominations which the Senate held over pending Adams' inauguration. "Efforts had been made by some of the Senators," Adams wrote as he entered the White House, "to obtain different nominations, and to introduce a principle of change or rotation in office at the expiration of these commissions; which would make the Government a perpetual and unintermitting scramble for office." [14] The term of the marshal of Indiana had expired and the incumbent, against whom no complaints were made, had been renominated by Monroe. The brother of Senator Noble of Indiana wanted the office, and a member of the Indiana delegation came to Adams to recommend him and to secure withdrawal of the nomination of the incumbent. Neither Monroe nor Adams took the hint. A member of the House from Rhode Island offered himself as a candidate for the Providence collectorship, the term having expired. The reappointment of the collector of Wilmington was protested.

Adams saw clearly enough the danger. "I determined," he said, "to renominate every person against whom there was no complaint which would have warranted his removal; and renominated every person nominated by Mr. Monroe, and upon

11 Madison, *Letters* (Congressional ed.), III, 196 (Dec. 10, 1820).
12 Adams, *Memoirs*, VI, 521 (March 5, 1825).
13 *Ibid.*, V, 287 (Feb. 21, 1821).
14 *Ibid.*, VI, 520–21 (March 5, 1825).

whose nomination the Senate had declined acting. Mr. Monroe always acted on this principle of renomination." [15]

Two years later, when the 1828 campaign was already in full swing, Adams renominated James R. Pringle, collector of the port at Charleston, South Carolina, although he was "devoted to the opposition."

. . . My system has been, and continues to be, to nominate for re-appointment all officers for a term of years whose commissions expire, unless official or moral misconduct is charged and substantiated against them. This does not suit the Falstaff friends "who follow for the reward," and I am importuned to serve my friends and reproached for neglecting them, because I will not dismiss, or drop from Executive offices, able and faithful political opponents to provide for my own partisans.[16]

In the winter of 1828 Adams was still holding strictly to his rule, despite the fact that a violent contest for the presidency was in motion in which many subordinate officials were believed openly to favor Jackson. "I have proceeded upon the principle established by Mr. Monroe, and have renominated every officer, friend or foe, against whom no specific charge of misconduct has been brought." [17] Adams held sternly to principle, but his resolution may have lost him a second term. His sense of right was tougher than could ordinarily be expected of officials living in the midst of the political struggle of persons, groups, parties, and sections. For the time being, however, Monroe and Adams held the patronage pressure at arms length, although their task was made much more difficult by Crawford's venture in statecraft.

BENTON'S REPORT

Perhaps as portentous as the Tenure of Office Act was Senator Thomas H. Benton's Report on the Reduction of Executive Patronage, delivered to the Senate in 1826.[18] This attack on executive power was primarily a part of the campaign of Jack-

15 *Ibid.*, VI, 521. Among the nominations were officers of the customs, land agents, and navy agents.

16 *Ibid.*, VII, 390 (Dec. 28, 1827).

17 *Ibid.*, VII, 425 (Feb. 7, 1828).

18 Benton's Report, Senate Doc. 88, 19th Cong., 1st sess. (May 4, 1826).

son's friends against Adams. We need not take too seriously the implied doctrine of legislative supremacy; the authors were not fighting a battle of a constitutional order, but one of factional advantage. On the other hand the declarations and assumptions of Benton's Report on the role of patronage in the winning of elections are of profound importance. They comprised the first systematic and public recognition of a new order of partisan warfare on the national scene which had the gravest consequences for the administrative system.

Beginning with a measured paragraph on the traditional American jealousy of power, Benton plunged into an analysis of the volume of patronage and its potential influence in elections. "The patronage of the Federal Government at the beginning," he wrote, "was founded upon a revenue of two millions of dollars. It is now operating upon twenty-two millions, and, within the life time of many now living, must operate upon fifty." The conclusion of payments on interest and principal of the debt, he figured, would turn this amount of revenue into new current expenditures and more patronage.

. . . Thus, the reduction of the public debt, and the increase of revenue, will multiply in a four fold degree the number of persons in the service of the Federal Government, the quantity of public money in their hands, and the number of objects to which it is applicable; but as each person employed will have a circle of greater or less diameter, of which he is the centre and soul . . . the actual increase of federal power and patronage . . . will be, not in the arithmetical ratio, but in geometrical progression, an increase almost beyond the power of the mind to calculate or to comprehend.[19]

To drive home his point, Benton listed the names and compensation of the customs officers at New York, then numbering 174.

A formidable list indeed! Formidable in numbers, and still more so from the vast amount of money in their hands. The action of such a body of men, supposing them to be animated by one spirit, must be tremendous in election; and that they will be so animated, is a proposition too plain to need demonstration. *Power* over a man's *support,* has always been held and admitted to be *power* over

[19] *Ibid.,* p. 3.

his *will.* The President has "power" over the "support" of all these officers; and they again have "power" over the "support" of debtor merchants to the amount of ten millions of dollars *per annum,* and over the daily support of an immense number of individuals, professional, mechanical, and day-laboring, to whom they *can* and *will* extend, or deny a valuable private as well as public patronage, according to the part which they shall act in *State,* as well as in *Federal* elections.[20]

Benton magnified the patronage power to the point where, as he alleged, it was upsetting the constitutional balance between the federal government and the states.

> . . . The power of patronage, unless checked by the vigorous interposition of Congress, must go on increasing, until Federal influence, in many parts of this Confederation, will predominate in elections. . . .
>
> . . . the power and influence of *Federal* patronage . . . is an overmatch for the power and influence of *State* patronage . . . its workings will . . . enable the Federal Government, eventually, to govern throughout the States, as effectually as if they were so many provinces of one vast empire.[21]

What did Benton propose to do to save the purity of American institutions? Did he, as sound Republican doctrine would have prescribed and as Jefferson, Randolph, Macon, and other great figures of the party would have directed, propose to reduce the patronage, curtail the activities of the federal government, and restore responsibility to the threatened states? Not at all; he accepted without argument a steady augmentation of federal expenditures and patronage. He simply proposed to transfer this patronage, with all the baneful influence that he had so eloquently described, to Congress. To this end he introduced six bills.[22] One would give the Senators and Representatives of each state the duty of selecting newspapers for the public printing. A second required the discharge of all delinquent collectors and disbursers of public revenue at the end of their four-year term, and in addition required the President to state the reasons for every removal at the time of submitting the nomina-

20 *Ibid.,* p. 7.
21 *Ibid.,* pp. 9, 10.
22 *Ibid.,* pp. 13–15.

tion of a successor. This provision looked toward reversal of the great decision of 1789 on the removal power. A third required Senate confirmation of postmasters. A fourth and fifth required the apportionment of cadets and midshipmen, one to each congressional district and two from the state at large; the last forbade the President to remove army or navy officers except after a court martial or upon an address to the President from the two Houses of Congress.

The tenor of Benton's Report bore more directly on elections than on presidential power. The influence of a well-organized phalanx of federal officials on elections, state as well as federal, was the underlying theme of this prophetic document. Federal patronage had not, in fact, been an important influence in federal elections to the presidency throughout either the Federalist or Republican eras. The congressional caucus had designated Madison and Monroe and neither carried on a public campaign. Crawford sought some advantage in such appointments as occurred by death or resignation, but Monroe certainly gave him no encouragement so far as presidential offices were concerned; and he, too, counted heavily on the caucus. John Quincy Adams was opposed to the use of the appointing power to influence elections. So far as the federal scene has been disclosed, therefore, we must conclude that the danger to the "purity" of democratic institutions that ostensibly disturbed Benton so much did not exist in fact and lay, if at all, in the irresponsible use of patronage that might reasonably be anticipated if it were turned over to Congress. Benton's Report nevertheless suggested a dark cloud on the horizon. So also did the development of political habits in some of the states, and the confusion caused by the collapse of the two-party system.

PATRONAGE PORTENTS

Many circumstances doubtless conspired to inject partisanship into the American administrative system. One of them was the gradual fading-away of the two-party system that was so marked a feature of political life in the first decade of the century and its replacement by personal factionalism.

The presidential election of 1800 was a close contest and although parties were not coherently organized the issue was clean-cut between national parties, each standing for well-defined and well-understood differences of foreign and domestic policy. The Federalists, although defeated, remained a well-disciplined party of opposition. Jefferson's overwhelming victory in 1804 might have destroyed the Federalists if he had not provided them with a solidifying issue in the embargo. They did better in 1808, and even better in 1812, but their weight as a party of opposition was undermined by their obstructive tactics in the War of 1812. In 1816 they carried only a negligible minority in the electoral college and by 1820 the party had disappeared.

From 1816 to 1828 only one effective party existed, the Republicans. There was no organized opposition, and no stable differences of opinion on public policy developed around which a new party could arise. Personal politics replaced party politics. Lacking great issues of public policy on which to appeal to the country, politicians sought success in personal combinations. The promise of office became a partial substitute for the support that had earlier come from convictions of principle.

Rotation and patronage in the state governments. The political and administrative habits of federal, state, and local governments are bound to resemble each other in considerable measure. They develop from the same community attitudes about public life; they are formed by men who move from one level of government to another; what is found useful in one situation may prove to be valuable in another. A politician who has learned certain ways of success in his career in a state is not likely to abandon them if he is raised to the federal scene.

This is not to say that political and administrative habits were the same in all the American states that comprised the Union under the Jeffersonians. New York and Virginia were obviously governed under the influence of widely divergent traditions; South Carolina and Pennsylvania were far apart in the patterns that made for success in public life. The tradition of the general government under the Jeffersonians was inevitably an amalgam or balance of these differences. The fact of difference in itself made it easier for Jefferson and Madison, Monroe and Adams to cling to the Virginia-Massachusetts ideal of government by gentlemen, free from the annoyance and interference of partisanship.[23]

Virginia had been steadily under the political control of the large plantation owners, who had developed a deep-rooted sense of responsibility for active participation in public affairs. They went to the meetings of the county court; they sat in the General Assembly; they became governors of the state—Jefferson, Monroe, Page, Macon, and other distinguished figures in the early history of the state and the nation. State and county offices were relatively few in a commonwealth heavily agricultural in its economy, and such offices had interest to the governing class only as places of honor, not of profit. Virginia nurtured a remarkable tradition of political *noblesse oblige.*

The same tradition, although threatened in Massachusetts, nevertheless prevailed through the Jeffersonian years. The first Republican governor, James Sullivan, refused to make political removals. The second, Elbridge Gerry, stood by the nonpartisan tradition in his first term (1810), but was driven to a course of political removals and appointments in his second. He was defeated at the next election. The incoming Federalist governor by one order discharged all Gerry's appointments to vacancies caused by removals and reinstated the old officers.[24] No more was heard of the misuse of patronage for many years. "Of the northern states, Massachusetts was perhaps the most exemplary in the conduct of the civil service. . . ."[25]

More significant of future events was the record in New York and Pennsylvania. The early history of appointments in New York closely followed that of the national government. George Clinton, governor from 1777 to 1795 and Republican Vice President under Jefferson and Madison, pursued a policy in many respects similar to that of Washington.[26] Each initiated

[23] Cf. Carl Russell Fish, *The Civil Service and the Patronage.*

[24] *Ibid.,* pp. 97–98. Fish quotes the text of a Republican sermon directed toward the reluctant governor: "But if ye will not drive out the inhabitants of the land from before you, then it shall come to pass that those that ye let remain of them shall be pricks in your eyes and thorns in your sides, and shall vex you in the land wherein ye dwell."

[25] *Ibid.,* p. 95.

[26] Howard Lee McBain, *DeWitt Clinton and the Origin of the Spoils System in New York,* p. 41.

a new government; each governed while political parties were in their formative years; each appointed principally on the basis of merit and without regard to political or factional allegiance. Clinton's Federalist successor, John Jay, made no removals for partisan reasons, but adopted the general policy of appointing only Federalists. He finished five successive annual terms in a complete deadlock with the council of appointment, comprising four senators and himself, a body which was controlled by Republicans.[27]

The dominating personality in New York politics after 1801 was DeWitt Clinton, nephew of Governor George Clinton. As a member of the council of appointment, he announced the rule of equal participation.[28] Party control of patronage thus became established in New York. Any "sense of shame soon disappeared, and all parties acted openly on the belief that they were held together by the cohesive power of public office. . . ." [29] The reforms of 1820 abolishing the council did not extend to a reform of the state spoils system.

The Pennsylvania constitution of 1790 was the outcome of a contest between the radical and conservative elements within the state, in which the latter undid some of the work of the former by improving the governor's status and increasing his authority to appoint subordinate officials. Thomas Mifflin, governor from 1790 to 1799, became a Federalist and confined most of his appointments to that party.[30] When the Republicans took the state in 1799 the new governor, Thomas McKean, started in, as he said, "to cleanse the Augean stable." He wrote to Jefferson in 1801:

. . . the anti-Republicans, even those in office, are as hostile as ever, though not so insolent. To overcome them they must be shaven, for in their offices (like Samson's hair-locks) their great strength lieth; their disposition for mischief may remain, but their power of doing it will be gone. It is out of the common order of

---

27 *Ibid.*, pp. 71–96.
28 *Ibid.*, pp. 103–4, 114–15.
29 Fish, *Civil Service and the Patronage*, p. 90.
30 *Ibid.*, p. 93.

nature, to prefer enemies to friends; the despisers of the people should not be their rulers.[31]

In making appointments, McKean was alleged to have been guilty of nepotism and favoritism as well as of party regularity, and after a party split in 1805 he removed members of the Duane branch of the Republican party whom he had himself appointed. ". . . henceforth the spoils system was accepted in Pennsylvania." [32]

Neither the south nor the west, for different reasons, went so rapidly in the direction of partisan patronage. The south tended toward the Virginia tradition; in the west politics were apt to be based on personal sympathy and local issues. The use of patronage to maintain the party organization was less conspicuous in these sections than to gain personal or local advantage.

The gradual extension of party patronage was facilitated by the constantly wider acceptance of democratic doctrine after 1801. One aspect of democracy was the idea of fixed terms and rotation in office. The custom of rotation was indigenous to Pennsylvania, where William Penn's "frame of government" prescribed in 1682 that no councilor should hold his office for more than three years continuously. The rule was introduced into the Pennsylvania constitution of 1776, and was followed by Maryland and New Hampshire. By 1830 fifteen states required rotation of the office of governor and nineteen states followed the rule with various lesser offices.[33]

The original intent was to limit the number of years a man might hold *elective* office. The idea gradually spread to *appointive* positions, at first those from which some danger to public liberties might be apprehended, such as sheriffs and justices of the peace. This extension was facilitated by the related idea of specific terms for appointive office, making it easier to replace by avoiding the necessity of removal. Formal requirement of rotation by law, by limiting the number of

31 Quoted in *ibid.,* p. 93.
32 *Ibid.,* p. 94.
33 *Ibid.,* pp. 80, 81–82.

years a person could hold office, was less widely extended than the statutory fixed term. Both conspired to the same end; the increase of opportunity for larger numbers to become educated by experience in the mysteries of government. These arrangements were inspired on the whole by devotion to democratic dogma, not to partisan advantage. They produced consequences of both orders.

By 1828, then, the practice of making appointments to state offices for partisan benefit, of making removals to secure places for partisan office seekers, and of causing vacancies to develop automatically by fixed terms had become standard in New York and Pennsylvania and was actively pushed as the correct treatment for party enemies in others. The popular movement was knocking on the door of the national government with increasing insistence. At the close of John Quincy Adams' administration it was an open question whether the public service ideals of Washington and his Republican successors would continue to prevail against the general criticism of elderly officeholders, the concept of rotation in office, the demands of Congressmen, the hostile intentions of Benton, and the well-organized machines in some important states. Monroe and Adams withstood great pressure, and the latter great temptation, in maintaining with no substantial breach the high ideals which Washington had bequeathed to his fellow citizens. The people seemed to be more and more restive as the memory of Washington receded and the task of organizing millions of voters for political action emerged.

CHAPTER TWENTY-SEVEN

Jonathan Chooses to Live Snug

The tradition of parsimony that the Republicans had succeeded in imposing upon the Federalists in the days of Washington and John Adams was naturally continued when Jefferson took over the reins of government. It was a tradition congenial to the time. In one of his lighter moments John Quincy Adams described perfectly the temper of his fellow citizens.

. . . Our Yankee countrymen will argue that a man is not a dollar's worth the better for the governor of a state because he can draw down thunder from Heaven. They would be apt shrewdly to suspect him not so good for it. They have no relish for a government of thunderbolts. Jonathan chooses to live snug and at small cost. He chooses to have no useless servants at great expense, and if now and then any of his men tells him it is impossible to live upon the wages he gives and asks for his discharge, Jonathan gives it, and the next day he finds an hundred solicitors storming his doors to get the place at the same wages that he gave before, aye, and the thunderbolt man as eager as any of the rest. When you talk to Jonathan about the necessity of maintaining his dignity, he laughs, casts a sly look across the waters at Brother John and says, there's dignity enough for both of us.[1]

EXECUTIVE AND LEGISLATIVE PAY POLICY

Department heads had the responsibility of getting work done, and they generally realized that good work would be done only by competent clerks, who in turn could be secured and retained only if adequately paid. The paymaster general of the War Department, referring to his clerks, put the matter in a

[1] Adams, *Writings*, V, 456–57 (Jan. 1, 1816).

nutshell when he declared, "The pay of the gentlemen should be equal to the labour required. . . ." [2] Albert Gallatin, although an economizer, did not intend to economize at this point. "Good clerks," he wrote Comptroller John Steele, "cannot be too well paid; so far as may depend on me you may rest assured that I will agree to everything relative thereto which you will think reasonable. . . ." [3] In 1806 Gallatin wrote the House Committee on Ways and Means, with reference to the collection of revenue, that "the capacity, attention, and integrity of the inspectors, particularly, forms one of its principal guards; and, it is undoubtedly important that the compensation may be sufficient to engage, as heretofore, the services of men of that description." [4]

These were the normal views of responsible officials, of whatever party complexion. The normal reply of Congress was found in its response to Gallatin's statement: "the Committee are of opinion that it would not be advisable, at this time, to incur additional expenditures in collecting the revenue, by increasing the compensation of the officers engaged therein." [5] The usual disposition was to deny requests for better pay in language such as that in the case of the Fredericksburg, Virginia, postmaster: "The compensation . . . does not seem adequate . . . but . . . the Department is struggling to support itself. . . ." [6] According to Niles, there were

. . . very few offices in the U. States, the salary or emoluments of which make it a *pecuniary* object for persons fitted to fill them to accept of them—if they have any thing else to do. There are tens of

2 House Report 105, 17th Cong., 1st sess., p. 9 (June 26, 1821).

3 John Steele, *Papers,* I, 243 (1801?).

4 *American State Papers: Finance,* II, 256 (Jan. 14, 1806).

5 *Ibid.,* II, 255. The following figures give a preliminary summary view of actual amounts; these and other cases are discussed below. The President's salary remained at $25,000 a year. Heads of departments went up from $5,000 ($4,500 in two cases) to $6,000. Principal Treasury officers were fixed at $3,000, except the first comptroller, $3,500. This was also the salary of the Attorney General. The ceiling on postmasters was $2,000. Clerical salaries stopped at $1,600; chief clerks ran somewhat higher. Surveyors general took $2,000 a year. Indian agents ran from $1,200 to $1,800. Figures for 1790–1820 are available in *American State Papers: Miscellaneous,* II, 640–42; for 1828 in the appropriation act for that year, 4 Stat. 247 (Feb. 12, 1828).

6 House Report 93, 18th Cong., 1st sess. (March 24, 1824).

thousands of farmers and mechanics . . . who live well, and yet save more money at the end of a year than either of the secretaries of the great departments of the government *can* save. . . .[7]

Congress was extremely sensitive to public reaction to official salaries, taught caution by popular wrath against the increase of congressional salaries in 1816. As a part of a general improvement in salary levels, Congress abandoned its previous per diem of eight dollars and voted Senators and Representatives an annual sum of $1,500 plus traveling expenses.[8] Jefferson described the sequence of events. "There has never been an instant before of so unanimous an opinion of the people, and that through every State in the Union. . . . almost the entire mass [of Congressmen] will go out, not only those who supported the law or voted for it, or skulked from the vote, but those who voted against it or opposed it actively, if they took the money; and the examples of refusals to take it were very few. The next Congress . . . will be almost wholly of new members." [9] After the fall elections, he wrote Gallatin, then abroad, about "almost an entire change in the body of Congress. . . . I have never known so unanimous a sentiment of disapprobation." And then in good Republican orthodoxy he added, "I confess I was highly pleased with this proof of the innate good sense, the vigilance, and the determination of the people to act for themselves." [10] The salary act was promptly repealed in 1817, but in such form as to preserve its benefits to members for the second session of the fourteenth Congress.[11] A new bill went on the books in 1818, fixing compensation for both Houses at the rate of eight dollars a day plus traveling expenses.[12]

This experience only confirmed a strong traditional disposition on the part of Congressmen to keep official pay under control. The salaries of the officers of state were fixed by law and annual appropriation and could be changed only by agreement of the two Houses. In 1801 they stood at $5,000 for the Secre-

[7] *Niles Register*, XXX, 427 (August 19, 1826).
[8] 3 Stat. 257 (March 19, 1816).
[9] Jefferson, *Works* (Federal ed.), XII, 35–37 (Sept. 8, 1816).
[10] *Ibid.*, XII, 70–71 (June 16, 1817).
[11] 3 Stat. 345 (Feb. 6, 1817).
[12] 3 Stat. 404 (Jan. 22, 1818).

taries of State and Treasury and $4,500 for War and Navy; by 1828 they were established uniformly at $6,000, including the Postmaster General. The salaries of "public ministers" abroad were set in 1800 at not over $9,000 a year to a minister pleni-potentiary; $4,500 to a chargé des affaires.[13] The "value" of these levels of compensation is suggested by the comment of Joseph Story as he abandoned a private practice amounting to over $5,000 annually for a seat on the Supreme Court at $3,500. Describing his reasons for accepting the appointment, he wrote, "The high honor attached to it, the permanence of tenure, the respectability, if I may say so, of the salary, and the opportunity it will allow me to pursue, what of all things I admire, juridical studies, have combined to urge me to this result." [14]

The methods of fixing the pay of clerks reveal how closely Congress kept its hands on expenditures. The Federalists, after a few years experience with precise statutory enumeration of pay allowed to each clerk, gave a slight discretion to department heads to apportion salaries within a fixed annual total.[15] In their first enactment on the subject, in 1806, the Republicans continued this policy.[16]

After the War of 1812 Congress went back to the first Fed-eralist practice, specifying by law how many clerks every depart-ment and office could employ and setting the exact salary for each one.[17] By way of example, the Secretary of State was au-thorized to employ one chief clerk at not over $2,000 a year; two clerks at not over $1,600 a year; four clerks at not over $1,400 a year; one, at not over $1,000; and two at not over $800. The law concluded with the injunction that "no higher or other allowance" should be made. This remained the basic type of legislation on the subject throughout the period. There was no salary range along which a clerk might expect to ad-vance at regular intervals, and no classification of duties to dif-ferentiate the work at various pay levels.

[13] 2 Stat. 78 (May 10, 1800). In 1819 J. Q. Adams called diplomatic salaries "excessively inadequate." Adams, *Memoirs*, IV, 477.

[14] Story, *Life and Letters*, I, 201 (Nov. 30, 1811).

[15] White, *The Federalists*, p. 297.

[16] 2 Stat. 396 (April 21, 1806).

[17] 3 Stat. 445 (April 20, 1818).

Congressmen had always been intuitively committed to the principle of equal pay for equal work, a rule sought to be secured in practice by the specific pay allowed to clerks and agents of particular descriptions. The principle was enunciated in a House committee letter to the heads of departments in 1818 on the pay of clerks, "having regard to an equalization, as near as practicable, of the compensation among clerks of equal responsibility, in the several departments of government." [18]

An early description of the duties of clerks, something quite different from a classification, was given as a consequence of this House committee letter. The State Department reported that it was impossible to define with precision the work of any of its clerks, but it gave as good an account as feasible. Richard Forrest copied letters, made out personal passports and ciphers, filled up certificates for the Secretary's signature, had charge of the abstracts of registered seamen, and made out and recorded exequaturs for foreign consuls. For these varied duties he received $1,250 a year. For the same amount Colvin prepared the acts of Congress for publication, collated the laws after newspaper publication, distributed the statutes and public documents, made out and recorded pardons and remission of fines, and arranged the papers relating to claims of individuals on foreign governments. [19]

Most of the field service staff was paid from fees for services performed to individuals, the amount of which was carefully prescribed by law. The schedule of fees of the collectors, naval officers, and surveyors, one of the largest and most important branches of the field organization, had been revised in 1799. [20] In the larger ports the fees brought in handsome earnings. The Republicans quickly imposed a limitation on these undemocratic privileges by fixing a ceiling of $5,000 for collectors, $3,500 for naval officers, and $3,000 for surveyors. [21] The economy drive of 1820–22 brought distress to the principal customs officers. The ceilings fixed in 1802 were substantially reduced.

18 House Doc. 194, 15th Cong., 1st sess., p. 3 (April 13, 1818).
19 *Ibid.*, p. 5. A full roster of clerks and duties is included in this document—a modest beginning of an elaborate process!
20 1 Stat. 704 (March 2, 1799).
21 2 Stat. 172 (April 30, 1802).

For the seven largest ports, collectors were limited to $4,000, naval officers to $3,000, and surveyors to $2,500; in all others, $3,000 for the collector, $2,500 for the naval officer, and $2,000 for the surveyor.[22]

Another important group of fee officers were the registers and receivers of the land offices. They received a base pay of $500 a year but their income arose chiefly from fees paid by purchasers. Congress looked into their compensation in 1818. Crawford's report showed two offices, Cincinnati and Vincennes, in which the total compensation exceeded $5,000, and Meigs, the land commissioner, suggested the advisability of fixing a maximum of $3,000.[23] The postmasters comprised a third large group of officers paid by fees. For them Congress set a ceiling of $2,000 net, a figure which in 1820 was reached only by four officers.

The fee system was regulated directly by Congress. What considerations governed its decisions? Economy and the avoidance of extravagance counted for much. Balancing this was the necessity of paying enough to get the service performed; but if persons could be found at rates that were admittedly low, no improvement was likely to be forthcoming. In recommending fees for customs officers, Crawford cited as criteria for judgment the expense of living and the salubrity or unhealthiness of the climate in which the duties were to be performed.[24] Although there were exceptions, the tendency of Congress by the late 1820's was to deal with compensation matters on the basis of a general rule, not individual treatment of hardship cases. "If any remedy is applied, it must be by a general act, founded upon information from the Treasury."[25]

THE RULE OF PUBLICITY

For various reasons the Republicans introduced a strict regime of publicity with respect to salaries of officials and employees. Early evidence of this policy was the declaration made by Jefferson in his first annual message:

[22] 3 Stat. 693, secs. 9–10 (May 7, 1822).
[23] House Doc. 142, 15th Cong., 1st sess. (March 9, 1818).
[24] House Doc. 26, 16th Cong., 2d sess., p. 3 (Dec. 8, 1820).
[25] House Report 35, 20th Cong., 1st sess. (Dec. 27, 1827).

. . . we may well doubt whether our organization is not too complicated, too expensive; whether offices and officers have not been multiplied unnecessarily and sometimes injuriously to the service they were meant to promote. I will cause to be laid before you an essay toward a statement of those who, under public employment of various kinds, draw money from the Treasury or from our citizens. . . . Considering the general tendency to multiply offices and dependencies and to increase expense to the ultimate term of burthen which the citizen can bear, it behooves us to avail ourselves of every occasion which presents itself for taking off the surcharge. . . .[26]

A substantially complete roster of federal officials and agents was delivered to Congress on February 17, 1802, constituting an invaluable source of information on the public service as the Republicans took over.[27]

The next step in the publicity program occurred in 1806 when the Republicans settled the amount of money available to the departments and offices for clerk hire. Department heads were required to report the names of the clerks employed year by year, the sum given to each, and "whether the business for clerks increases or diminishes . . . that Congress may be enabled to make further arrangements by law, respecting clerk hire."[28] In 1816 the *Official Register*, a biennial compilation of all civil and military personnel, was initiated in the State Department.

These regular annual reports were supplemented by special reports required from time to time by Congress. Thus in 1820 Congress asked for a report of the names and compensations of persons employed in building and supplying lighthouses for a five-year period, and a list of persons employed as agents for marine hospitals.[29] In 1821 the House called for a special report of payments made to subordinate customs officials for the years 1816–1820.[30] Shortly afterward it required reports on names and emoluments of naval constructors, storekeepers, timber in-

---

[26] Richardson, *Messages*, I, 328–29 (Dec. 8, 1801).

[27] *American State Papers: Miscellaneous*, I, 260–319.

[28] 2 Stat. 396, sec. 5 (April 21, 1806); reenacted in 1818, 3 Stat. 445, sec. 9 (April 20, 1818).

[29] House Doc. 77, 16th Cong., 2d sess. (Jan. 29, 1821).

[30] House Doc. 112, 16th Cong., 2d sess. (March 1, 1821).

spectors, and clerks of yards; [31] on superintendents, agents, sub-agents, interpreters, and blacksmiths in the Indian department; [32] and on receivers and registers of the land offices.[33] These and other special reports were occasioned by the retrenchment drive of 1820–1822.

The main object of these calls for names and compensation was clearly to reduce expenses. Publicity served, however, to enable Congress to check on compliance with the law governing "clerk hire." It also gave critics of the Administration ammunition for hostile demonstrations, justified or otherwise. No evidence has come to hand that the lists were used, even after the Tenure of Office Act, as convenient handbooks of potential patronage.

THE EXTRA COMPENSATION PROBLEM

A bothersome problem that came in for considerable attention in the decade 1820–1830 was that of extra compensation for official work not in exact line of duty. It arose in the civilian departments, in the army, and in the navy.

The case of Attorney General William Wirt has already been noticed.[34] The record of extra compensation for the district attorneys ran back to 1794 and was substantially continuous.[35] The 1794 precedent arose in Virginia, when the district attorney went to Norfolk to take depositions respecting the alleged capture of a British vessel by a French privateer. William Rawle of Pennsylvania was paid for "sundry opinions and other services" to the Treasury and for attorney fees "in various suits at law with individuals" initiated by the government. He attended President Washington on the expedition against the whiskey rebels and was paid $608.83 for this service.

The Attorney General and the district attorneys were not the only beneficiaries of extra compensation. When the Jackson Democrats came into power they looked into such payments for the years 1828 and 1829 made to officers employed in the civil

---

31 House Doc. 70, 17th Cong., 1st sess., Table, p. 8 (Feb. 18, 1822).
32 House Doc. 110, 17th Cong., 1st sess. (April 12, 1822).
33 House Doc. 95, 17th Cong., 2d sess. (March 3, 1823).
34 See above, ch. 23.
35 *American State Papers: Miscellaneous*, II, 932–33.

departments.[36] Over this two-year period thirty-four such cases were disclosed. Edward Jones, chief clerk in the office of the Secretary of the Treasury, served as secretary to the commissioners of the sinking fund, for which he received $250; he also earned $150 for transmitting passports and sea letters. John Woodside, clerk in the office of the first comptroller, served as superintendent of the State and Treasury buildings at $500 a year. James Rush, treasurer of the Mint, took a commission of $243.34 for distributing cents to banks and customhouses. John Lamb, chief clerk in the office of the first comptroller, was paid $433.33 for a digest of decisions on the revenue laws. In almost every case the specific additional service could be identified, whatever its claims to recognition.

On the other hand there was no expectation of pay for such overtime as might be necessary. In the State Department one or more clerks were always in attendance until five or six o'clock, although three o'clock was closing time.[37] In the register's office it was the rule to keep the records up to date; "when additional business requires more time than is usually devoted, the clerks are engaged in finishing their business at all hours. . . ." [38] One overworked clerk put in a claim for overtime pay, but this was instantly rejected by the Committee on Claims. "The Committee clearly entertain the opinion, that the Clerks are not entitled to extra pay for extra services performed when business presses on their respective Departments." [39]

The custom of extra compensation was relied upon for relief by two high officials removed by Jackson: Stephen Pleasonton, formerly fifth auditor, and Joseph Nourse, the register of the Treasury. Pleasonton asked for extra compensation as Treasury agent for prosecuting suits against delinquent accounting officers from 1820 to 1829, a duty that had been added to his regular position of fifth auditor.[40] The Senate Judiciary Committee accepted his claim,[41] but the House Committee on Claims

36 House Doc. 126, 21st Cong., 2d sess. (March 2, 1831).
37 *American State Papers: Miscellaneous*, II, 979.
38 *Ibid.*, II, 983.
39 House Report 11, 19th Cong., 2d sess., p. 2 (Dec. 20, 1826).
40 See above, ch. 12.
41 Senate Doc. 157, 23d Cong., 1st sess. (March 10, 1834).

resisted, and stated an important theory of the duties of public officers.

The claim to relief . . . is founded on the idea that all the duties assigned to the Fifth Auditor, not enumerated in the act establishing the office, gives the incumbent a claim on the United States to compensation for discharging these new assigned duties. . . .

The committee believe the grounds of this application to be a misconception of the duties of the several officers of the Treasury, by supposing them to be a sort of job work under a contract, the items of which work were designated in the law creating and organizing the Treasury Department. This must be erroneous, or every law that increases or diminishes these duties, or changes them relatively among the several branches, would change the contract, and furnish cause for new rules of compensation. In fact, the officers of the Treasury are salary officers, and are bound, in consideration of their yearly salaries, to discharge such duties as may, by law, and the necessary regulations of the department, be assigned them.[42]

The committee pointed out also that Pleasonton had given no notice that he expected any additional compensation, but accepted the office and discharged its duties for nine years without making any claim. So far as precedents were concerned the committee remarked, "they are bad precedents, and should not be followed."[43] Pleasonton was finally defeated in 1836 when the House Committee on Judiciary made an equally adverse report.[44]

Joseph Nourse had a different course imposed upon him, and was more successful. After his removal as register of the Treasury in 1829, the comptroller found him liable for certain expenditures on different accounts amounting to $11,769.13. Nourse disputed the settlement, refused to pay, was subjected to summary action, and took the matter to the district court of the District of Columbia. Here he presented a claim for extra services as a set-off against his balance as register, which the comptroller had declined to accept. The district court sustained Nourse's claim, and appointed auditors who found that from

---

[42] House Report 511, 22d Cong., 1st sess., pp. 1, 2 (July 5, 1832).

[43] The Senate committee on the case appended a long list of extra compensation cases to its report.

[44] House Report 541, 24th Cong., 1st sess. (April 15, 1836); cf. *U. S.* v. *George McDaniel,* 7 Peters 1 (1833), and *U. S.* v. *Fillebrown,* 7 Peters 28 (1833).

1789 to 1829 he had disbursed in other capacities than that of register over $940,000 on which he was entitled to a commission of two and one-half per cent or $23,582.72. The government appealed to the circuit court, which affirmed the judgment of the district court, and thence to the Supreme Court. Here it was held that no appeal lay from the decision of the district court to any higher court.[45] Nourse was thus triumphantly vindicated in his encounter with the accounting officers. Ironically enough it was Pleasonton who had the duty of initiating the proceedings against his old colleague. The House Committee on Claims, presented with these judicial proceedings, reported a bill to reimburse Nourse. Despite repeated committee reports favorable to Nourse, a hostile Democratic Congress refused to grant relief to him or to his widow. His heirs finally secured payment in 1848.[46]

The House of Representatives found much to criticize in extra compensation made to army officers detailed to clerical and accounting duties in Washington. The quartermaster general was opposed to the employment of men "who were *professionally clerks*," and insisted upon men who knew army practice and custom. He also intended the assignment to be in the nature of a training school in which "young gentlemen of the army . . . should have an opportunity . . . of educating themselves for the various duties of the staff." [47] The policy was well designed, but it skirted the issue of extra compensation.

The House Committee on Military Affairs was in no way impressed. ". . . however long this practice may have continued they have no hesitation in saying it appears to them highly improper. . . . when they perform no duties as officers, but merely act as clerks, it seems unreasonable to pay them as officers, and at the same time compensation as clerks." [48] "If the

---

[45] 6 Peters 470 (1832).

[46] House Report 372, 23d Cong., 1st sess. (March 28, 1834); Adams, *Memoirs*, XII, 214–15 (Sept. 19, 1845); 9 Stat. 720 (June 28, 1848).

[47] House Report 61, 16th Cong., 2d sess., p. 11 (Feb. 3, 1821).

[48] *Ibid.*, p. 3 (Feb. 13, 1821). The committee was particularly incensed by the case of Major Roberdeau, who took charge of certain mathematical instruments, kept them in his office for less than a year, and "for this service received from government $418.75 on the supposition that he had rendered important extra duties." Roberdeau was also drawing extra compensation as a clerk.

word salary has an appropriate meaning," the committee continued, "it certainly must be a stated or settled hire to the person who performs the duties of the office to which the salary is attached; no authority in this government, except the legislature, is deemed competent to increase or diminish it. . . . no precedent contrary to law ought or can have a binding influence." [49]

Secretary of the Navy Southard was put on the carpet in 1826 on shore allowances for naval officers. He defended navy practice vigorously.

There is active and very important employment for officers on shore, at Stations and Navy Yards—where, by their orders, they are compelled to remain, and are subjected to great expense. . . . The principle, therefore, and rule of the Government, since the original establishment of the Navy, in such cases, has been, to make an allowance sufficient to pay such of these expenses as were indispensably and absolutely necessary, to enable them to do their duty. . . . an officer . . . must have *lodgings, candles,* and *firewood* . . . and if he have not servants to aid him in his labor, both public and private, he cannot constantly attend to his duty. . . . If he were obliged to procure them for himself, it would consume the whole of his pay; and no man but he who had a private fortune, and chose to bestow both it and his time upon the public, could remain in the Navy.[50]

The issue was a perplexing one, and no clear-cut answer was found by the Republicans. Congressmen were disturbed when they discovered these apparent violations of the law and appropriation acts. Executives were upset when long-established customs, essential in their view to efficient operation, were endangered by persons unfamiliar with administrative necessities. There was, no doubt, danger of abuse but it was difficult to discover a suitable remedy.

The Republicans did not think deeply about the general considerations on which the pay of officials and employees should rest. The public documents and the private letters are almost devoid of discussion of rules or principles, although there is considerable material on particular cases. James Barbour, Sec-

[49] *Ibid.*, p. 4.
[50] House Doc. 87, 19th Cong., 1st sess., p. 6 (Feb. 4, 1826).

retary of War under Adams, contributed a thoughtful analysis growing out of the inadequacy of clerical pay scales.[51]

As to the just compensation for public employment, it is one of the most difficult problems in political science, and about which much difference of opinion prevails. Even the standard of compensation is yet to be settled. Shall it be confined to a support of the officer? Or shall it embrace that of his family, and beyond their support, enable the incumbent to make for them a reasonable provision? Shall he be enabled to practice the courtesies of hospitality, or be a mere isolated beast of burden? Were we to judge this question by the anxiety to obtain appointments, indicated by the number of candidates for office, and the zeal with which they pursue their object, we should be justified in inferring that the salaries were full high, if not exorbitant. On the contrary, if we advert to the impoverished condition of those, generally, who devote their time to the public service, we should be led to conclude that poverty is almost an inevitable effect of such devotion; and, as a consequence, the salaries, instead of being extravagant were penurious. Although there are occasional exceptions to this general result, effected by rigid economy, and great skill in the investment of money, yet the larger proportion of public servants die in poverty, and leave their families in the most bereaved condition.[52]

At higher levels Adams' judgment appeared sound. He wrote:

. . . To say the truth I do not know that Jonathan ever lost any important service, though he has lost many good servants, by the smallness of his wages. Money is not the only inducement or reward to important service. Men of spirit and of honor serve their country for fame, for glory, for patriotism; and believe me, my dear sir, whatever Jonathan may pay for his servants he is and will be well served. . . .[53]

51 Cf. a New York City memorial of 1816 on the inadequacy of customs officers compensation, *Annals,* 14th Cong., 1st sess., pp. 1712–14 (March 8, 1816).
52 House Report 259, 20th Cong., 1st sess., pp. 67–68 (March 3, 1828).
53 Adams, *Writings,* V, 457 (Jan. 1, 1816).

CHAPTER TWENTY-EIGHT

Public Service Ethics

The standard of official behavior approved by the Republicans was as laudable as that established by the Federalists. It was put in unmistakable terms by Secretary of the Treasury William H. Crawford: "It is extremely desirable that the conduct of officers of the government, especially those who have charge of the public money, should not only be correct, but that there should be no possible cause of suspecting them to be incorrect." [1] Given the frailties of human nature, this standard of behavior was maintained with few exceptions. The most extraordinary of these exceptions was without doubt Tobias Watkins, fourth auditor and close friend of President John Quincy Adams.

Circumstances within government favored sound canons of official ethics. Great care in making appointments was exercised not only by Presidents and Secretaries, but by lesser figures when called upon for advice. William Thornton, head of the Patent Office, asked Adams to consider the appointment of a workman to care for models of inventions. ". . . I would take the liberty," he wrote, "of recommending Mr. Keller, who is a very worthy, honest, and industrious man, a very ingenious and excellent workman, with a large family of helpless children." [2] Persons of dubious character were automatically excluded from consideration. The tone of government office, already well set by Washington, John Adams, and their immediate associates, was equally acceptable to the Virginia gentlemen who succeeded them. Personal integrity was taken as a matter of course.

[1] House Doc. 130, 17th Cong., 1st sess., p. 7 (March 24, 1819).
[2] *American State Papers: Miscellaneous*, II, 979 (August 21, 1822).

The stability of officeholding made its own contribution. Men working together year after year molded each others' values, habits, and dispositions. Newcomers, appearing in an office at infrequent intervals, and one by one, were readily assimilated to the unwritten but effective code of ethics that a few short years had fixed. Competition for vacancies in clerkships, always keen, reminded incumbents of the goods they possessed in their own holding and confirmed them in their intention to pursue a course of action above reproach.

External circumstances also favored high official standards. The pressures on officials were light. The general government had relatively few contacts with citizens. It dispensed few favors and interfered with no established ways of life. Conversely, citizens had little to ask of government. They were usually content to be let alone. Generally speaking, the commercial class had its own adequate standards of business ethics, which in turn protected officials from temptation from this quarter. The scale of affairs, public and private, was small; transactions of all sorts were widely known and talked about; anonymity was not yet attained.

It is an arresting fact that complaints of official favoritism, neglect, oppression, or malfeasance, while not unknown, were rare. The temper of American officialdom on the whole was accommodating, tended toward a leniency that in some cases became negligence, and was undisturbed by a sense of bureaucratic power. Officials were drawn from respectable circles of society, remained neighbors and participants in community life, and as officials maintained the reputation for integrity that had brought them to their stations.

The comments of Representative William Irving on the character of the customs officers of the port of New York bore testimony to these foundations on which official rectitude was based.

The officers of the customs in the city of New York are a very reputable class of men, many of them old Revolutionary officers; many of them persons who once were in comfortable, and even elevated circumstances, and who, owing to adverse fortune, have had to take refuge, in advanced life, in the scanty shelter from want that the *per diem* of a custom-house officer affords; and all of them, as far as my knowledge extends, possess the character of being up-right and exemplary. They are remarked for their official integrity; so much so, that I have never heard a lisp of such a thing as cor-ruption having been found among them.[3]

John Quincy Adams once described his views on the duty of the Chief Executive to maintain the ethical standards of the public service. "It is, in theory," he wrote, "one of the duties of a President of the United States to superintend in some de-gree the moral character of the public officers who hold their places at his pleasure. But the difficulty of carrying it into prac-tice is great. . . ."[4] "The censorial power of the President of the United States over the moral and official conduct of the officers appointed and subject to removal by him, is one of those the exercise of which is of the most extreme delicacy."[5] The record would suggest that while Presidents and Secretaries of departments were diligent in inquiring into the character of persons at the time of appointment and while they never knowingly appointed one whose ethical standards were doubt-ful, they were much less diligent in correcting their mistakes. Executive superintendence of the morals of subordinates was in fact a theory.

LOYALTY TO THE ADMINISTRATION

During the Republican period the problem of official loyalty came up under varying circumstances. One important case arose in connection with the obligation of collectors and attorneys to enforce the embargo in communities where public opinion was violent in opposition. Duty was clear, but interest and in-clination among New England officials might lead in another direction. There was without doubt some sabotage among cus-toms officers, and some deliberate refusal to cooperate by one or two United States attorneys, notably Blake of Massachusetts.[6] There were a few but not many reluctant officials who sought to resolve the conflict between official duty and personal prefer-ence by offering to resign. The embargo was the principal in-

---

[3] *Annals*, 14th Cong., 1st sess., p. 1712 (March 8, 1816).
[4] Adams, *Memoirs*, V, 151 (June 14, 1820).
[5] *Ibid.*, V, 158 (June 23, 1820).
[6] See ch. 30.

stance where this hard choice was put to executive officers.

Political loyalty, as the evidence already presented demonstrates, was not required or expected. At the same time, while Monroe and Adams were standing on ground of high principle, a body of opinion was taking shape that looked in the opposite direction. Many of Adams' friends urged him to get rid of his factional opponents in the minor as well as the higher offices. Henry Clay was one of these, and the doctrine of party loyalty was persuasively elaborated by Edward Everett in his correspondence with John McLean.[7] The dominant official view stood fast where Jefferson had planted it. No one in public office was to be disturbed for difference of political opinion.[8]

The duty of subordinates to refrain from anonymous political attacks upon their superiors, while generally accepted, was poorly understood by a few restless or ambitious clerks. Philip M. Freneau had furnished an example in his attacks on Hamilton while employed in Jefferson's office. Newspaper "leaks" were suspected from time to time to be traceable to clerks in the departmental offices, but none of them were made object lessons.[9] For most government agents, however, the problem of loyalty either to policy or person did not arise. Their obligation was one to perform well and honestly their daily task, and this duty was steadily carried forward.

THE CLERKS: INSIDE AGENCIES AND OUTSIDE EMPLOYMENT

The conduct of clerks in government offices came to public notice in 1818 in a congressional investigation which provided one of the principal sources of information on the standards of official behavior during the first thirty years of the century.[10] It had the useful effect of clearing the air as well as bringing to an end some minor abuses. Niles wrote that he had no personal

[7] See above, ch. 21.

[8] Abraham Bradley, assistant postmaster general, was placed in an awkward position when President John Quincy Adams called him to the White House to question him on the political activities of the Postmaster General. Bradley was apparently not reluctant to inform on his immediate superior. McLean on his part told Adams that Bradley was responsible for the acts that disturbed the President. Adams, *Memoirs*, VII, 537; VIII, 25.

[9] *Ibid.*, VI, 47 (July 28, 1822).

[10] *American State Papers: Miscellaneous*, II, 495–509 (March 30, 1818).

knowledge of any corruption, "but charges of it have been familiar to me for nearly twenty years past, and almost every body seems to believe that it exists extensively there." [11] Corruption was not discovered, but it was found that at some points clerical ethics needed reconstruction, although no offenses were found to be serious.

A number of Treasury clerks, contrary to specific prohibitions in the law, were discovered to have been acting as agents for claimants, a service for which they took fees. The committee declared that the "subordinate officers should have no interest in any account or claim which they might be called upon to inspect or examine." [12]

Aaron T. Crane was a clerk in the General Post Office. It was proved that he had been "very extensively concerned as agent for claimants against the United States, and in purchasing soldiers' lands" (a form of speculation); that he attended to these matters during hours at various departmental offices for a considerable portion of his time; and that he took fees amounting to about $1,500 a year. The committee was severe with Crane. "The temptation to indifference or neglect, when *private duties* pressed him, would be too strong to be resisted; and we apprehend that the public have little reason to expect fidelity from an officer whose *unofficial labors* are the principal object of his attention." [13] Crane defended himself on the ground that his salary of $1,000 a year was inadequate.

Messrs. Edwards and Stuart were clerks in the War Department who acted as agents for Canadian volunteers in securing land claims for a compensation. ". . . the tendency of the practice," declared the committee, "renders it necessary that it should be prevented. . . . Claims passing through *interested hands* would be likely to succeed, without the proper scrutiny." [14]

Benjamin Homans was chief clerk of the Navy Department. He became trustee of a fund of $12,000 (the *Epervier* fund)

[11] *Niles Register*, XIII, 345 (Jan. 24, 1818).
[12] *American State Papers: Miscellaneous*, II, 497.
[13] *Ibid.*, II, 495.
[14] *Ibid.*, II, 495-96.

appropriated by Congress to the widows and heirs of persons lost in this ship. Homans gave bond for its faithful application, and no beneficiary had been delayed in receiving his payments. It appeared, however, that Homans "had in one or two instances accommodated a friend with money from this fund." The committee expressed the opinion that Homans was a faithful officer and a responsible man, but also were "strongly inclined" to the belief that "public money should never be touched by the trustee, but for the purposes of executing the trust." [15]

Ezekiel MacDaniel, a clerk in the Navy Department, acted for an unfaithful navy purser, George Beale, Jr., who held about $290,000 prize money as agent of the principals. MacDaniel himself was guilty of no irregularity, but the committee took occasion to make an important statement. ". . . it will be perceived," they said, "that when clerks in the Departments are permitted to connect themselves with men like Beale, the public confidence will be impaired. . . ." [16]

While these cases of departure from law and proper official behavior were criticized and condemned, the committee on the whole cleared the public service of infidelity to its trust. They absolved the heads of departments of any fault but reminded them that "much must depend on a prompt execution of the laws by the principal officers of the Department. . . . public opinion holds them responsible for the performance of their duties, and that those duties should not be perverted by practices dangerous to the fidelity of the clerks and the interests of the public." [17] As to the public interest the committee thought it had not suffered materially from the practices they condemned. As to the clerks, the committee expressed satisfaction that "among so many public agents so few instances of conduct of dangerous tendency have yet been discovered. The gentlemen whose cases are here reported were notified and heard. . . . It is but justice to state that their conduct was frank, candid, and honorable, and that they did not appear to be conscious that the acts proved were incompatible with their duty." The

[15] *Ibid.*, II, 496.
[16] *Ibid.*, II, 496.
[17] *Ibid.*, II, 497.

committee nevertheless concluded that the practices discovered by their inquiry were "improper and inadmissible." [18]

Corrective action was taken at once by the four departments in a general public notice, the essential portion of which follows.

The employment of an Agent or Attorney is *not necessary* in any claim against the government. It is most generally attended with *expense* and sometimes with *actual loss*.

Claims will be promptly settled, when the accounts, and vouchers with which they are connected, are transmitted to the proper office.[19]

Hezekiah Niles thought this an excellent regulation: "it will do much good," and balanced the clerical ledger by writing these words of commendation. "Among the clerks employed at Washington, are many real gentlemen, of high and honorable minds, fine talents, and *truly* republican principles. . . ." [20]

Four years later Congress asked for a report showing whether any officers were "engaged in other pursuits or professions in nowise relating to the public service." [21] The replies showed that the lesson of 1818 had been taken to heart. A number of outside pursuits or professions were reported, but they were for the most part obviously innocent, and in every case were defended by the heads of the departments. Two clerks in the State Department owned farms in the vicinity of Washington, "to which they occasionally resort in person to pass the Sunday." Another was a clergyman. In the office of the Secretary of the Treasury were two clerks serving also as justices of the peace, and one as a notary. The third auditor reported one clerk who was a member of the city council, one a notary, one a bank director, and one who was a partner in a stage line, conducted by an agent. The General Land Office had two clergymen, one of

[18] The statements and defense of the clerks are printed in *ibid.*, II, 497–509. They make interesting reading.
[19] Reprinted in *Niles Register*, XIV, 256 (June 6, 1818). The notice, signed by Adams, Crawford, Calhoun, and Crowninshield, was dated May 27, 1818. Later in the year the *National Intelligencer* invited citizens who needed aid to seek help from their Congressmen. *Niles Register*, XV, 176 (Nov. 7, 1818).
[20] *Ibid.*, XIV, 413 (August 15, 1818).
[21] *American State Papers: Miscellaneous*, II, 978–85 (Dec. 3, 1822).

whom had been engaged with the understanding that he would be allowed Saturday to prepare his sermons—truly an invidious distinction! It also had an agent who was surveyor for the District of Columbia, and one who superintended a farm. Ministers of the Gospel were found in numerous offices. One War Department clerk conducted a bookstore, through an agent, in Georgetown; one in the Post Office boarded members of Congress. No case of outside employment was reported that caused criticism from the legislative branch.

MISUSE OF PUBLIC FUNDS

The disorganization of public offices during the War of 1812 and the large amount of public funds and naval prize money then available put special temptation in the way of fiscal agents. Some of them yielded, and in general there was much irregularity in accounting for money collected and disbursed. It is reasonably certain that government funds in the hands of its agents were used for private gain, although perhaps eventually accounted for in full.[22] Prize money, the property of ships crews, was a particularly vulnerable object, and some prize agents made a sorry record of faithlessness to their trust.[23] It required remedial legislation and years of hard work to correct this situation, but by the end of Monroe's second administration the task was substantially accomplished. Promptness and completeness in reporting financial transactions became general, so excellent, indeed, as to call for congressional approval of the system.

Some spectacular cases of embezzlement by public agents marred a generally good record. One such involved the clerk of the district court in the southern district of New York, Theron Rudd, and gave rise to such suspicion of the district judge, Van Ness, that the House Judiciary Committee investigated his affairs with a view to impeachment. Rudd absconded with $64,906.15 of public money, and with $52,400.86 belonging to litigants before the court. The Judiciary Committee found that the funds of the district court had been "most grossly and

22 See above, ch. 20.
23 House Doc. 153, 18th Cong., 1st sess., p. 7 (April 23, 1824), presents data of cases unsettled since 1815 or earlier.

nefariously purloined." Rudd's transactions were facilitated by orders of the court concerning the deposit of money, but sufficient grounds for impeachment were lacking.[24]

The case of John Brahan, receiver of public money at Huntsville, Alabama, suggested negligence as much as dishonesty. He was late in sending in his accounts. Crawford admonished him in November 1818, and again in March 1819. On June 28, 1819, Brahan wrote the Secretary of the Treasury, "I have the mortification to inform you that there is a considerable deficiency in my cash account." He was short about $80,000. "This circumstance," he continued, "has given me more concern than any occurrence of my life, and the deficiency shall be made up as quick as possible, at any sacrifice. . . . I have been in public service upwards of twenty years, and this is the first time in my life that my accounts have ever exhibited any loss of public money."[25] When the files of the comptroller's office were searched for Brahan's bond, none could be found. The form had been sent to him, but never returned; no one seemed to have been the wiser. The case was closed with a deed of trust conveying all of Brahan's property to the government and with the transfer of notes amounting to $46,000. Brahan had apparently been speculating in cotton.[26]

The defalcation of Dr. Tobias Watkins was the most spectacular of official derelictions. After a long and respectable record as a physician, army surgeon, and assistant surgeon general of the United States, he was appointed fourth auditor on January 3, 1825, with the best possible endorsements. He was a personal and intimate friend of John Quincy Adams. In 1829 he was replaced by Jackson's friend, Amos Kendall. To the consternation of the late Administration, Kendall discovered that Watkins had embezzled over $7,000 and upon imminent discovery had fled the scene. He was captured and after a long trial, convicted and imprisoned.[27] The case was used effectively by the Democratic press to demonstrate the necessity of an of-

24 *American State Papers: Claims*, pp. 587–88 (March 5, 1818).

25 House Doc. 130, 17th Cong., 1st sess., p. 8 (June 28, 1819).

26 *Ibid.*, p. 11.

27 *American State Papers: Naval Affairs*, III, 735; John Quincy Adams, *Memoirs*, VIII, 141, 144, 290; *Niles Register*, XXXVI (1829), *passim*.

ficial house cleaning. It was a hard blow to John Quincy Adams, who was more shocked by the news of Watkins' flight than he could have been "at the loss of ten elections." [28] On another occasion he wrote,

. . . That an officer under my Administration, and appointed partly at my recommendation, should have embezzled any part of the public moneys is a deeper affliction to me than almost anything else that has happened; that he was personally and warmly my friend aggravates the calamity. . . .[29]

These cases, it may be repeated, were as exceptional as they were conspicuous. Others could be cited, but the record still remains one distinguished on the whole by integrity and responsibility. The war years and those immediately following witnessed some departure from good standards that was due perhaps as much to overexacting and cumbersome procedures of settlement as to misconduct. Public service ethics in the handling of money were sound.

Not yet over the horizon were some important ethical problems that were to vex later official generations. The conflict between devotion to the public interest and to special interest had no meaning before powerful special interests had been formed. The problem of harmonizing a party responsibility and an official responsibility was on the edge of the immediate future, but it did not perplex the Republicans. The acceptance of public employment for a short period of professional training to be used in private practice was unknown. The issues that came under attention were principally simple ones of personal honor and integrity, and the prevailing standards of gentlemen were usually sufficient to the day.

In short, we may conclude that the standards of official behavior under Republican Presidents were a credit to themselves and to the service of which they were members. Subordinate personnel, middle and lower ranks alike, were selected on grounds of character and standing rather than on grounds of technical skill or managerial efficiency. Tenure was permanent during good behavior, and interest thus combined with expecta-

---

28 Adams, *Memoirs*, VIII, 141 (April 21, 1829).
29 *Ibid.*, VIII, 290 (Jan. 22, 1831).

tion to produce a moral elite. There were departures from these commendable standards, to be sure; and it was not difficult to detect a laxness among officials handling money that had to be counteracted after the War of 1812. Individuals occasionally proved unable to resist temptation, but these lapses can always be expected. It was taken for granted, and on the whole with full justification, that government men were honest and trustworthy.

CHAPTER TWENTY-NINE

The Embargo: An Experiment
in Peaceable Coercion

Three days before Christmas 1807, Congress adopted Thomas Jefferson's recommendation to impose an embargo upon all American vessels sailing for foreign ports. After only four days' debate, behind closed doors, the Republican majority thus committed the executive branch to a greater test of its moral authority and administrative capacity than it had yet endured. A President, bound by theory and personal preference to the restriction and dispersion of power, was driven by events to an extraordinary expansion and concentration of power. Receptive in his youth to a revolution every twenty years, he had to yield before one growing under his own hand. Opposed to the use of force against citizens reluctant to pay the excise tax on whiskey in 1794, he marshaled force of every available sort in 1808 against citizens reluctant to forego what they considered their right to sail the high seas.

Jefferson conceived the embargo as an alternative, indeed the only available alternative, to war.[1] It was an attempt at peaceable coercion of the greatest naval power and the greatest land power of his generation. It could be defended not merely by what might have been thought the intrinsic merit of peaceable coercion, but also by the utter impossibility in the late autumn of 1807 of deciding whether to declare war against the

[1] John Quincy Adams took the same view. Adams, *Writings*, IV, 160 (July 31, 1811). Cf. a contemporary analysis in the *American Register*, III (1808), 67–77.

greatest naval power, or the greatest land power, or both; for each was equally guilty of assault on American rights and interests.

Although the President thought of the embargo as an attempt to coerce these two great European powers by commercial pressure, in fact the embargo drove his Administration into an attempt to coerce a large, powerful, active, and hostile part of his fellow citizens. To this intermediate end, essential for the attainment of his greater purposes, Jefferson asked for power and more power; and upon the use of the authority which his Republican friends yielded, he became more and more insistent, asking commerce, agriculture, and industry to be as nothing before the great object he set himself.

In the end he was defeated in his major purpose of securing concessions from England or France; and in the application of force to his fellow citizens he drove resistance almost to the point of rebellion in New England and upper New York. The effort was a tragic one, the tragedy enhanced by the greatness of the goal that might have been attained. Jefferson was broken spiritually by his failure. He became, as he said himself, a mere spectator of events after December 1808, and finally was obliged to sign the bill abandoning the great experiment three days before he left public life forever.[2]

THE EMBARGO ACTS

Jefferson's brief message of December 18, 1807, merely suggested that Congress would "doubtless perceive all the advantages which may be expected from an inhibition of the departure of our vessels from the ports of the United States." [3] His intention was "to keep our seamen and property from capture, and to starve the offending nations." [4] He hoped to gain time, to call commerce home to safety, "to put the towns

2 For the political and economic aspects of the embargo, see two able monographs: Louis Martin Sears, *Jefferson and the Embargo* (Durham, No. Car.; Duke University Press, 1927); Walter Wilson Jennings, *The American Embargo, 1807–1809* (Iowa City: University of Iowa, 1921). See also the account in Henry Adams, *History of the United States*, Vol. IV, *passim*.

3 Richardson, *Messages*, I, 433.

4 Jefferson, *Writings* (Memorial ed.), XII, 27 (April 8, 1808).

and harbors . . . into a condition of defence," and to prepare for the restoration of the freedom of the seas.[5]

The wisdom and efficiency of the means to the end were not so apparent to Jefferson's advisers as they were to the President himself, whose naturally sanguine temperament discounted any serious problem of enforcement. Gallatin, who had to carry the main burden, told Jefferson plainly that he had no confidence in the enterprise. He notified the President:

. . . In every point of view, privations, sufferings, revenue, effect on the enemy, politics at home, &c., I prefer war to a permanent embargo.

Governmental prohibitions do always more mischief than had been calculated; and it is not without much hesitation that a statesman should hazard to regulate the concerns of individuals as if he could do it better than themselves.

. . . As to the hope that it may . . . induce England to treat us better, I think it entirely groundless.[6]

Robert Smith, Secretary of the Navy, opposed the embargo, calling it "this mischief-making busybody." [7] No evidence of Madison's private views on the embargo has come to hand nor is there any indication that he took part in working out enforcement policy or in applying enforcement measures. His correspondent, Morgan Lewis, warned him that the influence of the embargo on domestic affairs "will be unpleasant," and that a section of the Republicans were using the embargo as a means of putting George Clinton in the White House—disquieting news to an heir apparent.[8] Monroe, not then in the government but watching events closely from near-by Virginia, referred to "many impolitick measures," the context suggesting the embargo and its successor policies.[9] He declared that "the embargo supported a very dangerous conflict at home, hazarding the republican cause, union, &c. . . ." [10] Vice President George Clinton was reported in January 1809 as "most outrageous

[5] Jefferson, *Works* (Federal ed.), XI, 85 (Jan. 14, 1809).

[6] Gallatin, *Writings,* I, 368 (Dec. 18, 1807); cf. *ibid.,* I, 428.

[7] Adams, *Life of Gallatin,* p. 373.

[8] Madison Papers, Library of Congress, XXXIII, 85 (Jan. 9, 1808).

[9] Monroe, *Writings,* V, 115 (Feb. 25, 1810).

[10] Massachusetts Historical Society, *Proceedings,* XLII (1908–9), 329 (Oct. 25, 1810).

against the Embargo. Says 'tis damning the principle of Republicanism." [11] Governor Sullivan of Massachusetts, a staunch Republican, warned Jefferson of the danger to internal peace in case of conflict with England.[12] But as between war and the experiment of peaceable coercion, Jefferson did not waver. ". . . it was better," he said, "to take the chance of one year by the embargo, within which the orders & decrees producing it may be repealed, or peace take place in Europe, which may secure peace to us." [13]

The first embargo act. The policy of bringing pressure upon the European belligerents had been initiated by an act of 1806 prohibiting the importation of certain goods from Great Britain.[14] This legislation however was not put into effect until December 1807, on the eve of the first embargo act (December 22, 1807). A series of enactments followed: a second embargo act (January 9, 1808); a third (March 12, 1808); an enforcement act (April 25, 1808); a second enforcement act (January 9, 1809); and finally the repeal of the embargo (March 1, 1809). The content and bearing of these statutes appear in the pages that follow.[15]

The embargo act of December 22, 1807, was directed only against American vessels in the foreign trade known as *registered*, or *sea-letter, vessels*. It was assumed that they might be employed temporarily in the coastwise trade; but to discourage any of them from touching at a foreign port while at sea, the master, owner, consignee, or factor was required to give bond in a sum double the value of the vessel and cargo to land the goods in some port of the United States, "dangers of the sea excepted." Foreign vessels lying in port were allowed to depart,

[11] C. Savage to Samuel Savage, Jan. 23, 1809, *ibid.*, XLIX (1915–16), 90.

[12] Sears, *op. cit.*, p. 58.

[13] Jefferson, *Works* (Federal ed.), XI, 32 (May 20, 1808).

[14] 2 Stat. 379 (April 18, 1806). See an informing article on the practice of coercion by nonimportation (as opposed to embargo on exports) by Herbert Heaton, "Non-Importation, 1806–1812" in *Journal of Economic History*, I (1941), 178–98.

[15] The successive embargo acts were supplemented by Treasury circulars of instruction to the collectors, which in themselves provide a characteristic example of the interplay between statute and executive implementation. They are recorded in a manuscript volume in the National Archives entitled Circulars, Office, Secretary of the Treasury, September 14, 1789, to February 21, 1828, "T"; hereafter cited as Embargo Circulars.

with such cargo as they might have had on board. The collectors were forbidden to clear any American vessel to a foreign port or place except under the immediate direction of the President.[16] Thus simple was the prologue to a complex sequence of events.

The immediate administrative problem was to handle applications for permission to depart to a foreign port. By mid-January they were coming in, and Jefferson expected them to "overwhelm us." [17] In March he suggested advising merchants that on a certain day they could dispatch a vessel to designated ports, "and that no other will ever be permitted afterwards." [18] He finally resolved this problem by a determination not to use the authority for any private transactions whatever, but only for public purposes.[19] This simple solution, however, merely forced Congress to prescribe another means to enable merchants to get home their property lying abroad in the various ports of the world.

The second embargo act. The embargo act of January 9, 1808, was more explicit than its predecessor and was more directly concerned with the problem of enforcement. *Coasting vessels* were put under bond not to proceed to any foreign port; *fishing and whaling ships* were put under bond to steer clear of foreign ports and places and to land their fishing fare in the United States. Departures without clearance or touching at a foreign port were heavily penalized; the vessel and goods were wholly forfeited, but if they could not be seized, the owner or agent forfeited for every offense double the value of ship and cargo and was forever debarred from customs credit on goods imported. The master and every person knowingly concerned

16 2 Stat. 451. Gallatin promptly cancelled all leaves of absence on the revenue cutters and warned their commanders that "the utmost vigilance" was expected on their part. MS. National Archives, Treasury Department, Letters on Revenue Cutter Service, Oct. 1, 1790–April 2, 1833, pp. 58–59. Gallatin sent his first circular to the collectors on the day the act was signed, enclosing a copy and requiring their "particular and immediate attention." His second circular, December 31, 1807, contained the foreboding sentence, "Force may be used to detain vessels," a directive issued before the statutory power to detain had made its way on the books. Embargo Circulars, p. 217.

17 Gallatin, *Writings*, I, 369 (Jan. 14, 1808).

18 *Ibid.*, I, 376 (March 11, 1808).

19 *Ibid.*, I, 447 (Dec. 28, 1808).

were subject to a fine from $1,000 to $20,000 and the master's oath was forever thereafter inadmissible before any collector of customs.[20] The effect of these personal penalties would be to drive a convicted merchant from his import business, and a shipmaster from his profession.

The third embargo act. The third embargo act (March 12, 1808) was principally designed to correct certain hardship cases. Most of the transportation of goods at this time took place by water. Firewood and provisions came into New York City from Connecticut via the Sound, and from upstate New York on the Hudson; small vessels plied in swarms from port to neighboring port carrying potatoes, fish, baskets, woodwork, and scores of articles and supplies used in the daily round of domestic life. By this act these vessels were now exempted from the severe bonding requirements to which they, like registered vessels, had been subject under the second act. This exemption lasted only six weeks.

A more dangerous relaxation introduced by this enactment was the provision authorizing the President to grant permission to clear vessels in ballast to a foreign port to bring home goods of American citizens. Permission was subject to bond not to export any goods, to return to the United States, and to import no goods other than property held before the first embargo act. This authority was pushed upon the Administration by Congress. It gave Jefferson much trouble, compelling him to face the problem which he thought he had avoided under the first embargo act, by refusing to use his authority to grant permission to depart.

Although this, the third embargo act, was designed principally to ameliorate certain hardships, it also contained some added penalties. Foreign vessels engaged in the coastwise trade were bonded to four times the value of vessel and cargo to avoid foreign ports and reland cargoes in American ports. All bonds of vessels owned by citizens to ensure unloading in home ports had to be matched within four months by a collector's certificate of discharge of cargo sent in to the Treasury. Finally it was made

[20] 2 Stat. 453. Foreign vessels taking on any specie or goods were made liable to seizure.

unlawful, for the first time, to export by any means, land or sea, any goods, wares, or merchandise, subject to a fine of $10,-000 for each offense and forfeiture of the goods. Jefferson thus moved directly toward his major objective: to starve the enemy powers.[21]

The immediate enforcement problem again lay in the policy and procedure involved in presidential permission to authorize merchants to send vessels abroad to return their overseas property. The day after he signed the bill, Jefferson asked Gallatin for a consultation: "I received many petitions yesterday, all proposing to send their own vessels. I imagine they will come in bales every day. I understand there is scarcely a merchant in the United States who has not property somewhere beyond sea."[22] Gallatin's reply was full of good administrative sense. He declared for a general rule and meticulously analyzed the language of the statute to show Jefferson what the rule must contain.

For prudential reasons, hardly justified by the law, Gallatin sought to restrict the permission to the West Indies, and with few exceptions this became the rule.[23] He was embarrassed, however, by an imprudent permit given directly by Jefferson to a Chinese merchant, Punga Wingchong, to send a ship to the Far East.[24] Promptly other applications of the same kind came in from Americans, and with the demand that they be seen by the President. Experience demonstrated to Gallatin that it was impossible to prevent abuse of permits to send abroad;[25] personal solicitation became very embarrassing to the President;[26]

[21] 2 Stat. 473.
[22] Gallatin, *Writings*, I, 377 (March 13, 1808).
[23] *Ibid.*, I, 404.
[24] *Ibid.*, I, 404. The embarrassment became greater when the facts appeared. The story is told by Robert G. Albion. ". . . At the time when the embargo was prohibiting all American ships from making foreign voyages, New York was amazed to see the *Beaver* clear and sail for Canton. Astor had received permission from President Jefferson in the interest of 'international comity,' to carry home a distinguished 'mandarin' stranded in this country. Amazement gave way to indignation when it developed that the 'mandarin' was a very ordinary Chinaman dressed up for the purpose and envy was well mixed with admiration when the *Beaver* returned with a profit of $200,000 from a voyage in which all American competition had been legally debarred." Robert G. Albion with Jennie B. Pope, collaborator, *The Rise of New York Port, 1815-1860*, p. 197.
[25] Gallatin, *Writings*, I, 435.
[26] Jefferson, *Writings* (Memorial ed.), XII, 210 (Dec. 7, 1808).

and at Jefferson's own suggestion the authority was terminated in 1809.[27]

Jefferson apparently made a personal decision on each application to send a vessel abroad to bring back property. Late in May 1808 Gallatin wrote the President, then relaxing at Monticello after the late session of Congress: "I have on file about twenty applications for permission to send vessels in ballast, which I have concluded to keep till your return." [28] The whole purpose of the embargo was in a fair way to be frustrated.[29] From December 22, 1807, to September 30, 1808, no less than 594 vessels were authorized to sail for foreign ports, mostly in the West Indies. Of these 137 had not returned on the latter date, although presumably many of them were en route to their home ports. The value of property authorized to be brought back was approximately $7,000,000.[30]

In the face of much evidence of a determination to evade the embargo laws, Jefferson concluded by the end of March 1808 that more power must be granted the executive to keep evasion under control. He was specially concerned about the long Canadian border, and about two very sensitive ports—Passamaquoddy, Maine, just across the Canadian line, and St. Marys, Georgia, adjacent to the Spanish colony of Florida. He was also disturbed about the movement of provisions and lumber. The latitude of Jefferson's willingness to receive and employ power was revealed in his proposal to Gallatin that collectors be authorized to take into custody any collection of provisions or lumber anywhere in the United States that the collector might suspect was intended for export.[31] Gallatin could not stomach this scheme and told Jefferson both that it "could not pass," and that it would be "very oppressive" and "very embarrassing" in its administration.[32] In modified form, however, Congress soon gave the collectors the power that Jefferson proposed.

27 2 Stat. 506 (Jan. 9, 1809).
28 Gallatin, *Writings*, I, 393 (May 28, 1808).
29 Sears, *Jefferson and the Embargo*, pp. 66–67.
30 *Message of the President of the United States transmitting list of vessels permitted to depart from the United States since 22d December, 1807*. Printed by order of the Senate (Washington City: Roger Chew Weightman, 1808).
31 Gallatin, *Writings*, I, 379–80 (March 30, 1808).
32 *Ibid.*, I, 381 (April 1, 1808).

THE FIRST ENFORCEMENT ACT

The first enforcement act, April 25, 1808, was drastic. The March relaxations with reference to vessels confined to bays, sounds, rivers, and lakes were terminated; every one of them, large or small, was required to produce a manifest, secure a clearance, and furnish a certificate of landing. No vessel could receive a clearance, unless laden under the immediate inspection of a revenue officer. No ship with cargo was allowed to depart for an American port *adjacent to* foreign territory without special permission of the President. Commanders of public armed vessels and gunboats were authorized to stop any ship on suspicion. Foreign ships were barred from the coastwise trade. Collectors were authorized to detain any coasting vessel whenever in their opinion there was reason to suspect its intention, "until the decision of the President of the United States be had thereupon." [33] Finally the collectors were authorized to take into custody any unusual deposits of provisions, lumber, or other articles of domestic growth or manufacture *in any port adjacent to foreign territory* (without even the necessity to find or declare suspicion to evade the embargo) and to hold them for bond to ensure their delivery to a port or place in the United States.[34]

Immediately after the passage of this law, Congress adjourned. Jefferson was thus left in personal command of the enforcement of the embargo from April 25 to November 7, 1808. He moved with energy, determination, and confidence. "Congress," he wrote the Attorney General, "has just passed an additional embargo law, on which if we act as boldly as I am disposed to do, we can make it effectual." [35]

Before relating the story of the long struggle between merchants and the government, it is useful to pause for a moment to make clear the administrative situation created by the four enactments whose provisions have been summarized. The man-

[33] This extraordinary power was construed in *Otis* v. *Watkins,* 9 Cranch 339 (1815), and in *Opinions of the Attorneys General* (1841 ed.), pp. 227-29 (Oct. 8, 1819).

[34] 2 Stat. 499.

[35] Jefferson, *Works* (Federal ed.), XI, 29 (April 24, 1808).

date of Congress to citizens was simple and straightforward: the movement of American ships in foreign commerce was to stop; exports of specie and goods by land or sea were to cease. To enforce this mandate a number of administrative weapons were made available.

1. Formal clearance of all coastwise vessels, large or small, with heavy bond on coastwise, fishing, and whaling vessels not to touch at foreign ports.
2. Prohibition of coastwise trade to American ports adjacent to foreign territory, except individual voyages specifically authorized by the President; exclusion of foreign vessels from the coastwise trade.
3. Lading of vessels only under the immediate inspection of a revenue officer.
4. Authority vested in commanders of revenue cutters and naval vessels to stop a vessel on suspicion, even on the high seas.
5. Authority vested in collectors to detain a vessel on suspicion; release could be granted only by specific direction of the President.
6. Authority vested in collectors to take into custody unusual deposits of goods adjacent to foreign territory.

To the mandate of Congress bidding all foreign voyages to cease there were two exceptions. These exceptions, placed in personal custody of Thomas Jefferson, were:

1. To proceed to a foreign port under the act of December 22, 1807. As already indicated, Jefferson allowed no private vessel this permission.
2. To send a vessel in ballast to a foreign port to bring back property of American citizens held before December 22, 1807.

Before Congress adjourned in late April 1808, it gave the President power to suspend the embargo in the event of such changes in the foreign situation as would in his judgment render safe the commerce of the United States. This act of high discretion was debated at length in Congress on constitutional and prudential grounds and was limited to a period not over twenty days after the next meeting of Congress.[36] Jefferson had no occasion to exercise this responsibility.

[36] 2 Stat. 490 (April 22, 1808).

ADMINISTRATIVE POLICY

We may now look at Jefferson's administrative policy in the employment of these several authorities. It was dominated by a problem of theory: to what extent could peaceable coercion upon foreign nations through economic pressure be depended upon to secure national ends? Jefferson wanted an answer not only to the particular case, but as a guide to all the distant future. ". . . I place immense value," he confided to Gallatin, "in the experiment being fully made, how far an embargo may be an effectual weapon in future as well as on this occasion." [37] Referring particularly to the highly discretionary act of detention, he declared, ". . . I am clear we ought to use it freely that we may, by a fair experiment, know the power of this great weapon, the embargo." [38] With this long perspective, matching the long view of the Blue Ridge Mountains that spread before him as he wrote these lines from Monticello, we may understand better why he matched power against mounting resistance for fifteen anxious months.

"The crisis," wrote Henry Adams, "was peculiarly his own; and he assumed the responsibility for every detail of its management." [39] On May 6, 1808, Jefferson put in writing for the guidance of Albert Gallatin his view of general strategy. "The great leading object of the Legislature was, and ours in execution of it ought to be, to give complete effect to the embargo laws. They have bidden agriculture, commerce, navigation, to bow before that object, to be nothing when in competition with that." [40] Three weeks later he again wrote Gallatin, who had encountered trouble with coasting vessels: "With respect to the coasting trade, my wish is only to carry into full effect the intentions of the embargo laws. I do not wish a single citizen in any of the States to be deprived of a meal of bread, but I set down the exercise of commerce, merely for profit, as nothing when it carries with it the danger of defeating the objects of the embargo." [41] In midsummer when things were going badly, he

---

[37] Jefferson, *Writings* (Memorial ed.), XII, 56 (May 15, 1808).

[38] *Ibid.*, XII, 52–53 (May 6, 1808).

[39] Henry Adams, *History of the United States*, IV, 251.

[40] Jefferson, *Writings* (Memorial ed.), XII, 52–53.

[41] *Ibid.*, XII, 66 (May 27, 1808).

declared his "extreme anxiety to give a full effect to the important experiment of the embargo, at any expense within the
bounds of reason. . . . My principle is that the conveniences
of our citizens shall yield reasonably, and their taste greatly to
the importance of giving the present experiment so fair a trial
that on future occasions our legislators may know with certainty
how far they may count on it as an engine for national purposes." [42]

CONTROL OF THE COASTWISE TRADE

The successful use of this "great national engine" was condi-
tioned on finding answers to two problems. One was how to
control the coastwise trade. It dominated the provisions of the
enforcement act of April 25, 1808. The second was how to close
the long Canadian frontier, especially where it touched Vermont, New York, and the Great Lakes. The problem of the
frontier dominated the provisions of the second enforcement
act of January 9, 1809.

The hard dilemma put by the coasting trade was well stated
by Henry Adams.

. . . If the embargo was to coerce England or France, it must
stop supplies to the West Indian colonies, and prevent the escape
of cotton or corn for the artisans of Europe. The embargo aimed at
driving England to desperation, but not at famishing America; yet
the President found himself at a loss to do the one without doing
the other. Nearly all commerce between the States was by coasting-
vessels. If the coasting-trade should be left undisturbed, every
schooner that sailed from an American port was sure to allege that
by stress of weather or by the accidents of navigation it had been
obliged to stop at some port of Nova Scotia or the West Indies, and
there to leave its cargo. Only the absolute prohibition of the coasting-trade could prevent these evasions; but to prohibit the coasting-
trade was to sever the Union. The political tie might remain, but
no other connection could survive. [43]

In the first instance coastwise trade was secured against the
temptation to break the embargo by heavy bond and stiff personal penalties. For the rest, principal reliance was placed on

[42] *Ibid.*, XII, 82–83 (July 12, 1808).
[43] Henry Adams, *History of the United States*, IV, 250.

the power to detain vessels on suspicion of intent to evade the law. This act of high discretion was placed in the hands of the collectors, but each case was required to be reported to the President for his instructions and decision. This procedure left untouched those cases in which the collector should decide that the evidence of suspicion was not enough to detain or that the risks were too great.

The decision of the collectors to detain a vessel on suspicion was obviously one that required standards. Gallatin supplied a preliminary set of guidelines in a circular of April 28, 1808, transmitting the causes that the President deemed sufficient for action. They were four: direct evidence either from the declarations of the parties or "the suggestions of others"; unusual shipments either as to species or quantity or price, particularly provisions, masts, timber and lumber, naval stores and all articles consumed in the West Indies; former evasions by owners, captains, freighters, or pursers of navigation laws; and business connections with agents of foreign nations. The circular ended with the warning that these enumerated cases were not exclusive: "but that on the contrary, it seems proper that you should detain, investigate, and refer in all doubtful cases." [44] Gallatin sought to encourage the collectors to act with vigor. In a circular of April 26, 1808, he wrote them that the frequent and gross violations of the embargo had made necessary the enforcement act of April 25 and added, "the authority now vested puts it altogether in your power to prevent their recurrence." [45] In the circular of April 28 he concluded, "the President confidently expects that it will be carried into effect with fidelity, vigilance, and strictness. . . ." [46]

Detention of vessels and cargoes. The process of detention became in itself an administrative experiment of the greatest interest. It will consequently be convenient at this point to observe the evolution of administrative policy on detentions, and on certain other powers closely related thereto. The policy is contained in Jefferson's letters to Gallatin and in the latter's circulars to the collectors. These documents show the charac-

[44] Embargo Circulars, pp. 241–42.
[45] *Ibid.*, p. 237.
[46] *Ibid.*, p. 240.

teristic process by which administrative policy gradually becomes defined, and in this instance reveal the great lengths to which Jefferson was finally ready to go in the exercise of administrative power.

Jefferson's initial declarations of detention policy appeared in a letter to Gallatin.[47] "In the outset of the business of detentions, I think it impossible to form precise rules. After a number of cases shall have arisen, they may probably be thrown into groups and subjected to rules." He continued, however, by suggesting a number of guides. (1) ". . . to propositions to carry flour or other provisions into the Chesapeake, the Delaware, the Hudson, and other *exporting* places, we should say boldly it is not wanted there for consumption, and the carrying it there is too suspicious to be permitted." (2) With respect to flour, unless a governor certified the need, it "must not be carried." [48] (3) "As to shuffling of cotton, tobacco, flaxseed, tar, &c., from one port to another . . . it is not of a farthing's benefit to the nation at large, and risks their great object in the embargo." (4) "Dry goods of Europe, coal, bricks, &c., are articles entirely without suspicion." He concluded with a sweeping generalization, "I really think it would be well to recommend to every collector to consider every shipment of provisions, lumber, flaxseed, tar, cotton, tobacco, &c., enumerating the articles, as sufficiently suspicious for detention and reference here." Considering the means on which Jefferson could draw for enforcement, this was indeed an extraordinary proposal.

In this same letter, Jefferson delegated to Gallatin full authority to instruct collectors on individual cases of detention—contrary to his practice in deciding personally upon requests to send vessels abroad to bring back American property. "You will be so good as to decide these cases yourself, without forwarding them to me. Wherever you are clear either way, so decide. Where you are doubtful, consider me as voting for detention, being satisfied that individuals ought to yield their private interests to this great public object." He recognized the necessity

47 Gallatin, *Writings*, I, 385–86 (May 6, 1808).
48 The role of the governors is developed below.

of consistency in decisions and when cases came to his attention, as many did, he cleared them through Gallatin.[49]

The problem of consistency, however, proved a perplexing one. Jefferson had to recognize that the suspicious character of a shipment, or movement of a vessel, could be determined better by an official on the spot than by an executive working on a paper record at a distance. He concluded, therefore, to rely on the judgment of the collector as a general rule. "Wherever, therefore, the collector is impressed with suspicion, from a view of all circumstances, which are often indescribable, I think it proper to confirm his detention. It would be only where, from his own showing, or other good information, prejudice or false views biassed his judgment, that I should be disposed to countermand his detention."[50]

The net result of these directions was to confirm the judgment of the individual collector, a practice which of course abandoned the rule of consistency in favor of the rule of energy. Collectors were aware of the need for consistency among themselves, for their own protection. In the smaller ports along the eastern coast they wrote frequently to the collector of the port of Boston for information concerning his rules and procedure, hoping thus to find a standard that was lacking elsewhere.

The achievement of consistency in the detention of vessels and cargoes in fact eluded the government during nearly the whole experience of the embargo. Even the opinion of the President on detentions was construed by the Treasury not to be mandatory upon the collectors, and local pressures apparently were stronger than distant opinions. Gallatin admitted in November 1808 that much diversity in practice existed, and asked for presidential authority to make general rules binding on the collectors.[51] Such authority was eventually granted by Congress in the second enforcement act of January 9, 1809, and a variety of rules were worked out to guide the collectors.

These rules were relatively harmless in comparison with the policy envisaged by Jefferson late in 1808, proposing to cut off whole communities. Such a policy apparently was never ac-

---

[49] For example, his letter of May 15, 1808, *Writings* (Memorial ed.), XII, 56.
[50] *Ibid.*, XII, 81–82 (July 12, 1808).
[51] Gallatin, *Writings*, I, 429 (Nov. 24, 1808).

tually instituted, but it crept into the President's letters. Writing Gallatin about a request from Buckstown on the Penobscot, he asserted:

. . . Where every attempt, the Collector says, has been made and still continues to be made to evade the embargo laws, the nature of the cargo is sufficient to refuse the permit, being wholly of provisions and lumber. This is the first time the character of the place has been brought under consideration as an objection. Yet a general disobedience to the laws in any place must have weight towards refusing to give them any facilities to evade. In such a case we may fairly require positive proof that the individual of a town tainted with a general spirit of disobedience, has never said or done anything himself to countenance that spirit. But the first cause of refusal being sufficient, an inquiry into character and conduct is unnecessary.[52]

The same disposition appeared in a letter of the same date to Governor Lincoln asking his advice on Nantucket. "Our opinion here is, that that place has been so deeply concerned in smuggling, that if it wants, it is because it has illegally sent away what it ought to have retained for its own consumption." [53] These opinions are understandable in the light of the trouble Jefferson had experienced, but they went far toward the doctrine of guilt by association which in principle the President would have been the first to reject.

Governors' certificates and the flour trade. One of the principal objects of commerce in defiance of the embargo was flour, a product that commanded prices either in Nova Scotia or the West Indies irresistible to unscrupulous American traders. But flour was also a commodity normally carried in large amounts in the coastwise trade, and it had to be moved in some degree even during an embargo. To assist the collectors in deciding when a shipment of flour was an object of suspicion, Jefferson hit upon the device of a governor's certificate of necessity. Shipments covered by such a certificate were presumably innocent; others suspicious. In May 1806 Jefferson sent the following letter to the governors of the Territory of New Orleans, Georgia, South Carolina, Massachusetts, and New Hampshire.

[52] Jefferson, *Writings* (Memorial ed.), XII, 194 (Nov. 13, 1808).
[53] Jefferson, *Works* (Federal ed.), XI, 73–74 (Nov. 13, 1808).

The evasions of the preceding embargo laws went so far towards defeating their objects, and chiefly by vessels clearing out coast-wise, that Congress, by their act of April 25th, authorized the absolute detention of all vessels bound coast-wise with cargoes exciting suspicions of an intention to evade those laws. There being few towns on our seacoast which cannot be supplied with flour from their interior country, shipments of flour became generally suspicious and proper subjects of detention. Charleston is one of the few places on our seaboard which need supplies of flour by sea for its own consumption. That it may not suffer by the cautions we are obliged to use, I request of your Excellency, whenever you deem it necessary that your present or any future stock should be enlarged, to take the trouble of giving your certificate in favor of any merchant in whom you have confidence, directed to the collector of any port, usually exporting flour, from which he may choose to bring it, for any quantity which you may deem necessary for consumption beyond your interior supplies, enclosing to the Secretary of the Treasury at the same time a duplicate of the certificate as a check on the falsification of your signature. In this way we may secure a supply of the real wants of our citizens, and at the same time prevent those wants from being made a cover for the crimes against their country which unprincipled adventurers are in the habit of committing.[54]

This arrangement coincided with Jefferson's attachment to the states as partners in the federal system, but it offered administrative risks of a substantial order. It assumed that each governor would be both well informed and well intentioned. One weak link in the chain might be disastrous, and the discretion once delegated would be difficult to withdraw. Gallatin, who apparently had not been consulted, saw these risks immediately and wrote to Jefferson:

. . . I have been induced to believe that the system of licenses by the governors was unnecessary; and permit me to add that it will, I think, be less efficient than our own regulations. For we transfer thereby a limited discretion, which was vested in collectors responsible to ourselves and subject to our continual control, to men not under our control, afraid of clamor and of popularity, and transfer it without any limitation. The best mode certainly would have been, if recourse must be had to the governors, merely to call on

---

[54] Jefferson, *Writings* (Memorial ed.), XII, 51–52 (May 6, 1808). A similar letter was sent soon afterward to all the governors, Gallatin, *Writings*, I, 389–90.

them for information. Knowing Governors Sullivan and Charles
Pinckney as we do, we can have no confidence in the last, and must
rest assured that the other will refuse no certificates. They begin
already to arrive, and for large quantities.[55]

Jefferson was disturbed and, although he expressed confidence
in the governors, admitted that if he had thought of the collectors first he would have preferred that mode of execution.[56]

Gallatin's fears were justified so far as Governor Sullivan of
Massachusetts was concerned, but proved groundless elsewhere.
In mid-July Gallatin reported to Jefferson that no certificates
had been transmitted except by Sullivan and Langdon of New
Hampshire.[57] Jefferson complimented Langdon on his modera-
tion and circumspection.[58] Sullivan was a problem.

Gallatin wrote Jefferson in late May, "Governor Sullivan
dares not refuse flour certificates. One mail alone brought me
permits for eleven thousand barrels, exclusively of corn and rye
meal; as we must let those go at all events and without restriction, there is really more danger from that quarter than from
any other." [59] By mid-July Sullivan's certificates that had turned
up at the Treasury covered almost 50,000 barrels of flour, nearly
100,000 bushels of corn, and considerable quantities of rice and
rye, "some are for persons resident in Alexandria or Georgetown, of whom he could know nothing." [60]

The governor of the old Bay State, according to Jefferson,
"has been entirely distempered." He was out of sympathy with
the embargo policy, and in addition had an easygoing temperament. His Federalist son, William, wrote long after the event
that the governor "gave permits to every one who asked for
them." [61] Benjamin Weld, the deputy collector at Boston, told
Gallatin, "It is well known here that the Governor from his
ignorance of the wants of the inhabitance [*sic*] in the diferent
districts has been imposed upon by impropper applicants. . . .

55 *Ibid.*, I, 391 (May 23, 1808).
56 Jefferson, *Writings* (Memorial ed.), XII, 66–67 (May 27, 1808).
57 Gallatin, *Writings*, I, 394 (July 15, 1808).
58 Jefferson, *Works* (Federal ed.), XI, 39 (August 2, 1808).
59 Gallatin, *Writings,* I, 393 (May 28, 1808).
60 *Ibid.*, I, 394 (July 15, 1808).
61 William Sullivan, *The Public Men of the Revolution* (Philadelphia: Carey
and Hart, 1847), p. 290.

this is an abuse which had the application been made to this office where the Law placed it would not have occured, but for the impositions we are not accountable." [62] Sears concluded, "What Sullivan perhaps meant in kindness, but certainly continued in weakness, had thus assumed the proportions of a national scandal, contributing greatly to the ineffectiveness of the embargo and the embarrassment of the President." [63]

Immediately after receiving Gallatin's summary of the volume of certified trade to Massachusetts, the President took steps to close this open drain on his system. He wrote Sullivan that he assumed the governor had called for a year's supply in two months and since the state was now well furnished he asked Sullivan to issue no more certificates. Furthermore he asked Sullivan to supply the estimates of consumption against which the certificates had been issued.[64]

This pointed request was not effective. In September Gallatin had to write Jefferson again on Sullivan's dereliction.

... I am again compelled to address you on the subject of Governor Sullivan's certificates, which he continues, as I am informed from several quarters, pertinaciously to issue. Whether he still sends duplicates to the Treasury I do not know, but, from the new form which he has adopted, rather think that he does not. ... of the effect I can speak with certainty. Those permissions do not only create dissatisfaction and operate unequally in favor of those who obtain them, but they materially interfere with the execution of the embargo laws. ... The provisions imported into Massachusetts in large quantities are intended for exportation, and are the foundation of the violations of the embargo there.

... I think it really necessary that some efficient measure should be adopted to put an end to his certificates, or to prevent their being respected by the collectors.[65]

Jefferson was not forced to invent the efficient measures that the Treasury called for since Sullivan conveniently died on December 10, 1808, and was succeeded by the lieutenant governor, Levi Lincoln. In November Sullivan's certificates were

[62] MS. National Archives, Treasury Department, Letters from the Collector, Boston, April 15, 1790, to Dec. 21, 1812, I, 222–23 (Nov. 15, 1808).

[63] Sears, *Jefferson and the Embargo*, p. 89.

[64] Jefferson, *Writings* (Memorial ed.), XII, 95–96 (July 16, 1808).

[65] Gallatin, *Writings*, I, 418 (Sept. 16, 1808).

reported to be openly bought and sold in Alexandria and else-where.[66]

The experiment of sharing responsibility with governors for deciding when a shipment was open to suspicion thus faltered at the very point that Gallatin had predicted. It came near to success, but one weak governor was enough to justify Gallatin's preference for reliance on the collectors. Sullivan could not be controlled, but collectors could be removed. Jefferson came nearer success in this particular experiment than circumstances would have foretold, but it must be concluded that Gallatin's administrative judgment on this point was superior to that of Jefferson.

Gallatin was forced, indeed, to seek another guide for the col-lectors than the governors' certificates to determine when a cargo was suspicious, finding it personally "utterly impossible to decide on the multiplied applications." He directed the collec-tors to authorize any shipment coastwise (except to ports ad-jacent to foreign territory) when the value of the provisions amounted to less than one-eighth the value of the bond.[67] The "one-eighth rule" permitted the free transportation of small amounts of provisions and flour, thus meeting the needs of the country; it gave the collectors a clean-cut basis of judgment, and, as Gallatin observed, it "places us on a much safer footing, and at the same time much less exceptionable, than the permission from the governors. . . ." [68] The order did not *limit* cargoes of provisions to one-eighth of the bond, but it did free such small shipments from suspicion. Larger shipments were by Jefferson's policy suspicious per se unless accompanied by a governor's certificate. Since, apart from Sullivan and Langdon, no such certificates were issued, the collectors had to reach conclusions as best they might on cargoes exceeding the one-eighth rule.

The enforcement of the embargo on the coastwise trade might readily have raised another criterion of judgment, i.e., the political reliability of owners, masters, and shippers. There

66 Jefferson, *Works* (Federal ed.), XI, 74 (Nov. 13, 1808).

67 He apparently acted without getting Jefferson's prior consent: "You will find it in the annexed circular. . . ." Gallatin to Jefferson, May 23, 1808. Gallatin, *Writings*, I, 392; cf. *ibid.*, I, 401. Embargo Circulars, p. 247 (May 20, 1808).

68 Gallatin, *Writings*, I, 392.

is some ground to suspect that occasionally permits were recommended to supporters of the Administration and denied to its opponents. The ardent Republican collector, Joseph Whipple of Portsmouth, gave Gallatin information concerning the political reliability of shippers and owners as a part of the evidence to govern detentions and permits. On a request to ship a cargo to New Orleans, Whipple wrote, "Of the present applicants I have no cause to suspect illicit intentions." [69] In a later and similar case, he became more explicit: "The petitioners are not opposers of the law and are warm friends to the government." [70] Shortly afterward he reported, in another case, "The owners in this concern are known to me to be correct observers of the laws & faithful friends to the government." [71] No data have come to hand to show whether Gallatin was influenced by these considerations.

RESISTANCE TO CONTROL

News of the embargo went rapidly to every port of entry and to every producer of goods "of domestic growth or manufacture." Christmas week, 1807, was a week of tense excitement, of gloom, and of feverish planning for the emergency. In many parts of the country, acceptance of the congressional edict and compliance with it were the order of the day: the middle states generally, Virginia, North and South Carolina. But even here there were adventurous spirits ready to take the chance of huge profits by evading the embargo with cargoes of provisions, lumber, naval stores, or cotton. In New York and New England ruin stared the merchants and shipowners in the face—ruin imposed by a foreign policy they believed not only wrong but disastrous. Interest thus combined with party opposition to try the temper of the new measure.

Boston. Evasion of the embargo began as soon as ships could be loaded, and in January letters came to Gallatin from harassed collectors along the exposed seacoast they were expected to

[69] MS. National Archives, Treasury Department, Letters from the Collector, Portsmouth, N. H. (Dec. 18, 1808). Pages in this volume are unnumbered and letters will be identified only by date.
[70] *Ibid.* (Dec. 21, 1808).
[71] *Ibid.* (Jan. 4, 1809).

guard. Boston was both a leading port and the center of the opposition party. Its experience, as revealed in the letters of the deputy collector, Benjamin Weld, is full of interest.

Weld was a conscientious and diligent officer. On January 4, 1808, less than two weeks after the embargo had been imposed, he wrote Gallatin that he had seized several vessels and that he suspected many others, "but our vigilance will I hope prevent the escape." [72] By March his optimism had departed. He wrote Gallatin:

The Embargo Law which doubtless it was intended should have a general and equal operation doth not so operate here[.] vessels are daily loading here for Eastport with Flour, Beef Pork &c where they can land their Cargoes. The British waters mingle with ours just at the said Port. The articles can conveniently [be] put acrost the line in the night after. . . . in fact we have reason to think the law is very much evaded and we have no means to prevent it.[73]

By midsummer his reports were even darker. "It is painfull to me to relate that notwithstanding the care of the Custom House to prevent all abuses against the embargo laws we have failed of the wishes for success. We have reason to suspect that the smaller vessels load in the night after obtaining a permit to pass the Fort and drop down into the Bay where vessels are ready prepared to receive the Cargoes and depart to such ports as best suits their designs. . . ." [74] In a long letter in August he told Gallatin that, although he had armed and manned two swift sailing boats to stop and board any vessel going out of port, he could not prevent evasion—especially

small crafts which are much in the habit of carrying out small quantities of Flour and provisions even to three or four Barrells for which they obtain a premium of three dollars per Barrell delivered on board vessells that are laying off in the Bay to obtain their supplies. in fact we are crowded with small vessells from Novascotia &c who all of them obtain cargoes more or less, and who can have no other motive here than to haul freight outward. . . . if the President is desirous that the embargo Laws should be executed eastward of Connecticut Some more efficient step must be

72 Letters from the Collector, Boston, I, 193.
73 Ibid., I, 195 (March 22, 1808).
74 Ibid., I, 203 (July 19, 1808).

taken or he will be completely disappointed. I have been diffused already, but I know not how to stop. instances crowd upon me of evasions of the Laws which perhaps would be vain to detail.[75]

Three days later Weld had to report "a most flagrant breach of our laws." He directed the marshal to take possession of the ship *Marion*, under the power to detain. The marshal was opposed by an armed force who swore they would fire if he attempted to board. ". . . they used likewise much abusive language against this Government and the authorities thereof." The ship was eventually taken into custody.[76]

Trouble continued to press in, and the very next day he had to ask Gallatin for further advice.

Perhaps you know the Geography of the harbor of Boston. There is an Island below the Light House open to the sea which is called the Brewsters the owner of that place puts the Laws at defyance. He is in the habit of carrying down Flour and Fish from this Port and declares that he has a right so to do being within our harbor. This Flour we have good information is shiped on board Foreign vessells from thence by lighters. . . . I find that the Collectors are only authorised on *suspicion* to stop or detain property in places contaguous to the teritories of a foreign power. . . . I wish much for your direction in this business. are we authorised to prevent this outrage if we are, direct us how to do it. there is now an armed Ship in our Bay loading from this place and we have no force to prevent it. I will support the Laws if I have force as well as constitutional powers. otherways I must give it up.[77]

Weld stuck it out, despite murmurings against his activity, but he had to continue reports of evasions despite increased revenue and naval forces. At the end of November he reported two vessels that loaded at Cohassett and "run off with their cargoes to some foreign Port." [78] On January 14, 1809, the schooner *Charles* cleared from Boston for Charleston in ballast, but turned up at Lisbon. The master alleged that stress of weather had forced him "to bear away" for that distant port.[79]

[75] *Ibid.*, I, 211–12 (August 22, 1808).
[76] *Ibid.*, I, 214 (August 25, 1808).
[77] *Ibid.*, I, 215 (August 26, 1808).
[78] *Ibid.*, I, 228 (Nov. 30, 1808).
[79] MS. National Archives, Treasury Department, Office of the Secretary, Jan. 1, 1809, to March 31, 1818, p. 48 (May 10, 1809).

The north shore. The north shore of Massachusetts, the New Hampshire coast, and the thousands of bays and inlets of the district of Maine opened endless opportunities to defeat the embargo. The task of the revenue officers along this stretch of coast line was made more difficult by the temper of the population, bitterly anti-Administration and ready to break the embargo by any possible means. In the center of this reach stood Joseph Whipple, collector of Portsmouth, New Hampshire, once removed by John Adams for his intemperate dislike of Federalists and promptly restored by Jefferson to his old office. His loyalty to the embargo could be counted on, but he had to deal with a fractious people.

Whipple apparently kept his home port under firm control. He made an arrangement with the commander of the fort to require every outward bound vessel to exhibit permission from the customhouse: "this check has proved the most effectual," he told Gallatin, "in preventing evasions practised in some of the neighbouring ports." [80] Whipple was pleased with the success of his own efforts. In May he wrote Gallatin that although it was known that large quantities of flour and provisions had been shipped to Passamaquoddy, none had been shipped from Portsmouth to any district adjoining a foreign territory exceeding the quantity necessary for the families of the seamen and the owners of vessels.[81] In forwarding Governor Langdon's single certificate to import flour, he told Gallatin, "No certificates of the kind now transmitted, will ever go from hence under the smallest doubt of the truth of the facts stated by the parties." [82]

Whipple also kept a watchful eye on the collectors in neighboring ports, and had plenty to report to the Treasury. Writing in September 1808, he declared, "At Newburyport they exceed all bounds. . . . Newburyport is now in a high spirit of violent opposition to the laws, I have again dispatched the Cutter to the assistance of the Officers and government." [83]

The town of York, Maine, was, however, the object of his greatest indignation. He accused all the inhabitants of a disposi-

---

[80] Letters from the Collector, Portsmouth, N.H. (July 22, 1808).
[81] *Ibid.* (May 22, 1808).
[82] *Ibid.* (May 23, 1808).
[83] *Ibid.* (Sept. 1808).

tion to violate the embargo laws, and deeply suspected the collector. The case of the ship *Rhoda* amply confirmed his suspicions. This sloop loaded in Portsmouth but Whipple refused a clearance, "being myself confident from the nature of her Cargo that it is intended to be put on board some Vessel out of the reach of a Custom House." [84] The cargo was consequently taken off by the owner, the empty sloop cleared for near-by York, and the goods were taken by land to this neighboring town. Whipple promptly sent a cutter to watch the course of events. On February 3 the cutter's crew discovered that the disputed cargo had been taken on board during the previous night. The captain of the cutter put four men aboard the *Rhoda*, and, being refused any assistance by the collector of York, hastened to Portsmouth for directions. The sequel can best be reported in Whipple's own words:

. . . I directed him to return without delay with one hand, who was ready, and I dispatched immediately after him 4 men, Masters of Vessels, who volunteered their services on this occasion, they took a sleigh at the ferry and the snow being deep it was 1 o clock in the night before they reached Cape Neddick, where they found that 40 or 50 men had overcome the guard, placed on board the Rhoda, the Vessel afloat and put off.[85]

This affair prompted Whipple to accuse the collector at York. He wrote Gallatin, "I am impelled by a sense of duty, but with pain and *regret* to state to you, that the proceedings in the District of York under the collectorship of Jeremiah Clarke Esq have every appearance of Collusions with the violators of the law. . . . But . . . no overt act has yet been stated to me which would justify an open complaint." [86]

Passamaquoddy, Maine, and Barnstable, Massachusetts, were two other weak links in the embargo chain. The former had a trustworthy but not too capable collector who proved unable to deal with his exposed position; the latter had agents who could not cover the shore line within their district. The collector on the Maine frontier was L. F. Delesdernier, whose name

[84] *Ibid.* (Dec. 31, 1808).
[85] *Ibid.* (Feb. 14, 1809).
[86] *Ibid.* (Feb. 22, 1809).

suggests the antiquity of the French-Canadian migration to the United States. Of him Gallatin wrote to Jefferson, "The collector of Passamaquoddy is, as you will perceive, a very bad writer, but he is a man of great integrity, zeal, and activity, and full reliance may be placed on his facts as on his exertions." [87] Delesdernier was at one of the critical transfer points for goods moving in illicit channels from the United States to Great Britain, and there is much indirect evidence suggesting that the flow of commerce was beyond his power to control.[88] Gallatin sent the district attorney of Maine to Passamaquoddy in late spring 1808,[89] and by September could report to Jefferson that this officer had "restored order in that quarter." [90]

The middle and southern ports. With variations the same type of reports came in from collectors up and down the sea coast. William Duane was not too trustworthy a source of information but as an old newspaperman he probably knew a good deal of what was going on in the port of Philadelphia. He sent his opinions directly to Jefferson:

. . . much abuse of the Embargo has been committed in this port; I communicated to the Custom house information last week, of provisions and other articles put on board a vessel at one of our wharves; and instances have been frequent and notorious. The inability of Genl. Shee for a long time past, to give energy to the office; and the indecent hostility of Mr. Graaf the deputy Collector to the general administration and its public policy have combined to relax the due force of the law in a manner that is inconceivable unless on the scene of action. Indeed the Custom house is proverbially a den of disorganization and has been constantly one of the most fatal means of distraction and division between the friends of public policy, and the professed friends.[91]

---

[87] Gallatin, *Writings*, I, 388 (May 16, 1808).

[88] See for example Whipple to Gallatin, May 22, 1808, Letters from the Collector, Portsmouth, N. H.; see also Joseph Otis of Barnstable to Benjamin Lincoln, May 31, 1808, referring to the schooner *Amazon* loaded with flour, fish, cheese, rice, pork, and bacon for Provincetown: ". . . she there with great expedition augmented her cargo with shipments of flour, from your port, and cleared for Passamaquoddy." Letters from the Treasury, Collectors, &c., Vol. S (unpaged), in National Archives.

[89] Gallatin, *Writings*, I, 388 (May 16, 1808).

[90] *Ibid.*, I, 417 (Sept. 14, 1808).

[91] Massachusetts Historical Society, *Proceedings*, 2d series. XX (1906-7), 310-11 (August 9, 1808).

The collector at Baltimore, Gabriel Christie, sent Gallatin word of cargoes of flour going out to the West Indies on board schooners lying up the Chesapeake Bay.[92] There was loud talk by a notorious character who boasted that he "would smuggle as much as he pleased without detection from the Custom House officers whom he frequently cursed as well as the Government." [93] In April 1808 the new collector, James H. McCulloch, sent Gallatin a cryptic but significant letter:

Foreign vessels arrive and land their Cargoes, depart or seem to depart in Ballast, return and clear out to return again. how long or by what means a trade can be supported that deposits great properties in successive Voyages without returning any thing to the course from which it proceeds, may be a problem deserving some attempt to solve.

The barren sand and stones of an Indian traders ballast, may like the earth of that region be fertile in gold and silver for any thing we know.[94]

A month later he reported "appearances of much foul business being done in some of the Rivers down the Bay. . . ." [95]

Collector Bessent of St. Marys, Georgia, called for help and in December 1808 Gallatin sent him additional gunboats.[96] This need for aid was confirmed by a letter to Jefferson from a southern friend, "From every information I have received their appears to be a very shameful Traffic carried on about St. Marys River, it is said . . . that English ships go there, & take in on the Spanish side cargoes of Cotton, Rice, &c. . . . I am fearful it will have a very bad tendency. . . ." [97] At the very close of 1808, Gallatin was obliged to write Jefferson that "the system of illegal exportations is carried on the largest scale, and embraces all the sea-coast of Georgia. . . . Cotton at this moment is the great object. . . . Even to the northward similar plans are in operation. All the cotton in New York has been purchased by

92 MS. National Archives, Treasury Department. Letters to and from Collectors, Baltimore, May 24, 1807, to March 18, 1838, p. 17 (Feb. 11, 1808).
93 *Ibid.*, p. 19 (April 4, 1808).
94 *Ibid.*, p. 20 (April 19, 1808).
95 *Ibid.*, p. 23 (May 18, 1808).
96 Letters on Revenue Cutter Service, p. 64 (Dec. 27, 1808). Name also spelled Bissent.
97 Thomas Lehré to Jefferson, Jan. 21, 1809, quoted in Sears, *Jefferson and the Embargo*, p. 133.

speculators in Boston, and they want to transport it. . . . I have written to Mr. Gelston not to permit the shipment of one bale. . . ." [98]

Resistance thus raised its head from St. Marys to Passamaquoddy, most powerfully eastward from Connecticut. On the coast the government relied on its collectors and revenue officers, its revenue cutters, gunboats, and naval vessels. Resistance also was encountered on the Canadian border, where the problem of effective policing was at the time almost impossible. The crisis in upper New York and Lake Champlain was most severe, but it was also grave along Lake Ontario. It came to a head early along the northern land frontier of New York.

The northern frontier. Prohibition of export by land came only with the third embargo act of March 12, 1808.[99] On April 19, the anniversary of the battle of Concord and Lexington, the situation had become so serious along Lake Champlain and the adjacent frontier that Jefferson declared a state of insurrection, "too powerful to be suppressed by the ordinary course of judicial proceedings or by the powers vested in the marshals," and called upon all civil and military officers to "quell and subdue" the disorders.[100] The proclamation was ineffective.

Rafts carrying the produce of Vermont and New York were moved up to the head of Lake Champlain to meet Canadian conspirators. They were sometimes intercepted, and sometimes escaped amidst rifle fire between the boatmen and the militia. At St. Albans in northern Vermont, thirty men fought twelve soldiers to regain twelve barrels of potash, and succeeded in their attempt.[101] In May Gallatin reported to Jefferson that large quantities of potash had arrived at Montreal.[102] On July 19 Jefferson wrote Gallatin about the "habitual breaches" of the embargo on the Canadian line, and at the end of the month confessed, "To prevent it is I suppose beyond our means, but we must try to harass the unprincipled agents and punish as many as we can." [103]

[98] Gallatin, *Writings,* I, 448 (Dec. 28, 1808).
[99] 2 Stat. 473, sec. 4.
[100] Richardson, *Messages,* I, 450–51.
[101] Jennings, *The American Embargo,* p. 115.
[102] Gallatin, *Writings,* I, 389 (May 16, 1808).
[103] Sears, *op. cit.,* p. 92.

In early August Governor Tompkins reported an insurrection at Oswego. Gallatin told Jefferson it was no more an insurrection than there had been on Lake Champlain or at Passamaquoddy, but agreed that there was "certainly a forcible violation of the embargo" such as would justify calling out the militia.[104]

In September a revenue cutter on Lake Champlain intercepted a batteau, the *Black Snake*, and pursued it up a small river where its crew abandoned ship. The revenue men went ashore and engaged in battle; a citizen was killed, and the captain of the batteau and one of the crew were convicted and executed.[105] Shortly thereafter both militia and a detachment of regulars arrived on the lake, and open violations diminished. The long frontier was, however, almost impossible to close, with sections of New England practically at war with the government authorities.[106]

Resistance to the embargo was therefore substantial and violations were frequent. The spectacular success of adventurous violators, however, ought not to conceal the fact that the embargo came much closer to success than failure so far as the immediate object of keeping American ships in harbor and American goods out of foreign hands was concerned. Despite all the trouble on the New England coast and elsewhere, despite defiance on the Canadian border, the agents of the federal government made a remarkable record in shutting off foreign commerce by sea and by land. In the spring and summer of 1808 goods and merchandise were smuggled out in considerable quantities, but even at the height of this illegal exportation, the bulk of American shipping lay idle in port, under the effective control of the government. Contemporary data from Newburyport, the seat of disaffection, a town in a "violent spirit" of resistance, speak to the point. As of April 5, 1808, "The following is a correct list of vessels now laying in this port embargoed: 15 ships, 27 brigs, 1 barque, 27 schooners. Total, 70 vessels." As of July 12, 1808, "There are now collected in our harbor 24 ships 28 brigs and 27 schs" As of July 15, 1808, "Our wharves have now the stillness of the grave,—indeed nothing flourishes

104 Gallatin, *Writings,* I, 402–3 (August 9, 1808).
105 Sears, *op. cit.,* p. 170.
106 Jennings, *op. cit.,* p. 115.

on them but vegetation." [107] The game between collectors and
merchants was by no means won by the latter.

[107] John J. Currier, *History of Newburyport, Mass., 1764–1905* (2 vols., Newburyport, Mass.: Author, 1906–9), I, 649. Data taken from contemporary *Newburyport Semi-Weekly Herald*. Cf. Sears, *op. cit.*, p. 96. No evidence has come
to attention that either Jefferson or Gallatin gave any thought to ways and
means of alleviating the hardships caused by the embargo.

CHAPTER THIRTY

End of the Experiment

The events that have been related make it clear that the federal government faced an administrative crisis of first magnitude. The situation was far more difficult to manage than that set by the Whiskey Rebellion in 1794. Then only a small number of farmers across the mountains were in discontent; now a large mass of merchants, shipowners, importers and exporters and their employees on land and sea, concentrated in New England but spread along the whole seacoast, were aroused. Then no party spirit sustained the rebellious; now the Federalist party, still thought to be a formidable opponent, was in full sympathy with the foes of the embargo. Then it was feasible, despite Jefferson's misgivings, to quell the disorder by sending a contingent of militia to the seat of discontent; now it was clear that no such simple remedy could be employed. How to enforce the law under the circumstances that Jefferson faced was a novel and perplexing problem.

THE RECORD OF THE ENFORCEMENT AGENCIES

Against the resistance springing up on seaboard and inland frontiers the government had various means of coercion, and sooner or later used them all. The first line of defense comprised the normal enforcement agencies—collectors, captains of the revenue cutters, marshals, and district attorneys, backed by the courts. The second line of defense was the navy. The third line was the militia and the regular army.

The collectors. The record of the normal enforcement agencies was on the whole highly creditable. Most of the collectors were faithful in the enforcement of the embargo, diligent and

[453]

active in their efforts; no evidence has come to hand suggesting
indifference on the part of the captains of the revenue cutters;
and most of the district attorneys prosecuted the seizures made
at the direction of the collectors. Henry Adams exaggerated
exceptional cases when he wrote that "the collectors shut their
eyes to smuggling," [1] and that Gallatin's "agents and instruments broke down in every direction." [2] The letters from collectors to the Secretary of the Treasury during 1808 and the
early months of 1809 breathe determination to enforce the law,
difficult or at times impossible as it seemed to them. They asked
Gallatin for help, but did not yield to their adversaries even
when they became the object of suit for personal damages.[3]
"No better story of loyalty in administrative work can be told—
and that under trying circumstances—than that which may be
found in the efforts of forgotten revenue and naval officers.
While others grumbled, these men worked. . . ." [4]

To these general observations there were individual exceptions. The collector at York was probably in collusion with
smugglers. The collector at New Bedford was removed.[5] The
collector at Sackett's Harbor resigned, as Gallatin believed,
"from fear, or at least from a wish not to lose his popularity
with the people." [6] There was want of energy in the collectors
on Lake Ontario,[7] and Pease of Edgartown, on Martha's Vine-

---

[1] Adams, *History of the United States*, IV, 259.

[2] Adams, *Life of Albert Gallatin*, p. 370. Walter W. Jennings asserted that
"In the North, cases of collusion were frequent. Officers winked at smuggling or
made only half hearted attempts to prevent it." He cited in evidence however
only the *Boston Gazette* of May 19, 1808. *The American Embargo*, p. 117.

[3] The record of the port of New York has been summarized from an examination of the district court records. During 1808, 28 vessels were seized for violating
the embargo, as well as nearly 60 consignments of prohibited imports. In the
early part of 1809, 55 embargo breakers were caught. From 1806 to 1812, including both nonimportation and embargo years, the New York agents caught
not less than 170 vessels and at least 300 consignments of goods. Herbert Heaton,
"Non-Importation, 1806–1812," *Journal of Economic History*, I, 184–85. This
article also gives data for other ports. There is an incomplete statement of fines
and forfeitures arising out of the embargo and nonimportation laws in *American
State Papers: Finance*, II, 490 (March 2, 1811).

[4] W. Freeman Galpin, "The American Grain Trade under the Embargo of
1808," *Journal of Economic and Business History*, II (1929–30), 71–100, at p. 85.

[5] Jennings, *op. cit.*, p. 117.

[6] Gallatin, *Writings*, I, 389.

[7] *Ibid.*, I, 397.

yard, was characterized by Gallatin as "a bad collector." [8] But
Weld of Boston was steadfast and active; Whipple of Portsmouth was a near fanatic in his work; Gelston of New York
had "nerve and zeal"; [9] Samuel Tredwell of Edenton, North
Carolina, was strict "in complying with instructions"; [10] the
collector of Barnstable and his son, who acted as deputy, "faithfully used their best endeavors to carry the laws into effect." [11]
Hodge, the surveyor at Newburyport, where sentiment rose so
violently against the embargo, was, in Gallatin's words, "a Federalist, who had always done his duty." [12] The drastic enforcement act of 1809, however, induced a flurry of resignations from
collectors who could take no more.[13]

The district attorneys. Among the district attorneys George
Blake of Massachusetts was the only one who was clearly disloyal to his official duties. In August 1808 Gallatin reported to
the President that he did "not seem zealous, or even active," [14]
and later in the same month Gallatin received a complaint from
the acting collector at Boston: "the Attorney of this District is
absent and we suffer much for want of advise. . . ." [15] Gallatin
repeated his observations to Jefferson ". . . I fear that there
has been a laxity on the part of the district attorney, Mr. Blake.
He is often absent, has answered none of my letters, and I have
been obliged to authorize the collectors, in several instances, to
employ other counsel." [16] Jefferson declined to remove Blake,
but after he had retired from office he wrote President Madison,
"Blake calls himself republican, but never was one at heart. His
treachery to us under the embargo should put him by forever." [17]

The published correspondence of Jefferson and of Gallatin

8 *Ibid.*, I, 404.

9 *Ibid.*, I, 397.

10 *Ibid.*, I, 400.

11 *Ibid.*, I, 427.

12 *Ibid.*, I, 451.

13 Jennings, *op. cit.*, p. 117, noting Lincoln, Weld, Olney and his brother at
Providence, and Hodge.

14 Gallatin, *Writings*, I, 404 (August 9, 1808).

15 Letters from the Collector, Boston, I, 212 (August 22, 1808).

16 Gallatin, *Writings*, I, 414 (Sept. 2, 1808). In November Gallatin again stated
that Blake refused to answer his letters on the embargo. *Ibid.*, I, 427.

17 Jefferson, *Works* (Federal ed.), XI, 152 (Oct. 15, 1810).

during the embargo crisis contains adverse references only to Blake. Silas Lee, district attorney for Maine, was commended by Gallatin for his efforts at enforcement.[18] A. J. Dallas, district attorney for the eastern district of Pennsylvania, was vigorous and attentive to all his duties and a firm Republican. George Hay of Virginia was no friend of Jefferson in later years, but at this time he was "a confirmed Jeffersonian Republican." [19] No complaint was entered against Bullock of Georgia, Stephen of Maryland, Sandford of New York, or Huntington of Connecticut. The evidence, such as it is, suggests that with a single exception the district attorneys did their duty.

The courts and trial juries. Jefferson had little complaint to make of the courts. In July 1808 there was an adverse decision from the circuit judge of South Carolina, William Johnson, in which a section of one of Gallatin's circulars was declared not well founded in law.[20] But Johnson was a Republican, a friend of Jefferson and one of his own appointments. Balancing this check was a decision by District Judge John Davis of Massachusetts, an Adams appointee and a Federalist, sustaining the constitutionality of the embargo law.[21]

Two serious problems nevertheless raised their heads around the courts. One was the reluctance of juries to convict, the other was the appearance of harassing suits brought in court against the collectors. Both hampered operations. Failure of a jury to convict in the face of evidence, like refusal of a district attorney to prosecute, is a sign of the breakdown of authority, and it occurred both in upper New York and in Massachusetts. Gallatin told Jefferson in the summer of 1808 that, "As to judiciary redress there is very little hope," in New York. Even a Republican jury refused to find bills against Canadian prisoners who had been captured on a smuggling raft on Lake Champlain.[22]

In September Gallatin complained of difficulty in starting prosecutions in northern New York.[23] John Quincy Adams

---

[18] Gallatin, *Writings*, I, 417.

[19] *Dictionary of American Biography*, VIII, 430.

[20] Jennings, *op. cit.*, p. 123.

[21] *Ibid.*, p. 124. For citations to Supreme Court cases involving the embargo, see Cummings and McFarland, *Federal Justice*, pp. 73–74.

[22] Gallatin, *Writings*, I, 397.

[23] *Ibid.*, I, 417.

wrote privately to William B. Giles in January 1809, stating that the district court of Massachusetts, after trying upward of forty cases of embargo law violations, had adjourned without a single conviction. One juror was reputed to have declared that he would never agree to a conviction, whatever might be the facts.[24] What with the disaffection of District Attorney Blake, the ability of the Federalist bar in defense of violators, and the unwillingness of juries to convict, enforcement through the New England courts was far from successful where it was most needed. But Adams, in the letter just cited, cleared the district judge of any partiality: "The judge has been firm and decided in support of the laws. . . ."

Liability of collectors. Suits against collectors by shipowners whose vessels were under detention were well calculated to undermine the vigor of enforcement of the embargo, for the unhappy collector not only stood in danger of social ostracism but also of financial ruin. As early as July 1808 Gallatin informed Jefferson that "we cannot expect that the collectors generally will risk all they are worth in doubtful cases. . . ."[25] These suits, he admitted later, "not only perplex faithful officers, but have the effect of intimidating others, and prevent an energetic performance of their duties."[26]

It was the plain duty of collectors to seize any vessel guilty of violating the customs, navigation, or embargo acts. At the same time, if a collector made a mistake and seized a vessel that in fact had not broken the law, or could not be proved in court to have broken the law, he was liable to damages for trespass in a state common-law court. To encourage collectors to perform their duty, Congress had provided in the original collection act that in case of seizure the federal district judge in his discretion could issue a certificate of reasonable cause which gave full protection to the collector against damage suits.[27] No such protection was afforded in cases of detention under the embargo laws until it had nearly run its course. A collector who thus might find himself under the awkward necessity of paying dam-

24 Adams, *Writings*, III, 287–88 (Jan. 16, 1809).
25 Gallatin, *Writings*, I, 397 (July 29, 1808).
26 *Ibid.*, I, 433 (Nov. 24, 1808).
27 1 Stat. 627, sec. 89 (March 2, 1799).

ages to shipowners where the judge would not protect him had no recourse except to petition Congress for relief in accordance with the customary claims procedure.

Benjamin Weld of Boston put the problem directly to the Secretary of the Treasury in early autumn, 1808. Suit had been brought against him, the marshal of his district, the captain of his revenue cutter, and the collector of Barnstable, upon the refusal of the district attorney to libel a vessel under detention and suspected of smuggling flour. "These circumstances are stated to you," wrote Weld, "under the expectation of being supported by the Government and held harmless. . . . otherways in performing the duties of the Collector, I may be involved in law suits that may be perplexing or even serious. Your answer to this is earnestly requested with explicit information of the extent of the support I may expect." [28]

Gallatin had no sufficient answer. He had no authority to issue instructions to the district attorneys and no means of ensuring their professional attention to the protection of the collectors. "I can do no more than to give general assurances of support," he wrote Jefferson. "Both as relates to the suits against the collector and the question of replevy, which, if submitted to, will defeat the operation of any law we can pass, I wish that the President would . . . give an opinion which I may, in his name, communicate to the district attorney." [29] The resisting shipowners had discovered a weak spot in the enforcement machinery which must have operated to stay the government's hand except in the strongest of cases.

Intervention of the state courts. A bold attempt to defeat the embargo by calling upon state courts to free property seized or detained by the collectors originated in Newport, Rhode Island. Gallatin promptly directed the collector to pay no obedience "to such efforts to defeat the law, as the State courts have no shadow of jurisdiction in such cases." "Still," he sighed, "this increases our difficulties. . . ." [30] The federal statutes provided

[28] Letters from the Collector, Boston, I, 217 (Sept. 13, 1808). Weld was subject to repeated suits; see *ibid.*, I, 228, 229. Whipple was threatened with suit at Portsmouth. Letters from the Collector, Portsmouth, N. H. (Dec. 31, 1808).

[29] Gallatin, *Writings*, I, 427 (Nov. 8, 1808).

[30] *Ibid.*, I, 401 (August 6, 1808). Jefferson promptly supported Gallatin in this

no easy way of dealing with such invasions. The sheriff executing a state court order could only be considered as a trespasser, and be resisted accordingly. Gallatin told Giles that "there is no other way at present to resist such illegal process but actual force," and recommended additional legislation.[31] Congress, however, deemed the matter too delicate and the second enforcement act of 1809 was silent on this issue.

The navy. It could hardly have been supposed by Jefferson when he recommended the embargo in December 1807 that within three months he would propose putting the navy to work to stop American vessels on the high seas on suspicion of violating the law.[32] Such was, however, the case, and in April Congress authorized commanders of public armed vessels and gunboats, as well as revenue cutters, to stop and examine any American vessel, and to send it into port under custody if found open to suspicion.[33]

Gallatin was the only person with the information needed to deploy the naval force to best advantage but he had no control over the disposition of ships. He consequently had to initiate his plans through Jefferson, asking him to instruct Robert Smith, the Secretary of the Navy.[34] Jefferson responded immediately. His letter to the Secretary of the Navy is an interesting administrative document.

Complaints multiply upon us of evasions of the embargo laws, by fraud and force. These come from Newport, Portland, Machias, Nantucket, Martha's Vineyard, etc., etc. As I do consider the severe enforcement of the embargo to be of an importance, not to be measured by money, for our future government as well as present objects, I think it will be advisable that during this summer all the gunboats, actually manned and in commission, should be distributed through as many ports and bays as may be necessary to assist the embargo. On this subject I will pray you to confer with Mr. Gallatin, who will call on you on his passage through Baltimore,

matter, Jefferson, *Writings* (Memorial ed.), XII, 134 (August 15, 1808); "No civil officer of the States can take cognizance of a federal case."

31 Gallatin, *Writings*, I, 433 (Nov. 24, 1808).

32 *Ibid.*, I, 379–80 (March 30, 1808).

33 2 Stat. 499, sec. 7 (April 25, 1808). On the gunboats see Harold and Margaret Sprout, *Rise of American Naval Power*, pp. 58–61.

34 Gallatin, *Writings*, I, 394 (July 15, 1808).

and to communicate with him hereafter, *directly,* without the delay
of consulting me, and generally to aid this object with such means
of your department as are consistent with its situation.[35]

With this clearance Gallatin asked Smith "to send north-
wardly all the force that can be spared either in gunboats or
cruising vessels. . . ."[36] The Navy Department took the *Wasp*
off the Passamaquoddy Station where she had been cruising,
and sent her to the Massachusetts coast, where she was joined by
the *Argus,* the *Chesapeake,* and the *Revenge.* Gallatin could secure only three gunboats, which he stationed at Newport, New
Bedford, and Barnstable. "This," he reported to Jefferson, "with
the revenue cutters, is all we can do, and of course we must
remain satisfied with the result, whatever it may be."[37] Within
a week a mob interfered with the customhouse officers at Newburyport, and the *Argus* and *Wasp* were dispatched to this seat
of opposition. The *Chesapeake,* off Block Island, had already
sent in eight vessels.[38] On the Georgia coast Gallatin could only
send gunboats.[39]

The navy was alert and active, in no way affected by domestic
differences of opinion. There is a hint that there was some
rivalry between revenue cutters and naval ships in the seizure
of suspects, a rivalry probably induced by the prospect of the
crew's share of proceeds of condemned vessels.[40] So far as it
could reach, the navy was energetic and effective.

The militia and regulars were also put to work during 1808,
but the provisions for calling out the militia contained in the
second enforcement act were so exceptional that this aspect of
the enforcement problem will be noticed in the following section.

THE SECOND ENFORCEMENT ACT, 1809

Resistance thus induced coercion, step by step. Every power
granted by Congress was put in motion—the punitive bonds

[35] Jefferson, *Writings* (Memorial ed.), XII, 93 (July 16, 1808).
[36] Gallatin, *Writings*, I, 397 (July 29, 1808).
[37] *Ibid.*, I, 403-4 (August 9, 1808).
[38] *Ibid.*, I, 406 (August 17, 1808).
[39] *Ibid.*, I, 448 (Dec. 28, 1808).
[40] *Ibid.*, I, 448.

and penalties, the restraint of vessels in the coastwise trade, the prohibition of all exports to foreign places, the detention of ships, the seizure of unusual deposits, the deployment of the navy, the assignment of militia, and the use of the regulars. Seizures and forfeitures multiplied despite the indisposition of New England juries to convict and the hostile intervention of the state courts, despite the harassing suits against collectors and occasional outbreaks of violence. But evasion, too, continued, although on a lesser scale than in the spring and summer of 1808. Jefferson determined to apply more force and more rigorous means of restraint. The course of Jefferson and Gallatin during the late summer and autumn of 1808 is a fascinating record of doctrinal disorder as the two greatest defenders of liberty in their age put the screws on their fellow American citizens.

The dilemma of these two liberal minds, faced with official responsibilities which Jefferson had imposed upon the government, is admirably revealed in their correspondence. Gallatin was in near despair as the summer months brought trouble to his desk in a never-ending stream. In late July he dispatched a remarkable letter to Jefferson.

> . . . I am perfectly satisfied that if the embargo must be persisted in any longer, two principles must necessarily be adopted in order to make it sufficient: 1st, that not a single vessel shall be permitted to move without the special permission of the Executive; 2d, that the collectors be invested with the general power of seizing property anywhere, and taking the rudders or otherwise effectually preventing the departure of any vessel in harbor, though ostensibly intended to remain there; and that without being liable to personal suits. I am sensible that such arbitrary powers are equally dangerous and odious.
>
> . . . I mean generally to express an opinion founded on the experience of this summer, that Congress must either invest the Executive with the most arbitrary powers and sufficient force to carry the embargo into effect, or give it up altogether. And in this last case I must confess that, unless a change takes place in the measures of the European powers, I see no alternative but war. But with whom? . . .[41]

41 *Ibid.*, I, 398–99 (July 29, 1808).

This declaration for arbitrary power beyond the control of the courts, or for war, brought forth an explicit answer from Jefferson accepting the peaceful horn of the dilemma. "This embargo law," he replied to his unhappy Secretary of the Treasury, "is certainly the most embarrassing one we have ever had to execute. I did not expect a crop of so sudden & rank growth of fraud & open opposition by force could have grown up in the U. S. I am satisfied with you that if orders & decrees are not repealed, and a continuance of the embargo is preferred to war (which sentiment is universal here), Congress must legalize all *means* which may be necessary to obtain it's *end*." [42] Jefferson's determination did not weaken even in view of all the summer's problems. Only two days before he penned the preceding letter to Gallatin he had written in uncompromising terms to Henry Dearborn: "The tories of Boston openly threaten insurrection if their importation of flour is stopped. The next post will stop it." [43]

After returning from Monticello the President followed up this correspondence by asking Gallatin to prepare a new enforcement bill to present to Congress, and noted some of its heads.[44] It is a fair inference from one of Gallatin's letters to Jefferson that the President had suggested the actual destruction of vessels to prevent evasion of the embargo. Gallatin wrote Jefferson, "We cannot destroy the boats, &c., at St. Mary's without being authorized by law so to do; and Congress shows so much reluctance in granting powers much less arbitrary, that there is no expectation of their giving this." [45]

Following Jefferson's lead, Gallatin proposed a discerning, if alarming, list of new official authorities to William B. Giles, the Republican Senate leader, that formed the basis of new and more rigorous legislation.[46] The enforcement act of January 9, 1809, was the climax toward which the long accumulation of power in executive hands had been moving. The climax having been reached, the resolution was not long delayed.

42 Jefferson, *Works* (Federal ed.), XI, 41 (August 11, 1808).

43 *Ibid.*, XI, 40 (August 9, 1808).

44 Gallatin, *Writings*, I, 420 (Oct. 25, 1808).

45 *Ibid.*, I, 447 (Dec. 28, 1808).

46 *Ibid.*, I, 428–35 (Nov. 24. 1808); *American State Papers: Commerce and Navigation*, I, 730–32.

The act of 1809 was especially remarkable because it was the product of the Republican party, enacted by a Republican House and Senate at the request of a Republican President, a party whose historic significance had been its fear of power and its opposition to the grant of power to executive hands. Congress followed closely Gallatin's recommendations, but omitted giving collectors power to seize suspicious goods at any point in the United States. The law opened by forbidding, for the first time, the act of loading a vessel or vehicle with intent to evade the embargo.[47] The collectors were given absolute authority to refuse a permit to load upon suspicion of an intent to violate the embargo, and the President was authorized to single out specific vessels to which no permit could be issued.[48] No vessel could be loaded, even with good intent, except by prior permission of the collector specifying the articles that could be put on board, and requiring as formerly an inspector to supervise the loading. Coastwise vessels were denied the right to plead capture, distress, or any accident whatever as an excuse for failure to deliver their cargoes to an American port, except under the most rigorous conditions. If capture was offered as a defense, it had to be expressly proved to have been hostile; if distress or accident, it had to be proved without negligence or deviation; and every living officer and mariner aboard had to be produced in court and sworn as a witness.[49]

Collectors were authorized to take into custody any cargo when there was reason to suspect an intention to export, and any articles in carts, wagons, sleighs, or other vehicles "or in any manner apparently on their way towards the territories of a foreign nation, or the vicinity thereof." Even more, they were authorized to designate the place to which such goods could be removed, under bond, "whence, in the opinion of the collector, there shall not be any danger of such articles being exported."[50]

Three powers vested in the collectors—to refuse permission to put cargo on board a vessel, to detain a vessel, and to take goods into custody on suspicion—were henceforth to be exer-

47 2 Stat. 506, sec. 1.
48 *Ibid.*, sec. 2.
49 *Ibid.*, sec. 7.
50 *Ibid.*, sec. 9.

cised in conformity with instructions given by the President.[51] This provision was a commendable effort to secure some degree of uniformity and consistency among the collectors, hitherto wanting. The Federalists, however, assailed it as merely another concentration of power in the hands of the Chief Executive.

Some protection was given to the collectors against suit by authorizing them to plead in their defense this new enforcement act and the instructions of the President; the district court was given summary powers to hear and adjudge such cases "as law and justice may require"; and if the court sustained the collector, he was entitled to treble costs from his accuser. The President was authorized to arm thirty vessels to be employed under the direction of the Secretary of the Treasury,[52] and the authority to permit vessels to go abroad to return property of American citizens was terminated.[53]

The most extraordinary power conferred by the second enforcement act was, however, that concerning the state militia. Congress, following the plan of Jefferson and Gallatin,[54] enacted that "it shall be lawful for the President of the United States, or such other person as he shall have empowered for that purpose, to employ such part of the land or naval forces or militia of the United States . . . as may be judged necessary" to enforce the embargo laws.[55] A Federalist Congress had already authorized the President to call out the militia in case of invasion, insurrection, or opposition to the execution of the laws too powerful to be suppressed by the usual means, but under careful safeguards involving the intervention of a federal district judge.[56] Now a Republican Congress not only gave the President power to act without these formalities, but also authority to delegate this high responsibility to others.

ARMED FORCE

To use the navy against American citizens offended sufficiently against true Republican doctrine, but even greater

[51] *Ibid.,* sec. 10.
[52] *Ibid.,* sec. 13.
[53] *Ibid.,* sec. 14.
[54] Gallatin, *Writings,* I, 431 (Nov. 24, 1808).
[55] 2 Stat. 506, sec. 11.
[56] 1 Stat. 264 (May 2, 1792).

offense was implicit in the employment of the militia and the regulars. In 1794 Jefferson had held that the grand jury was the proper means of coercing a turbulent citizenry and had opposed calling the militia to compel the whiskey distillers to pay the excise tax. Now he was to fall back on both the militia and the regulars to try to close the Canadian frontier, and to consider expedients for calling out the militia that had not been imagined by the Federalists.

Jefferson's proclamation of April 19, 1808, against insurrection around Lake Champlain, calling on all civil and military authorities to quell any such combination, was apparently met with contemptuous silence. The experience was so depressing that when trouble broke out again in August 1808, Jefferson had not dared issue another proclamation of the same sort. Instead Gallatin conferred privately with Governor Daniel Tompkins of New York to induce him to call out the militia on his own responsibility, but with assurance of reimbursement by the federal government.[57] Tompkins was reluctant, both because he feared that the militia officers, if selected at random, would be "imprudent or disaffected," [58] and because he wanted to try judicial prosecution before a resort to armed force.[59] After some hesitation he yielded and in September 1808 parties of militia, as well as some regulars, were stationed at various key points in upper New York.[60]

The second enforcement act authorized use of the militia with the slightest of formalities. No sooner was it on the books than Gallatin asked Jefferson for instructions concerning the employment of the militia. "I perceive," he said, "no other mode than that you should authorize each collector, *in the cases stated in the section,* to call either on military force of United States, if any within his district, or on such part of the militia as he may himself select. Some general caution may be added." Gallatin did not overlook the probability that governors might resist

57 Gallatin, *Writings*, I, 402–3 (August 9, 1808); see Jefferson to Tompkins, August 15, 1808, Jefferson, *Writings* (Memorial ed.), XII, 132, confirming Gallatin's proposition.

58 Gallatin, *Writings*, I, 403.

59 Tompkins to Jefferson, August 22, 1808, quoted in Sears, *Jefferson and the Embargo*, p. 94.

60 Gallatin, *Writings*, I, 417 (Sept. 14, 1808).

such a derogation of their own dignity and of their own authority over the militia: ". . . it is necessary to know whether, at
any time, militia has been called without first applying to the
governor; and how far it may be eligible, if it has never been
done, to do it in this instance." [61]

Jefferson wisely decided not to by-pass the governors. Instead,
the Secretary of War sent a circular letter to each governor on
January 17, 1809, the essential terms of which follow.

. . . To put an end to this scandalous insubordination to the
laws, the Legislature has authorized the President to empower
proper persons to employ militia, for preventing or suppressing
armed or riotous assemblages of persons resisting the customhouse
officers. . . . He therefore requests you, as commanding officer of
the militia of your State, to appoint some officer of the militia, of
known respect for the laws, in or near to each port of entry within
your State, with orders, when applied to by the collector of the
district, to assemble immediately a sufficient force of his militia,
and to employ them efficaciously to maintain the authority of the
laws respecting the embargo. . . . He has referred this appointment
to your Excellency, because your knowledge of characters, or means
of obtaining it, will enable you to select one who can be most confided in to exercise so serious a power, with all the discretion, the
forbearance, the kindness even, which the enforcement of the law
will possibly admit,—ever to bear in mind that the life of a citizen
is never to be endangered, but as the last melancholy effort for the
maintenance of order and obedience to the laws. [62]

The first emergency broke through this prudent procedure.
Jefferson himself authorized the collector at near-by Alexandria,
Colonel Charles Simms, to apply for aid of the Virginia militia. [63]

Governor Lincoln of Massachusetts proceeded to follow the
War Department circular, selecting officers whom he thought
reliable and writing directly to them rather than transmitting
orders, as was normally the case, through the adjutant general. [64]

61 *Ibid.*, I, 450 (Jan. 10, 1809).

62 Jefferson, *Works* (Federal ed.), XI, 88–89.

63 Jefferson, *Writings* (Memorial ed.), XII, 239 (Jan. 22, 1809).

64 William Sullivan, *The Public Men of the Revolution*, pp. 294–95. From
Lincoln's circular, as reproduced by Sullivan, is taken the following passage:
"The President of the United States has directed the Secretary of War to
request me to appoint some officer of the militia, *of known respect for the laws,*
in, or near each port of entry in this state, with orders, *when applied to by the*

He got a prompt and hostile reaction from the Massachusetts House of Representatives, which resolved "that these orders were irregular, illegal, and inconsistent with the principles of the constitution; tending to the destruction of military discipline; an infringement of the rights and derogatory to the honor of both officers and soldiers; subversive of the militia system, and highly dangerous to the liberties of the people." [65]

The governor's orders nevertheless prevailed, but in some communities they ran against an immovable local opposition. A company of militia stood on the deck of the brig *Betsey* in obedience to the summons of the collector of York, despite "very harsh language" of the owner, until the tide had ebbed. They were promptly haled before the magistrate at Kennebunk, twenty miles distant, and held to the superior court for trial for trespass, the local justice declaring the embargo laws unconstitutional. The superior court released the worried militiamen, but the incident was not conducive to martial energy.[66]

Federalist-minded William Sullivan, over twenty years later, could still recall the impression made on Lincoln's resisting contemporaries by his invidious appeal to the reliable part of the militia. "*This service* was *force* by one class of citizens, distinguished by a political creed and by subserviency to Thomas Jefferson's will, against another class who considered him as depriving them of rights guaranteed by the constitution, with no other motive than to aid Napoleon to enforce his continental system." [67]

These were indeed "the most arbitrary powers" that Gallatin had foretold would be necessary. Collectors became despots in

---

Collector of the District, to assemble a sufficient force of his militia, and to employ them *efficaciously,* to maintain the authority of the laws respecting the embargo. *The President is peculiarly anxious, that the officers selected should be such, who can be best confided in to exercise so serious a power."*

[65] *Ibid.,* pp. 295–96.

[66] *American State Papers: Claims,* pp. 382–83.

[67] Sullivan, *op. cit.,* p. 295. Sullivan wrote this in 1833, and to make his point clear he added, "The legality of this measure and its effect can best be comprehended, by imagining *selected* bodies of militia to be placed at the disposal of President Jackson's collectors of ports; and by imagining, that these bodies might be called into action against the citizens, whenever these collectors might be of opinion, that their agency was necessary in maintaining the majesty of the Presidents will!" *Ibid.,* p. 296.

their respective districts, and the President had powers so vast that in fact no vessel could sail if he specified that it should swing at anchor. All that was left was for Congress to authorize the collectors to seize the rudders and put them under lock and key. Of this act, Henry Adams wrote, "It was a terrible measure, and in comparison with its sweeping grants of arbitrary power, all previous enactments of the United States Congress sank into comparative insignificance." [68] It was the death blow to the embargo.[69]

COLLAPSE

The embargo was a terminable policy, an experiment which had to have a conclusion, successful or otherwise, within a brief period of time. Jefferson acknowledged in the early summer of 1808, writing to Thomas Leib: "It is true, the time will come when we must abandon it. But if this is before the repeal of the orders of council, we must abandon it only for a state of war. The day is not distant, when that will be preferable to a longer continuance of the embargo." [70] By midsummer Robert Smith, Secretary of the Navy, privately told Gallatin that the embargo should be abandoned. "Most fervently ought we to pray," he wrote, "to be relieved from the various embarrassments of this said embargo." [71] By the end of the year Gallatin himself prophesied that the Republican majority would not adhere to the embargo much longer.[72]

However, in his eighth annual message, November 8, 1808, Jefferson gave no sign of bringing it to an end.[73] He recognized

---

[68] Henry Adams, *Life of Gallatin,* pp. 378–79.

[69] Jennings, *The American Embargo,* p. 59.

[70] Jefferson, *Works* (Federal ed.), XI, 34–35 (June 23, 1808). He repeated this view in July, *ibid.,* XI, 38 (July 17, 1808).

[71] Adams, *Life of Gallatin,* p. 373 (August 1, 1808).

[72] Gallatin, *Writings,* I, 449 (Dec. 29, 1808).

[73] Indeed Joseph Story, a Republican who was well informed, said that he knew Jefferson was determined to protract the embargo "for an indefinite period, even for years." It was Story who led the break in Republican ranks. His account of the crisis is found in a letter to Edward Everett: "The whole influence of the Administration was directly brought to bear upon Mr. Ezekiel Bacon and myself, to seduce us from what we considered a great duty to our country, and especially to New England. We were scolded, privately consulted, and argued with, by the Administration and its friends, on that occasion. I knew, at the time, that Mr. Jefferson had no ulterior measure in view, and

that the suspension of foreign commerce was a subject of concern, but praised the consequent growth of manufactures. On the problem of enforcement he noted that some "small and special detachments" of militia had been required, but asserted that, "By the aid of these and of the armed vessels called into service in other quarters the spirit of disobedience and abuse, which manifested itself early and with sensible effect while we were unprepared to meet it, has been considerably repressed." [74] The initial response of Congress was not to move toward repeal, but toward more rigorous enforcement.

The storm was nevertheless gathering strength and in a sudden burst late in the session swept all before it. On November 25, 1808, there had been read in the Senate the Resolutions of the Massachusetts General Court, speaking ominously of the extreme and increasing pressure upon the people and of the danger to "our domestic peace, and the union of these States." The Resolutions instructed the Massachusetts Senators, and requested the Representatives, to use their "most strenuous exertions" to secure repeal.[75]

Governor Trumbull of Connecticut, responding to the circular asking for militia to be put at the disposal of the collectors, told Jefferson that he had no constitutional power to make such a request and that he (Trumbull) "deemed it peculiarly and highly improper for a state executive to contribute his *volunteer* aid in support of laws bearing such an aspect." [76] At a special session of the Connecticut legislature the General Assem-

---

was determined on protracting the embargo for an indefinite period, even for years. I was well satisfied, that such a course would not and could not be borne by New England, and would bring on a direct rebellion. It would be ruin to the whole country. Yet Mr. Jefferson, with his usual visionary obstinacy, was determined to maintain it; and the New England Republicans were to be made the instruments. Mr. Bacon and myself resisted, and measures were concerted by us, with the aid of Pennsylvania, to compel him to abandon his mad scheme. For this he never forgave me. The measure was not carried until I left Congress for home. The credit of it is due to the firmness and integrity of Mr. Bacon." Story, *Life and Letters,* I, 187. But Jefferson confided to Dr. William Eustis on January 14, 1809, that the embargo was then "near its term." *Works* (Federal ed.), XI, 85.

[74] Richardson, *Messages,* I, 455.

[75] *Annals,* 10th Cong., 2d sess., pp. 128–30; *American State Papers: Commerce and Navigation,* I, 776–78.

[76] Jennings, *op. cit.,* p. 146.

bly "highly approved" Trumbull's conduct and directed all persons holding executive office under the state to refrain from any official aid in the execution of the embargo.[77] Rhode Island joined Massachusetts and Connecticut, and the Delaware House of Representatives fell in with these northern states. At the same time New Hampshire rejected a motion hostile to the embargo, and a number of states passed resolutions in support of it. Sentiment in most of New England was hardening, however, and the drastic terms of the enforcement act of January 9, 1809, made opposition more bitter. Disunion was feared by statesmen such as John Quincy Adams and Joseph B. Varnum, Speaker of the House,[78] and Jefferson himself recorded that Congress fell under the belief that the alternative was civil war or repeal.[79]

The patience of the merchants also was giving out. Ships had been loaded in the fall of 1808 in the expectation that the embargo would be terminated when Congress met in December.[80] Instead Congress put on the books "the ferocious amending act" of January 9, 1809, which forced owners either to unload their cargoes or give heavy bonds. "This," said Heaton, "was the last straw." [81] By the end of March 1809 there were forty ships, embargo breakers, in Liverpool, and more expected. Rumors were circulating in January 1809 that undermined whatever moral authority the embargo then possessed: "Have just got accounts tis coming off very fast Eastward." [82] Gallatin had already sensed

[77] Feb. 23, 1809. This and other documents on the embargo are reprinted in Herman V. Ames, ed., *State Documents on Federal Relations: The States and the United States* (Philadelphia: University of Pennsylvania, 1900–1906), No. I, pp. 26–44.

[78] Sears, *Jefferson and the Embargo*, pp. 183–84.

[79] Jefferson to William Pinkney, July 15, 1810, Massachusetts Historical Society, *Proceedings*, 2d series, XII, 268.

[80] This anticipatory loading was the occasion of another Treasury circular. Those concerned were required to make a declaration of their purpose and if suspicion of intent to evade the law was aroused in the mind of the collector he was directed not to put an inspector on board—which made any lading illegal. If, however, the owners declared that their object was merely to use the vessels as stores, their intent was perfectly legal and could not be stopped. MS. National Archives, Embargo Circulars, pp. 252–53 (Nov. 15, 1808).

[81] Heaton, "Non-Importation, 1806–1812," *Journal of Economic History*, I, 191.

[82] C. Savage to Samuel Savage, Jan. 23, 1809, in Massachusetts Historical Society, *Proceedings*, XLIX (1915–16), 90.

the advancing crisis and in November 1808 had exhorted his forces. "I rely at this critical moment," he wrote the collectors, "equally on your vigilance in carrying that object [i.e., enforcement of the embargo] into effect, and on your discretion in doing it in such a manner as will give no grounds of complaint to any but those who intend to disregard the law." [83]

Spring optimism thus faded into summer despair, autumn determination was followed by winter crisis. On March 1, 1809, Jefferson signed a bill repealing the embargo and substituting nonintercourse with England, France, and their possessions. His great experiment collapsed, as he said, "in a kind of panic" among his own party members in Congress.[84] Within three days he left public office. At the close of his life, he recorded: "I saw the necessity of abandoning it [the embargo], and instead of effecting our purpose by this peaceful weapon, we must fight it out, or break the Union." [85]

Jefferson believed, nevertheless, that peaceable coercion in the form of the embargo would have succeeded, given time and determination. He realized, as he wrote William Short when he was packing for Monticello, "Our embargo has worked hard." [86] But as conflict with Britain came to an end in 1815, he declared that "a continuance of the embargo for two months longer would have prevented our war. . . ." [87] He believed the margin was always narrow between an accommodation induced by want in England and war, and he clung to the prospect of peace.

William Pinkney doubtless spoke for many when he declared in the summer of 1809:

The embargo was a noble and magnificent effort, suited to the extraordinary occasion by which it was suggested, and adequate if persevered in to all its purposes. . . .

. . . Any other measure than the embargo would . . . have been madness or cowardice. For no others were in our choice but war with both aggressors, or submission to both; with the certainty too,

83 Embargo Circulars, p. 253 (Nov. 15, 1808).

84 Jefferson, *Works* (Federal ed.), XI, 97 (Feb. 7, 1809). The repeal is contained in the Nonintercourse Act, 2 Stat. 528, sec. 12 (March 1, 1809).

85 *Works* (Federal ed.), XII, 423 (Dec. 25, 1825).

86 *Ibid.*, XI, 104 (March 8, 1809).

87 *Ibid.*, XI, 478 (June 12, 1815).

that that submission would in its progress either lead to war, or to a state of abject degradation.[88]

Pinkney believed that the embargo was on the point of success when it was abandoned. Contemporary judgment is to the contrary.

Success or failure has to be measured by two different considerations: was the embargo successful in stopping American exports; was it successful in bringing either England or France to terms, the real objective? Measured by the latter criterion, the embargo was not a success. Neither France nor England was seriously embarrassed by the lack of American flour, provisions, and other goods. Jennings concluded on this aspect of the matter, "The embargo as an economic means of forcing the European nations to rescind their obnoxious orders and decrees was consequently a failure." [89]

The embargo was more nearly successful from the point of view of stopping the movement of American ships and goods to foreign ports, although even here administrative means were not wholly adequate to the immediate end. The major administrative question was whether the government possessed a system strong enough, reliable enough, and equipped with the necessary legal authority and physical power to enforce the embargo. The record showed that such a system existed, had been given adequate powers by the emergency legislation, and had discovered within itself the moral authority and determination to reach a substantial degree of success.

The very means of securing this measure of administrative success, however, raised larger questions of a political order: the danger inherent in the concentration of power, the control of official discretion, the means of protecting citizens against their government while ensuring obedience to its legitimate directions.

The concentration of administrative power was very great. Thomas Jefferson could in fact do what Gallatin said must be done: refuse any ship permission to move upon suspicion of its

[88] William Pinkney, *The Life of William Pinkney* (New York: D. Appleton and Co., 1853), pp. 148–49.
[89] Jennings, *op. cit.*, p. 93.

motives. Congress put in his hands power to authorize a ship to depart for a foreign port or to keep it at home; to authorize a merchant to send a vessel abroad to return his property or to require him to leave it in a foreign warehouse; to instruct a collector whether to allow a vessel under detention to sail or not; to permit or refuse shipments of flour from port to port; and, in his judgment of the safety of the seas, to suspend the embargo at pleasure. Jefferson asked for these harsh means of coercion and used them fully, to know, "by fair experiment . . . the power of this great weapon, the embargo." His contemporaries were convinced of the reality of the power, but were far from satisfied as to the wisdom of its use.

Apart from these broader considerations the country discovered that the general government possessed power and the will and capacity to use it against the most active and influential portion of the population. It discovered also that an administrative system organized for the normal tasks of daily routine could be mobilized effectively for an emergency and vested with discretionary authority adequate to the demands of a crisis. For the most part these vast discretionary powers slumbered peacefully for a half century after the repeal of the embargo in 1809.

CHAPTER THIRTY-ONE

Internal Improvements

The central domestic problem facing the Jeffersonians in 1801, apart from the payment of the debt, was the improvement of the means of communication. Sailing vessels and small boats sufficed for the transportation of goods and persons along the coast and up and down the water courses, but the movement of produce and supplies from the coast inland and from the back country to the towns was laborious, time-consuming, and expensive.[1]

Political as well as economic considerations emphasized the gravity of the problem of communications. The uneasy West moved on its rivers. The rivers flowed away from the east, westward along the Ohio and the Tennessee, south along the Mississippi. The danger of separation and independence of the country over the mountains was in men's minds even after the purchase of Louisiana, and thoughtful persons knew that unless roads and canals could connect the interests of these great regions, the future of the Union might remain uncertain. Gallatin put effectively what many men believed.

The early and efficient aid of the *Federal* Government is recommended by still more important considerations. The inconveniences, complaints, and perhaps dangers, which may result from a vast ex-

1 There is no satisfactory general account of the internal improvement movement in both its national and state aspects. The subject is discussed shrewdly in Henry Adams, *History of the United States,* Vol. III especially. See also Balthasar Henry Meyer, ed., *History of Transportation in the United States before 1860* (Washington: Carnegie Institution of Washington, 1917); Seymour Dunbar, *A History of Travel in America* (4 vols., Indianapolis: Bobbs-Merrill, 1915); Edward Kirkland, *Men, Cities, and Transportation* (2 vols., Cambridge: Harvard University Press, 1948).

tent of territory, can no otherwise be radically removed or prevented than by opening speedy and easy communications through all its parts. Good roads and canals will shorten distances, facilitate commercial and personal intercourse, and unite, by a still more intimate community of interests, the most remote quarters of the United States. No other single operation, within the power of Government, can more effectually tend to strengthen and perpetuate that Union which secures external independence, domestic peace, and internal liberty.[2]

The fertile mind and glowing imagination of the inventor, Robert Fulton, saw all this in more vivid colors. He had invented a torpedo for the defense of ports and had convinced himself that navies were henceforth useless. He urged his countrymen accordingly to dispense with warships, and instead to build bridges and canals and support education. "Canals," he wrote, "bending round the hills would irrigate the grounds beneath, and convert them into luxuriant pasturage. They would bind a hundred millions of people in one inseparable compact —alike in habits, in language, and in interest; one homogeneous brotherhood, the most invulnerable, powerful, and respectable, on earth."[3]

In 1783 there was not a single "artificial road" west of the Alleghenies.[4] People across the mountains were living in an age of pack-horse travel. Indeed an overwhelming part of the land traffic of the country, except between the principal eastern cities, was carried on by pack horses as late as 1790. The enterprisers in pack trains in fact resisted the making of roads that were suitable for the use of wagons.[5] Even in the cities the number of privately owned vehicles was astonishingly small. Costs of transportation were great, and prices consequently high.

[2] *American State Papers: Miscellaneous*, I, 725 (April 4, 1808).

[3] *American State Papers: Naval Affairs*, I, 225–26 (Feb. 26, 1810).

[4] An "artificial road" was distinguished from a tote-road or pack road, i.e., trails for horses and foot passage, and from a common road, i.e., ruts worn by the successive passage of wagons across the countryside. From Alexandria to Mt. Vernon there was a maze of such common "roads" wandering through the woods, a new route being taken when an old one became impassable.

[5] Dunbar, *op. cit.*, I, 194.

PLANS AND PORTENTS

As the population of the west increased, the demand for federal expenditures for internal improvements grew. The western farmers knew that federal money was being spent for eastern shipowners and merchants in the form of lighthouses, buoys and beacons, and harbor works. They thought it appropriate for federal money to be spent also for roads and canals over which they could send their produce to the eastern market.

The Jeffersonians agreed in principle. They were held back only by their desire to get rid of the debt, and by a conviction that they needed additional constitutional authority. Led by Thomas Jefferson himself, however, they looked forward to the time when it would be constitutionally correct and financially practicable to embark upon great public works of national importance. In his second inaugural address, Jefferson declared that surplus revenue should be applied to rivers, canals, roads, arts, manufactures, education, and other great objects.[6] He repeated this sentiment in his annual message of 1806 and again in 1808, following Gallatin's great report on public works.[7]

Gallatin's plan. From the beginning of his public life Gallatin had favored internal improvements, and he was not vexed by constitutional worries.[8] "The General Government," he declared, "can alone remove these obstacles." [9] He waited only until the debt was out of the way, and by 1807 that auspicious event seemed sufficiently close to warrant the preparation of plans. His closest friend in the Senate, Thomas Worthington of Ohio, aided and abetted by John Quincy Adams, brought about the passage of a resolution asking him for a report. This state paper, on which Gallatin worked for nearly a year, became a landmark. It was the first great plan for the physical development of the country, as Hamilton's report on manufactures was the first plan for its economic development. It was bold, shrewd, farseeing, and thoroughly national in scope and design. It was,

[6] Richardson, *Messages,* I, 379 (March 4, 1805).

[7] See Charles E. Merriam and Frank P. Bourgin, "Jefferson as a Planner of National Resources," *Ethics,* LIII (1943), 284–92.

[8] Adams, *Life of Albert Gallatin,* pp. 85, 156–57.

[9] *American State Papers: Miscellaneous,* I, 725.

moreover, practical, and easily within the technical and financial resources of the time, had those resources not been drained by war with Great Britain. Its major outlines remained valid until, just as the Republican period came to a close, they were rendered in large part out of date by the invention of the steam railroad.

The magnitude of the plan and its enormous consequences for the future of the country become clear in even a brief summary of its principal features.[10] Gallatin proposed two great means of communication north and south, one by inland waters and one by land. The water channel stretched from Boston to St. Marys, Georgia, and required construction of only four short canals—Boston to Buzzards Bay (in preference to the Cape Cod canal); a New Jersey canal from the Raritan to the Delaware River; the Delaware and Chesapeake Canal leading into the head of Chesapeake Bay; and the Chesapeake and Albemarle Canal leading southward through the Dismal Swamp, Albemarle Sound, and Pamlico Sound to the protected natural waterway along the southern coast. Gallatin estimated canal construction of only ninety-eight miles at a probable cost of $3,050,000.[11] The second line, the great turnpike from Maine to Georgia traversing routes already well established in large part, he estimated to cost $4,800,000.[12]

Of even greater consequence were Gallatin's proposals for lines of communication east and west. He proposed to establish four routes to the west, utilizing the rivers on either side of the mountains and connecting each pair of rivers with a highway. These pairs were (from north to south), the Susquehanna and the Allegheny, the Potomac and the Monongahela, the James and the Kanawha, and the Santee and the Tennessee.[13] These routes would serve the interests of the whole middle and southern sections of the original states supplemented by a canal at the falls of the Ohio, at Louisville.

The connections of New York and New England with the west were clearly designated by nature along the Hudson and

---

10 *Ibid.,* I, 724–921 (April 4, 1808).
11 *Ibid.,* I, 725.
12 *Ibid.,* I, 746.
13 *Ibid.,* I, 732.

Mohawk Rivers, and New York State already had under contemplation a canal to the Great Lakes. Gallatin included in his
plan a canal from the Hudson to Lake Ontario, another to
Lake Champlain to open up northern New England, and a canal
around Niagara Falls. The estimated cost of all these national
improvements, north and south, east and west, was $16,600,000.
He sought to forestall objections from parts of the Union less
immediately benefited by his program, i.e., New England and
the extreme South, by proposing, on the grounds of "policy not
less than justice," the construction of either canals or roads of
primarily local benefit, amounting to $3,400,000, bringing his
total estimated cost to $20,000,000.

Gallatin did not, however, fall into the error of trying to apportion federal money among the states on the basis of population. "Arithmetical precision cannot, indeed, be attained in
objects of that kind; nor would an apportionment of the moneys
applied according to the population of each State be either just
or practicable, since roads and particularly canals are often of
greater utility to the States which they unite, than to those
through which they pass." [14]

This bold and imaginative program of the old Republicans
was destined to be blocked by war. The new Republicans, led
by Calhoun, Clay, and others, were as fully committed to the
task. In 1818 the House of Representatives directed Calhoun, as
Secretary of War, to report a plan "for the purpose of opening
and constructing such roads and canals, as may deserve and
require the aid of the government, with a view to military operations in time of war." In 1819 Calhoun presented a second
major plan for internal improvements.[15]

Calhoun's plan. Calhoun immediately seized upon the proposition that a road good for military purposes would normally
also be good for commercial and postal purposes: "A judicious
system of roads and canals, constructed for the convenience of
commerce, and the transportation of the mail only" would be

14 *Ibid.,* I, 740. This is one of the first statements, if not the first, on the
vexing problem of the standards upon which federal grants to states may
justly rest.

15 House Doc. 87, 15th Cong., 2d sess. (Jan. 7, 1819); also in *American State
Papers: Miscellaneous,* II, 533–37; and with Gallatin's report reprinted in House
Report 8, 17th Cong., 1st sess.

"with few exceptions, precisely those which would be required for the operations of war, such a system, by consolidating our Union, and increasing our wealth and fiscal capacity, would add greatly to our resources in war." [16] "The road or canal can scarcely be designated, which is highly useful for military operations, which is not equally required for the industry or political prosperity of the community." [17]

In his report Calhoun emphasized the importance of the great north-south artery, at all times a most important object of the nation, and, in a war with a naval power, "almost indispensable to our military, commercial, and financial operations." "It must be perfected by the General Government, or not be perfected at all, at least for many years. No one or two States have a sufficient interest." [18] He urged again the inland water course already proposed by Gallatin, and in addition a "durable and well-finished road" from Maine to Louisiana. So far as the western lines of communication were concerned, he argued that the interest of commerce and the spirit of rivalry between the great Atlantic cities would suffice to ensure their construction; but he approved federal contributions to the expense involved in connecting Albany with the Lakes; Philadelphia, Baltimore, Washington, and Richmond with the Ohio; and Charleston and Augusta with the Tennessee.

These far-reaching plans were doomed to contemporary failure. The puny expenditures on the construction of military roads and post roads were a slight contribution indeed to the great central need of the American people before the days of the railroad. Leadership passed to the states. In the Erie Canal New York was to demonstrate the national advantage that the general government found it impossible to achieve.

FRUSTRATION

The fatal impediment to action was the theory of strict construction of the Constitution. As part of their warfare against the Federalists, the Republicans had steadfastly opposed reading implied powers into the authority of the general government,

---

16 *American State Papers: Miscellaneous*, II, 534.
17 *Ibid.*, II, 536.
18 *Ibid.*, II, 534.

believing that the liberty of the people demanded the restriction of national power. No section of the Constitution expressly delegated power to undertake a program of public improvements. Jefferson, indeed, had warmly protested Madison's apparent willingness in 1796 to build post roads, even with the specific right of Congress to establish post offices and post roads.[19] Since no authority had been delegated, it could be exercised only by new powers secured by a constitutional amendment.

Jefferson stood squarely on this proposition in each of his recommendations to Congress. He favored internal improvements, but he intended to protect the integrity of the federal system. Gallatin, in deference to Jefferson's views, said little in his report about the constitutional problem. Calhoun felt no such restraints and entertained no shadow of doubt that the general government possessed adequate constitutional power. In 1817 he asked a question for which no Republican had an answer: "If we are restricted in the use of our money to the enumerated powers, on what principle can the purchase of Louisiana be justified?" [20]

The movement of events, however, was to prove the stubbornness of old ideas. The Second Bank of the United States was chartered in 1816 [21] and for its privileges paid the United States a bonus of $1,500,000. Calhoun introduced a bill to use this sum and dividends arising from governmental shares in the Bank as a permanent fund for the construction of roads and canals in each state, with its consent, finding constitutional warrant in the "general welfare" clause. After a hot debate the bill squeaked through the House, 86 to 84, passed the Senate, and went to Madison. On the last day of his second term he vetoed the bill.[22] The first "real internal-improvement bill, based on broad construction of the constitution, was dead." [23]

Monroe endorsed Madison's constitutional views and told Congress in his first annual message that he had reached "a settled conviction" that Congress did not possess the right to

19 Jefferson, *Works* (Federal ed.), VIII, 226–27 (March 6, 1796).
20 *Annals*, 14th Cong., 2d sess., p. 856 (Feb. 4, 1817).
21 3 Stat. 267 (April 10, 1816).
22 Richardson, *Messages*, I, 584 (March 3, 1817).
23 Jeremiah Simeon Young, *A Political and Constitutional Study of the Cumberland Road* (Chicago: University of Chicago Press, 1904), p. 54.

establish a system of internal improvements.[24] He had no doubt, however, of their value and urged a constitutional amendment.

The issue next came to a head in 1822. To provide money for repairs on the Cumberland Road, Congress authorized the President to erect tollgates and apply the proceeds for this purpose. Implicit in the bill was the assumption of jurisdiction over the road to enforce payment of the tolls. On May 4, 1822, Monroe vetoed this bill on the ground that Congress lacked constitutional authority to exercise jurisdiction over internal improvements.[25]

Despite this veto, Monroe had modified his early constitutional position, declaring in a long statement accompanying the veto message that Congress had an unlimited power to raise money and a discretionary power to appropriate it for purposes of "general, not local, national, not State benefit." [26] He did not explain how public works were to be built, maintained, and policed under this theory of the spending power, but there were three possibilities. Public works of a national character might be built by direct application of federal funds, either by the government itself or by contract, jurisdiction remaining with the states. Fortifications and harbor works provided precedents, although in these cases jurisdiction was regularly ceded by the states to the general government. Or federal funds could be granted to the states for the construction of public works under their jurisdiction, either directly or by contract. Or the federal government might provide funds for the use of private corporations engaged in building public works by purchasing a block of their shares, a plan already suggested by Gallatin.

Following Monroe's lead Congress made a direct appropriation for the repair of the Cumberland Road,[27] for making surveys of projects of national benefit,[28] for subscribing to the stock of the Chesapeake and Delaware Canal Company,[29] and for the construction of river and harbor improvements in an omnibus

24 Richardson, *Messages*, II, 18 (Dec. 2, 1817).
25 *Ibid.*, II, 142.
26 *Ibid.*, II, 144–83, at p. 173.
27 3 Stat. 728 (Feb. 28, 1823).
28 4 Stat. 22 (April 30, 1824).
29 4 Stat. 124 (March 3, 1825).

rivers and harbors act.[30] Ample precedent existed for the latter,
but the Survey Act seemed to promise a new era. This legislation authorized a comprehensive survey of routes for such roads
and canals as the President might deem of national importance,
"in a commercial or military point of view, or necessary for the
transportation of the public mail." [31] A House committee of the
21st Congress made the following comment on this act.

The survey bill was considered as the precursor to all future improvements. Its design was to obtain an accurate knowledge of the
topography of the country, by the examination of scientific men,
under the direction of the President, who were to make plans, &c.
of such objects as the President should direct, reserving to Congress
to select in succession the routes which they might deem the most
urgent, and of the highest national importance, to be first executed.
. . . The proceedings of the engineers produced effects of salutary
importance. . . .[32]

It appeared in 1825 that the curtain was about to rise on a substantial federal program of public improvements, especially in
the light of the views of John Quincy Adams. Early in the first
session of Congress under his administration, a member came
to the White House to report plans for an amendment to the
Constitution. Adams declared he did not agree with the necessity for additional authority. "I thought the power of making
roads and canals given by the Constitution; and . . . an amendment . . . impracticable and useless." [33]

The federal program was destined, however, not to advance
much beyond the stage of survey and report. Jefferson, Crawford, and others still thought Adams' doctrines unconstitutional.
The program was opposed by Senator Benton and the Jackson
men, who asserted that the selection of routes under the Survey
Act degenerated "from national to sectional, from sectional to
local, and from local to mere neighborhood improvements." [34]
No appropriation was made after 1828.[35]

---

[30] 4 Stat. 175 (May 20, 1826).
[31] 4 Stat. 22 (April 30, 1824).
[32] House Report 77, 21st Cong., 2d sess., p. 5 (Feb. 10, 1831).
[33] Adams, *Memoirs*, VII, 80 (Dec. 14, 1825).
[34] Benton, *Thirty Years' View*, I, 26.
[35] 4 Stat. 275 (May 19, 1828).

In his own view his failure to bring Congress to embark energetically on internal improvements was Adams' greatest disappointment.

. . . The great effort of my administration was to mature into a permanent and regular system the application of all the superfluous revenue of the Union to internal improvement. . . . With this system in ten years from this day [1837] the surface of the whole Union would have been checkered over with railroads and canals. . . .

. . . I fell and with me fell, I fear never to rise again, certainly never to rise again in my day, the system of internal improvement by means of national energies. The great object of my life therefore, as applied to the administration of the government of the United States, has failed.[36]

Thus stood the constitutional position. The political branches of the government were dominated by two successive vetoes which the friends of internal improvements in Congress were unable to overcome. The willingness of the judicial branch to support a broad interpretation of the Constitution that was clearly wide enough to permit the construction of roads and canals was of no practical help. For nearly thirty years everyone agreed that internal improvements were essential and that only the federal government could supply the funds and the general plan. This sentiment encountered first the obstacle of the debt, then the blockade of constitutional objections, finally, under the second Adams, the confusion of factional politics.

So the country stood for three decades, hamstrung in the achievement of its greatest need. The clash of economic interest and constitutional doctrine resulted for the time being in a victory for the lawyers. The Jeffersonians, looking backward with a sense of frustration as the term of John Quincy Adams drew to a close, could not have imagined how near was the answer to their problem. The solution was to be found not in the exertions of the general government, but in the invention of the railroad and the steam locomotive, and in the application of private capital. Jackson's final veto of federal appropriations for internal improvements rang down the curtain on one stage,

36 Adams to the Reverend Charles W. Upham, Feb. 2, 1837, in Brooks Adams, "The Heritage of Henry Adams," in Henry Adams, *The Degradation of the Democratic Dogma* (New York: Macmillan, 1919), pp. 24–25.

but another curtain was rising on a far more magnificent scene.

THE CUMBERLAND ROAD

Due to the inventive genius of Albert Gallatin a constitutional means was discovered to permit Congress to appropriate money for the construction of the great east-west highway known as the Cumberland Road, or the National Highway.[37] As a part of the compact for the admission of Ohio as a state, Congress enacted that 5 per cent of the net proceeds of the sale of public lands in Ohio after June 30, 1802, should be applied "to the laying out and making public roads, leading from the navigable waters emptying into the Atlantic, to the Ohio, to the said state, and through the same," under the authority of Congress and with the consent of the states through which the road passed.[38] By subsequent agreement the amount was reduced to 2 per cent and became known as the "two per cent fund." The first appropriation was made in 1806. Eventually appropriations were made as an "advance" on future collections, a legal fiction that was sufficient to extend the Cumberland Road well into Illinois, as corresponding compacts were made with Indiana and her western neighbor.

The Cumberland Road was the single great internal improvement that the general government was able to construct. Its governmental and administrative history is instructive. The initial legislation, enacted three years after Ohio had been admitted, vested full authority in the President.[39] With the advice and consent of the Senate he was directed to appoint three commissioners to lay out the road and after the consent of the states had been secured to proceed with its construction. Congress specified that the road should be cleared the whole width of four rods, should be raised in the middle with stone, earth, gravel, or sand, supplied with ditches, and built with an elevation of not over five degrees with the horizon. At every quarter mile and every angle Congress required "a plain and distinguishable

[37] For a full account of the constitutional and administrative phases of this enterprise, see Jeremiah S. Young, *Political and Constitutional Study of the Cumberland Road.*

[38] 2 Stat. 173, sec. 7 (3) (April 30, 1802).

[39] 2 Stat. 357 (March 29, 1806).

mark on a tree," or some stake or monument. In every other particular the manner of making the road was left to the President. Jefferson proceeded without delay, but soon found that Pennsylvania intended to dictate the course of the road through its boundaries. He was annoyed but yielded in part, influenced by Gallatin's warning that otherwise "we will infallibly lose the State of Pennsylvania at the next election." [40]

Progress was slow, and was further delayed by the War of 1812. Contracts were let from time to time for short sections of the road proceeding from Cumberland westward.[41] In 1813 ten miles of the road had been finished, and eleven more were under contract. In 1818 it was opened for traffic to Wheeling on the Ohio River.[42] From 1806 to 1820 slightly over $1,500,000 had been expended on surveys and construction.[43]

Delay and administrative problems failed to discourage the congressional friends of the Cumberland Road. In 1816 a House committee spoke its determination: "Good roads have an influence over physical impossibilities. . . . They increase the value of lands and the fruits of the earth in remote situations. . . . They promote a free intercourse among the citizens of remote places, by which unfounded prejudices and animosities are dissipated, local and sectional feelings are destroyed, and a nationality of character, so desirable to be encouraged, is universally inculcated." [44]

Repairs. The use of the Cumberland Road was so heavy that repairs became necessary almost as rapidly as sections were completed. Superintendent Shriver's first report, dated January 14, 1812, called attention to the need for legislation to authorize repairs, and suggested tolls as the means of finance.[45] Gallatin

---

40 Gallatin, *Writings*, I, 395 (July 27, 1808).

41 A sample contract may be examined in *American State Papers: Miscellaneous*, II, 175, signed by Gallatin and approved by Madison.

42 Young, *op. cit.*, p. 32; there is an account of the Cumberland Road in Thomas B. Searight, *The Old Pike* (Uniontown, Pa.: author, 1894). See also Seymour Dunbar, *History of Travel in America*, II, 691–740; Archer Butler Hulbert, *The Cumberland Road* (Cleveland: Arthur H. Clark, 1904).

43 House Doc. 99, 16th Cong., 1st sess., p. 7. A detailed statement of amounts appropriated and expended, 1806–1829, is available in House Report 850, 24th Cong., 1st sess. (July 2, 1836).

44 *American State Papers: Miscellaneous*, II, 302 (March 23, 1816).

45 *Ibid.*, II, 177.

endorsed the idea of tolls but stated they could be levied only under the authority of the state of Maryland.[46] A House committee also endorsed the plan of tolls, but no action was forthcoming.[47]

There ensued a stalemate between the general and the state governments. Neither wanted to assume the cost of maintenance; each hoped to force the other to act through its own inaction. Congress finally took the lead and in 1822 passed the tollgate act for the repair of the road. Monroe, as we have already seen, vetoed this bill. He suggested, however, that he could accept a direct appropriation for repairs, and Congress adopted this means.

That repairs were needed was abundantly clear. The Postmaster General reported in 1823 that the western part of the road was "in a ruinous state, and becoming rapidly impaired. . . . The Cumberland road, so interesting to the nation, will (in my opinion, formed by observation when upon it,) cease to be useful unless repaired." [48] In 1824 David Shriver, having now been appointed superintendent of repairs, went upon the road, "and discovered it to be in a ruinous condition." [49] In 1826, a House committee declared, "At present, this road, owing to the great and increasing travel upon it, its total neglect, and exposure to the destructive operation of the elements, is in a state of rapid dilapidation, and, unless some remedy be soon applied, total destruction must be the speedy and inevitable result. . . ." [50] In 1827 the superintendent of the road then under construction west of Zanesville, Ohio, wrote the chief engineer of the War Department with reference to the older sections, ". . . the road has become by long neglect, too bad to be mended: It must in a great degree be renewed." [51] In 1828 McLean declared that in many places the road was impassable to mail stages, which were forced to take to the adjacent woods.[52]

46 *Ibid.*, II, 175.
47 *Ibid.*, II, 182 (April 14, 1812). This endorsement was renewed in 1816, in face of alleged constitutional prohibition. *Ibid.*, II, 301.
48 House Doc. 16, 17th Cong., 2d sess., p. 3 (Jan. 7, 1823).
49 House Doc. 154, 18th Cong., 1st sess., p. 7 (Feb. 27, 1824).
50 House Report 143, 19th Cong., 1st sess., p. 1 (March 27, 1826).
51 Senate Doc. 1, 20th Cong., 1st sess., p. 66 (Nov. 16, 1827).
52 House Doc. 269, 20th Cong., 1st sess., p. 3 (May 10, 1828).

In 1823 Congress made an initial appropriation of $25,000 for repairs.[53] After it had been spent the need for repairs seemed as great as ever. Four years passed by before any more money was wrung from a reluctant Congress. In 1827 it allowed $30,-000, and in 1829, $100,000 for repairs east of Wheeling.[54] The struggle between the states and the general government to avoid the costs of maintenance was thus won in the first instance by the former. Eventually Congress escaped from the problem of repairs and maintenance by ceding the Cumberland Road to the states through which it passed. Of the sole alternatives that were seriously discussed during the 1820's, i.e., repairs financed by federal tollgates, and cession of the road and all the responsibilities that went with it to the states, the latter finally prevailed.[55]

Gallatin's great plan for internal improvements under the stimulus and direction of the federal government thus remained unfulfilled. Not even Calhoun's dynamic energy could muster, through the war power, the resources needed for the internal system of communications which he saw so clearly would serve the needs of commerce as well as of defense. The House Committee on Roads and Canals was too optimistic in 1826 when it rejoiced "in the contemplation of the period as not far distant" which would soon make it the interest and duty of the national government to adopt a general system of internal improvements under the constitutional authority to regulate commerce among the several states, to establish post offices and post roads, and to provide for the common defense.[56] The strict construction theory of the Constitution prevailed in the White House until the days of John Quincy Adams, and the opposition of New England, the far South, and the Jackson men remained thereafter. The House committee was doubtless correct in noting that "the general sentiment of the country is decidedly in favor of this policy—a sentiment which is rapidly extending itself throughout the country, and prevails almost universally in the *young and growing States* of the Union, while the opposition

---

53 3 Stat. 728 (Feb. 28, 1823).
54 4 Stat. 228 (March 2, 1827); 4 Stat. 363 (March 3, 1829).
55 Young, *op. cit.*, ch. 7.
56 House Report 228, 19th Cong., 1st sess., pp. 12–13 (May 22, 1826).

to it is confined almost exclusively to those States, whose relative
strength in the Union is either *declining* or stationary." [57] The
need for roads and canals and bridges was urgent, but it was the
states, not the general government, which proved able and
willing to carry the load of meeting the need.[58]

INTERNAL IMPROVEMENTS IN THE STATES

No constitutional handicaps prevented the construction of
roads, canals, bridges, and other public works under the authority of the state government. Roads had traditionally been
built by the towns and counties, and maintained by a road tax,
usually worked out by farmers with shovels and wagons. The
roads were as good—or indifferent—as local initiative and
interest prescribed. They were used principally for local travel,
since the rivers and sea provided more comfortable means for
long journeys.

The need for internal transportation led to much state activity, for the most part subsequent to 1800 and so far as canals
were concerned after the War of 1812.[59] The war was the great
dividing line of the Republican years from many points of view,
and affected the states in much the same way as the national
government. From the economic viewpoint it marked "the shift-
ing of the centre of interest in our economic activity from the
ocean and foreign commerce to the interior and internal commerce. It was . . . the beginning of what has been the chief
object of our economic activity ever since; namely, the application of capital to the settlement of the interior and the development of its natural resources." [60]

The earliest activity of the states came before the great era
of canals in the form of incorporation of and assistance to turn-

[57] *Ibid.*, p. 13.

[58] There were occasional direct appropriations to open roads in territories.
See, for example, 2 Stat. 396, sec. 7 (April 21, 1806).

[59] For a valuable early account see Henry S. Tanner, *A Description of the
Canals and Rail Roads of the United States, comprehending Notices of all the
Works of Internal Improvement throughout the Several States* (New York: T. R.
Tanner and J. Disturnell, 1840).

[60] G. S. Callender, "The Early Transportation and Banking Enterprises of the
States in Relation to the Growth of Corporations," *Quarterly Journal of Eco-
nomics*, XVII (1902-3), 111-62 at 115.

pike companies. The experience of Pennsylvania, which encouraged the improvement of internal communication largely
through the instrumentality of the mixed corporation, is of
special interest.[61] Precedent had been established in 1793 with
a state subscription to the stock of the Bank of Pennsylvania.
By 1815, the state had invested over $2,000,000 in stock of var-
ious banks. In 1806 the bank precedent was put to work in the
construction of roads, by state subscriptions to the funds of
turnpike companies. By 1820 over $1,000,000 had thus been
invested in better roads. In 1815 a beginning was made in bridge
construction; by 1820 eleven bridge companies had received
state aid. Ten years later the state, deeply concerned about the
prospective loss of the western trade to New York through the
Erie Canal, made contributions to private corporations for the
great line of communication between Philadelphia and Pittsburgh.

This line contemplated the construction of a railroad (originally using horses as motive power) from Philadelphia to the
Susquehanna, thence up this river to the Juniata, along which
a canal would lead to the foot of the mountains at Hollidaysburg. Here the canal boats would take to land, be pulled up to
the summit on inclined planes by stationary steam engines and
let down again to the Conemaugh River at Johnstown, which
in turn led directly by water route to Pittsburgh. The work was
completed in 1834.[62] In October 1834 the keelboat, *Hit or Miss,*
was taken from the Susquehanna waters at Hollidaysburg "and
laid safely in Allegheny waters at Johnstown," the first craft to
leap the Alleghenies.[63]

The administration of public works in Pennsylvania proved
to be a perplexing and unsolved problem. The Board of Canal
Commissioners had a hectic history. It was originally appointed
by the governor but in 1829 the legislature itself made the appointments of the nine commissioners. Political trading ensued
and the power of appointment was returned to the governor. In

61 Louis Hartz, *Economic Policy and Democratic Thought: Pennsylvania, 1776–
1860* (Cambridge: Harvard University Press, 1948). The following paragraphs on
Pennsylvania are based on this able work.

62 See map in *ibid.,* p. 154, and in Archer Butler Hulbert, *The Great American
Canals* (2 vols., Cleveland: Arthur H. Clark, 1904), I, 185–86.

63 *Ibid.,* I, 206.

1844 the board was elected directly by the voters. There was much fear that it would become "an engine of almost unlimited power." In fact it seems to have had too little power, and to have been too dependent on the state legislature. The assembly was torn by local interests, and was as lax as Congress in providing money for repairs. The board was unable to give effective supervision to the section superintendents and to the contractors. Despite these administrative handicaps, perhaps inevitable in a generation without experience in large-scale affairs, this work was brought to a successful conclusion.[64]

New York provided the object lesson that Pennsylvania admired and feared. In 1816 the state assembly authorized the preparation of surveys and plans for a canal from the Hudson River to Lake Erie. Construction began near Rome, New York, in 1817 and the whole canal of over four hundred miles was completed in 1825. This was easily the greatest public work yet produced in America and one which was destined to play a fundamental role in the political as well as the economic history of the country. It immediately became the favorite route to the west.[65] It was largely responsible for the rapid development of the northern tier of states leading beyond the Great Lakes to Wisconsin and Minnesota. It favored not only the settlement of this rich empire but also the preponderance of the country north of the Ohio as compared with the regions to the south. Within New York State itself the consequences were impressive, exem-

[64] A valuable account of this route is in *ibid.*, I, 169–215.

[65] Cf. the testimony of Dr. William Beaumont: "A more useful & Stupendeous work could not have been *conceived, planned* & put *into execution* than this Canal. . . . Nothing can be pleasanter than to pass through the canal in the passage boats for you have nothing to disturb the most plasant feeling—being perfectly safe from every apprehension of danger of any kind—gliding smothily [*sic*] along upon the surface of still water at the rate of 5 miles an hour through a most delightful country. . . ." *William Beaumont's Formative Years: Two Early Notebooks, 1811–1821* (New York: Henry Schuman, 1946), pp. 52–53. The canal became the favorite route to Niagara Falls, and was traversed in 1825 by Justice Story. "These packet boats," he wrote a friend, "are almost thirty-five feet long, with a single deck or story, in which there are two cabins, one for ladies, and the other for gentlemen. . . . They are drawn by three horses . . . on a brisk walk, of about four miles an hour. Except when you pass a lock, not the slightest motion is felt in the boat, though the rapidity with which the surrounding objects pass by you, is very apt at first to make you a little dizzy." Story, *Life and Letters*, I, 459 (July 10, 1825).

plified by the rise of the chain of cities along the Mohawk and beyond, from Albany to Buffalo. The canal ensured the commercial supremacy of New York City; Boston never recovered a competitive position, nor did Philadelphia or Baltimore.

In Massachusetts reliance was put on private capital to develop the communications between the coast and the interior. The Middlesex Canal, leading from the Merrimac River to Boston, was one of the earliest large-scale improvements in New England. The Blackstone Canal, connecting Worcester with Providence, Rhode Island, gave the fathers of the Old Bay State much concern as they saw Providence drawing away business from Boston. Their concern found expression in serious plans (1826) for a canal from Boston across the Berkshire Mountains by means of a tunnel to the Hudson. Before construction began the problem was solved by the building of railroads.

Virginia made its first bid for the western trade in 1816 when it established a board of internal improvements. In 1820 work began on a canal to connect the James River with the Kanawha, flowing on the west side of the mountains down to the Ohio near Gallipolis.[66] In 1828 Virginia and Maryland joined forces to construct the Chesapeake and Ohio Canal, and were successful in securing federal aid through a stock subscription. This project was originally set on foot by George Washington, and had been supported by Virginia and Maryland in identical legislation of 1785.[67] As soon as it appeared that the prohibitive cost of crossing the mountains would make Cumberland the western terminus of the canal, thus denying Baltimore access to the western trade, the Baltimore interests threw themselves behind a railroad. They secured the incorporation of the Baltimore and Ohio Rail Road Company, expecting to use horse-drawn vehicles moving on iron rails. Both canal and railroad companies inaugurated construction on July 4, 1828, with grand celebrations. President Adams turned the first shovel of earth for the

---

[66] Wayland Fuller Dunaway, *History of the James River and Kanawha Company* (New York: Columbia University, 1922).

[67] For basic data on the Chesapeake and Ohio Canal, see House Report 228, 19th Cong., 1st sess. (May 22, 1826) and House Report 90, 19th Cong., 2d sess. (Jan. 30, 1827). See also Walter S. Sanderlin, *The Great National Project: A History of the Chesapeake and Ohio Canal* (Baltimore: Johns Hopkins Press, 1946).

canal; the venerable Charles Carroll of Carrollton, the only
surviving signer of the Declaration of Independence, performed
a similar service for the railroad. The canal was eventually completed to Cumberland. The railroad, soon equipped with steam
locomotives, successfully crossed the mountains and maintained
Baltimore as an important commercial center. It ended the
potential usefulness of its rival.[68]

The new states across the Alleghenies were also busy with
their own canal projects, at times favored by federal land grants.
A packet line improved travel on the Ohio River as early as
1793, making a round trip from Pittsburgh to Cincinnati in four
weeks. This advance over flatboats floating downstream still left
something to be desired, despite the optimistic advertisement of
the packet proprietors:

> No danger need be apprehended from the enemy, as every person
> on board will be under cover, made proof against rifle or musquet
> balls, and convenient port holes for firing out of. Each of the boats
> are armed with six pieces, carrying a pound ball; also a number of
> good musquets and amply supplied with plenty of ammunition,
> strongly manned with choice hands, and the masters of approved
> knowledge.[69]

In 1811 Fulton put into operation the steamboat *New Orleans*,
running from Louisville to Cincinnati. It was sunk in 1814, a
frequent fate of these early vessels, but by 1818 steamboat service on the Ohio and the Mississippi was established.

The basic need of Ohio was twofold. The first was a line of
communication to the east, which was fulfilled by the Cumberland Road and shortly thereafter by the Erie Canal. The second was a line from the Ohio to Lake Erie. National military
needs also suggested the importance of a line from Pittsburgh
to Lake Erie. The state legislature established a canal commission in 1822 and began construction of a north-south route from
Cleveland through Akron to Newark and thence to Portsmouth

---

[68] North Carolina also looked longingly across the mountains. An account of
its plans and frustrations, in part arising out of the impossibility of securing
a chief engineer, is found in Archibald D. Murphey, *Papers*, II, 96, 103.

[69] Ohio State Archaeological and Historical Society, *Publications*, III (1895),
104, quoted in Ernest Ludlow Bogart, *Internal Improvements and State Debt in
Ohio* (New York: Longmans, Green, 1924), pp. 5–6.

on the Ohio. Governor Clinton of New York was the guest of the state at the ground-breaking ceremonies. The whole work was completed in 1833.[70]

Ohio made a clean record in this large enterprise. The surveys and the supervision of construction were in the hands of state agents, but the work was performed by private contractors. "No fraud or even scandal was associated with the early construction or financial administration of the canals of Ohio, and while some credit should be given to the method of control, most is due to the honesty and integrity of those entrusted with the expenditures of the state funds." [71]

These references to a few of the larger undertakings by or within the states suggest the very substantial effort that was forthcoming with the assistance of states and localities, or through the energies of private entrepreneurs. While the federal government was bending every effort to pay off its debt, the states were creating a funded debt of over $200,000,000—"a larger debt than the federal government had ever owed, and the first large funded debt created by the government of any country for purely industrial purposes." [72]

The mixed corporation was the favorite device for financing these internal improvements, recommended by Gallatin and employed by both the federal and state governments. Financial considerations were largely responsible for its use. The credit of the federal government abroad was at a high point, due to its debt payment policy; that of the state governments also was generally excellent. Foreign investors, whose funds were needed to supplement domestic savings, were readily attracted to enterprises in which government was a partner.[73] In the major public improvements there was also some sentiment that the public interest was best served by full government responsibility. The first report of the New York Canal Commission contained this passage: "Too great a national interest is at stake. It must not become the subject of a job or a fund for speculation. . . .

[70] *Ibid., passim.*

[71] *Ibid.*, pp. 32-33.

[72] Callender, *op. cit.*, p. 114. The principal objects were banks, turnpikes, canals, river improvements, bridges, and after 1830 railroads.

[73] *Ibid.*, pp. 139 ff.

Moreover, such large expenditures can be more economically made under public authority than by the care and vigilance of any company." [74] A corresponding view was expressed by the Ohio Canal Commissioners in 1825. They declared:

. . . It does not consist with the dignity, the interest, or the convenience of the State that a private company of citizens or foreigners (as may happen) should have the management and control of them [i.e., the great navigable ways]. . . . Besides, such works should be considered with a view to the greatest possible accommodation to our citizens; as a public work, the public convenience is the paramount object; and a private company will look only to the best means for increasing their profits.[75]

This was not, as Louis Hartz has so effectively demonstrated, an era of laissez faire. Through joint ownership of mixed corporations, through public works programs, and through the statutory regulation of many economic activities the states played an important role in the economy. Benjamin F. Wright suggests, indeed, that "governmental participation was as great, perhaps greater, in Pennsylvania in 1830 as in 1930, if one takes into account the scale and range of economic development." [76]

The Republicans never resolved on a national scale the dilemma put by their recognition of the urgent need for national public works and by their commitment to the necessity of a constitutional amendment to authorize the general government to build them. This quarter century thus missed what might have been fertile administrative experimentation either in the direction of large-scale national public works or in joint operations with the states. Much engineering experience was gained in the extensive program of coast fortifications, but this, of course, excluded administrative relations with the states. It was sufficient, nevertheless, to establish firmly the army engineer corps, and the operations under the Survey Act brought the army engineers into direct contact with civilian public works.

The country was destined to secure its great civilian public works through state enterprise in part, but above all through

74 Quoted in *ibid.*, p. 155.
75 *Ibid.*, pp. 155–56.
76 Hartz, *op. cit.*, Foreword, p. ix.

the exertions of private capital and the ingenuity of American inventors. Insofar as the national government was concerned with the field of internal improvements the War Department was the beneficiary. Its major enterprises were the system of fortifications, the coast survey, and the expansion of its own means of military transport along the rivers of the Mississippi Valley.

The Republicans were not only handicapped by their constitutional doctrine; they were divided by sectional rivalries that almost ruined the usefulness of the one major internal improvement they pushed to completion, the Cumberland Road. Refusal to appropriate money for repairs, and the tardy grant of inadequate amounts in the 1820's caused the road to yield to the Erie Canal as the primary artery of east-west traffic. The bottled-up impetus to build was released, not through the instrumentalities of the nation, but through those of the states and their turnpike and canal companies. The state of New York, not the general government, pioneered with the greatest internal improvement of the age.

CHAPTER THIRTY-TWO

"In Regions Wide and Wild":
The Management of
Indian Affairs

The character of the Indian problem changed radically during the first three decades of the nineteenth century. In Washington's day the Indians had been a military danger. By the time of John Quincy Adams the Indians had become an uneasy moral charge on the public conscience. The Indians themselves had descended from defiance to submission. Their old savage culture, within which they had been able to lead an independent, if rude existence, had disintegrated. They had become dependent on the white man's guns, traps, and axes, and had been demoralized by the white man's whiskey. The Indians were no longer a military danger but they had become a moral problem of national dimensions.

Indian policy under the Jeffersonians was consequently a varying mixture of four ingredients: military control of the red men and protection of the whites; regulation of trade; cession of land and removal of the tribes beyond the Mississippi; and the civilization of the aborigines, with some vague expectation of integrating them into the domestic economy. The military ingredient tended to diminish; efforts to civilize the Indian tended to increase, but never exceeded very modest dimensions.

The driving force which had brought about the transformation of these years was the irresistible pressure of the white population on Indian lands. "From the first discovery of America to the present time, one master passion, common to all mankind—that of acquiring land—has driven, in ceaseless succession, the white man on the Indian." [1] Despite good intentions the Great White Father had never been able to keep his sons from trespassing on the valleys and prairies to which Indian title was fully recognized. The Federalists had tried, by marking boundary lines, by requiring passports to step across into Indian territory, and by directing army squads to remove trespassers. They had tried also to regulate trade with the Indians for their own protection, but they had failed in large measure before the steady march across the mountains. The defiant resistance of the Indians to these encroachments broke out in massacre and warfare; submission was symbolized in treaties ceding land and eventually in agreements to migrate west, in the vain hope of settling beyond the reach of the white man.

The administrative procedure underlying land cession was simple. The federal government retained the sole right to deal with the Indian tribes in the matter. Commissioners proceeded by treaty, by the terms of which the two parties bargained until agreement was reached, if possible. The Indians had possession. They were warmed to the occasion by presents and speeches—not, let it be said, by liquor—but there were no means of compelling agreement if the Indians proved stubborn. It was, indeed, a complaint that the native owners would not yield some especially desirable lands. [2]

Treaty after treaty was nevertheless negotiated, and territory after territory was ceded for a price. [3] The terms were various, but usually included purchase money or merchandise, and an annuity. Occasionally the United States agreed to erect mills and provide millers, to furnish salt or implements of husbandry, or to build a house for the chief of the tribe. The execution of

---

[1] *American State Papers: Indian Affairs,* II, 647.

[2] Barbour commented that the "obstinacy of the Indians . . . whose removal we most wish, fully equals the zeal of those who wish to procure their lands. . . ." *Ibid.,* II, 648.

[3] A list of Indian treaties, with annotations, is printed in *ibid.,* I, 816. Monroe's resettlement program is found in House Doc. 64, 18th Cong., 2d sess. (Jan. 27, 1825); at this time there were nearly 130,000 Indians residing within the states and territories, who claimed over 77,000,000 acres of land.

these obligations became a duty of the Indian agent assigned to the tribe or territory.

Eventually the pressure for land became so great that wholesale emigration beyond the Mississippi was brought to pass. The agreement to emigrate was made by treaty. The emigration itself was carried out by the army with the assistance of an Indian agent.[4]

The central administrative problem was the regulation of Indian trade. The pattern set up by the Federalists, including both licensed traders and publicly owned and managed trading houses, was finally terminated in 1822 despite the warm objections of the superintendent of Indian trade, Thomas L. McKenney. The liquidation of the trading houses signified impatience with public undertakings of a commercial order and the dominance of private enterprise philosophy. The moral responsibility of the nation to protect the Indians against the avarice of private traders yielded to these prevailing impulses.

THE REGULATION OF INDIAN TRADE

Congress had established in 1795 the system of Indian trade that was to endure until 1822. It was a combination of licensed private traders and government trading houses or factories.[5] Both private and public trading went on side by side, and with

[4] The process of dispossession of the Indian is not pursued here, since it was a political rather than an administrative problem. See J. P. Kinney, *A Continent Lost—A Civilization Won: Indian Land Tenure in America* (Baltimore: Johns Hopkins Press, 1937), and Grant Foreman, *The Last Trek of the Indians* (Chicago: University of Chicago Press, 1946). For a valuable collection of colonial and state laws relating to the Indians, see House Report 319, 21st Cong., 1st sess. (March 19, 1830).

[5] The principal documents are found in *American State Papers: Indian Affairs*, Vols. I and II. There are two excellent secondary works, George Dewey Harmon, *Sixty Years of Indian Affairs: Political, Economic, and Diplomatic, 1789–1850* (Chapel Hill: University of North Carolina Press, 1941); and Edgar B. Wesley, "The Government Factory System among the Indians, 1795–1822," in *Journal of Economic and Business History*, IV (1931–32), 487–511. See also Frederick J. Turner, "The Character and Influence of the Indian Trade in Wisconsin," in *Johns Hopkins University Studies in Historical and Political Science*, IX (1891), 541–615. There is a mass of valuable original material in three collections edited by Reuben Gold Thwaites, "Fur-Trade on the Upper Lakes, 1778–1815," in State Historical Society of Wisconsin, *Collections*, XIX (1910), 234–374; "The Fur-Trade in Wisconsin, 1815–1817," *ibid.*, XIX, 375–488; and "The Fur-Trade in Wisconsin, 1812–1825," *ibid.*, XX (1911), I, 1–395.

ever sharper competition. The struggle was the first major conflict between public and private enterprise, although the friends
of the government trading houses freely declared that their
system was suitable only for this special case.

The system was launched by an appropriation of $50,000 for
the purchase of goods to be sold to the Indians at places designated by the President.[6] Washington selected a spot on the St.
Marys River in Georgia, at Coleraine; and a site in East Tennessee, across the mountains, at Tellico. This tentative plan was
confirmed by law in 1796.[7] Congress authorized the President to
establish trading houses "for the purpose of carrying on a liberal trade with the several Indian nations," and directed the
appointment of an agent for each trading house who, with his
clerks, was excluded from all private trading. Congress appropriated $150,000 as a trading capital, and an annual amount of
$8,000 to pay the salaries of agents and clerks. The price of
goods was to be regulated so as not to make a profit, but to protect the capital investment. The purposes to be achieved were
multiple: to help control the native tribes, to take trade away
from the British and Spanish, to diminish their influence over
the savages, to encourage the friendship of the Indians to the
United States, and, by supplying them with good merchandise
at reasonable prices, to protect them against the greed of the
private traders.[8] The system was completed in 1806 with the
creation of the office of superintendent of Indian trade.[9]

The War of 1812 caused heavy losses. Three factories were
destroyed by the British and one by the American army to prevent its capture; over $40,000 of goods and furs were destroyed
elsewhere, and nearly $20,000 worth of debts were accumulated
by the Indians. Peace, however, ended British competition in
the fur trade, and the factories were restored.

[6] 1 Stat. 443 (March 3, 1795).

[7] 1 Stat. 452 (April 18, 1796).

[8] Harmon, *op. cit.*, p. 99. Cf. Thomas Jefferson writing in 1802: "every thing
satisfies me that the Traders are the people who disturb our peace with the
Indians, & that we can exclude them peaceably no otherwise than by an extension of our trade & underselling them." *Territorial Papers*, VII, 72 (August 30,
1802).

[9] 2 Stat. 402 (April 21, 1806); the first published report is in *American State
Papers: Indian Affairs*, I, 756 (Jan. 16, 1809).

In 1818 eight factories were in operation.[10] The general plan of business had become well established. The superintendent of Indian trade, with headquarters first at Philadelphia and later at Georgetown, sent out order blanks; the factors sent in their requisitions; the superintendent purchased the supplies and forwarded them to the factories. The factors sent their furs and peltries to the superintendent, who held public sales in the best domestic market for their disposition. A typical shipment of factory goods included such items as blankets, strouds, guns, powder, lead, axes, knives, bottles, wampum, trinkets, coffee, and food supplies. The Indians traded furs, skins, beeswax, tallow, bear oil, feathers, and other products.[11]

The end of foreign competition after 1815 was the signal for a drive by the great fur companies to destroy government competition. A campaign of misrepresentation against the factors was launched among the Indians, who were told that they were given credit as an excuse to seize their land, that the factors sold goods intended for presents, and that they stole half the presents.[12] The principal attack on the trading houses turned, however, on charges of mismanagement and incompetency. It was alleged, and later demonstrated, that the system had not been able to maintain its capital unimpaired despite the fact that no interest was charged on it, that the pay of the agents and clerks was found in a special annual appropriation, that the army helped to build the stores, and that a mark-up ranging from 50 to 68 per cent was standard practice.[13] One of Senator Benton's correspondents, an important agent of the American Fur Company named Ramsay Crooks, put the point in these terms: "I confess that, to me, it appears inexplicable how any trade can possibly fail to maintain itself, when it maintains all its means of operation, both fiscal and executive, free of every charge; and the wonder increases when we recollect that the sales are at an

10 House Doc. 25, 15th Cong., 2d sess., p. 5 (Dec. 5, 1818). There is a good historical sketch of the factory system in this report.

11 Wesley, *op. cit.*, pp. 497-99.

12 Harmon, *op. cit.*, p. 124.

13 The House Committee on Indian Affairs stated in 1824 that 68 per cent was the standard advance. House Report 129, 18th Cong., 1st sess., p. 2 (May 25, 1824).

average of forty per cent. clear gain." [14] Harmon stated that "the agents employed in the factory system were the worst foes of the experiment, for they were unacquainted with the Indians and the nature of their trade; and they received their salaries regardless of the success or failure of the system." [15]

The appointment of such a person as Joseph Varnum gave weight to this judgment, for however honest Varnum may have been, he was completely without experience. The Secretary of War described him in this passage, announcing his assignment to Chicago. "Mr Varnum has for about one year been a Clerk in my Office; he is the Son of Genl Varnum Member of Congress from Massachusetts. No young man possess' more purity of morals or integrity of Character than Mr Varnum, and I am confident he will do his duty with perfect fidelity." [16]

While there was some talk of fraud, the evidence cleared both McKenney and the factors. Crooks, whose criticism has just been quoted, added these words: "I cannot close the answer to this query without stating my conviction that the factors are every where industrious, persevering, and as much devoted to their business as any men ought to be." [17] Another critic testified: "With regard to the character of the factors, I know nothing disadvantageous." The inefficiency of the system was declared to rest upon "the wretched character of the supplies, the high prices at which they have been purchased, and the unreasonable advance which has been put upon them." [18]

There were some genuine handicaps to this government enterprise. The trading houses were at fixed points, not always the most convenient; the Indians had to come to them while the private traders went to the Indians. As already noted, heavy financial losses occurred as a consequence of the War of 1812, for

[14] *American State Papers: Indian Affairs*, II, 331 (Jan. 23, 1822). Ramsay Crooks was a noted fur trader associated with Astor. He was a man of the highest character in a business where standards were often low under fierce competition. In addition to his own standing in the fur trade, he married a member of the Chouteau family, the great fur traders of St. Louis. *Dictionary of American Biography*, IV, 565.

[15] Harmon, *op. cit.*, p. 131.

[16] *Territorial Papers*, VII, 460 (June 6, 1807).

[17] *American State Papers: Indian Affairs*, II, 331.

[18] *Ibid.*, II, 327.

which the management was in no way responsible. The fact remained, however, that the capital had not been maintained undiminished. The final reckoning showed that of $290,000 actually advanced, about $269,000 was recovered. There was apparently some laxness in disposing of furs in the eastern market. On one occasion they were kept in a cellar where a considerable portion was spoiled by moths and worms.[19] The superintendent was handicapped in his sales policy by being forbidden to sell in the foreign market.

The stoutest defender of the trading houses was Thomas L. McKenney. From 1818 to 1822 he fought for the retention of the factories and for the humane policy that he deemed implied in them. In 1820 he reminded the Senate Committee on Indian Affairs that gain was "not one of the characteristics of this system."

. . . Greater objects than such as are included in making gains out of an impoverished people were in the view of those who originated this intercourse with our Indians; nor has the time that has elapsed since its commencement diminished any of their importance. The same justice is to be consulted, the same humanity exercised, and the same political influence is to be sustained, now, as then; and the civilization and preservation of these helpless people are to be accomplished. *A well-organized commercial intercourse . . . must form the basis of all these important objects.*[20]

On the eve of the termination of the factories, McKenney warned Congress of the consequences of a free field to private traders. Granting that private capital was competent to meet all the needs of the Indians, he argued that the laws could never compel observance of either justice or humanity on the part of the traders.

. . . It is one thing to enact laws, and another to enforce their violated provisions . . . it is not so much to what the law threatens that offenders look, as to the probable chances which promise their safety from its punishment. In regions wide and wild, like those inhabited by our Indians, laws are of little more importance in regulating the conduct of the avaricious, who go there for the pur-

19 Harmon, *op. cit.*, p. 119.
20 *American State Papers: Indian Affairs*, II, 222 (Nov. 30, 1820).

pose of trade, than would be the testimony of the Indian for the security of whose person and property they might be enacted.[21]

Senator Benton proved too powerful to resist. He put forward, as he said, "a strenuous exertion" to overthrow the system.[22] Harmon concluded on the evidence that it was difficult "to escape the suspicion that Benton was serving Clark, Hempstead, Chouteau, and other influential fur dealers who were his constituents." [23] Benton collected a substantial amount of testimony against the system, much of it from interested parties but impressive in mass.[24] He put his own views in these terms, "The experience of the Indian factory system is an illustration of the unfitness of the federal government to carry on any system of trade, the liability of the benevolent designs of the government to be abused, and the difficulty of detecting and redressing abuses in the management of our Indian affairs." [25] Congress directed that the factory system should be liquidated as of June 3, 1822.[26]

The factory system fell less from its own incompetence than from the opposition of its competitors and from the underlying sentiment that government trading houses were an anomaly in a free competitive society. Congress had never been more than lukewarm in support of the policy, periodically renewing it sometimes for three years, sometimes for two, sometimes for one, and sometimes neglecting to renew and forcing the system to continue in extralegal tolerance for short periods. Some of the objects sought by the first establishment of the trading houses were achieved with the passage of time: the greater security of the frontier, the control of the fur trade against British and Spanish competition, the more certain adherence of the Indians to American rather than British policy. The objects of which

21 *Ibid.*, II, 261 (Dec. 27, 1821). For good measure he added the following passage: "For the want of a controlling power over the licentious, they riot in every sort of enormity which human depravity can contrive, and the Indians are the perpetual victims of their speculations and frauds." *Ibid.*, II, 264.

22 Benton, *Thirty Years' View*, I, 21.

23 Harmon, *Sixty Years of Indian Affairs*, p. 129.

24 Reprinted in *American State Papers: Indian Affairs*, II, 326–64.

25 Benton, *op. cit.*, I, 20–21.

26 3 Stat. 679 (May 6, 1822). For reports on the process of liquidation, see House Report 129, 18th Cong., 1st sess. (May 25, 1824); and House Doc. 61, 18th Cong., 2d sess. (Oct. 25, 1824).

McKenney made so much, the protection of the Indians against the rapacity of the traders and their more rapid civilization, were not achieved, but some denied that the factories were either necessary or useful to these ends.

The contemporary judgment of Calhoun concerning the factory system was temperate and balanced.

. . . It was commenced, and has been continued from motives both of prudence and humanity; and though it may not have fully realized the expectations of its friends, it has no doubt produced beneficial effects. If wars have not been entirely prevented by it, they, probably without it, would have been more frequent; and, if the Indians have made but little advances in civilization, they probably without it, would have made less.[27]

THE CIVILIZATION OF THE INDIANS

As the fear of Indian wars receded, the long-range problem of the relation of Indians to the white population and to the government emerged. Some would have taken the view that the white men had no responsibility, that the westward movement of the Indians to the unknown mountains and deserts beyond the Mississippi should be pressed forward relentlessly, and that the ultimate extinction of the race was to be contemplated with equanimity.[28] This was never the view of most responsible statesmen, but they were deeply perplexed to find a course of action that would combine justice and humanity with the evident destiny of white predominance through the length and breadth of the country.

Secretary of War Crawford expressed the general philosophy of public policy toward the Indians.

. . . it is the true policy and earnest desire of the Government to draw its savage neighbors within the pale of civilization. If I am mistaken in this point—if the primary object of the Government is to extinguish the Indian title, and settle their lands as rapidly as possible, then commerce with them ought to be entirely abandoned to individual enterprise, and without regulation. The result would be continual warfare, attended by the extermination or expulsion

[27] House Doc. 25, 15th Cong., 2d sess., p. 5 (Dec. 8, 1818).
[28] Henry Clay was one who privately held this view; see Adams, *Memoirs*, VII, 90 (Dec. 22, 1825).

of the aboriginal inhabitants of the country to more distant and less hospitable regions. The correctness of this policy cannot for a moment be admitted. The utter extinction of the Indian race must be abhorrent to the feelings of an enlightened and benevolent nation. The idea is directly opposed to every act of the Government, from the declaration of independence to the present day.[29]

Congress had inaugurated the policy of cultivating the Indians in 1793 when it authorized the President, "in order to promote civilization among the friendly Indian tribes, and to secure the continuance of their friendship," to furnish them useful domestic animals and implements of husbandry, and with goods or money as he might deem proper.[30] The Republicans reenacted this policy in 1802, and the annual giving of presents continued.[31] The motive was less to civilize the red man than to cultivate his friendship.

The first clear intent to civilize the Indians appeared in 1819. Congress then made available $10,000 annually "for the purpose of providing against the further decline and final extinction of the Indian tribes . . . and for introducing among them the habits and arts of civilization." [32] These ends were to be sought through education. The President was authorized to employ "capable persons of good moral character" to instruct the Indians, with their consent, in agriculture, and to teach their children reading, writing, and arithmetic. Monroe applied the money by making grants to benevolent associations or individuals who were prepared to devote themselves to this task. Calhoun circularized interested persons and groups, suggesting in addition to the three R's practical agriculture and mechanics for the Indian boys, and spinning, weaving, and sewing for the girls. He offered aid both in erecting school buildings and in current expenses.[33]

The program was well under way in 1822. There were then in operation eleven principal schools and three subordinate ones, with three more in preparation. The number of scholars

---

29 *American State Papers: Indian Affairs*, II, 28 (March 13, 1816). Calhoun even went so far as to suggest intermarriage if other means of assimilation failed.

30 1 Stat. 329 (March 1, 1793).

31 2 Stat. 139 (March 30, 1802).

32 3 Stat. 516 (March 3, 1819).

33 House Doc. 46, 16th Cong., 1st sess., p. 4 (Sept. 3, 1819).

was 508. Something over $7,000 had been expended on buildings, and over $8,000 on tuition.[34] The Cherokees had been particularly receptive. By 1824 thirty-two schools were in operation, with 916 children in attendance. McKenney, then head of the office of Indian affairs, optimistically declared that "an entire reformation may be effected . . . in the course of the present generation." [35] Calhoun was less confident, but he was looking farther ahead than McKenney.

Congress maintained the policy of civilizing the Indians through education, at the rate of $10,000 a year. It also maintained the policy of westward migration and of commerce by private traders with little governmental control. The result was not conducive to the integration of a savage culture with that of its dispossessors. James Barbour had a plan, too, for the happiness of the Indians, and their civilization; but he closed its presentation with the somber words that if these efforts "should even fail, by the overruling influence of an inscrutable destiny whose fulfilment requires their extinction, however it may fill us with sorrow, we shall be relieved from remorse." [36]

THE MANAGEMENT OF INDIAN AFFAIRS

The Federalists had placed responsibility for Indian matters in the War Department, an inevitable decision when border raids and open warfare were the principal problems. Out in the Indian country, two sets of authorities disputed with each other, although both were subordinate to the War Department. One was civilian, and comprised the territorial governors, ex officio superintendents of Indian affairs, the Indian agents subordinate to them, and the factors and their small staffs. The second authority was military and comprised the commandants of the scattered garrisons and posts throughout the western country. The latter tended to aggress on the former despite the division

[34] House Doc. 59, 17th Cong., 1st sess., p. 5 (Feb. 8, 1822).

[35] Senate Doc. 1, 18th Cong., 2d sess., p. 107 (Nov. 24, 1824). In view of what had happened to the public trading houses Calhoun thought it prudent to tell Congress in 1822 that no teachers or agriculturalists had been employed by the War Department in connection with the program of education. House Doc. 110, 17th Cong., 1st sess., p. 3 (April 11, 1822).

[36] *American State Papers: Indian Affairs*, II, 647–49 (Feb. 3, 1826). For Calhoun's views on Indian policy, see Wiltse, *John C. Calhoun: Nationalist*, pp. 168–70.

of responsibility established by Hamilton and McHenry in 1799.[37] The Jeffersonians continued responsibility in the War Department, and continued to divide it in the field between military commanders and Indian superintendents, although the authority of the civilian officers tended gradually to increase.

In due course of time the War Department established two separate civilian offices for the two distinct phases of its responsibilities, broadly conceived as control and trade respectively. The first, originating at the outset of Washington's administration, was the so-called Indian department to which substantial appropriations had been regularly made.[38] In 1824 Calhoun designated this office the Bureau of Indian Affairs, and defined its duties under five heads: to handle the Indian annuities; to give first review of the accounts and vouchers showing expenditures; to administer the fund for the civilization of the Indians; to examine claims arising out of intercourse with the tribes; and to carry on the ordinary correspondence with the superintendents of Indian affairs (i.e., the territorial governors) and agents.[39]

The bureau was established by mere departmental direction of the Secretary of War, and when it was discovered in 1826 by John Cocke, chairman of the House Committee on Indian Affairs, the transaction called forth a somewhat arrogant inquiry: "you mention a Bureau where the affairs of the Government with the several Indian tribes appear to be transacted—they have searched in vain for the law establishing that office. . . . The Committee have directed me to inquire when, and by what law, the said Bureau is authorized. . . ."[40] The title of bureau was discreetly dropped for the moment in deference to the sentiments of the chairman of the House committee but had reappeared in 1828.[41]

---

37 White, *The Federalists*, pp. 375–80. For evidence of later difficulties see by way of example, *Territorial Papers*, X, 509 (Feb. 17, 1815), and *ibid.*, X, 597 (Sept. 27, 1815).

38 See Senate Doc. 15, 16th Cong., 2d sess. for appropriations and expenditures on account of the Indian department, 1789–1819.

39 Instruction of March 11, 1824, printed in House Doc. 146, 19th Cong., 1st sess., p. 6 (March 21, 1826).

40 House Doc. 146, 19th Cong., 1st sess., p. 3 (March 21, 1826).

41 See *Territorial Papers*, XI, 1195.

The second civilian office dealing with Indian affairs was that of superintendent of Indian trade, noted in the preceding pages. He reported directly to the Secretary of War and was not responsible to the superintendents of Indian affairs in the field. In 1822 Calhoun recommended that the office be subordinated to the Indian department,[42] but the liquidation of the factory system solved the problem by abolishing the office of Indian trade. Thenceforward all Indian business went through the office (or bureau) of Indian affairs.

The field service of the Indian office comprised the superintendents of Indian affairs, the agents and subagents, and a number of employees such as interpreters, blacksmiths, and other artisans. The educational staff for the civilization of the Indians was retained in a private capacity by the benevolent associations that received grants. From a statement presented in 1822 the size and variety of the field service can be stated with precision.[43]

Three territorial governors were ex officio superintendents of Indian affairs, Lewis Cass of Michigan, James Miller of Arkansas, and William Clark of Missouri, recently become a state. The hazards in the life of a territorial governor discharging his duties as Indian superintendent were sometimes considerable. Lewis Cass asked for a sentinel at his quarters:

. . . at Detroit my situation is at all times very unpleasant and sometimes very unsafe. Surrounded by drunken lawless Indians, doubtful friends and secret enemies, without any physical force at my disposal, and breaking in upon me at all hours of the day; their conduct and demands may easily be conceived. It is a literal fact, that I have been compelled, more than twenty times to hide myself, to avoid their importunities.[44]

There were seventeen Indian agents, appointed by the President at salaries ranging from $1,200 to $1,800 a year. They included some well-known names, such as Return J. Meigs, father of the Postmaster General, and Benjamin O'Fallon, a frontier figure of wide renown. There were also twenty-five subagents, a number of them acting as interpreters, usually appointed by the Secretary of War but occasionally by a superintendent or an

42 House Doc. 146, 19th Cong., 1st sess., p. 12.
43 House Doc. 110, 17th Cong., 1st sess. (April 8, 1822).
44 *Territorial Papers*, X, 510 (Feb. 17, 1815).

agent. In addition there were thirty-four interpreters, appointed either by the superintendents or agents with the approval of the War Department. Twenty-one blacksmiths were employed for the benefit of various tribes, often in accordance with treaty stipulations. The total pay roll amounted to over $67,000. Agents and subagents were responsible in principle to the Indian superintendents and through them to the Department of War.

The volume of Indian business was great. Crawford complained about it in 1816, and in 1828 Peter B. Porter, for a short time Secretary of War, repeated Crawford's views.

In the few weeks that have elapsed since I had the honor to be called to this Department, I have found no portion of its extensive and complicated duties so perplexing, and the performance of which has been less welcome, than those which appertain to the Bureau of Indian Affairs. Scarcely a day passes when there is not a call upon the head of the Department, if not on the President himself, to pass upon some controverted principle or doubtful evidence in the settlement of an account. . . .

These difficulties . . . are, evidently, the effects of the want of a well digested system of principles and rules for the administration of our Indian concerns.[45]

Calhoun had tried to relieve himself of the burden by proposing to transfer the work to the new Home Department, jointly recommended in the 1816 Report of the Four Secretaries. His successor, James Barbour, tried another solution by supporting McKenney's recommendation in favor of delegating authority by law to the office of Indian affairs. Neither plan was successful.

The management of Indian affairs by the end of the Jeffersonian period had thus become an enterprise of considerable magnitude and much perplexity. Trading policy had been reversed, military policy had declined in importance, treaty negotiations for land cession were frequent, and almost no one felt either satisfied or confident with regard to the future of the native tribes. The War Department was involved in modest expenditures to civilize them, but the heavy costs of the Indian office went for annuities, presents, and the maintenance of a far-

[45] *Ibid.*, XI, 1194 (July 28, 1828).

flung establishment, one of whose duties was to license traders, without possessing means to control them.

TWO INDIAN AGENTS

Two figures stand out in the little world of Indian affairs, Henry Rowe Schoolcraft and Thomas L. McKenney. Schoolcraft was one of the earliest American ethnologists. Born in Albany County, New York, in 1793, his life spanned the years from George Washington to Abraham Lincoln (1864). His first explorations took him to the mineral regions of Missouri and Arkansas in 1817–1818 and resulted in a report published in 1819 with the title, *A View of the Lead Mines of Missouri.* In 1820 he accompanied an expedition to the upper Mississippi and the Lake Superior copper region. Here he made an intimate acquaintance with the Indians, and in 1822 he was appointed Indian agent for the tribes of Lake Superior, serving as such for almost twenty years. In 1823 he married a quarter-blood Chippewa girl. For the rest of his life he was engaged in administrative and scholarly work concerned with Indian life. He became superintendent of Indian affairs for Michigan in 1836 and served in the Indian department until 1841. One of the founders of the Historical Society of Michigan in 1828, he published many literary and some scientific works in his special field.[46] He was one of the early Americans with a scholarly reputation who found a career in the public service.

Thomas Loraine McKenney was born in Maryland in 1785 and died in 1859. After completing his schooling he entered commercial life and settled in Washington and Georgetown. His business ventures were interrupted by the War of 1812 in which he served as adjutant to militia companies. Madison appointed him superintendent of Indian trade in 1816, a post that he occupied until its termination in 1822. He had high ideals of business rectitude, but was indiscreet in permitting a merchant from whom he bought large quantities of goods for the Indian

---

[46] *Dictionary of American Biography,* XVI, 456–57. A complete bibliography of his writings is contained in Chase S. Osborn and Stellanova Osborn, *Schoolcraft, Longfellow, Hiawatha* (Lancaster, Penn.: Jacques Cattell, 1942), pp. 624–53. Schoolcraft's book, *The Myth of Hiawatha* (Philadelphia: J. B. Lippincott, 1856), provided the source material for Longfellow's *Hiawatha.*

trade to endorse his notes.[47] He also had high ideals of public service. He found in the office of Indian trade clerks "whose integrity and experience made them of great value," and without a thought of replacement continued them in office. "To dismiss from office, in those days, without cause," he declared, "would have been deemed an outrage, not less against the public interests, than the party proscribed. Hence, competency, zeal, and honesty, being the characteristics of the clerks I found in the office of Indian trade, when I succeeded to its management, it no more occurred to me to turn them out, than it did to cut their throats."[48]

McKenney had a shrewd sense of the need of a public officer for self-protection, and carefully locked in his own safe a triplicate copy of every voucher. The auditor later refused to clear McKenney's accounts for lack of vouchers, which had mysteriously disappeared. McKenney was able to clear his accounts completely with the triplicate set; but it was obvious that he believed, possibly with justice, that skulduggery lurked in the office of the auditor. He refused to allow the triplicate vouchers to pass out of his clerk's hands except as, one by one, they were accepted by the auditor.

After a brief interval following the liquidation of the trading houses Monroe appointed him superintendent of the bureau of Indian affairs, where he worked until removed by Jackson. McKenney, too, had a taste for writing. In 1827 he published *Sketches of a Tour to the Lakes,* material for which came to hand in connection with an Indian treaty that he negotiated with Lewis Cass. His *Memoirs,* written toward the end of his life, revealed a personality tending toward hero worship of his favorites, including John Jacob Astor, Monroe, and Adams, and abuse of his aversions, of whom Andrew Jackson was perhaps the principal.

The good will of the general government toward its Indian wards during the early Jeffersonian period was repeated in one official document after another. The instructions to Silas Dinsmoor, agent to the Choctaw nation, recited that the motives of the government were the cultivation of peace and harmony and

47 *Dictionary of American Biography,* XII, 89–90.
48 McKenney, *Memoirs,* I, 22, 24.

the introduction of husbandry and domestic manufactures. Dins-moor was urged to encourage the use of the plow and the cultivation of cotton and grain, and was directed to discourage the use of spirituous liquors by precept and example.[49] Nicolas Boilvin, setting out for the villages of the Sac Indians, was instructed to conciliate the friendship of the Indians, to procure garden seeds, apple seeds, and peach stones, to organize a garden, and to encourage the cultivation of potatoes.[50] Young Varnum was urged to let every transaction with the Indians be so conducted as to inspire them with full confidence in the honor, integrity, and good faith of the government.[51]

These evidences of good will, honored by many agents and factors, were overbalanced by events that the government could not control. The traders, once licensed, were disregardful of rules seeking to protect the natives. The lead miners along the Mississippi paid little attention to trespass on Indian lands. The settlers pressed upon the heels of the westward moving red men and gave them no peace. Army officers were not usually tender of Indian rights. And the Indians themselves gave plenty of provocation for the disregard of the good intentions of the Great White Father. Adverse circumstances defeated the hope of absorbing the native population into an advanced European culture.

[49] *Territorial Papers*, V, 146 (May 8, 1802).
[50] Thwaites, "Fur-Trade on the Upper Lakes," *op. cit.*, pp. 315–16 (April 10, 1806).
[51] *Ibid.*, p. 327 (Sept. 9, 1808).

CHAPTER THIRTY-THREE

Disposition of the Public Lands

One of the most complicated administrative jobs that the general government had to undertake was to survey and sell the public lands. A system had been set up by the Federalists in 1796 which experience proved to be sound. Its smooth and efficient operation was handicapped by congressional parsimony and by the impetuous advance of settlers who were not disposed to wait on the orderly procedure of government acquisition of Indian titles, survey, and official sale. The land office was always behind the event, but the system remained substantially intact from 1796 to the end of the Republican period.

The operation was an immense one. By 1826 the general government had acquired since its organization, free from all Indian claims, over 261,000,000 acres of land.[1] Other millions still lay beyond the frontier. The original Northwest Territory had been doubled by the lands south of the Ohio, and both of these more than doubled by the Louisiana Purchase and the acquisition of Florida. Never before in all recorded history had there been a task of surveying, recording, and selling real estate on such an imperial scale.

LAND POLICY

Early land policy had been dominated by expectation of substantial revenue, but Federalist experience had demonstrated that funds from land sales were both unreliable and inadequate.[2]

---

[1] *American State Papers: Public Lands,* IV, 912.

[2] There is a considerable and valuable body of writing on land policy, giving some attention to administrative problems. See Payson Jackson Treat, *The National Land System, 1785–1820* (New York: E. B. Treat, 1910); Milton Con-

To increase volume the act of 1796 introduced a credit system by which the purchaser paid down only 5 per cent, with a year's credit (later extended to five years) for the remainder.[3] By 1804 over $1,000,000 was due the government on postponed payments on the part of nearly 2,000 purchasers, and Gallatin feared grave difficulty in collection.[4]

By 1820 the amount due the government was well over $21,-000,000 and Gallatin's recommendations were finally adopted by Congress.[5] On and after July 1, 1820, sales were allowed for cash only; the minimum price was reduced from $2.00 to $1.25 per acre, and tracts as small as eighty acres were offered to purchasers.[6] This important change in policy was due both to alarm over the amount of outstanding credit and to a desire to facilitate settlement by persons expecting to cultivate the soil and establish a permanent residence.

From 1787 to 1825 inclusive, about nineteen millions of acres had been sold to individuals.[7] While this was a remarkable achievement, it failed to satisfy the people pouring into the Mississippi Valley. They complained bitterly about the lack of progress in opening up their country.[8] Administrative problems were involved: the surveys were slow; procedure in clearing old claims was tedious; and no land could be purchased below the statutory figure of $2.00, later $1.25 an acre, a requirement that caused only the best land to be bought. There were also strong political overtones in the complaints of the West, reflected in a

---

over, *The General Land Office* (Baltimore: Johns Hopkins Press, 1923); Benjamin Horace Hibbard, *A History of the Public Land Policies* (New York: Macmillan, 1924); Roy M. Robbins, *Our Landed Heritage: the Public Domain, 1776–1936* (Princeton: Princeton University Press, 1942).

[3] 1 Stat. 464, sec. 7 (May 18, 1796).

[4] *American State Papers: Public Lands,* I, 183 (Jan. 2, 1804).

[5] For an account of the steps taken to facilitate collection of this sum, see Treat, *op. cit.,* ch. 6.

[6] 3 Stat. 566 (April 24, 1820). Treat comments on policy prior to 1820 in these words, "If the land system had developed toward a reduction in the size of the tracts and toward concessions in favor of the actual settler, a great amount of bad business and cheap politics might have been saved." *Op. cit.,* p. 141.

[7] *American State Papers: Public Lands,* IV, 909 (Feb. 14, 1827). Net sales, including credit extended, amounted to slightly over $40,000,000.

[8] Senator Benton assailed the whole policy of sale, Thomas Hart Benton, *Thirty Years' View,* I, 102–7.

report of the House Committee on Public Lands that spoke of "the anomaly of the exercise, on the part of a powerful Government of sovereignty in fact, over about twelve-thirteenths of the whole territory of seven States, declared to be sovereign and independent by treaties, compacts, and constitutions of Government." [9]

In the disposition of the public lands it had been the traditional policy of the government to reserve the mineral lands, and to lease rights of exploitation. [10] The major problem arose with regard to the lead mines near Potosi, in the Territory of Missouri, viz., to prevent unauthorized working of the mines, and to secure the payment of 10 per cent of the output, under the standard terms of lease. The leasing provision had long been ineffectual. The interests of the government suffered also because the only lands reserved were those noted by the surveyor on his survey line; any lands not falling under his eye were left open for acquisition by private parties. Intruders, more resourceful than law-abiding, harassed proper leaseholders with vexatious lawsuits.

In 1821 the supervision of the lead mines was turned over to the War Department. Colonel George Bomford of the ordnance department sent out an able and enterprising young officer, Martin Thomas, to serve as government agent. Lieutenant Thomas arrived early in 1825 and discovered much confusion and little attention to what he called "the true interests of the Government." "Any system . . . would be preferable to the present uncertainty. The losses of the Government, by trespassers on the mine lands, has been enormous, and to a person unacquainted with the country, almost incredible." [11] He set about dispossessing "a large population having had undisturbed possession of all the public mines for a number of years," not an

9 House Report 125, 20th Cong., 1st sess., p. 2 (Feb. 5, 1828). Of 16 million acres in Indiana, 12 million remained unsold in 1826; of 29 million acres in Illinois, 24 million were unsold. For these and other figures, see *American State Papers: Public Lands*, IV, 912 ff.

10 Act of May 20, 1785, reserving one-third part of all gold, silver, lead, and copper mines; 2 Stat. 440, sec. 4 (March 3, 1807), reserving lead mines and salt springs; and 2 Stat. 445, sec. 2 (March 3, 1807), authorizing leases for a term not over three years.

11 Senate Doc. 38, 19th Cong., 1st sess., p. 17 (Jan. 21, 1825).

easy matter which at the end of a year was still in process. His trouble came, as he put it, from "the most worthless and abandoned part of the community . . . equally disposed to plunder the private, as public mines." [12] He proposed a new form of lease to encourage the concentration of smelting establishments in the interest of greater efficiency.[13] Colonel Bomford approved with the hopeful notation: "And, if practicable, such men only should be employed as are of good character, and from whom the government would be likely to meet with the least trouble and difficulty." [14] Despite Thomas' industry and ability, which were the object of a special commendation, he was defeated by the unsatisfactory system of leasing and by the discovery of much richer deposits of lead on the upper Mississippi. In 1827 he recommended that the Missouri mines be sold,[15] and in 1829 Congress gave the necessary authority.[16]

SETTLEMENT OF PRIVATE LAND CLAIMS

When the United States acquired title to lands across the Alleghenies by the Treaty of Peace with Great Britain, by the Louisiana Purchase in 1803, and by the acquisition of Florida in 1819, it secured sovereignty over areas in which private ownership had already been established at scattered points. Such ownership was, of course, recognized by the new sovereign when properly validated, and these lands were excluded from public sales.

Unfortunately neither France nor Spain had well-established procedures for making private land grants, and British titles in the Northwest Territory were often incomplete, transfers of ownership were often not recorded, and claims often rested merely on the fact of settlement. It became, therefore, a complicated problem to determine what land was "public land," quite apart from the fraudulent claims that multiplied on every side. It was essential to protect bona fide grants by previous

[12] Senate Doc. 45, 19th Cong., 1st sess., p. 7 (Feb. 18, 1826).
[13] Senate Doc. 38, 19th Cong., 1st sess., p. 15.
[14] *Ibid.*, p. 16.
[15] House Doc. 45, 20th Cong., 1st sess. (Sept. 30, 1827).
[16] 4 Stat. 364 (March 3, 1829).

governments under a loose and careless system, while defeating fraudulent speculators.

Two courses of action might have been suggested. One would have referred the validation of all doubtful prior claims to the courts for judicial determination. This plan was subject to serious objections. The judicial system in the territories was imperfectly organized and would have been overwhelmed with the volume of business, to say nothing of the inconvenience to claimants. Furthermore judicial process was slow and speed was essential, for until the private claims were cleared up, the land could not be opened for sale.

Congress therefore turned to the alternative course, administrative adjudication, subject in many instances to final congressional action.[17] The procedure established for clearing titles in the land south of Tennessee provides a satisfactory example.[18] Persons resident in Mississippi on October 27, 1795, holding a grant, not complete, from either the British or Spanish governments; persons occupying land in Mississippi in 1797; and persons occupying land on the date of the act of 1803 were confirmed in their titles, or in the latter case given a preference as purchasers. Two commissions were established to hear and adjudicate claims under these provisions, each consisting of the register of the land office and two persons appointed by the President. The boards were given authority to hear and decide in a summary manner all matters respecting claims and "to determine thereon according to justice and equity." Their decision was final.[19] By a subsequent act of 1804 the summary powers were discontinued, and the commissioners were directed to transmit to Congress for final action all claims disallowed on suspicion of fraud. The Secretary of the Treasury was authorized to appoint an agent to investigate claims brought to the commissioners and to oppose all that seemed to him fraudulent or unfounded.[20]

In view of the state of the records of land ownership it was

17 For a detailed account of procedure in the Northwest Territory, see Treat, *National Land System*, ch. 9.

18 2 Stat. 229 (March 3, 1803). For a different system effective in Indiana Territory, see 2 Stat. 277 (March 26, 1804).

19 2 Stat. 229, sec. 6.

20 2 Stat. 303, secs. 3, 4 (March 27, 1804).

impossible for Congress to provide a more definite rule for adjudication than that of "justice and equity." After twenty years' experience the House Committee on Public Lands recorded its conviction that, "In all legislation, much must necessarily be left to construction, and the sound discretion of those charged with the administration of the laws." [21]

Preference for administrative determination was strongly stated in 1828 by the Senate Committee on Private Land Claims.

. . . in the opinion of the Committee, a special tribunal . . . liberally compensated and judiciously selected, so as to ensure the requisite integrity, talents, and industry, for the faithful, intelligent, and prompt discharge of its duties, holding its sessions in the City of Washington, where access can be had to the public records and where competent agents can be most easily obtained to represent the rights of the respective claimants . . . will most effectually advance the purposes of justice, and will best promote the interests of the public, while it will effectually protect the just rights of the claimants.[22]

Administrative agencies similar to that set up south of Tennessee were established in other regions. The validation of titles in Florida was especially difficult. Congress took an active part in final disposition, on the basis of findings made by the boards, and generally proved to be more lenient than their agents.[23] The task was a wearing one. Robbins concluded, "Without doubt the adjustment of foreign titles was one of the most complicated administrative problems which the government of the United States has ever encountered." [24]

ADMINISTRATIVE ORGANIZATION FOR THE SALE OF LANDS

The organic land act of 1796 provided for the survey of the public domain, for the continuation of the six-mile square township and the 640 acre section, for the method of sale and of payment by the purchaser, and for the grant of title by land patent signed by the President and countersigned by the Secre-

[21] House Report 130, 18th Cong., 1st sess. (May 26, 1824).
[22] Senate Doc. 22, 20th Cong., 1st sess., p. 5 (Jan. 9, 1828).
[23] Treat, *op. cit.*, p. 228.
[24] Robbins, *Our Landed Heritage*, p. 24.

tary of State.[25] Surveying began under the first surveyor general, Rufus Putnam; sales of sections were authorized at Pittsburgh and Cincinnati, all under the general direction of the Treasury Department. The Land Act of 1800 perfected the administrative machinery for sales by establishing local land offices, four of which were authorized within the limits of what was soon to become the state of Ohio.[26]

General Land Office. Business soon reached a volume that required a more elaborate Treasury organization at headquarters than had hitherto prevailed, limited as it had been to the designation of a clerk to be responsible for the land transactions. The General Land Office was established in 1812 to consolidate functions formerly performed by the Secretary and the register of the Treasury, the Secretary of State, and the Secretary of War.[27] The commissioner of the General Land Office was placed in charge of all land matters under the general direction of the Secretary of the Treasury. Pressure of business had thus imposed the rule of single responsibility in place of the checks and balances provided by the Federalists in 1796.

The importance of the office was attested by the character and experience of its incumbents. Madison appointed Edward Tiffin, president of the Ohio Constitutional Convention, twice governor of Ohio, and United States Senator. He remained in the office only two years (1812–14) when he exchanged places with Josiah Meigs, then surveyor general stationed in Cincinnati. Tiffin held this field office until 1829, dying shortly after his removal by President Jackson.[28]

His successor, Josiah Meigs, was a colorful character, one of the first to combine an academic and a public service career. Meigs was a Connecticut Yankee, Yale 1778, who returned to his

25 1 Stat. 464 (May 18, 1796). The Treasury circulars and instructions, including the basic instructions of 1796, are listed and summarized in Robert Mayo, *A Synopsis of the Commercial and Revenue System of the United States . . .* (Washington: J. and G. S. Gideon, 1847), ch. 8.

26 2 Stat. 73 (May 10, 1800).

27 2 Stat. 716 (April 25, 1812).

28 William Edward Gilmore, *Life of Edward Tiffin, First Governor of Ohio* (Chillicothe: Horney and Son, 1897); *Dictionary of American Biography,* XVIII, 535–36.

alma mater in 1781 as tutor. He was admitted to the bar in
1783 and in 1784 became the first city clerk of New Haven, an
office that he held for five years. In the same year he resigned his
appointment at Yale and began publication of a Federalist
weekly, *The New Haven Gazette,* a journal that expired in
1788. From 1789 to 1794, he was in Bermuda representing Connecticut clients in claims cases. His quick temper and outspoken
tongue eventually got him into trouble, and he returned to
Yale as professor of mathematics and natural philosophy. He
had now become an ardent Jeffersonian and the climate both of
Yale and New Haven was more than unpleasant. He "went into
exile" by moving to Georgia where he became president of
Franklin College, but after some early success his temper diminished his usefulness. He withdrew to a professorship and within
a year was discharged for criticizing the college trustees. At this
point (1812) he became surveyor general of the territory north
of the Ohio and in 1814 commissioner of the General Land Office. He held this post until his death in 1822. His interest in
the academic world did not lessen; he served as president of the
Columbian Institute in Washington from 1819 to 1822 and was
one of the first trustees of Columbia College, now George Washington University. His daughter married John Forsyth, Secretary of State under Jackson and Van Buren.[29] His nephew, Return Jonathan Meigs, only seven years his junior, was Postmaster General.[30]

Meigs' successor, George Graham, a member of the Brent
clan, belonged to the rising official class. A graduate of Columbia (1790) and a practicing lawyer, he became commander of
the Fairfax Light Horse in the War of 1812, and in 1813 chief
clerk of the War Department, an office he held for a decade. In
1823 he became the third incumbent of the General Land Office,
a position he held until his death in 1830.[31] It took him three
years' hard work to bring arrearages up to date, but in 1826 he
was current with the surveyors and land offices except in Mississippi and Louisiana.

29 William M. Meigs, *Life of Josiah Meigs* (Philadelphia, 1887); *Dictionary of
American Biography,* XII, 506–7.
30 See ch. 21.
31 *Lamb's Biographical Dictionary of the United States,* III, 348.

The General Land Office was in large measure a clerical office. In 1826 Graham declared that he could manage with "seventeen competent Clerks, seven of those being good and efficient Book Keepers. . . ."[32] Six clerks were employed in making out and recording land patents, copying, and indexing. The nature of the business appeared in its normal routine. The surveyors' township plats were recorded in the field office of the surveyor general and a copy sent to the General Land Office. This office thereupon gave public notice of the time of sale. The highest bidder, after depositing 5 per cent of the purchase price, received a certificate, and upon final payment a patent. The clerks of the General Land Office kept a record of all such certificates, price of sale, partial and subsequent payments, and eventually they made out and delivered the patent to the purchaser. In financial matters the General Land Office occupied a unique position since it settled the accounts of the land offices on its own responsibility and reported its settlements directly to the comptroller without the preliminary inspection of an auditor.[33]

Survey. The task of surveying was committed to a surveyor general, who in 1826 was in direct personal charge of the surveys in Ohio, Indiana, and Michigan. He also had broad supervision of four surveyors, one, south of Tennessee; one in Illinois, Missouri, and Arkansas; one in Alabama; and one in Florida. There was a vacancy in the office of surveyor of Mississippi and Louisiana.[34] Each of these appointed deputy surveyors for particular assignments, and each was allowed one clerk. The duties of this staff were strictly limited to making the survey and preparing plats.

Land offices. The principal field agency was the land office, of which there were thirty-nine in 1824, including six across the Mississippi.[35] Each office was in charge of a register, who in a way was the central figure in the whole organization. The register was "the public broker for the sale of lands," with whom all and sundry seeking property for settlement or speculation had

32 Senate Doc. 1, 19th Cong., 2d sess., Part IV, p. 139 (Dec. 1, 1826).
33 2 Stat. 716, sec. 9 (April 25, 1812).
34 House Doc. 55, 19th Cong., 2d sess., pp. 5-8 (Jan. 16, 1827).
35 House Doc. 46, 18th Cong., 2d sess. (Nov. 12, 1824).

to deal. The importance of the office was suggested by the congressional ceiling on its compensation, set at $3,000 as the equivalent in terms of cost of living of the $5,000 maximum fixed for collectors of customs.[36] In each land office there was also a fiscal agent, the receiver of public money. He, too, was an important figure as indicated by his salary ceiling of $3,000.[37] From his salary, however, he had to pay office rent and such clerk hire as he found necessary.[38]

The work of registers and receivers was technical in character and required an accurate understanding of law, regulations, instructions, and practice.[39] Few of them entered upon their duties with any preparation. They learned the job as they exercised their duties, tutored by a clerk, by their immediate associate, register or receiver as the case might be, and by the persons with whom they did business.

There is some indication that land offices were becoming politically important to the Congressmen in whose districts they were located. In 1827 John Quincy Adams complained about reading a multitude of letters "about the removal of a land-office from Delaware to Tiffin, in the State of Ohio—a distracting question of state, upon which perhaps depend the political standing and election of two or three members of Congress." [40]

The administrative system for the sale of public land thus fell into three parts: the General Land Office in Washington which was the central directing agency; the surveying staff in the field; and the local land offices extending farther and farther westward across the prairies. The relation of the surveyors to the General Land Office was obscure and at times inharmonious. It was not until 1836 that they were definitely subordinated to the land commissioner.[41] The land offices were always inferior posts, receiving instructions from Washington. They were sub-

---

[36] 3 Stat. 466 (April 20, 1818); House Doc. 142, 15th Cong., 1st sess. (Feb. 17, 1818).

[37] 3 Stat. 466.

[38] MS. in National Archives, General Land Office, Miscellaneous Letters, VIII, 511 (March 22, 1819).

[39] For a dramatic account of the troubles of the land office at St. Helena, Louisiana, see *American State Papers: Public Lands*, III, 631.

[40] Adams, *Memoirs*, VII, 220–21 (Feb. 4, 1827).

[41] 5 Stat. 107 (July 4, 1836).

ject to regular annual inspection, so far as known the first established element of the civilian inspectional system of the general government.

From the point of view of administration, the chief interest of the land office organization lay in the adjudication procedures just described and in the arrangements for central inspection of land offices. The system of inspection originated in 1804 when Congress directed the Secretary of the Treasury to cause "the books of the officers of the land-offices to be examined," and their balances ascertained once a year.[42] At first inspection was carried out by persons selected by the Treasury Department who resided in the vicinity of the land offices.[43] The results were purely formal. The examiners were generally the friends and neighbors of the officers whose books were under inspection, and often unacquainted with the form of accounts. If the person designated was unable to act, he was asked to name a proper person in his place. Secretary Crawford later reported that the annual examination was made in compliance with the injunctions of the law, rather than from "a conviction that the information obtained was of any intrinsic value to the public service."

In 1816 Secretary Dallas directed that the land offices in Ohio and further west should be examined by one of the clerks in the General Land Office, Nicholas B. Van Zandt. His printed instructions were presumably the same that had been sent earlier to local examiners.[44] He was directed to examine the book of entries to ascertain that no blank spaces had been left between entries, and that no blotter (i.e., a temporary daybook) had been used. He was not expected to make a very minute examination of the journal and ledger; it was sufficient to examine "whether

[42] 2 Stat. 277, sec. 14 (March 26, 1804); instructions to the land agents for what was probably the first inspection are found in a volume in the National Archives entitled Secretary of the Treasury, Miscellaneous Letters Sent, Public Lands, I, 360–61. They enjoined the agents to afford every facility to the examiner.

[43] *American State Papers: Public Lands,* III, 511–14. This document includes the names of all inspectors from 1805 to 1817 inclusive.

[44] A copy dated June 5, 1816, is preserved in the records of the General Land Office, Miscellaneous Letters, VI, 619.

they have the appearance of fairness and regularity," and to ascertain whether they were up to date. He was directed to count the money in hand and see whether it agreed with the books. Two or three days were thought adequate in ordinary cases. Van Zandt received his instructions on June 5, 1816, and on August 17 was back again in Washington.

His report was transmitted to the Secretary of the Treasury,[45] but Land Commissioner Meigs began sending out letters of instruction and correction without delay. A circular ordered all registers and receivers to report on the status of the posting of their books.[46] Nicholas Gray was warned not to keep a rough book of entries, since the act of May 10, 1800, prohibiting blank spaces would be "nugatory if a blotter is kept." [47] Jesse Spencer, register at Chillicothe, was admonished by the General Land Office, which had just learned that his books had never been balanced.[48] Symmes and Findlay at Cincinnati read a short letter from the General Land Office in these words:

The report of the Gentleman who was appointed to examine your books, states, that the posting, is considerably in arrears; this report must go to the Secretary of the Treasury: I recommend that you have the books posted forthwith, & that you advise me as soon as this is done.[49]

Special examinations of particular offices followed this first inspection from headquarters, John Crumbacker of Wooster, Ohio, examined the land office at that place.[50] Governor David Holmes of the Mississippi Territory was asked to investigate complaints of the land office at Washington and to report "whether the business of the Land Office is conducted so as to give *general* satisfaction—to give *universal* satisfaction is the fortunate lot of but few public Officers." [51] The collector and district attorney in Mobile were asked to count the money held

45 *Ibid.*, VII, 6 (August 17, 1816).
46 *Ibid.*, VII, 15 (August 23, 1816).
47 *Ibid.*, VII, 14 (August 22, 1816).
48 *Ibid.*, VII, 46 (Sept. 23, 1816).
49 *Ibid.*, VII, 6 (August 17, 1816).
50 *Ibid.*, VII, 67 (Oct. 30, 1816).
51 *Ibid.*, VII, 128 (Dec. 23, 1816).

by the receiver of St. Stephens, with the instruction, "It is *not* necessary that you should give Mr. Smith previous notice of this examination." [52]

Regular inspections from headquarters became, however, an annual custom. Van Zandt was sent out again in 1817; John Dickins in 1818 and 1819, Dickins and Richard B. Lee in 1820; but in 1821 two western men were sent on a general commission: Alexander Anderson of Tennessee for offices in Mississippi and Alabama, and Senator Jesse B. Thomas of Illinois for offices in Ohio, Indiana, and Illinois.[53]

Dickins' inspection report for 1818 disclosed various irregularities. A deficit of about $3,500 appeared in the Marietta office. The Chillicothe office was "not in the habit of Balancing its Books" and could not account for over $25,000. Apparently the registers generally were not "in the habit of balancing their Books," and Meigs asked Secretary Crawford whether "the labour of balancing the Books of the Registers for eighteen years past, must be encountered." [54]

The introduction of headquarters inspection in 1816 was significant, and the improvement in inspection was recorded by Crawford in no uncertain terms.

From the experience which has been acquired on this subject, no doubt is entertained that the mode of examination, which has been pursued since the year 1815, is decidedly preferable to that which had been previously pursued. When a different person is employed to examine each office, the judgment which is formed of the manner and style in which the books are kept will depend upon the intelligence, the prejudices, or partialities, of the different examiners: but, when the same person examines a number of offices, the same intelligence is exercised in each case, exempt, too, from partiality or prejudice, when the examiner is not a neighbor or connexion of the officer. . . . An examination now is not a matter of form. The time the examiner is to arrive is unknown. When he does

[52] *Ibid.*, VII, 276 (April 10, 1817).

[53] This assignment became the cause of an investigation to determine whether Thomas had not vacated his senatorial seat by accepting an executive office. He had received over $1,000 for examining eighteen offices. He kept his seat. *American State Papers: Public Lands*, III, 538.

[54] General Land Office, Miscellaneous Letters, VIII, 287 (Oct. 10, 1818).

arrive, the examination immediately commences, and is continued without relaxation until it is completed. . . .

It is also an object of some importance that the examiner should communicate, confidentially, many things that he would not be willing to incorporate in his report, and which it would even be improper to incorporate. The value of such communications will depend entirely upon the knowledge which the head of the Department has of the character of the person who makes them.[55]

Crawford missed few of the essential characteristics of a sound inspectional system.

As a landlord the general government failed to meet the expectations of its clients. Whether settlers or speculators, the customers were impatient, unruly, and prepared if necessary to take possession without formality. The government was slow, its procedures were involved, and complications of law often delayed it beyond reason. In 1808 Gallatin sent a sharp letter to Madison complaining that after the Treasury clerks had done all the work, land patents were held interminably in the State Department.[56] From the point of view of the settler, the formalities of securing a title must often have seemed interminable.

The essential elements of the process were nevertheless conducive to order, system, and security, if not to speed. They included (1) acquisition of title as part of the public domain, usually by treaty; (2) survey; (3) public sale; (4) payment in full or by installments; (5) ultimate grant of a land patent validated by the signature of the President himself. The process was tedious by reason of the niggardly appropriations for surveyors and land offices; bottlenecks in Washington where all the papers had to be sent, recorded, and acted upon; and the formalities of signature and approval by busy officials including the Chief Executive. Security was prized officially more highly than expedition; but on the frontier official precautions were hard to understand, with an almost endless stretch of rich unoccupied prairie waiting for the settler to turn the soil.

The land operation would have been an immense one even

[55] *American State Papers: Public Lands*, III, 512 (Jan. 28, 1822).
[56] Library of Congress, Madison Papers, XXXV, No. 93 (Dec. 21, 1808).

with all the administrative resources of a later age. That it was accomplished literally by hand, with the compass and chain, quill pen and ink, illuminated by candlelight in rough hewn prairie offices, was in itself a herculean performance, even though too slow to keep up with the westward migration.

CHAPTER THIRTY-FOUR

Administrative Dualism:
The Case of the Militia

The pattern of organization established by the Federalists presupposed few official relations between the two sets of governments concerned with the interests of the American people. Members of the first Congress who became Federalists insisted that the general government be independent of state officials for the conduct of its own domestic affairs; and conversely the states continued to perform their own tasks without interference or aid from the new government. At a few points mutual convenience led to mutual services that were continued in the Republican era. The prevailing pattern of separateness and independence, however, overshadowed these arrangements of accommodation. No Republican after 1801 proposed to turn over collection of the customs and tonnage dues to state officials, or to execute the decisions of federal courts by state sheriffs instead of federal marshals. The heads of the various departments of the general government intended to do their own jobs, whether they were Federalists or Republicans. The Jeffersonians diminished the weight of the general government by reducing its expenses, but not by abnegating its operations.

Neither government lived in a vacuum and politically each was dependent on the other. The states were the electoral agents for the members of Congress; the general government guaranteed a republican form of government for its constituent members. The electoral college, comprising electors chosen by the various states, was the formal means for selecting the President;

new states were admitted by consent of Congress. The political branches of both sets of governments were manned through the activities of political parties organized by states and counties; the same party organization served both state and nation.

At one point the general and the state governments could not avoid each other. The Constitution deliberately divided responsibility for the militia, assigning some duties to the former and reserving others to the latter. Here was to be spelled out the first great experiment in federal-state relations at the administrative level, and here was first to appear the principle that some central means of securing compliance were essential to produce energy, uniformity, or even cooperation among the states. The general government lacked such means, and all efforts to secure a "well-ordered" militia were fruitless.[1]

THE NATURE OF THE PROBLEM

The problem was essentially an administrative one, but not entirely. The constitutional division of authority was at the bottom of the administrative difficulties. Congress could call forth the militia to execute the laws of the Union, to suppress insurrections, and repel invasions; and it could provide for organizing, arming, and disciplining the militia and for governing such parts of them as might be employed by the United States. The states respectively had the right to appoint the officers and the authority to train the militia according to the discipline prescribed by Congress.[2] As the House Committee on the Militia declared in 1827:

. . . the obvious truth forces itself on the mind, that "the jealousy of concentrated power which existed at the adoption of the constitution, caused the States, when they granted to the Federal Govern-

---

[1] After two years of war Governor William Jones of Rhode Island wrote the Secretary of War, Sept. 8, 1814, "I am ready . . . to call out the militia . . . but we are destitute of almost every necessary for the comfort and subsistence of those men, and for making them effective, as soldiers. We are without tents, equipage, and provisions, and have a very inadequate supply of cannon, muskets, and ammunition. I have attempted to raise a corps of five hundred men. . . . In this I have not yet succeeded, having been able to enlist only about one hundred and fifty men, notwithstanding a bounty was offered by the State." *American State Papers: Military Affairs*, I, 622.

[2] Art. I, sec. 8.

ment the unlimited power to maintain armies, build navies, and
raise revenues, to reserve to themselves the militia force. . . . This
power then must be considered as the grand physical characteristic
of State sovereignty. . . ." [3]

The same committee, after wrestling for another two years with
the means of creating a well-ordered militia, had to admit that
the "division of constitutional powers . . . was not without its
embarrassing effects." [4]

Behind these constitutional provisions there was an almost
universal myth which identified the militia as the only safe
means of protecting a republic, a conviction that induced a
naive confidence in its capacity to meet any danger. The myth
was stated over and over again in official papers, and may be
illustrated here by a single example written by the Secretary of
War in 1826: "Among the political maxims which the experience of the people of the United States has adopted as unques-
tionable, there is no one more universally subscribed to than
that a well-organized and well-disciplined militia is the natural
defence of a free people." [5] Nothing could destroy the myth, not
even the painful facts of the War of 1812.[6]

Failure of the militia system was also due in part to the lack
of a professional military tradition in this, a frontier country,
and to an unwillingness on the part of a restless population to
endure discipline. This reluctant spirit was acknowledged by a
House committee after the War of 1812. The committee reported:

[3] House Report 92, 19th Cong., 2d sess., p. 3 (Feb. 27, 1827).
[4] House Report 68, 20th Cong., 2d sess., p. 1 (Feb. 4, 1829).
[5] *American State Papers: Military Affairs*, III, 393 (July 11, 1826). This excerpt may be compared with one written in 1827: "Again, under our constitution, the Militia must ever be estimated as the bulwark of our civil and individual liberty. Directed by public sentiment, it will guard us from the oppression of power; regulated by wisdom and patronized by the Government, it will
secure us from anarchy; officered, trained, and supported by the States, it is
the guaranty of their sovereignty and Union; and properly armed and disciplined, in conjunction with the Army and Navy, it forms an impenetrable
barrier to the invader." House Report 92, 19th Cong., 2d sess., p. 11 (Feb. 27,
1827).
[6] This illusion did not blind regular army officers. See *American State Papers:
Military Affairs*, I, 263, for the caustic remarks of General Ebenezer Huntington
(Jan. 5, 1810).

. . . The sentiments and habits of a free country necessarily produce amongst the citizens a superior restlessness under restraint than is to be met with in the subjects of a monarchy. This spirit frequently manifests itself even in a career of military services. . . . There can scarcely be a restraint more vexatious and disgusting to a grown man, than the initiatory lessons of the military art. . . . It is believed that to this cause is to be attributed the little progress which has been made in training the militia of the United States.[7]

To the informed the militia had always been recognized as having doubtful military value. As early as 1803 the House of Representatives was told that "the deficiency . . . of the militia, which is too apparent in some of the States, does not arise from any defect in that part of the system which is under the control of Congress, but from omission on the part of the State Governments." The only remedy that occurred to the committee at this early date was to invite the President to urge upon the governors "the importance and indispensable necessity of vigorous exertions" to render the militia "a sure and permanent bulwark of national defence." [8] Exhortation proved inadequate.

FAILURE OF NATIONAL AUTHORITY

The reform of the militia was on the docket of both Federalist and Republican leaders from 1789 to 1829, but no President was able to convince Congress or persuade the states to take even modest steps toward its improvement.

Washington had sought authority to appoint the officers composing militia courts martial, a device that would have been steadily advantageous in maintaining discipline and standards. The states realized the strength of this weapon and declined to yield it.[9] Another form of compulsion upon the individual militiaman might have been the collection of fines for refusing to answer summons for enrollment or for absence from muster. No authority was delegated to Congress to regulate fines for

---

7 *Ibid.*, I, 664 (Jan. 17, 1817).

8 *Ibid.*, I, 163 (Feb. 7, 1803).

9 The act of 1792 providing for calling forth the militia declared categorically that "courts martial for the trial of militia shall be composed of militia officers only." 1 Stat. 264 (May 2, 1792). These officers were sometimes elected by their companies and always under state authority.

nonattendance,[10] and, as will be seen in a later section, the means possessed by the federal government to collect fines levied by the states were incompetent to the task. Jefferson sought to strengthen the militia by classifying it according to age groups, and by relying on the younger men for the most active service.[11] Congressmen were unconvinced, in the light of "the prejudices against such a mode of organization" that they discovered among their constituents.[12] Not even adequate reports could be extorted from the states concerning the condition of the militia, despite the law of 1803 requiring such periodic statements. The returns were imperfect, delayed, or entirely missing.[13]

The provision of arms to the militia illustrates the difficulties experienced in the dual system. It was the duty of the general government to provide for arming militiamen. Congress discharged this duty in the act of 1792, effective during the Republican period, by requiring every citizen enrolled in the militia to provide himself with suitable arms and accoutrements.[14] As the prospect of war with Great Britain loomed in the midst of the embargo, Congress concluded that this form of armament might be inadequate and in 1808 authorized an annual appropriation of $200,000 to provide arms and military equipment to the militia of each state, to be distributed within the state as each legislature should prescribe.[15]

[10] American State Papers: Military Affairs, I, 256 (March 6, 1810).

[11] Jefferson, Works (Federal ed.), X, 392 (May 5, 1807); cf. his fifth annual message to Congress, December 3, 1805, Richardson, Messages, I, 385.

[12] American State Papers: Military Affairs, I, 256 (March 6, 1810).

[13] The enactment was in 2 Stat. 207 (March 2, 1803). In 1819 the adjutant general of Maryland wrote General Daniel Parker on this matter as follows. "It is impossible for me to say when a return of the militia of the state may be expected. I have exerted myself to procure a return ever since my appointment, but have not yet succeeded, nor is it probable that I shall while our militia laws remain so defective." House Doc. 104, 16th Cong., 2d sess., p. 8 (Nov. 11, 1819). The adjutant general of Delaware told Parker that his state had repealed military fines for nonattendance of the militia on parade days, that "a total neglect of every appearance of military duty" had resulted, and that he was confronted with "the utter inability . . . to comply with the requisition" of returns. Ibid., pp. 8–9. These were extreme cases, and many returns, not too precise, came in without too great delay. As late as 1826 there was a lack of uniformity. House Doc. 95, 19th Cong., 1st sess., p. 4 (Feb. 10, 1826).

[14] 1 Stat. 271 (May 8, 1792).

[15] 2 Stat. 490 (April 23, 1808). A report dated 1813 showed extraordinary lack of energy in pursuing this policy. One million dollars had then been made

This policy, supplementing the obligation of the militiaman to provide his own musket for drill, remained in effect through John Quincy Adams' administration.[16] Its results were reported in 1824 by Colonel George Bomford. "The arms are delivered to the respective governors, or to other executive officers, duly authorised to receive them. When the arms are thus delivered, they become the property of the state; and the officers of the General Government no longer exercise any control over them." Colonel Bomford commented on the various modes of distribution within the states and on the harmful consequences of putting equipment in the hands of the militiamen. Arms so distributed, he declared, "must in the course of a few years, be greatly injured, if not irreparably damaged and lost:—and even, if it were possible, under such circumstances, to preserve them uninjured, their wide dispersion would be almost equivalent to a total loss to the state, from the difficulty of collecting them upon urgent occasions." [17] Bomford argued, sensibly enough, that in time of danger sole reliance would have to be placed on arms deposited in the public depots. He therefore recommended that Congress require arms for the militia to be deposited in arsenals, there to be kept until needed for actual service.[18] This modest requirement was one too delicate for Congress to approve, and arms continued to be distributed as each state thought best, beyond even the official knowledge of the War Department.

The provision of military instruction was definitely reserved to the states. Such training was crucial to an effective militia and the War Department sought for means to bring its influence to bear. A competent board of army officers, constituted by the Secretary of War in 1826, was able to get no further than to

---

available but only $94,792 had been expended and only 26,000 stands of arms had been delivered to the states. *American State Papers: Military Affairs*, I, 337 (July 8, 1813).

16 The personal requirement to furnish arms, originally inspired by need for governmental economy, was condemned by the House Committee on the Militia in 1827. The committee stated that "the experience of many years proves the law to be useless and unavailing. As well might Congress require the Militia to furnish their own subsistence. . . ." House Report 92, 19th Cong., 2d sess., p. 8 (Feb. 27, 1827).

17 House Report 83, 18th Cong., 1st sess., p. 2 (Feb. 19, 1824).

18 *Ibid.*, p. 4.

recommend that each state provide camps of instruction for its militia officers, and that it become the duty of the Secretary of War, "on applications made by the executives of the several States, to provide competent instructors." [19] The House Committee on the Militia, however, thought it immaterial whether the general government or the state furnished the instructors, but exhorted the states to require applicants for officer appointments to "undergo the most rigid examination by a tribunal eminently qualified for the purpose; an examination that will defy imposition." [20] It can hardly be said that the House committee was speaking in realistic terms. Training remained securely in the jurisdiction of the states, under such instructors as they saw fit to provide.

At the direction of Congress, the Secretary of War prepared manuals of instruction for the militia in 1826 but the War Department had no control over their use by the states.[21] These manuals were nevertheless one of the most efficient instruments of progress available to the general government, even though the House Committee on the Militia was overoptimistic in expecting "the most favorable and beneficial results." The committee was certainly justified in concluding, at that time, that they were "at a loss to conceive of any other plan that could have been devised, so likely to attain the grand object in view." [22]

The War Department, indeed, was not properly organized to deal effectively with the various state authorities concerned with the militia. "The President," reported a board of army officers in 1826, "has now no officer to call upon for answers to his inquiries respecting the militia except the Secretary of War, who, under the existing organization, possesses no official information other than such as is afforded by the present incomplete abstracts of the Annual Returns of the States and Territories,

[19] *American State Papers: Military Affairs,* III, 392.

[20] House Report 92, 19th Cong., 2d sess., p. 11.

[21] In 1829 the House Committee on the Militia expressed the opinion that "an implicit observance" of this system of tactics "should be imperatively required," but how to do this escaped their attention. House Report 68, 20th Cong., 2d sess., p. 3.

[22] House Report 92, 19th Cong., 2d sess., p. 2 (Feb. 27, 1827).

some of which have not made any for several years." [23] Congress was invited to improve the overhead by appointing an adjutant general for the single purpose of corresponding with the states and collecting information: "such an officer is indispensable to the enlightened reformation and efficiency of the system. . . ." [24] Whether or not Congress was animated by "disastrous and withering parsimony," as an indignant House Committee on the Militia charged, it failed to provide this needed assistance.

The general government in fact lacked most of the normal means of securing compliance from the states. It could not threaten to withdraw benefits, because none were offered. It could not inspect and advise, because such power was not granted by the Constitution. It had not learned to set standards beyond the provision of manuals of instruction that might be disregarded. It could not provide officers of instruction. It could not specify the periods of instruction to officers or men. It could not control discipline through the militia courts martial, nor control the imposition of fines for nonperformance of militia duty. In these matters the general government could act effectively upon neither the states nor its citizens.

The efforts of the national military authorities, beginning with President Washington and General Knox and continuing without interruption for forty years, were thus broken on the constitutional division of powers, the jealousy of the states, and the absence of administrative means of action. No way was found to exhort, intrigue, or compel the states to establish a uniform and well-disciplined citizen army. The general government before the War of 1812 became resigned to its situation. "If the States," reported a Senate committee, "are anxious for an effective militia, to them belong the power, and to them too belong the means of rendering the militia truly our bulwark in war, and our safeguard in peace. . . ." [25] The miserable record made by the militia in the War of 1812 revived efforts to improve its competence, but without substantial results. At the

[23] Senate Doc. 1, 19th Cong., 2d sess., p. 491.
[24] House Report 92, 19th Cong., 2d sess., p. 3.
[25] *American State Papers: Military Affairs,* I, 256 (March 6, 1810).

principal point where administrative relationships were imposed by the Constitution, it proved as yet impossible to invent effective means of coordination.

COLLECTION OF MILITIA FINES

The handicaps of the dual system of dealing with militia matters were amply illustrated in the extraordinary fiasco in collecting fines imposed upon militiamen during the War of 1812. The facts were revealed piece by piece from 1820 to 1823.[26]

The system of fines provided by the militia acts of 1792 and 1795 was the sanction on the basis of which militia duty rested. Any officer or private failing to obey the orders of the President when called into federal service was subjected to a fine of not less than one month's nor more than one year's pay, and in case of failure to hand over the penalty was liable to one month imprisonment for every five dollars fine.[27] The method of assessing and collecting the fine involved both state and federal agencies. Liability was assessed by militia courts martial, composed exclusively of militia (i.e., state) officers. The amount was reported to the United States marshal or one of his deputies, who was directed to proceed with the distress and sale of goods of the delinquent as provided by state law. The marshal, as the law was subsequently modified, was directed to pay recoveries into the Treasury within two months, after paying from proceeds the costs of the courts martial.[28] In case of failure to account on his part, the comptroller was required to notify the district attorney of the United States, who brought the delinquent marshal into court.[29]

In the course of the war nearly 10,000 militiamen were fined, principally for failing to respond to summons. The total amount assessed was about $500,000, of which approximately one-half originated in Pennsylvania and about two-fifths in New York.[30]

---

[26] The principal documents are Calhoun's report of 1821, *ibid.*, II, 314; Crawford's report of 1822, *ibid.*, II, 329; the select committee report of 1822, *ibid.*, II, 389; and Crawford's report of 1823, *ibid.*, II, 527.

[27] 1 Stat. 264 (May 2, 1792); 1 Stat. 424 (Feb. 28, 1795).

[28] 2 Stat. 797 (Feb. 2, 1813).

[29] The act of 1795 and supporting legislation in Pennsylvania are construed in *Houston* v. *Moore*, 5 Wheaton 1 (1820).

[30] *American State Papers: Military Affairs*, II, 316.

In 1820 Congress began to inquire what part of this large sum
had been collected and in 1822 a select committee revealed that
the whole machinery had broken down. "After the lapse of
almost seven years from the time when these militia fines were
assessed, your committee are under the painful necessity of
stating that not one cent of their amount has yet reached the
Treasury of the United States. Instead of receiving any money
from this source, the United States have paid the sum of $24,-
241.08 out of the public Treasury, towards defraying the expenses of the courts-martial by which those very fines were
assessed." [31] To make matters worse, the marshal of Pennsylvania, John Smith, had collected over $75,000 and defaulted on
the whole sum, for the recovery of which no hope was held,
both Smith and his sureties being insolvent.[32]

The causes of this breakdown involved both the federal and
state governments. Fundamentally the fault lay in the dual system. The state assessed the fines but had no interest in or responsibility for collecting them. The general government had
to collect, but its record of delinquents came from the states.
The machinery of collection and payment into the Treasury
was cumbersome. The states were better adapted to collection,
for, as the select committee found, somewhat ruefully, "The
experience of the past has shown how little calculated officers of the United States are to collect small sums of money
from delinquents scattered over the surface of an extensive
State." [33]

The administrative task was made more difficult by popular
resistance. The United States marshal in Pennsylvania reported
in 1814, "This measure has excited much attention and irritation on the part of the delinquents; they aver the proceedings
illegal, and have instituted a suit against me for having committed one of them to prison. . . ." [34] The marshal of Virginia
reported in 1815 that he had collected all the fines in four
counties but was then confronted by a court decision that the

---

[31] *Ibid.*, II, 391–92 (April 25, 1822). A report in 1820 disclosed that the total
cost of militia courts martial in the three states of New Hampshire, New York,
and Pennsylvania for 1812–15 inclusive was over $97,000. *Ibid.*, II, 315.

[32] *Ibid.*, II, 389 ff.

[33] *Ibid.*, II, 394.

[34] *Ibid.*, II, 332.

courts martial were irregular, the fines illegally imposed, and he subject to damages.[35]

The marshal of Maryland reported in 1817 that he found so many difficulties he "thought it best to suspend any further collections for the present."

. . . When I seized their property, they got a replevin out of Baltimore County Court, and took the property out of my possession. I then seized their persons; to prevent their going to jail they paid me the fine, but immediately brought suit in the County Court to recover it back again. Some of the Society of Friends went to jail; they were pardoned by the President. Mr. Monroe, while acting as Secretary of State, directed me not to execute any more of the Society of Friends, or others whose families would be distressed by the payment of the fines. . . . The Society of Friends, the very poor people and those improperly fined, take in nearly the whole. . . .[36]

The collector of New York confirmed these difficulties in 1820. ". . . the time, which has elapsed since they [i.e., the fines] were imposed, the death of many of the parties, the insolvency of others, the scarcity of money, and total inability to raise it even among many of those who have property, and the spirit of litigation which, in some counties, has been infused into the delinquents . . . have all united to embarrass and delay the collections, and have given rise to a variety of suits against the deputy marshals. . . ."[37]

Laxness on the part of the comptroller was involved, as well as these multiplied troubles on the citizen front. Lists of fines assessed in the amount of $243,000 had been certified to the comptroller during the years 1814, 1815, and 1816. It became his duty to note whether the marshals paid in these sums within two months, and if not to notify the district attorneys. Not until May 5, 1818, did Comptroller Anderson send out a circular to the marshals asking for a report. No marshal paid any attention. Over two years later Anderson followed up with a second circular, but only a part of the marshals replied.[38] On the best

35 *Ibid.*, II, 527–28.
36 *Ibid.*, II, 318.
37 *Ibid.*, II, 317.
38 *Ibid.*, II, 316.

showing Anderson was much less than diligent in the matter.
The fact seems to be that no one had ever foreseen thousands
of militiamen would be fined nearly half a million dollars under
the terms of an act passed in 1792 to deal with the occasional
individual case. The mass of discontent equaled the volume of
business, and no one in the executive branch cared to press the
law to its conclusion. Monroe pardoned; the comptroller directed no militiaman to be committed to close confinement, or
taken into custody for want of property; [39] the marshals rested
on their oars; the district attorneys received no instructions from
the Treasury to proceed. The states had no incentive to press
the general government, and its executive officers had every
incentive to let sleeping dogs lie. Congressmen might scold the
executive branch for failure to do its duty, but their own solution suggested prudence rather than valor.

Their answer was not to repeal the statute that was causing
the trouble but to offer the accumulated fines and the problem
of collecting them to the states. Pennsylvania received this
Pandora box in 1822; Virginia in 1823. [40] Neither state pursued
its citizens.

THE MASSACHUSETTS MILITIA CLAIMS

One further episode illustrates the cumbersome and unsatisfactory character of federal-state relations in military affairs,
the reimbursement of the states for militia and other expenditures incurred during the War of 1812. A number of states were
involved in disputes with the federal authorities, most of them
arguments over the settlement of accounts by the comptroller.
They were annoying, but concerned principles of settlement
rather than relations between two administrative systems. [41] The

[39] *Ibid.,* II, 529.

[40] 3 Stat. 678 (May 4, 1822); 3 Stat. 777 (March 3, 1823).

[41] South Carolina was one of the most persistent claimants. The bad temper
that was induced on both sides is illustrated in this selection from the state's
correspondence: "And it cannot be a very consoling reflection to those who are
the real friends of our Union, that the States, after having surrendered the
power, and the means of making and carrying on war, should, when the hour
of danger comes, have to defend themselves, and afterwards, for years, become
petitioners at the doors of the Departments, or of Congress Hall, for the settlement of their accounts. The nation owes it to her own honor, as well as to the
dignity of the States, that these things shall not be permitted." House Doc. 38,
20th Cong., 1st sess., p. 7 (Jan. 3, 1828).

claims of Massachusetts stood on a different footing.

The governors of both Massachusetts and Connecticut, when faced with Madison's call for militia, took the ground that they, not the President, had the authority to decide whether the circumstances actually existed, as enumerated in the Constitution, to permit the commander in chief to call forth the state forces. They also claimed that once in service, the militia contingents were subject only to the orders of the President as commander in chief and could not be put under the direction of any regular army officer.[42]

Governor Caleb Strong of Massachusetts received his first notice of requisition on April 15, 1812, calling for 10,000 militia. In August he wrote the Secretary of War, William Eustis, that the people of Massachusetts were under no apprehension of an invasion, that to detach the militia and put it under federal command would limit its usefulness, and that both the executive council of the state and the justices of the state supreme court had advised him that only the governor, as commander in chief of the militia, had the right to decide whether any of the constitutional exigencies actually existed to call forth the militia: i.e., to execute the laws of the Union, to suppress insurrection, and to repel invasion.[43] Strong therefore declined to obey the requisition of the War Department, except for three companies sent to Passamaquoddy on the Canadian border.

In the course of the war substantial bodies of the Massachusetts militia were in service, sometimes "detached" and put under command of the regular army, sometimes operating independently under the orders of the governor. Thus Governor Strong wrote the War Department on September 7, 1814, that he had recently put 1,100 militia under General Dearborn's command for the defense of the seacoast; "but such objections and inconveniences have arisen from that measure, that it cannot now be repeated." He called out an additional force but put it under the independent command of a major general of

---

42 The principal documents may be consulted in *American State Papers: Military Affairs*, I, 319–26 (1812); *ibid.*, I, 604–23 (1815); *ibid.*, I, 675 (1818); and House Report 18, 19th Cong., 1st sess. (Jan. 3, 1826).

43 *American State Papers: Military Affairs*, I, 321–24.

militia. A month later he refused to obey a requisition from General Dearborn for 300 militia to guard prisoners of war at Pittsfield.[44]

The operating consequences of these high views of the governor of Massachusetts were fatal to military efficiency. The regular army officers were never sure what troops they could command, nor indeed whether a militia officer of higher rank, "detached" to the United States Army, might not take over the whole force in the military district. Brigadier General Cushing of the regular army, in command of the second military district with headquarters in New London, called for 3,000 Connecticut militia in August 1814. Governor Smith complied but insisted on placing a major general at their head—an officer outranking Cushing. In confusion the latter wrote to the Secretary of War, "if he should persist, how is the difficulty to be gotten over?"[45] A stalemate ensued, which was apparently resolved by retaining the militia under exclusive state control.

When the War of 1812 came to an end, the Senate Committee on Military Affairs asked James Monroe, then head of the War Department, for his views on the position taken by the governor of Massachusetts. Monroe prepared an able and convincing statement sustaining the full power of the President and denying any capacity for discretion on the part of the governors.

The power . . . to provide for calling forth the militia, for the purposes specified in the constitution, is unconditional. . . . If it was dependent on the assent of the Executives of the individual States, it might be entirely frustrated. The character of the Government would undergo an entire and radical change. . . .

. . . A necessary consequence of so complete and absolute a restraint on the power of the General Government over the militia, would be to force the United States to resort to standing armies for all national purposes. A policy so fraught with mischief, and so absurd, ought not to be imputed to a free people in this enlightened age. . . .

When the militia are called into the service of the United States, all State authority over them ceases.[46]

[44] *Ibid.*, I, 613.
[45] *Ibid.*, I, 617.
[46] *Ibid.*, I, 605–6 (Feb. 11, 1815).

The Senate committee endorsed these views. A House committee in 1818 approved the practice of circumventing governors by means of presidential calls directly to some officer of the militia, not the executive: "The Governor of a State is not a militia officer, bound to execute the orders of the President; he cannot be tried for disobedience of orders, and punished by the sentence of a court martial." [47] This plan was not, however, put into effect, although validated in principle by the Supreme Court in 1820.[48]

In 1823 the Commonwealth of Massachusetts recanted and disavowed the doctrine of 1812.[49] The issue was finally put to rest by the Supreme Court which confirmed the position stated by Monroe.[50]

There remained the controversial issue of responsibility for payment of the costs of the Massachusetts militia called out by the governor but never placed under the command of the United States Army. When Governor Strong refused in 1814 to place a body of militia under General Dearborn, he asked whether their expenses would nevertheless be paid by the general government.[51] Monroe, Secretary of War, gave a decisive answer: "if this force has been called into service by the authority of the State, independently of Major General Dearborn, and be not placed under him, as commander of the district . . . the State of Massachusetts is chargeable with the expense, and not the United States." [52] Massachusetts was not prepared to abide by such a ruling and in 1817 her commissioners presented a claim for reimbursement.[53]

This claim stirred hot indignation in quarters that had seen with dismay the noncooperative and defiant spirit of Massachu-

---

[47] Ibid., I, 675 (Jan. 9, 1818).

[48] Houston v. Moore, 5 Wheaton 1 (1820).

[49] The Republican party won the state elections and put in the governor's chair the same William Eustis who had been Secretary of War when defied by Governor Strong. Governor Eustis' disavowal and the confirming answers of the Massachusetts House and Senate (May 1823) are reprinted in House Report 18, 19th Cong., 1st sess., pp. 111–18 (Jan. 5, 1826).

[50] Martin v. Mott, 12 Wheaton 19 (1827).

[51] American State Papers: Military Affairs, I, 613.

[52] Ibid., I, 614.

[53] Reprinted with other relevant documents in House Report 18, 19th Cong., 1st sess., pp. 121–30.

setts and Connecticut during the war. Niles expressed his astonishment in these words: "we were not prepared for this—to use a sheer Yankee phrase, 'it bangs everything'—first, to disobey the orders of the general government and then claim an indemnity for the cost of the act of disobedience!" [54] "The money claimed *cannot* be paid . . . without a violation of *principle* that will cause the most of those that vote for it to be hurled from their seats by the suffrages of an indignant and justly offended people. . . ." [55]

The federal executive stood firm and there the matter rested for several years despite a select committee report of 1818 favorable to the state.[56] In 1819 the governor of Massachusetts called on John Quincy Adams, then Secretary of State, to enlist his aid. Adams was disgusted with his fellow citizens for their course of action during the war, "for which," he said, "nothing but the depraving and stupefying influence of faction can account. . . ." [57] The issue was one on which the President alone could give an answer, and Monroe gave no answer until Massachusetts disavowed the position it had taken during the war. He then laid the matter before Congress in a conciliatory but firm message. To emphasize the importance of the renunciation, he reminded Congress of the situation in 1812, and of the importance of the issue.

. . . The public mind throughout the Union was much excited by that occurrence, and great solicitude was felt as to its consequences. . . . The executive of the State was warned . . . of the light in which its conduct was viewed. . . . Under these circumstances the power of the Executive of the United States to settle any portion of this claim seems to be precluded. It seems proper, also, that this claim should be decided on full investigation before the public, that the principle on which it is decided may be thoroughly understood by our fellow-citizens of every State, which can be done by Congress alone, who alone, also, possess the power to pass laws which may be necessary to carry such decision into effect.[58]

54 *Niles Register*, XI, 337 (Jan. 18, 1817).
55 *Ibid.*, XIII, 209 (Nov. 29, 1817).
56 House Report 18, 19th Cong., 1st sess., p. 169.
57 Adams, *Memoirs*, IV, 422 (Oct. 8, 1819).
58 Richardson, *Messages*, II, 229 (Feb. 23, 1824).

Monroe recommended that a penitent Massachusetts be placed on the same footing as other states.

During 1824 the claims were audited by Peter Hagner, the third auditor, and in 1825, just as he was leaving office, Monroe recommended their payment.[59] Thus was settled another phase of the perplexing adjustments between two constitutional and administrative systems.

We may conclude that for twenty-eight years after the fall of the Federalists the general government and state governments had little to do with each other in the conduct of the public business except in the single field where the Constitution required them to work together, the militia. The general government came close to Jefferson's ideal: the common agent of the people for the conduct of foreign affairs and matters arising between the states. The scope of public business was narrow at best, and the domestic part of it was absorbed by the states, acting under their own constitutions and administrative systems. The limited activities of government reduced the points at which the two administrative systems might have been thrown in each other's way. Where they were required to join hands in the organization, training, and maintenance of the militia, they made much trouble for each other.

The administrative calm which generally prevailed by reason of the separateness and independence of the two systems was in perilous contrast to the political disputation that filled many of these years and cast a foreboding shadow over the future. In an anxious moment, a select committee of the Senate wrote these words:

. . . the only security for the permanent union of these States, is to be found in the principle of common affection, resting on the basis of common interest. The sanctions of the Constitution would be impotent to retain, in concerted and harmonious action, twenty-four sovereignties, hostile in their feelings towards each other, and acting under the impulse of a real, or imagined diversity of interest. The resort to force would be alike vain and nugatory.[60]

59 *Ibid.*, II, 286 (Feb. 21, 1825). The House Committee on Military Affairs was still stoutly opposed in 1824 to paying any claims for militia service not under the general government. House Report 120, 18th Cong., 1st sess. (May 3, 1824).
60 Senate Doc. 69, 19th Cong., 2d sess., p. 6 (March 1, 1827).

Three major issues threatened this common affection. One, the authority to call forth the militia, was conclusively and amicably settled by the passage of time and the good sense of the parties. A second, the status of slavery in the states erected from the territories, came to its first climax and was quieted by compromise, but not withdrawn from the political arena. The third, the proper interpretation of the powers of the general government and the proper means of resistance by the states, was inherent in the federal system and was coming to a new crisis as the Republicans left the stage. John C. Calhoun was about to abandon his devotion to national interests and to furnish the philosophical foundation for a defense of states' rights that was overcome only by war. The administrative and the political scenes could hardly have been in sharper contrast.

CHAPTER THIRTY-FIVE

Republican Achievements
in Administration

Toward the end of his long life Thomas Jefferson wrote his friend, Judge Spencer Roane, that "the revolution of 1800 . . . was as real a revolution in the principles of our government as that of 1776 was in its form. . . ." [1] His mind was filled with the conviction that he had wrung power from impending monarchy, and that in this sense he had saved the Republic.[2] However this may be, the Republicans brought no revolution in administration. They found a system in full order; the people were familiar with its operations; it was well adapted to the work to be done; and it was taken over with hardly a ripple and maintained substantially intact for over a quarter century.

That no revolution could have occurred was evident from the situation of the American people immediately before and after Jefferson's election. The country was prosperous and the prospect of war with either France or England seemed to have disappeared. The basic economy was successfully centered on agriculture; the population was heavily rural despite the growth of older cities on the seaboard and new ones along the inland rivers and canals. Even the cities retained the atmosphere of rural villages. Josiah Quincy, mayor of Boston, was arrested for galloping his horse through the city streets on official business. This was not an environment out of which revolution was likely to be born.

1 Jefferson, *Works* (Federal ed.), XII, 136 (Sept. 6, 1819).
2 Henry Adams, *History of the United States*, I, 209.

Jefferson, of course, was thinking in terms of a revolution in public sentiment that had finally abandoned hope of a monarchy and at last permanently accepted republican institutions. Even here he exaggerated both the extent of royal inclination and the shift of opinion reflected in the election of 1800. The fact that Jefferson and Burr received 71 votes in the electoral college while John Adams won 65 did not suggest a fundamental change of opinion on either high matters of state or the character and functions of the administrative system.

The continuation of Federalist methods of administration was natural, if not inevitable, and could be traced at almost every point. The role of the President in single command of all branches of government business was unquestioned. The structure of the four great departments, as well as that of the post office, the office of the Attorney General, and the field service was untouched. The procedures of administration were unaltered. Mail contractors continued to be selected on the basis of competitive bids approved by the Postmaster General; letters were handed to the public for the most part by the same deputy postmasters in the same buildings. Public officers were bonded under the same surety, and required to make the same accounting. After a brief period of transition, during which new men took over most of the important posts, the same expectation of nonpartisan, lifetime service prevailed.

In short, to the master of a ship entering and clearing from an American port, to the merchant paying customs dues, to the lawyer appearing in federal cases, to the planter sending letters to friends or business connections, to the supplier selling rations to the army or navy, to the Indians receiving annuities and gifts, to the citizen buying land in the wilderness, to the invalid Revolutionary soldier getting his modest pension, little change was apparent as a consequence of the momentous political shift of 1801. The same laws were on the books; the same motions occurred within the administrative system.

I

The projection of Federalist administrative institutions into the Republican years was due to other factors than stability in the economic and social structure and the satisfaction of Americans with an inexpensive and restricted government. One circumstance of special importance was the uninterrupted control of government and the administrative system after 1801 by gentlemen. The same social class that had set up the new system in 1789 carried it forward under Jefferson and Gallatin and their successors in the White House and the departments of state. The basic outlook, predispositions, habits, and ways of life of men in the public service were unchanged; and the ethical standards of the civil servants of 1820 were identical with those of 1800. Beneath the political shift that Jefferson emphasized so greatly was a solid and unchanged official substructure anchored deeply in the mores of the American people.

This dominant class of gentlemen who bridged the gap between Federalists and Republicans could be defined from one point of view by the state laws fixing qualifications for voting and for officeholding. These requirements generally excluded from active participation in public affairs those who lacked substantial property qualifications. The mere possession of property, however, did not in itself constitute a gentleman in either Federalist or Republican views.

The concept of a gentleman was drawn from Elizabethan England.[3] Its principal elements were virtue, learning, and wealth. The central theme was virtue, which was understood to connote justice, prudence, temperance, fortitude, courtesy, and liberality. The English gentleman accepted an obligation to govern his country: the great aristocrats were occupied in the foreign service and the high offices of state, the lesser gentry were engaged in the conduct of local affairs as justices of the peace. The Virginia gentleman, of whom Washington and Jefferson were prototypes, recognized the same moral obligation. Virginia was governed by the landholding gentry. Other states also were governed by persons drawn from the well-to-do, educated classes.

The Federalist view of a gentleman put emphasis upon wealth and social position; Jefferson, however, talked and wrote about the *natural* gentleman. Most Federalists would have accepted John Adams' description of a gentleman in his *Defence of the*

[3] Edwin Harrison Cady, *The Gentleman in America: A Literary Study in American Culture* (Syracuse: Syracuse University Press, 1949).

Constitutions of Government of the United States of America.

. . . The people, in all nations, are naturally divided into two sorts, the gentlemen and the simplemen, a word which is here chosen to signify the common people. By gentlemen are not meant the rich or the poor, the high-born or the low-born, the industrious or the idle; but all those who have received a liberal education, an ordinary degree of erudition in liberal arts and sciences, whether by birth they be descended from magistrates and officers of government, or from husbandmen, merchants, mechanics, or laborers; or whether they be rich or poor. We must, nevertheless, remember that *generally* those who are rich, and descended from families in public life, will have the best education in arts and sciences, and therefore the gentlemen will ordinarily, notwithstanding some exceptions to the rule, be the richer, and born of more noted families.[4]

John Adams' wife, Abigail, put the matter in a nutshell in her advice to her young son, John Quincy, "Great learning and superior abilities, should you ever possess them, will be of little value and small estimation, unless virtue, honor, truth, and integrity are added to them." [5]

Jefferson could not accept a class of gentlemen by birth in wealthy families, but he fully recognized the existence of a body of men superior to their fellows and he fully intended to base government upon them. In his correspondence with John Adams, he wrote:

. . . For I agree with you that there is a natural aristocracy among men. The grounds of this are virtue and talents. . . . The natural aristocracy I consider as the most precious gift of nature, for the instruction, the trusts, and government of society. . . . May we not even say, that the form of government is the best, which provides the most effectually for a pure selection of these natural *aristoi* into the offices of government? [6]

Here is the implication of the Republican insistence upon respectability as the criterion of appointment to public office.

---

[4] *The Works of John Adams* (Charles Francis Adams, ed., 10 vols., Boston: Little, Brown, 1850–56), VI, 185.

[5] *Letters of Mrs. Adams* (Charles Francis Adams, ed., 2 vols., 3d ed., Boston: Charles C. Little and James Brown, 1841), I, 126 (June 1778).

[6] Jefferson, *Works* (Federal ed.), XI, 343–44 (Oct. 28, 1813).

Republicans, like their predecessors, intended to choose only men of virtue and honor, who had standing in their community and were recognized as gentlemen. "Not only competent talents," wrote Jefferson in 1801, "but respectability in the public estimation are to be considered." [7] In filling a vacancy in the Richmond post office, he declared to Monroe his desire to appoint "a gentleman of respectable standing in society; and to such I would wish to give office, because they would add respect and strength to the administration." [8]

The concept of gentleman was entirely independent of party affiliation or geographical location. A Federalist gentleman differed only in his political views from a Republican gentleman. The basic ideal of behavior was the same in both, and carried with it a sense of obligation to serve the state when called to public office. Since the government was in the hands of Republican gentlemen from 1801 to 1829, it was inevitable that its character should remain the same as in the previous decade when it had been in the hands of Federalist gentlemen. The qualities of integrity, restraint, deference, responsibility, and honor that characterized gentlemen also characterized their government and administrative system.

II

The Federalists had worked out a systematic theory of government and administration to which they consistently adhered while in office. The Republicans were ambivalent both in theory and practice, and even their greatest leader, Thomas Jefferson, abandoned his philosophy when hard circumstances prescribed a contrary course. The theory of strict construction of the Constitution yielded to the purchase of Louisiana in 1803 and to the establishment of the second United States Bank in 1816, but it held fast in preventing a national system of internal improvements. The Republicans cherished a sensitive fear of governmental power, especially in offices as remote from the people as those in Washington, and had denounced the authority vested in the President by the Alien and Sedition Acts of 1798. Despite

7 *Ibid.*, IX, 255 (May 17, 1801).
8 Dec. 13, 1801, quoted in Edward Channing, *A History of the United States* (6 vols., New York: Macmillan Co., 1916–25), IV, 248, n. 1.

this antipathy to the concentration of power, Jefferson secured from a Republican Congress a grant of authority to enforce the embargo acts exceeding any that the Federalists had dared put on the books, and he used these powers with all the energy that some of his early partisans had declared was the mark of tyranny.

Within the framework of government the Republicans defended the dominance of the legislative branch, but Jefferson and Gallatin exercised an executive influence and control that equaled that of Hamilton. When Congress later asserted itself, it was not in conscious pursuit of sound Republican theory but by reason of the lapse of executive leadership which gave opportunity to able men in the legislative branch. The Republicans in theory objected to referring policy matters to the executive and to receiving drafts of bills from the departments; in practice they did not hesitate to take advantage of these conveniences. The Republicans declared that an appropriation was binding in its terms upon the executive departments, but their War and Navy Departments never accepted this doctrine. The Republicans had claimed an unqualified right to call for executive papers when in opposition, but Republican Presidents exercised their judgment as to what papers the public interest required to be submitted.

The Republicans were committed in theory to the restriction of the federal government and to reliance on the states for the major part of the task of government, but they declined to undo the work of their predecessors or to delegate some branches of federal administration, such as the collection of customs or excise taxes, to the states. They respected the integrity of the states, however, refusing to build the Cumberland Road and other public works until the consent of the interested commonwealths had been received. Reliance upon the states to help enforce the embargo proved partly unsuccessful, and to invigorate the militia proved entirely vain. On the whole in their relations with the states the Republicans managed to keep practice and theory in close harmony, each system going its independent way without interference from the other.

At other points also the Jeffersonians were successful in aligning theory and practice. Republican Congresses were more energetic in their effort to control administration than had been their predecessors. The standing committees on expenditures, the special committees of investigation, the reports of committees on claims, the drive for retrenchment in 1820, the attempts to control transfers of funds, all signified a recognition of the duty of Congress to regulate the conduct of administration. The Republicans were committed to frugality in government, and so far as the scales of official pay and the number of clerks were concerned they held their own. The government really "lived snug."

In the matter of large expenditures for public works, however, the Republicans broke into two opposing groups. The old Republicans, symbolized by John Randolph and Nathaniel Macon, stood firmly against federal commitments. The new Republicans, led by Calhoun, were ready to spend money liberally for roads and canals. Jefferson could have been cited by either wing of the party. The trend away from early doctrine had gone so far by 1825 that John Quincy Adams seemed almost more a Federalist than a Republican. He was in fact a Republican and had been since 1808; but he belonged (with Calhoun and Rush and others) to a faction of the party that was privately repudiated by many leading members such as Monroe and Crawford.

Despite numerous Republican departures from doctrine, which could be matched by Federalist vagaries as the party of the opposition, there remained nevertheless a point of view that Republicans could claim as their own. They emphasized the responsibility of the executive branch and the administrative system to Congress. They activated Congress to the better discharge of this function. They respected the integrity of the states and depended upon them for the better system of internal communications that was so badly needed. They departed with extreme reluctance from the course of judicial proceedings designed to protect officials in their fiscal relations to government. At the same time they left open means for citizens to safeguard themselves against arbitrary official action. They declined to intervene in the economic scene, except for protective tariffs. They instinctively steered away from the interferences of a bureaucracy such as Crawford described when he landed in France in 1813.

. . . The formalities, the parade and the delay which was incident to every act of office made me feel that I was now in a country where the rulers were everything and the people nothing. In the United States we are insensible of the existence of Government except in the granting of benefits.[9]

The attitude of Republicans in Congress and in the executive offices was more tender to the citizen than that which on the whole the Federalists had developed.

III

While, therefore, the Federalist structure of administration was accepted by the Republicans, and while the spirit in which it was operated was governed by the common attitudes of gentlemen both before and after 1801, there were some changes in emphasis that resulted by reason of the Republican victory in 1800. There was also, as a matter of course, a change in personnel. New men appeared at the heads of departments, and with the passage of time new men took over the subordinate posts. They were men whose character and talents would generally have been recognized by open-minded Federalists, however unacceptable their politics.

It may fairly be said that the Republicans discovered as ample a supply of administrative talent as had been employed by their predecessors. Gallatin was hardly less an administrative genius than Hamilton, and was much more adapted to teamwork. John Quincy Adams was an abler Secretary of State than Timothy Pickering, and John Calhoun stood head and shoulders above any Federalist Secretary of War. John McLean was the ablest Postmaster General during the first forty years of postal history. William Wirt was the first to put the office of Attorney General on its feet. Southard was an able Secretary of the Navy. At lesser levels the Republicans took advantage of solid administrative talent among such persons as McKenney in the Indian office, Goldsborough in the Navy, Abraham Bradley in the Post Office, Thayer at West Point, and others. These men gave an impulse to the conduct of affairs quite equal to that which had prevailed earlier in "the reign of energy."

9 Shipp, *Giant Days*, pp. 105–6 (July 12, 1813).

The passage of twenty-eight years from 1801 to 1829 inevitably left its mark upon the administrative system, quite apart from the theoretical views of either party. The changes that took place were indigenous. No influence from abroad played upon American administrative institutions. Officials dealt with their problems on the basis of American experience and outlook. The foundations of the administrative system were English, but this fact did not imply that Americans were affected by subsequent experience in the mother country, even after the War of 1812 had receded into the distance.

The major developments of the period grew out of the crisis caused by war. The embargo left no permanent changes in normal procedures, although it provided some extraordinary precedents, and the depression of 1819–1822 was neither long nor severe enough to leave a mark on the administrative system. The incompetence of the defense departments and of civilian administration revealed by the war with Great Britain was so impressive, however, that it caused the first major reorganization of the federal administrative system. The principal elements will be recalled: the establishment of the army General Staff, the formation of the Board of Navy Commissioners, and the reconstruction of the accounting organization and system of accountability. Other significant reforms and developments also took place after 1815. West Point was reorganized and put on a high professional standard. Ship construction was standardized. A system of inspection of land offices was introduced, the first of its kind. The procedures of the State Department were greatly improved by John Quincy Adams. The Post Office was energized by John McLean.

Of special importance was the establishment of professional assistance to the heads of the two defense departments by means of the General Staff of the army and the Board of Navy Commissioners. The full significance of this innovation was probably not understood at the time, since each institution was proposed and defended as a means of relieving the head of the department from an impossible burden of detail. The Secretaries did benefit to some extent in this respect, although detail kept crowding its way to their desks. Much more important was the availability of professional advice on army and navy affairs, hitherto lacking on any systematic or orderly basis. The Navy Board was particularly useful in bringing its judgment to bear on naval construction and on the management of navy yards and posts. Both agencies were successful in elaborating a body of regulations for the government of the uniformed forces.

The State Department remained throughout the period with no professional officer to assist the Secretary. Treasury had enjoyed the services of men above the rank of chief clerk from the beginning: the commissioner of revenue, the register, and the head of the General Land Office in particular, but like the comptrollers and auditors, they brought no relief to the Secretary in the discharge of his own duties. The Post Office had two officers of general competence aiding the Postmaster General: the first and second assistant postmasters general. These modest advances were significant of later developments.

The Republican years confirmed Federalist ideas about permanent service in the general government. Tenure, although not protected by law, was in fact during good behavior, both in Washington and in the field. Clerks might end their official work in the same office, indeed in the same position in which they began, but the expectation of life service was high. The army and navy offered somewhat greater freedom of movement than the civilian agencies, but both uniformed services suffered from successive statutory reductions that forced many career officers into civilian life.

One of the most interesting innovations during the Republican period was the requirement of examinations for entrance into certain branches of the public service: West Point, navy midshipmen, and the medical services of both the army and the navy. The examinations were taken seriously, and represented the first effort to establish formal standards of competence and character in government circles. They suggest a degree of stability and institutional maturity that could have been reached only with the passage of the years.

From one point of view it could be argued that by the end of the Republican era a modest bureaucracy was growing up in the general government. Clerks and officials tended to come from an identifiable section of the population; they were not infrequently succeeded by their sons, and they often found places for their relatives; they organized a Provident Society for their mutual benefit; they sometimes developed their own small cliques; and they grew old in office. A few statesmen began to sense the problems arising out of these circumstances, but no one seriously considered how they could be managed. The advent of President Jackson was to supply one type of solution.

The Republicans did not enrich the literature of public administration. There were no writings of the nature of the *Federalist Papers,* either by officials or citizens. The central interests of public men were political and constitutional. The writings of Thomas Jefferson are singularly barren of views or comments on the art of conducting public business. Gallatin more frequently stated a rule or precept in a sentence or two, but he seldom developed the type of reasoned argument in explanation of his administrative doctrine that appeared so abundantly in the writings of Alexander Hamilton. Of all the Republicans John Quincy Adams had perhaps the greatest sensitivity to administrative matters. During the years of his service as Secretary of State and President, he put into his diary a steady stream of observations, comments, and generalizations which, if drawn together, would form a coherent body of administrative doctrine. Adams never found time, and probably did not have the interest to undertake this task. The attention of most executive, administrative, and middle management officers was confined to the particular duties that were assigned to them, and to the disposition of the business that automatically came to their attention, instructed by law, regulation, and common sense. The art of public administration continued to be practiced, but not to be written about.

Beyond official circles, also, there was no writing on the subject matter of the administrative art. At the same time the substantive tasks of government were attracting attention in the periodical literature that began to take its place in American life. *Niles' Weekly Register,* first published in 1811, kept up a commentary on contemporary affairs. Niles wrote his own column, politically independent but leaning toward the ideals of the old Republicans in many instances, and he reprinted newspaper items from home and abroad dealing with public matters.

The *North American Review,* founded in 1815, carried a

whole series of informative articles on public issues, such as the abuses of political discussion; [10] university education; [11] slavery and the Missouri question; [12] internal improvements of North Carolina; [13] the American penitentiary system; [14] the militia; [15] and a review of a paper by Charles J. Ingersoll read before the American Philosophical Society, "A Communication on the Improvement of Government." [16] To the *North American Review* goes the honor of publishing the first article that was reprinted in a congressional document, dealing with privateering.[17] Americans were turning to the considered discussion of their public policy in the magazines of opinion and enlightenment, but the art of administration went unnoticed.

In some respects the Republicans failed to make advances that circumstances might have suggested. Both Presidents and department heads were badly overburdened with official work, but neither of the two obvious remedies—delegation or provision of administrative assistants—were grasped. Department heads were cut off from direct personal contact with their field services but none of them, excepting the General Land Office and the War Department, visualized the advantages of an inspection service. The accounting branches were characterized by pettifogging meticulous precision in settling accounts, but neither Congress nor the President showed any concern to ameliorate such annoyances. The explanation of these failures is to be found in part in the dogma of parsimony, in part in the distrust of officials possessed of public funds.

In considerable measure, however, the defaults were due to the prevailing state of the art of administration. Each generation uses the wisdom and technique that it has acquired from its predecessor, and makes some advances of its own. The Republicans employed effectively what their time could give them, but

---

10 *North American Review*, IV (1816–17), 193–201.

11 *Ibid.*, X (1820), 115–37.

12 *Ibid.*, X (1820), 137–68.

13 *Ibid.*, XII (1821), 16–37.

14 *Ibid.*, XIII (1821), 417–40.

15 *Ibid.*, XIX (1824), 275–97.

16 *Ibid.*, XX (1825), 227–29.

17 *Ibid.*, XI (1820), 166–96; House Doc. 76, 16th Cong., 2d sess. Note also "A Cursory Inquiry into the Embargo Policy of the American Government," in the *American Review of History and Politics*, III (1812), 306–32.

they, like others, were unable to think, plan, or execute with means beyond their age.

The closing years of the Republican period showed tension between the established tradition of nonpartisanship in the middle and lesser offices and the increasing insistence of new political leaders for partisan use of public patronage. Some states had already demonstrated what could be done, and on the national scene Van Buren and Benton joined from the east and west to threaten official neutrality. Monroe and Adams held fast, but the event was to bring defeat to their ideals. Power was to pass from the gentlemen who had carried on the business of the Republic for more than a generation to other hands.

IV

The role of the Jeffersonians in the field of administration was not and indeed could hardly have been that of innovation and creation which fell to the Federalists. Their function was to direct an existing governmental mechanism toward the objectives that were imposed by their views of public policy: peace, economy, discharge of the debt, reduction of the army and navy, protection of the rights of the states and of the citizen. The policy was in considerable measure negative in character, and as a consequence gave even less opportunity for constructive experimentation. The changes that time brought in the administrative system were largely the product of mere growth of population and area, and of the impact of the war crisis of 1812–1815. In both cases circumstances forced the hand of the government, rather than Republican antipathy to Federalist patterns of organization and administration.

The Jeffersonians in fact carried the Federalist administrative machine forward without substantial alteration in form or in spirit for nearly three decades. Under their direction the American people gained invaluable experience in the management of their national affairs. A system of government that for the first twelve years was an admitted experiment became in the next thirty years a stable and accepted institution. The good sense of the Republicans in conserving an administrative organization which, in the first instance, they would probably have planned on different principles was a major contribution to the

young federation. A new generation arose amidst its revolutionary elders to hold intact the governmental system and to direct
it from the past to the never-ending struggle with the problems
of an emerging future. It was well that these added years of
consolidation and maturity were possible before the vast changes
that the steam locomotive was to launch burst upon the country.
Forty years of stable performance and experience, from 1789 to
1829, set the first pattern of national administration firmly in
the American inheritance.

INDEX

Accountability, case of David Gelston, 153–56; system of, 162–65; breakdown of, 165–69; reform of, 169–80; treasury agent, 180–82; of foreign agents, 191–94; of navy agents, 292; of postmasters, 327–29; case of Stephen Pleasonton, 407–8; case of Joseph Nourse, 408–9; in land offices, 525–26

Accounting officers, 163–65

Accounts, of persons insolvent, 167; procedure for requiring submission of, 167–69, 177–80; administrative examination of, 174; progress in clearing, 175–77

Adams, Abigail, 549

Adams, Henry, quoted, 7, 8, 10, 50; on Monroe, 221; on Jefferson and the embargo, 433; on coastwise trade, 434; on enforcement act of 1809, 468

Adams, John, on gentlemen in government, 548–49

Adams, John Quincy, on Republican victory, 13; on progress in America, 16; on free enterprise, 24–25; on Jefferson, 34; on Clay, 39–40; and presidency, 41–42; on Burwell, 47; on veto power, 52; on congressional nominating caucus, 54; on election of Speaker, 57–59; on administrative position of President, 61–62; on duty of department heads, 62, 68; relations with McLean, 67, 314–19; on President's relation to estimates, 69; and Todson, 72–74; on Cabinet, 82; preparation of messages, 84–86; on office seeking by Congressmen, 92; on Tenure of Office Act, 129, 387, 388, 389, 390; on Gallatin, 136; and settlement of accounts, 164–65, 193; and diplomatic appointments, 186; on business of State Department, 189, 190; on system, 194; on reforms in State Department, 194–95; on press of business, 195; on himself, 195–98; on office seeking, 197, 366–67; on the

presidential campaign, 198–99; on publication of laws, 200–2; on pardons, 202–3; and report on weights and measures, 203–4; and census, 204–5; and Patent Office, 206; on naval policy in 1816, 269; on appointment of postmasters, 324–25; conducts postal contractors on tour of White House, 333–34; on party and appointments, 355; appointment policy, 357; on nepotism, 358, 359; on limited terms in foreign service, 373; personal appeals to, 377; on Monroe, 380; number of removals by, 380; refuses to remove for political reasons, 380–81; on renomination policy, 390; on government pay policy, 399, 411; on Massachusetts militia claims, 543; on President's duty to maintain ethical standards of public service, 414; on Tobias Watkins, 421; on failure of juries to convict for violation of embargo, 457; on internal improvements, 482, 483

Adjudication, administrative, in land claims, 517–18

Administration, public, political background of, 7–15; social background of, 16–28; and presidency, 29 ff.; and Congress, 89 ff.; Calhoun on, 246–50; personnel management, 347 ff.; and the embargo, 423 ff.; literature of, 557–58

Administrative art, improvement in, 11–12, 117 ff.; Presidents and, 34–44; congressional relations, 45–59, 89 ff.; Presidents and heads of departments, 60 ff., 77 ff.; in finance, 108 ff., 140–47; in Treasury, 156 ff., 180–82; in State, 188–91, 200 ff.; in War, 216–23, 228–31, 238–45, 263–64; in Navy, 276–81, 287–92, 296–97; in Post Office, 306–10, 320–25, 329–34; in personnel, 354 ff.; ethical standards in, 412 ff.; law enforcement: the embargo,

423 ff.; in trading houses, 500–4; in land management, 523–26; foundations of, 547 ff.

Administrative careers, Thomas Jefferson, 1–7; William A. Burwell, 47–48; Albert Gallatin, 135–36; John Q. Adams, 195–99; William Thornton, 207–10; John C. Calhoun, 246–50; Charles W. Goldsborough, 281–82; S. L. Southard, 281; John Rodgers, 282; John McLean, 313–19; Theodorus Bailey, 321; Solomon Van Rensselaer, 320–21, 323–25; Joseph Nourse, 371; Brent family, 371–73; H. R. Schoolcraft, 510; Thomas L. McKenney, 510–11

Administrative families, 357

Administrative power, *see* embargo, executive power

Agents, army, 224–25; for settlement of claims, 417–18; trading houses, 501; Indian, 501, 510–11

Allocation of funds, Gallatin and war expenditures, 146

Anderson, Joseph, on settlement of accounts, 168

Appointment policy and practice, case of Claiborne, 33; case of Gallatin, 36; department heads, 60, 62–64, 80–81; John Q. Adams on, 62; Madison on, 83, n. 17; case of members of Congress, 90–92; Senate confirmation, 125–31; Tenure of Office Act, 129; Benton's Report, 130–31; in Post Office, 305; Jefferson on, 347–54; procedure, 354–55

Apportionment of appointments, 128–29; West Point cadets, 256; in Cabinet, 360; in subordinate offices, 360–61; of midshipmen, 361; of army medical officers, 361–62

Appropriation procedure, 108–13; enacting clause, 112

Armstrong, John, Madison on, 37; removed as Secretary of War, 65; evaluation of, 218

Army engineers, establishment, 260; and coast fortifications, 260–61; and internal improvements, 261–62; prestige of, 263

Army officers, claim for extra pay for civilian duties, 409–10

Army organization, General Staff, 236–40; staff and line, 240–45

Assistant Secretaries, denied to War Department, 235–36

Attorney General, residence in Washington, 336–37; records of, 337–38; duties of, 338–40; and district attorneys, 340–42; private income, 342–43; Levi Lincoln, 343; William Pinkney, 343–44; William Wirt, 344–46

Auditor, 164, 166, 173–77

Bailey, Theodorus, postmaster of New York, 321

Balances, ascertainment of, 163–65; of persons insolvent, 167; collection by lawsuit, 167–69; by summary process, 177–82

Barbour, James, on government pay scales, 411

Benton, Thomas H., on John Rodgers, 282; opposes Indian trading houses, 503

Benton's Report, 374, 390–93

Bernard, General Simon, 261

Bill drafting, 51–52

Blake, George, district attorney, neglects to enforce embargo, 455

Board of Canal Commissioners, Pa., 489–90

Board of Engineers, 260–61

Board of Engineers for Internal Improvements, 261–62

Board of Navy Commissioners, on discretion in use of appropriations, 113; organization of, 276–79; evaluation of, 280

Board of Surgeons, 296

Boston, enforcement of embargo act, 443–45

Brahan, John, 420

Brent, Daniel, 189–90, 372

Brent family, careers in government, 371–73

Brent, Robert, 372, 377

Bureaus, in Treasury, 139–40; accounting offices, 173–74; Patent Office, 205–6; in War Department, 236–40; Board of Navy Commissioners, 276–77; in Post Office, 304–6; of Indian affairs, 507; General Land Office, 519–22

Burwell, William A., John Q. Adams on, 47

Cabinet, Jefferson's Cabinet, 8–9; problem of unity of policy within, 62–64, 79–83; Monroe on, 63–64; Crawford on, 64; procedure in, 77–78; Jefferson on, 77–78; Madison's Cabinet, 80–81; Monroe's Cabinet, 81–82; Adams' Cabinet, 82–83; geographical representation in, 83; political and administrative aspects, 83–84; business of: messages, 84–86; secrecy in, 86–88; case of Solomon Van Rensselaer, 323–25

Calhoun, John C., relations with Monroe on report on internal improvements, 67–68; on Crawford's violation of secrecy of Cabinet discussions, 86–87; on War Department accounts, 175–76; on regular army, 214–15; and Andrew Jackson, 244–45; administrative career of, 246–50; basic ideas on administration, 246; on responsibility, 247; on achievements, 248–49; plan for internal improvements, 478–79; sponsors bill for internal improvements, 480; on Indian trading houses, 504

Canals, Robert Fulton on, 475; Gallatin on, 477–78; Calhoun on, 478–79; subscriptions to, 481; in Pennsylvania, 489; in New York, 490–91; in Massachusetts, 491; in Virginia, 491–92; in Ohio, 492–93

Career officials, *see* administrative careers

Career service, tenure, 369–70; Nourse family, 371; Brent family, 371–72; Graham family, 372; in diplomacy, 373; among district attorneys, 373–74; among subordinate staff, 374–75

Caucus, 49–51; congressional nominating, 53–54

Census, 204–5

Character, a prerequisite to officeholding, 351–52, 356–57, 369 ff.

Civil-military relations, 74–75, 240–45, 287

Claiborne, William C. C., 33

Claims, case of David Gelston, 153–56; case of John Q. Adams, 164–65; case

of John H. Piatt, 230–31; private land claims, 516–18; Massachusetts militia claims, 539–44

Classification, State Department clerks, 403

Clay, Henry, J. Q. Adams on, 39; as Speaker, 55; on removals for political reasons, 380

Clerks, efficiency of, 122–24; John B. Colvin, 190; number in Post Office, 303; tenure of, 374–75; superannuation, 377–78; ethical standards of, 415–19; outside employment of, 416–19; in General Land Office, 521

Collection districts, 119–20

Collectors of customs, functions, 148–49; party membership, 149–50, 151; character qualifications, 152–53; compensation, 153; David Gelston, 153–56; relations with Treasury, 156–57; Jefferson on, 161; superannuation of, 376–77; and embargo, 431, 432, 435, 439–40; and enforcement of embargo, 443 ff., 463–64; Benjamin Weld, 443–44; Joseph Whipple, 446; Jeremiah Clarke, 447; L. F. Delesdernier, 448–49; Gabriel Christie, 449; James H. McCulloch, 449; Bessent, 449; record of during embargo, 453–54; liability of, 457–58

Collectors of public money, recovery from, 178–79

Commissioners of Naval Hospitals, 293–95

Committee of the Whole, 45–46

Committee on Foreign Relations, 186

Committee on Ways and Means, 46, 120, 154, 400

Committees, and legislative-executive relations, 46–47, 50–51, 56–57, 92–93, 122, 165–66, 407–9

Committees of investigation, 99–101, 311–12, 415–19, 500–1

Committees on expenditures, functions, 101–3; War Department, 103–4; Navy Department, 104–5, 120; arduous character of work, 105–6

Communications, 11, 23–24, 229 ff., 474 ff.

Compensation, *see* fees, pay policy, salaries

Comptroller, duties, 164, 173–74; and

arrearages, 166; and settlement of foreign accounts, 191–92; and collection of militia fines, 538–39

Congress, call for papers, 94–95; annual reports to, 95–97; special reports, 97–101; committees on expenditures, 101–6; control of expenditures, 108–16; itemization, 109–12; binding character of appropriation, 112–13; restrictions on transfers, 113–15; deficiencies, 115–16; reduction of salaries, 122; and army supply system, 225–26; reform of supply system, 231–32; relations with Post Office, 311–13; investigations, 311–12; neglects problem of superannuation, 378; and official compensation, 399–411; and internal improvements, 480–82; and Cumberland Road, 484–87; and militia, 529–44

Congressmen, and contracts, 91–92; and constituents, 100–1; *see also* Congress

Constitution, on appointment of Congressmen to public office, 90; and internal improvements, 479–83

Contractors, War Department, 227–31; John H. Piatt, 230–31; army officers on contract system, 231; in Post Office, 329–35; procedure, 330–31; terms of, 331–32; local residence required of, 332–33; penalties, 333; and John Q. Adams, 333–34

Contracts, 91–92

Courts, and settlement of accounts, 167, 168; and enforcement of embargo, 456–57, 458–59

Crawford, William H., on freedom from regulation, 24; on Cabinet, 64; relations with Monroe, 65–66; disability of, 69–70; on secrecy in Cabinet, 86–88; on efficiency of clerks, 123; on settlement of accounts, 168–69; on reorganization of accounting system, 171; on General Staff of 1813, 218, 238; and Tenure of Office Act, 387–88; on official ethical standards, 412; on system of inspection of land offices, 525–26; on formalities of French administration, 552–53

Cumberland Road, establishment and construction, 484–85; repairs on, 485–88

Customs officers, ethical standards of, 413–14; *see also* collectors of customs

Customs service, tenure in, 375

Dallas, Alexander J., on appointment of veterans, 360

Deficiency appropriations, 115–16

Department heads, relations to President, 60–76; John Q. Adams on, 61–62; policy views and President, 62–64, 67–68; removal of, 64–67; case of Crawford, 66; disability of, 69–70; Robert Smith on, 75

Detention, of ships under embargo acts, 431, 434–38

Disability of department head, 69–70

Disbursing officers, accounts of, 178–79

Discretion, administrative, 153–57; Republican and Federalist views on, 29–30; among naval officers, 74–75; in application of appropriations, 108–9, 112–13; among collectors, 153–57, 426 ff., 435 ff.

District attorneys, duties and responsibilities, 340–42; Jefferson on, 353–54; tenure of, 373–74; and enforcement of embargo, 455–56

Dry docks, 289–90

Duane, William, on enforcement of embargo, 448

Economy and efficiency, Jefferson on, 2–3; Congress and, 94–106; reorganization, 117–25, 171–77, 236–40, 272–80, 307–8, 314; Gallatin and, 140–46

Edwards, Senator Ninian, 127

Embargo, objects of, 423–24; embargo acts, 424–30; enforcement acts, 431–32; administrative policy, 433–34; coastwise trade, 434–43; resistance to, 443–52; Boston, 443–45; north shore, 446–48; middle and southern ports, 448–50; northern frontier, 450–51; enforcement agencies, 453–60; second enforcement act, 460–67; collapse, 467–72; evaluation of, 472–73

Embezzlement, 419–21

Emoluments, *see* fees, pay policy, salaries

Employment, expansion of, 25–26; in Treasury Department, 139; in State, 187; in War, 234; in Navy, 269; in

Post Office, 303; in office of Attorney General, 337; in Bureau of Indian Affairs, 508

Engineers, shortage of, 262–63

Equipment, in Post Office, 306–8; steamboats, 307–8

Erie Canal, 490–91

Estimates, relation of President to, 68–69; in Navy Department, 113; Treasury influence on, 140–46; procedure in preparing, 141–42, 145–46; quality of, 145; committee revision, 145–46

Ethics, see public service ethics

Eustis, William, as Secretary of War, 217–18; on Military Academy, 253

Everett, Alexander H., and settlement of accounts, 193

Examinations, for navy surgeons, 296, 297, 362–63; army medical corps, 362; West Point, 363; midshipmen, 363–64; Southard on, 364

Executive-legislative relations, see legislative-executive relations

Executive power, Jefferson and, 5–6, 31; Republican theory of, 29–30, 108–9, 131–33, 546 ff.; and presidency, 60–61, 75–76; and Congress, 119 ff.; and appointments, 125 ff.; and embargo, 423 ff.; and militia, 528 ff.

Expenditures, Congress and, 94–100; committees on, 101–6; itemization, 109–12; appropriation act, 112–13; transfers, 113–15; deficiencies, 115–16; retrenchment in, 119–25; Treasury control of, 140–47; accounting for, 162 ff., 191 ff.

Federal-state relations, effect of patronage on, 392; in maintaining Cumberland Road, 485–87; see also militia

Federalist theory of administration, relation to Republican, 547

Fees, in field service, 403–4; basis of, 404; for outside employment, 416–19

Field services, in Treasury, 148 ff., 443 ff., 453–55; in State, 187–88, 191–93; in War, 234 ff., 260 ff.; in Navy, 285 ff.; in Post Office, 306–8, 320 ff.; district attorneys, 340–42, 455–56; Indian service, 498 ff.; land offices, 518–23

Floor leader, 48–49

Forms and procedures, in Cabinet, 77 ff.; call for papers, 94–95; reports, 95–98; investigations, 98–101; committees on expenditures, 101–6; in budget, 109–12; in appropriation act, 112–15; in appointments, 125–30, 354 ff.; in customs service, 156–60; in accounting, 164 ff., 191 ff.; in army supply, 224 ff.; in Navy, 277–79, 290–92; in Post Office, 306–10, 330–33; in legal matters, 340–41; in fixing emoluments, 399 ff.; in enforcing embargo, 431–32; in land policy, 516–18, 523–26; in control of militia, 531 ff.

Fortifications, 260–61

Fouchee, William, postmaster at Richmond, 321

Four Secretaries, Report of, 171–73

Fulton, Robert, on canals, 475

Functions, of Treasury, 137–40; of collectors of customs, 148–49; of accounting officers, 163–64, 173–74; of Treasury agent, 180–82; of State Department, 187–88, 200 ff.; of War Department, 234–35; of army engineers, 260–62; of Navy Department, 285 ff.; of Post Office, 303–4; of Bureau of Indian Affairs, 507; of General Land Office, 519

Functions, public, Jefferson on, 2–5; scope of, 21–26

Gallatin, Albert, on nationalism, 10; and Congress, 32; resignation, 36–37; financial leader of House, 1795, 46; and House, 51–52; observes appropriation language, 112–13; on reduction of debt, 140–41; evaluation of 135–36, 147; influence on estimates 140–46; role as Secretary of Treasury, 144; on William Smith, 158; on regular army, 213–14; on peace and naval policy, 266–67; on embargo, 425 ff.; on pay policy, 400; on internal improvements by federal government, 474–75; plan for internal improvements, 476–78; and Cumberland Road, 484; on land policy, 514

Gelston, David, career as collector of customs, 153–56

General Land Office, 519–21

General Staff, members of, 237; Crawford on, 238; Calhoun on, 238, 239;
staff and line, 240–45; members in
1812, 218–19

Gentlemen, social class in control of
government, 547–50

Gerry, Elbridge, on standing army, 213;
brother removed by Jefferson, 353

Goldsborough, Charles Washington,
chief clerk, Navy Department, 281–
82; president, Provident Association
of Clerks, 384

Gordon, Samuel, 375–76

Government enterprise, stage lines, 329–
30; Indian trading houses, 498–504

Governors, and embargo, 438–42

Graham, George, 521–22

Graham, John, 372

Granger, Gideon, on significance of
post office, 299; career of, 301; investigated by Congress, 311–12; on
removals in post office, 326

Green, Duff, mail contractor, 332–33

Gunboats, 267–68

Hagner, Peter, 174–75

Hamilton, Alexander, Rush on, 15; on
Jefferson and the executive power,
31; views of Treasury function, 134

Hamilton, Paul, 271

Hartz, Louis, 494

Home Department, 172, 188

Hospitals, naval, deductions for, 293;
commissioners of, 293; misapplication
of funds, 294–95

Huger, Benjamin, report on accounts,
165–66

Humphreys, Joshua, 286

Impeachment, 99

Indian affairs, nature of, 496–98; regulation of Indian trade, 498–504; civilization of Indians, 504–6; schools for
Indians, 505–6; organization for,
507–9; Indian agents, 509–11

Indian trade, trading houses established, 498–500; opposition to, 500–1;
defense of trading houses, 502–3;
termination of, 503–4

Inspection, lack of in Treasury, 157; of
land offices, 523–26

Internal improvements, and army en-

gineers, 261–62; projects in 1828, 262;
plans for, 476–79; frustration of, 479–
84; Cumberland Road, 484–88; in
states, 488–94

Investigation, in connection with im-
peachments, 99; means of control of
executive, 99–101; committees on
public expenditures, 101–6; of post
office, 311–12

Itemization of appropriations, 109–12

Jackson, Andrew, relations with War
Department, 240–45

Jefferson, Thomas, character and personality, 1–3; on scope of public
functions, 2–6; on administration, 4;
on long-range policy, 4–5; on power,
5–6; on farming, 21; on individual
enterprise, 22–23; on Missouri Compromise, 27; presidential leadership,
32–35; John Q. Adams on, 34; Pickering on, 35; and House leadership,
48–49; and bill drafting, 51–52; and
detail, 71; on Cabinet procedure, 77–
78; on unity in Cabinet, 79–80; on
written instead of oral opinions, 80–
81; on itemization of appropriations,
109, 111–12; on Senate confirmation of appointments, 125–26; on
preparation of estimates, 143–44; on
Hamilton's financial system, 146–47;
military policy, 212; on War Department, 222; on navy, 266, 267–68;
on gunboats, 268; on appointment of
postmasters, 322; on appointment
policy, 347–54; on political harmony,
350–51; on freedom of speech among
officeholders, 351; doctrine of due
proportion, 352–53; on respectability
as prerequisite to appointment, 356–
57; on nepotism, 358; on apportionment, 360; on office seeking, 365;
number of removals by, 379; on congressional salary act, 401; and embargo, 34, 423 ff.; on internal improvements, 480; and militia, 532; on
revolution of 1800, 546; on gentlemen
in government, 549; ambivalence in
theory and practice, 551–52

Jesup, Thomas, and War Department,
226–27

Jones, William, on warehousing, 160;

Secretary of the Navy, 271–72; on navy reorganization, 273–75

Land claims, procedure by administrative adjudication, 517–18
Land offices, 521–23
Law enforcement, embargo acts, 426 ff.
Lawyers in public service, 381–82
Lead mines, 515–16
Lee, Light-horse Harry, 184–85
Legislative-executive relations, Federalist and Republican theories, 29–30; under Jefferson, 32–35; under Madison, 35–38; under Monroe, 38–41; under John Q. Adams, 41–42; role of committees, 46–47; congressional independence, 90–92; congressional dependence, 92–94; congressional supervision, 94–98; congressional investigations, 98–106; in administrative reform, 117–19; in retrenchment, 119–25; in appointments, 125–31
Library, State Department, 202
Lincoln, Levi, Attorney General, 343; orders Massachusetts militia to enforce embargo, 466–67
Local residence rule, postal contractors, 332–33; Jefferson on, 362
Louisiana, 32
Lovell, Joseph, 247–48
Loyalty, official, to position, 414; to the Administration, 415

McKenney, Thomas L., on clerks, 376; superintendent of Indian trade, 502, 510–11; defends trading houses, 502–3
McLean, John, relations with John Q. Adams, 67, 315–19; on use of postal surplus, 303; on insurance of mail, 308; on removals in post office, 327; on standards of efficiency, 334–35; career of, 313–14; success as Postmaster General, 314; political interests, 314–15; letters on patronage, 316–18; and Jackson, 318; evaluation of, 318–19
Macon, Nathaniel, 91
Madison, James, ineptitude for executive office, 36; and Smith faction, 36; and War of 1812, 37; removes Robert Smith, 64–65; removes General Armstrong, 65; incompetence in selecting

generals, 219–20; at Battle of Bladensburg, 220–21; as commander in chief, 221; on Board of Navy Commissioners, 277–78; number of removals by, 379; vetoes bill for internal improvements, 480
Marshals, Jefferson on, 353–54; and collection of militia fines, 537–38
Massachusetts, patronage in, 395; use of militia to enforce embargo, 466–67; Resolution opposing embargo, 469; internal improvements in, 491
Medical service, see hospitals, navy surgeons
Meigs, Josiah, 519–20
Meigs, Return Jonathan, Postmaster General, 302; on guards for mail, 309
Military instruction, West Point, 251–58; artillery school, 258–59; militia, 533–34
Militia, in defense of Washington, 221–22; and enforcement of embargo, 464–68; division of authority over, 529–31; militia myth, 530; failure to secure effective militia, 530–31; failure of national authority over, 531–36; Washington's program, 531; Jefferson's program, 532; provision of arms for, 532–33; military instruction, 533–34; collection of militia fines, 536–39; Massachusetts militia claims, 539–44; refusal to supply militia, 539–41; Monroe on, 541–42; Niles on, 543
Mixed corporation, 493–94
Money bills, 46
Monroe, James, Van Buren on, 38, 40; and presidency, 38–41; and Congress, 38–39; J. Q. Adams on, 39–40; election of Speaker, 57–58; correspondence on entering Cabinet, 63–64; quarrels with Crawford, 66; on estimates, 69; and duties of detail, 72; on integration of responsibility, 74; on control of army, 241–45; and postmaster appointments, 323–25; appointment policy, 357; on local residence, 362; number of removals by, 379–80; and renomination policy, 390; on internal improvements, 480–81; on Massachusetts militia claims, 541–42, 543, 544

National Highway, *see* Cumberland Road

Nationalism, 10–11

Naval academy, 284–85

Naval constructors, 288

Navy agents, duties of, 290–92; tenure of, 374

Navy Department, Committee on Expenditures in, 104–5; character of appropriations, 110–11; on estimates, 113; retrenchment in, 120–21; estimates reduced by Gallatin, 142–43; early naval policy, 265–66; Republican views on, 266–69; organization, 269–72; reorganization, 272–80; naval personalities, 281–83; shore organization, 284–98; navy yards, 285–89; dry docks, 289–90; navy agents, 290–92; naval hospitals, 292–96; naval medical personnel, 296–97; officers pay for shore duty, 410; and enforcement of embargo, 459–60

Navy surgeons, organization of, 296–97; tenure of, 374

Navy yards, Paul Hamilton on Washington yard, 271; Federalist origins, 285–86; excessive number of, 286–87; civilian heads, 287; competence in, 288; threatened strike in, 288–89

Nepotism, Jefferson on, 358; Adams on, 358, 359; Niles on, 359

Newburyport, enforcement of embargo in, 451

New Haven remonstrance, 351–52

New York, internal improvements in, 490–91; patronage in, 395–96

Nicholas, Wilson C., and Jefferson, 49

Niles, Hezekiah, *see* Niles Register

Niles, John M., on navy, 272

Niles Register, on machinery of government, 12; on manufacturing, 21; on self-government, 27–28; on army engineers, 261–62; on Board of Navy Commissioners, 280; on post office, 308–9; on nepotism, 359; on professional education, 381; on government salaries, 400–1; on official ethics, 415–16, 418; on Massachusetts militia claims, 543

North American Review, on military policy, 211; on West Point, 258; on engineers, 262–63

Nourse, Joseph, asks for estimates, 141; career in government, 371; and nepotism, 358–59; claim for extra compensation, 408–9

Officeholding, party qualification, collectors, 149–52; ethical standards in, 412–14

Office seeking, by Congressmen, 92; Jefferson on, 365; case of Joseph Whipple, 366; case of Solomon Southwick, 366; case of Horatio Turpin, 366; John Q. Adams on, 366–67

Official Register, 405

Ohio, internal improvements in, 492–93

Organization, of government, 11–12; of presidency, 29 ff., 70–74; of Congress, 45 ff., 101–6; of Cabinet, 77 ff.; reorganization, 117–19; of Treasury, 137–40; of State, 188–91; of War, 234–36; of General Staff, 236–40; of Navy, 269–72; reorganization of Navy, 272–78; of navy surgeons, 296–97; of Post Office, 304–6; of office of Attorney General, 337–38; for Indian management, 506–10; land offices, 518–23

Organizations of employees, navy surgeons, 383; army captains, 383–84; clerks, 384–85

Overtime, 407

Pardons, 202–3

Parties, political, 12–15, 29–30, 47–49, 53–55, 265–67, 348–54, 547–53

Party affiliation, and appointment to office, 347–54, 355–56

Patent Office, 205–10

Patronage, and leadership in legislation, 43; and publication of laws, 200–2; McLean on, 316–18; and post office, 322–25; Josiah Quincy on, 386; Benton's Report, 390–93; and elections, 393; in Virginia, 395; in Massachusetts, 395; in New York, 395–96; in Pennsylvania, 396–97

Paullin, Charles O., on Board of Navy Commissioners, 280; on naval officers, 282–83

Pay policy, executive and legislative views, 399–402; methods, 402–4; fees, 403–4; rule of publicity, 404–6; extra compensation problem, 406–10; *see also* fees, salaries

Pennsylvania, patronage in, 396–97; internal improvements in, 489–90

Personnel administration, Republican dilemma, 347–48; interim period of adjustment, 348–54; Republican practice, 354–64; party affiliation, 355–56; respectability, 356–57; nepotism, 357–59; veterans, 359–60; apportionment, 360–62; local residence, 362; examinations, 362–64; office seekers, 364–68; public service careers, 369–75; problem of superannuation, 375–78; removal, 379–81; professional foundations, 381–83; employee organizations, 383–85; Tenure of Office Act, 387–90; Benton's Report, 390–93; patronage in states, 393–98

Pinkney, William, 336; Attorney General, 343–44; on embargo, 471–72

Planning, *see* internal improvements

Pleasonton, Stephen, Treasury agent, 180–82; claim for extra compensation, 407–8

Plumer, Senator William, quoted, 33

Political activity, removal for, 350–51, 353–54, 380–81

Porter, Peter B., on press of Indian business, 509

Postmasters, Solomon Southwick, 320; Solomon Van Rensselaer, 320–21, 323–25; Theodorus Bailey, 321; William Fouchee, 321; appointment of, 321–25; Jefferson on appointment of, 322; party regularity of, 322–23; appointment by Postmaster General, 323; compensation of, 400

Postmasters General, Granger, 301; Meigs, 302; duties of, 304–5; McLean, 313–19

Post Office, political significance of, 299–301; Postmasters General, 301–2; expansion, 1801–1829, 302–4; organization of, 304–6; equipment and procedures, 306–8; regularity and security of mail, 308–10; Congress and, 311–13; John McLean, 313–19; postmasters, 320–25; tenure of postmasters, 326–27; accountability of postmasters, 327–29; contractors, 329–

34; case of Samuel Gordon, 375–76

Post roads, Jefferson on, 2–3

Power, *see* executive power

Presidency, Federalist and Republican theories, 29–30; Jefferson's leadership, 32–35; Madison and, 35–38; Monroe and, 38–41; John Q. Adams and, 41–42; under Jeffersonians, 42–44; and relations with Congress, 45–59; nomination to, 53–54; and the administrative system, 60–76; dominance of Presidents, 61; and heads of departments, 61–70; and estimates, 68–69; and detail, 70–74; and lack of secretarial aid, 74; Robert Smith on, 75; and Cabinet, 77–88; and foreign affairs, 183–86; and appointment of postmasters, 322–25; and patronage (Benton's Report), 390–93; and embargo acts, 426 ff.

Prestige, of army engineers, 263

Professional foundations of public service, law, 381–82; medicine, 382; engineering, 382

Promotion, *see* administrative careers

Provident Association of Clerks, 384–85

Public lands, land policy, 513–16; private land claims, 516–18; organization for sale of, 518–23; system of inspection, 523–66

Public service ethics, Crawford on, 412; foundations of, 412–13; in customs service, 413–14; John Q. Adams on, 414; loyalty to Administration, 414–15; outside employment, 415–19; misuse of public funds, 419–21

Public works, *see* canals, fortifications, internal improvements, roads

Publication of laws, 200–2

Publicity, of accounts, 169–71, 173; of official compensation, 404–6; Jefferson on, 404–5; *Official Register*, 1816, 405; reports, 405–6

Pursers, tenure of, 374

Qualifications for office, *see* appointment policy and practice

Quartermaster general, 225, 226–27

Quincy, Josiah, on patronage, 386

Railroads, in Pennsylvania, 489

Randolph, John, on constitutional powers, 33–34

Regulation, freedom from government, 23–24

Removals, case of Robert Smith, Secretary of State, 64–65; case of General Armstrong, 65; case of John McLean, 67; case of William Smith, 158; for failure to submit accounts, 179; Granger on, 326; McLean on, 326–27; during interim period, 1801–1803, 352–53; for pernicious political activity, 353–54; reluctance to use power of, 379; by Presidents, 379–80; Clay on removals for political activity, 380; John Q. Adams on same, 380–81; case of William Blake, 455

Reorganization, general view, 117–19; retrenchment program, 119–25; in accounting staff, 171–77; of General Staff, 236–40; Navy Department, 272–80; report of Secretary Jones, 1814, 273–75; navy captains on, 275–76; act of 1815, 276–78; operations under, 278–80; in post office, 307–8, 314

Reports to Congress, 92–94

Republican party, general attitude of, 12–15; military policy, 212–15; naval policy, 265–66; change of attitude on navy, 272–73; and appointment policy, 347–54; and internal improvements, 479–83, 494–95; administrative achievements of, 546–59

Republican theory of administration, dualism of Thomas Jefferson, 2–6; dualism of old and new Republicans, 10–15, 26–27; on presidency, 29–30, 42–44; on executive-legislative relations, 45–47, 59, 131–33; on President and department heads, 74–76, 88; on congressional control of administration, 89–90, 94, 106–7; on financial administration, 108–15

Residence, local, and appointment, 362

Respectability, prerequisite to appointment, 356–57

Responsibility, Calhoun on, 247

Retrenchment, Treasury, 119–20, 123; Navy, 120–21; of congressional salaries, 122; War Department, 123–24

Rhoda, case of ship *Rhoda*, 447

Rivers and harbors, improvements in, 481–82

Roads, Gallatin's plan for, 477–78; Calhoun's plan for, 478–79; surveys of, 482; Cumberland Road, 484–88; in states, 488

Rodgers, John, 277, 282

Rodney, Caesar A., Jefferson on, 48–49

Rotation, in elective and appointive office, 397–98

Rudd, Theron, 419–20

Rush, Richard, on Alexander Hamilton, 15; on Washington, D.C., 17

Safety, regulation of, 23

Salaries, withholding of, 178–79; of postmasters, 400; of Congressmen, 401; of executive officers, 401–2; of clerks, 402, 403; of field officers, 403–4; ceilings, 403–4; publicity of, 404–6; extra compensation problem, 406–10; adequacy of, 410–11

Schoolcraft, Henry R., Indian agent, 510

Schools, for Indians, 505–6

Secrecy, Cabinet discussions, 86–88

Senate and appointments, Jefferson on, 125–26, 322; practice, 126–31; Monroe's views, 128; case of Van Rensselaer, 128; West Point cadets, 128; Benton's Report, 130–31

Senatorial courtesy, *see* Senate and appointments

Shipping industry, freedom from regulation of, 24

Shriver, David, 485, 486

Smith, Robert, removed as Secretary of State, 64–65; on presidential control of departments, 75; and navy estimates, 142–43; Secretary of Navy, 269–71; on threatened strike in navy yard, 288–89; on embargo, 468, 475

Smith, William S., surveyor of New York Port, 157–58

Southard, Samuel L., Secretary of the Navy, 281; on navy yards, 286–87; on dry docks, 290; on appropriations for naval hospitals, 295; on examinations for naval officers, 364; on shore pay for naval officers, 410

Southwick, Solomon, postmaster at Albany, 320, 366

Speaker, House of Representatives, election, 54; center of influence, 55; Monroe and election of, 57–58

Standards, among collectors, 157, 161; in auditing, 174–77; in military administration, 213–19, 228–31, 248–49, 263–64; at West Point, 257–58; in the navy, 280, 288, 295–96; in the post office, 307–9, 314; in appointments, 354 ff.; of compensation, 399 ff.; of official ethics, 412 ff.; in militia, 529–31; Republican foundations, 547–50, 553; see also public service ethics

State Department, subordinate to President, 184–86; organization and activities, 187–91; administrative affairs, 191–94; John Q. Adams and, 194–99; domestic business of, 200 ff.; publication of laws, 200–2; library, 202; pardons, 202–3; weights and measures, 203–4; census, 204–5; Patent Office, 205–10

State of the nation, expansion, 18–19; rural and urban population, 19–21; manufacturing, 21; freedom from regulation, 23–24

States, internal improvements in, 488–94

Steamboats, safety on, 23–24; and carriage of mail, 307–8

Story, Joseph, on careers in government, 370–71

Strikes, in navy yard, 288–89

Sullivan, Governor William, and embargo, 440–41

Summary process, in settlement of accounts, 172–73, 178

Superannuation, case of Samuel Gordon, 375–76; among collectors, 376–77; among clerks, 377–78

Superintendent general of military supplies, 226–27

Supervision, by Congress, 89, 94–106, 111–16, 119–25, 311–13, 390–93, 415–19; by Treasury over estimates, 141–44; of collectors, 156–57, 435–37; in War Department, 215, 234–35, 240 ff.; of West Point, 257–58; in Navy Department, 278–79; in Post Office, 304–6, 327–29, 333; of district attorneys, 340–41; of Indian affairs,

506–10; of land offices, 523–26; of militia, 534–35

Supply, breakdown of army, 227–30; reform of, 231–32

Tennessee, settlement of land claims in, 517

Tenure, of collectors, 149–51; of postmasters, 326–27; career service, 369–75

Tenure of Office Act, drafted by Crawford, 387–88; terms of, 387; Monroe on, 388; Jefferson on, 388; Madison on, 389; John Q. Adams on, 389

Thayer, Major Sylvanus, 256–57

Thornton, William, 206, 207–10

Tiffin, Edward, 519

Tingey, Captain Thomas, 287–88

Todson, Dr. George P., and John Q. Adams, 72–74

Trading houses, Indian, 498–504

Training, West Point, 251–58; artillery school, 258–59; of midshipmen, 363

Transfers of appropriations, 113–15

Treasury agent, 180–82

Treasury Department, and estimates, 68–69; collection districts, 119–20; retrenchment in, 119–20, 123; and public policy, 134–37; organization, 137–40; control of estimates and expenditures, 140–46; and settlement of accounts, 172, 173–74; the "octogenarian" department, 377

Trinidad Gazette, quoted, 28

Turpin, Horatio, 366

Van Buren, Martin, on Monroe, 38, 40; and appointment of Solomon Van Rensselaer, 323–25

Van Rensselaer, Solomon, 320–21; appointment of, 128, 323–25

Veterans, preference in appointments, 359–60

Veto, use of, 52; of bill for internal improvements, 480; of tollgate bill, 481

Virginia, patronage in, 395; internal improvements in, 491–92

War Department, Committee on Expenditures in, 103–4; retrenchment in, 123–24; accounts of, 174–75, 179–80; lack of system in, 215–16; reorganization of, 224–27, 231–32, 235–36,

238–39, 246–49, 254–55, 263–64; Republican military policy, 211–16; civil and military leadership in (War of 1812), 216–23; supply system, 224–32; civilian organization, 233–36; General Staff, 236–40; staff and line, 240–45; John C. Calhoun, 246–50; Joseph Lovell, 247; medical service, 247, n.; West Point, 251–60; army corps of engineers, 260–64; artillery school, 258–59; and militia, 534–35

Warehousing, 160

Warrant of distress, 178

Washington, D.C., description of, 16–18; capture of, 220–22

Washington, George, and militia, 531

Watkins, Tobias, 420–21

Weights and measures, 203–4

Weld, Benjamin, and enforcement of embargo, 444–45; on liability as collector, 458

West Point, apportionment of cadets, 128–29, 256; Hamilton on, 252; establishment of, 252–53; course of study, 252, 254; selection of cadets, 255–56; Board of Visitors, 257–58; discipline in, 253, 257; evaluation of, 259–60

Whipple, Joseph, seeks customs office, 366; on embargo shipments, 443; and enforcement of embargo, 446–47

Winder, William, accounts of, 181; military incapacity, 219

Wirt, William, on Washington, D.C., 17; on use of facsimile of official signature, 70; on secrecy of Cabinet discussions, 87; on public contract law, 92; on records of Attorney General, 337–38; on duties of Attorney General, 338–40; and district attorneys, 340–42; income of, 342; as Attorney General, 344–46